PROFESSIONAL

# Visual Basic® 2012 and .NET 4.5 Programming

# PROFESSIONAL VISUAL BASIC® 2012 AND .NET 4.5 PROGRAMMING

PROFESSIONAL

# Visual Basic® 2012 and .NET 4.5 Programming

Bill Sheldon
Billy Hollis
Rob Windsor
David McCarter
Gastón C. Hillar
Todd Herman

WILEY

John Wiley & Sons, Inc.

## Professional Visual Basic® 2012 and .NET 4.5 Programming

Published by
John Wiley & Sons, Inc.
10475 Crosspoint Boulevard
Indianapolis, IN 46256
www.wiley.com

Copyright © 2013 by John Wiley & Sons, Inc., Indianapolis, Indiana

Published simultaneously in Canada

ISBN: 978-1-118-31445-6
ISBN: 978-1-118-33213-9 (ebk)
ISBN: 978-1-118-33542-0 (ebk)
ISBN: 978-1-118-39638-4 (ebk)

Manufactured in the United States of America

10 9 8 7 6 5 4 3 2 1

For general information on our other products and services please contact our Customer Care Department within the United States at (877) 762-2974, outside the United States at (317) 572-3993 or fax (317) 572-4002.

Wiley publishes in a variety of print and electronic formats and by print-on-demand. Some material included with standard print versions of this book may not be included in e-books or in print-on-demand. If this book refers to media such as a CD or DVD that is not included in the version you purchased, you may download this material at http://booksupport.wiley.com. For more information about Wiley products, visit www.wiley.com.

**Library of Congress Control Number:** 2012946061

*This book is dedicated to Tracie, Billy, and Johnny, who had to put up with me locking myself away in my home office and not spending as much time with them as I'd like and they deserved.*

*—BILL SHELDON*

*I'd like to dedicate this book to those in the software development community who put users first. I've watched with regret as our profession has become inwardly focused, worrying far more about technology and process than what we can accomplish for our users and the businesses for which they work. I salute those who invest the time and effort to deliver compelling and wonderful experiences to their users, and I hope the material I contributed to this book will help them do that.*

*—BILLY HOLLIS*

*This book is dedicated to you, the reader. Unless you didn't pay for the book—in that case it's dedicated to my Mom (love ya, Mom).*

*—ROB WINDSOR*

*To my son, Kevin.*

*—GASTÓN C. HILLAR*

*For my wife, Amy. Thank you for your support while I worked on this project. I must also thank my son, Aidan, and daughter, Alaina, for their support and understanding while I was busy in my office rather than spending time with them. I love all of you. Thank you.*

*—TODD HERMAN*

# ABOUT THE AUTHORS

**BILL SHELDON** is a software architect and engineer, originally from Baltimore, Maryland. Holding a degree in computer science from the Illinois Institute of Technology (IIT), Bill has worked in the IT industry since resigning his commission with the United States Navy. He is the Vice President of Information Technology for Rubio's Restaurants (www.rubios.com) and has eight years as a Microsoft MVP for Visual Basic. Bill lives in Oceanside, California, with his wife and two sons. Bill is an avid cyclist and is active in the fight against diabetes. You can track Bill down via Twitter: @NerdNotes.

**BILLY HOLLIS** is a developer and user-experience designer based in Nashville, Tennessee. His consulting company, Next Version Systems, offers design and development on software applications requiring innovative and intuitive user experiences. He speaks regularly at major industry conferences, usually on design concepts and user experience technologies. He is also available for training in XAML technologies and in user experience design concepts.

**ROB WINDSOR** is a Lead SharePoint Consultant with Portal Solutions—a Microsoft Gold Partner based in Washington, D.C., and Boston. He has 20 years' experience developing rich-client and web applications with Delphi, VB, C#, and VB.NET, and is currently spending a majority of his time working with SharePoint. Rob is a regular speaker at conferences, code camps, and user groups across North America and Europe. He regularly contributes articles and videos to MSDN, TechNet, and the Pluralsight On-Demand library, and is the coauthor of *Professional Visual Basic 2010 and .NET 4*. Rob is the founder and past president of the North Toronto .NET User Group and has been recognized as a Microsoft Most Valuable Professional for his involvement in the developer community. You can follow Rob on Twitter at @robwindsor.

**DAVID MCCARTER** is a Microsoft MVP and a principal software engineer/architect in San Diego. He is the editor-in-chief of dotNetTips.com, a website dedicated to helping programmers in all aspects of programming. David has written for programming magazines and has published four books, the latest of which is *David McCarter's .NET Coding Standards*, and is available at: http://codingstandards.notlong.com. He is one of the founders and directors of the 18-year-old San Diego .NET Developers Group (www.sddotnetdg.org). In 2008 David won the INETA Community Excellence Award for his involvement in the .NET community. David is also an inventor of a software printing system that was approved by the U.S. Patent Office in May 2008.

**GASTÓN C. HILLAR** is an Italian living in Argentina. He has been working with computers since he was eight years old. He began programming with the legendary Texas TI-99/4A and Commodore 64 home computers in the early '80s. He has worked as developer, architect, project manager, and IT consultant for many companies around the world. He is always looking for new adventures around the world. Gastón has written four books in English, contributed chapters to three other books, and has written more than 40 books in Spanish. He contributes to Dr. Dobbs at `http://drdobbs.com`, and is a guest blogger for Intel Software Network at `http://software.intel.com`. In 2009, 2010, 2011, and 2012, he received the Intel® Black Belt Software Developer award. In 2011, he received the Microsoft MVP on Technical Computing award.

Gastón lives in Argentina with his wife, Vanesa, and his son, Kevin. When not tinkering with computers, he enjoys developing and playing with wireless virtual reality devices and electronic toys with his father, his son, and his nephew Nico. You can reach him at `gastonhillar@hotmail.com`. You can follow him on Twitter at `http://twitter.com/gastonhillar`. Gastón's blog is at `http://csharpmulticore.blogspot.com`

**TODD HERMAN** works for APX Labs as a senior software engineer. His current focus is developing a robust library to support the XMPP standard. He has been programming since he received his first computer, a Commodore 64, on his 11th birthday. His experience ranges from developing data entry software in FoxPro for a water research laboratory, to writing biometric applications in Visual Basic for NEC. He lives in Virginia with his wife and children, spending his free time programming, playing computer games, and watching the SyFy Channel or reruns of *Firefly*.

# ABOUT THE TECHNICAL EDITORS

**DOUG WATERFIELD** has been a software developer and architect for over 20 years and has been working with .NET languages and related technologies since their first release. He has designed and constructed solutions for Fortune 500 and Defense Department clients through Chameleon Consulting, and he is a Senior Software Engineer with Interactive Intelligence, Inc. Doug graduated from Rose-Hulman Institute of Technology in 1988 and recently earned PMP (Project Management Professional) certification from PMI. Doug and his family are very active in the Avon, Indiana, community through the Boy Scouts of America and other organizations. He can be reached at djw@iquest.net.

**DOUG PARSONS** lives in Northeast Ohio and has been developing software professionally for over 15 years. He has a diverse background, having worked in the political, financial, medical, and manufacturing sectors over the course of his career. He is currently employed as a Senior .NET Developer with Harley-Davidson Motor Company. In his free time he tinkers with his various motorcycles, sits on the advisory committee of a High School Technology program, and spends time with his family.

# CREDITS

**ACQUISITIONS EDITOR**
Mary James

**PROJECT EDITOR**
Christina Haviland

**TECHNICAL EDITORS**
Doug Waterfield
Doug Parsons

**PRODUCTION EDITOR**
Daniel Scribner

**COPY EDITOR**
Christina Haviland

**EDITORIAL MANAGER**
Mary Beth Wakefield

**FREELANCER EDITORIAL MANAGER**
Rosemarie Graham

**ASSOCIATE DIRECTOR OF MARKETING**
David Mayhew

**MARKETING MANAGER**
Ashley Zurcher

**BUSINESS MANAGER**
Amy Knies

**PRODUCTION MANAGER**
Tim Tate

**VICE PRESIDENT AND EXECUTIVE GROUP PUBLISHER**
Richard Swadley

**VICE PRESIDENT AND EXECUTIVE PUBLISHER**
Neil Edde

**ASSOCIATE PUBLISHER**
Jim Minatel

**PROJECT COORDINATOR, COVER**
Katie Crocker

**PROOFREADER**
Mark Steven Long

**INDEXER**
Robert Swanson

**COVER DESIGNER**
LeAndra Young

**COVER IMAGE**
© dan_prat / iStock

# ACKNOWLEDGMENTS

**MANY THANKS TO ALL OF THE PEOPLE** associated with getting this book together and out the door. More so than any other edition, there seemed to be a real struggle as we made some truly major changes to much of the content. Thanks to those who stepped up and met the challenges that we were presented with during the production cycle.

—BILL SHELDON

**THANKS TO BETH MASSI** for being too busy to work on this project and thanks to the people at Wrox for accepting Beth's suggestion that I would be a suitable replacement. I'd also like to thank those who helped me advance professionally to the point that this opportunity was even possible: Craig Flanagan, Sasha Krsmanovic, Jean-Rene Roy, Mark Dunn, Carl Franklin, Richard Campbell, Barry Gervin, Dave Lloyd, Bruce Johnson, Donald Belcham, and everyone at Portal Solutions.

—ROB WINDSOR

# CONTENTS

# INTRODUCTION

**WELCOME TO THE NEXT ERA** in .NET development. .NET has moved from a set of developer-focused tools and a runtime environment to the core of the latest Microsoft operating system. In 2002, Microsoft released .NET and introduced developers to a new paradigm for building applications. For Visual Basic it was not only a new environment, but really a new language.

Visual Basic .NET (as it was initially called) went beyond an overhaul. .NET changed core elements of the syntax affecting every aspect of development with Visual Basic. The entire runtime model shifted to a new common language runtime (CLR) environment and the language went from object-based to object-oriented. Although most people didn't recognize it, we were moving to a new language.

Now with the introduction of Windows RT, Microsoft has again shifted the paradigm. Not so much at the language level, but as it relates to how user interfaces are developed and work. The original runtime environment, although enhanced for .NET 4.5, risks being flagged as being on the path to that fatal "legacy" designator. Windows 8 introduces the concept of Windows Store applications, which are built on a version of the CLR that has different features, and that's important. Because while client applications may view the core CLR as legacy, server-based applications have probably never been in a position to leverage it more.

This book provides details about not only the latest version of Visual Basic and the new .NET Framework 4.5. More important, it carries this coverage to a new platform, Windows RT, and a new class of Windows Store applications. As a result the contents of this book have been turned upside down. This book doesn't just indicate that there are new Windows Store applications, but focuses in directly on how to build and deploy this new class of applications. The result is a very different book from the previous edition.

If you compare this edition to an older edition you'll immediately realize that this edition is visibly smaller. Just as you saw Visual Basic evolve nearly 10 years ago, .NET is going through an evolution of its own. The result was a need to refocus on what this book covers. This has resulted in a sea change with regard to where to focus coverage for Visual Basic.

The most noticeable omission from the book is in fact the original smart client development model—Windows Forms. When Microsoft introduced WPF it informally announced that the era of Windows Forms was ending. It has taken some time, and certainly support will continue for many more years, but the reality is that the evolution of Windows Forms is complete. The information around Windows Forms provided in past editions of this book is essentially complete. While one or two of the chapters do still reference Windows Forms in their samples, by and large the book has moved beyond the use of this technology.

The result was that Billy Hollis, who has a passion for user interface design, agreed to take on the rather significant task of re-imagining how to approach user interface design in a world that includes Windows RT. The new XAML-based interface design chapters are completely redone from the ground up and focused on teaching developers how to approach XAML development from the ground up. The last version of the book approached the user interface model from Windows Forms and transitioning to XAML. However, in this version the approach takes on XAML as the primary user interface development model. As such these chapters address Windows Store application development head-on, not as an afterthought.

However, Windows Forms wasn't alone in being moved into the past. We've eliminated several appendices, Microsoft Office (both VSTO and SharePoint) integration, and references to classic COM. Some, for example, development around Microsoft Office, is facing its own set of changes as Microsoft Office prepares to evolve. Others, such as classic COM and Windows Forms, are no longer technologies that developers should be targeting. We also found ourselves needing to change out how we addressed larger topics such as ASP.NET and Silverlight. The result is that this book is much more focused on building applications using Visual Basic that target Microsoft's core next generation of technologies.

## THE FUTURE OF VISUAL BASIC

Early in the adoption cycle of .NET, Microsoft's new language, C#, got the lion's share of attention. However, as .NET adoption has increased, Visual Basic's continuing importance has also been apparent. Microsoft has publicly stated that it considers Visual Basic to be the language of choice for applications for which developer productivity is one of the highest priorities.

In the past, it was common for Microsoft and others to "target" different development styles; with Visual Studio 2010, Microsoft announced that VB and C# will follow a process of coevolution. As new language features are developed, they will be introduced to both Visual Basic and C# at the same time. This release is the first step in that process, although it's not complete at this time.

Coevolution does not mean that the languages will look the same, but rather that they will support the same capabilities. For example, Visual Basic has XML literals, but that doesn't mean C# will get exactly the same functionality, as C# has the capability to work with XML through the existing framework classes. The old process of first introducing a feature in Visual Basic and then in the next release having C# catch up, and vice versa, is over. As new capabilities and features are introduced, they are being introduced to both Visual Basic and C# at the same time.

This leads to a discussion of the "Roslyn" compiler implementation. It seems like almost five years ago that the first whispers of a new 64-bit Visual Basic compiler implemented with Visual Basic started. Considered the standard for a serious language, implementing a language compiler in the language it compiles has become something of a standard.

However, over time this project evolved. Microsoft, seeing commonalities across the C# and Visual Basic compilation projects, realized that once the core syntax had been consumed the remainder of the compilation process was common across languages. While each implementation language needed a custom solution to handle parsing and interpreting the raw "code," once that code had been converted to Intermediate Language (IL) the remaining compiler steps were essentially the same.

Suddenly a new concept—the compiler as a service—was created. Code-named Roslyn, this is the future for both Visual Basic and C# compilation. Roslyn takes the traditional compiler as a "black-box" and provides an interface that for interacting with the creation of .NET assemblies. Introducing an API that exposes your components during the compilation process is a powerful tool. Roslyn has been in a technology preview model since well before the release of Visual Studio

2012 and .NET 4.5—however, Microsoft isn't quite ready to declare it ready for prime time. As a result it's still an optional add-on with Visual Studio 2012.

However, even though Roslyn isn't part of Visual Studio 2012, Visual Studio 2012 includes a few paradigm shifts. For starters you'll find that you can now work on projects that targeted older versions of Visual Studio without breaking backward compatibility in those projects. Visual Studio 2012 was designed so that those people who move to the latest tools are limited when working with a team that hasn't fully migrated to that new version.

More important, Visual Studio 2012 comes with a promise of updates. It'll be interesting to see how this plays out over the coming months, but the Visual Studio team has indicated that they will be releasing regular updates to Visual Studio. Update 1 has already been announced as this book goes to print, and the team has indicated that they would like to continue with updates on a quarterly basis. This goes beyond what we've seen in the past, with Power Pack style updates that occurred out of the standard release cycle. Instead we see that Microsoft is committing to keeping Visual Studio on the cutting edge of evolving technology. As the environments we developers need to support change, we can expect that Visual Studio will be adapting and incrementally improving to help us.

While these changes may not involve changes to the core of the .NET framework, we can expect .NET to remain the most productive environment for custom applications. One of the most important advantages of the .NET Framework is that it enables applications to be written with dramatically less code then other alternatives. Originally this was in comparison to older technologies, but today the comparison is as opposed to writing native solutions that support the many different platforms and operating systems you need to support. In the world of business applications, the goal is to concentrate on writing business logic and to eliminate routine coding tasks as much as possible. In other words, of greatest value in this new paradigm is writing robust, useful applications without churning out a lot of code.

Visual Basic is an excellent fit for this type of development, which makes up the bulk of software development in today's economy. Moreover, it will grow to be an even better fit as it is refined and evolves for exactly that purpose.

## WHO THIS BOOK IS FOR

This book was written to help experienced developers learn Visual Basic. For those who are just starting the transition from other languages or earlier versions to those who have used Visual Basic for a while and need to gain a deeper understanding, this book provides information on the most common programming tasks and concepts you need.

*Professional Visual Basic 2012 and .NET 4.5 Programming* offers a wide-ranging presentation of Visual Basic concepts, but the .NET Framework is so large and comprehensive that no single book can cover it all. The focus in this book is providing a working knowledge of key technologies that are important to Visual Basic developers. It provides adequate knowledge for a developer to work across both Windows Store applications through WCF services. This book is meant to provide a breadth of knowledge about how to leverage Visual Basic when developing applications. For certain specific technologies, developers may choose to add to their knowledge by following this book with a book dedicated entirely to a single technology area.

# WHAT THIS BOOK COVERS

This book covers Visual Basic from start to finish. It starts by introducing Visual Studio 2010. As the tool you'll use to work with Visual Basic, understanding Visual Studio's core capabilities is key to your success and enjoyment with building .NET applications. In these pages, you have the opportunity to learn everything from database access, Language Integrated Queries (LINQ), and the Entity Framework, to integration with other technologies such as WPF, WCF, and service-based solutions. Along with investigating new features in detail, you'll see that Visual Basic 10 has emerged as a powerful yet easy-to-use language that enables you to target the Internet just as easily as the desktop. This book covers the .NET Framework 4.

# HOW THIS BOOK IS STRUCTURED

**Part I, "Language Constructs and Environment"**—The first six chapters of the book focus on core language elements and development tools used by Visual Basic developers. This section introduces Visual Studio 2012, objects, syntax, and debugging.

➤ **Chapter 1, "Visual Studio 2012"**—Start with the environment where you will work with Visual Basic. This chapter looks at the Visual Studio development environment. Introducing a simple WPF application project and reviewing key capabilities like the debugger, this chapter will help you to prepare for and become comfortable with this powerful environment.

➤ **Chapter 2, "The Common Language Runtime"**—This chapter examines the core of the .NET platform: the common language runtime (CLR). The CLR is responsible for managing the execution of code compiled for the .NET platform, as well as on the Windows RT platform. This chapter introduces you to how the different versions of the CLR are in fact closer to different operating systems than to a common environment. You'll learn about versioning and deployment, memory management, cross-language integration, metadata, and the IL Disassembler. The chapter also introduces namespaces and their hierarchical structure. An explanation of namespaces and some common examples are provided. In addition, you learn about custom namespaces, and how to import and alias existing namespaces within projects. This chapter also looks at the My namespace available in Visual Basic.

➤ **Chapter 3, "Objects and Visual Basic"**—This is the first of two chapters that explore object-oriented programming in Visual Basic. This chapter introduces the basics of objects, types, type conversion, reference types, and the key syntax which make up the core of Visual Basic.

➤ **Chapter 4, "Custom Objects"**—This chapter examines creating objects, and describes how they fit within Visual Basic. Starting with inheritance, you create simple and abstract classes and learn how to create base classes from which other classes can be derived. This chapter puts the theory of object-oriented development into practice. The four defining object-oriented concepts (abstraction, encapsulation, polymorphism, inheritance) are described, and you will learn how these concepts can be applied in design and development to create effective object-oriented applications.

➤ **Chapter 5, "Advanced Language Constructs"**—This chapter looks at some of the more advanced language concepts such as lambda expressions, the new Async keyword, and Iterators. Each of these provides key capabilities that are new to Visual Basic 2012, and this new chapter provides details on how you can leverage these new language constructs.

➤ **Chapter 6, "Exception Handling and Debugging"**—This chapter covers how error handling and debugging work in Visual Basic by discussing the CLR exception handler and the `Try...Catch...Finally` structure. Also covered are error and trace logging, and how you can use these methods to obtain feedback about how your program is working.

**Part II, "Business Objects and Data Access"**—The next five chapters, Chapter 7 through Chapter 11, look at common structures used to contain and access data. This includes framework elements such as arrays and collections, XML, database access, and Windows Communication Foundation (WCF) services. These chapters focus on gathering data for use within your applications.

➤ **Chapter 7, "Arrays, Collections, Generics"**—This chapter focuses on introducing arrays and collections as a baseline for having a set of related items. It then expands on these basic structures by exploring generics. Introduced with version 2.0 of the .NET Framework, generics enable strongly typed collections.

➤ **Chapter 8, "Using XML with Visual Basic"**—This chapter presents the features of the .NET Framework that facilitate the generation and manipulation of XML. We describe the .NET Framework's XML-related namespaces, and a subset of the classes exposed by these namespaces is examined in detail.

➤ **Chapter 9, "ADO.NET and LINQ"**—This chapter focuses on what you need to know about the ADO.NET object model in order to build flexible, fast, and scalable data-access objects and applications. The evolution of ADO into ADO.NET is explored, and the main objects in ADO.NET that you need to understand in order to build data access into your .NET applications are explained. Additionally, this chapter delves into LINQ to SQL. LINQ offers the capability to easily access underlying data—basically a layer on top of ADO.NET. Microsoft has provided LINQ as a lightweight façade that provides a strongly typed interface to the underlying data stores.

➤ **Chapter 10, "Data Access with the Entity Framework"**—The EF represents Microsoft's implementation of an Entity Relationship Modeling (ERM) tool. Using EF, developers can generate classes to represent the data structures that are defined within SQL Server, and leverage these objects within their applications.

➤ **Chapter 11, "Services (XML/WCF)"**—This chapter looks at how to build service-oriented components that allow for standards-based communications over a number of protocols. WCF is Microsoft's answer for component communications within and outside of the enterprise.

**Part III, "Specialized Topics and Libraries"**—Chapters 12 through Chapter 14 focus on creating client applications. These chapters address Windows Store applications, which are exclusive to the Windows RT CLR. In parallel it discusses building applications for WPF that are compatible with earlier versions of Windows and which represent the majority of corporate applications. Chapter 14 moves to looking at web-based applications and interfaces. Chapters 15 through 20 then focus on topics such as localization, windows services, security, multi-threaded applications, and deployment.

➤ **Chapter 12, "XAML Essentials"**—Introduced in .NET 3.0, XAML is the syntax originally associated with the Windows Presentation Foundation. With the transition to Windows Store applications, XAML is still applicable, although it behaves slightly differently. This chapter introduces you to building applications focused on the XAML model of user interface declaration.

➤ **Chapter 13, "Creating XAML Applications for Windows 8"**—In this chapter you go deeper into the specifics around building Windows Store applications. The chapter looks at specific conventions around Windows 8 user interfaces, new features specific to Windows 8, and leveraging the visual designer that is part of Visual Studio 2012. This chapter gets into the nuts-and-bolts steps for handling things like Live Tiles and contracts for Windows 8 integration.

➤ **Chapter 14, "Applications with ASP.NET, MVC, JavaScript, and HTML"**—This chapter goes through web-based application development. It covers examples of everything from ASP.NET with AJAX and CSS to MVC (Model-View-Controller) applications.

➤ **Chapter 15, "Localization"**—This chapter looks at some of the important items to consider when building your applications for worldwide use. It looks closely at the System. Globalization namespace and everything it offers your applications.

➤ **Chapter 16, "Application Services"**—This chapter examines how Visual Basic is used in the production of Windows Services. The creation, installation, running, and debugging of Windows Services are covered.

➤ **Chapter 17, "Assemblies and Reflection"**—This chapter examines assemblies and their use within the CLR. The structure of an assembly, what it contains, and the information it contains are described. In addition, you will look at the manifest of the assembly and its role in deployment, and how to use remoting.

➤ **Chapter 18, "Security in the .NET Framework"**—This chapter examines the System .Security.Permissions namespace including how it relates to managing permissions. You also look at the System.Security.Cryptography namespace and run through some code that demonstrates its capabilities.

➤ **Chapter 19, "Parallel Programming Using Tasks and Threads"**—This chapter explores threading and explains how the various objects in the .NET Framework enable any of its consumers to develop multithreaded applications. You will learn how threads can be created, how they relate to processes, and the differences between multitasking and multithreading.

➤ **Chapter 20, "Deploying XAML Applications via the Windows 8 Windows Store"**—This chapter takes a close look at using the Windows Store to deploy applications. You will see the new Windows 8 deployment options and how to set up an account with the Windows Store for deploying your applications. It also looks at how enterprise developers will deploy custom internal line-of-business applications on Windows 8.

# WHAT YOU NEED TO USE THIS BOOK

Although it is possible to create Visual Basic applications using the command-line tools contained in the .NET Framework, you'll want Visual Studio 2012, which includes the .NET Framework 4.5, to get the most out of this book. In addition, note the following:

➤ You'll need .NET Framework 4.5, which is installed with whatever version of Visual Studio 2012 you select.

➤ Some chapters make use of SQL Server 2008. You can run the example code using Microsoft's SQL Express, which is a free download.

➤ To build Windows Store applications you'll need to be running Windows 8 or Windows Server 2012. Visual Studio 2012 doesn't require this operating system but building these applications does.

Several chapters make use of Internet Information Services (IIS). IIS is part of every operating system released by Microsoft since Windows XP, but on newer operating systems you'll need to run as administrator to develop against it. Alternatively, you can leverage the development server that ships with Visual Studio 2012.

The source code for the samples is available for download from the Wrox website at:

```
www.wrox.com/remtitle.cgi?isbn=9781118314456
```

# CONVENTIONS

To help you get the most from the text and keep track of what's happening, we've used a number of conventions throughout the book.

> **WARNING** *Boxes like this one hold important, not-to-be forgotten information that is directly relevant to the surrounding text.*

> **NOTE** *Tips, hints, tricks, and asides to the current discussion are offset and placed in italics like this.*

As for styles in the text:

➤ We *italicize* new terms and important words when we introduce them.

➤ We show keyboard strokes like this: Ctrl+A.

➤ We show filenames, URLs, and code within the text like so: `persistence.properties`.

➤ We present code in two different ways:

```
We use a monofont type with no highlighting for most code examples.
We use bold to emphasize code that is particularly important in the present
context or to show changes from a previous code snippet.
```

## SOURCE CODE

As you work through the examples in this book, you may choose either to type in all the code manually, or to use the source code files that accompany the book. All the source code used in this book is available for download at `www.wrox.com`. Specifically for this book, the code download is on the Download Code tab at:

```
www.wrox.com/remtitle.cgi?isbn=9781118314456
```

You can also search for the book at www.wrox.com by ISBN (the ISBN for this book is 978-1-118-31445-6) to find the code. And a complete list of code downloads for all current Wrox books is available at `www.wrox.com/dynamic/books/download.aspx`.

At the beginning of each chapter that contains downloadable code, we've provided a reminder of the link you can use to find the code files. Throughout the chapter, you'll also find references to the names of code files in the listing titles or the text.

Most of the code on `www.wrox.com` is compressed in a .ZIP, .RAR archive, or similar archive format appropriate to the platform. Once you download the code, just decompress it with an appropriate compression tool.

> **NOTE** *Because many books have similar titles, you may find it easiest to search by ISBN; this book's ISBN is 978-1-118-31445-6.*

Once you download the code, just decompress it with your favorite compression tool. Alternately, you can go to the main Wrox code download page at `www.wrox.com/dynamic/books/download .aspx` to see the code available for this book and all other Wrox books.

## ERRATA

We make every effort to ensure that there are no errors in the text or in the code. However, no one is perfect, and mistakes do occur. If you find an error in one of our books, like a spelling mistake or a faulty piece of code, we would be very grateful for your feedback. By sending in errata, you may save another reader hours of frustration, and at the same time, you will be helping us provide even higher-quality information.

To find the errata page for this book, go to

```
www.wrox.com/remtitle.cgi?isbn=9781118314456
```

and click the Errata link. On this page you can view all errata that has been submitted for this book and posted by Wrox editors.

If you don't spot "your" error on the Book Errata page, go to `www.wrox.com/contact/ techsupport.shtml` and complete the form there to send us the error you have found. We'll check the information and, if appropriate, post a message to the book's errata page and fix the problem in subsequent editions of the book.

## P2P.WROX.COM

For author and peer discussion, join the P2P forums at `http://p2p.wrox.com`. The forums are a Web-based system for you to post messages relating to Wrox books and related technologies and interact with other readers and technology users. The forums offer a subscription feature to e-mail you topics of interest of your choosing when new posts are made to the forums. Wrox authors, editors, other industry experts, and your fellow readers are present on these forums.

At `http://p2p.wrox.com`, you will find a number of different forums that will help you, not only as you read this book, but also as you develop your own applications. To join the forums, just follow these steps:

1. Go to `http://p2p.wrox.com` and click the Register link.

2. Read the terms of use and click Agree.

3. Complete the required information to join, as well as any optional information you wish to provide, and click Submit.

4. You will receive an e-mail with information describing how to verify your account and complete the joining process.

> **NOTE** *You can read messages in the forums without joining P2P, but in order to post your own messages, you must join.*

Once you join, you can post new messages and respond to messages other users post. You can read messages at any time on the Web. If you would like to have new messages from a particular forum e-mailed to you, click the Subscribe to this Forum icon by the forum name in the forum listing.

For more information about how to use the Wrox P2P, be sure to read the P2P FAQs for answers to questions about how the forum software works, as well as many common questions specific to P2P and Wrox books. To read the FAQs, click the FAQ link on any P2P page.

# PART I
# Language Constructs and Environment

# 1

# Visual Studio 2012

## WHAT'S IN THIS CHAPTER?

- ➤ Versions of Visual Studio
- ➤ An introduction to key Visual Basic terms
- ➤ Targeting a runtime environment
- ➤ Creating a baseline Visual Basic Windows Form
- ➤ Project templates
- ➤ Project properties—application, compilation, debug
- ➤ Setting properties
- ➤ IntelliSense, code expansion, and code snippets
- ➤ Debugging
- ➤ The Class Designer

## WROX.COM CODE DOWNLOADS FOR THIS CHAPTER

The wrox.com code downloads for this chapter are found at `www.wrox.com/remtitle .cgi?isbn=9781118314456` on the Download Code tab. The code is in the chapter 1 download and individually named according to the code filenames listed in the chapter.

You can work with Visual Basic without Visual Studio. In practice, however, most Visual Basic developers treat the two as almost inseparable; without a version of Visual Studio, you're forced to work from the command line to create project files by hand, to make calls to the associated compilers, and to manually address the tools necessary to build your application. While Visual Basic supports this at the same level as C#, F#, C++, and other .NET languages, this isn't the typical focus of a Visual Basic professional.

Visual Basic's success rose from its increased productivity in comparison to other languages when building business applications. Visual Studio 2012 increases your productivity and provides assistance in debugging your applications and is the natural tool for Visual Basic developers.

Accordingly this book starts off by introducing you to Visual Studio 2012 and how to build and manage Visual Basic applications. The focus of this chapter is on ensuring that everyone has a core set of knowledge related to tasks like creating and debugging applications in Visual Studio 2012. Visual Studio 2012 is used throughout the book for building solutions. Note while this is the start, don't think of it as an "intro" chapter. This chapter will intro key elements of working with Visual Studio, but will also go beyond that. You may find yourself referencing back to it later for advanced topics that you glossed over your first time through. Visual Studio is a powerful and, at times, complex tool, and you aren't expected to master it on your first read through this chapter.

This chapter provides an overview of many of the capabilities of Visual Studio 2012. The goal is to demonstrate how Visual Studio makes you, as a developer, more productive and successful.

## VISUAL STUDIO 2012

For those who aren't familiar with the main elements of .NET development there is the common language runtime (CLR), the .NET Framework, the various language compilers and Visual Studio. Each of these plays a role; for example, the CLR—covered in Chapter 2—manages the execution of code on the .NET platform. Thus code can be targeted to run on a specific version of this runtime environment.

The .NET Framework provides a series of classes that developers leverage across implementation languages. This framework or Class Library is versioned and targeted to run on a specific minimum version of the CLR. It is this library along with the language compilers that are referenced by Visual Studio. Visual Studio allows you to build applications that target one or more of the versions of what is generically called .NET.

In some cases the CLR and the .NET Framework will be the same; for example, .NET Framework version 1.0 ran on CLR version 1.0. In other cases just as Visual Basic's compiler is on version 10, the .NET Framework might have a newer version targeting an older version of the CLR.

The same concepts carry into Visual Studio. Visual Studio 2003 was focused on .NET 1.1, while the earlier Visual Studio .NET (2002) was focused on .NET 1.0. Originally, each version of Visual Studio was optimized for a particular version of .NET. Similarly, Visual Studio 2005 was optimized for .NET 2.0, but then along came the exception of the .NET Framework version 3.0. This introduced a new Framework, which was supported by the same version 2.0 of the CLR, but which didn't ship with a new version of Visual Studio.

Fortunately, Microsoft chose to keep Visual Basic and ASP.NET unchanged for the .NET 3.0 Framework release. However, when you looked at the .NET 3.0 Framework elements, such as Windows Presentation Foundation, Windows Communication Foundation, and Windows Workflow Foundation, you found that those items needed to be addressed outside of Visual Studio. Thus, while Visual Studio is separate from Visual Basic, the CLR, and .NET development, in practical terms Visual Studio was tightly coupled to each of these items.

When Visual Studio 2005 was released, Microsoft expanded on the different versions of Visual Studio available for use. Earlier editions of this book actually went into some of the differences between these versions. This edition focuses on using Visual Studio's core features. While some of the project types require Visual Studio Professional, the core features are available in all versions of Visual Studio.

In Visual Studio 2008, Microsoft loosened the framework coupling by providing robust support that allowed the developer to target any of three different versions of the .NET Framework. Visual Studio 2010 continued this, enabling you to target an application to run on .NET 2.0, .NET 3.0, .NET 3.5, or .NET 4.

However, that support didn't mean that Visual Studio 2010 wasn't still tightly coupled to a specific version of each compiler. In fact, the new support for targeting frameworks is designed to support a runtime environment, not a compile-time environment. This is important, because when projects from previous versions of Visual Studio are converted to the Visual Studio 2010 format, they cannot be reopened by a previous version.

The reason for this was that the underlying build engine used by Visual Studio 2010 accepts syntax changes and even language feature changes, but previous versions of Visual Studio do not recognize these new elements of the language. Thus, if you move source code written in Visual Studio 2010 to a previous version of Visual Studio, you face a strong possibility that it would fail to compile. However, Visual Studio 2012 changed this, and it is now possible to open projects associated with older versions of Visual Studio in Visual Studio 2012, work on them, and have someone else continue to work in an older version of Visual Studio.

Multitargeting support continues to ensure that your application will run on a specific version of the framework. Thus, if your organization is not supporting .NET 3.0, .NET 3.5, or .NET 4, you can still use Visual Studio 2012. The compiler generates byte code based on the language syntax, and at its core that byte code is version agnostic. Where you can get in trouble is if you reference one or more classes that aren't part of a given version of the CLR. Visual Studio therefore manages your references when targeting an older version of .NET, allowing you to be reasonably certain that your application will not reference files from one of those other framework versions. Multitargeting is what enables you to safely deploy without requiring your customers to download additional framework components they don't need.

Complete coverage of all of Visual Studio's features warrants a book of its own, especially when you take into account all of the collaborative and Application Lifecycle Management features introduced by Team Foundation Server and its tight integration with both Team Build and SharePoint Server.

## VISUAL BASIC KEYWORDS AND SYNTAX

Those with previous experience with Visual Basic are already familiar with many of the language keywords and syntax. However, not all readers will fall into this category, so this introductory section is for those new to Visual Basic. A glossary of keywords is provided, after which this section will use many of these keywords in context.

Although they're not the focus of the chapter, with so many keywords, a glossary follows. Table 1-1 briefly summarizes most of the keywords discussed in the preceding section, and provides a short description of their meaning in Visual Basic. Keep in mind there are two commonly used terms that aren't Visual Basic keywords that you will read repeatedly, including in the glossary:

1. **Method**—A generic name for a named set of commands. In Visual Basic, both subs and functions are types of methods.

2. **Instance**—When a class is created, the resulting object is an instance of the class's definition.

**TABLE 1-1:** Commonly Used Keywords in Visual Basic

| KEYWORD | DESCRIPTION |
| --- | --- |
| Namespace | A collection of classes that provide related capabilities. For example, the System .Drawing namespace contains classes associated with graphics. |
| Class | A definition of an object. Includes properties (variables) and methods, which can be Subs or Functions. |
| Sub | A method that contains a set of commands, allows data to be transferred as parameters, and provides scope around local variables and commands, but does not return a value. |
| Function | A method that contains a set of commands, returns a value, allows data to be transferred as parameters, and provides scope around local variables and commands. |
| Return | Ends the currently executing Sub or Function. Combined with a return value for functions. |
| Dim | Declares and defines a new variable. |
| New | Creates an instance of an object. |
| Nothing | Used to indicate that a variable has no value. Equivalent to null in other languages and databases. |
| Me | A reference to the instance of the object within which a method is executing. |
| Console | A type of application that relies on a command-line interface. Console applications are commonly used for simple test frames. Also refers to a .NET Framework Class that manages access of the command window to and from which applications can read and write text data. |
| Module | A code block that isn't a class but which can contain Sub and Function methods. Used when only a single copy of code or data is needed in memory. |

Even though the focus of this chapter is on Visual Studio, during this introduction a few basic elements of Visual Basic will be referenced and need to be spelled out. This way, as you read, you can understand the examples. Chapter 2, for instance, covers working with namespaces, but some examples and other code are introduced in this chapter that will mention the term, so it is defined here.

Let's begin with namespace. When .NET was being created, the developers realized that attempting to organize all of these classes required a system. A namespace is an arbitrary system that the .NET developers used to group classes containing common functionality. A namespace can have multiple levels of grouping, each separated by a period (.). Thus, the System namespace is the basis for classes that are used throughout .NET, while the Microsoft.VisualBasic namespace is used for classes in the underlying .NET Framework but specific to Visual Basic. At its most basic level, a namespace does not imply or indicate anything regarding the relationships between the class implementations in that namespace; it is just a way of managing the complexity of both your custom application's classes, whether it be a small or large collection, and that of the .NET Framework's thousands of classes. As noted earlier, namespaces are covered in detail in Chapter 2.

Next is the keyword Class. Chapters 3 and 4 provide details on object-oriented syntax and the related keywords for objects and types, but a basic definition of this keyword is needed here. The Class keyword designates a common set of data and behavior within your application. The class is the definition of an object, in the same way that your source code, when compiled, is the definition of an application. When someone runs your code, it is considered to be an instance of your application. Similarly, when your code creates or instantiates an object from your class definition, it is considered to be an instance of that class, or an instance of that object.

Creating an instance of an object has two parts. The first part is the New command, which tells the compiler to create an instance of that class. This command instructs code to call your object definition and instantiate it. In some cases you might need to run a method and get a return value, but in most cases you use the New command to assign that instance of an object to a variable. A variable is quite literally something which can hold a reference to that class's instance.

To declare a variable in Visual Basic, you use the Dim statement. *Dim* is short for "dimension" and comes from the ancient past of Basic, which preceded Visual Basic as a language. The idea is that you are telling the system to allocate or dimension a section of memory to hold data. As discussed in subsequent chapters on objects, the Dim statement may be replaced by another keyword such as Public or Private that not only dimensions the new value, but also limits the accessibility of that value. Each variable declaration uses a Dim statement similar to the example that follows, which declares a new variable, winForm:

```
Dim winForm As System.Windows.Forms.Form = New System.Windows.Forms.Form()
```

In the preceding example, the code declares a new variable (winForm) of the type Form. This variable is then set to an instance of a Form object. It might also be assigned to an existing instance of a Form object or alternatively to Nothing. The Nothing keyword is a way of telling the system that the variable does not currently have any value, and as such is not actually using any memory on the heap. Later in this chapter, in the discussion of value and reference types, keep in mind that only reference types can be set to Nothing.

A class consists of both state and behavior. State is a fancy way of referring to the fact that the class has one or more values also known as properties associated with it. Embedded in the class definition are zero or more Dim statements that create variables used to store the properties of the class. When you create an instance of this class, you create these variables; and in most cases the class contains logic to populate them. The logic used for this, and to carry out other actions, is the *behavior*. This behavior is encapsulated in what, in the object-oriented world, are known as *methods*.

However, Visual Basic doesn't have a "method" keyword. Instead, it has two other keywords that are brought forward from Visual Basic's days as a procedural language. The first is Sub. Sub, short for "subroutine," and it defines a block of code that carries out some action. When this block of code completes, it returns control to the code that called it without returning a value. The following snippet shows the declaration of a Sub:

```
Private Sub Load(ByVal object As System.Object)

End Sub
```

The preceding example shows the start of a Sub called Load. For now you can ignore the word Private at the start of this declaration; this is related to the object and is further explained in the next chapter. This method is implemented as a Sub because it doesn't return a value and accepts one parameter when it is called. Thus, in other languages this might be considered and written explicitly as a function that returns Nothing.

The preceding method declaration for Sub Load also includes a single parameter, object, which is declared as being of type System.Object. The meaning of the ByVal qualifier is explained in chapter 2, but is related to how that value is passed to this method. The code that actually loads the object would be written between the line declaring this method and the End Sub line.

Alternatively, a method can return a value; Visual Basic uses the keyword Function to describe this behavior. In Visual Basic, the only difference between a Sub and the method type Function is the return type.

The Function declaration shown in the following sample code specifies the return type of the function as a Long value. A Function works just like a Sub with the exception that a Function returns a value, which can be Nothing. This is an important distinction, because when you declare a function the compiler expects it to include a Return statement. The Return statement is used to indicate that even though additional lines of code may remain within a Function or Sub, those lines of code should not be executed. Instead, the Function or Sub should end processing at the current line, and if it is in a function, the return value should be returned. To declare a Function, you write code similar to the following:

```
Public Function Add(ByVal ParamArray values() As Integer) As Long
    Dim result As Long = 0
    'TODO: Implement this function
    Return result
    'What if there is more code
    Return result
End Function
```

In the preceding example, note that after the function initializes the second line of code, there is a Return statement. There are *two* Return statements in the code. However, as soon as the first Return statement is reached, none of the remaining code in this function is executed. The Return statement immediately halts execution of a method, even from within a loop.

As shown in the preceding example, the function's return value is assigned to a local variable until returned as part of the Return statement. For a Sub, there would be no value on the line with the Return statement, as a Sub does not return a value when it completes. When returned, the return value is usually assigned to something else. This is shown in the next example line of code, which calls a function:

```
Dim ctrl = Me.Add(1, 2)
```

The preceding example demonstrates a call to a function. The value returned by the function Add is a Long, and the code assigns this to the variable ctrl. It also demonstrates another keyword that you should be aware of: Me. The Me keyword is how, within an object, you can reference the current instance of that object.

You may have noticed that in all the sample code presented thus far, each line is a complete command. If you're familiar with another programming language, then you may be used to seeing a specific character that indicates the end of a complete set of commands. Several popular languages use a semicolon to indicate the end of a command line.

Visual Basic doesn't use visible punctuation to end each line. Traditionally, the BASIC family of languages viewed source files more like a list, whereby each item on the list is placed on its own line. At one point the term was *source listing*. By default, Visual Basic ends each source list item with the carriage-return line feed, and treats it as a command line. In some languages, a command such as X = Y can span several lines in the source file until a semicolon or other terminating character is reached. Thus previously, in Visual Basic, that entire statement would be found on a single line unless the user explicitly indicates that it is to continue onto another line.

To explicitly indicate that a command line spans more than one physical line, you'll see the use of the underscore at the end of the line to be continued. However, one of the features of Visual Basic, originally introduced in version 10 with Visual Studio 2010, is support for an implicit underscore when extending a line past the carriage-return line feed. However, this feature is limited, as there are still places where underscores are needed.

When a line ends with the underscore character, this explicitly tells Visual Basic that the code on that line does not constitute a completed set of commands. The compiler will then continue to the next line to find the continuation of the command, and will end when a carriage-return line feed is found without an accompanying underscore.

In other words, Visual Basic enables you to use exceptionally long lines and indicate that the code has been spread across multiple lines to improve readability. The following line demonstrates the use of the underscore to extend a line of code:

```
MessageBox.Show("Hello World", "A Message Box Title",  _
    MessageBoxButtons.OK, MessageBoxIcon.Information)
```

Prior to Visual Basic 10 the preceding example illustrated the only way to extend a single command line beyond one physical line in your source code. The preceding line of code can now be written as follows:

```
MessageBox.Show("Hello World", "A Message Box Title",
    MessageBoxButtons.OK, MessageBoxIcon.Information)
```

The compiler now recognizes certain key characters like the "," or the "=" as the type of statement where a line isn't going to end. The compiler doesn't account for every situation and won't just look for a line extension anytime a line doesn't compile. That would be a performance nightmare;

however, there are several logical places where you, as a developer, can choose to break a command across lines and do so without needing to insert an underscore to give the compiler a hint about the extended line.

Finally, note that in Visual Basic it is also possible to place multiple different statements on a single line, by separating the statements with colons. However, this is generally considered a poor coding practice because it reduces readability.

## Console Applications

The simplest type of application is a *console application*. This application doesn't have much of a user interface; in fact, for those old enough to remember the MS-DOS operating system, a console application looks just like an MS-DOS application. It works in a command window without support for graphics or input devices such as a mouse. A console application is a text-based user interface that displays text characters and reads input from the keyboard.

The easiest way to create a console application is to use Visual Studio. For the current discussion let's just look at a sample source file for a Console application, as shown in the following example. Notice that the console application contains a single method, a Sub called Main. By default, if you create a console application in Visual Studio, the code located in the Sub Main is the code which is by default started. However, the Sub Main isn't contained in a class; instead, the Sub Main that follows is contained in a Module:

```
Module Module1
    Sub Main()
        Console.WriteLine("Hello World")
        Dim line = Console.ReadLine()
    End Sub
End Module
```

A Module isn't truly a class, but rather a block of code that can contain methods, which are then referenced by code in classes or other modules—or, as in this case, it can represent the execution start for a program. A Module is similar to having a Shared class. The Shared keyword indicates that only a single instance of a given item exists.

For example, in C# the static keyword is used for this purpose, and can be used to indicate that only a single instance of a given class exists. Visual Basic doesn't support the use of the Shared keyword with a Class declaration; instead, Visual Basic developers create modules that provide the same capability. The Module represents a valid construct to group methods that don't have state-related or instance-specific data.

Note a console application focuses on the Console Class. The Console Class encapsulates Visual Basic's interface with the text-based window that hosts a command prompt from which a command-line program is run. The console window is best thought of as a window encapsulating the older nongraphical style user interface, whereby literally everything was driven from the command prompt. A Shared instance of the Console class is automatically created when you start your application, and it supports a variety of Read and Write methods. In the preceding example, if you were to run the code from within Visual Studio's debugger, then the console window would open and close immediately. To prevent that, you include a final line in the Main Sub, which executes a Read statement so that the program continues to run while waiting for user input.

# Creating a Project from a Project Template

While it is possible to create a Visual Basic application working entirely outside of Visual Studio, it is much easier to start from Visual Studio. After you install Visual Studio, you are presented with a screen similar to the one shown in Figure 1-1. Different versions of Visual Studio may have a different overall look, but typically the start page lists your most recent projects on the left, some tips for getting started, and a headline section for topics on MSDN that might be of interest. You may or may not immediately recognize that this content is HTML text; more important, the content is based on an RSS feed that retrieves and caches articles appropriate for your version of Visual Studio.

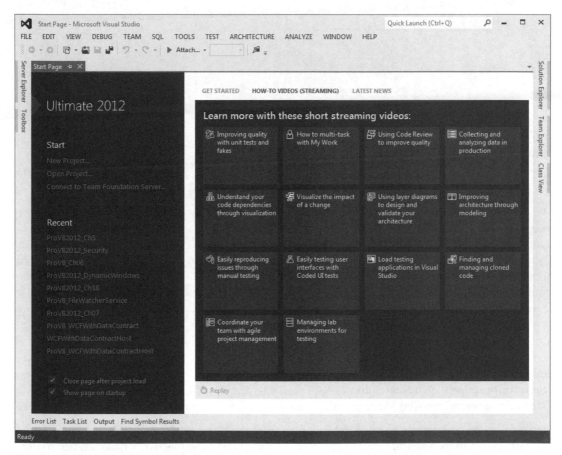

**FIGURE 1-1:** Visual Studio 2012 Start screen

The start page provides a generic starting point either to select the application you intend to work on, to quickly receive vital news related to offers, as shown in the figure, or to connect with external resources via the community links.

Once here, the next step is to create your first project. Selecting File ⇨ New ⇨ Project opens the New Project dialog, shown in Figure 1-2. This dialog provides a selection of templates customized by application type. One option is to create a Class Library project. Such a project doesn't include a user interface; and instead of creating an assembly with an .exe file, it creates an assembly with a .dll file. The difference, of course, is that an .exe file indicates an executable that can be started by the operating system, whereas a .dll file represents a library referenced by an application.

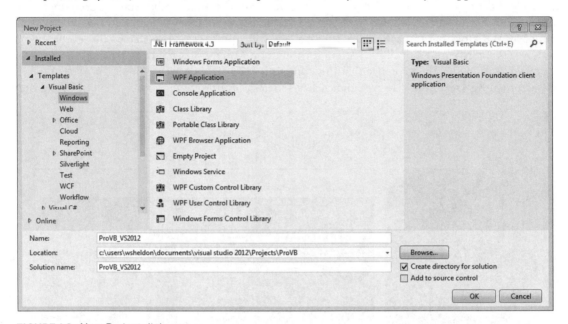

**FIGURE 1-2:** New Project dialogue

Figure 1-2 includes the capability to target a specific .NET version in the drop-down box located above the list of project types. If you change this to .NET 2.0, you'll see the dialog change to show only six project types below the selection listed. For the purposes of this chapter, however, you'll want .NET 4.5 selected, and the template list should resemble what is shown in Figure 1-2. Note this chapter is going to create a Windows .NET application, not a Windows Store application. Targeting keeps you from attempting to create a project for WPF without recognizing that you also need at least .NET 3.0 available on the client. Although you can change your target after you create your project, be very careful when trying to reduce the version number, as the controls to prevent you from selecting dependencies don't check your existing code base for violations. Changing your targeted framework version for an existing project is covered in more detail later in this chapter.

Not only can you choose to target a specific version of the framework when creating a new project, but this window has a new feature that you'll find all over the place in Visual Studio. In the upper-right corner, there is a control that enables you to search for a specific template. As you work through more of the windows associated with Visual Studio, you'll find that a context-specific search capability has often been added to the new user interface.

Reviewing the top level of the Visual Basic tree in Figure 1-2 shows that a project type can be further separated into a series of categories:

➤ **Windows**—These are projects used to create applications that run on the local computer within the CLR. Because such projects can run on any operating system (OS) hosting the framework, the category "Windows" is something of a misnomer when compared to, for example, "Desktop."

➤ **Web**—You can create these projects, including Web services, from this section of the New Project dialog.

➤ **Office**—Visual Studio Tools for Office (VSTO). These are .NET applications that are hosted under Office. Visual Studio 2010 includes a set of templates you can use to target Office 2010, as well as a separate section for templates that target Office 2007.

➤ **Cloud Services**—These are projects that target the Azure online environment model. These projects are deployed to the cloud and as such have special implementation and deployment considerations.

➤ **Reporting**—This project type enables you to create a Reports application.

➤ **SharePoint**—This category provides a selection of SharePoint projects, including Web Part projects, SharePoint Workflow projects, and Business Data Catalog projects, as well as things like site definitions and content type projects. Visual Studio 2010 includes significant new support for SharePoint.

➤ **Silverlight**—With Visual Studio 2010, Microsoft has finally provided full support for working with Silverlight projects. Whereas in the past you've had to add the Silverlight SDK and tools to your existing development environment, with Visual Studio 2010 you get support for both Silverlight projects and user interface design within Visual Studio.

➤ **Test**—This section is available only to those using Visual Studio Team Suite. It contains the template for a Visual Basic Unit Test project.

➤ **WCF**—This is the section where you can create Windows Communication Foundation projects.

➤ **Workflow**—This is the section where you can create Windows Workflow Foundation (WF) projects. The templates in this section also include templates for connecting with the SharePoint workflow engine.

Not shown in that list is a Windows Store project group. That option is available only if you are running Visual Studio 2012 on Windows 8. The project group has five different project types under Visual Basic, but they are available only if you aren't just targeting Windows 8, but are actually using a Windows 8 computer.

This chapter assumes you are working on a Windows 7 computer. The reason for this is that it is expected the majority of developers will continue to work outside of Windows RT. If you are working in a Windows 8 or Windows RT environment, then what you'll look for in the list of Visual Basic templates is a Windows Store application. Keep in mind, however, that those projects will only run on Windows 8 computers. Details of working with Windows Store applications are the focus of Chapters 14 and 15.

Visual Studio has other categories for projects, and you have access to other development languages and far more project types than this chapter has room for. When looking to create an application you will choose from one or more of the available project templates. To use more than a single project to create an application you'll leverage what is known as a solution. A solution is created by default whenever you create a new project and contains one or more projects.

When you save your project you will typically create a folder for the solution, then later if you add another project to the same solution, it will be contained in the solution folder. A project is always part of a solution, and a solution can contain multiple projects, each of which creates a different assembly. Typically, for example, you will have one or more Class Libraries that are part of the same solution as your Windows Form or ASP.NET project. For now, you can select a WPF Application project template to use as an example project for this chapter.

For this example, use ProVB_VS2012 as the project name to match the name of the project in the sample code download and then click OK. Visual Studio takes over and uses the Windows Application template to create a new WPF Application project. The project contains a blank form that can be customized, and a variety of other elements that you can explore. Before customizing any code, let's first look at the elements of this new project.

## The Solution Explorer

The Solution Explorer is a window that is by default located on the right-hand side of your display when you create a project. It is there to display the contents of your solution and includes the actual source file(s) for each of the projects in your solution. While the Solution Explorer window is available and applicable for Express Edition users, it will never contain more than a single project. Visual Studio provides the ability to leverage multiple projects in a single solution. A .NET solution can contain projects of any .NET language and can include the database, testing, and installation projects as part of the overall solution. The advantage of combining these projects is that it is easier to debug projects that reside in a common solution.

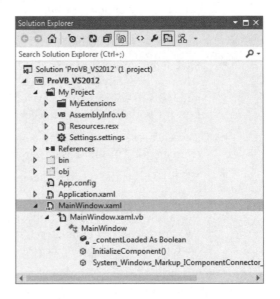

**FIGURE 1-3:** Visual Studio Solution Explorer

Before discussing these files in depth, let's take a look at the next step, which is to reveal a few additional details about your project. Hover over the small icons at the top of the Solution Explorer until you find the one with the hint "Show All Files." Click that button in the Solution Explorer to display all of the project files, as shown in Figure 1-3. As this image shows, many other files make up your project. Some of these, such as those under the My Project grouping, don't require you to edit them directly. Instead, you can double-click the My Project entry in the Solution Explorer and open the pages to edit your project settings. You do not need to change any of the default settings for this project, but the next section of this chapter walks you through the various property screens.

Additionally, with Visual Studio 2012 the Solution Explorer goes below the level of just showing files. Notice how in Figure 1-3 that below the reference to the VB file, the display transitions into one that gives you class-specific information. The Solution Explorer is no longer just a tool to take you to the files in your project, but a tool that allows you to delve down into your class and jump directly to elements of interest within your solution.

The `bin` and `obj` directories shown are used when building your project. The `obj` directory contains the first-pass object files used by the compiler to create your final executable file. The "binary" or compiled version of your application is then placed in the `bin` directory by default. Of course, referring to the Microsoft intermediate language (MSIL) code as binary is something of a misnomer, as the actual translation to binary does not occur until runtime, when your application is compiled by the just-in-time (JIT) compiler. However, Microsoft continues to use the bin directory as the default output directory for your project's compilation.

Figure 1-3 also shows that the project contains an app.config file by default. Most experienced ASP.NET developers are familiar with using web.config files. app.config files work on the same principle in that they contain XML, which is used to store project-specific settings such as database connection strings and other application-specific settings. Using a .config file instead of having your settings in the Windows registry enables your applications to run side-by-side with another version of the application without the settings from either version affecting the other.

For now however, you have a new project and an initial XAML Window, MainWindows, available in the Solution Explorer. In this case, the MainWIndows.xaml file is the primary file associated with the default window. You'll be customizing this window shortly, but before looking at that, it would be useful to look at some of the settings available by opening your Project Properties. An easy way to do this is to right-click on the My Project heading shown in Figure 1-3.

## Project Properties

Visual Studio uses a vertically tabbed display for editing your project settings. The Project Properties display shown in Figure 1-4 provides access to the newly created ProVB_VS2012 project settings. The Project Properties window gives you access to several different aspects of your project. Some, such as Signing, Security, and Publish, are covered in later chapters.

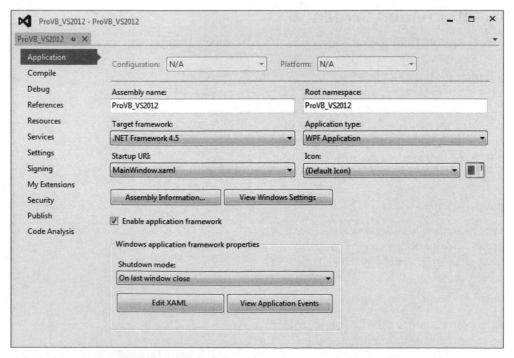

**FIGURE 1-4:** Project Properties—Application tab

You can customize your assembly name from this screen, as well as your root namespace. In addition, you can now change the target framework for your application and reset the type of application and object to be referenced when starting your application. However, resetting the application type is not typically recommended. In some cases, if you start with the wrong application type, it is better to create a new application due to all of the embedded settings in the application template.

In addition, you can change attributes such as the class, which should be called when starting your project. Thus, you could select a screen other than the default `MainWindow.xaml` as the startup screen. You can also associate a given default icon with your form (refer to Figure 1-4).

Near the middle of the dialogue are two buttons. Assembly Information is covered in the next section. The other button, labeled `View Windows Settings`, refers to your `app.manifest` file. Within this file are application settings for things like Windows compatibility and User Access Control settings, which enable you to specify that only certain users can successfully start your application. In short, you have the option to limit your application access to a specific set of users. The UAC settings are covered in more detail in Chapter 18.

Finally, there is a section associated with enabling an application framework. The application framework is a set of optional components that enable you to extend your application with custom events and items, or access your base application class, with minimal effort. Enabling the framework is the default, but unless you want to change the default settings, the behavior is the same—as if the framework weren't enabled. The third button, View Application Events, adds a new source file, `ApplicationEvents.vb`, to your project, which includes documentation about which application events are available.

## Assembly Information Screen

Selecting the Assembly Information button from within your My Project window opens the Assembly Information dialogue. Within this dialogue, shown in Figure 1-5, you can define file properties, such as your company's name and versioning information, which will be embedded in the operating system's file attributes for your project's output. Note these values are stored as assembly attributes in `AssemblyInfo.vb`.

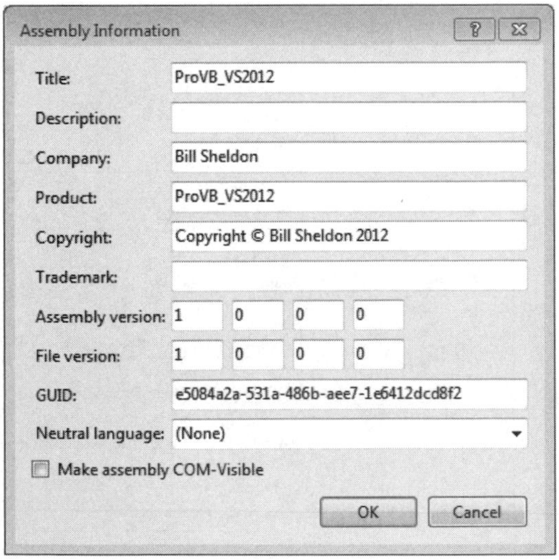

### Assembly Attributes

The `AssemblyInfo.vb` file contains attributes that are used to set information about the assembly. Each attribute has an *assembly modifier*, shown in the following example:

```
<Assembly: AssemblyTitle("")>
```

All the attributes set within this file provide information that is contained within the assembly metadata. The attributes contained within the file are summarized in Table 1-2:

**FIGURE 1-5:** Project Properties Assembly Information dialogue

**TABLE 1-2:** Attributes of the AssemblyInfo.vb File

| ATTRIBUTE | DESCRIPTION |
| --- | --- |
| Assembly Title | This sets the name of the assembly, which appears within the file properties of the compiled file as the description. |
| Assembly Description | This attribute is used to provide a textual description of the assembly, which is added to the `Comments` property for the file. |
| Assembly Company | This sets the name of the company that produced the assembly. The name set here appears within the Version tab of the file properties. |
| Assembly Product | This attribute sets the product name of the resulting assembly. The product name appears within the Version tab of the file properties. |
| Assembly Copyright | The copyright information for the assembly. This value appears on the Version tab of the file properties. |
| Assembly Trademark | Used to assign any trademark information to the assembly. This information appears on the Version tab of the file properties. |
| Assembly Version | This attribute is used to set the version number of the assembly. Assembly version numbers can be generated, which is the default setting for .NET applications. This is covered in more detail in Chapter 17. |
| Assembly File Version | This attribute is used to set the version number of the executable files. |
| COM Visible | This attribute is used to indicate whether this assembly should be registered and made available to COM applications. |
| Guid | If the assembly is to be exposed as a traditional COM object, then the value of this attribute becomes the ID of the resulting type library. |
| NeutralResourcesLanguageAttribute | If specified, provides the default culture to use when the current user's culture settings aren't explicitly matched in a localized application. Localization is covered further in Chapter 15. |

## Compiler Settings

When you select the Compile tab of the Project Properties, you should see a window similar to the one shown in Figure 1-6. At the top of the display you should see your Configuration and Platform settings. By default, these are for Debug and Any CPU.

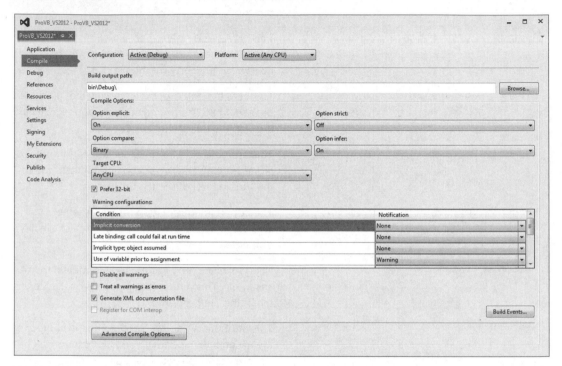

**FIGURE 1-6:** Project Properties—Compile tab

If you don't see these drop-downs in your display, you can restore them by selecting Tools ⇨ Options, and then turning on the Advanced compile options. The main reason to restore these options has to do with being able to properly target the output of your application build.

Before getting to the top four drop-downs related to compile options, let's quickly discuss the fifth drop-down for the Target CPU. In Visual Studio, the default is to target AnyCPU, but this means that on a 64-bit developer workstation, Visual Studio will target a 64-bit assembly for your debug environment. When working on a 64-bit workstation, you must explicitly target an x86 environment in order to enable both Edit and Continue as well as COM-Interop. COM is a 32-bit, so you are required to target a 32-bit/x86 environment to support COM-Interop.

Aside from your default project file output directory and Target CPU, this page contains several compiler options. The Option Explicit, Option Infer, and Option Strict settings directly affect your variable usage. Each of the following settings can be edited by adding an `Option` declaration to the top of your source code file. When placed within a source file each of the following settings applies to all of the code entered in that source file, but only to the code in that file:

➤ **Option Explicit**—This option has not changed from previous versions of Visual Basic. When enabled, it ensures that every variable is explicitly declared. Of course, if you are using Option Strict, then this setting doesn't matter because the compiler won't recognize the type of an undeclared variable. To my knowledge, there's no good reason to ever turn this option off unless you are developing pure dynamic solutions, for which compile time typing is unavailable.

➤ **Option Strict**—When this option is enabled, the compiler must be able to determine the type of each variable, and if an assignment between two variables requires a type conversion—for example, from `Integer` to `Boolean`—then the conversion between the two types must be expressed explicitly.

➤ **Option Compare**—This option determines whether strings should be compared as binary strings or whether the array of characters should be compared as text. In most cases, leaving this as binary is appropriate. Doing a text comparison requires the system to convert the binary values that are stored internally prior to comparison. However, the advantage of a text-based comparison is that the character "A" is equal to "a" because the comparison is case-insensitive. This enables you to perform comparisons that don't require an explicit case conversion of the compared strings. In most cases, however, this conversion still occurs, so it's better to use binary comparison and explicitly convert the case as required.

➤ **Option Infer**—This option was new in Visual Studio 2008 and was added due to the requirements of LINQ. When you execute a LINQ statement, you can have returned a data table that may or may not be completely typed in advance. As a result, the types need to be inferred when the command is executed. Thus, instead of a variable that is declared without an explicit type being defined as an object, the compiler and runtime attempt to infer the correct type for this object.

Existing code developed with Visual Studio 2005 is unaware of this concept, so this option will be off by default for any project that is migrated to Visual Studio 2012. New projects will have this option turned on, which means that if you cut and paste code from a Visual Studio 2005 project into a Visual Studio 2012 project, or vice versa, you'll need to be prepared for an error in the pasted code because of changes in how types are inferred.

From the properties page Option Explicit, Option Strict, Option Compare, and Option Infer can be set to either On or Off for your project. Visual Studio 2012 makes it easy for you to customize specific compiler conditions for your entire project. However, as noted, you can also make changes to the individual compiler checks that are set using something like Option Strict.

Notice that as you change your Option Strict settings in particular, the notifications with the top few conditions are automatically updated to reflect the specific requirements of this new setting. Therefore, you can literally create a custom version of the Option Strict settings by turning on and off individual compiler settings for your project. In general, this table lists a set of conditions that relate to programming practices you might want to avoid or prevent, and which you should definitely be aware of. The use of warnings for the majority of these conditions is appropriate, as there are valid reasons why you might want to use or avoid each but might also want to be able to do each.

Basically, these conditions represent possible runtime error conditions that the compiler can't detect in advance, except to identify that a possibility for that runtime error exists. Selecting a Warning for a setting bypasses that behavior, as the compiler will warn you but allow the code to remain. Conversely, setting a behavior to Error prevents compilation; thus, even if your code might be written to never have a problem, the compiler will prevent it from being used.

An example of why these conditions are noteworthy is the warning of an instance variable accessing a Shared property. A Shared property is the same across all instances of a class. Thus, if a specific instance of a class is updating a Shared property, then it is appropriate to get a warning to that effect. This action is one that can lead to errors, as new developers sometimes fail to realize that a Shared property value is common across all instances of a class, so if one instance updates the value, then the new value is seen by all other instances. Thus, you can block this dangerous but certainly valid code to prevent errors related to using a Shared property.

As noted earlier, option settings can be specific to each source file. This involves adding a line to the top of the source file to indicate to the compiler the status of that Option. The following lines will override your project's default setting for the specified options. However, while this can be done on a per-source listing basis, this is not the recommended way to manage these options. For starters, consistently adding this line to each of your source files is time-consuming and potentially open to error:

```
Option Explicit On
Option Compare Text
Option Strict On
Option Infer On
```

Most experienced developers agree that using Option Strict and being forced to recognize when type conversions are occurring is a good thing. Certainly, when developing software that will be deployed in a production environment, anything that can be done to help prevent runtime errors is desirable. However, Option Strict can slow the development of a program because you are forced to explicitly define each conversion that needs to occur. If you are developing a prototype or demo component that has a limited life, you might find this option limiting.

If that were the end of the argument, then many developers would simply turn the option off and forget about it, but Option Strict has a runtime benefit. When type conversions are explicitly identified, the system performs them faster. Implicit conversions require the runtime system to first identify the types involved in a conversion and then obtain the correct handler.

Another advantage of Option Strict is that during implementation, developers are forced to consider every place a conversion might occur. Perhaps the development team didn't realize that some of the assignment operations resulted in a type conversion. Setting up projects that require explicit conversions means that the resulting code tends to have type consistency to avoid conversions, thus reducing the number of conversions in the final code. The result is not only conversions that run faster, but also, it is hoped, a smaller number of conversions.

Option Infer is a powerful feature. It is used as part of LINQ and the features that support LINQ, but it affects all code. In the past, you needed to write the AS <type> portion of every variable definition in order to have a variable defined with an explicit type. However, now you can dimension a variable and assign it an integer or set it equal to another object, and the AS Integer portion of your declaration isn't required; it is inferred as part of the assignment operation. Be careful with Option Infer; if abused it can make your code obscure, since it reduces readability by potentially hiding the true type associated with a variable. Some developers prefer to limit Option Infer to per-file declarations to limit its use to when it is needed, for example with LINQ.

In addition, note that Option Infer is directly affected by Option Strict. In an ideal world, Option Strict Off would require that Option Infer also be turned off or disabled in the user interface. That isn't the case, although it is the behavior that is seen; once Option Strict is off, Option Infer is essentially ignored.

Also note in Figure 1-6 that below the grid of individual settings is a series of check boxes. Two of these are self-explanatory; the third is the option to generate XML comments for your assembly. These comments are generated based on the XML comments that you enter for each of the classes, methods, and properties in your source file.

Finally, at the bottom is the Advanced Compile Options button. This button opens the Advanced Compiler Settings dialogue shown in Figure 1-7. Note a couple of key elements on this screen, the first being the "Remove integer overflow checks" check box. When these options are not enabled, the result is a performance hit on Visual Basic applications in comparison to C#. The compilation constants are values you shouldn't need to touch normally. Similarly, the generation of serialization assemblies is something that is probably best left in auto mode.

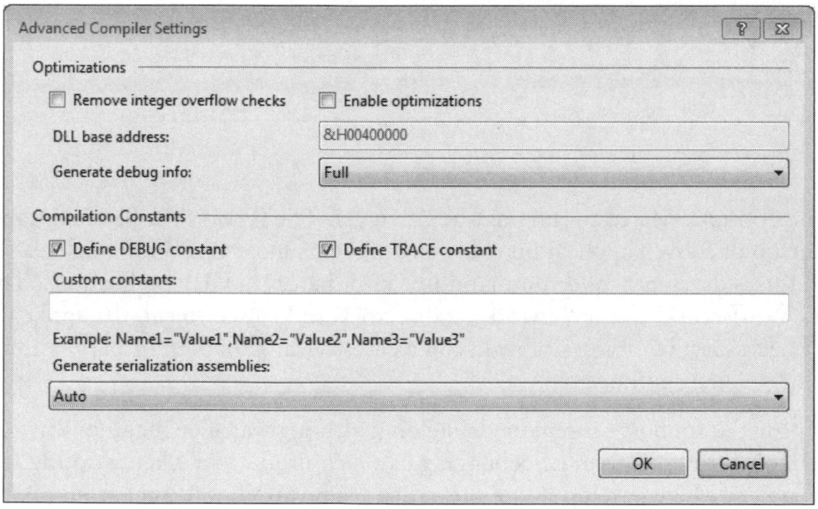

**FIGURE 1-7:** Advanced Compiler Settings

## Debug Properties

Figure 1-8 shows the project debugger startup options from Visual Studio 2012. The default action is to start the current project. However, developers have two additional options. The first is to start an external program. In other words, if you are working on a DLL or a user control, then you might want to have that application start, which can then execute your assembly. Doing this is essentially a shortcut, eliminating the need to bind to a running process. Similarly, for Web development, you can reference a specific URL to start that Web application.

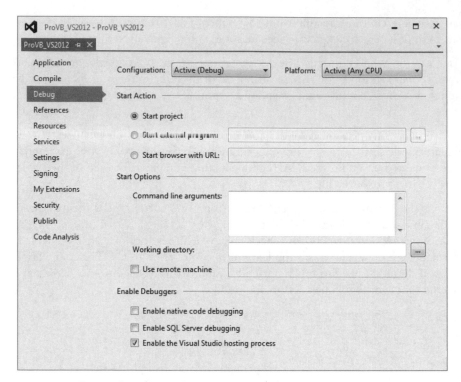

**FIGURE 1-8:** Project Properties—Debug Tab

Next developers have three options related to starting the debugger. The first is to apply command-line arguments to the startup of a given application. This, of course, is most useful for console applications, but in some cases developers add command-line parameters to GUI applications. The second option is to select a different directory, a working directory, to be used to run the application. Generally, this isn't necessary; but it's desirable in some cases because of path or permission requirements or having an isolated runtime area.

As noted, Visual Studio provides support for remote debugging, although such debugging is involved and not configured for simple scenarios. Remote debugging can be a useful tool when working with an integration test environment where developers are prevented from installing Visual Studio but need to be able to debug issues. However, you shouldn't be limited by just using the debugger for understanding what is occurring in your application at runtime.

Finally, as might be expected, users of Visual Studio who work with multiple languages, and who use tools that are tightly integrated with SQL Server, have additional debuggers. Within the Enable Debuggers section of this display are three check boxes. The first of these is for native code debugging and turns on support for debugging outside of the CLR—what is known as *unmanaged code*. As a Visual Basic developer, the only time you should be using unmanaged code is when you are referencing legacy COM components. The developers most likely to use this debugger work in C++.

The next option turns on support for SQL Server debugging, a potentially useful feature. In short, it's possible, although the steps are not trivial, to have the Visual Studio debugging engine step directly into T-SQL stored procedures so that you can see the interim results as they occur within a complex stored procedure.

Finally, the last check box is one you should typically leave unchanged. When you start an application for debugging the default behavior—represented by this check box—it hosts your running application within another process. Called the Visual Studio host, this application creates a dynamic environment controlled by Visual Studio within which your application runs. The host process allows Visual Studio to provide enhanced runtime features. For some items such as debugging partial trust applications, this environment is required to simulate that model. Because of this, if you are using reflection, you'll find that your application name references this host process when debugging.

# References

It's possible to add additional references as part of your project. Similar to the default code files that are created with a new project, each project template has a default set of referenced libraries. Actually, it has a set of imported namespaces and a subset of the imported namespaces also referenced across the project. This means that while you can easily reference the classes in the referenced namespaces, you still need to fully qualify a reference to something less common. For example, to use a `StringBuilder` you'll need to specify the fully qualified name of `System.Text` `.StringBuilder`. Even though the `System.Text` namespace is referenced it hasn't been imported by default.

Keep in mind that changing your target framework does not update any existing references. If you are going to attempt to target the .NET 2.0 Framework, then you'll want to remove references that have a version higher than 2.0.0.0. References such as `System.Core` enable new features in the `System` namespace that are associated with .NET 4.0.

To review details about the imported and referenced namespaces, select the References tab in your Project Properties display, as shown in Figure 1-9. This tab enables you to check for unused references and even define reference paths. More important, it is from this tab that you select other .NET Class Libraries and applications, as well as COM components. Selecting the Add drop-down button gives you the option to add a reference to a local DLL or a Web service.

When referencing DLLs you have three options: reference an assembly from the GAC, reference an assembly based on a file path, or reference another assembly from within your current solution. Each of these options has advantages and disadvantages. The GAC is covered in more detail in Chapter 17.

In addition you can reference other assemblies that are part of your solution. If your solution consists of more than a single project, then it is straightforward and highly recommended to use project references in order to enable those projects to reference each other. While you should avoid circular references—Project A references Project B which references Project A—using project references is preferred over file references. With project references, Visual Studio can map updates to these assemblies as they occur during a build of the solution.

This is different from adding a reference to a DLL that is located within a specified directory. When you create a reference via a path specification, Visual Studio can check that path for an updated copy of the reference, but your code is no longer as portable as it would be with a project reference. More important, unless there is a major revision, Visual Studio usually fails to detect the types of changes you are likely to make to that file during the development process. As a result, you'll need to manually update the referenced file in the local directory of the assembly that's referencing it.

One commonly used technique with custom references is to ensure that instead of referencing third-party controls based on their location, add the property "copy local" for some references so that the version-specific copy of the control deploys with the code that depends on it.

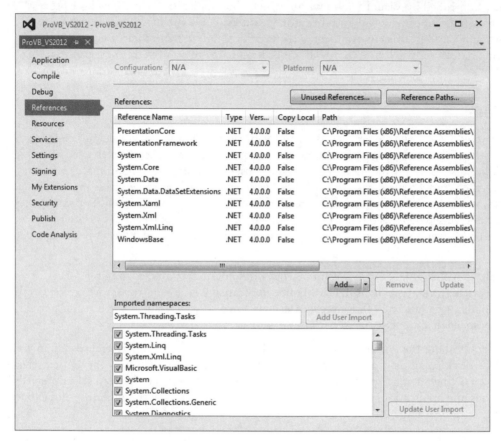

**FIGURE 1-9:** Project Properties—References tab

# Resources

In addition to referencing other assemblies, it is quite common for a .NET application to need to reference things such as images, icons, audio, and other files. These files aren't used to provide application logic but are used at runtime to provide support for the look, feel, and even text used to communicate with the application's user. In theory, you can reference a series of images associated with your application by looking for those images based on the installed file path of your application. Doing so, however, places your application's runtime behavior at risk, because a user might choose to replace or delete your files.

This is where project references become useful. Instead of placing the raw files onto the operating system alongside your executable, Visual Studio will package these files into your executable so that they are less likely to be lost or damaged. Figure 1-10 shows the Resources tab, which enables you to review and edit all the existing resources within a project, as well as import files for use as resources in your project. It even allows you to create new resources from scratch.

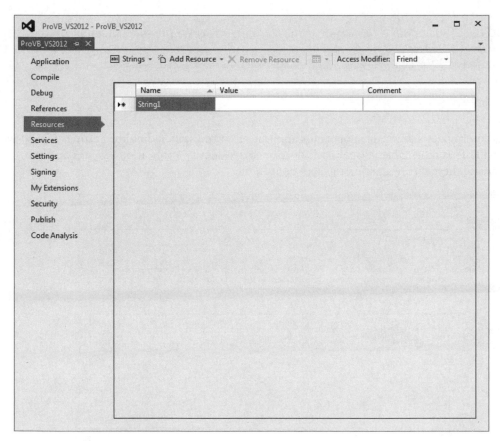

**FIGURE 1-10:** Project Properties—Resources tab

Note one little-known feature of this tab: Using the Add Resource drop-down button and selecting an image (not an existing image but one based on one of the available image types) will create a new image file and automatically open an image editor; this enables you to actually create the image that will be in the image file.

Additionally, within the list of Add Resource items, Visual Studio users can select or create a new icon. Choosing to create a new icon opens Visual Studio's icon editor, which provides a basic set of tools for creating custom icons to use as part of your application. This makes working with .ico files easier because you don't have to hunt for or purchase such files online; instead, you can create your own icons.

However, images aren't the only resources that you can embed with your executable. Resources also apply to the fixed text strings that your application uses. By default, people tend to embed this text directly into the source code so that it is easily accessible to the developer. Unfortunately, this leaves the application difficult to localize for use with a second language. The solution is to group all of those text strings together, thereby creating a resource file containing all of the text strings, which is still part of and easily accessible to the application source code. When the application is converted for use in another language, this list of strings can be converted, making the process of localization easier. Localization is covered in detail in Chapter 15.

> **NOTE** *The next tab is the Services tab. This tab is discussed in more detail in Chapter 11, which addresses services.*

## Settings

Visual Studio provides significant support for application settings, including the Settings tab, shown in Figure 1-11. This tab enables Visual Basic developers to identify application settings and automatically create these settings within the app.config file.

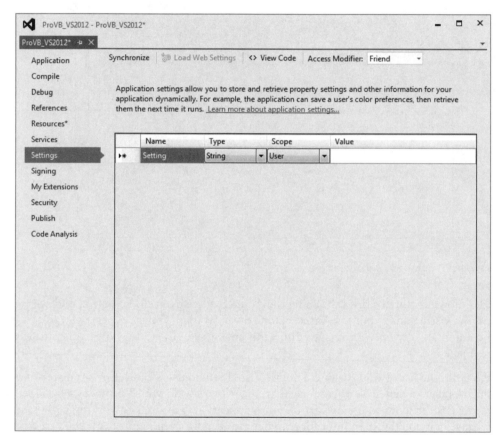

**FIGURE 1-11:** Project Properties—Settings tab

Figure 1-11 illustrates several elements related to the application settings capabilities of Visual Basic. The first setting is of type String. Under .NET 1.x, all application settings were seen as strings, and this was considered a weakness. Accordingly, the second setting, LastLocation, exposes the Type drop-down, illustrating that under you can now create a setting that has a well-defined type.

However, strongly typed settings are not the customizable attribute related to application settings. The very next column defines the scope of a setting. There are two possible options: application wide or user specific. The settings defined with application scope are available to all users of the application.

The alternative is a user-specific setting. Such settings have a default value; in this case, the last location defaults to 0,0. However, once a user has read that default setting, the application generally updates and saves the user-specific value for that setting. As indicated by the LastLocation setting, each user of the application might close it after having moved it to a new location on the screen; and the goal of such a setting would be to reopen the application where it was last located. Thus, the application would update this setting value, and Visual Basic makes it easy to do this, as shown in the following code:

```
My.Settings.LastLocation = Me.Location
My.Settings.Save()
```

That's right—Visual Basic requires only two lines of code that leverage the My namespace in order for you to update a user's application setting and save the new value.

Visual Studio automatically generated all the XML needed to define these settings and save the default values. Note that individual user settings are not saved back into the config file, but rather to a user-specific working directory. In fact, it is possible not only to update application settings with Visual Basic, but also to arrange to encrypt those settings, although this behavior is outside the scope of this chapter.

# Other Project Property Tabs

In addition to the tabs that have been examined in detail, there are other tabs which are more specific. In most cases these tabs are used only in specific situations that do not apply to all projects.

## Signing

This tab is typically used in conjunction with deployment. If you are interested in creating a commercial application that needs to be installed on client systems, you'll want to sign your application. There are several advantages to signing your application, including the capability to publish it via ClickOnce deployment. Therefore, it is possible to sign an application with a developer key if you want to deploy an application internally.

## My Extensions

The My Extensions tab enables you to create and leverage extensions to Visual Basic's My namespace. By default, Visual Studio 2012 ships with extensions to provide My namespace shortcuts for key WPF and Web applications.

## Security

The Secutiry tab enables you to define the security requirements of your application for the purposes of ClickOnce deployment.

## Publish

The Publish tab is used to configure and initiate the publishing of an application. From this tab you can update the published version of the application and determine where to publish it.

## Code Analysis

This Code Analysis tab enables the developer to turn on and configure the static code analysis settings. These settings are used after compilation to perform automated checks against your code. Because these checks can take significant time, especially for a large project, they must be manually turned on.

# PROJECT PROVB_VS2012

The Design view opens by default when a new project is created. If you have closed it, you can easily reopen it using the Solution Explorer by right-clicking `MainWindow.xaml` and selecting View Designer from the pop-up menu. Figure 1-12 illustrates the default view you see when your project template completes. On the screen is the design surface upon which you can drag controls from the Toolbox to build your user interface and update properties associated with your form.

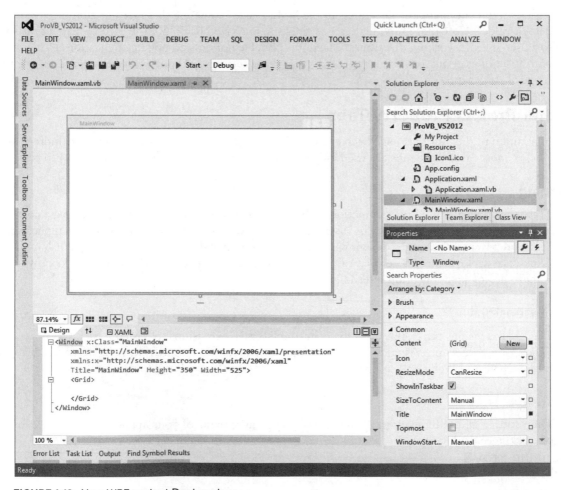

**FIGURE 1-12:** New WPF project Design view

The Properties pane, shown in more detail in Figure 1-13, is by default placed in the lower-right corner of the Visual Studio window. Like many of the other windows in the IDE, if you close it, it can be accessed through the View menu. Alternatively, you can use the F4 key to reopen this window. The Properties pane is used to set the properties of the currently selected control, or for the Form as a whole.

Each control you place on your form has its own distinct set of properties. For example, in the Design view, select your form. You'll see the Properties window adjust to display the properties of MainWindow (refer to Figure 1-13). This is the list of properties associated with your window. If you want to limit how small a user can reduce the display area of your form, then you can now define this as a property.

For your sample, go to the Title property and change the default of MainWindow to "ProVB 2012" Once you have accepted the property change, the new value is displayed as the caption of your form. In addition to your window frame, WPF has by default populated the body of your window with a Grid control. As you look to customize your new window, this grid will allow you to define regions of the page and control the layout of items within the window.

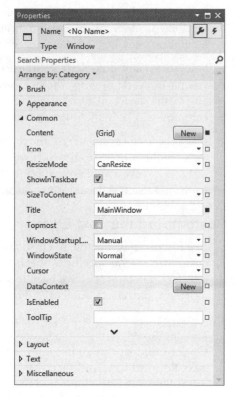

**FIGURE 1-13:** Properties for Main Window

## Tear-Away Tabs

You may have noticed in Figure 1-12 that the Code View and Form Designer windows open in a tabbed environment. This environment is the default for working with the code windows inside Visual Studio, but you can change this. As with any other window in Visual Studio, you can mouse down on the tab and drag it to another location.

What makes this especially useful is that you can drag a tab completely off of the main window and have it open as a standalone window elsewhere. Thus, you can take the current source file you are editing and drag it to a monitor that is separate from the remainder of Visual Studio—examples of this are the Project Properties shown earlier in this chapter in Figures 1-4 through 1-11. If you review those images you'll see that they are not embedded within the larger Visual Studio frame but have been pulled out into their own window. This feature can be very useful when you want to have another source file from your application open either for review or reference while working in a primary file.

## Running ProVB_VS2012

You've looked at the form's properties, so now is a good time to open the code associated with this file by either double clicking the file MainWindow.xaml.vb, or right-clicking MainWindow in the

Solution Explorer and selecting Code view, or right-clicking the form in the Design view and selecting View Code from the pop-up menu. The initial display of the code is simple. There is no implementation code beyond the class definition in the `MainWindows.xaml.vb` file.

So before continuing, let's test the generated code. To run an application from within Visual Studio, you have several options; the first is to click the Start button, which looks like the Play button on any media device. Alternatively, you can go to the Debug menu and select Start. Finally, the most common way of launching applications is to press F5.

Once the application starts, an empty form is displayed with the standard control buttons (in the upper-right corner) from which you can control the application. The form name should be ProVB 2012, which you applied earlier. At this point, the sample doesn't have any custom code to examine, so the next step is to add some simple elements to this application.

## Customizing the Text Editor

In addition to being able to customize the overall environment provided by Visual Studio, you can customize several specific elements related to your development environment. Visual Studio's user interface components have been rewritten using WPF so that the entire display provides a much more graphical environment and better designer support.

Visual Studio provides a rich set of customizations related to a variety of different environment and developer settings. To leverage Visual Studio's settings, select Tools ➪ Options to open the Options dialog, shown in Figure 1-14. To match the information shown in Figure 1-14 select the Text Editor folder, and then the All Languages folder. These settings apply to the text editor across every supported development language. Additionally, you can select the Basic folder, the settings (not shown) available at that level are specific to how the text editor behaves when you edit VB source code.

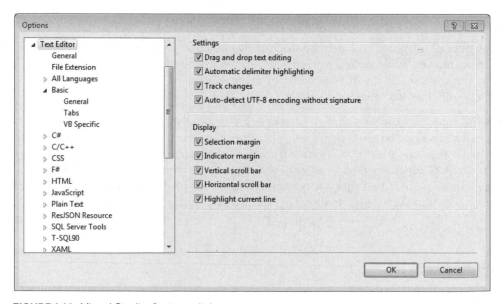

**FIGURE 1-14:** Visual Studio Options dialogue

From this dialogue, it is possible to modify the number of spaces that each tab will insert into your source code and to manage several other elements of your editing environment. Within this dialogue you see settings that are common for all text editing environments, as well as the ability to customize specific settings for specific languages. For example, the section specific to Visual Basic includes settings that allow for word wrapping and line numbers. One little-known but useful capability of the text editor is line numbering. Checking the Line numbers check box will cause the editor to number all lines, which provides an easy way to unambiguously reference lines of code.

Visual Studio also provides a visual indicator so you can track your changes as you edit. Enabling the Track changes setting under the Text Editor options causes Visual Studio to provide a colored indicator in places where you have modified a file. This indicator appears as a colored bar at the left margin of your display. It shows which portions of a source file have been recently edited and whether those changes have been saved to disk.

## ENHANCING A SAMPLE APPLICATION

Switch your display to the Design view. Before you drag a control onto the WPF design surface you are first going to slightly customize the Grid control that is already part of your window. The goal is to define a row definition in the default grid that was generated with your baseline WPF class. As noted, the default window that was created has a Grid that fills the display area. Using your mouse, click on a spot just to the left of the Grid, but about a finger's width below the top of the Grid. This should create a thin horizontal line across your window. In your XAML below the design surface you'll see some new XML that describe your new row.

Once you have defined this row, go over to the properties for your Grid and change the background color of the Grid to black. To do this first make sure the Grid is selected in the designer. Then move to the top of the list of property categories where you should find the 'Brush' category, and select it. To change the value of this property from No Brush, which you'll see is the current selection, select the next rectangle icon for a solid brush. The display will dynamically change within the properties window and you'll see a full color selector. For simplicity, just assign a black brush to the background.

To add more controls to your application, you are going to use the control Toolbox. The Toolbox window is available whenever a form is in Design view. By default, the Toolbox (see Figure 1-15) is docked to the left side of Visual Studio as a tab. When you click this tab, the control window expands, and you can drag controls onto your form. Alternatively, if you have closed the Toolbox tab, you can go to the View menu and select Toolbox.

If you haven't set up the Toolbox to be permanently visible, it will slide out of the way and disappear whenever focus is moved away from it. This helps maximize the available screen real estate. If you don't like this feature (and you won't while working to add controls) you can make the Toolbox permanently visible by clicking the pushpin icon on the Toolbox's title bar.

By default the Toolbox contains the standard controls. All controls loaded in the Toolbox are categorized so it's easier to find them. Before customizing the first control added to this form, take a closer look at the Visual Studio Toolbox. The tools are broken out by category, but this list of categories isn't static. Visual Studio allows you to create your own custom controls. When you create such controls, the IDE will—after the controls have been compiled—automatically add them to the display when you are working in the same solution as the controls. These would be local references to controls that become available within the current solution.

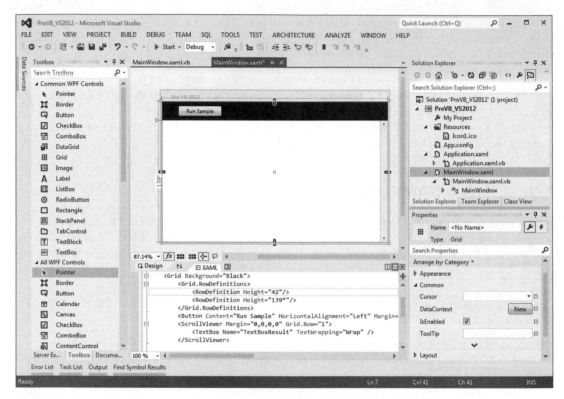

**FIGURE 1-15:** Visual Studio with sample ProVB_VS2012 in the designer

Additionally, depending on whether you are working on a Web or a Windows Forms application, your list of controls in the Toolbox will vary. Windows Forms has a set of controls that leverages the power of the Windows operating system. Web applications, conversely, tend to have controls oriented to working in a disconnected environment.

It's also possible to have third-party controls in your environment. Such controls can be registered with Visual Studio and are then displayed within every project you work on. When controls are added to the Toolbox they typically appear in their own custom categories so that they are grouped together and therefore easy to find.

Next, go to the Toolbox and drag a button onto the top row of the display that you created earlier. Now take a scroll viewer and deposit it within the bottom section of the grid. For the next step you're going to go to the XAML, which is below your Design view. The design will have assigned a group of properties, and your first task is to remove most of these. Your XAML should include a line similar to the following:

```
<ScrollViewer HorizontalAlignment="Left" Height="100" Margin="138,80,0,0"
        Grid.Row="1" VerticalAlignment="Top" Width="100"/>
```

You want to transform that line into one that looks like the following:

```
<ScrollViewer  Margin="0,0,0,0" Grid.Row="1"></ScrollViewer>
```

Notice that you've modified the values for the Margin to be all zero. Additionally, instead of the XML being a self-terminating declaration, you've separated out the termination of the XML.

You'll see that the border of the control now fills the lower section of your display. That means the scroll view control is now ready to have a textbox placed on it. Drag and drop one from the Toolbox, and you'll see your XAML transform to include the following line—and it should have appeared before the start and end tags for the scroll viewer you just added.

```
<TextBox Height="23" TextWrapping="Wrap" Text="TextBox" Width="120"/>
```

Once again you are going to edit this line of XML to simplify it. In this case you want to remove the size attributes and default contents and provide a name for your textbox control so you can reference it from code. The result should be something similar to the following line of XML.

```
<TextBox Name="TextBoxResult" TextWrapping="Wrap" />
```

Finally, select the button you originally dropped on the form. Go to the Properties window and select the Common category. The first property in that category should be Content, and you want to set the label to "Run Sample." Once you've done this, resize the button to display your text. At this point your form should look similar to what is seen in Figure 1-15, introduced earlier in this chapter.

Return to the button you've dragged onto the form. It's ready to go in all respects—however, Visual Studio has no way of knowing what you want to happen when it is used. Having made these changes, double-click the button in the Display view. Double-clicking tells Visual Studio that you want to add an event handler to this control, and by default Visual Studio adds an On_Click event handler for buttons. The IDE then shifts the display to the Code view so that you can customize this handler. Notice that you never provided a name for the button. It doesn't need one—the hook to this handler is defined in the XAML, and as such there is no reason to clutter the code with an extra control name.

## Customizing the Code

With the code window open to the newly added event handler for the Button control, you can start to customize this handler. Although the event handler can be added through the designer, it's also possible to add event handlers from Code view. After you double-clicked the button, Visual Studio transferred you to Code view and displayed your new event handler. Notice that in Code view there are drop-down lists on the top of the edit window. The boxes indicate the current "named" object on the left—in this case, your main window—and the current method on the right—in this case, the click event handler. You can add new handlers for other events for the selected object using these drop-down lists.

The drop-down list on the left side contains only those objects which have been named. Thus, your button isn't listed, but the first named parent for that control is selected: MainWindow. While you can create events for unnamed controls, you can only create handlers in code for named objects. The drop-down list on the right side contains all the events for the selected object only. For now, you have created a new handler for your button's click event, so now you can customize the code associated with this event. Figure 1-16 shows the code for this event handler with generated XML Comments.

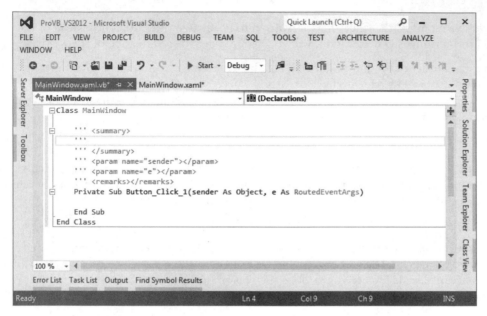

**FIGURE 1-16:** Button_Click_1 event handler

## Adding XML Comments

One of Visual Studio's features is the capability to generate an XML comments template for Visual Basic. XML comments are a much more powerful feature than you might realize, because they are also recognized by Visual Studio for use in IntelliSense. To add a new XML comment to your handler, go to the line before the handler and type three single quotation marks: '''. This triggers Visual Studio to replace your single quotation marks with the following block of comments. You can trigger these comments in front of any method, class, or property in your code.

```
''' <summary>
'''
''' </summary>
''' <param name="sender"></param>
''' <param name="e"></param>
''' <remarks></remarks>
```

Visual Studio provides a template that offers a place to include a summary of what this method does. It also provides placeholders to describe each parameter that is part of this method. Not only are the comments entered in these sections available within the source code, when it's compiled you'll also find an XML file in the project directory, which summarizes all your XML comments and can be used to generate documentation and help files for the said source code. By the way, if you refactor a method and add new parameters, the XML comments also support IntelliSense for the XML tags that represent your parameters.

## IntelliSense, Code Expansion, and Code Snippets

One of the reasons why Microsoft Visual Studio is such a popular development environment is because it was designed to support developer productivity. People who are unfamiliar with Visual Studio might just assume that "productivity" refers to organizing and starting projects. Certainly, as shown by the project templates and project settings discussed so far, this is true, but those features don't speed your development after you've created the project.

This section covers three features that target your productivity while writing code. They are of differing value and are specific to Visual Studio. The first, IntelliSense, has always been a popular feature of Microsoft tools and applications. The second feature, code expansion, is another popular feature available since Visual Studio 2005. It enables you to type a keyword, such as "select," and then press the Tab key to automatically insert a generic select-case code block which you can then customize. Finally, going beyond this, you can use the right mouse button and insert a code snippet at the location of your mouse click. As you can tell, each of these builds on the developer productivity capabilities of Visual Studio.

### IntelliSense

Early versions of IntelliSense required you to first identify a class or property in order to make uses of the IntelliSense feature. Now IntelliSense is activated with the first letter you type, so you can quickly identify classes, commands, and keywords that you need.

Once you've selected a class or keyword, IntelliSense continues, enabling you to not only work with the methods of a class, but also automatically display the list of possible values associated with an enumerated list of properties when one has been defined. IntelliSense also provides a tooltip-like list of parameter definitions when you are making a method call.

Figure 1-17 illustrates how IntelliSense becomes available with the first character you type. Also note that the drop-down window has two tabs on the bottom: one is optimized for the items that you are likely to want, while the other shows you everything that is available. In addition, IntelliSense works with multiword commands. For example, if you type **Exit** and a space, IntelliSense displays a drop-down list of keywords that could follow Exit. Other keywords that offer drop-down lists to present available options include Goto, Implements, Option, and Declare. In most cases, IntelliSense displays more tooltip information in the environment than in past versions of Visual Studio, and helps developers match up pairs of parentheses, braces, and brackets.

Finally, note that IntelliSense is based on your editing context. While editing a file, you may reach a point where you are looking for a specific item to show up in IntelliSense, but when you repeatedly type slightly different versions, nothing appears. IntelliSense recognizes that you aren't in a method or you are outside of the scope of a class, so it removes items that are inappropriate for the current location in your source code from the list of items available from IntelliSense.

### Code Expansion

Going beyond IntelliSense is code expansion. Code expansion recognizes that certain keywords are consistently associated with other lines of code. At the most basic level, this occurs when you declare a new `Function` or `Sub`: Visual Studio automatically inserts the `End Sub` or `End Function` line once you press Enter. Essentially, Visual Studio is expanding the declaration line to include its matching endpoint.

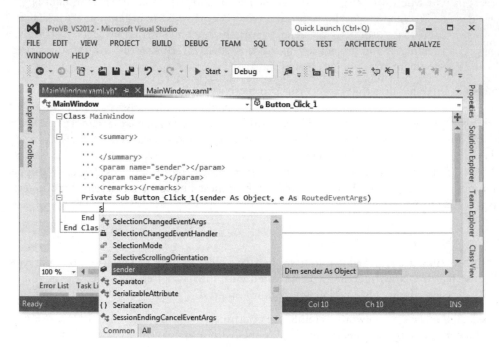

**FIGURE 1-17:** IntelliSense in action

However, true code expansion goes further than this. With true code expansion, you can type a keyword such as `For`, `ForEach`, `Select`, or any of a number of Visual Basic keywords. If you then use the Tab key, Visual Studio will attempt to recognize that keyword and insert the block of code that you would otherwise need to remember and type yourself. For example, instead of needing to remember how to format the control values of a `Select` statement, you can just type the first part of the command **Select** and then press Tab to get the following code block:

```
Select Case VariableName
    Case 1
    Case 2
    Case Else
End Select
```

Unfortunately, this is a case where just showing you the code isn't enough. That's because the code that is inserted has active regions within it that represent key items you will customize. Thus, Figure 1-18 provides a better representation of what is inserted when you expand the `Select` keyword into a full `Select Case` statement.

When the block is inserted, the editor automatically positions your cursor in the first highlighted block—`VariableName`. When you start typing the name of the variable that applies, the editor automatically clears that static `VariableName` string, which is acting as a placeholder. Once you have entered the variable name you want, you can just press Tab. At that point the editor automatically jumps to the next highlighted item. This capability to insert a block of boilerplate code and have it automatically respond to your customization is extremely useful. However, this code isn't needed in the sample. Rather than delete, it use the Ctrl+Z key combination to undo the addition of this Select statement in your code.

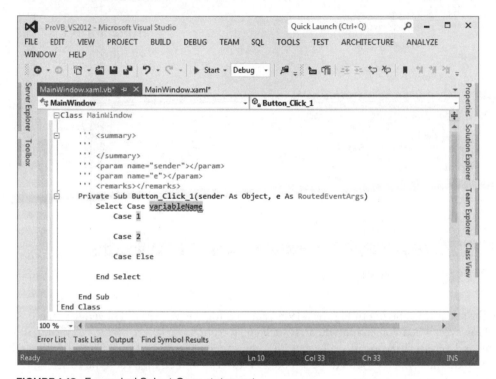

**FIGURE 1-18:** Expanded Select Case statement

Code expansion enables you to quickly shift between the values that need to be customized, but these values are also linked where appropriate, as in the next example. Another code expansion shortcut creates a new property in a class. Position the cursor above your generated event handler to add a custom property to this form. Working at the class level, when you type the letters **prop** and then press the Tab key twice, code expansion takes over. After the first tab you'll find that your letters become the word "Property," and after the second tab the code shown in Figure 1-19 will be added to your existing code. On the surface this code is similar to what you see when you expand the `Select` statement. Note that although you type **prop**, even the internal value is part of this code expansion. Furthermore, Visual Basic implemented a property syntax that is dependent on an explicit backing field. For simplicity, you may not use a backing field on every property, but it's good to see how this expansion provides the more robust backing-field-supported syntax for a property.

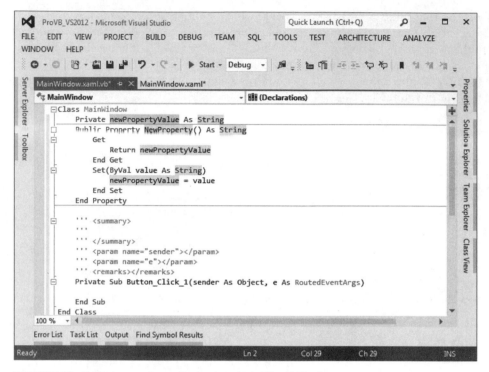

**FIGURE 1-19:** Editing a newly created property in Visual Studio

Notice how the same value String in Figure 1-19 is repeated for the property. The value you see is the default. However, when you change the first such entry from String to Integer, Visual Studio automatically updates all three locations because it knows they are linked. Using the code shown in Figure 1-19, update the property value to be m_Count. Press Tab and change the type to Integer; press Tab again and label the new property Count. Keep in mind this is a temporary state—once you've accepted this template, the connections provided by the template are lost. Once you are done editing, you now have a simple property on this form for use later when debugging.

The completed code should look like the following block:

```
Private m_Count As Integer
Public Property Count() As Integer
    Get
        Return m_Count
    End Get
    Set(ByVal value As Integer)
        m_Count = value
    End Set
End Property
```

This capability to fully integrate the template supporting the expanded code with the highlighted elements, helping you navigate to the items you need to edit, makes code expansion such a valuable tool.

## Code Snippets

With a click of your mouse you can browse a library of code blocks, which, as with code expansion, you can insert into your source file. However, unlike code expansion, these snippets aren't triggered by a keyword. Instead, you right-click and—as shown in Figure 1-20—select Insert Snippet from the context menu. This starts the selection process for whatever code you want to insert.

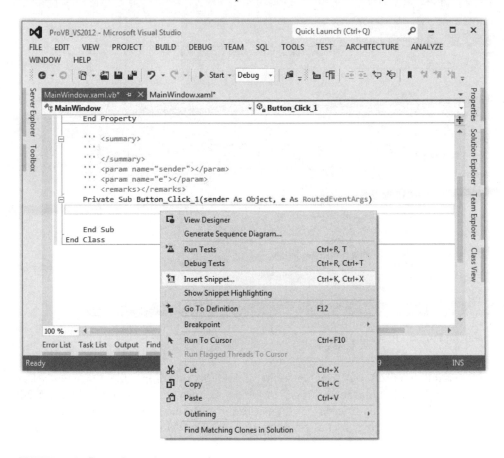

**FIGURE 1-20:** Preparing to insert a snippet

The snippet library, which is installed with Visual Studio, is fully expandable, as discussed later in this chapter. Snippets are categorized by the function on which each is focused. For example, all the code you can reach via code expansion is also available as snippets, but snippets go well beyond that list. There are snippet blocks for XML-related actions, for operating system interface code, for items related to Windows Forms, and, of course, a lot of data-access-related blocks. Unlike code expansion, which enhances the language in a way similar to IntelliSense, code snippets are blocks of code focused on functions that developers often write from scratch.

As shown in Figure 1-21, the insertion of a snippet triggers the creation of a placeholder tag and a context window showing the categories of snippets. Each of the folders can contain a combination of snippet files or subdirectories containing still more snippet files. In addition, Visual Studio includes the folder My Code Snippets, to which you can add your own custom snippet files.

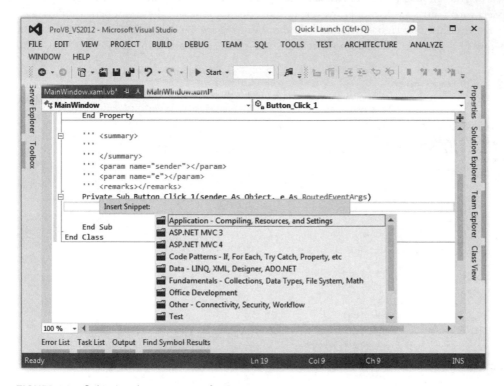

**FIGURE 1-21:** Selecting the category of snippet

Selecting a folder enables you to select from one of its subfolders or a snippet file. Once you select the snippet of interest, Visual Studio inserts the associated code into your source file. Figure 1-22 shows the result of adding an operating system snippet to some sample code. The selected snippet was Windows System—Logging, Processes, Registry, Services Í Windows—Event Logs ➪ Read Entries Created by a Particular Application from the Event Log.

As you can see, this code snippet is specific to reading the Application Log. This snippet is useful because many applications log their errors to the Event Log so that they can be reviewed either locally or from another machine in the local domain. The key, however, is that the snippet has pulled in the necessary class references, many of which might not be familiar to you, and has placed them in context. This reduces not only the time spent typing this code, but also the time spent recalling exactly which classes need to be referenced and which methods need to be called and customized.

Finally, it is also possible to shortcut the menu tree. Specifically, if you know the shortcut for a snippet, you can type that and then press Tab to have Visual Studio insert the snippet. For example, typing **evReadApp** followed by pressing Tab will insert the same snippet shown in Figure 1-22.

Tools such as code snippets and especially code expansion are even more valuable when you work in multiple languages. Keep in mind, however, that Visual Studio isn't limited to the features that come in the box. It's possible to extend Visual Studio not only with additional controls and project templates, but also with additional editing features. Once again this code was merely for demonstration, and you shouldn't keep this snippet within your event handler.

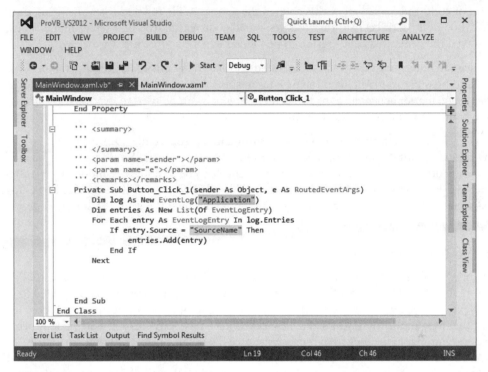

**FIGURE 1-22:** Viewing the snippet code

## Code Regions

Source files in Visual Studio allow you to collapse blocks of code. The idea is that in most cases you can reduce the amount of onscreen code, which seems to separate other modules within a given class, by collapsing the code so it isn't visible; this feature is known as *outlining*. For example, if you are comparing the load and save methods and you have several other blocks of code, then you can effectively "hide" this code, which isn't part of your current focus.

By default, there is a minus sign next to every method (sub or function). This makes it easy to hide or show code on a per-method basis. If the code for a method is hidden, the method declaration is still shown and has a plus sign next to it indicating that the body code is hidden. This feature is very useful when you are working on a few key methods in a module and you want to avoid scrolling through many screens of code that are not relevant to the current task.

It is also possible to create custom regions of code so you can hide and show portions of your source files. For example, it is common to see code where all of the properties are placed in one region, and all of the public methods are placed in another. The #Region directive is used for this within the IDE, though it has no effect on the actual application. A region of code is demarcated by the #Region directive at the beginning and the #End Region directive at the end. The #Region directive that is used to begin a region should include a description that appears next to the plus sign shown when the code is minimized.

The outlining enhancement was in part inspired by the fact that the original Visual Studio designers generated a lot of code and placed all of this code in the main .vb file for that form. It wasn't until Visual Studio 2005 and partial classes that this generated code was placed in a separate file. Thus, the region allowed the generated code section to be hidden when a source file was opened.

Being able to see the underpinnings of your generated UI does make it is easier to understand what is happening, and possibly to manipulate the process in special cases. However, as you can imagine, it can become problematic; hence the #Region directive, which can be used to organize groups of common code and then visually minimize them.

Visual Studio developers can also control outlining throughout a source file. Outlining can be turned off by selecting Edit ⇨ Outlining ⇨ Stop Outlining from the Visual Studio menu. This menu also contains some other useful functions. A section of code can be temporarily hidden by highlighting it and selecting Edit ⇨ Outlining ⇨ Hide Selection. The selected code will be replaced by ellipses with a plus sign next to it, as if you had dynamically identified a region within the source code. Clicking the plus sign displays the code again.

## Customizing the Event Handler

At this point you should customize the code for the button handler, as this method doesn't actually do anything yet. Start by adding a new line of code to increment the property Count you added to the form earlier. Next, use the System.Windows.MessageBox class to open a message box and show the message indicating the number of times the Hello World button has been pressed. Fortunately, because that namespace is automatically imported into every source file in your project, thanks to your project references, you can reference the MessageBox.Show method directly. The Show method has several different parameters and, as shown in Figure 1-23, not only does the IDE provide a tooltip for the list of parameters, it also provides help regarding the appropriate value for individual parameters.

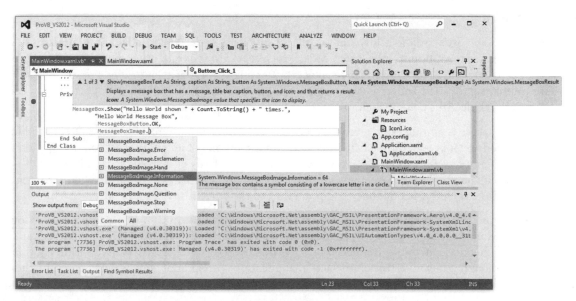

**FIGURE 1-23:** Using IntelliSense to the fullest

The completed call to `MessageBox.Show` should look similar to the following code block. Note that the underscore character is used to continue the command across multiple lines. In addition, unlike previous versions of Visual Basic, for which parentheses were sometimes unnecessary, in .NET the syntax best practice is to use parentheses for every method call:

```
Private Sub Button_Click_1(sender As Object, e As RoutedEventArgs)
    Count += 1
    MessageBox.Show("Hello World shown " + Count.ToString() + " times.",
        "Hello World Message Box",
        MessageBoxButton.OK,
        MessageBoxImage.Information)

End Sub
```

Once you have entered this line of code, you may notice a squiggly line underneath some portions of your text. This occurs when there is an error in the line you have typed. The Visual Studio IDE works more like the latest version of Word—it highlights compiler issues while allowing you to continue working on your code. Visual Basic is constantly reviewing your code to ensure that it will compile, and when it encounters a problem it immediately notifies you of the location without interrupting your work.

## Reviewing the Code

The custom code for this project resides in two source files. The first is the definition of the window, `MainWindows.xaml`. Listing 1-1 displays the final XAML for this file. Note your `Grid.RowDefinition` probably varies from what you'll see in the final listing.

**LISTING 1-1: XAML for main window—MainWindow.xaml**

```xml
<Window x:Class="MainWindow"
    xmlns="http://schemas.microsoft.com/winfx/2006/xaml/presentation"
    xmlns:x="http://schemas.microsoft.com/winfx/2006/xaml"
    Title="Pro VB 2012" Height="350" Width="525">
    <Grid Background="Black">
        <Grid.RowDefinitions>
            <RowDefinition Height="42"/>
            <RowDefinition Height="139*"/>
        </Grid.RowDefinitions>
        <Button Content="Run Sample" HorizontalAlignment="Left"
Margin="37,10,0,0" VerticalAlignment="Top"
Width="100" Height="22" Click="Button_Click_1"/>
        <ScrollViewer Margin="0,0,0,0" Grid.Row="1">
            <TextBox Name="TextBoxResult" TextWrapping="Wrap" />
        </ScrollViewer>
    </Grid>
</Window>
```

This XAML reflects the event handler added for the button. The handler itself is implemented in the accompanying code-behind file `MainWindow.xaml.vb`. That code is shown in Listing 1-2 and contains the custom property and the click event handler for your button.

**LISTING 1-2:** Visual Basic code for main window—MainWindow.xaml.vb

```vb
Class MainWindow
    Private m_Count As Integer
    Public Property Count() As Integer
        Get
            Return m_Count
        End Get
        Set(ByVal value As Integer)
            m_Count = value
        End Set
    End Property

    ''' <summary>
    '''
    ''' </summary>
    ''' <param name="sender"></param>
    ''' <param name="e"></param>
    ''' <remarks></remarks>
    Private Sub Button_Click_1(sender As Object, e As RoutedEventArgs)
        Count += 1
        MessageBox.Show("Hello World shown " + Count.ToString() + " times.",
                "Hello World Message Box",
                MessageBoxButton.OK,
                MessageBoxImage.Information)
    End Sub
End Class
```

At this point, you can test the application, but to do so let's first look at your build options.

## Building Applications

For this example, it is best to build your sample application using the Debug build configuration. The first step is to ensure that Debug is selected as the active configuration. As noted earlier in this chapter around Figure 1-7, you'll find the setting available on your project properties. It's also available from the main Visual Studio display as a drop-down list box that's part of the Standard Toolbar. Visual Studio provides an entire Build menu with the various options available for building an application. There are essentially three options for building applications:

**1.** **Build**—This option uses the currently active build configuration to build the project or solution, depending upon what is available.

**2.** **Rebuild**—By default for performance, Visual Studio attempts to leave components that haven't changed in place. However, in the past developers learned that sometimes Visual Studio wasn't always accurate about what needed to be built. As a result this menu item allows you to tell Visual Studio to do a full build on all of the assemblies that are part of your solution.

**3.** **Clean**—This does what it implies—it removes all of the files associated with building your solution.

The Build menu supports building for either the current project or the entire solution. Thus, you can choose to build only a single project in your solution or all of the projects that have been defined as part of the current configuration. Of course, anytime you choose to test-run your application, the compiler will automatically perform a compilation check to ensure that you run the most recent version of your code.

You can either select Build from the menu or use the Ctrl+Shift+B keyboard combination to initiate a build. When you build your application, the Output window along the bottom edge of the development environment will open. As shown in Figure 1-24, it displays status messages associated with the build process. This window should indicate your success in building the application.

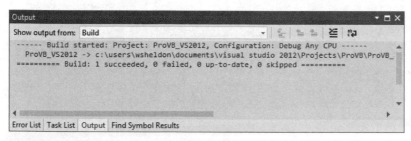

**FIGURE 1-24:** Build window

If problems are encountered while building your application, Visual Studio provides a separate window to help track them. If an error occurs, the Task List window will open as a tabbed window in the same region occupied by the Output window (refer to Figure 1-24). Each error triggers a separate item in the Task List. If you double-click an error, Visual Studio automatically repositions you on the line with the error. Once your application has been built successfully, you can run it, and you will find the executable file located in the targeted directory. By default, for .NET applications this is the \bin subdirectory of your project directory.

## Running an Application in the Debugger

As discussed earlier, there are several ways to start your application. Starting the application launches a series of events. First, Visual Studio looks for any modified files and saves those files automatically. It then verifies the build status of your solution and rebuilds any project that does not have an updated binary, including dependencies. Finally, it initiates a separate process space and starts your application with the Visual Studio debugger attached to that process.

When your application is running, the look and feel of Visual Studio's IDE changes, with different windows and button bars becoming visible (see Figure 1-25). Most important, and new to Visual Studio 2012, the bottom status bar goes from blue to orange to help provide a visual indicator of the change in status.

While your code remains visible, the IDE displays additional windows—by default, the Immediate Window appears as a new tabbed window in the same location as the Output Window. Others, such as the Call Stack, Locals, and Watch windows, may also be displayed over time as you work with the debugger. These windows are used by you, the real debugger, for reviewing the current value of variables within your code.

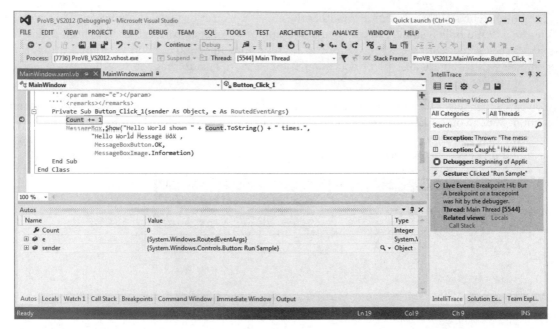

**FIGURE 1-25:** Stopped at a breakpoint while debugging

The true power of the Visual Studio debugger is its interactive debugging. To demonstrate this, with your application running, select Visual Studio as the active window. Change your display to the `MainWindow.xaml.vb` Code view (not Design view) and click in the border alongside the line of code you added to increment the count when the button is clicked. Doing this creates a breakpoint on the selected line (refer to Figure 1-25). Return to your application and then click the "Run Sample" button. Visual Studio takes the active focus, returning you to the code window, and the line with your breakpoint is now selected.

**FIGURE 1-26:** IntelliTrace display at a breakpoint

Visual Studio 2010 introduced a new window that is located in the same set of tabs as the Solution Explorer. As shown in Figure 1-25, the IntelliTrace window tracks your actions as you work with the application in Debug mode. Figure 1-26 focuses on this new feature available to the Ultimate edition of Visual Studio. Sometimes referred to as *historical debugging*, the IntelliTrace window provides a history of how you got to a given state.

When an error occurs during debugging, your first thought is likely to be "What just happened?" But how do you reproduce that error? As indicated in Figure 1-26, the IntelliTrace window tracks the steps you have taken—in this case showing that you had used the Run Code button a second time since the steps shown in Figure 1-26. By providing a historical trail, IntelliTrace enables you to reproduce a given set of steps through your application. You can also filter the various messages either by message type or by thread.

The ability to select these past breakpoints and review the state of variables and classes in your running application can be a powerful tool for tracking down runtime issues. The historical debugging capabilities are unfortunately only available in Visual Studio Ultimate, but they take the power of the Visual Studio debugger to a new level.

However, even if you don't have the power of historical debugging, the Visual Studio debugger is a powerful development ally. It is, arguably, more important than any of the other developer productivity features of Visual Studio. With the execution sitting on this breakpoint, it is possible to control every aspect of your running code. Hovering over the property Count, as shown in Figure 1-27, Visual Studio provides a debug tooltip showing you the current value of this property. This "hover over" feature works on any variable in your local environment and is a great way to get a feel for the different values without needing to go to another window.

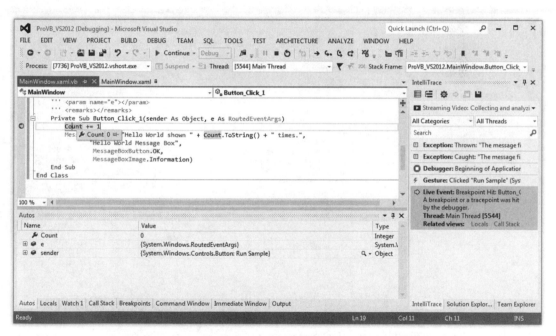

FIGURE 1-27: Using a debug tooltip to display the current value of a variable

Windows such as Locals and Autos display similar information about your variables, and you can use these to update those properties while the application is running. However, you'll note that the image in Figure 1-27 includes a small pin symbol. Using this, you can keep the status window for this variable open in your Code view. Using this will allow you to see the information in the debug window update to show the new value of Count every time the breakpoint is reached.

This isn't the end of it. By clicking on the down arrows you see on the right-hand side of your new custom watch window, just below the pin, you can add one or more comments to your custom watch window for this value. You also have the option to unpin the initial placement of this window and move it off of your Code view display. Not only that, but the custom watch window is persistent in Debug mode. If you stop debugging and restart, the window is automatically restored and remains available until you choose to close it using the close button.

Next, move your mouse and hover over the parameter sender. This will open a window similar to the one for count and you can review the reference to this object. However, note the small plus sign on the right-hand side, which if clicked expands the pop-up to show details about the properties of this object. As shown in Figure 1-28, this capability is available even for parameters like sender, which you didn't define. Figure 1-28 also illustrates a key point about looking at variable data. Notice that by expanding the top-level objects you can eventually get to the properties inside those objects. Within some of those properties on the right-hand side is a little magnifying glass icon. That icon tells you that Visual Studio will open the potentially complex value in any one of up to four visualization tool windows. When working with complex XML or other complex data, these visualizers offer significant productivity benefits by enabling you to review data.

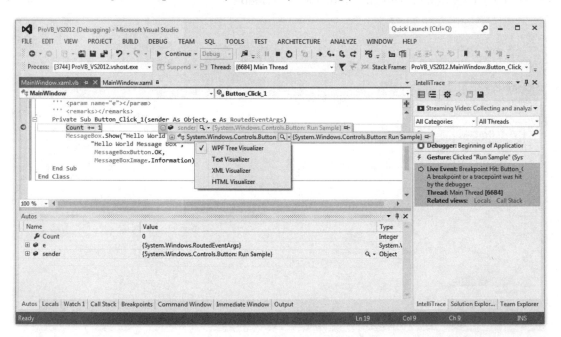

**FIGURE 1-28:** Delving into sender and selecting a visualizer

Once you are at a breakpoint, you can control your application by leveraging the Debug buttons on the Standard toolbar. These buttons, shown in Figure 1-29, provide several options for managing the flow of your application. One of the main changes to Visual Studio 2012 is in fact the layout of the buttons and options visible within the IDE. This is one of those situations: in the past the debug buttons were grouped, but now there are several other buttons that sit between the various actions. From the left you see the Start/Continue button. Then a little further over in about the center of the image is the square that represents stop. It's colored red, and next to it is the icon to restart debugging. Finally, on the far right the last three buttons that use arrows represent Step-In, Step Over, and Step Out, respectively.

**FIGURE 1-29:** Toolbar buttons used in debugging

Step-In tells the debugger to jump to whatever line of code is first within the next method or property you call. Keep in mind that if you pass a property value as a parameter to a method, then the first such line of code is in the Get method of the parameter. Once there, you may want to step out. Stepping out of a method tells the debugger to execute the code in the current method and return you to the line that called the method. Thus, you could step out of the property and then step in again to get into the method you are actually interested in debugging.

Of course, sometimes you don't want to step into a method; this is where the Step-Over button comes in. It enables you to call whatever method(s) are on the current line and step to the next sequential line of code in the method you are currently debugging. The final button, Step-Out, is useful if you know what the code in a method is going to do, but you want to determine which code called the current method. Stepping out takes you directly to the calling code block.

Each of the buttons shown on the debugging toolbar in Figure 1-29 has an accompanying shortcut key for experienced developers who want to move quickly through a series of breakpoints.

Of course, the ability to leverage breakpoints goes beyond what you can do with them at runtime. You can also disable breakpoints that you don't currently want to stop your application flow, and you can move a breakpoint, although it's usually easier to just click and delete the current location, and then click and create a new breakpoint at the new location.

Visual Studio provides additional properties for managing and customizing breakpoints. As shown in Figure 1-30, it's also possible to add specific properties to your breakpoints. The context menu shows several possible options.

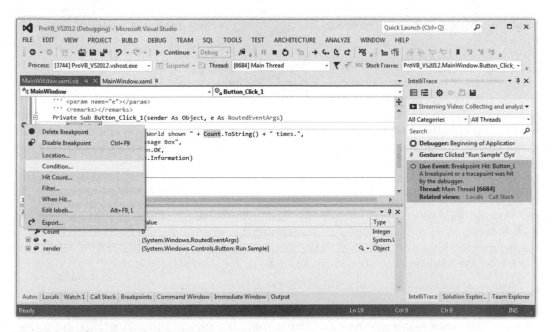

**FIGURE 1-30:** Customizing a breakpoint

More important, it's possible to specify that a given breakpoint should execute only if a certain value is defined (or undefined). In other words, you can make a given breakpoint conditional, and a pop-up window enables you to define this condition. Similarly, if you've ever wanted to stop, for example, on the thirty-seventh iteration of a loop, then you know the pain of repeatedly stopping at a breakpoint inside a loop. Visual Studio enables you to specify that a given breakpoint should stop your application only after a specified number of hits.

The next option is one of the more interesting options if you need to carry out a debug session in a live environment. You can create a breakpoint on the debug version of code and then add a filter that ensures you are the only user to stop on that breakpoint. For example, if you are in an environment where multiple people are working against the same executable, then you can add a breakpoint that won't affect the other users of the application.

Similarly, instead of just stopping at a breakpoint, you can also have the breakpoint execute some other code, possibly even a Visual Studio macro, when the given breakpoint is reached. These actions are rather limited and are not frequently used, but in some situations this capability can be used to your advantage.

Note that breakpoints are saved when a solution is saved by the IDE. There is also a Breakpoints window, which provides a common location for managing breakpoints that you may have set across several different source files.

Finally, at some point you are going to want to debug a process that isn't being started from Visual Studio—for example, if you have an existing website that is hosting a DLL you are interested in debugging. In this case, you can leverage Visual Studio's capability to attach to a running process and debug that DLL. At or near the top (depending on your settings) of the Tools menu in Visual Studio is the Attach to Process option. This menu option opens a dialog showing all of your processes. You could then select the process and have the DLL project you want to debug loaded in Visual Studio. The next time your DLL is called by that process, Visual Studio will recognize the call and hit a breakpoint set in your code. This is covered in more detail in Chapter 16.

## Other Debug-Related Windows

As noted earlier, when you run an application in Debug mode, Visual Studio can open a series of windows related to debugging. Each of these windows provides a view of a limited set of the overall environment in which your application is running. From these windows, it is possible to find things such as the list of calls (stack) used to get to the current line of code or the present value of all the variables currently available. Visual Studio has a powerful debugger that is fully supported with IntelliSense, and these windows extend the debugger.

### Output

Recall that the build process puts progress messages in this window. Similarly, your program can also place messages in it. Several options for accessing this window are discussed in later chapters, but at the simplest level the Console object echoes its output to this window during a debug session. For example, the following line of code can be added to your sample application:

```
Console.WriteLine("This is printed in the Output Window")
```

This line of code will cause the string "This is printed in the Output Window" to appear in the Output window when your application is running. You can verify this by adding this line in front of the command to open the message box. Then, run your application and have the debugger stop on the line where the message box is opened. If you check the contents of the Output window, you will find that your string is displayed.

Anything written to the Output window is shown only while running a program from the environment. During execution of the compiled module, no Output window is present, so nothing can be written to it. This is the basic concept behind other objects such as Debug and Trace, which are covered in more detail in Chapter 6.

## Call Stack

The Call Stack window lists the procedures that are currently calling other procedures and waiting for their return. The call stack represents the path through your code that leads to the currently executing command. This can be a valuable tool when you are trying to determine what code is executing a line of code that you didn't expect to execute.

## Locals

The Locals window is used to monitor the value of all variables currently in scope. This is a fairly self-explanatory window that shows a list of the current local variables, with the value next to each item. As in previous versions of Visual Studio, this display enables you to examine the contents of objects and arrays via a tree-control interface. It also supports the editing of those values, so if you want to change a string from empty to what you thought it would be, just to see what else might be broken, then feel free to do so from here.

## Watch Windows

There are four Watch windows, numbered Watch 1 to Watch 4. Each window can hold a set of variables or expressions for which you want to monitor the values. It is also possible to modify the value of a variable from within a Watch window. The display can be set to show variable values in decimal or hexadecimal format. To add a variable to a Watch window, you can either right-click the variable in the Code Editor and then select Add Watch from the pop-up menu, or drag and drop the variable into the watch window.

## Immediate Window

The Immediate window, as its name implies, enables you to evaluate expressions. It becomes available while you are in Debug mode. This is a powerful window, one that can save or ruin a debug session. For example, using the sample from earlier in this chapter, you can start the application and press the button to stop on the breakpoint. Go to the Immediate window and enter `?TextBoxResult.Text = "Hello World"` and press Enter. You should get a response of false as the Immediate window evaluates this statement.

Notice the preceding ?, which tells the debugger to evaluate your statement, rather than execute it. Repeat the preceding text but omit the question mark: `TextBoxResult.Text = "Hello World"`. Press F5 or click the Run button to return control to your application, and notice the text now shown in the window. From the Immediate window you have updated this value. This window can be very useful if you are working in Debug mode and need to modify a value that is part of a running application.

Autos

Finally, there is the Autos window. The Autos window displays variables used in the statement currently being executed and the statement just before it. These variables are identified and listed for you automatically, hence the window's name. This window shows more than just your local variables. For example, if you are in Debug mode on the line to open the `MessageBox` in the ProVB_ VS2012 sample, then the `MessageBox` constants referenced on this line are shown in this window. This window enables you to see the content of every variable involved in the currently executing command. As with the Locals window, you can edit the value of a variable during a debug session.

## Reusing Your First Windows Form

As you proceed through the book and delve further into the features of Visual Basic, you'll want a way to test sample code. Chapter 2 in particular has snippets of code which you'll want to test. One way to do this is to enhance the ProVB_VS2012 application. Its current use of a `MessageBox` isn't exactly the most useful method of testing code snippets. So let's update this application so it can be reused in other chapters and at random by you when you are interested in testing a snippet.

At the core you'll continue to access code to test where it can be executed from the ButtonTest Click event. However, instead of using a message box, you can use the resulting text box to hold the output from the code being tested.

## USEFUL FEATURES OF VISUAL STUDIO 2012

The focus of most of this chapter has been on using Visual Studio to create a simple application. It's now time to look at some of the less commonly recognized features of Visual Studio. These features include, but are not limited to, the following items.

When Visual Studio 2012 is first started, you configure your custom IDE profile. Visual Studio enables you to select either a language-specific or task-specific profile and then change that profile whenever you desire.

Configuration settings are managed through the Tools ⇨ Import and Export Settings menu option. This menu option opens a simple wizard, which first saves your current settings and then allows you to select an alternate set of settings. By default, Visual Studio ships with settings for Visual Basic, Web development, and C#, to name a few, but by exporting your settings you can create and share your own custom settings files.

The Visual Studio settings file is an XML file that enables you to capture all your Visual Studio configuration settings. This might sound trivial, but it is not. This feature enables the standardization of Visual Studio across different team members. The advantages of a team sharing settings go beyond just a common look and feel.

## The Task List

The Task List is a great productivity tool that tracks not only errors but also pending changes and additions. It's also a good way for the Visual Studio environment to communicate information that the developer needs to know, such as any current errors. The Task List is displayed by selecting Task List from the View menu. It offers two views, Comments and User Tasks, and it displays either group of tasks based on the selection in the drop-down box that is part of this window.

The Comment option is used for tasks embedded in code comments. This is done by creating a standard comment with the apostrophe and then starting the comment with the Visual Studio keyword TODO. The keyword can be followed with any text that describes what needs to be done. Once entered, the text of these comments shows up in the Task List. Note that users can create their own comment tokens in the options for Visual Studio via Tools ⇨ Options ⇨ Environment ⇨ Task List. Other predefined keywords include HACK and UNDONE.

Besides helping developers track these pending coding issues as tasks, leveraging comments embedded in code results in another benefit. Just as with errors, clicking a task in the Task List causes the Code Editor to jump to the location of the task without hunting through the code for it. Also of note is that the Task List is integrated with Team Foundation Server if you are using this for your collaboration and source control.

The second type of tasks is user tasks. These may not be related to a specific item within a single file. Examples are tasks associated with resolving a bug, or a new feature. It is possible to enter tasks into the Task List manually. Within the Task List is an image button showing a red check mark. Pressing this button creates a new task in the Task List, where you can edit the description of your new task.

## Server Explorer

As development has become more server-centric, developers have a greater need to discover and manipulate services on the network. The Server Explorer feature in Visual Studio makes working with servers easier. The Server Explorer enables you to explore and alter your application's database or your local registry values. For example, it's possible to fully explore and alter an SQL Server database.

If the Server Explorer hasn't been opened, it can be opened from the View menu. Alternatively it should be located near the control Toolbox. It has behavior similar to the Toolbox in that if you hover over or click the Server Explorer's tab, the window expands from the left-hand side of the IDE. Once it is open, you will see a display similar to the one shown in Figure 1-31. Note that this display has three top-level entries. The first, Data Connections, is the starting point for setting up and configuring the database connection. You can right-click on the top-level Data Connections node and define new SQL Server connection settings that will be used in your application to connect to the database. The Server Explorer window provides a way to manage and view project-specific database connections such as those used in data binding.

The second top-level entry, Servers, focuses on other server data that may be of interest to you and your application. When you expand the list of available servers, you have access to several server resources. The Server Explorer even provides the capability to stop and restart services on the server. Note the wide variety of server resources that are available for inspection or use in the project. Having the Server Explorer available means you don't have to go to an outside resource to find, for example, what message queues are available.

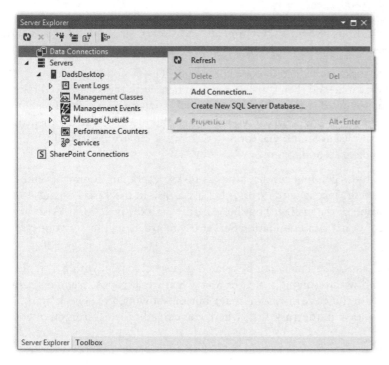

**FIGURE 1-31:** Server Explorer window

By default, you have access to the resources on your local machine; but if you are in a domain, it is possible to add other machines, such as your Web server, to your display. Use the Add Server option to select and inspect a new server. To explore the Event Logs and registry of a server, you need to add this server to your display. Use the Add Server button in the button bar to open the dialog and identify the server to which you would like to connect. Once the connection is made, you can explore the properties of that server.

The third top-level node, SharePoint Connections, enables you to define and reference elements associated with one or more SharePoint servers for which you might be creating solutions.

## Class Diagrams

One of the features introduced with Visual Studio 2005 was the capability to generate class diagrams. A *class diagram* is a graphical representation of your application's objects. By right-clicking on your project in the Solution Explorer, you can select View Class Diagram from the context menu. Alternatively, you can choose to Add a New Item to your project. In the same window where you can add a new class, you have the option to add a new class diagram. The class diagram uses a .cd file extension for its source files. It is a graphical display, as shown in Figure 1-32.

Adding such a file to your project creates a dynamically updated representation of your project's classes. As shown in Figure 1-32, the current class structures for even a simple project are immediately represented when you create the diagram. It is possible to add multiple class diagrams to your project. The class diagram graphically displays the relationships between objects—for example, when one object contains another object or even object inheritance. When you change your source code the diagram is also updated. In other words, the diagram isn't something static that you create once at the start of your project and then becomes out-of-date as your actual implementation changes the class relationships.

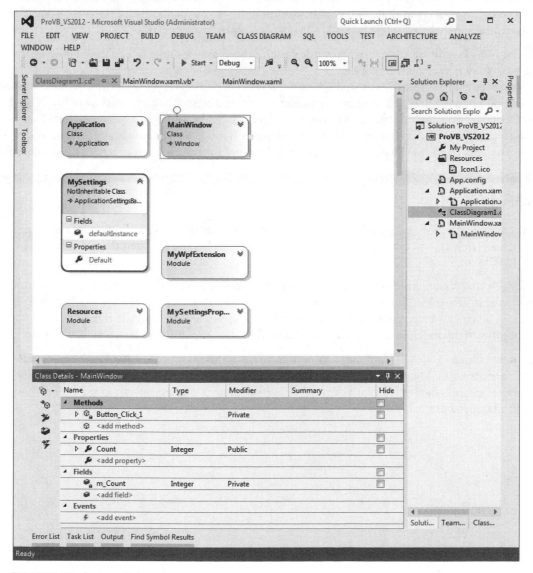

**FIGURE 1-32:** A class diagram

More important, you can at any time open the class diagram, make changes to one or more of your existing objects, or create new objects and define their relationship to your existing objects, and when done, Visual Studio will automatically update your existing source files and create new source files as necessary for the newly defined objects.

As shown in Figure 1-32, the class diagram files (*.cd) open in the same main display area used for the Visual Studio UI designer and viewing code. They are, however, a graphical design surface that behaves more like Visio than the User Interface designer. You can compress individual objects or expose their property and method details. Additionally, items such as the relationships between classes can be shown graphically instead of being represented as properties.

In addition to the editing surface, when working with the Class Designer a second window is displayed. As shown at the bottom of Figure 1-32, the Class Details window is generally located in the same space as your Output, Tasks, and other windows. The Class Details window provides detailed information about each of the properties and methods of the classes you are working with in the Class Designer. You can add and edit methods, properties, fields, and even events associated with your classes. While you can't write code from this window, you can update parameter lists and property types. The Class Diagram tool is an excellent tool for reviewing your application structure.

## SUMMARY

In this chapter, you have taken a dive into the versions and features of Visual Studio. This chapter was intended to help you explore the new Visual Studio IDE. It demonstrated the powerful features of the IDE.

You've seen that Visual Studio is highly customizable and comes in a variety of flavors. As you worked within Visual Studio, you've seen how numerous windows can be hidden, docked, or undocked. They can be layered in tabs and moved both within and beyond the IDE. Visual Studio also contains many tools, including some that extend its core capabilities.

In the next chapter you will learn more about the runtime environment for .NET, which provides a layer of abstraction above the operating system. Your application runs within this runtime environment. The next chapter looks at how functions like memory management and operating system compatibility are handled in .NET.

# The Common Language Runtime

**WROX.COM CODE DOWNLOADS FOR THIS CHAPTER**

The wrox.com code downloads for this chapter are found at www.wrox.com/remtitle .cgi?isbn=9781118314456 on the Download Code tab. The code is in the chapter 2 download and individually named according to the code file names throughout the chapter.

You started with a quick jump straight into getting your hands on Visual Studio. Most developers want to feel something, but before you start diving into syntax this chapter is going to take a look at the bigger picture of how .NET runs in relation to the operating system (OS). While at really low levels for graphics some implementations of the common language runtime (CLR) and the OS may be indistinguishable, at its core the CLR provides the environment in which your application runs.

The architects of .NET realized that all procedural languages require certain base functionality. For example, many languages ship with their own runtime that provides features such as memory management, but what if, instead of each language shipping with its own runtime implementation, all languages used a common runtime? This would provide languages with a standard environment and access to all of the same features. This is exactly what the CLR provides.

The CLR manages the execution of code on the .NET platform. Its common features provide support for many advanced features, including operator overloading, implementation inheritance, threading, and the ability to marshal objects. Building such features is not trivial. The CLR enabled Microsoft to concentrate on building this plumbing one time and then reuse it across different programming languages. As a result the runtime environment used by Visual Basic is the equal of every other .NET language, with the CLR eliminating many of the shortcomings of the previous versions of Visual Basic.

Visual Basic developers can view the CLR as a better Visual Basic runtime. However, this runtime, unlike the old standalone Visual Basic runtime, is common across all of .NET regardless of the underlying operating system. Thus, the functionality exposed by the CLR is available to all .NET languages; more important, all of the features available to other .NET languages via the CLR are available to Visual Basic developers. Additionally, as long as you develop using managed code — code that runs in the CLR — you'll find that it doesn't matter whether your application is installed on a Windows XP client, a Vista client, or a Windows 7 client; your application will run. The CLR provides an abstraction layer separate from the details of the operating system.

This chapter gets down into the belly of the application runtime environment — not to examine how .NET enables this abstraction from the operating system, but instead to look at some specific features related to how you build applications that run against the CLR. This includes an introduction to several basic elements of working with applications that run in the CLR, including the following:

➤ Framework Profiles

➤ Elements of a .NET application

➤ Integration across .NET languages

➤ Memory management and the garbage collector (GC)

➤ Namespaces

## FRAMEWORK PROFILES AND PLATFORMS

When .NET was initially launched, Microsoft released a single copy of the .NET Framework. This version ran with the one and only CLR that was released at the same time. As new versions of .NET were released, these two things tended to stay in step. A new version of the framework was matched with a new version of the CLR. However, as we moved from version 1 through version 4, the framework started becoming ever larger.

For part of .NET 3.5, Microsoft decided to create a subset of the full framework called the .NET 3.5 Client Profile. This wasn't a major change, but it created a subset of the full framework that could omit certain server-focused libraries. The result is a smaller deployment package for most client computers. The disadvantage, of course, is that it means you need to consider which .NET profile you will target, because the client profile contains only a subset of the full framework.

Now as we look at Windows 8 we see that Microsoft has added another framework platform specifically targeting Windows Metro style applications. In this case, however, the change isn't just to create a focused subset of features; it is designed with the idea that Metro as an alternate platform will have a different runtime and different features provided by the .NET Framework. With .NET 4.5 we are seeing an introduction of a completely different set of capabilities between the frameworks on these two platforms.

## Client and Full Framework Profiles

As noted it is possible to state that the client profile available for .NET 3.5 (or later) is in fact a subset of the full framework. These represent what most developers who have been developing for the Windows environment see as the traditional .NET Framework. It should be noted that when we think about the version of .NET framework that will be available on versions of Windows prior to Windows 8, these represent what those machines will have.

The client profile is a subset within the traditional Windows environment that provides a subset of .NET Framework capabilities. It omits things like ASP.NET, the MSBuild engine, third party data-access, and even advanced WCF capabilities. By eliminating these capabilities the deployment of the .NET Framework is made easier.

However, keep in mind that although it is called a client profile, the client isn't limited to only installing this version. Both the client profile and the full version of the .NET 3.5 (or later) frameworks can be installed on any Windows computer. While the features available in each version 3.5 vs. 4 vs. 4.5 for the client profile may change the focus on having a subset of the full version, not a different platform.

## Framework for Metro

There is a temptation to state that the .NET Framework for Metro breaks backward compatibility. However, that statement would imply that things written for the Metro environment would also run on version 4.5 of the CLR and leverage the same framework outside of Metro. That statement isn't true. The introduction of the .NET Framework for Metro is a branch in .NET to another platform. The CLR used on Metro does not integrate to the Windows 8 operating system in the same way that the non-Metro version of .NET does.

This is important because it helps explain why applications written against this branch of the .NET Framework will not run unless the Windows 8 operating system is available. In fact you can't even build against this framework unless you are developing on a Windows 8 machine. The .NET framework for Metro prevents actions that are difficult to monitor for security. For example COM-Interop isn't available within the Metro environment.

Applications typically aren't going to just need a minor rewrite in order to move from the existing .NET Framework to Metro. While the underlying features are similar, the Metro framework will have new namespaces and features that are not currently and probably never will be part of the traditional Windows framework. At the same time some of the underlying capabilities of the traditional Windows framework will not be part of the Metro framework. A good way to think of it is that the .NET Framework for Metro will be a client implementation on steroids that leverages WCF to communicate with server-based solutions.

As such the Metro platform will include features such as built-in support for GPS location data, multitouch interfaces, etc. These features in many cases are not going to be made available in the Windows platform. Similarly the Metro platform will have more in common with the .NET Framework Client Profile in that it doesn't support server-side capabilities like ASP.NET or classes that are focused on server-side WCF capabilities.

## Silverlight, Windows Phone, and Others

If you've done any development for Silverlight or Windows Phones, you realize that each of these environments is in fact a separate platform. Traditionally, because they were on out-of-cycle release schedules, these platforms weren't part of the core .NET Framework releases.

However, just as Metro is being approached as a separate platform, these platforms have always hosted a custom version of the CLR. If you've done any work with either Silverlight or Windows Phone you know that classes created in a library project that targets the Windows version of the .NET Framework can't be referenced. Instead you've spent a lot of time copying code that exists in one project over to another project that targets one of these platforms.

The goal of this section isn't to break out the common and unique features across each platform. Instead you should now recognize that we need a solution that allows us to write code one time and have it function on multiple different .NET platforms. This is where the new project type within Visual Studio 2012 comes in.

## .NET 4.5 Portable Class Library

With a plethora of different .NET Frameworks now in play, it potentially becomes more difficult to reuse your business objects across environments. After all, who wants to rewrite the same business logic for every different platform on which your application needs to function? This doesn't just mean the full application; it means that the `Person` object you create within the client is the same `Person` object that you need on the server. Having to rewrite your code potentially breaks interfaces.

You will use a Portable Class Library project, to create a solution that can move across different .NET Framework profiles. In this case the portable designation has nothing to do with a mobile device. The portability is focused on moving between different versions of the CLR. Applications built as a portable class library are limited to features common across each different .NET Framework that is included. In essence they target the lowest common denominator of .NET Framework features across these platforms.

Creating a Portable Class Library project allows you to choose two or more platforms. Table 2-1 shows the available platforms as of this writing. Note that since a profile is a subset of a platform, you'll actually be limited to the features for the client profile of the .NET Framework.

**TABLE 2-1:** Portable Class Library Targets

| PLATFORM | VERSIONS |
|---|---|
| `.NET Framework` | .NET Framework 4 and later (default) |
| | .NET Framework 4, update 4.0.3 or later |
| | .NET Framework 4.5 |
| `Silverlight` | Silverlight 4 and later (default) |
| | Silverlight 5 |
| `Windows Phone` | Windows Phone 7 and later (default) |
| | Windows Phone 7.5 and later |
| | Windows Phone 8 |
| `.NET for Metro style apps` | .NET Framework for Metro style (default) |
| `Xbox 360` | Not currently selected by default |

## ELEMENTS OF A .NET APPLICATION

A .NET application is composed of four primary entities:

1. **Types**—The common unit of transmitting data between modules running in the CLR
2. **Classes**—The basic units that encapsulate data and behavior
3. **Modules**—The individual files that contain the intermediate language (IL) for an assembly
4. **Assemblies**—The primary unit of deployment of a .NET application

Classes are covered in detail in the next two chapters, As such we are going to limit the discussion here to clarify that they are defined in the source files for your application or class library. Upon compilation of your source files, you produce a module. The code that makes up an assembly's modules may exist in a single executable (.exe) file or as a dynamic link library (.dll).

A module, is in fact, a Microsoft intermediate language (MSIL) file, which is then used by the CLR when your application is run. However, compiling a .NET application doesn't produce only an MSIL file; it also produces a collection of files that make up a deployable application or assembly. Within an assembly are several different types of files, including not only the actual executable files, but also configuration files, signature keys, and related resources.

## Types

The type system provides a template that is used to describe the encapsulation of data and an associated set of behaviors. It is this common template for describing data that provides the basis for the metadata that .NET uses when classes interoperate at runtime.

All types are based on a common system that is used across all .NET languages, profiles and platforms. Similar to the MSIL code, which is interpreted by the CLR based upon the current runtime environment, the CLR uses a common metadata system to recognize the details of each type. The result is that all .NET languages are built around a common type system. Thus it isn't necessary to translate data through a special notation to enable transfer of data types between different .exe and .dll files.

A type has fields, properties, and methods:

➤ **Fields**—Variables that are scoped to the type. For example, a Pet class could declare a field called Name that holds the pet's name. In a well-engineered class, fields are typically kept private and exposed only as properties or methods.

➤ **Properties**—Properties look like fields to clients of the type but can have code behind them (which usually performs some sort of data validation). For example, a Dog data type could expose a property to set its gender. Code could then be placed within the property definition so that only "male" or "female" are accepted values. Internally the selected value might be transformed and stored in a more efficient manner using a field in the Dog class.

➤ **Methods**—Methods define behaviors exhibited by the type. For example, the Dog data type could expose a method called Sleep, which would suspend the activity of the Dog.

The preceding elements are just part of each class. Note that some types are defined at the application level, and others are defined globally. With .NET it is not only possible but often encouraged that the classes and types defined in your modules be visible only at the application level. The advantage of this is that you can run several different versions of an application side by side.

## Modules

A module contains Microsoft intermediate language (MSIL, often abbreviated to IL) code, associated metadata, and the assembly's manifest. IL is a platform-independent way of representing managed code within a module. Before IL can be executed, the CLR must compile it into the native machine code. The default method is for the CLR to use the JIT (just-in-time) compiler to compile the IL on a method-by-method basis. At runtime, as each method is called for the first time, it is passed through the JIT compiler for compilation to machine code. Similarly, for an ASP.NET application, each page is passed through the JIT compiler the first time it is requested.

Additional information about the types declared in the IL is provided by the associated metadata. The metadata contained within the module is used extensively by the CLR. For example, if a client and an object reside within two different processes, then the CLR uses the type's metadata to marshal data between the client and the object. MSIL is important because every .NET language compiles down to IL. The CLR doesn't care about or even need to know what the implementation language was; it knows only what the IL contains. Thus, any differences in .NET languages exist at the level where the IL is generated; but once compiled to IL; all .NET languages have the same runtime characteristics. Similarly, because the CLR doesn't care in which language a given module was originally written, it can leverage modules implemented in entirely different .NET languages.

A question that always arises when discussing the JIT compiler and the use of a runtime environment is "Wouldn't it be faster to compile the IL language down to native code before the user asks to run it?" Although the answer is not always yes, the answer is that combined with the flexibility of changes to the machine and other advantages related to evaluation of the environment when the code is accessed, this is the most robust solution.

However, because sometimes the only consideration is speed, Microsoft has provided a utility to handle this compilation: the Native Image Generator, or Ngen.exe. This tool enables you to essentially run the JIT compiler on a specific assembly, which is then installed into the user's application cache in its native format. The obvious advantage is that now when the user asks to execute something in that assembly, the JIT compiler is not invoked, saving a small amount of time. Unlike the JIT compiler, which compiles only those portions of an assembly that are actually referenced, Ngen .exe needs to compile the entire code base. This is important because the time required for NGEN compilation is not the same as what a user actually experiences with the JIT compiler.

Ngen.exe is executed from the command line. The utility was updated as part of .NET 2.0 and now automatically detects and includes most of the dependent assemblies as part of the image-generation process. To use Ngen.exe, you simply reference this utility followed by an action; for example, install followed by your assembly reference. Several options are available as part of the generation process, but that subject is beyond the scope of this chapter, given that Ngen.exe itself is a topic that generates heated debate regarding its use and value.

Where does the debate begin about when to use Ngen.exe? Keep in mind that in a server application, where the same assembly will be referenced by multiple users between machine restarts, the difference in performance on the first request is essentially lost. This means that compilation to native code is more valuable to client-side applications. Unfortunately, using Ngen.exe requires running it on each client machine, which can become cost prohibitive in certain installation scenarios, particularly if you use any form of self-updating application logic.

Another issue relates to using reflection, which enables you to reference other assemblies at runtime. Of course, if you don't know what assemblies you will reference until runtime, then the Native Image Generator has a problem, as it won't know what to reference, either. You may have occasion to use Ngen.exe for an application you've created, but you should fully investigate this utility and its advantages and disadvantages beforehand, keeping in mind that even native images execute within the CLR. Native image generation changes only the compilation model, not the runtime environment.

## Assemblies

An assembly is the primary unit of deployment for .NET applications. It is either a dynamic link library (.dll) or an executable (.exe). An assembly is composed of a manifest, one or more modules, and (optionally) other files, such as .config, .ASPX, .ASMX, images, and so on. By default, the Visual Basic compiler creates an assembly that combines both the assembly code and the manifest.

The manifest of an assembly contains the following:

➤ Information about the identity of the assembly, including its textual name and version number.

➤ If the assembly is public, then the manifest contains the assembly's public key. The public key is used to help ensure that types exposed by the assembly reside within a unique namespace. It may also be used to uniquely identify the source of an assembly.

➤ A declarative security request that describes the assembly's security requirements (the assembly is responsible for declaring the security it requires). Requests for permissions fall into three categories: required, optional, and denied. The identity information may be used as evidence by the CLR in determining whether or not to approve security requests.

➤   A list of other assemblies on which the assembly depends. The CLR uses this information to locate an appropriate version of the required assemblies at runtime. The list of dependencies also includes the exact version number of each assembly at the time the assembly was created.

➤   A list of all types and resources exposed by the assembly. If any of the resources exposed by the assembly are localized, the manifest will also contain the default culture (language, currency, date/time format, and so on) that the application will target. The CLR uses this information to locate specific resources and types within the assembly.

The manifest can be stored in a separate file or in one of the modules. By default, for most applications, it is part of the `.dll` or `.exe` file, which is compiled by Visual Studio. For ASP.NET applications, you'll find that although there is a collection of ASPX pages, the actual assembly information is located in a DLL referenced by those ASPX pages.

## Better Support for Versioning

Managing component versions was challenging prior to .NET's ability to associate a manifest and use application-level references. Often, even though the version number of the component could be set, it was not used by the runtime.

For many applications, .NET has removed the need to identify the version of each assembly in a central registry on a machine. However, some assemblies are installed once and used by multiple applications. .NET provides a global assembly cache (GAC), which is used to store assemblies that are intended for use by multiple applications. The CLR provides global versioning support for all components loaded in the GAC.

The CLR provides two features for assemblies installed within the GAC:

**1.**   **Side-by-side versioning**—Multiple versions of the same component can be simultaneously stored in the GAC.

**2.**   **Automatic Quick Fix Engineering (QFE)**—Also known as hotfix support; if a new version of a component, which is still compatible with the old version, is available in the GAC, the CLR loads the updated component. The version number, which is maintained by the developer who created the referenced assembly, drives this behavior.

The assembly's manifest contains the version numbers of referenced assemblies. The CLR uses the assembly's manifest at runtime to locate a compatible version of each referenced assembly. The version number of an assembly takes the following form:

```
Major.Minor.Build.Revision
```

## Major.Minor.Build.Revision

Changes to the major and minor version numbers of the assembly indicate that the assembly is no longer compatible with the previous versions. The CLR will not use versions of the assembly that have a different major or minor number unless it is explicitly told to do so. For example, if an assembly was originally compiled against a referenced assembly with a version number of 3.4.1.9, then the CLR will not load an assembly stored in the GAC unless it has major and minor numbers of 3 and 4, respectively.

Incrementing the revision and build numbers indicates that the new version is still compatible with the previous version. If a new assembly that has an incremented revision or build number is loaded into the GAC, then the CLR can still load this assembly for applications that were compiled referencing a previous version.

For .NET applications running outside of Metro, most components should not be registered. The external assemblies are referenced locally, which means they are carried in the application's local directory structure. Using local copies of external assemblies enables the CLR to support the side-by-side execution of different versions of the same component.

Except when looking to add an application to Metro, the only requirement for installing a .NET application is to copy it to the local machine. A .NET application can be distributed using a simple command like this:

```
xcopy \\server\appDirectory "C:\Program Files\appDirectory" /E /O /I
```

However, because Metro has introduced the concept of a Windows Application Store details of deployment are being focused on in Chapter 22.

## CROSS-LANGUAGE INTEGRATION

Prior to .NET, interoperating with code written in other languages was challenging. There were pretty much two options for reusing functionality developed in other languages: COM interfaces or DLLs with exported C functions.

Visual Basic is built on top of the CLR. As such it interoperates with code written in other .NET languages. It's even able to derive from a class written in another language. To support this type of functionality, the CLR relies on a common way of representing types, as well as rich metadata that can describe these types.

## The Common Type System

Each programming language seems to bring its own island of data types with it. To help resolve this problem, C, an operating-system-level implementation language, became the lowest common denominator for interfacing between programs written in multiple languages. An exported function written in C that exposes simple C data types can be consumed by a variety of other programming languages. In fact, the Windows API is exposed for .NET developers as a set of C functions. Note this changes for those building Metro applications, but this does not change the value of the common type system (CTS) across .NET.

Unfortunately, to access a C interface, you must explicitly map C data types to a language's native data types. This is not only cumbersome, but also error prone due to the complexity. Accidentally mapping a variable declared as Long to lpBuffer wouldn't generate any compilation errors, but calling the function at runtime would result in difficult-to-diagnose, intermittent access violations at runtime.

The .NET CTS provides a set of common data types for use across all programming languages. It provides every language running on top of the .NET platform with a base set of types, as well as mechanisms for extending those types. These types are derived from a common `System.Object` class definition.

Because every type supported by the CTS is derived from `System.Object`, every type supports a common set of methods, as shown in Table 2-2.

**TABLE 2-2:** Common Type Methods

| METHOD | DESCRIPTION |
|---|---|
| `Boolean Equals(Object)` | Used to test equality with another object. Reference types should return `True` if the `Object` parameter references the same object. Value types should return `True` if the `Object` parameter has the same value. |
| `Int32 GetHashCode()` | Generates a number corresponding to the value of an object. If two objects of the same type are equal, then they must return the same hash code. |
| `Type GetType()` | Gets a `Type` object that can be used to access metadata associated with the type. It also serves as a starting point for navigating the object hierarchy exposed by the Reflection API (discussed shortly). |
| `String ToString()` | The default implementation returns the fully qualified name of the object's class. This method is often overridden to output data that is more meaningful to the type. For example, all base types return their value as a string. |

# Metadata

Metadata is the information that enables components to be self-describing. It describes many aspects of .NET components including classes, methods, and fields, and the assembly itself. Metadata is used by the CLR to facilitate behavior, such as:

➤ Validating an assembly before it is executed, or performing garbage collection while managed code is being executed.

➤ Visual Basic developers use metadata to instruct the CLR how to behave at runtime.

➤ Components referenced within applications have accompanying type libraries that contain metadata about the components, their methods, and their properties. You can use the Object Browser to view this information. (The information contained within the type library is what is used to drive IntelliSense.)

## Better Support for Metadata

.NET refines the use of metadata within applications in three significant ways:

1. .NET consolidates the metadata associated with a component.

2. Because a .NET component does not have to be registered, installing and upgrading the component is easier and less problematic.

3. .NET makes a clear distinction between attributes that should only be set at compile time and those that can be modified at runtime.

> **NOTE** *All attributes associated with Visual Basic components are represented in a common format and consolidated within the files that make up the assembly.*

Because all metadata associated with a .NET component must reside within the file that contains the component, no global registration of components is required. When a new component is copied into an application's directory, it can be used immediately. Because the component and its associated metadata cannot become out of sync, upgrading the component is not an issue.

.NET makes a much better distinction between attributes that should be set at compile time and those that should be set at runtime. For example, whether a .NET component is serializable is determined at compile time. This setting cannot be overridden at runtime.

## Attributes

Attributes are used to decorate entities such as assemblies, classes, methods, and properties with additional information. Attributes can be used for a variety of purposes. They can provide information, request a certain behavior at runtime, or even invoke a particular behavior from another application. An example of this can be demonstrated by using the Demo class defined in the following code block (code file: ProVB_Attributes\Module1.vb):

```
Module Module1
  <Serializable()>
  Public Class Demo
    <Obsolete("Use Method2 instead.")>
    Public Sub Method1()
      ' Old implementation …
    End Sub
    Public Sub Method2()
      ' New implementation …
    End Sub
  End Class

  Public Sub Main()
    Dim d = New Demo()
    d.Method1()
  End Sub
End Module
```

Create a new console application for Visual Basic by selecting File ⇨ New Project and selecting Windows Console Application and then add a class into the file module1 by copying the previous code into Module1. A best practice is to place each class in its own source file, but in order to simplify this demonstration, the class Demo has been defined within the main module.

The first attribute on the Demo class marks the class with the Serializable attribute. The base class library will provide serialization support for instances of the Demo type. For example, the ResourceWriter type could be used to stream an instance of the Demo type to disk.

Method1 is prefaced by the Obsolete attribute. Method1 has been marked as obsolete, but it is still available. When a method is marked as obsolete, it is possible to instruct Visual Studio to prevent applications from compiling. However, a better strategy for large applications is to first mark a method or class as obsolete and then prevent its use in the next release. The preceding code causes Visual Studio to display a warning if `Method1` is referenced within the application, as shown in Figure 2-1. Not only does the line with `Method1` have a visual hint of the issue, but a warning message is visible in the Error List, with a meaningful message on how to correct the issue.

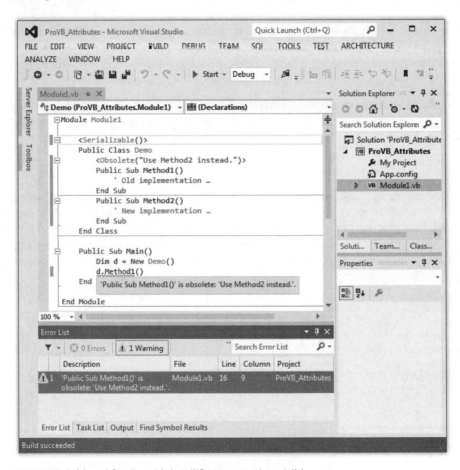

**FIGURE 2-1:** Visual Studio with IntelliSense warning visible

If the developer leaves this code unchanged and then compiles it, the application will compile correctly.

Sometimes you might need to associate multiple attributes with an entity. The following code shows an example of using both of the attributes from the previous example at the class level:

```
<Serializable(), Obsolete("No longer used.", True)>
Public Class Demo
   ' Implementation …
End Class
```

Note in this case the `Obsolete` attribute has been modified to cause a compilation error by setting its second parameter to `True`. As shown in Figure 2-2, the compilation fails.

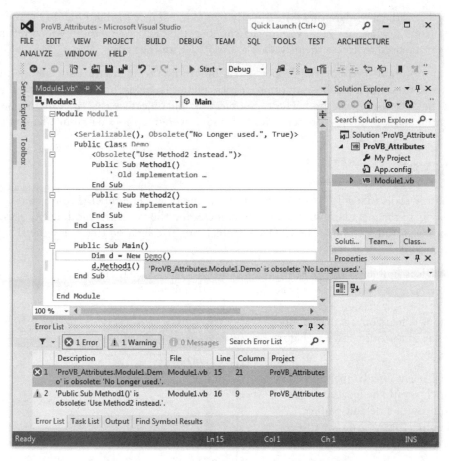

**FIGURE 2-2:** Visual Studio illustrating an obsolete class declaration error

Attributes play an important role in the development of .NET applications, particularly XML Web Services. As you'll see in Chapter 11, the declaration of a class as a Web service and of particular methods as Web methods are all handled through the use of attributes.

## The Reflection API

Leveraging the presence of metadata throughout assemblies and classes, the .NET Framework provides the Reflection API. You can use the Reflection API to examine the metadata associated with an assembly and its types, even to examine the currently executing assembly or an assembly you would like to start while your application is running.

The `Assembly` class in the `System.Reflection` namespace can be used to access the metadata in an assembly. The `LoadFrom` method can be used to load an assembly, and the `GetExecutingAssembly` method can be used to access the currently executing assembly. The `GetTypes` method can then be used to obtain the collection of types defined in the assembly.

It's also possible to access the metadata of a type directly from an instance of that type. Because every object derives from System.Object, every object supports the GetType method, which returns a Type object that can be used to access the metadata associated with the type.

The Type object exposes many methods and properties for obtaining the metadata associated with a type. For example, you can obtain a collection of properties, methods, fields, and events exposed by the type by calling the GetMembers method. The Type object for the object's base type can also be obtained by calling the DeclaringType property. Reflection is covered in more detail in Chapter 17.

## IL DISASSEMBLER

One of the many handy tools that ships with Visual Studio is the IL Disassembler (ildasm.exe). It can be used to navigate the metadata within a module, including the types the module exposes, as well as their properties and methods. The IL Disassembler can also be used to display the IL contained within a module.

You can find the IL Disassembler in the SDK installation directory for Visual Studio 2012; the default path is C:\Program Files (x86)\Microsoft SDKs\Windows\v8.0A\bin\NETFX 4.0 Tools. Note there is a 64-bit version in a sub folder of this location. When you start the application a window similar to the one shown in Figure 2-3 will be displayed.

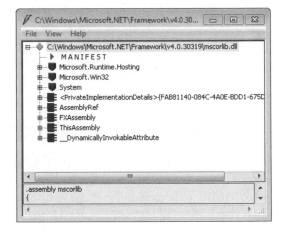

Within this window, select File ⇨ Open. Open mscorlib.dll, which should be located in your system directory with a default path of C:\Windows\Microsoft.NET\Framework\ v4.0.30319\mscorlib.dll.

Once mscorlib.dll has been loaded, ILDasm will display a set of folders for each namespace in this assembly. Expand the System namespace, then the ValueType namespace, and finally double-click the Equals method.

**FIGURE 2-3:** ILDasm window

Figure 2-4 shows the IL for the Equals method. Notice how the Reflection API is used to navigate through the instance of the value type's fields in order to determine whether the values of the two objects being compared are equal.

The IL Disassembler is a useful tool for learning how a particular module is implemented, but it could jeopardize your company's proprietary logic. After all, what's to prevent someone from using it to reverse-engineer your code? Fortunately, Visual Studio 2012, like previous versions of Visual Studio, ships with a third-party tool called an *obfuscator*. The role of the obfuscator is to ensure that the IL Disassembler cannot build a meaningful representation of your application logic.

A complete discussion of the obfuscator that ships with Visual Studio 2012 is beyond the scope of this chapter, but to access this tool, select the Tools menu and choose PreEmptive Dotfuscator and Analytics. The obfuscator runs against your compiled application, taking your IL file and stripping out many of the items that are embedded by default during the compilation process.

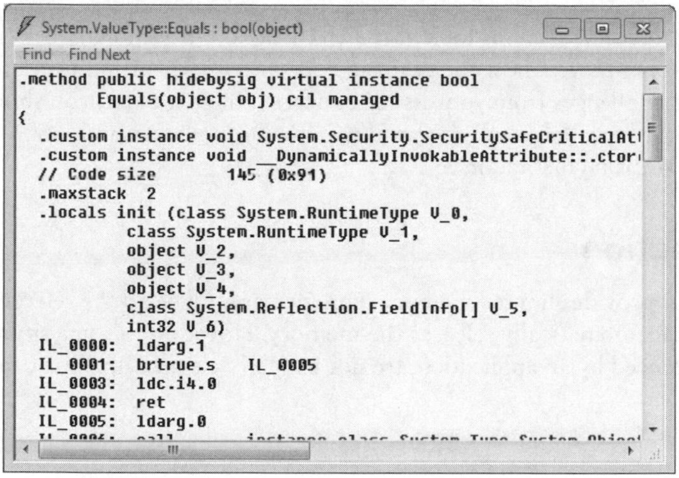

```
System.ValueType::Equals : bool(object)

Find   Find Next

.method public hidebysig virtual instance bool
        Equals(object obj) cil managed
{
  .custom instance void System.Security.SecuritySafeCriticalAt
  .custom instance void __DynamicallyInvokableAttribute::.ctor
  // Code size       145 (0x91)
  .maxstack  2
  .locals init (class System.RuntimeType V_0,
          class System.RuntimeType V_1,
          object V_2,
          object V_3,
          object V_4,
          class System.Reflection.FieldInfo[] V_5,
          int32 V_6)
  IL_0000:  ldarg.1
  IL_0001:  brtrue.s    IL_0005
  IL_0003:  ldc.i4.0
  IL_0004:  ret
  IL_0005:  ldarg.0
```

**FIGURE 2-4:** IL code for method Equals

## MEMORY MANAGEMENT

This section looks at one of the larger underlying elements of managed code. One of the reasons why .NET applications are referred to as "managed" is that memory deallocation is handled automatically by the system. Developers are accustomed to worrying about memory management only in an abstract sense. The basic rule has been that every object created and every section of memory allocated needs to be released (destroyed). The CLR introduces a garbage collector (GC), which simplifies this paradigm. Gone are the days when a misbehaving component—for example, one that fails to properly dispose of its object references or allocates and never releases memory—could crash a machine.

However, the use of a GC introduces new questions about when and if objects need to be explicitly cleaned up. There are two elements in manually writing code to allocate and deallocate memory and system resources. The first is the release of any shared resources, such as file handles and database connections. This type of activity needs to be managed explicitly and is discussed shortly. The second element of manual memory management involves letting the system know when memory is no longer in use by your application. Developers in unmanaged languages like C are accustomed to explicitly disposing of memory references. While you can explicitly show your intent to destroy the object by setting it to Nothing manually, this is not good practice.

The .NET GC automatically manages the cleanup of allocated memory. You don't need to carry out memory management as an explicit action. The GC will reclaim objects, at times in the middle of executing the code in a method. Fortunately, the system ensures that collection happens only as long as your code doesn't reference the object later in the method.

For example, you could actually end up extending the amount of time an object is kept in memory just by setting that object to Nothing. Thus, setting a variable to Nothing at the end of the method prevents the garbage collection mechanism from proactively reclaiming objects, and therefore is discouraged.

Given this change in paradigms, the next few sections look at the challenges of traditional memory management and peek under the covers to reveal how the garbage collector works, including a quick look at how the GC eliminates these challenges from your list of concerns. In particular, you should understand how you can interact with the garbage collector and why the Using command, for example, is recommended over a finalization method in .NET.

## Traditional Garbage Collection

An unmanaged runtime environment provides limited memory management. Once all the references are released on an object, the runtime automatically releases the memory. However, in some situations objects that are no longer referenced by an application are not properly cleaned up. One cause of this is the *circular reference*.

### Circular References

One of the most common situations in which the unmanaged runtime is unable to ensure that objects are no longer referenced by the application is when these objects contain a circular reference. An example of a circular reference is when object A holds a reference to object B and object B holds a reference to object A.

Circular references are problematic because the unmanaged environment typically relies on a reference counting mechanism to determine whether an object can be deactivated. Each object may be responsible for maintaining its own reference count and for destroying itself once the reference count reaches zero. Clients of the object are responsible for updating the reference count appropriately.

However, in a circular reference scenario, object A continues to hold a reference to object B, and vice versa, so the internal cleanup logic of these components is never triggered. In addition, problems can occur if the clients do not properly maintain the object's reference count.

The application can invalidate its references to A and B by setting the associated variables equal to Nothing. However, even though objects A and B are no longer referenced by the application, the unmanaged runtime isn't notified to remove them because A and B still reference each other.

The CLR garbage collector solves the problem of circular references because it looks for a reference from the root application or thread to every class, and all classes that do not have such a reference are marked for deletion, regardless of any other references they might still maintain.

### The CLR's Garbage Collector

The .NET garbage collection mechanism is complex, and the details of its inner workings are beyond the scope of this book, but it is important to understand the principles behind its operation. The GC is responsible for collecting objects that are no longer referenced.

At certain times, and based on internal rules, a task will run through all the objects looking for those that no longer have any references from the root application thread or one of the worker threads. Those objects may then be terminated; thus, the garbage is collected.

As long as all references to an object are either implicitly or explicitly released by the application, the GC will take care of freeing the memory allocated to it. Managed objects in .NET are not responsible for maintaining their reference count, and they are not responsible for destroying themselves. Instead, the GC is responsible for cleaning up objects that are no longer referenced by the application. The GC periodically determines which objects need to be cleaned up by leveraging the information the CLR maintains about the running application. The GC obtains a list of objects that are directly referenced by the application. Then, the GC discovers all the objects that are referenced (both directly and indirectly) by the "root" objects of the application. Once the GC has identified all the referenced objects, it is free to clean up any remaining objects.

The GC relies on references from an application to objects; thus, when it locates an object that is unreachable from any of the root objects, it can clean up that object. Any other references to that object will be from other objects that are also unreachable. Thus, the GC automatically cleans up objects that contain circular references.

Note just because you eliminate all references to an object doesn't mean that it will be terminated immediately. It just remains in memory until the garbage collection process gets around to locating and destroying it, a process called *nondeterministic finalization.*

This nondeterministic nature of CLR garbage collection provides a performance benefit. Rather than expend the effort to destroy objects as they are dereferenced, the destruction process can occur when the application is otherwise idle, often decreasing the impact on the user

It is possible to explicitly invoke the GC, but this process takes time and bypasses the automated optimization built into the CLR, so it is not the sort of behavior to invoke in a typical application. For example, you could call this method each time you set an object variable to Nothing, so that the object would be destroyed almost immediately, but this forces the GC to scan all the objects in your application — a very expensive operation in terms of performance.

It's far better to design applications such that it is acceptable for unused objects to sit in memory for some time before they are terminated. That way, the garbage collector can also run based on its optimal rules, collecting many dereferenced objects at the same time. This means you need to design objects that don't maintain expensive resources in instance variables. For example, database connections, open files on disk, and large chunks of memory (such as an image) are all examples of expensive resources. If you rely on the destruction of the object to release this type of resource, then the system might be keeping the resource tied up for a lot longer than you expect; in fact, on a lightly utilized Web server, it could literally be days.

The first principle is working with object patterns that incorporate cleaning up such pending references before the object is released. Examples of this include calling the close method on an open database connection or a file handle. In most cases, it's possible for applications to create classes that do not risk keeping these handles open. However, certain requirements, even with the best object design, can create a risk that a key resource will not be cleaned up correctly. In such an event, there are two occasions when the object could attempt to perform this cleanup: when the final reference to the object is released and immediately before the GC destroys the object.

One option is to implement the IDisposable interface. When implemented, this interface ensures that persistent resources are released. This is the preferred method for releasing resources. The second option is to add a method to your class that the system runs immediately before an object is destroyed. This option is not recommended for several reasons, including the fact that many developers fail to remember that the garbage collector is nondeterministic, meaning that you can't, for example, reference an SQLConnection object from your custom object's finalizer.

Finally, as part of .NET 2.0, Visual Basic introduced the Using command. The Using command is designed to change the way that you think about object cleanup. Instead of encapsulating your cleanup logic within your object, the Using command creates a window around the code that is referencing an instance of your object. When your application's execution reaches the end of this window, the system automatically calls the IDisposable interface for your object to ensure that it is cleaned up correctly.

## The Finalize Method

Conceptually, the GC calls an object's Finalize method immediately before it collects an object that is no longer referenced by the application. Classes can override the Finalize method to perform any necessary cleanup. The basic concept is to create a method that fills the same need as what in other object-oriented languages is referred to as a destructor. A Finalize method is recognized by the GC, and its presence prevents a class from being cleaned up until after the finalization method is completed. The following example shows the declaration of a finalization method:

```
Protected Overrides Sub Finalize()
    ' clean up code goes here
    MyBase.Finalize()
End Sub
```

This code uses both Protected scope and the Overrides keyword. Notice that not only does custom cleanup code go here (as indicated by the comment), but this method also calls MyBase.Finalize, which causes any finalization logic in the base class to be executed as well. Any class implementing a custom Finalize method should always call the base finalization class.

Be careful, however, not to treat the Finalize method as if it were a destructor. A destructor is based on a deterministic system, whereby the method is called when the object's last reference is removed. In the GC system, there are key differences in how a finalizer works:

➤ Because the GC is optimized to clean up memory only when necessary, there is a delay between the time when the object is no longer referenced by the application and when the GC collects it. Therefore, the same expensive resources that are released in the Finalize method may stay open longer than they need to be.

➤ The GC doesn't actually run Finalize methods. When the GC finds a Finalize method, it queues the object up for the finalizer to execute the object's method. This means that an object is not cleaned up during the current GC pass. Because of how the GC is optimized, this can result in the object remaining in memory for a much longer period.

➤ The GC is usually triggered when available memory is running low. As a result, execution of the object's Finalize method is likely to incur performance penalties. Therefore, the code in the Finalize method should be as short and quick as possible.

➤ There's no guarantee that a service you require is still available. For example, if the system is closing and you have a file open, then .NET may have already unloaded the object required to close the file, and thus a Finalize method can't reference an instance of any other .NET object.

## The IDisposable Interface

In some cases, the Finalize behavior is not acceptable. For an object that is using an expensive or a limited resource, such as a database connection, a file handle, or a system lock, it is best to ensure that the resource is freed as soon as the object is no longer needed.

One way to accomplish this is to implement a method to be called by the client code to force the object to clean up and release its resources. This is not a perfect solution, but it is workable. This cleanup method must be called directly by the code using the object or via the use of the Using statement. The Using statement enables you to encapsulate an object's life span within a limited range, and automate the calling of the IDisposable interface.

The .NET Framework provides the IDisposable interface to formalize the declaration of cleanup logic. Be aware that implementing the IDisposable interface also implies that the object has over-ridden the Finalize method. Because there is no guarantee that the Dispose method will be called, it is critical that Finalize triggers your cleanup code if it was not already executed.

All cleanup activities should be placed in the Finalize method, but objects that require timely cleanup should implement a Dispose method that can then be called by the client application just before setting the reference to Nothing:

```
Class DemoDispose

  Private m_disposed As Boolean = False

  Public Sub Dispose()
    If (Not m_disposed) Then
      ' Call cleanup code in Finalize.
      Finalize()
      ' Record that object has been disposed.
      m_disposed = True
      ' Finalize does not need to be called.
      GC.SuppressFinalize(Me)
    End If
  End Sub

  Protected Overrides Sub Finalize()
    ' Perform cleanup here
    End Sub
End Class
```

The DemoDispose class implements a Finalize method but uses a Dispose method that calls Finalize to perform any necessary cleanup. To ensure that the Dispose method calls Finalize only once, the value of the private m_disposed field is checked. Once Finalize has been run, this value is set to True. The class then calls GC.SuppressFinalize to ensure that the GC does not call the Finalize method on this object when the object is collected. If you need to implement a Finalize method, this is the preferred implementation pattern.

Having a custom finalizer ensures that once released, the garbage collection mechanism will eventually find and terminate the object by running its Finalize method. However, when handled correctly, the IDisposable interface ensures that any cleanup is executed immediately, so resources are not consumed beyond the time they are needed.

Note that any class that derives from System.ComponentModel.Component automatically inherits the IDisposable interface. This includes all of the forms and controls used in a Windows Forms UI, as well as various other classes within the .NET Framework. Because this interface is inherited, you will review a custom implementation of the IDisposable interface. You can leverage the code download or preferably create a new Windows Console project. Add a new class to your project and name it Person. Once your new class has been generated, go to the editor window and below the class declaration add the code to implement the IDisposable interface:

```
Public Class Person
    Implements IDisposable
```

This interface defines two methods, Dispose and Finalize, that need to be implemented in the class. However, what's important is that Visual Studio automatically inserts both these methods into your code (code file: ProVB_Disposable\Person.vb):

```
#Region " IDisposable Support "
    Private disposedValue As Boolean ' To detect redundant calls

    ' IDisposable
    Protected Overridable Sub Dispose(ByVal disposing As Boolean)
        If Not Me.disposedValue Then
            If disposing Then
                ' TODO: dispose managed state (managed objects).
            End If
            ' TODO: free unmanaged resources (unmanaged objects)
            '    and override Finalize() below.
            ' TODO: set large fields to null.
        End If
        Me.disposedValue = True
    End Sub

    ' TODO: override Finalize() only if Dispose(ByVal disposing As Boolean) above
    '       has code to free unmanaged resources.
    Protected Overrides Sub Finalize()
        ' Do not change this code.  Put cleanup code in
        '    Dispose(ByVal disposing As Boolean) above.
        Dispose(False)
        MyBase.Finalize()
    End Sub

    ' This code added by Visual Basic to correctly implement the disposable
  pattern.
    Public Sub Dispose() Implements IDisposable.Dispose
        ' Do not change this code.  Put cleanup code in
        '    Dispose(ByVal disposing As Boolean) above.
        Dispose(True)
        GC.SuppressFinalize(Me)
    End Sub
#End Region
```

Notice the use of the Overridable and Overrides keywords. The automatically inserted code is following a best-practice design pattern for implementation of the IDisposable interface and the

`Finalize` method. The idea is to centralize all cleanup code into a single method that is called by either the `Dispose` method or the `Finalize` method as appropriate.

Accordingly, you can add the cleanup code as noted by the `TODO:` comments in the inserted code. As mentioned in Chapter 1, the `TODO:` keyword is recognized by Visual Studio's text parser, which triggers an entry in the task list to remind you to complete this code before the project is complete.

Generally, it is up to your client code to call the dispose method at the appropriate time to ensure that cleanup occurs. Typically, this should be done as soon as the code is done using the object.

This is not always as easy as it might sound. In particular, an object may be referenced by more than one variable, and just because code in one class is done with the object doesn't mean that it isn't referenced by other variables. If the `Dispose` method is called while other references remain, then the object may become unusable and cause errors when invoked via those other references.

## Using IDisposable

One way to work with the `IDisposable` interface is to manually insert the calls to the interface implementation everywhere you reference the class (code file: `ProVB_Disposable\Module1.vb`):

```
CType(mPerson, IDisposable).Dispose()
```

Note that because the `Dispose` method is part of a secondary interface, use of the `CType` method to access that specific interface is needed in order to call the method.

This solution works fine for patterns where the object implementing `IDisposable` is used within a method, but it is less useful for other patterns—for example, an open database connection passed between methods or when the object is used as part of a Web service. In fact, even for client applications, this pattern is somewhat limited in that it requires the application to define the object globally with respect to its use.

For these situations, .NET 2.0 introduced a new command keyword: `Using`. The `Using` keyword is a way to quickly encapsulate the life cycle of an object that implements `IDisposable`, and ensure that the `Dispose` method is called correctly (code file: `ProVB_Disposable\Module1.vb`):

```
Using mPerson As Person = New Person
    'Use the mPerson in custom method calls

End Using
```

The preceding statements allocate a new instance of the `mPerson` object. The `Using` command then instructs the compiler to automatically clean up this object's instance when the `End Using` command is executed. The result is a much cleaner way to ensure that the `IDisposable` interface is called.

# Faster Memory Allocation for Objects

The CLR introduces the concept of a *managed heap*. Objects are allocated on the managed heap, and the CLR is responsible for controlling access to these objects in a type-safe manner. One of the advantages of the managed heap is that memory allocations on it are very efficient. When unmanaged code allocates memory on the unmanaged heap, it typically scans through some sort of data structure in search of a free chunk of memory that is large enough to accommodate the allocation.

The managed heap maintains a reference to the end of the most recent heap allocation. When a new object needs to be created on the heap, the CLR allocates memory starting from the end of the heap, and then increments the reference to the end of heap allocations accordingly. Figure 2-5 illustrates a simplification of what takes place in the managed heap for .NET.

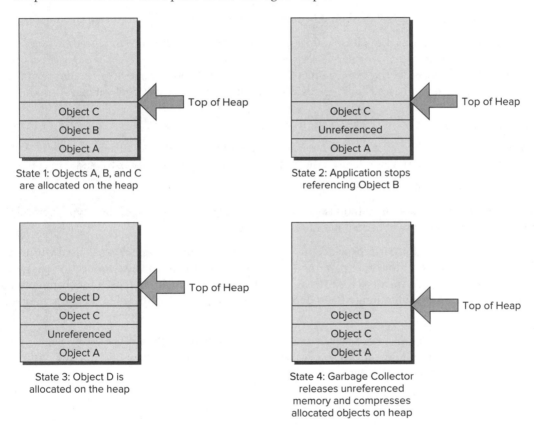

**FIGURE 2-5:** Memory Map State diagram

➤ State 1—A compressed memory heap with a reference to the endpoint on the heap.

➤ State 2—Object B, although no longer referenced, remains in its current memory location. The memory has not been freed and does not alter the allocation of memory or other objects on the heap.

➤ State 3—Even though there is now a gap between the memory allocated for object A and object C, the memory allocation for object D still occurs on the top of the heap. The unused fragment of memory on the managed heap is ignored at allocation time.

➤ State 4—After one or more allocations, before there is an allocation failure, the garbage collector runs. It reclaims the memory that was allocated to object B and repositions the remaining valid objects. This compresses the active objects to the bottom of the heap, creating more space for additional object allocations (refer to Figure 2-5).

This is where the power of the GC really shines. Before the CLR reaches a point where it is unable to allocate memory on the managed heap, the GC is invoked. The GC not only collects objects that are no longer referenced by the application, but also has a second task: compacting the heap. This is important, because if the GC only cleaned up objects, then the heap would become progressively more fragmented. When heap memory becomes fragmented, you can wind up with the common problem of having a memory allocation fail—not because there isn't enough free memory, but because there isn't enough free memory in a contiguous section of memory. Thus, not only does the GC reclaim the memory associated with objects that are no longer referenced, it also compacts the remaining objects. The GC effectively squeezes out all of the spaces between the remaining objects, freeing up a large section of managed heap for new object allocations.

## Garbage Collector Optimizations

The GC uses a concept known as *generations*, the primary purpose of which is to improve its performance. The theory behind generations is that objects that have been recently created tend to have a higher probability of being garbage-collected than objects that have existed on the system for a longer time.

To understand generations, consider the analogy of a mall parking lot where cars represent objects created by the CLR. People have different shopping patterns when they visit the mall. Some people spend a good portion of their day in the mall, and others stop only long enough to pick up an item or two. Applying the theory of generations to trying to find an empty parking space for a car yields a scenario in which the highest probability of finding a parking space is a function of where other cars have recently parked. In other words, a space that was occupied recently is more likely to be held by someone who just needed to quickly pick up an item or two. The longer a car has been parked, the higher the probability that its owner is an all-day shopper and the lower the probability that the parking space will be freed up anytime soon.

Generations provide a means for the GC to identify recently created objects versus long-lived objects. An object's generation is basically a counter that indicates how many times it has successfully avoided garbage collection. An object's generation counter starts at zero and can have a maximum value of two, after which the object's generation remains at this value regardless of how many times it is checked for collection.

You can put this to the test with a simple Visual Basic application. From the File menu, select either File ➪ New ➪ Project, or open the sample from the code download. Select a console application, provide a name and directory for your new project, and click OK. Within the Main module, add the following code snippet (code file: ProVB_Memory\Module1.vb):

```
Module Module1
  Sub Main()
    Dim myObject As Object = New Object()
    Dim i As Integer
      For i = 0 To 3
        Console.WriteLine(String.Format("Generation = {0}", _
                          GC.GetGeneration(myObject)))
        GC.Collect()
```

```
            GC.WaitForPendingFinalizers()
        Next i
        Console.Read()
    End Sub
End Module
```

This code sends its output to the .NET console. For a Windows application, this console defaults to the Visual Studio Output window. When you run this code, it creates an instance of an object and then iterates through a loop four times. For each loop, it displays the current generation count of myObject and then calls the GC. The GC.WaitForPendingFinalizers method blocks execution until the garbage collection has been completed.

As shown in Figure 2-6, each time the GC was run, the generation counter was incremented for myObject, up to a maximum of 2.

**FIGURE 2-6:** Progression of generations

Each time the GC is run, the managed heap is compacted, and the reference to the end of the most recent memory allocation is updated. After compaction, objects of the same generation are grouped together. Generation-2 objects are grouped at the bottom of the managed heap, and generation-1 objects are grouped next. New generation-0 objects are placed on top of the existing allocations, so they are grouped together as well.

This is significant because recently allocated objects have a higher probability of having shorter lives. Because objects on the managed heap are ordered according to generations, the GC can opt to collect newer objects. Running the GC over a limited portion of the heap is quicker than running it over the entire managed heap.

It's also possible to invoke the GC with an overloaded version of the Collect method that accepts a generation number. The GC will then collect all objects no longer referenced by the application that belong to the specified (or younger) generation. The version of the Collect method that accepts no parameters collects objects that belong to all generations.

Another hidden GC optimization results from the fact that a reference to an object may implicitly go out of scope; therefore, it can be collected by the GC. It is difficult to illustrate how the optimization occurs only if there are no additional references to the object and the object does not have a finalizer. However, if an object is declared and used at the top of a module and not referenced again in a method, then in the release mode, the metadata will indicate that the variable is not referenced in the later portion of the code. Once the last reference to the object is made, its logical scope ends; and if the garbage collector runs, the memory for that object, which will no longer be referenced, can be reclaimed before it has gone out of its physical scope.

## NAMESPACES

Even if you did not realize it, you have been using namespaces since the beginning of this book. For example, `System`, `System.Diagnostics`, and `System.Data.SqlClient` are all namespaces contained within the .NET Framework. Namespaces are an easy concept to understand; in short, the .NET Framework is built using a collection of libraries. These libraries allow for both a hierarchy of classes that are related to a given topic and horizontally for classes that fill in unrelated capabilities.

Namespaces are important to the CLR in that depending on which version of the .NET Framework you are targeting, which class libraries are available may change. As noted different .NET Platforms and Profiles provide an implementation for different features. As such when selecting which version of the .NET Framework and CLR your application will run against, you are selecting which namespaces should be available to it.

## What Is a Namespace?

Namespaces are a way of organizing the vast number of classes, structures, enumerations, delegates, and interfaces that a version of the .NET Framework class library provides. They are a hierarchically structured index into a class library, which is available to all of the .NET languages, not only the Visual Basic 2012 language (with the exception of the `My` namespace). The namespaces, or object references, are typically organized by function. For example, the `System.IO` namespace contains classes, structures, and interfaces for working with input/output streams and files. The classes in this namespace do not necessarily inherit from the same base classes (apart from `Object`, of course).

A namespace is a combination of a naming convention and an assembly, which organizes collections of objects and prevents ambiguity about object references. A namespace can be, and often is, implemented across several physical assemblies, but from the reference side, it is the namespace that ties these assemblies together. A namespace consists of not only classes, but also other (child) namespaces. For example, `IO` is a child namespace of the `System` namespace.

Namespaces provide identification beyond the component name. With a namespace, it is possible to use a more meaningful title (for example, `System`) followed by a grouping (for example, `Text`) to group together a collection of classes that contain similar functions. For example, the `System.Text` namespace contains a powerful class called `StringBuilder`. To reference this class, you can use the fully qualified namespace reference of `System.Text.StringBuilder`, as shown here:

```
Dim sb As New System.Text.StringBuilder()
```

The structure of a namespace is not a reflection of the physical inheritance of classes that make up the namespace. For example, the System.Text namespace contains another child namespace called RegularExpressions. This namespace contains several classes, but they do not inherit or otherwise reference the classes that make up the System.Text namespace.

Figure 2-7 shows how the System namespace contains the Text child namespace, which also has a child namespace, called RegularExpressions. Both of these child namespaces, Text and RegularExpressions, contain a number of objects in the inheritance model for these classes, as shown in the figure.

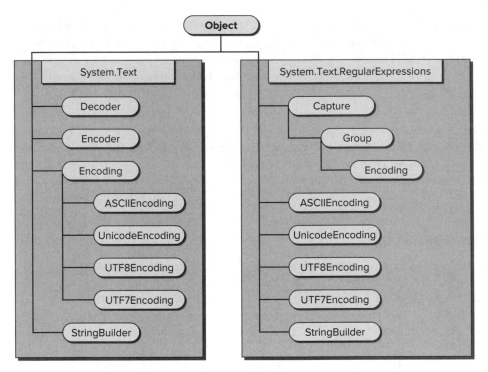

**FIGURE 2-7:** Logical class relationships in namespace

As shown in Figure 2-7, while some of the classes in each namespace do inherit from each other, and while all of the classes eventually inherit from the generic Object, the classes in System.Text .RegularExpressions do not inherit from the classes in System.Text.

To emphasize the usefulness of namespaces, we can draw another good example from Figure 2-7. If you make a reference to System.Drawing.Imaging.Encoder in your application, then you are making a reference to a completely different Encoder class than the namespace shown in Figure 2-7—System.Text.Encoder. Being able to clearly identify classes that have the same name but very different functions, and disambiguate them, is yet another advantage of namespaces.

The System namespace, imported by default as part of every project created with Visual Studio, contains not only the default Object class, but also many other classes that are used as the basis for every .NET language.

What if a class you need isn't available in your project? The problem may be with the references in your project. For example, by default, the System.DirectoryServices namespace, used to get programmatic access to the Active Directory objects, is not part of your project's assembly. Using it requires adding a reference to the project assembly.

In fact, with all this talk about referencing, it is probably a good idea to look at an example of adding an additional namespace to a project. Before doing that, though, you should know a little bit about how a namespace is actually implemented.

Namespaces are implemented within .NET assemblies. The System namespace is implemented in an assembly called System.dll provided with Visual Studio. By referencing this assembly, the project is capable of referencing all the child namespaces of System that happen to be implemented in this assembly. Using the preceding table, the project can import and use the System.Text namespace, because its implementation is in the System.dll assembly. However, although it is listed, the project cannot import or use the System.Data namespace unless it references the assembly that implements this child of the System namespace, System.Data.dll.

You will now create a sample project so you can examine the role that namespaces play within it. Using Visual Studio 2012, create a new Visual Basic Console Application project; for the download this project was called ProVB_Namespaces.

The System.Collections library is not, by default, part of Visual Basic 2012 console applications. To gain access to the classes that this namespace provides, you need to add it to your project. You can do this by using the Add Reference dialog (available by right-clicking the Project Name node within the Visual Studio Solution Explorer). The Add Reference dialog has four tabs, each containing elements that can be referenced from your project:

1. **Assemblies**—Contains .NET assemblies that can be found in the GAC. In addition to providing the name of the assembly, you can also get the version of the assembly and the version of the framework to which the assembly is compiled. This tab actually has two categories: those libraries which are part of your targeted framework, and those which are extensions to that framework.

2. **Solution**—Custom .NET assemblies from any of the various projects contained within your solution.

3. **COM**—This tab displays all the available COM components. It provides the name of the component and the TypeLib version.

4. **Browse**—Allows you to search for any component files (.dll, .tlb, .olb, .ocx, .exe, or .manifest) on the network.

The Add Reference dialog is shown in Figure 2-8. The available .NET namespaces are listed by component name. This is the equivalent of the namespace name.

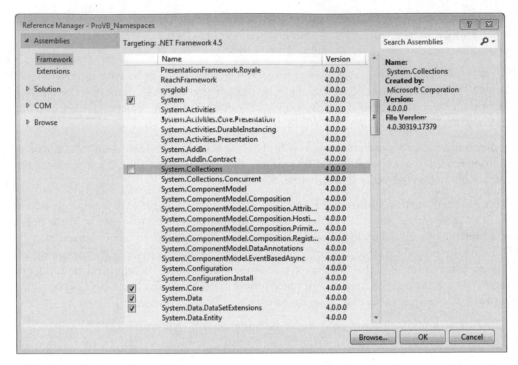

**FIGURE 2-8:** Reference Manager

## Namespaces and References

The list of default references automatically included varies depending on the type of project. By right-clicking on your project and going to the References tab you see the list shown in Figure 2-9. If the project type were an ASP.NET Web service (not shown), then the list would include references to the System.Web and System.Web.Services namespaces.

In addition to making the namespaces available, references play a second important role in your project. One of the advantages of .NET is using services and components built on the common language runtime (CLR), which enables you to avoid DLL conflicts. The various problems that can occur related to DLL versioning, commonly referred to as *DLL hell*, involve two types of conflict.

The first situation occurs when you have a component that requires a minimum DLL version, and an older version of the same DLL causes your product to break. The alternative situation is when you require an older version of a DLL, and a new version is incompatible. In either case, the result is that a shared file, outside of your control, creates a system-wide dependency that affects your software. With .NET, it is possible, but not required, to indicate that a DLL should be shipped as part of your project to avoid an external dependency.

To indicate that a referenced component should be included locally, you can select the reference in the Solution Explorer and then examine the properties associated with that reference. One editable property is called Copy Local. You will see this property and its value in the Properties window within Visual Studio 2012. For those assemblies that are part of a Visual Studio 2012 installation, this value defaults to `False`, as shown in Figure 2-9. However, for custom references, this property defaults to `True` to indicate that the referenced DLL should be included as part of the assembly. Changing this property to `True` changes the path associated with the assembly. Instead of using the path to the referenced file's location on the system, the project copies the referenced DLL into your application's runtime folder.

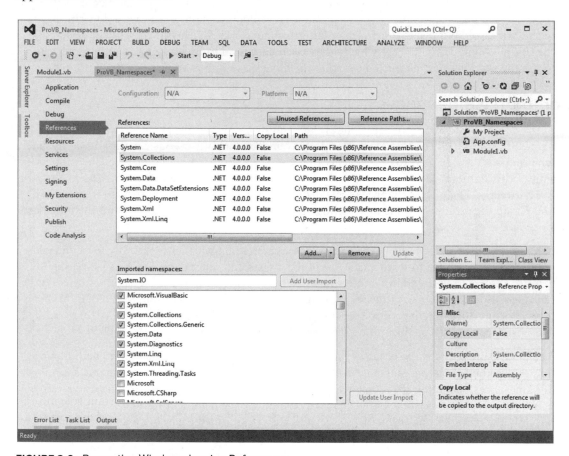

**FIGURE 2-9:** Properties Window showing References

The benefit of this is that even when another version of the DLL is later placed on the system, your project's assembly will continue to call its local copy. However, this protection from a conflicting version comes at a price: Future updates to the namespace assembly to fix flaws will be in the system version, but not in the private version that is part of your project's assembly.

To resolve this, Microsoft's solution is to place new versions in directories based on their version information. If you examine the path information for all of the Visual Studio 2012 references, you will see that it includes a version number. As new versions of these DLLs are released, they are installed in a separate directory. This method allows for an escape from DLL hell by keeping new versions from overwriting old versions, and it enables old versions to be easily located for maintenance updates. Therefore, it is often best to leave alone the default behavior of Visual Studio 2012, which is set to copy only locally custom components, until your organization implements a directory structure with version information similar to that of Microsoft.

Visual Studio 2012 will not allow you to add a reference to your assembly if the targeted implementation includes a reference that is not also referenced in your assembly. The good news is that the compiler will help. The compiler will flag references to invalid namespaces with underlining, similar to the Microsoft Word spelling or grammar error underlines. When you click the underlined text, the compiler will either tell you which other assemblies need to be referenced in the project in order to use the class in question, or indicate that the namespace isn't available.

## Common Namespaces

Every Visual Basic 2012 project includes the namespace `Microsoft.VisualBasic`. This namespace is part of the Visual Studio project templates for Visual Basic 2012 and is, in short, what makes Visual Basic 2012 different from C# or any other .NET language. The implicit inclusion of this namespace is the reason why you can call `IsDBNull` and other methods of Visual Basic 2012 directly. The only difference in the default namespaces included with Visual Basic 2012 and C# application projects is that the former use `Microsoft.VisualBasic` and the latter use `Microsoft.CSharp`.

Figure 2-9 shows an example of the namespaces that are imported automatically for a console application. Of course, to really make use of the classes and other objects in this list, you need more detailed information. In addition to resources such as Visual Studio 2010's help files, the best source of information is the Object Browser, available directly in the Visual Studio 2012 IDE. You can find it by selecting View ⇨ Object Browser if you are using Visual Studio 2012, 2010, 2005, or 2003. The Visual Studio 2012 Object Browser is shown in Figure 2-10.

The Object Browser displays each of the referenced assemblies and enables you to drill down into the various namespaces. Figure 2-10 illustrates how the `System.dll` implements a number of namespaces, including some that are part of the `System` namespace. By drilling down into a namespace, you can see some of the classes available. By further selecting a class, the browser shows not only the methods and properties associated with the selected class, but also a brief outline of what that class does.

Using the Object Browser is an excellent way to gain insight into which classes and interfaces are available via the different assemblies included in your project, and how they work. Clearly, the ability to actually see which classes are available and know how to use them is fundamental to being able to work efficiently. Working effectively in the .NET CLR environment requires finding the right class for the task.

## Importing and Aliasing Namespaces

Not all namespaces should be imported at the global level. Although you have looked at the namespaces included at this level, it is much better to import namespaces only in the module where they will be used. As with variables used in a project, it is possible to define a namespace at the module level. The advantage of this is similar to using local variables in that it helps to prevent different namespaces from interfering with each other. As this section shows, it is possible for two different namespaces to contain classes or even child namespaces with the same name.

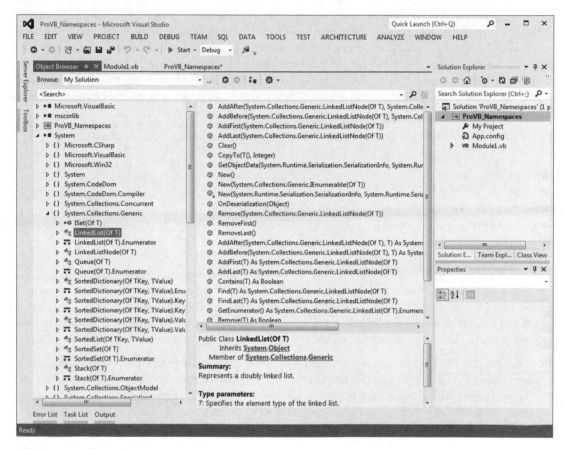

**FIGURE 2-10:** Object Browser

## Importing Namespaces

The development environment and compiler need a way to prioritize the order in which namespaces should be checked when a class is referenced. It is always possible to unequivocally specify a class by stating its complete namespace path. This is referred to as fully qualifying your declaration. The following example fully qualifies a `StringBuilder` object:

```
Dim sb = New System.Text.StringBuilder
```

However, if every reference to every class needed its full namespace declaration, then Visual Basic 2010 and every other .NET language would be very difficult to program in. After all, who wants to type `System.Collections.ArrayList` each time an instance of the `ArrayList` class is wanted? If you review the global references, you will recall we added a reference to the

`System.Collections` namespace. Thus, you can just type **ArrayList** whenever you need an instance of this class, as the reference to the larger `System.Collections` namespace has already been made by the application.

In theory, another way to reference the `StringBuilder` class is to use `Text.StringBuilder`, but with all namespaces imported globally, there is a problem with this, caused by what is known as *namespace crowding*. Because there is a second namespace, `System.Drawing`, that has a child called `Text`, the compiler does not have a clear location for the `Text` namespace and, therefore, cannot resolve the `StringBuilder` class. The solution to this problem is to ensure that only a single version of the `Text` child namespace is found locally. That way, the compiler will use this namespace regardless of the global availability of the `System.Drawing.Text` namespace.

`Imports` statements specify to the compiler those namespaces that the code will use:

```
Imports Microsoft.Win32
Imports System
Imports SysText = System.Text
```

Once they are imported into the file, you are not required to fully qualify your object declarations in your code. For instance, if you imported the `System.Data.SqlClient` namespace into your file, then you would be able to create a `SqlConnection` object in the following manner:

```
Dim conn As New SqlConnection
```

Each of the preceding `Imports` statements illustrates a different facet of importing namespaces. The first namespace, `Microsoft.Win32`, is not imported at the global level. Looking at the reference list, you may not see the Microsoft assembly referenced directly. However, opening the Object Browser reveals that this namespace is actually included as part of the `System.dll`.

As noted earlier, the `StringBuilder` references become ambiguous because both `System.Text` and `System.Drawing.Text` are valid namespaces at the global level. As a result, the compiler has no way to determine which `Text` child namespace is being referenced. Without any clear indication, the compiler flags `Text.StringBuilder` declarations in the command handler. However, using the `Imports System` declaration in the module tells the compiler that before checking namespaces imported at the global level, it should attempt to match incomplete references at the module level. Because the `System` namespace is declared at this level, if `System.Drawing` is not, then there is no ambiguity regarding to which child namespace `Text.StringBuilder` belongs.

This sequence demonstrates how the compiler looks at each possible declaration:

➤ It first determines whether the item is a complete reference, such as `System.Text` `.StringBuilder`.

➤ If the declaration does not match a complete reference, then the compiler tries to determine whether the declaration is from a child namespace of one of the module-level imports.

➤ Finally, if a match is not found, then the compiler looks at the global-level imports to determine whether the declaration can be associated with a namespace imported for the entire assembly.

While the preceding logical progression of moving from a full declaration through module-level to global-level imports resolves the majority of issues, it does not handle all possibilities.

Specifically, if you import `System.Drawing` at the module level, the namespace collision would return. This is where the third `Imports` statement becomes important—this `Imports` statement uses an alias.

## Aliasing Namespaces

Aliasing has two benefits in .NET. First, aliasing enables a long namespace such as `System .EnterpriseServices` to be replaced with a shorthand name such as `COMPlus`. Second, it adds a way to prevent ambiguity among child namespaces at the module level.

As noted earlier, the `System` and `System.Drawing` namespaces both contain a child namespace of `Text`. Because you will be using a number of classes from the `System.Drawing` namespace, it follows that this namespace should be imported into the form's module. However, were this namespace imported along with the `System` namespace, the compiler would again find references to the `Text` child namespace ambiguous. By aliasing the `System.Drawing` namespace to `SysDraw`, the compiler knows that it should check the `System.Drawing` namespace only when a declaration begins with that alias. The result is that although multiple namespaces with the same child namespace are now available at the module level, the compiler knows that one (or more) of them should be checked at this level only when they are explicitly referenced.

Aliasing as defined here is done in the following fashion:

```
Imports SysText = System.Text
```

## Referencing Namespaces in ASP.NET

Making a reference to a namespace in ASP.NET is quite similar to working with Windows applications, but you have to take some simple, additional steps. From your ASP.NET solution, first make a reference to the assemblies from the References folder, just as you do with Windows Forms. Once there, import these namespaces at the top of the page file in order to avoid having to fully qualify the reference every time on that particular page.

For example, instead of using `System.Collections.Generic` for each instance, use the `< %# Import % >` page directive at the top of the ASP.NET page (if the page is constructed using the inline coding style) or use the `Imports` keyword at the top of the ASP.NET page's code-behind file (just as you would with Windows Forms applications). The following example shows how to perform this task when using inline coding for ASP.NET pages:

```
<%# Import Namespace="System.Collections.Generic" %>
```

Now that this reference is in place on the page, you can access everything this namespace contains without having to fully qualify the object you are accessing. Note that the `Import` keyword in the inline example is not missing an "s" at the end. When importing in this manner, it is `Import` (without the "s") instead of `Imports`—as it is in the ASP.NET code-behind model and Windows Forms.

In ASP.NET 1.0/1.1, if you used a particular namespace on each page of your application, you needed the `Import` statement on each and every page where that namespace was needed. ASP.NET 3.5 introduced the ability to use the `web.config` file to make a global reference so that you don't need to make further references on the pages themselves, as shown in the following example:

```
<pages>
   <namespaces>
      <add namespace="System.Drawing" />
      <add namespace="Wrox.Books" />
   </namespaces>
</pages>
```

In this example, using the <namespaces> element in the web.config file, references are made to the System.Drawing namespace and the Wrox.Books namespace. Because these references are now contained within the web.config file, there is no need to again reference them on any of the ASP.NET pages contained within this solution.

## CREATING YOUR OWN NAMESPACES

Every assembly created in .NET is part of some root namespace. By default assemblies are assigned a namespace that matches the project name. In .NET it is possible to change this default behavior. Just as Microsoft has packaged the system-level and CLR classes using well-defined names, you can create your own namespaces. Of course, it is also possible to create projects that match existing namespaces and extend those namespaces, but that is typically a poor programming practice.

Namespaces can be created at one of two levels in Visual Basic. Similar to C# it is possible to explicitly assign a namespace within a source file using the Namespace keyword. However, Visual Basic provides a second way of defining your custom namespace. By default one of your project properties is the root namespace for your application in Visual Basic. This root namespace will be applied to all classes that don't explicitly define a namespace. You can review your project's default namespace by accessing the project properties. This is done through the assembly's project pages, reached by right-clicking the solution name in the Solution Explorer window and working off the first tab (Application) within the Properties page that opens in the document window, as shown in Figure 2-11.

The next step is optional, but, depending on whether you want to create a class at the top level or at a child level, you can add a Namespace command to your code. There is a trick to being able to create top-level namespaces or multiple namespaces within the modules that make up an assembly. Instead of replacing the default namespace with another name, you can delete the default namespace and define the namespaces only in the modules, using the Namespace command.

The Namespace command is accompanied by an End Namespace command. This End Namespace command must be placed after the End Class tag for any classes that will be part of the namespace. The following code demonstrates the structure used to create a MyMetaNamespace namespace, which contains a single class:

```
Namespace MyMetaNamespace
    Class MyClass1
        ' Code
    End Class
End Namespace
```

You can then utilize the MyClass1 object simply by referencing its namespace, MyMetaNamespace .MyClass1. It is also possible to have multiple namespaces in a single file, as shown here:

```
Namespace MyMetaNamespace1
    Class MyClass1
        ' Code
    End Class
 End Namespace
Namespace MyMetaNamespace2
    Class MyClass2
        ' Code
    End Class
 End Namespace
```

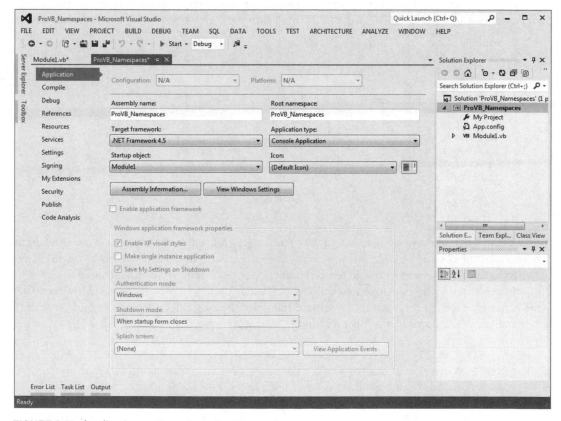

**FIGURE 2-11:** Application settings in project properties

Using this kind of structure, if you want to utilize `MyClass1`, then you access it through the namespace `MyMetaNamespace.MyClass1`. This does not give you access to `MyMetaNamespace2` and the objects that it offers; instead, you have to make a separate reference to `MyMetaNamespace2.MyClass2`. Note typically it is best practice to place each class into a separate file; similarly, having multiple namespaces in a single file is not considered best practice.

The `Namespace` command can also be nested. Using nested `Namespace` commands is how child namespaces are defined. The same rules apply — each `Namespace` must be paired with an `End Namespace` and must fully encompass all of the classes that are part of that namespace. In the following example, the `MyMetaNamespace` has a child namespace called `MyMetaNamespace.MyChildNamespace`:

```
Namespace MyMetaNamespace
    Class MyClass1
        ' Code
    End Class
    Namespace MyChildNamespace
        Class MyClass2
            ' Code
        End Class
    End Namespace
End Namespace
```

This is another point to be aware of when you make references to other namespaces within your own custom namespaces. Consider the following example:

```
Imports System
Imports System.Data
Imports System.Data.SqlClient
Imports System.IO
Namespace MyMetaNamespace1
    Class MyClass1
        ' Code
    End Class
End Namespace
Namespace MyMetaNamespace2
    Class MyClass2
        ' Code
    End Class
End Namespace
```

In this example, a number of different namespaces are referenced in the file. The four namespaces referenced at the top of the code listing—the `System`, `System.Data`, and `System.Data.SqlClient` namespace references—are available to every namespace developed in the file. This is because these three references are sitting outside of any particular namespace declarations. However, the same is not true for the `System.IO` namespace reference. Because this reference is made within the `MyMetaNamespace2` namespace, it is unavailable to any other namespace in the file.

> **NOTE** *When you create your own namespaces, Microsoft recommends that you use a convention of* `CompanyName.TechnologyName` *— for example,* `Wrox.Books`. *This helps to ensure that all libraries are organized in a consistent way.*

Sometimes when you are working with custom namespaces, you might find that you have locked yourself out of accessing a particular branch of a namespace, purely due to naming conflicts. Visual Basic includes the `Global` keyword, which can be used as the outermost root class available in the .NET Framework class library. Figure 2-12 shows a diagram of how the class structure looks with the `Global` keyword.

This means that you can make specifications such as:

```
Global.System.String
```

or

```
Global.Wrox.System.Titles
```

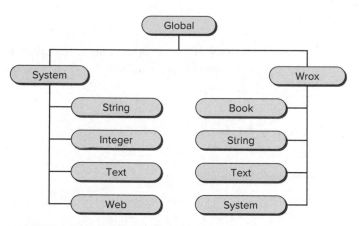

**FIGURE 2-12:** Visual Basic's Global keyword's namespace hierarchy

# THE MY KEYWORD

The My keyword is a novel concept that was introduced in the .NET Framework 2.0 to quickly give you access to your application, your users, your resources, the computer, or the network on which the application resides. The My keyword has been referred to as a way of speed-dialing common but complicated resources to which you need access. Using the My keyword, you can quickly access a wide variety of items, such as user details or specific settings of the requester browser.

Though not really considered a true namespace, the My object declarations that you make work in the same way as the .NET namespace structure you are used to working with. To give you an example, first look at how you get the user's machine name using the traditional namespace structure:

```
Environment.MachineName.ToString()
```

For this example, you simply need to use the Environment class and use this namespace to get at the MachineName property. The following shows how you would accomplish this same task using the My keyword:

```
My.Computer.Info.MachineName.ToString()
```

Looking at this example, you may be wondering what the point is if the example that uses My is lengthier than the first example, which just works off of the Environment namespace. Remember that the point is not the length of what you type to access specific classes, but a logical way to find frequently accessed resources without spending a lot of time hunting for them. Would you have known to look in the Environment class to get the machine name of the user's computer? Maybe, but maybe not. Using My.Computer.Info.MachineName.ToString is a tremendously more logical approach; and once compiled, this namespace declaration will be set to work with the same class as shown previously without a performance hit.

If you type the My keyword in your Windows Forms application, IntelliSense provides you with seven items to work with: Application, Computer, Forms, Resources, Settings, User, and WebServices. Though this keyword works best in the Windows Forms environment, there are still things that you can use in the Web Forms world. If you are working with a Web application, then you will have three items off the My keyword: Application, Computer, and User. Each of these is described further in the following sections.

# My.Application

The My.Application namespace gives you quick access to specific settings and points that deal with your overall application. Table 2-3 details the properties and methods of the My.Application namespace.

**TABLE 2-3:** My.Application Properties and Methods

| PROPERTY/METHOD | DESCRIPTION |
| --- | --- |
| ApplicationContext | Returns contextual information about the thread of the Windows Forms application. |
| ChangeCulture | A method that enables you to change the culture of the current application thread. |
| ChangeUICulture | A method that enables you to change the culture that is being used by the Resource Manager. |
| Culture | Returns the current culture being used by the current thread. |
| Deployment | Returns an instance of the ApplicationDeployment object, which allows for programmatic access to the application's ClickOnce features. |
| GetEnvironmentVariable | A method that enables you to access the value of an environment variable. |
| Info | Provides quick access to the assembly of Windows Forms. You can retrieve assembly information such as version number, name, title, copyright information, and more. |
| IsNetworkDeployed | Returns a Boolean value that indicates whether the application was distributed via the network using the ClickOnce feature. If True, then the application was deployed using ClickOnce—otherwise False. |
| Log | Enables you to write to your application's Event Log listeners. |
| MinimumSplashScreenDisplayTime | Enables you to set the time for the splash screen. |
| OpenForms | Returns a FormCollection object, which allows access to the properties of the forms currently open. |
| SaveMySettingsOnExit | Provides the capability to save the user's settings upon exiting the application. This method works only for Windows Forms and console applications. |
| SplashScreen | Enables you to programmatically assign the splash screen for the application. |
| UICulture | Returns the current culture being used by the Resource Manager. |

Much can be accomplished using the `My.Application` namespace. For an example of its use, you will focus on the `Info` property. This property provides access to the information stored in the application's `AssemblyInfo.vb` file, as well as other details about the class file. In one of your applications, you can create a message box that is displayed using the following code (code file: `ProVB_Namespaces\Module1.vb`):

```
System.Windows.Forms.MessageBox.Show("Company Name: " &
    My.Application.Info.CompanyName & vbCrLf &
    "Description: " & My.Application.Info.Description & vbCrLf &
    "Directory Path: " & My.Application.Info.DirectoryPath & vbCrLf &
    "Copyright: " & My.Application.Info.Copyright & vbCrLf &
    "Trademark: " & My.Application.Info.Trademark & vbCrLf &
    "Name: " & My.Application.Info.AssemblyName & vbCrLf &
    "Product Name: " & My.Application.Info.ProductName & vbCrLf &
    "Title: " & My.Application.Info.Title & vbCrLf &
    "Version: " & My.Application.Info.Version.ToString())
```

From this example, it is clear that you can get at quite a bit of information concerning the assembly of the running application. Running this code produces a message box similar to the one shown in Figure 2-13.

Another interesting property to look at from the `My.Application` namespace is the `Log` property. This property enables you to work with the log files for your application. For instance, you can easily write to the system's Application Event Log by first changing the application's `app.config` file to include the following (code file: `ProVB_Namespaces\app.config.txt`):

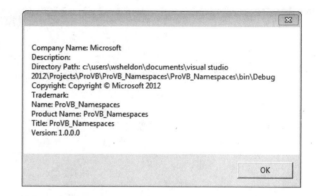

FIGURE 2-13: Project properties displayed in a message box

```
<?xml version="1.0" encoding="utf-8" ?>
<configuration>
    <startup>
        <supportedRuntime version="v4.0" sku=".NETFramework,Version=v4.5" />
    </startup>
    <system.diagnostics>
        <sources>
            <source name="DefaultSource" switchName="DefaultSwitch">
                <listeners>
                    <add name="EventLog"/>
                </listeners>
            </source>
        </sources>
        <switches>
            <add name="DefaultSwitch" value="Information" />
        </switches>
        <sharedListeners>
            <add name="EventLog"
              type="System.Diagnostics.EventLogTraceListener"
              initializeData="ProVBEventWriter" />
```

```
        </sharedListeners>
      </system.diagnostics>
    </configuration>
```

Once the configuration file is in place, you can record entries to the Application Event Log. Note that writing to the Application Event Log is a privileged action, and you need to have started Visual Studio 2012 as an administrator on your machine. However, the code shown in the following simple example can leverage the configuration settings previously shown to leave a message within the event log (code file: ProVB_Namespaces\Module1.vb):

```
My.Application.Log.WriteEntry("Entered Form1_Load", _
    TraceEventType.Information, 1)
```

You could also just as easily use the `WriteExceptionEntry` method in addition to the `WriteEntry` method. After running this application and looking in the Event Viewer, you will see the event shown in Figure 2-14.

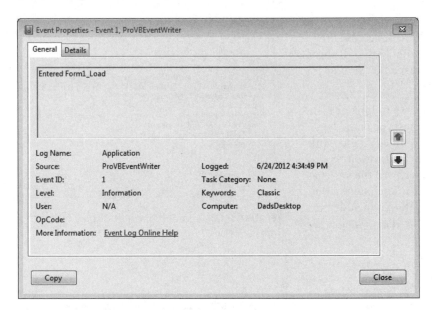

**FIGURE 2-14:** Details from the Event Log

The previous example shows how to write to the Application Event Log when working with the objects that write to the event logs. In addition to the Application Event Log, there is also a Security Event Log and a System Event Log. Note that when using these objects, it is impossible to write to the Security Event Log, and it is only possible to write to the System Event Log if the application does it under either the Local System or the Administrator accounts.

In addition to writing to the Application Event Log, you can just as easily write to a text file. As with writing to the Application Event Log, writing to a text file also means that you need to make changes to the `app.config` file (code file: `app.config to support writing to filelog`):

```
<?xml version="1.0" encoding="utf-8" ?>
<configuration>
```

```
<startup>
    <supportedRuntime version="v4.0" sku=".NETFramework,Version=v4.5" />
</startup>
<system.diagnostics>
    <sources>
        <source name="DefaultSource" switchName="DefaultSwitch">
            <listeners>
                <add name="EventLog"/>
                <add name="FileLog" />
            </listeners>
        </source>
    </sources>
    <switches>
        <add name="DefaultSwitch" value="Information" />
    </switches>
    <sharedListeners>
        <add name="EventLog"
         type="System.Diagnostics.EventLogTraceListener"
         initializeData="ProVBEventWriter" />
        <add name="FileLog"
         type="Microsoft.VisualBasic.Logging.FileLogTraceListener,
         Microsoft.VisualBasic, Version=8.0.0.0, Culture=neutral,
         PublicKeyToken=b03f5f7f11d50a3a, processorArchitecture=MSIL"
         initializeData="FileLogWriter"/>
    </sharedListeners>
</system.diagnostics>
</configuration>
```

Now with this `app.config` file in place, you simply need to run the same `WriteEntry` method as before. This time, however, in addition to writing to the Application Event Log, the information is also written to a new text file. You can find the text file at `C:\Users\`[*username*]`\AppData`
`\Roaming\`[*AssemblyCompany*]`\`[*AssemblyProduct*]`\`[*Version*]. For instance, in my example, the log file was found at `C:\Users\WSheldon\AppData\Roaming\Microsoft\ProVB_Namespaces`
`\1.0.0.0\`. In the `.log` file found, you will see a line such as the following:

```
DefaultSource    Information    1    Entered Form1_Load
```

By default, it is separated by tabs, but you can change the delimiter yourself by adding a delimiter attribute to the FileLog section in the `app.config` file:

```
<add name="FileLog"
    type="Microsoft.VisualBasic.Logging.FileLogTraceListener,
    Microsoft.VisualBasic, Version=8.0.0.0, Culture=neutral,
    PublicKeyToken=b03f5f7f11d50a3a, processorArchitecture=MSIL"
    initializeData="FileLogWriter" delimiter=";" />
```

In addition to writing to Event Logs and text files, you can also write to XML files, console applications, and more.

## My.Computer

The `My.Computer` namespace can be used to work with the parameters and details of the computer in which the application is running. Table 2-4 details the objects contained in this namespace.

**TABLE 2-4:** My.Computer Objects

| PROPERTY | DESCRIPTION |
| --- | --- |
| Audio | This object enables you to work with audio files from your application. This includes starting, stopping, and looping audio files. |
| Clipboard | This object enables you to read and write to the clipboard. |
| Clock | This enables access to the system clock to get at GMT and the local time of the computer running the application. You can also get at the tick count, which is the number of milliseconds that have elapsed since the computer was started. |
| FileSystem | This object provides a large collection of properties and methods that enable programmatic access to drives, folders, and files. This includes the ability to read, write, and delete items in the file system. |
| Info | This provides access to the computer's details, such as amount of memory, the operating system type, which assemblies are loaded, and the name of the computer itself. |
| Keyboard | This object provides information about which keyboard keys are pressed by the end user. Also included is a single method, SendKeys, which enables you to send the pressed keys to the active form. |
| Mouse | This provides a handful of properties that enable detection of the type of mouse installed, including details such as whether the left and right mouse buttons have been swapped, whether a mouse wheel exists, and how much to scroll when the user uses the wheel. |
| Name | This is a read-only property that provides access to the name of the computer. |
| Network | This object provides a single property and some methods that enable you to interact with the network to which the computer running the application is connected. With this object, you can use the IsAvailable property to first verify that the computer is connected to a network. If so, then the Network object enables you to upload or download files, and ping the network. |
| Ports | This object can provide notification when ports are available, as well as allow access to the ports. |
| Registry | This object provides programmatic access to the registry and the registry settings. Using the Registry object, you can determine whether keys exist, determine values, change values, and delete keys. |
| Screen | This provides the capability to work with one or more screens that may be attached to the computer. |

## My.Resources

The `My.Resources` namespace is a very easy way to get at the resources stored in your application. If you open the `MyResources.resx` file from the `My Project` folder in your solution, you can easily create as many resources as you wish. For example, you could create a single `String` resource titled `MyResourceString` and give it a value of St. Louis Rams.

To access the resources that you create, use the simple reference shown here:

```
My.Resources.MyResourceString.ToString()
```

Using IntelliSense, all of your created resources will appear after you type the period after the `MyResources` string.

## My.User

The `My.User` namespace enables you to work with the `IPrincipal` interface. You can use the `My.User` namespace to determine whether the user is authenticated or not, the user's name, and more. For instance, if you have a login form in your application, you could allow access to a particular form with code similar to the following:

```
If (Not My.User.IsInRole("Administrators")) Then
    ' Code here
End If
You can also just as easily get the user's name with the following:

My.User.Name
In addition, you can check whether the user is authenticated:

If My.User.IsAuthenticated Then
    ' Code here
End If
```

### My.WebServices

When not using the `My.WebServices` namespace, you access your Web services references in a lengthier manner. The first step in either case is to make a Web reference to some remote XML Web Service in your solution. These references will then appear in the Web References folder in the Solution Explorer in Visual Studio 2012. Before the introduction of the `My` namespace, you would have accessed the values that the Web reference exposed in the following manner:

```
Dim ws As New RubiosMenu.GetMenuDetails
Label1.Text = ws.GetLatestPrice.ToString()
```

This works, but now with the `My` namespace, you can use the following construct:

```
Label1.Text = My.WebServices.GetMenuDetails.GetLatestPrice.ToString()
```

## EXTENDING THE MY NAMESPACE

You are not limited to only what the My namespace provides. Just as you can with other namespaces, you can extend this namespace until your heart is content. To show an example of extending the My namespace so that it includes your own functions and properties, in your Console application, create a new module called CompanyExtensions.vb.

The code for the entire module and the associated class is presented here (code file: ProVB_Namespaces \CompanyExtensions.vb):

```
Namespace My
    <HideModuleName()> _
    Module CompanyOperations
        Private _CompanyExtensions As New CompanyExtensions
        Friend Property CompanyExtensions() As CompanyExtensions
            Get
                Return _CompanyExtensions
            End Get
            Set(ByVal value As CompanyExtensions)
                _CompanyExtensions = value
            End Set
        End Property
    End Module
End Namespace
Public Class CompanyExtensions
    Public ReadOnly Property CompanyDateTime() As DateTime
        Get
            Return DateTime.Now()
        End Get
    End Property
End Class
```

From this example, you can see that the module CompanyOperations is wrapped inside the My namespace. From there, a single property is exposed—CompanyExtensions. The class, CompanyExtensions, is a reference to the class found directly below in the same file. This class, CompanyExtensions, exposes a single ReadOnly Property called CompanyDateTime.

With this in place, build your application, and you are now ready to see the new expanded My namespace in action. Add the following code snippet to Module1.vb. As you type this you'll find that IntelliSense recognizes your custom extension to the My namespace.

```
System.Windows.Forms.MessageBox.Show(My.CompanyExtensions.CompanyDateTime)
```

The name of the module CompanyOperations doesn't also appear in the IntelliSense list because the <HideModuleName() > attribute precedes the opening module statement. This attribute signifies that you don't want the module name exposed to the My namespace.

The preceding example shows how to create your own sections within the My namespace, but you can also extend the sections that are already present (for example, Computer, User, etc.). Extending the My namespace is simply a matter of creating a partial class and extending it with the feature sets that you want to appear in the overall My namespace. An example of such an extension is presented in the following code sample (code file: ProVB_Namespaces\CompanyExtensions.vb):

```
Namespace My
    Partial Class MyComputer
        Public ReadOnly Property Hostname() As String
            Get
                Dim iphostentry As System.Net.IPHostEntry = _
                    System.Net.Dns.GetHostEntry(String.Empty)
                Return iphostentry.HostName.ToString()
            End Get
        End Property
    End Class
End Namespace
```

From this, you can see that this code is simply extending the already present `MyComputer` class:

```
Partial Class MyComputer
End Class
```

This extension exposes a single `ReadOnly` property called `Hostname` that returns the local user's hostname. After compiling or utilizing this class in your project, you will find the `Hostname` property available to you within the `My.Computer` namespace, as shown in Figure 2-15.

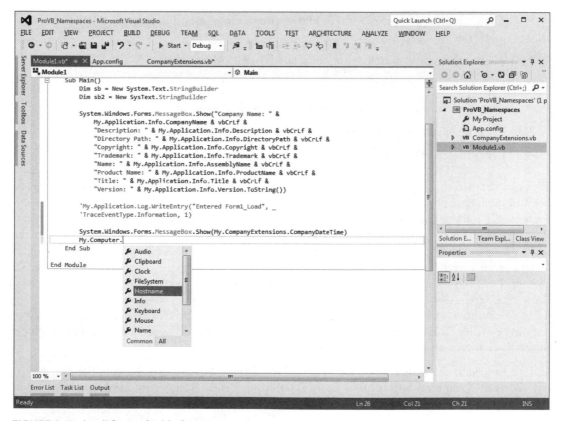

**FIGURE 2-15:** IntelliSense for My.Computer

# SUMMARY

This chapter introduced the CLR. You first looked at its memory management features, including how .NET uses namespaces to structure the classes available within the Framework. The chapter reviewed how the .NET Framework is handling multiple profiles and touched on the Visual Basic specific features of the My namespace. Chapter highlights include the following:

➤ Whenever possible, do not implement the Finalize method in a class.

➤ If the Finalize method is implemented, then also implement the IDisposable interface, which can be called by the client when the object is no longer needed.

➤ There is no way to accurately predict when the GC will collect an object that is no longer referenced by the application (unless the GC is invoked explicitly).

➤ The order in which the GC collects objects on the managed heap is nondeterministic. This means that the Finalize method cannot call methods on other objects referenced by the object being collected.

➤ Leverage the Using keyword to automatically trigger the execution of the IDisposable interface.

➤ The Portable Library project type allows you to target multiple different .NET Framework platforms.

➤ That namespace hierarchies are not related to class hierarchies.

➤ How to review and add references to a project.

➤ How to import and alias namespaces at the module level.

➤ Creating custom namespaces.

➤ Using the My namespace.

This chapter also examined the value of a common runtime and type system that can be targeted by multiple languages. This chapter illustrated how namespaces play an important role in the .NET Framework and your software development. They enable Visual Studio to manage and identify the appropriate libraries for use in different versions of .NET or when targeting different .NET platforms. Anyone who has ever worked on a large project has experienced situations in which a fix to a component was delayed because of the potential impact on other components in the same project. The CLR has the ability to version and support multiple versions of the same project. Regardless of the logical separation of components in the same project, developers who take part in the development process worry about collisions. With separate implementations for related components, it is not only possible to alleviate this concern, but also easier than ever before for a team of developers to work on different parts of the same project.

Having looked at the primary development tool in Chapter 1 and now reviewing the runtime environment, Chapter 3 will begin the process of using Visual Basic's core fundamental structure — the class.

# 3

# Objects and Visual Basic

**WROX.COM CODE DOWNLOADS FOR THIS CHAPTER**

The wrox.com code downloads for this chapter are found at www.wrox.com/remtitle .cgi?isbn=9781118314456 on the Download Code tab. The code is in the chapter 3 download and individually named according to the code filenames throughout the chapter.

This chapter takes you through the basic syntax of Visual Basic. With its transition many years ago to .NET, Visual Basic like all native .NET languages, became an object-oriented language. At the time this was a major transition, and even now you continue to talk about how Visual Basic supports the four major defining concepts required for a language to be fully object-oriented:

1. **Abstraction**—Abstraction is merely the ability of a language to create "black box" code, to take a concept and create an abstract representation of that concept within a program. A `Customer` object, for instance, is an abstract representation of a real-world customer. A `DataTable` object is an abstract representation of a set of data.

2. **Encapsulation**—Encapsulation is the concept of a separation between interface and implementation. The idea is that you can create an interface (public methods, properties, fields, and events in a class), and, as long as that interface remains consistent, the application can interact with your objects. This remains true even when you entirely rewrite the code within a given method—thus, the interface is independent of the implementation. The publicly exposed interface becomes what is known as a contract. It is this contract that you will look to limit changes to for those who consume your objects. For example, the algorithm you use to compute pi might be proprietary. You can expose a simple API to the end user, but hide all the logic used by the algorithm by encapsulating it within your class. Later if you change that algorithm, as long as the consumers of your object get the same results from your public interface, they won't need to make changes to support your updates. Encapsulation enables you to hide the internal implementation details of a class.

3. **Polymorphism**—Polymorphism is reflected in the ability to write one routine that can operate on objects from more than one class—treating different objects from different classes in exactly the same way. For instance, if both the `Customer` and the `Vendor` objects have a `Name` property and you can write a routine that calls the `Name` property regardless of whether you are using a `Customer` or `Vendor` object, then you have polymorphism.

   Visual Basic supports polymorphism in two ways—through late binding (much like Smalltalk, a classic example of a true object-oriented language) and through the implementation of multiple interfaces. This flexibility is very powerful and is preserved within Visual Basic.

4. **Inheritance**—Inheritance is the concept that a new class can be based on an existing class gaining the interface and behaviors of that base class. The child or subclass of that base or parent class is said to inherit the existing behaviors and properties. The new class can also customize or override existing methods and properties, as well as extending the class with new methods and properties. When inheriting from an existing class, the developer is implementing a process known as *subclassing*.

Chapter 4 discusses these four concepts in detail; this chapter focuses on the syntax that enables you to utilize classes that already implement these concepts. The concepts are then illustrated through a review of the core types that make up Visual Basic, as well as through the creation of a custom class that leverages these core concepts.

Visual Basic is also a component-based language. Component-based design is often viewed as a successor to object-oriented design, so component-based languages have some other capabilities. These are closely related to the traditional concepts of object orientation:

➤ **Multiple interfaces**—Each class in Visual Basic defines a *primary interface* (also called the *default* or *native interface*) through its public methods, properties, and events. Classes can also implement other, secondary interfaces in addition to this primary interface. An object based on this class has multiple interfaces, and a client application can choose with which interface it will interact with the object.

➤ **Assembly (component) level scoping**—Not only can you define your classes and methods as `Public` (available to anyone), `Protected` (available through inheritance), and `Private` (available only locally), you can also define them as `Friend`—meaning they are available only within the current assembly or component. This is not a traditional object-oriented concept, but is very powerful when used with component-based applications.

This chapter explains how to create and use classes and objects in Visual Basic. You won't get too deeply into code, but it is important that you spend a little time familiarizing yourself with basic object-oriented terms and concepts.

## OBJECT-ORIENTED TERMINOLOGY

To begin, you will take a look at the word *object* itself, along with the related *class* and *instance* terms. Then you will move on to discuss the four terms that define the major functionality in the object-oriented world: abstraction, encapsulation, polymorphism, and inheritance.

## Objects, Classes, and Instances

An *object* is a code-based abstraction of a real-world entity or relationship. For instance, you might have a `Customer` object that represents a real-world customer, such as customer number 123, or you might have a `File` object that represents `C:\config.sys` on your computer's hard drive.

A closely related term is *class*. A class is the code that defines an object, and all objects are created based on a class. A class is the definition which explains the properties and behavior of an object. It provides the basis from which you create instances of specific objects. For example, in order to have a `Customer` object representing customer number 123, you must first have a `Customer` class that contains all of the code (methods, properties, events, variables, and so on) necessary to create `Customer` objects. Based on that class, you can create any number of Customer instances. Each instance of the object Customer is identical to the others, except that it may contain different data. This means that each object represents a different customer.

## Composition of an Object

You use an *interface* to get access to an object's data and behaviors. This defines a contract for the object to follow. This is much like a real-world legal contract that binds the object to a standard definition of data and behaviors, where in your interface you can define what is needed to fulfill a contract. The object's data and behaviors are defined by the object, so a client application can treat the object like a black box, accessible only through its interface. This is a key object-oriented concept called *encapsulation*. The idea is that any program that makes use of this object will not have direct access to the behaviors or data; rather, those programs must make use of your object's interface.

## Interface

The interface is defined as a set of methods (Sub and Function methods), properties (property methods), events, and fields (also known as variables) that are declared public in scope.

You can also have private methods and properties in your code. While these methods may be called by code within your object, they are not part of the interface and cannot be called by programs written to use your object. Other keywords such as `Friend` may be used to define a portion of your interface that is not hidden but limits who can access that interface. These keywords are looked at more in Chapter 4, along with inheritance.

As a baseline example however, you might have the following code in a class:

```
Public Function CalculateValue() As Integer

End Function
```

Because this method is declared with the `Public` keyword, it is part of the interface and can be called by client applications that are using the object. You might also have a method such as this:

```
Private Sub DoSomething()

End Sub
```

This method is declared as being `Private`, so it is not part of the interface. This method can only be called by code within the class — not by any code outside the class, such as code in a program that's using one of the objects.

## Implementation or Behavior

The code inside a class is called the *implementation*. Sometimes in the case of methods it is also called *behavior*. This code that actually makes the object do useful work. For instance, you might have an `Age` property as part of the object's interface similar to the following:

```
Public ReadOnly Property Age() As Integer
```

In this case, the property simply returns a value as opposed to using code to calculate the value based on a birth date. The code necessary to call the `Age` property would look something like this:

```
theAge = myObject.Age
```

At some point you might find the object's data more accurate if it did calculate the age based on a fixed birth date. The key point is to understand that calling applications can use the object's property even if you change the implementation. As long as you do not change the public interface, callers are oblivious to how you compute the Age value. As long as this basic interface is unchanged, then you can change the implementation any way you want.

Fortunately, you can change the implementation without changing the client code:

```
Private _BirthDate As Date

Public ReadOnly Property Age() As Integer
  Get
     Return CInt(DateDiff(DateInterval.Year, _BirthDate, Now))
  End Get
End Property
```

You have changed the implementation behind the public interface, effectively changing how it behaves without changing the interface itself.

Additionally, to implement this change you've moved from one of the new features of Visual Basic 2010—auto-implemented properties—to a traditional property with a backing field implementation. Much of the existing .NET code you'll see in Visual Basic will use a backing field for properties.

Keep in mind that encapsulation is a *syntactic* tool—it enables the calling code to continue to run without change. However, it is not *semantic*, meaning that just because the code continues to run, that does not mean it continues to do what you actually want it to do.

## Fields or Instance Variables

The third key part of an object is its data, or state. In fact, it might be argued that the most important part of an object is its data. After all, every instance of a class is absolutely identical in terms of its interface and its implementation; the only thing that can vary at all is the data contained within that particular object.

Fields are variables that are declared so that they are available to all code within the class. They are also sometimes referred to as *instance variables* or *member variables*. Fields that are declared Private in scope are available only to the code in the class itself. Typically fields are not exposed, as this makes your underlying implementation part of the class's interface.

Don't confuse fields with properties. In Visual Basic, a property is a type of method geared to retrieving and setting values, whereas a field is a variable within the class that may hold the value exposed by a property. For instance, you might have a class that has these fields:

```
Public Class TheClass

    Private _Name As String
    Private _BirthDate As Date
End Class
```

Each instance of the class—each object—will have its own set of these fields in which to store data. Because these fields are declared with the Private keyword, they are only available to code within each specific object.

While fields can be declared as Public in scope, this makes them available to any code using the objects in a manner you cannot control. This directly breaks the concept of encapsulation, as code outside your object can directly change data values without following any rules that might otherwise be set in the object's code.

Consider the Age property shown in the previous section. You'll notice that by using a property, the underlying implementation was hidden to the outside world. When you decided to change the implementation to use a dynamically generated age, you could change that implementation without changing your interface.

If you want to make the value of a field available to code outside of the object, you should instead use a property:

```
Public Class TheClass
   Private _Name As String
   Private _BirthDate As Date

   Public ReadOnly Property Name() As String
     Get
       Return _Name
     End Get
   End Property

End Class
```

Because the Name property is a method, you are not directly exposing the internal variables to client code, so you preserve encapsulation of the data. Using properties allows you to encapsulate your implementation, so if later you choose to store the name as an array of characters or as a reference to a web service method, the code using your class isn't effected.

Note that even though you may use a property, there is, as you saw earlier, still a hidden backing field that you can declare explicitly without changing the external interface. Properties do not break the concept of encapsulation.

Now that you have a grasp of some of the basic object-oriented terminology, you are ready to explore the creation of classes and objects. First you will see how Visual Basic enables you to interact with objects and provides core types (all of which are objects), and then you will dive into the actual process of authoring those objects.

## System.Object

For now, the one key to remember is that all classes in Visual Basic—all classes in .NET, for that matter—inherit from the base class System.Object. The parent class for all other classes is System .Object. All other classes from Strings and Integers to Windows and custom classes developed by you. When a Class doesn't explicitly state its parent, .NET will automatically have the class inherit from System.Object. This also means that even if a Class does explicitly inherit from another Class, it will still inherit from System.Object. There was an old saying about how all roads lead to Rome. Well, in .NET all object hierarchies lead to System.Object.

This is where the term *polymorphism* becomes important. Since you can cast any object to a type from which it inherits, any type of object can be cast to the base class of System.Object. Casting is the name for code which takes an object of, for example, type Integer and assigns it to a variable of type System.Object. As you'll see as you work with Visual Basic or another object-oriented language, this means that you'll see many methods that are written to handle a parameter of type Object. This has several advantages for code reuse, but you'll learn that reuse can come at a cost.

The thing you'll want to keep in mind is that when an object is cast to its parent class it causes the methods of only the parent class to be available. While the object can be cast back to its original type, because it knows what that type is, it doesn't make all of its data and behavior available until it is cast back to its original type. You can cast to any type in an object's inheritance hierarchy; however, you can't cast down to an object which inherits from a base class. Inheritance will be covered in more detail in Chapter 4.

`System.Object` provides a member in which you will be interested. The method `ToString` provides a way to get a string representation of any object. The default implementation of this method will return the type of that object; however, many types provide a custom implementation of this method, and doing so is considered best practice.

## WORKING WITH VISUAL BASIC TYPES

Having introduced a combination of keywords and concepts for objects in Visual Basic, it is time to start exploring specific types. In order to ensure this is hands on, you need a project in Visual Studio 2012. The first chapter focused on Visual Studio 2012 and many of its features as your primary development tool. This chapter is much more focused on the Visual Basic language, and to limit its size you are going to reference the project created in the first chapter. As this chapter introduces some of the core types of Visual Basic classes provided by the .NET Framework, you will use the test code snippets from this chapter in that project.

You can create a new project based on the ProVB2012 project from Chapter 1 and use it to host the example snippets throughout this chapter. The code download for this chapter includes the final version of the samples in a project titled ProVB2012_Ch03. This means that as you progress through the chapter, you can either look in the sample download for the same code, or step-by-step build up your own copy of the sample, using the sample when something doesn't seem quite right in your own code. One change from the previous chapter's code is that the custom property and message box used in that chapter have already been removed from this project.

At this point, you have a display that allows you to show the results from various code snippets simply by updating the `Text` property on the `TextBox1` control of your window. The display for the baseline Windows Form application is shown in Figure 3-1.

The baseline is simply a button to initiate the sample code combined with a text box. To test a snippet, you add a new method to MainWindow, and then call this method from the Click event handler for the button. The sample download shows these methods in place, and then when you are ready to test the next method, remove the single quote to activate that method. Once you are done with one sample, comment out that method call and move to the next.

## Value and Reference Types

Experienced developers generally consider integers, characters, Booleans, and strings to be the basic building blocks of any language. As noted previously in .NET, all objects share a logical inheritance from the base `Object` class. This enables all of .NET to build on a common type system. As noted in Chapter 2, Visual Basic builds on the common type system shared across all .NET languages.

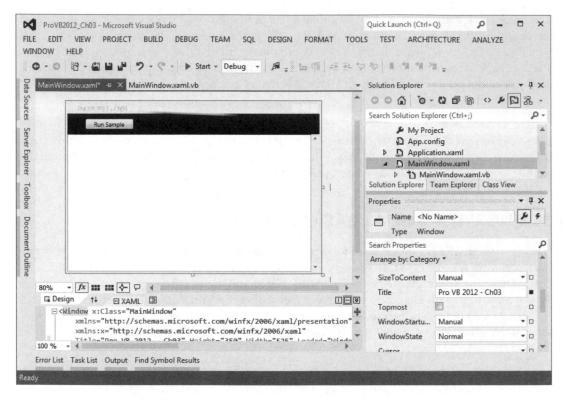

**FIGURE 3-1:** Baseline test frame

Because all data types are based on the core `Object` class, every variable you dimension can be assured of having a set of common characteristics. However, this logical inheritance does not require a common physical implementation for all variables. This is important because while everything in .NET is based on the `Object` class, under the covers .NET has two major implementations of types: value and reference.

For example, what most programmers consider to be some of the basic underlying types, such as `Integer`, `Long`, `Character`, and even `Byte`, are not implemented as classes. This is important, as you'll see when you look at boxing and the cost of transitioning between value types and reference types. The difference between value types and reference types is an underlying implementation difference:

➤   Value types represent simple data storage located on the stack. The stack is used for items of a known size, so items on the stack can be retrieved faster than those on the managed heap.

➤   Reference types are based on complex classes with implementation inheritance from their parent classes, and custom storage on the managed heap. The managed heap is optimized to support dynamic allocation of differently sized objects.

Note that the two implementations are stored in different portions of memory. As a result, value types and reference types are treated differently within assignment statements, and their memory management is handled differently. It is important to understand how these differences affect the software you will write in Visual Basic. Understanding the foundations of how data is manipulated in the .NET Framework will enable you to build more reliable and better-performing applications.

Consider the difference between the stack and the heap. The stack is a comparatively small memory area in which processes and threads store data of fixed size. An integer or decimal value needs the same number of bytes to store data, regardless of the actual value. This means that the location of such variables on the stack can be efficiently determined. (When a process needs to retrieve a variable, it has to search the stack. If the stack contained variables that had dynamic memory sizes, then such a search could take a long time.)

Reference types do not have a fixed size—a string can vary in size from two bytes to nearly all the memory available on a system. The dynamic size of reference types means that the data they contain is stored on the heap, rather than the stack. However, the address of the reference type (that is, the location of the data on the heap) does have a fixed size, and thus can be (and, in fact, is) stored on the stack. By storing a reference only to a custom allocation on the stack, the program as a whole runs much more quickly, as the process can rapidly locate the data associated with a variable.

Storing the data contained in fixed and dynamically sized variables in different places results in differences in the way variables behave. Rather than limit this discussion to the most basic of types in .NET, this difference can be illustrated by comparing the behavior of the `System.Drawing.Point` structure (a value type) and the `System.Text.StringBuilder` class (a reference type).

The `Point` structure is used as part of the .NET graphics library, which is part of the `System.Drawing` namespace. The `StringBuilder` class is part of the `System.Text` namespace and is used to improve performance when you're editing strings.

First, you will examine how the `System.Drawing.Point` structure is used. To do this, you'll create a new method called `ValueType()` within your ProVB2012_Ch03 application. This new private `Sub` will be called from the `ButtonTest` click event handler. The new method will have the following format (code file: `MainWindow.xaml.vb`):

```
Private Sub ValueType()
    Dim ptX As System.Drawing.Point = New System.Drawing.Point(10, 20)
    Dim ptY As System.Drawing.Point
    ptY = ptX
    ptX.X = 200
    TextBox1.Text = "Pt Y = " & ptY.ToString()
End Sub
```

The output from this operation will be `Pt Y = {{X = 10, Y = 20}}`, is shown in Figure 3-2.

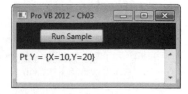

When the code copies `ptX` into `ptY`, the data contained in `ptX` is copied into the location on the stack associated with `ptY`. Later, when the value of `ptX` changes, only the memory on the stack associated with `ptX` is altered. Changing `ptX` has no effect on `ptY`. This is not the case with reference types. Consider the following code, a new method called `RefType`, which uses the `System.Text.StringBuilder` class (code file: `MainWindow.xaml.vb`):

**FIGURE 3-2** Output Pt Y value

```
Private Sub RefType()
    Dim objX As System.Text.StringBuilder =
            New System.Text.StringBuilder("Hello World")
    Dim objY As System.Text.StringBuilder
    objY = objX
    objX.Replace("World", "Test")
    TextBox1.Text = "objY = " & objY.ToString()
End Sub
```

The output from this operation will be ObjY = Hello Test, as shown in Figure 3-3, not ObjY = Hello World.

The first example using point values demonstrated that when one value type is assigned to another, the data stored on the stack is copied. This example demonstrates that when objY is assigned to objX, the address associated with objX on the stack is associated with objY on the stack. However, what is copied in this case isn't the actual data, but rather the address on the managed heap where the data is actually located. This means that objY and objX now reference the same data. When that

**FIGURE 3-3** Output of the ObjY value

data on the heap is changed, the data associated with every variable that holds a reference to that memory is changed. This is the default behavior of reference types, and is known as a *shallow copy*. Later in this chapter, you'll see how this behavior varies for strings.

The differences between value types and reference types go beyond how they behave when copied, and later in this chapter you'll encounter some of the other features provided by objects. First, though, take a closer look at some of the most commonly used value types and learn how .NET works with them.

## Primitive Types

Visual Basic, in common with other development languages, has a group of elements such as integers and strings that are termed *primitive types*. These primitive types are identified by keywords such as String, Long, and Integer, which are aliases for types defined by the .NET class library. This means that the line

```
Dim i As Long
```

is equivalent to the line

```
im i As System.Int64
```

The reason why these two different declarations are available has to do with long-term planning for your application. In most cases (such as when Visual Basic transitioned to .NET), you want to use the Short, Integer, and Long designations. If at some point your system decides to allow an integer to hold a larger 64 bit value you don't need to change your code.

On the other hand Int16, Int32, and Int64 specify a physical implementation; therefore, if your code is someday migrated to a version of .NET that maps the Integer value to Int64, then those values defined as `Integer` will reflect the new larger capacity, while those declared as `Int32` will not. This could be important if your code were manipulating part of an interface where changing the physical size of the value could break the interface.

Table 3-1 lists the primitive types that Visual Basic 2012 defines, and the structures or classes to which they map:

**TABLE 3-1:** Primitive Types in .NET

| PRIMITIVE TYPE | .NET CLASS OR STRUCTURE |
|---|---|
| Byte | System.Byte (structure) |
| Short | System.Int16 (structure) |
| Integer | System.Int32 (structure) |
| Long | System.Int64 (structure) |
| Single | System.Single (structure) |
| Double | System.Double (structure) |
| Decimal | System.Decimal (structure) |
| Boolean | System.Boolean (structure) |
| Date | System.DateTime (structure) |
| Char | System.Char (structure) |
| String | System.String (class) |

> **NOTE** *The* `String` *primitive type stands out from the other primitives. Strings are implemented as a class, not a structure. More important, strings are the one primitive type that is a reference type.*

You can perform certain operations on primitive types that you can't on other types. For example, you can assign a value to a primitive type using a literal:

```
Dim i As Integer = 32
Dim str As String = "Hello"
```

It's also possible to declare a primitive type as a constant using the `Const` keyword, as shown here:

```
Dim Const str As String = "Hello"
```

The value of the variable `str` in the preceding line of code cannot be changed elsewhere in the application containing this code at run time. These two simple examples illustrate the key properties of primitive types. As noted, most primitive types are, in fact, value types. The next step is to take a look at core language commands that enable you to operate on these variables.

## COMMANDS: CONDITIONAL

Unlike many programming languages, Visual Basic has been designed to focus on readability and clarity. Many languages are willing to sacrifice these attributes. Visual Basic is designed under the paradigm that the readability of code matters, so commands in Visual Basic tend to spell out the exact context of what is being done.

Literally dozens of commands make up the Visual Basic language, so there isn't nearly enough space here to address all of them. Moreover, many of the more specialized commands are covered later in this book. However, in case you are not familiar with Visual Basic or are relatively new to programming, this book will touch on a few of these. In this chapter, it makes the most sense to review the syntax of conditional statements.

Each of these statements has the ability to literally encapsulate a block of code. Of course the preferred way of embedding code within the scope of a conditional or loop is to call another method. Using a method within your loop or conditional helps keep your structure apparent and simple to view, and allows for code reuse if the same actions need to be accomplished from another location within your code.

Note that the variables declared within the context of a conditional statement (between the If and End If lines) are available only up until the End If statement. After that, these variables go out of scope. The concept of scoping is discussed in more detail later in this chapter.

### If Then

The conditional is one of two primary programming constructs (the other being the loop) that is present in almost every programming language. Visual Basic supports the If- Then statement as well as the Else statement, and unlike some languages, the concept of an ElseIf statement. The ElseIf and Else statements are totally optional, and it is not only acceptable but common to use conditionals that do not utilize either of these code blocks. The following example illustrates a simple pair of conditions that have been set up serially:

```
If i > 1 Then
    'Code A1
ElseIf i < 1 Then
    'Code B2
Else
    'Code C3
End If
```

If the first condition is true, then code placed at marker A1 is executed. The flow would then proceed to the End If, and the program would not evaluate any of the other conditions. Note that for best performance, it makes the most sense to have your most common condition first in this structure, because if it is successful, none of the other conditions need to be tested.

If the initial comparison in the preceding example code were false, then control would move to the first Else statement, which in this case happens to be an ElseIf statement. The code would therefore test the next conditional to determine whether the value of i were less than 1. If so, then the code associated with block B2 would be executed.

However, if the second condition were also false, then the code would proceed to the Else statement, which isn't concerned with any remaining condition and just executes the code in block C3. Not only is the Else optional, but even if an ElseIf is used, the Else condition is still optional. It is acceptable for the Else and C3 block to be omitted from the preceding example.

## Comparison Operators

Essentially, the code between the If and Then portions of the statement must eventually evaluate out to a Boolean. At the most basic level, this means you can write If True Then, which results in a valid statement that would always execute the associated block of code with that If statement. The idea, however, is that for a basic comparison, you take two values and place between them a comparison operator. Comparison operators include the following symbols: =, >, <, >=, <=.

Additionally, certain keywords can be used with a comparison operator. For example, the keyword Not can be used to indicate that the reversal of a Boolean result. Note that with Visual Basic the Not conditional is simply placed before the comparions to which it will be applied. An example of this is shown in the next example:

```
If Not i = 1 Then
    'Code A1
End If
```

In this case, the result is only reversed so code at marker A1 is executed whenever i does not equal 1. The If statement supports complex comparisons and leveraging boolean statements such as And and Or. These statements enable you to create a complex condition based on several comparisons, as shown here:

```
If Not i = 1 Or i < 0 And str = "Hello" Then
    'Code A1
Else
    'Code B2
End If
```

The And and Or conditions are applied to determine whether the first comparison's results are true or false along with the second value's results. The And conditional means that both comparisons must evaluate to true in order for the If statement to execute the code in block A1, and the Or statement means that if the condition on either side is true, then the If statement can evaluate code block A1. However, in looking at this statement, your first reaction should be to pause and attempt to determine in exactly what order all of the associated comparisons occur.

Visual Basic applies conditions based on precedence. First, any numeric style comparisons are applied, followed by any unary operators such as Not. Finally, proceeding from left to right, each Boolean comparison of And and Or is applied. However, a much better way to write the preceding statement is to use parentheses to identify in what order you want these comparisons to occur. The first If statement in the following example illustrates the default order, while the second and third use parentheses to force a different priority on the evaluation of the conditions:

```
If ((Not i = 1) Or i < 0) And (str = "Hello") Then
If (Not i = 1) Or (i < 0 And str = "Hello") Then
If Not ((i = 1 Or i < 0) And str = "Hello") Then
```

All three of the preceding If statements are evaluating the same set of criteria, yet their results are potentially very different. It is always best practice to enclose complex conditionals within parentheses to indicate the desired order of evaluation. Of course, these comparisons have been rather simple; you could replace the variable value in the preceding examples with a function call that might include a call to a database. In such a situation, since the method execution might have a higher performace cost you might want to use one of the shortcut comparison operators.

Typically Visual Basic always evaluates both sides of a condition. But you know that for an And statement both sides of the If statement must be true. Thus there are times when knowing that the first condition is false means you don't need to evaluate the other side of the And statement. Bypassing this could save processing time; you would not bother executing the second condition. Similarly, if the comparison involves an Or statement, then once the first part of the condition is true, there is no reason to evaluate the second condition, because you know that the net result is success. In these cases, Visual Basic provides the AndAlso and OrElse conditionals to allow for performance optimization:

```
If ((Not i = 1) Or i < 0) AndAlso (MyFunction() = "Success") Then
If Not i = 1 OrElse (i < 0 And MyFunction() = "Success") Then
```

The preceding code illustrates that instead of using a variable your condition might call a function you've written that returns a value. In the preceding statements, each conditional statement has been optimized so that there are situations where the code associated with MyFunction won't be executed.

This is potentially important, not only from a performance standpoint, but also in a scenario where, given the first condition, your code might throw an error. For example, it's not uncommon to first determine whether a variable has been assigned a value and then to test that value. Once you know the value doesn't exist it is erroneous to check that value.

However, not all values are primitive types; thus to determine if a reference type has a value Visual Basic provides an additional pair of conditional elements: the Is and IsNot conditionals.

Using Is and IsNot enables you to determine whether a variable has been given a value, or to determine its type. In the past it was common to see nested If statements, with the first determining whether the value was Nothing, followed by a separate If statement to determine whether the value was valid. Starting with .NET 2.0, the short-circuit conditionals enable you to check for a value and then check whether that value meets the desired criteria. The short-circuit operator prevents the check for a value from occurring and causing an error if the variable is undefined, so both checks can be done with a single If statement:

```
Dim mystring as string = Nothing
If mystring IsNot Nothing AndAlso mystring.Length > 100 Then
    'Code A1
ElseIf mystring.GetType Is GetType(Integer) Then
    'Code B2
End If
```

The preceding code will fail on the first condition because mystring has been initialized to Nothing, meaning that by definition it doesn't have a length. Note also that the second condition will fail because you know that myString isn't of type Integer.

## Select Case

The preceding section makes it clear that the If statement is the king of conditionals. However, in another scenario you may have a simple condition that needs to be tested repeatedly. For example, suppose a user selects a value from a drop-down list and different code executes depending on that value. This is a relatively simple comparison, but if you have 20 values, then you would potentially need to string together 20 different If Then and ElseIf statements to account for all of the possibilities.

A cleaner way of evaluating such a condition is to leverage a Select Case statement. This statement was designed to test a condition, but instead of returning a Boolean value, it returns a value that is then used to determine which block of code, each defined by a Case statement, should be executed:

```
Select Case i
    Case 1
        'Code A1
    Case 2
        'Code B2
    Case Else
        'Code C3
End Select
```

The preceding sample code shows how the Select portion of the statement determines the value represented by the variable i. Depending on the value of this variable, the Case statement executes the appropriate code block. For a value of 1, the code in block A1 is executed; similarly, a 2 results in code block B2 executing. For any other value, because this Case statement includes an Else block, the Case statement executes the code represented by C3. Note that while in this example each item has its own block, it is also possible to have more than a single match on the same Case. Thus Case 2, 3 would match if the value of i were either a 2 or a 3. Finally, the next example illustrates that the cases do not need to be integer values, and can, in fact, even be strings:

```
Dim mystring As String = "Intro"
Select Case mystring
    Case "Intro"
        'Code A1
    Case "Exit"
        'Code A2
    Case Else
        'Code A3
End Select
```

Now that you have been introduced to these two control elements that enable you to specify what happens in your code, your next step is to review details of the different variable types that are available within Visual Basic 2012, starting with the value types.

## VALUE TYPES (STRUCTURES)

Value types aren't as versatile as reference types, but they can provide better performance in many circumstances. The core value types (which include the majority of primitive types) are Boolean, Byte, Char, DateTime, Decimal, Double, Guid, Int16, Int32, Int64, SByte, Single, and

`TimeSpan`. These are not the only value types, but rather the subset with which most Visual Basic developers consistently work. As you've seen, value types by definition store data on the stack.

Value types can also be referred to by their proper name: structures. The underlying principles and syntax of creating custom structures mirrors that of creating classes, covered in the next chapter. This section focuses on some of the built-in types provided by the .NET Framework — in particular, the built-in types known as *primitives*.

## Boolean

The .NET `Boolean` type represents true or false. Variables of this type work well with the conditional statements that were just discussed. When you declare a variable of type `Boolean`, you can use it within a conditional statement directly. Test the following sample by creating a `Sub` called `BoolTest` within ProVB2012_Ch03 (code file: `MainWindow.xaml.vb`):

```
Private Sub BoolTest()
    Dim blnTrue As Boolean = True
    Dim blnFalse As Boolean = False
    If (blnTrue) Then
        TextBox1.Text = blnTrue & Environment.NewLine
        TextBox1.Text &= blnFalse.ToString
    End If
End Sub
```

The results of this code are shown in Figure 3-4. There are a couple things outside of the Boolean logic to review within the preceding code sample. These are related to the update of `Textbox1``.Text`. In this case, because you want two lines of text, you need to embed a new line character into the text. There are two ways of doing this in Visual Basic. The first is to use the `Environment``.Newline` constant, which is part of the core .NET Framework. Alternatively, you may find a Visual Basic developer leveraging the Visual Basic–specific constant `vbCRLF`, which does the same thing.

**FIGURE 3-4** Boolean results

The second issue related to that line is that you are concatenating the implicit value of the variable `blnTrue` with the value of the `Environment.Newline` constant. Note the use of an ampersand (`&`) for this action. This is a best practice in Visual Basic, because while Visual Basic does overload the plus (+) sign to support string concatenation, in this case the items being concatenated aren't necessarily strings. This is related to not setting `Option Strict` to `On`. In that scenario, the system will look at the actual types of the variables, and if there were two integers side by side in your string concatenation you would get unexpected results. This is because the code would first process the "+" and would add the values as numeric values.

Thus, since neither you nor the sample download code has set `Option String` to `On` for this project, if you replace the preceding `&` with a `+`, you'll find a runtime conversion error in your application. Therefore, in production code it is best practice to always use the `&` to concatenate strings in Visual Basic unless you are certain that both sides of the concatenation will always be a string. However, neither of these issues directly affect the use of the `Boolean` values, which when interpreted this way provide their `ToString()` output, not a numeric value.

> **NOTE** *Always use the* `True` *and* `False` *constants working with* `Boolean` *variables.*

Unfortunately, in the past developers had a tendency to tell the system to interpret a variable created as a `Boolean` as an `Integer`. This is referred to as *implicit conversion* and is related to `Option Strict`. It is not the best practice, and when .NET was introduced, it caused issues for Visual Basic, because the underlying representation of `True` in other languages doesn't match those of Visual Basic.

Within Visual Basic, `True` has been implemented in such a way that when converted to an integer, Visual Basic converts a value of `True` to -1 (negative one). This different from other languages, which typically use the integer value 1. Generically, all languages tend to implicitly convert `False` to 0, and `True` to a nonzero value.

To create reusable code, it is always better to avoid implicit conversions. In the case of Booleans, if the code needs to check for an integer value, then you should explicitly convert the Boolean and create an appropriate integer. The code will be far more maintainable and prone to fewer unexpected results.

## Integer Types

There are three sizes of integer types in .NET. The `Short` is the smallest, the `Integer` represents a 32-bit value, and the `Long` type is an eight-byte or 64-bit value. In addition, each of these types also has two alternative types. In all, Visual Basic supports the nine `Integer` types described in Table 3-2.

**TABLE 3-2:** Visual Basic Integer Types

| TYPE | ALLOCATED MEMORY | MINIMUM VALUE | MAXIMUM VALUE |
|---|---|---|---|
| Short | 2 bytes | –32768 | 32767 |
| Int16 | 2 bytes | –32768 | 32767 |
| UInt16 | 2 bytes | 0 | 65535 |
| Integer | 4 bytes | –2147483648 | 2147483647 |
| Int32 | 4 bytes | –2147483648 | 2147483647 |
| UInt32 | 4 bytes | 0 | 4294967295 |
| Long | 8 bytes | –9223372036854775808 | 9223372036854775807 |
| Int64 | 8 bytes | –9223372036854775808 | 9223372036854775807 |
| UInt64 | 8 bytes | 0 | 18446744073709551615 |

## Short

A Short value is limited to the maximum value that can be stored in two bytes, aka 16 bits, and the value can range between −32768 and 32767. This limitation may or may not be based on the amount of memory physically associated with the value; it is a definition of what must occur in the .NET Framework. This is important, because there is no guarantee that the implementation will actually use less memory than when using an Integer value. It is possible that in order to optimize memory or processing, the operating system will allocate the same amount of physical memory used for an Integer type and then just limit the possible values.

The Short (or Int16) value type can be used to map SQL smallint values when retrieving data through ADO.NET.

## Integer

An Integer is defined as a value that can be safely stored and transported in four bytes (not as a four-byte implementation). This gives the Integer and Int32 value types a range from −2147483648 to 2147483647. This range is adequate to handle most tasks.

The main reason to use an Int32 class designation in place of an Integer declaration is to ensure future portability with interfaces. In future 64-bit platforms, the Integer value might be an eight-byte value. Problems could occur if an interface used a 64-bit Integer with an interface that expected a 32-bit Integer value, or, conversely, if code using the Integer type is suddenly passed to a variable explicitly declared as Int32.

Unless you are working on an external interface that requires a 32-bit value, the best practice is to use Integer so your code is not constrained by the underlying implementation. However, you should be consistent, and if using Int32 use it consistently throughout your application.

The Visual Basic .NET Integer value type matches the size of an Integer value in SQL Server.

## Long

The Long type is aligned with the Int64 value. The Long has an eight-byte range, which means that its value can range from −9223372036854775808 to 9223372036854775807. This is a big range, but if you need to add or multiply Integer values, then you need a large value to contain the result. It's common while doing math operations on one type of integer to use a larger type to capture the result if there's a chance that the result could exceed the limit of the types being manipulated.

The Long value type matches the bigint type in SQL.

# Unsigned Types

Another way to gain additional range on the positive side of an Integer type is to use one of the unsigned types. The unsigned types provide a useful buffer for holding a result that might exceed an operation by a small amount, but this isn't the main reason they exist. The UInt16 type happens to have the same characteristics as the Character type, while the Uint32 type has the same characteristics as a system memory pointer on a 32-byte system.

However, never write code that attempts to leverage this relationship. Such code isn't portable, as on a 64-bit system the system memory pointer changes and uses the Uint64 type. However, when larger integers are needed and all values are known to be positive, these values are of use. As for the low-level uses of these types, certain low-level drivers use this type of knowledge to interface with software that expects these values, and they are the underlying implementation for other value types. This is why, when you move from a 32-bit system to a 64-bit system, you need new drivers for your devices, and why applications shouldn't leverage this same type of logic.

## Decimal Types

Just as there are several types to store integer values, there are three implementations of value types to store real number values, shown in Table 3-3.

**TABLE 3-3:** Memory Allocation for Real Number Types

| TYPE | ALLOCATED MEMORY | NEGATIVE RANGE | POSITIVE RANGE |
| --- | --- | --- | --- |
| Single | 4 bytes | −3.402823E38 to −1.401298E-45 | 1.401298E-45 to 3.402823E38 |
| Double | 8 bytes | −1.79769313486231E308 to −4.94065645841247E-324 | 4.94065645841247E-324 to 1.79769313486232E308 |
| Currency | Obsolete | — | — |
| Decimal | 16 bytes | −79228162514264 337593543950335 to 0.00000000000000 00000000000001 | 0.00000000000000 00000000000001 to 792281625142643 37593543950335 |

## Single

The Single type contains four bytes of data, and its precision can range anywhere from 1.401298E-45 to 3.402823E38 for positive values and from −3.402823E38 to −1.401298E-45 for negative values.

It can seem strange that a value stored using four bytes (like the Integer type) can store a number that is larger than even the Long type. This is possible because of the way in which numbers are stored; a real number can be stored with different levels of precision. Note that there are six digits after the decimal point in the definition of the Single type. When a real number gets very large or very small, the stored value is limited by its significant places.

Because real values contain fewer significant places than their maximum value, when working near the extremes it is possible to lose precision. For example, while it is possible to represent a Long with the value of 9223372036854775805, the Single type rounds this value to 9.223372E18. This seems like a reasonable action to take, but it isn't a reversible action. The following code demonstrates how this loss of precision and data can result in errors. To run it, a Sub called Precision is added to the ProVB2012_Ch03 project and called from the `Click` event handler for the `ButtonTest` control (code file: `MainWindow.xaml.vb`):

```
Private Sub Precision()
    Dim l As Long = Long.MaxValue
    Dim s As Single = Convert.ToSingle(l)
    TextBox1.Text = l & Environment.NewLine
    TextBox1.Text &= s & Environment.NewLine
    s -= 1000000000000
    l = Convert.ToInt64(s)
    TextBox1.Text &= l & Environment.NewLine
End Sub
```

The code creates a `Long` that has the maximum value possible, and outputs this value. Then it converts this value to a `Single` and outputs it in that format. Next, the value 1000000000000 is subtracted from the `Single` using the `-=` syntax, which is similar to writing `s = s – 1000000000000`. Finally, the code assigns the `Single` value back into the `Long` and then outputs both the `Long` and the difference between the original value and the new value. The results, shown in Figure 3-5, probably aren't consistent with what you might expect.

The first thing to notice is how the values are represented in the output based on type. The `Single` value actually uses an exponential display instead of displaying all of the significant digits. More important, as you can see, the result of what is stored in the `Single` after the math operation actually occurs is not accurate in relation to what is computed using the `Long` value. Therefore, both the `Single` and `Double` types have limitations in accuracy when you are doing math operations. These accuracy issues result from storage limitations and how binary numbers represent decimal numbers. To better address these issues for precise numbers, .NET provides the `Decimal` type.

**FIGURE 3-5** Showing a loss of precision

## Double

The behavior of the previous example changes if you replace the value type of `Single` with `Double`. A `Double` uses eight bytes to store values, and as a result has greater precision and range. The range for a `Double` is from 4.94065645841247E-324 to 1.79769313486232E308 for positive values and from –1.79769313486231E308 to –4.94065645841247E-324 for negative values. The precision has increased such that a number can contain 15 digits before the rounding begins. This greater level of precision makes the `Double` value type a much more reliable variable for use in math operations. It's possible to represent most operations with complete accuracy with this value. To test this, change the sample code from the previous section so that instead of declaring the variable s as a `Single` you declare it as a `Double` and rerun the code. Don't forget to also change the conversion line from `ToSingle` to `ToDouble`. The resulting code is shown here with the `Sub` called `PrecisionDouble` (code file: `MainWindow.xaml.vb`):

```
Private Sub PrecisionDouble()
    Dim l As Long = Long.MaxValue
    Dim d As Double = Convert.ToDouble(l)
    TextBox1.Text = l & Environment.NewLine
```

```
        TextBox1.Text &= d & Environment.NewLine
        d -= 1000000000000
        l = Convert.ToInt64(d)
        TextBox1.Text &= l & Environment.NewLine
        TextBox1.Text &= Long.MaxValue - 1
    End Sub
```

The results shown in Figure 3-6 look very similar to those from Single precision except they almost look correct. The result, as you can see, is off by just 1. On the other hand, this method closes by using the original MaxValue constant to demonstrate how a 64-bit value can be modified by just one and the results are accurate. The problem isn't specific to .NET; it can be replicated in all major development languages. Whenever you choose to represent very large or very small numbers by eliminating the precision of the least significant digits, you have lost that precision. To resolve this, .NET introduced the Decimal, which avoids this issue.

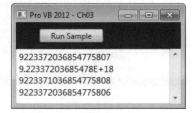

FIGURE 3-6 Precision errors with doubles

## Decimal

The Decimal type is a hybrid that consists of a 12-byte integer value combined with two additional 16-bit values that control the location of the decimal point and the sign of the overall value. A Decimal value consumes 16 bytes in total and can store a maximum value of 79228162514264337593543950335. This value can then be manipulated by adjusting where the decimal place is located. For example, the maximum value while accounting for four decimal places is 7922816251426433759354395.0335. This is because a Decimal isn't stored as a traditional number, but as a 12-byte integer value, with the location of the decimal in relation to the available 28 digits. This means that a Decimal does not inherently round numbers the way a Double does.

As a result of the way values are stored, the closest precision to zero that a Decimal supports is 0.0000000000000000000000000001. The location of the decimal point is stored separately; and the Decimal type stores a value that indicates whether its value is positive or negative separately from the actual value. This means that the positive and negative ranges are exactly the same, regardless of the number of decimal places.

Thus, the system makes a trade-off whereby the need to store a larger number of decimal places reduces the maximum value that can be kept at that level of precision. This trade-off makes a lot of sense. After all, it's not often that you need to store a number with 15 digits on both sides of the decimal point, and for those cases you can create a custom class that manages the logic and leverages one or more decimal values as its properties. You'll find that if you again modify and rerun the sample code you've been using in the last couple of sections that converts to and from Long values by using Decimals for the interim value and conversion, your results are accurate.

## Char and Byte

The default character set under Visual Basic is Unicode. Therefore, when a variable is declared as type Char, Visual Basic creates a two-byte value, since, by default, all characters in the Unicode character set require two bytes. Visual Basic supports the declaration of a character value in three ways. Placing a $c$ following a literal string informs the compiler that the value should be treated as a character, or the `Chr` and `ChrW` methods can be used. The following code snippet shows how all three of these options work similarly, with the difference between the `Chr` and `ChrW` methods being the range of available valid input values. The `ChrW` method allows for a broader range of values based on wide character input.

```
Dim chrLtr_a As Char = "a"c
Dim chrAsc_a As Char = Chr(97)
Dim chrAsc_b As Char = ChrW(98)
```

To convert characters into a string suitable for an ASCII interface, the runtime library needs to validate each character's value to ensure that it is within a valid range. This could have a performance impact for certain serial arrays. Fortunately, Visual Basic supports the `Byte` value type. This type contains a value between 0 and 255 that matches the range of the ASCII character set.

> **NOTE** *When interfacing with a system that uses ASCII, it is best to use a* `Byte` *array. The runtime knows there is no need to perform a Unicode-to-ASCII conversion for a* `Byte` *array, so the interface between the systems operates significantly faster.*

In Visual Basic, the `Byte` value type expects a numeric value. Thus, to assign the letter "a" to a `Byte`, you must use the appropriate character code. One option to get the numeric value of a letter is to use the `Asc` method, as shown here:

```
Dim bytLtrA as Byte = Asc("a")
```

# DateTime

You can, in fact, declare date values using both the `DateTime` and `Date` types. Visual Basic also provides a set of shared methods that provides some common dates. The concept of shared methods is described in more detail in the next chapter, which covers object syntax, but, in short, shared methods are available even when you don't create an instance of a class.

For the `DateTime` structure, the `Now` method returns a `Date` value with the local date and time. The `UtcNow` method works similarly, while the `Today` method returns a date with a zero time value. These methods can be used to initialize a `Date` object with the current local date, or the date and time based on Universal Coordinated Time (also known as Greenwich Mean Time), respectively. You can use these shared methods to initialize your classes, as shown in the following code sample (code file: `MainWindow.xaml.vb`):

```
Private Sub Dates()
    Dim dtNow = Now()
    Dim dtToday = Today()
    TextBox1.Text = dtNow & Environment.NewLine
    TextBox1.Text &= dtToday.ToShortDateString & Environment.NewLine
    TextBox1.Text &= DateTime.UtcNow() & Environment.NewLine
    Dim dtString = #12/13/2009#
    TextBox1.Text &= dtString.ToLongDateString()
End Sub
```

Running this code results in the output shown in Figure 3-7.

As noted earlier, primitive values can be assigned directly within your code, but many developers seem unaware of the format, shown previously, for doing this with dates. Another key feature of the Date type is the capability to subtract dates in order to determine a difference between them. The subtract method is demonstrated later in this chapter, with the resulting Timespan object used to output the number of milliseconds between the start and end times of a set of commands.

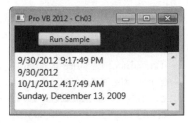

**FIGURE 3-7** Date formats

# REFERENCE TYPES (CLASSES)

A lot of the power of Visual Basic is harnessed in objects. An object is defined by its class, which describes what data, methods, and other attributes an instance of that class supports. Thousands of classes are provided in the .NET Framework class library.

When code instantiates an object from a class, the object created is a reference type. Recall that the data contained in value and reference types is stored in different locations, but this is not the only difference between them. A class (which is the typical way to refer to a reference type) has additional capabilities, such as support for protected methods and properties, enhanced event-handling capabilities, constructors, and finalizers; and it can be extended with a custom base class via inheritance. Classes can also be used to define how operators such as "=" and "+" work on an instance of the class.

The intention of this section is to introduce you to some commonly used classes, and to complement your knowledge of the common value types already covered. This section examines the features of the Object, String, DBNull, and Array classes, as well as briefly introduce the Collection classes found in the System.Collections namespace.

## The Object Class

As noted earlier, the Object class is the base class for every type in .NET, both value and reference types. At its core, every variable is an object and can be treated as such.

Because the Object class is the basis of all types, you can cast any variable to an object. Reference types maintain their current reference and implementation but are treated generically. On the other hand value types must have their data taken from its current location on the stack and placed into the heap with a memory location associated with the newly created Object. This process of moving value type data is called "boxing" because you are taking the value and shipping it from one location to another. Boxing is discussed in more detail in Chapter 7.

The key addition to your understanding of Object is that if you create an implementation of ToString in your class definition, then even when an instance of your object is cast to the type Object, your custom method will still be called. The following snippet shows how to create a generic object and cast it back to its original type to reference a property on the original class.

```
Dim objVar as Object

objVar = Me

CType(objVar, Form).Text = "New Dialog Title Text"
```

The object objvar is assigned a reference to the current instance of a Visual Basic form. In order to access the Text property of the original Form class, the Object must be cast from its declared type of Object to its actual type (Form), which supports the Text property. The CType command (covered later) accepts the object as its first parameter, and the class name (without quotes) as its second parameter. In this case, the current instance variable is of type Form; and by casting this variable, the code can reference the Text property of the current form.

# The String Class

Another class that plays a large role in most development projects is the String class. The String class is a special class within .NET because it is the one primitive type that is not a value type. To make String objects compatible with some of the underlying behavior in .NET, they have some interesting characteristics, the most important of which is immutability.

## String()

The String class has several different constructors for those situations in which you aren't simply assigning an existing value to a new string. The term *constructor* is expanded upon in Chapter 4. Constructors are methods that are used to create an instance of a class. String() would be the default constructor for the String class, but the String class does not expose this constructor publicly. The following example shows some of the most common methods for creating a String. This example method does not show the end of this Sub, because it will be used for all of the string-related examples, with the output from these methods shown together. The following code snippet is the start of a method; the End Sub is shown later. The full Sub in the code download is the concatenation of this snippet with the next five snippets. You can build and test these parts sequentially (code file: MainWindow.xaml.vb).

```
Private Sub StringSamples()
    Dim strSample As String = "ABC"
    Dim strSample2 = "DEF"
    Dim strSample3 = New String("A"c, 20)
    Dim line = New String("-", 80)
    '
```

A variable is declared of type String and as a primitive is assigned the value "ABC." The second declaration uses one of the parameterized versions of the String constructor. This constructor accepts two parameters: The first is a character and the second specifies how many times that character should be repeated in the string.

In addition to creating an instance of a string and then calling methods on your variable, the String class has several shared methods. A shared method refers to a method on a class that does not require an instance of that class. Shared methods are covered in more detail in relation to objects in Chapter 4; for the purpose of this chapter, the point is that you can reference the class String followed by a "." and see a list of shared methods for that class. For strings, this list includes the methods described in Table 3-4.

**TABLE 3-4:** Methods Available on the Class String

| SHARED METHOD | DESCRIPTION |
|---|---|
| Empty | This is actually a property. It can be used when an empty String is required. It can be used for comparison or initialization of a String. |
| Compare | Compares two objects of type String. |
| CompareOrdinal | Compares two Strings, without considering the local national language or culture. |
| Concat | Concatenates two or more Strings. |
| Copy | Creates a new String with the same value as an instance provided. |
| Equals | Determines whether two Strings have the same value. |
| IsNullorEmpty | This shared method is a very efficient way of determining whether a given variable has been set to the empty string or Nothing. |

Not only have creation methods been encapsulated, but other string-specific methods, such as character and substring searching, and case changes, are now available from String object instances.

## The SubString Method

The instance method SubString is a powerful method when you want to break out a portion of a string. For example, if you have a string "Hello World" and want only the first word, you would take the substring of the first five characters. There are two ways to call this method. The first accepts a starting position and the number of characters to retrieve, while the second accepts the starting location. The following code shows examples of using both of these methods on an instance of a String (code file: MainWindow.xaml.vb), and the resulting output is the first pair of strings shown in Figure 3-8:

```
' Sub String
Dim subString = "Hello World"
TextBox1.Text = subString.Substring(0, 5) & Environment.NewLine
TextBox1.Text &= subString.Substring(6) & Environment.NewLine
TextBox1.Text &= line & Environment.NewLine
```

## The PadLeft and PadRight Methods

These instance methods enable you to justify a String so that it is left- or right-justified. As with SubString, the PadLeft and PadRight methods are overloaded. The first version of these methods requires only a maximum length of the String, and then uses spaces to pad the String. The other version requires two parameters: the length of the returned String and the character that should be used to pad the original String (code file: MainWindow.xaml.vb):

```
' Pad Left & Pad Right
Dim padString = "Padded Characters"
TextBox1.Text &= padString.PadLeft("30") & Environment.NewLine
TextBox1.Text &= padString.PadRight("30", "_") &
    Environment.NewLine
TextBox1.Text &= line & Environment.NewLine
```

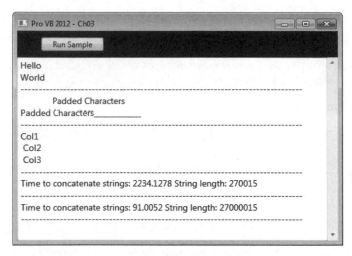

**FIGURE 3-8** String manipulation examples

Figure 3-8 shows the same string first with the left padded with spaces, then with the right padded with underscores. Note that because the default font on this screen isn't fixed size, the spaces are compacted and the two strings do not appear as the same length.

## The String.Split Method

This instance method on a string enables you to separate it into an array of components. For example, if you want to quickly find each of the different elements in a comma-delimited string, you could use the Split method to turn the string into an array of smaller strings, each of which contains one field of data. As shown in Figure 3-8, the csvString is converted to an array of three elements (code file: MainWindow.xaml.vb):

```
' String Split
Dim csvString = "Col1, Col2, Col3"
Dim stringArray As String() = csvString.Split(",")
TextBox1.Text &= stringArray(0) & Environment.NewLine
TextBox1.Text &= stringArray(1) & Environment.NewLine
TextBox1.Text &= stringArray(2) & Environment.NewLine
TextBox1.Text &= line & Environment.NewLine
```

## The String Class Is Immutable

To support the default behavior that people associate with the String primitive type, the String class doesn't function in the same way like most other classes. Strings in .NET do not allow editing of their data. When a portion of a string is changed or copied, the operating system allocates a new memory location and copies the resulting string to this new location. This ensures that when a string is copied to a second variable, the new variable references its own copy.

To support this behavior in .NET, the String class is defined as an *immutable class*. This means that each time a change is made to the data associated with a string, a new instance is created, and the original referenced memory is released for garbage collection. Garbage collection is covered in detail in Chapter 2. You should be aware that this can become a comparatively expensive operation.

However, having strings be immutable is important to ensure that the String class behaves as people expect a primitive type to behave. Additionally, when a copy of a string is made, the String class forces a new version of the data into the referenced memory. All of these immutable behaviors ensures that each instance of a string references only its own memory.

Next consider the following code (code file: MainWindow.xaml.vb):

```
' String Concatenation vs String Builder
Dim start = Now()
Dim strRedo = "A simple string"
For index = 1 To 10000 'Only 10000 times for concatenation
    strRedo &= "Making a much larger string"
Next
' The date processing below uses the built in capability
' to subtract one datetime from another to get the difference
' between the dates as a timespan. This is then output as a
' number of milliseconds.
TextBox1.Text &= "Time to concatenate strings: " &
    (Now().Subtract(start)).TotalMilliseconds().ToString() &
    " String length: " & strRedo.Length.ToString() &
    Environment.NewLine
TextBox1.Text &= line & Environment.NewLine
```

This code does not perform well. For each assignment operation on the strMyString variable, the system allocates a new memory buffer based on the size of the new string, and copies both the current value of strMyString and the new text that is to be appended. The system then frees its reference to the previous memory that must be reclaimed by the garbage collector. As this loop continues, the new memory allocation requires a larger chunk of memory. Therefore, operations such as this can take a long time.

To illustrate this, you'll note that the code captures the start time before doing the 10,000 concatenations, and then within the print statement uses the DateTime.Subtract method to get the difference. That difference is returned as an object of type Timespan, between the start time and the print time. This difference is then expressed in milliseconds (refer to Figure 3-8).

However, .NET offers an alternative in the System.Text.StringBuilder object, shown in the following snippet (code file: MainWindow.xaml.vb):

```
start = Now()
Dim strBuilder = New System.Text.StringBuilder("A simple string")
For index = 1 To 1000000 '1 million times....
    strBuilder.Append("Making a much larger string")
Next
TextBox1.Text &= "Time to concatenate strings: " &
    (Now().Subtract(start)).TotalMilliseconds().ToString() &
    " String length: " & strBuilder.ToString().Length.ToString() &
    Environment.NewLine
TextBox1.Text &= line & Environment.NewLine
End Sub
```

The preceding code works with strings but does not use the String class. The .NET class library contains the System.Text.StringBuilder class, which performs better when strings will be edited repeatedly. This class does not store strings in the conventional manner; it stores them as individual characters, with code in place to manage the ordering of those characters. Thus, editing or appending more characters does not involve allocating new memory for the entire string. Because the preceding code snippet does not need to reallocate the memory used for the entire string, each time another set of characters is appended it performs significantly faster.

Note that the same timing code is used in this snippet. However, for the `StringBuilder`, the loop executes one million times (versus ten thousand). The increase in the number of iterations was made in order to cause enough of a delay to actually show it requiring more than just one or two milliseconds to complete. Even with 100 times the number of iterations, Figure 3-8 still illustrates that this is a much more efficient use of system resources.

Ultimately, an instance of the `String` class is never explicitly needed, because the `StringBuilder` class implements the `ToString` method to roll up all of the characters into a string. While the concept of the `StringBuilder` class isn't new, because it is available as part of the Visual Basic implementation, developers no longer need to create their own string memory managers.

### String Constants

If you ever have to produce output based on a string you'll quickly find yourself needing to embed certain constant values. For example, it's always useful to be able to add a carriage-return line-feed combination to trigger a new line in a message box. One way to do this is to learn the underlying ASCII codes and then embed these control characters directly into your `String` or `StringBuilder` object.

Visual Basic provides an easier solution for working with these: the `Microsoft.VisualBasic.Constants` class. The `Constants` class, which you can tell by its namespace is specific to Visual Basic, contains definitions for several standard string values that you might want to embed. The most common, of course, is `Constants.VbCrLf`, which represents the carriage-return line-feed combination. Feel free to explore this class for additional constants that you might need to manipulate string output.

## The DBNull Class and IsDBNull Function

When working with a database, a value for a given column may be defined as Null. For a reference type this isn't a problem, as it is possible to set reference types to `Nothing`. However, for value types, it is necessary to determine whether a given column from the database or other source has an actual value prior to attempting to assign a potentially null value. The first way to manage this task is to leverage the `DBNull` class and the `IsDBNull` function.

This class is part of the `System` namespace, and you reference it as part of a comparison. The `IsDBNull` function accepts an object as its parameter and returns a `Boolean` that indicates whether the variable has been initialized. The following snippet shows two values, one a string being initialized to `Nothing` and the other being initialized as `DBNull.Value` (code file: `MainWindow.xaml.vb`):

```
Private Sub NullValues()
    Dim strNothing As String = Nothing
    Dim objectNull As Object = DBNull.Value
    TextBox1.Text = ""
    If IsDBNull(strNothing) Then
        TextBox1.Text = "But strNothing is not the same as Null."
```

```
        End If
        If System.DBNull.Value.Equals(objectNull) Then
            TextBox1.Text &= "objectNull is null." & Environment.NewLine
        End If
    End Sub
```

The output of this code is shown in Figure 3-9. In this code, the strNothing variable is declared and initialized to Nothing. The first conditional is evaluated to False, which may seem counterintuitive, but in fact VB differentiates between a local value, which might not be assigned, and the actual DBNull value. This can be a bit misleading, because it means that you need to separately check for values which are Nothing.

The second conditional references the second variable, object-Null. This value has been explicitly defined as being a DBNull .value as part of its initialization. This is similar to how a null value would be returned from the database. The second condition evaluates to True. While DBNull is available, in most cases, developers now leverage the generic Nullable class described in Chapter 7, rather than work with DBNull comparisons.

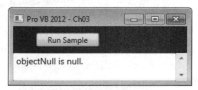

**FIGURE 3-9** The DBNull example

## PARAMETER PASSING

When an object's methods or an assembly's procedures and methods are called, it's often appropriate to provide input for the data to be operated on by the code. The values are referred to as *parameters*, and any object can be passed as a parameter to a Function or Sub.

When passing parameters, be aware of whether the parameter is being passed "by value" (ByVal) or "by reference" (ByRef). Passing a parameter by value means that if the value of that variable is changed, then when the Function/Sub returns, the system automatically restores that variable to the value it had before the call. Passing a parameter by reference means that if changes are made to the value of a variable, then these changes affect the actual variable and, therefore, are still present when the variable returns.

This is where it gets a little challenging for new Visual Basic developers. Under .NET, passing a parameter by value indicates only how the top-level reference (the portion of the variable on the stack) for that object is passed. Sometimes referred to as a *shallow copy operation*, the system copies only the top-level reference value for an object passed by value, and it is only this reference which is protected. This is important to remember because it means that referenced memory is not protected.

When you pass an integer by value, if the program changes the value of the integer, then your original value is restored. Conversely, if you pass a reference type, then only the location of your referenced memory is protected, not the data located within that memory location. Thus, while the reference passed as part of the parameter remains unchanged for the calling method, the actual values stored in referenced objects can be updated even when an object is passed by value.

In addition Visual Basic supports optional parameters. Optional parameters can be omitted by the calling code. This way, it is possible to call a method such as PadRight, passing either a single parameter defining the length of the string and using a default of space for the padding character, or with two parameters, the first still defining the length of the string but the second now replacing the default of space with a dash (code file: MainWindow.xaml.vb):

```
Public Sub PadRight(ByVal intSize as Integer, _
                        Optional ByVal chrPad as Char = " "c)
End Function
```

To use optional parameters, it is necessary to make them the last parameters in the function declaration. Visual Basic also requires that every optional parameter have a default value. It is not acceptable to merely declare a parameter and assign it the `Optional` keyword. In Visual Basic, the `Optional` keyword must be accompanied by a value that is assigned if the parameter is not passed in.

## ParamArray

In addition to passing explicit parameters, it is also possible to tell Visual Basic that you would like to allow a user to pass any number of parameters of the same type. This is called a *parameter array*, and it enables a user to pass as many instances of a given parameter as are appropriate. For example, the following code creates a function `Add`, which allows a user to pass an array of integers and get the sum of these integers (code file: `MainWindow.xaml.vb`):

```
Public Function Add(ByVal ParamArray values() As Integer) As Long
    Dim result As Long
    For Each value As Integer In values
        result += value
    Next
    Return result
End Function
```

The preceding code illustrates a function (first shown at the beginning of this chapter without its implementation) that accepts an array of integers. Notice that the `ParamArray` qualifier is preceded by a `ByVal` qualifier for this parameter. The `ParamArray` requires that the associated parameters be passed by value; they cannot be optional parameters.

You might think this looks like a standard parameter passed by value except that it's an array, but there is more to it than that. In fact, the power of the `ParamArray` derives from how it can be called, which also explains many of its limitations. The following code shows two ways this method can be called (code file: `MainWindow.xaml.vb`):

```
Private Sub CallAdd()
    Dim int1 As Integer = 2
    Dim int2 = 3
    TextBox1.Text = "Adding 3 integers: " & Add(1, int1, int2) &
        Environment.NewLine
    Dim intArray() = {1, 2, 3, 4}
    TextBox1.Text &= "Adding an array of 4 integers: " & Add(intArray)
End Sub
```

The output from running this `CallAdd` method is shown in Figure 3-10. Notice that the first call, to the `Add` function, doesn't pass an array of integers; instead, it passes three distinct integer values. The `ParamArray` keyword tells Visual Basic to automatically join these three distinct values into an array for use within this method. The second call, to the `Add` method, actually leverages using an actual array of integers to populate

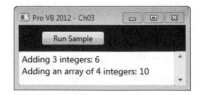

**FIGURE 3-10** Using the function Add

the parameter array. Either of these methods works equally well. Arrays are covered in more detail in Chapter 7.

Finally, note one last limitation of the `ParamArray` keyword: It can only be used on the last parameter defined for a given method. Because Visual Basic is grabbing an unlimited number of input values to create the array, there is no way to indicate the end of this array, so it must be the final parameter.

# Variable Scope

The concept of variable scope encapsulates two key elements. In the discussion so far of variables, you have not focused on the allocation and deallocation of those variables from memory. Chapter 2 covers the release of variables and memory once it is no longer needed by an application, so this section is going to focus on the allocation and to some extent the availability of a given variable.

In order to make clear why this is important, consider an allocation challenge. What happens when you declare two variables with the same name but at different locations in the code? For example, suppose a class declares a variable called `myObj` that holds a property for that class. Then, within one of that class's methods, you declare a different variable also named `myObj`. What will happen in that method is determined by a concept called: *Scope*. *Scope* defines the lifetime and precedence of every variable you declare, and provides the rules to answer this question.

The first thing to understand is that when a variable is no longer "in scope," it is available to the garbage collector for cleanup. This handles the deallocation of that variable and its memory. However, when do variables move in and out of scope?

.NET essentially defines four levels of variable scope. The outermost scope is *global*. Essentially, just as your source code defines classes, it can also declare variables that exist the entire time that your application runs. These variables have the longest lifetime because they exist as long as your application is executing. Conversely, these variables have the lowest precedence. Thus, if within a class or method you declare another variable with the same name, then the variable with the smaller, more local scope is used before the global version.

After global scope, the next scope is at the *class* or *module* level. When you add properties to a class, you are creating variables that will be created with each instance of that class. The methods of that class will then reference those member variables from the class, before looking for any global variables. Note that because these variables are defined within a class, they are visible only to methods within that class. The scope and lifetime of these variables is limited by the lifetime of that class, and when the class is removed from the system, so are those variables. More important, those variables declared in one instance of a class are not visible in other classes or in other instances of the same class (unless you actively expose them, in which case the object instance is used to fully qualify a reference to them).

The next shorter lifetime and smaller scope is that of method variables. When you declare a new variable within a method, such variables, as well as those declared as parameters, are only visible to code that exists within that module. Thus, the method `Add` wouldn't see or use variables declared in the method `Subtract` in the same class.

Finally, within a given method are various commands that can encapsulate a block of code (mentioned earlier in this chapter). Commands such as `If Then` and `For Each` create blocks of code within a method, and it is possible within this block of code to declare new variables. These variables then have a scope of only that block of code. Thus, variables declared within an `If Then` block or a `For` loop only exist within the constraints of the `If` block or execution of the loop. Creating variables in a `For` loop is a poor coding practice and performance mistake and should be avoided.

Variable scope is applicable whether you are working with one of the primitive types, a library class or a custom object. Recall that everything in .NET is represented as an object and all objects have scope, be it at the level of the application root or within a specific method.

## WORKING WITH OBJECTS

In the .NET environment in general and within Visual Basic in particular, you use objects all the time without even thinking about it. As noted earlier, every variable, every control on a form—in fact, every form—inherits from `System.Object`. When you open a file or interact with a database, you are using objects to do that work.

## Objects Declaration and Instantiation

Objects are created using the `New` keyword, indicating that you want a new instance of a particular class. There are numerous variations on how or where you can use the `New` keyword in your code. Each one provides different advantages in terms of code readability or flexibility.

The most obvious way to create an object is to declare an object variable and then create an instance of the object:

```
Dim obj As TheClass
obj = New TheClass()
```

The result of this code is that you have a new instance of `TheClass` ready for use. To interact with this new object, you use the `obj` variable that you declared. The `obj` variable contains a reference to the object, a concept explored later.

You can shorten the preceding code by combining the declaration of the variable with the creation of the instance, as illustrated here:

```
Dim obj As TheClass = New TheClass()
Dim obj As New TheClass()
Dim obj = New TheClass()
```

> **NOTE** *At run time there is no difference between the first example and this one, other than code length.*

The preceding code shows three ways to both declare the variable `obj` as data type `TheClass` and create an instance of the class. In all cases you are immediately creating an object that you can use. It is up to you how you create these instances, as it is really a matter of style.

Such flexibility is very useful when working with inheritance or multiple interfaces. You might declare the variable to be of one type — say, an interface — and instantiate the object based on a class that implements that interface. You will revisit this syntax when interfaces are covered in detail in Chapter 4.

So far, you've been declaring a variable for new objects, but sometimes you simply need to pass an object as a parameter to a method, in which case you can create an instance of the object right in the call to that method:

```
DoSomething(New TheClass())
```

This calls the DoSomething method, passing a new instance of TheClass as a parameter. This can be even more complex. Perhaps, instead of needing an object reference, your method needs an Integer. You can provide that Integer value from a method on the object:

```
Public Class TheClass
  Public Function GetValue() As Integer
    Return 42
  End Function
End Class
```

You can then instantiate the object and call the method all in one shot, thus passing the value returned from the method as a parameter:

```
DoSomething(New TheClass().GetValue())
```

Obviously, you need to carefully weigh the readability of such code against its compactness. At some point, having code that is more compact can detract from readability, rather than enhance it.

## Object References

Typically, when you work with an object, you are using a reference to the memory that contains that object's data. Conversely, when you are working with simple data types, such as Integer, you are working with the actual value, rather than a reference. Let's explore these concepts and see how they work and interact.

When you create a new object using the New keyword, you are allocated memory on the heap and store a reference to the memory for that object in a variable on the stack, as shown here:

```
Dim obj As New TheClass()
```

This code creates a new instance of TheClass. You gain access to this new object via the obj variable. This variable points to a memory location on the stack that holds a reference to the object. You might then do something like this:

```
Dim another As TheClass
another = obj
```

Now, you have a second variable, another, which also has a memory location on the stack that references the same object data on the heap. You can use either variable interchangeably, as they both reference the exact same object. Remember that the variable you have is not the object itself but just a reference, or pointer, to the object.

As noted earlier in this chapter, objects are reference type, meaning the values are stored on the managed heap with only pointers kept on the stack.

## Early Binding versus Late Binding

One of the strengths of Visual Basic has long been that it provides access to both early and late binding when interacting with objects. *Early binding* means that at compile time, the compiler recognizes the type of each variable and prepares the code to directly interact with a specific type of object by directly calling its methods. Because the Visual Basic compiler knows the object's data type ahead of time, it can directly compile code to invoke the methods on the object. Early binding also enables the IDE to use IntelliSense to aid development efforts by enabling the compiler to ensure that you are referencing methods that exist and are providing the proper parameter values.

*Late binding* means that your code interacts with an object dynamically at run time. This provides a great deal of flexibility, because the code doesn't care what type of object it is interacting with as long as the object supports the methods you want to call. Because the type of the object is not known by the IDE or compiler, neither IntelliSense nor compile-time syntax checking is possible, but in exchange you get unprecedented flexibility.

Visual Basic provides a switch for you to decide if you want to enable late binding within your application. Enabling strict type checking by using `Option Strict On` in the project's Properties dialogue or at the top of the code modules, disables late binding. When `Option Strict` is on, the IDE and compiler enforce early binding behavior.

By default, `Option Strict` is turned off, so you have easy access to the use of late binding within the code. Chapter 1 discusses `Option Strict`. You can change this default directly in Visual Studio 2012 by selecting Tools ⇨ Options from the VS menu. The Options dialog is shown in Figure 3-11. Expanding the Projects and Solutions node reveals the VB defaults. Feel free to change any of these default settings.

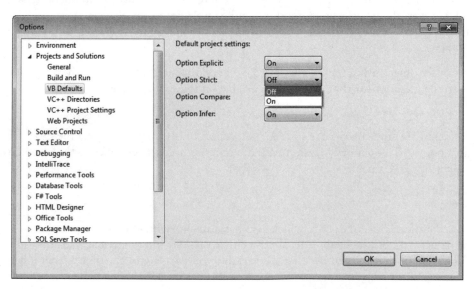

**FIGURE 3-11** Resetting the default settings for new projects in Visual Studio

## Implementing Late Binding

Late binding occurs when the compiler cannot determine the type of object that you'll be calling. This level of ambiguity can be achieved using the `Object` data type. A variable of data type `Object` can hold virtually any value, including a reference to any type of object. Thus, code such as the following could be run against any object that implements a `DoSomething` method that accepts no parameters:

```
Option Strict Off

Module LateBind
  Dim x as Integer = 20
  Dim y = DoWork(x)

  Public Function DoWork(ByVal obj As String) as String
   Return obj.substring(0, 3)
  End Function
End Module
```

If the object passed into this routine cannot be converted to a string then method, then an exception will be thrown. Note, however, that you are passing an integer into the method. Late binding allows Visual Basic to determine at run time that the inbound parameter needs to be converted to a string, and Visual Basic will automatically handle this conversion. Keep in mind, however, that late binding goes beyond what is done by `Option Strict`. For example, it plays into the ability to determine the exact type associated with a LINQ query at run time.

While late binding is flexible, it can be error prone and is slower than early-bound code. To make a late-bound method call, the .NET run time must dynamically determine whether the target object is actually compatible with what you are trying to do. It must then invoke that a conversion on your behalf. This takes more time and effort than an early-bound call, whereby the compiler knows ahead of time that the method exists and can compile the code to make the call directly. With a late-bound call, the compiler has to generate code to make the call dynamically at run time.

# Data Type Conversions

When developing software, it is often necessary to take a numeric value and convert it to a string to display in a text box. As you've seen this can be done implicitly via late binding. Similarly, it is often necessary to accept input from a text box and convert this input to a numeric value. These conversions, unlike some, can be done in one of two fashions: *implicitly* or *explicitly*.

Implicit conversions are those that rely on the runtime system to adjust the data via late binding to a new type without any guidance. Often, Visual Basic's default settings enable developers to write code containing many implicit conversions that the developer may not even notice.

Explicit conversions, conversely, are those for which the developer recognizes the need to change a variable's type and assign it to a different variable. Unlike implicit conversions, explicit conversions are easily recognizable within the code. Some languages such as C# require that all conversions that might be type unsafe be done through an explicit conversion; otherwise, an error is thrown.

It is therefore important to understand what a type-safe implicit conversion is. In short, it's a conversion that cannot fail because of the nature of the data involved. For example, if you assign the value of a smaller type, Short, into a larger type, Long, then there is no way this conversion can fail. As both values are integer-style numbers, and the maximum and minimum values of a Short variable are well within the range of a Long, this conversion will always succeed and can safely be handled as an implicit conversion:

```
Dim shortNumber As Short = 32767
Dim longNumber As Long = shortNumber
```

However, the reverse of this is not a type-safe conversion. In a system that demands explicit conversions, the assignment of a Long value to a Short variable results in a compilation error, as the compiler doesn't have any safe way to handle the assignment when the larger value is outside the range of the smaller value. It is still possible to explicitly cast a value from a larger type to a smaller type, but this is an explicit conversion. By default, Visual Basic supports certain unsafe implicit conversions. Thus, adding the following line will not, when Option Strict is Off, cause an error under Visual Basic:

```
shortNumber = longNumber
```

One of the original goals of Visual Basic is to support rapid prototyping. In a rapid prototyping model, a developer is writing code that "works" for demonstration purposes but may not be ready for deployment. This distinction is important because in the discussion of implicit conversions, you should always keep in mind that they are not a best practice for production software.

## Performing Explicit Conversions

Keep in mind that even when you choose to allow implicit conversions, these are allowed only for a relatively small number of data types. At some point you'll need to carry out explicit conversions. The following code is an example of some typical conversions between different integer types when Option Strict is enabled:

```
Dim myShort As Short
Dim myUInt16 As UInt16
Dim myInt16 As Int16
Dim myInteger As Integer
Dim myUInt32 As UInt32
Dim myInt32 As Int32
Dim myLong As Long
Dim myInt64 As Int64

myShort = 0
myUInt16 = Convert.ToUInt16(myShort)
myInt16 = myShort
myInteger = myShort
myUInt32 = Convert.ToUInt32(myShort)
myInt32 = myShort
myInt64 = myShort
myLong = Long.MaxValue

If myLong < Short.MaxValue Then
   myShort = Convert.ToInt16(myLong)
End If
myInteger = CInt(myLong)
```

The preceding snippet provides some excellent examples of what might not be intuitive behavior. The first thing to note is that you can't implicitly cast from Short to UInt16, or any of the other unsigned types for that matter. That's because with `Option Strict` the compiler won't allow an implicit conversion that might result in a value out of range or lead to loss of data. You may be thinking that an unsigned `Short` has a maximum that is twice the maximum of a signed `Short`, but in this case, if the variable `myShort` contained a -1, then the value wouldn't be in the allowable range for an unsigned type.

Just for clarity, even with the explicit conversion, if `myShort` were a negative number, then the `Convert.ToUInt32` method would throw a runtime exception. Managing failed conversions requires either an understanding of exceptions and exception handling, as covered in Chapter 6, or the use of a conversion utility such as `TryParse`, covered in the next section.

The second item illustrated in this code is the shared method `MaxValue`. All of the integer and decimal types have this property. As the name indicates, it returns the maximum value for the specified type. There is a matching `MinValue` method for getting the minimum value. As shared properties, these properties can be referenced from the class (`Long.MaxValue`) without requiring an instance.

Finally, although this code will compile, it won't always execute correctly. It illustrates a classic error, which in the real world is often intermittent. The error occurs because the final conversion statement does not check to ensure that the value being assigned to `myInteger` is within the maximum range for an integer type. On those occasions when `myLong` is larger than the maximum allowed, this code will throw an exception.

Visual Basic provides many ways to convert values. Some of them are updated versions of techniques that are supported from previous versions of Visual Basic. Others, such as the `ToString` method, are an inherent part of every class (although the .NET specification does not define how a `ToString` class is implemented for each type).

The following set of conversion methods is based on the conversions supported by Visual Basic. They coincide with the primitive data types described earlier; however, continued use of these methods is not considered a best practice. That bears repeating: While you may find the following methods in existing code, you should strive to avoid and replace these calls.

- ➤ `Cbool()`
- ➤ `Cchar()`
- ➤ `CDbl()`
- ➤ `Cint()`
- ➤ `Cobj()`
- ➤ `CSng()`
- ➤ `Cbyte()`
- ➤ `Cdate()`
- ➤ `Cdec()`
- ➤ `CLng()`
- ➤ `Cshort()`
- ➤ `CStr()`

Each of these methods has been designed to accept the input of the other primitive data types (as appropriate) and to convert such items to the type indicated by the method name. Thus, the `CStr` class is used to convert a primitive type to a `String`. The disadvantage of these methods is that they only support a limited number of types and are specific to Visual Basic. If you are working with developers who don't have a long Visual Basic history they will find these methods distracting. A more generic way to handle conversions is to leverage the `System.Convert` class shown in the following code snippet:

```
Dim intMyShort As Integer = 200
Dim int = Convert.ToInt32(intMyShort)
Dim dt = Convert.ToDateTime("9/9/2001")
```

The class `System.Convert` implements not only the conversion methods listed earlier, but also other common conversions. These additional methods include standard conversions for things such as unsigned integers and pointers.

All the preceding type conversions are great for value types and the limited number of classes to which they apply, but these implementations are oriented toward a limited set of known types. It is not possible to convert a custom class to an `Integer` using these classes. More important, there should be no reason to have such a conversion. Instead, a particular class should provide a method that returns the appropriate type. That way, no type conversion is required. However, when `Option Strict` is enabled, the compiler requires you to cast an object to an appropriate type before triggering an implicit conversion. Note, however, that the `Convert` method isn't the only way to indicate that a given variable can be treated as another type.

## Parse and TryParse

Most value types, at least those which are part of the .NET Framework, provide a pair of shared methods called `Parse` and `TryParse`. These methods accept a value of your choosing and then attempt to convert this variable into the selected value type. The `Parse` and `TryParse` methods are available only on value types. Reference types have related methods called `DirectCast` and `Cast`, which are optimized for reference variables.

The `Parse` method has a single parameter. This input parameter accepts a value that is the target for the object you want to create of a given type. This method then attempts to create a value based on the data passed in. However, be aware that if the data passed into the `Parse` method cannot be converted, then this method will throw an exception that your code needs to catch. The following line illustrates how the `Parse` function works:

```
result = Long.Parse("100")
```

Unfortunately, when you embed this call within a `Try-Catch` statement for exception handling, you create a more complex block of code. Note that exception handling and its use is covered in Chapter 6; for now just be aware that exceptions require additional system resources for your running code that impacts performance. Because you always need to encapsulate such code within a `Try-Catch` block, the .NET development team decided that it would make more sense to provide a version of this method that encapsulated that exception-handling logic.

This is the origin of the `TryParse` method. The `TryParse` method works similarly to the `Parse` method except that it has two parameters and returns a `Boolean`, rather than a value. Instead of assigning the value of the `TryParse` method, you test it as part of an `If-Then` statement to determine whether the conversion of your data to the selected type was successful. If the conversion was successful, then the new value is stored in the second parameter passed to this method, which you can then assign to the variable you want to hold that value:

```
Dim converted As Long
If Long.TryParse("100", converted) Then
    result = converted
End If
```

## Using the CType Function

Whether you are using late binding or not, it can be useful to pass object references around using the `Object` data type, converting them to an appropriate type when you need to interact with them. This is particularly useful when working with objects that use inheritance or implement multiple interfaces, concepts discussed in Chapter 4.

If `Option Strict` is turned off, which is the default, then you can write code using a variable of type `Object` to make an early-bound method call (code file: `MainWindow.xaml.vb`):

```
Public Sub objCType(ByVal obj As Object)
    Dim local As String
    local = obj
    local.ToCharArray()
End Sub
```

This code uses a strongly typed variable, `local`, to reference what was a generic object value. Behind the scenes, Visual Basic converts the generic type to a specific type so that it can be assigned to the strongly typed variable. If the conversion cannot be done, then you get a trappable runtime error.

The same thing can be done using the `CType` function. If `Option Strict` is enabled, then the previous approach will not compile, and the `CType` function must be used. Here is the same code making use of `CType` (code file: `MainWindow.xaml.vb`):

```
Public Sub CType1(ByVal obj As Object)
    Dim local As String
    local = CType(obj, String)
    local.ToLower()
End Sub
```

This code declares a variable of type `TheClass`, which is an early-bound data type that you want to use. The parameter you're accepting is of the generic `Object` data type, though, so you use the `CType` method to gain an early-bound reference to the object. If the object isn't of the type specified in the second parameter, then the call to `CType` fails with a trappable error.

Once you have a reference to the object, you can call methods by using the early-bound variable local. This code can be shortened to avoid the use of the intermediate variable. Instead, you can simply call methods directly from the data type (code file: `MainWindow.xaml.vb`):

```
Public Sub CType2(obj As Object)
    CType(obj, String).ToUpper()
End Sub
```

Even though the variable you are working with is of type `Object` and therefore any calls to it will be late bound, you use the `CType` method to temporarily convert the variable into a specific type — in this case, the type `String`.

> **NOTE** *If the object passed as a parameter is not of type specified as the second parameter, then you get a trappable error, so it is always wise to wrap this code in a* `Try...Catch` *block.*

As shown in Chapter 4, the `CType` function can also be very useful when working with objects that implement multiple interfaces. When an object has multiple interfaces, you can reference a single object variable through the appropriate interface as needed by using CType.

## Using DirectCast

Another function that is very similar to `CType` is the method `DirectCast`. The `DirectCast` call also converts values of one type into another type. It works in a more restrictive fashion than `CType`, but the trade-off is that it can be somewhat faster than `CType`:

```
Dim obj As TheClass

obj = New TheClass
DirectCast(obj, ITheInterface).DoSomething()
```

This is similar to the last example with `CType`, illustrating the parity between the two functions. There are differences, however. First, `DirectCast` works only with reference types, whereas `CType` accepts both reference and value types. For instance, `CType` can be used in the following code:

```
Dim int As Integer = CType(123.45, Integer)
```

Trying to do the same thing with `DirectCast` would result in a compiler error, as the value `123.45` is a value type, not a reference type.

Second, `DirectCast` is not as aggressive about converting types as `CType`. `CType` can be viewed as an intelligent combination of all the other conversion functions (such as `CInt`, `CStr`, and so on). `DirectCast`, conversely, assumes that the source data is directly convertible, and it won't take extra steps to convert it.

As an example, consider the following code:

```
Dim obj As Object = 123.45

Dim int As Integer = DirectCast(obj, Integer)
```

If you were using `CType` this would work, as `CType` uses `CInt`-like behavior to convert the value to an `Integer`. `DirectCast`, however, will throw an exception because the value is not directly convertible to `Integer`.

## Using TryCast

A method similar to `DirectCast` is `TryCast`. `TryCast` converts values of one type into another type, but unlike `DirectCast`, if it can't do the conversion, then `TryCast` doesn't throw an exception.

Instead, `TryCast` simply returns `Nothing` if the cast can't be performed. `TryCast` works only with reference values; it cannot be used with value types such as `Integer` or `Boolean`.

Using `TryCast`, you can write code like this (code file: `MainWindow.xaml.vb`):

```
Public Sub TryCast1 (ByVal obj As Object)
    Dim temp = TryCast(obj, Object)
    If temp Is Nothing Then
      ' the cast couldn't be accomplished
      ' so do no work
    Else
      temp.DoSomething()
    End If
End Sub
```

If you are not sure whether a type conversion is possible, then it is often best to use `TryCast`. This function avoids the overhead and complexity of catching possible exceptions from `CType` or `DirectCast` and still provides you with an easy way to convert an object to another type.

# CREATING CLASSES

Using objects is fairly straightforward and intuitive. It is the kind of thing that even the most novice programmers pick up and accept rapidly.

## Basic Classes

As discussed earlier, objects are merely instances of a specific template (a class). The class contains the code that defines the behavior of its objects, and defines the instance variables that will contain the object's individual data.

Classes are created using the `Class` keyword, and include definitions (declaration) and implementations (code) for the variables, methods, properties, and events that make up the class. Each object created based on this class will have the same methods, properties, and events, and its own set of data defined by the fields in the class.

### The Class Keyword

If you want to create a class that represents a person — a `Person` class — you could use the `Class` keyword:

```
Public Class Person
    ' Implementation code goes here
End Class
```

As you know, Visual Basic projects are composed of a set of files with the `.vb` extension. It is possible for each file to contain multiple classes, which means that within a single file you could have something like this:

```
Public Class Adult
  ' Implementation code goes here.
End Class

Public Class Senior
```

```
    ' Implementation code goes here.
End Class

Public Class Child
    ' Implementation code goes here.
End Class
```

The most common and preferred approach is to have a single class per file. This is because the Visual Studio 2012 Solution Explorer and the code-editing environment are tailored to make it easy to navigate from file to file to find code. To demonstrate why, choose the Project ⇨ Add Class menu option to add a new class module to the project, and call it `People.vb`. Next add in the various classes shown in the preceding snippet. When you create a single class file with all these classes, the Solution Explorer simply displays a single entry, as shown in Figure 3-12. However, with Visual Studio 2012, you can now expand that single entry and see the reference to the four different classes defined within that single file.

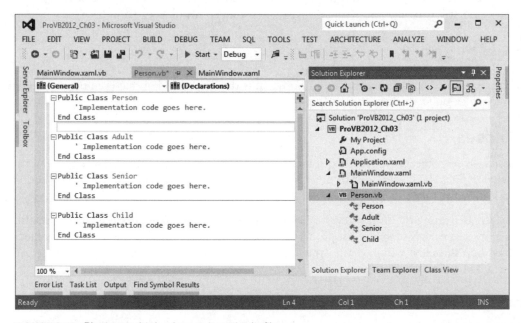

**FIGURE 3-12:** Placing multiple classes in a single file

This chapter uses one class per file in the examples, as this is the most common approach. Returning to the project again access the Project ⇨ Add Class menu option to add a new class module to the project. You'll be presented with the standard Add New Item dialog. Change the name to `Person.vb` and click Add. The result will be the following code, which defines the `Person` class:

```
Public Class Person

End Class
```

With the `Person` class created, you are ready to start adding code to declare the interface, implement the behaviors, and declare the instance variables.

## Fields

Fields are variables declared in the class. They will be available to each individual object when the application is run. Each object gets its own set of data — basically, each object gets its own copy of the fields.

Earlier, you learned that a class is simply a template from which you create specific objects. Variables that you define within the class are also simply templates — and each object gets its own copy of those variables in which to store its data.

Declaring member variables is as easy as declaring variables within the `Class` block structure. Add the following code to the `Person` class:

```
Public Class Person

    Private mName As String
    Private mBirthDate As Date
End Class
```

You can control the scope of the fields with the following keywords:

➤   `Private`—Available only to code within the class

➤   `Friend`—Available only to code within the project/component

➤   `Protected`—Available only to classes that inherit from the class (discussed in detail in Chapter 4)

➤   `Protected Friend`—Available to code within your project/component and classes that inherit from the class whether in the project or not (discussed in detail in Chapter 4)

➤   `Public`—Available to code outside the class and to any projects that reference the assembly

Typically, fields are declared using the `Private` keyword, making them available only to code within each instance of the class. Choosing any other option should be done with great care, because all the other options allow code outside the class to directly interact with the variable, meaning that the value could be changed and your code would never know that a change took place.

> **NOTE** *One common exception to making fields* `Private` *is to use the* `Protected` *keyword, discussed in Chapter 4.*

## Methods

Objects typically need to provide services (or functions) that can be called when working with the object. Using their own data or data passed as parameters to the method, they manipulate information to yield a result or perform an action.

Methods declared as `Public`, `Friend`, or `Protected` in scope define the interface of the class. Methods that are `Private` in scope are available to the code only within the class itself, and can be used to provide structure and organization to code. As discussed earlier, the actual code within each method is called an *implementation*, while the declaration of the method itself is what defines the interface.

Methods are simply routines that are coded within the class to implement the services you want to provide to the users of an object. Some methods return values or provide information to the calling code. These are called *interrogative methods*. Others, called *imperative methods*, just perform an action and return nothing to the calling code.

In Visual Basic, methods are implemented using Sub (for imperative methods) or Function (for interrogative methods) routines within the class module that defines the object. Sub routines may accept parameters, but they do not return any result value when they are complete. Function routines can also accept parameters, and they always generate a result value that can be used by the calling code.

A method declared with the Sub keyword is merely one that returns no value. Add the following code to the Person class:

```
Public Sub Walk()

    ' implementation code goes here

End Sub
```

The Walk method presumably contains some code that performs some useful work when called but has no result value to return when it is complete. To make use of this method, you might write code such as this:

```
Dim myPerson As New Person()
myPerson.Walk()
```

## Methods That Return Values

If you have a method that does generate some value that should be returned, you need to use the Function keyword:

```
Public Function Age() As Integer
   Return CInt(DateDiff(DateInterval.Year, mBirthDate, Now()))
End Function
```

Note that you must indicate the data type of the return value when you declare a function. This example returns the calculated age as a result of the method. You can return any value of the appropriate data type by using the Return keyword.

Optionally Visual Basic still allows you to return the value without using the Return keyword. Setting the value of the function name itself tells Visual Basic that this value should be used for the return:

```
Public Function Age() As Integer
    Age = CInt(DateDiff(DateInterval.Year, mBirthDate, Now()))
End Function
```

## Indicating Method Scope

Adding the appropriate keyword in front of the method declaration indicates the scope:

```
Public Sub Walk()
```

This indicates that Walk is a public method and thus is available to code outside the class and even outside the current project. Any application that references the assembly can use this method. Being public, this method becomes part of the object's interface.

The `Private` keyword indicates that a method is available only to the code within your particular class:

```
Private Function Age() As Integer
```

Private methods are very useful to help organize complex code within each class. Sometimes the methods contain very lengthy and complex code. In order to make this code more understandable, you may choose to break it up into several smaller routines, having the main method call these routines in the proper order. Moreover, you can use these routines from several places within the class, so by making them separate methods, you enable reuse of the code. These subroutines should never be called by code outside the object, so you make them `Private`.

## Method Parameters

You will often want to pass information into a method as you call it. This information is provided via parameters to the method. For instance, in the `Person` class, you may want the `Walk` method to track the distance the person walks over time. In such a case, the `Walk` method would need to know how far the person is to walk each time the method is called. The following code is a full version `Person` class (code file: `Person.vb`):

```
Public Class Person
  Private mName As String
  Private mBirthDate As Date
  Private mTotalDistance As Integer
  Public Sub Walk(ByVal distance As Integer)
     mTotalDistance += distance
  End Sub
  Public Function Age() As Integer
     Return CInt(DateDiff(DateInterval.Year, mBirthDate, Now()))
  End Function
End Class
```

With this implementation, a `Person` object sums all of the distances walked over time. Each time the `Walk` method is called, the calling code must pass an `Integer` value, indicating the distance to be walked. The code to call this method would be similar to the following:

```
Dim myPerson As New Person()
myPerson.Walk(42)
```

## Properties

The .NET environment provides for a specialized type of method called a *property*. A property is a method specifically designed for setting and retrieving data values. For instance, you declared a variable in the `Person` class to contain a name, so the `Person` class may include code to allow that name to be set and retrieved. This can be done using regular methods (code file: `Person.vb`):

```
Public Sub SetName(ByVal name As String)
  mName = name
End Sub

Public Function GetName() As String
  Return mName
End Function
```

Using methods like these, you write code to interact with the object:

```
Dim myPerson As New Person()

myPerson.SetName("Jones")
Messagebox.Show(myPerson.GetName())
```

While this is perfectly acceptable, it is not as nice as it could be with the use of a property. A `Property` style method consolidates the setting and retrieving of a value into a single structure, and makes the code within the class smoother overall. You can rewrite these two methods into a single property. The `Property` method is declared with both a scope and a data type. You could add the following code to the `Person` class (code file: `Person.vb`):

```
Public Property Name() As String
  Get
      Return mName
  End Get
  Set(ByVal Value As String)
   mName = Value
  End Set
End Property
```

However the preceding code can be written in a much simpler way:

```
Public Property Name() As String
```

This style of defining a property actually creates a hidden backing field called something similar to _Name, which is not defined in the source code but generated by the compiler. For most properties where you are not calculating a value during the get or set, this is the easiest way to define it.

By using a property method instead, you can make the client code much more readable:

```
Dim myPerson As New Person()

myPerson.Name = "Jones"
Messagebox.Show(myPerson.Name)
```

The return data type of the `Name` property is `String`. A property can return virtually any data type appropriate for the nature of the value. In this regard, a property is very similar to a method declared using the `Function` keyword.

By default, the parameter is named `Value`, but you can change the parameter name to something else, as shown here:

```
Set(ByVal NewName As String)
    mName = NewName
End Set
```

In many cases, you can apply business rules or other logic within this routine to ensure that the new value is appropriate before you actually update the data within the object. It is also possible to restrict the `Get` or `Set` block to be narrower in scope than the scope of the property itself. For instance, you may want to allow any code to retrieve the property value, but only allow other code in your project to alter the value. In this case, you can restrict the scope of the `Set` block to `Private`, while the `Property` itself is scoped as `Public`(code file: `Person.vb`):

```
Public Property Name() As String
  Get
    Return mName
  End Get
  Private Set(ByVal Value As String)
    mName = Value
  End Set
End Property
```

The new scope must be more restrictive than the scope of the property itself, and either the `Get` or `Set` block can be restricted, but not both. The one you do not restrict uses the scope of the `Property` method.

## Parameterized Properties

The `Name` property you created is an example of a single-value property. You can also create property arrays or parameterized properties. These properties reflect a range, or an array, of values. For example, people often have several phone numbers. You might implement a `PhoneNumber` property as a parameterized property, storing not only phone numbers, but also a description of each number. To retrieve a specific phone number you would write code such as the following (code file: `Person.vb`):

```
Dim myPerson As New Person()

Dim homePhone As String
homePhone = myPerson.Phone("home")
```

To add or change a phone number, you'd write the following code:

```
myPerson.Phone("work") = "555-9876"
```

Not only are you retrieving and updating a phone number property, you are also updating a specific phone number. This implies a couple of things. First, you can no longer use a simple variable to hold the phone number, as you are now storing a list of numbers and their associated names. Second, you have effectively added a parameter to your property. You are actually passing the name of the phone number as a parameter on each property call.

To store the list of phone numbers, you can use the `Hashtable` class. The `Hashtable` is very a standard object, but it allows you to test for the existence of a specific element. Add the following declarations to the `Person` class (code file: `Person.vb`):

```
Public Class Person
  Public Property Name As String
  Public Property BirthDate As Date
  Public Property TotalDistance As Integer
  Public Property Phones As New Hashtable
```

You can implement the `Phone` property by adding the following code to the `Person` class (code file: `Person.vb`):

```
Public Property Phone(ByVal location As String) As String
  Get
    Return CStr(Phones.Item(Location))
  End Get
```

```
    Set(ByVal Value As String)
      If Phones.ContainsKey(location) Then
        Phones.Item(location) = Value
      Else
        Phones.Add(location, Value)
      End If
    End Set
  End Property
```

The declaration of the `Property` method itself is a bit different from what you have seen.

```
Public Property Phone(ByVal location As String) As String
```

In particular, you have added a parameter, `location`, to the property itself. This parameter will act as the index into the list of phone numbers, and must be provided when either setting or retrieving phone number values.

Because the `location` parameter is declared at the `Property` level, it is available to all code within the property, including both the `Get` and `Set` blocks. Within your `Get` block, you use the `location` parameter to select the appropriate phone number to return from the `Hashtable`:

```
Get
    If Phones.ContainsKey(Location) Then
        Return Phones.Item(Location)
    End If
    Return ""
End Get
```

In this case, you are using the `ContainsKey` method of `Hashtable` to determine whether the phone number already exists in the list. When a value exists for a location you return it; however, if no value is stored matching the location, then you return `Nothing`. Similarly in the `Set` block that follows, you use the location to update or add the appropriate element in the `Hashtable`. If a location is already associated with a value, then you simply update the value in the list; otherwise, you add a new element to the list for the value (code file: `Person.vb`):

```
Set(ByVal Value As String)
  If Phones.ContainsKey(location) Then
    Phones.Item(location) = Value
  Else
    Phones.Add(location, Value)
  End If
End Set
```

This way, you are able to add or update a specific phone number entry based on the parameter passed by the calling code.

## Read-Only Properties

Sometimes you may want a property to be read-only so that it cannot be changed. In the `Person` class, for instance, you may have a read-write property, `BirthDate`, and a read-only property, `Age`. If so, the `BirthDate` property is a normal property, as follows (code file: `Person.vb`):

```
Public Property BirthDate() As Date
```

The Age value, conversely, is a derived value based on BirthDate. This is not a value that should ever be directly altered, so it is a perfect candidate for read-only status.

You could create all your objects without any Property routines at all, just using methods for all interactions with the objects. However, Property routines are obviously attributes of an object, whereas a Function might be an attribute or a method. By implementing all attributes as Properties, using the ReadOnly or WriteOnly attributes as necessary, and having any interrogative methods as Function routines, you create more readable and understandable code.

To make a property read-only, use the ReadOnly keyword and only implement the Get block:

```
Public ReadOnly Property Age() As Integer
  Get
    Return CInt(DateDiff(DateInterval.Year, BirthDate, Now()))
  End Get
End Property
```

Because the property is read-only, you will get a syntax error also known as a compile time error if you attempt to implement a Set block.

## Write-Only Properties

As with read-only properties, sometimes a property should be write-only, whereby the value can be changed but not retrieved.

Many people have allergies, so perhaps the Person object should have some understanding of the ambient allergens in the area. This is not a property that should be read from the Person object, as allergens come from the environment, rather than from the person, but it is data that the Person object needs in order to function properly. Add the following variable declaration to the class (code file: Person.vb):

```
Public WriteOnly Property AmbientAllergens() As Integer
  Set(ByVal Value As Integer)
    mAllergens = Value
  End Set
End Property
```

To create a write-only property, use the WriteOnly keyword and only implement a Set block in the code. Because the property is write-only, you will get a syntax error if you try to implement a Get block.

## The Default Property

Objects can implement a default property, which can be used to simplify the use of an object at times by making it appear as if the object has a native value. A good example of this behavior is the Collection object, which has a default property called Item that returns the value of a specific item, allowing you to write the following:

```
Dim mData As New HashTable()

Return mData(index)
```

Default properties must be parameterized properties. A property without a parameter cannot be marked as the default. Your `Person` class has a parameterized property — the `Phone` property you built earlier. You can make this the default property by using the `Default` keyword (code file: `Person.vb`):

```
Default Public Property Phone(ByVal location As String) As String
   Get
      If Phones.ContainsKey(Location) Then
          Return Phones.Item(Location)
      End If
      Return ""
   End Get
   Set(ByVal Value As String)
      If mPhones.ContainsKey(location) Then
        mPhones.Item(location) = Value
      Else
        mPhones.Add(location, Value)
      End If
   End Set
End Property
```

Prior to this change, you would have needed code such as the following to use the `Phone` property:

```
Dim myPerson As New Person()

MyPerson.Phone("home") = "555-1234"
```

Now, with the property marked as Default, you can simplify the code:

```
myPerson("home") = "555-1234"
```

As you can see, the reference to the property name `Phone` is not needed. By picking appropriate default properties, you can potentially make the use of objects more intuitive.

## Events

Both methods and properties enable you to write code that interacts with your objects by invoking specific functionality as needed. It is often useful for objects to provide notification, as certain activities occur during processing. You see examples of this all the time with controls, where a button indicates that it was clicked via a `Click` event, or a text box indicates that its contents have been changed via the `TextChanged` event.

Objects can raise events of their own, providing a powerful and easily implemented mechanism by which objects can notify client code of important activities or events. In Visual Basic, events are provided using the standard .NET mechanism of delegates; but before discussing delegates, let's explore how to work with events in Visual Basic.

## Handling Events

You are used to seeing code in a form to handle the `Click` event of a button, such as the following code:

```
Private Sub Button1_Click(ByVal sender As System.Object, _
    ByVal e As System.EventArgs) Handles Button1.Click

End Sub
```

Typically, you write your code in this type of routine without paying a lot of attention to the code created by the Visual Studio IDE. However, take a second look at that code, which contains some important things to note.

First, notice the use of the `Handles` keyword. This keyword specifically indicates that this method will be handling the `Click` event from the `Button1` control. Of course, a control is just an object, so what is indicated here is that this method will be handling the `Click` event from the `Button1` object.

Second, notice that the method accepts two parameters. The `Button` control class defines these parameters. It turns out that any method that accepts two parameters with these data types can be used to handle the `Click` event. For instance, you could create a new method to handle the event (code file: `MainWindow.vb`):

```
Private Sub MyClickMethod(ByVal s As System.Object, _
    ByVal args As System.EventArgs) Handles Button1.Click

End Sub
```

Even though you have changed the method name and the names of the parameters, you are still accepting parameters of the same data types, and you still have the `Handles` clause to indicate that this method handles the event.

## Handling Multiple Events

The `Handles` keyword offers even more flexibility. Not only can the method name be anything you choose, a single method can handle multiple events if you desire. Again, the only requirement is that the method and all the events being raised must have the same parameter list.

> **NOTE** *This explains why all the standard events raised by the .NET system class library have exactly two parameters—the sender and an* `EventArgs` *object. Being so generic makes it possible to write very generic and powerful event handlers that can accept virtually any event raised by the class library.*

One common scenario where this is useful is when you have multiple instances of an object that raises events, such as two buttons on a form (code file: `MainWindow.vb`):

```
Private Sub MyClickMethod(ByVal sender As System.Object, _
    ByVal e As System.EventArgs) _
    Handles Button1.Click, Button2.Click

End Sub
```

Notice that the `Handles` clause has been modified so that it has a comma-separated list of events to handle. Either event will cause the method to run, providing a central location for handling these events.

## The WithEvents Keyword

The `WithEvents` keyword tells Visual Basic that you want to handle any events raised by the object within the code:

```
Friend WithEvents Button1 As System.Windows.Forms.Button
```

The `WithEvents` keyword makes any event from an object available for use, whereas the `Handles` keyword is used to link specific events to the methods so that you can receive and handle them. This is true not only for controls on forms, but also for any objects that you create.

The `WithEvents` keyword cannot be used to declare a variable of a type that does not raise events. In other words, if the `Button` class did not contain code to raise events, you would get a syntax error when you attempted to declare the variable using the `WithEvents` keyword.

The compiler can tell which classes will and will not raise events by examining their interface. Any class that will be raising an event has that event declared as part of its interface. In Visual Basic, this means that you will have used the `Event` keyword to declare at least one event as part of the interface for the class.

## Raising Events

Your objects can raise events just like a control, and the code using the object can receive these events by using the `WithEvents` and `Handles` keywords. Before you can raise an event from your object, however, you need to declare the event within the class by using the `Event` keyword.

In the `Person` class, for instance, you may want to raise an event anytime the `Walk` method is called. If you call this event `Walked`, you can add the following declaration to the `Person` class (code file: `Person.vb`):

```
Public Class Person
    Private msName As String
    Private mBirthDate As Date
    Private mTotalDistance As Integer
    Private mPhones As New Hashtable()
    Private mAllergens As Integer
    Public Event Walked()
```

Events can also have parameters, values that are provided to the code receiving the event. A typical button's `Click` event receives two parameters, for instance. In the `Walked` method, perhaps you want to also indicate the total distance that has been walked. You can do this by changing the event declaration:

```
Public Event Walked(ByVal distance As Integer)
```

Now that the event is declared, you can raise that event within the code where appropriate. In this case, you'll raise it within the `Walk` method, so anytime a `Person` object is instructed to walk, it fires an event indicating the total distance walked. Make the following change to the `Walk` method (code file: `Person.vb`):

```
Public Sub Walk(ByVal distance As Integer)
    TotalDistance += distance
    RaiseEvent Walked(TotalDistance)
End Sub
```

The `RaiseEvent` keyword is used to raise the actual event. Because the event requires a parameter, that value is passed within parentheses and is delivered to any recipient that handles the event.

In fact, the `RaiseEvent` statement causes the event to be delivered to all code that has the object declared using the `WithEvents` keyword with a `Handles` clause for this event, or any code that has used the `AddHandler` method. The `AddHandler` method is discussed shortly.

If more than one method will be receiving the event, then the event is delivered to each recipient one at a time. By default, the order of delivery is not defined—meaning you can't predict the order in which the recipients receive the event—but the event is delivered to all handlers. Note that this is a serial, synchronous process. The event is delivered to one handler at a time, and it is not delivered to the next handler until the current handler is complete. Once you call the `RaiseEvent` method, the event is delivered to all listeners one after another until it is complete; there is no way for you to intervene and stop the process in the middle.

## Declaring and Raising Custom Events

As just noted, by default you have no control over how events are raised. You can overcome this limitation by using a more explicit form of declaration for the event itself. Rather than use the simple `Event` keyword, you can declare a custom event. This is for more advanced scenarios, as it requires you to provide the implementation for the event itself.

The concept of delegates is covered in detail later in this chapter, but it is necessary to look at them briefly here in order to declare a custom event. Note that creating a fully customized event handler is an advanced concept, and the sample code shown in this section is not part of the sample. This section goes beyond what you would normally look to implement in a typical business class.

A delegate is a definition of a method signature. When you declare an event, Visual Basic defines a delegate for the event behind the scenes based on the signature of the event. The `Walked` event, for instance, has a delegate like the following:

```
Public Delegate Sub WalkedEventHandler(ByVal distance As Integer)
```

Notice how this code declares a "method" that accepts an `Integer` and has no return value. This is exactly what you defined for the event. Normally, you do not write this bit of code, because Visual Basic does it automatically, but if you want to declare a custom event, then you need to manually declare the event delegate.

You also need to declare within the class a variable where you can keep track of any code that is listening for, or handling, the event. It turns out that you can tap into the prebuilt functionality of delegates for this purpose. By declaring the `WalkedEventHandler` delegate, you have defined a data type that automatically tracks event handlers, so you can declare the variable like this:

```
Private mWalkedHandlers As WalkedEventHandler
```

You can use the preceding variable to store and raise the event within the custom event declaration:

```
Public Custom Event Walked As WalkedEventHandler
  AddHandler(ByVal value As WalkedEventHandler)
    mWalkedHandlers = _
      CType([Delegate].Combine(mWalkedHandlers, value), WalkedEventHandler)
  End AddHandler
```

```
    RemoveHandler(ByVal value As WalkedEventHandler)
      mWalkedHandlers = _
        CType([Delegate].Remove(mWalkedHandlers, value), WalkedEventHandler)
    End RemoveHandler

    RaiseEvent(ByVal distance As Integer)
      If mWalkedHandlers IsNot Nothing Then
        mWalkedHandlers.Invoke(distance)
      End If
    End RaiseEvent
  End Event
```

In this case, you have used the `Custom Event` key phrase, rather than just `Event` to declare the event. A `Custom Event` declaration is a block structure with three subblocks: `AddHandler`, `RemoveHandler`, and `RaiseEvent`.

The `AddHandler` block is called anytime a new handler wants to receive the event. The parameter passed to this block is a reference to the method that will be handling the event. It is up to you to store the reference to that method, which you can do however you choose. In this implementation, you are storing it within the delegate variable, just like the default implementation provided by Visual Basic.

The `RemoveHandler` block is called anytime a handler wants to stop receiving your event. The parameter passed to this block is a reference to the method that was handling the event. It is up to you to remove the reference to the method, which you can do however you choose. In this implementation, you are replicating the default behavior by having the delegate variable remove the element.

Finally, the `RaiseEvent` block is called anytime the event is raised. Typically, it is invoked when code within the class uses the `RaiseEvent` statement. The parameters passed to this block must match the parameters declared by the delegate for the event. It is up to you to go through the list of methods that are handling the event and call each of those methods. In the example shown here, you are allowing the delegate variable to do that for you, which is the same behavior you get by default with a normal event.

The value of this syntax is that you could opt to store the list of handler methods in a different type of data structure, such as a `Hashtable` or `collection`. You could then invoke them asynchronously, or in a specific order based on some other behavior required by the application.

## Receiving Events with WithEvents

Now that you have implemented an event within the `Person` class, you can write client code to declare an object using the `WithEvents` keyword. For instance, in the project's MainWindow code module, you can write the following code:

```
Class MainWindow
  Private WithEvents mPerson As Person
```

By declaring the variable `WithEvents`, you are indicating that you want to receive any events raised by this object. You can also choose to declare the variable without the `WithEvents` keyword, although in that case you would not receive events from the object as described here. Instead, you would use the `AddHandler` method, which is discussed after `WithEvents`.

You can then create an instance of the object, as the form is created, by adding the following code (code file: `MainWindow.vb`):

```
Private Sub Window_Loaded_1 (sender As System.Object, _
    e As RoutedEventArgs)
  mPerson = New Person()

End Sub
```

At this point, you have declared the object variable using `WithEvents` and have created an instance of the `Person` class, so you actually have an object with which to work. You can now proceed to write a method to handle the `Walked` event from the object by adding the following code to the form. You can name this method anything you like; it is the `Handles` clause that is important, because it links the event from the object directly to this method, so it is invoked when the event is raised (code file: `MainWindow.xaml.vb`):

```
Private Sub OnWalk(ByVal Distance As Integer) Handles mPerson.Walked
  MessageBox.Show("Person walked a total distance of " & Distance)
End Sub
```

You are using the `Handles` keyword to indicate which event should be handled by this method. You are also receiving an `Integer` parameter. If the parameter list of the method doesn't match the list for the event, then you'll get a compiler error indicating the mismatch.

Finally, you need to call the `Walk` method on the `Person` object. Modify the `Click` event handler for the button (code file: `MainWindow.xaml.vb`):

```
Private Sub Button_Click_1(sender As Object, e As RoutedEventArgs)

  mPerson.Walk(42)

End Sub
```

When the button is clicked, you simply call the `Walk` method, passing an `Integer` value. This causes the code in your class to be run, including the `RaiseEvent` statement. The result is an event firing back into the window's code, because you declared the mPerson variable using the `WithEvents` keyword. The `OnWalk` method will be run to handle the event, as it has the `Handles` clause linking it to the event.

Figure 3-13 illustrates the flow of control, showing how the code in the button's `Click` event calls the `Walk` method, causing it to add to the total distance walked and then raise its event. The `RaiseEvent` causes the window's `OnWalk` method to be invoked; and once it is done, control returns to the `Walk` method in the object. Because you have no code in the `Walk` method after you call `RaiseEvent`, the control returns to the `Click` event back in the window, and then you are done.

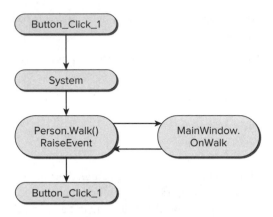

**FIGURE 3-13:** Flow of control from button click

> **NOTE** *Many people assume that events use multiple threads to do their work. This is not the case. Only one thread is involved in the process. Raising an event is like making a method call, as the existing thread is used to run the code in the event handler. Therefore, the application's processing is suspended until the event processing is complete.*

## Receiving Events with AddHandler

Now that you have seen how to receive and handle events using the `WithEvents` and `Handles` keywords, consider an alternative approach. You can use the `AddHandler` method to dynamically add event handlers through your code, and `RemoveHandler` to dynamically remove them.

> **NOTE** *The WithEvents and the Handles clause are typically the preferred method for handling events on an object. However, there are situations where you might need more flexibility.*

`WithEvents` and the `Handles` clause require that you declare both the object variable and event handler as you build the code, effectively creating a linkage that is compiled right into the code. `AddHandler`, conversely, creates this linkage at run time, which can provide you with more flexibility. However, before getting too deeply into that, let's see how `AddHandler` works.

In `MainWindow`, you can change the way the code interacts with the `Person` object, first by eliminating the `WithEvents` keyword:

```
Private mPerson As Person
```

And then by also eliminating the `Handles` clause:

```
Private Sub OnWalk(ByVal Distance As Integer)
  MsgBox("Person walked a total distance of " & Distance)
End Sub
```

With these changes, you've eliminated all event handling for the object, and the form will no longer receive the event, even though the Person object raises it.

Now you can change the code to dynamically add an event handler at run time by using the AddHandler method. This method simply links an object's event to a method that should be called to handle that event. Anytime after you have created the object, you can call AddHandler to set up the linkage (code file: MainWindow.xaml.vb):

```
Private Sub Window_Loaded_1 (sender As System.Object, _
    e As RoutedEventArgs)

    AddHandler mPerson.Walked, AddressOf OnWalk
  End Sub
```

This single line of code does the same thing as the earlier use of WithEvents and the Handles clause, causing the OnWalk method to be invoked when the Walked event is raised from the Person object.

However, this linkage is performed at run time, so you have more control over the process than you would have otherwise. For instance, you could have extra code to determine which event handler to link up. Suppose that you have another possible method to handle the event for cases when a message box is not desirable. Add this code to MainWindow:

```
Private Sub LogOnWalk(ByVal Distance As Integer)
  System.Diagnostics.Debug.WriteLine("Person walked a total distance of " &
                                      Distance)
End Sub
```

Rather than pop up a message box, this version of the handler logs the event to the output window in the IDE, or in the real world to a log file or event log as shown in Chapter 6. First add a new Setting to the application using the Project Properties. Name the property "NoPopup," give it the type Boolean and Application scope. You can accept the default value of false. Now you can enhance the AddHandler code to determine which handler should be used dynamically at run time (code file: MainWindow.xaml.vb):

```
Private Sub Window_Loaded_1 (sender As System.Object, _
    e As RoutedEventArgs)
  If My.Settings.NoPopup Then
    AddHandler mPerson.Walked, AddressOf LogOnWalk
  Else
    AddHandler mPerson.Walked, AddressOf OnWalk
  End If
End Sub
```

If the setting NoPopup is true, then the new version of the event handler is used; otherwise, you continue to use the message-box handler.

The counterpart to AddHandler is RemoveHandler. RemoveHandler is used to detach an event handler from an event. One example of when this is useful is if you ever want to set the mPerson variable to `Nothing` or to a new `Person` object. The existing `Person` object has its events attached to handlers, and before you get rid of the reference to the object, you must release those references:

```
If My.Settings.NoPopup Then
   RemoveHandler mPerson.Walked, AddressOf LogOnWalk
Else
   RemoveHandler mPerson.Walked, AddressOf OnWalk
End If
mPerson = New Person
```

If you do not detach the event handlers, the old `Person` object remains in memory because each event handler still maintains a reference to the object even after `mPerson` no longer points to the object. While this logic hasn't been implemented in this simple example, in a production environment you would need to ensure that when `mPerson` was ready to go out of scope you cleaned up any `AddHandler` references manually.

This illustrates one key reason why the `WithEvents` keyword and `Handles` clause are preferable in most cases. `AddHandler` and `RemoveHandler` must be used in pairs; failure to do so can cause memory leaks in the application, whereas the `WithEvents` keyword handles these details for you automatically.

# Constructor Methods

In Visual Basic, classes can implement a special method that is always invoked as an object is being created. This method is called the *constructor*, and it is always named `New`.

The constructor method is an ideal location for such initialization code, as it is always run before any other methods are ever invoked, and it is run only once for an object. Of course, you can create many objects based on a class, and the constructor method will be run for each object that is created.

You can implement a constructor in your classes as well, using it to initialize objects as needed. This is as easy as implementing a Public method named `New`. Add the following code to the `Person` class (code file: `Person.vb`):

```
Public Sub New()
   Phone("home") = "555-1234"
   Phone("work") = "555-5678"
End Sub
```

In this example, you are simply using the constructor method to initialize the home and work phone numbers for any new `Person` object that is created.

## Parameterized Constructors

You can also use constructors to enable parameters to be passed to the object as it is being created. This is done by simply adding parameters to the `New` method. For example, you can change the `Person` class as follows (code file: `Person.vb`):

```
Public Sub New(ByVal name As String, ByVal birthDate As Date)
   mName = name
   mBirthDate = birthDate
```

```
      Phone("home") = "555-1234"
      Phone("work") = "555-5678"
   End Sub
```

With this change, anytime a `Person` object is created, you will be provided with values for both the name and birth date. However, this changes how you can create a new `Person` object. Whereas you used to have code such as

```
Dim myPerson As New Person()
```

now you will have code such as

```
Dim myPerson As New Person("Bill", "1/1/1970")
```

In fact, because the constructor expects these values, they are mandatory—any code that needs to create an instance of the `Person` class must provide these values. Fortunately, there are alternatives in the form of optional parameters and method overloading (which enables you to create multiple versions of the same method, each accepting a different parameter list). These topics are discussed later in the chapter.

## OBJECT-ORIENTED CONCEPTS

So far, you have learned how to work with objects, how to create classes with methods, properties, and events, and how to use constructors. You have also learned how objects are destroyed within the .NET environment and how you can hook into that process to do any cleanup required by the objects.

Now you can move on to some more complex topics and variations on what has been discussed so far. First you'll look at some advanced variations of the methods you can implement in classes, including an exploration of the underlying technology behind events.

## Overloading Methods

Methods often accept parameter values. The `Person` object's `Walk` method, for instance, accepts an `Integer` parameter (code file: `Person.vb`):

```
Public Sub Walk(ByVal distance As Integer)
   mTotalDistance += distance
   RaiseEvent Walked(distance)
End Sub
```

Sometimes there is no need for the parameter. To address this, you can use the `Optional` keyword to make the parameter optional (code file: `Person.vb`):

```
Public Sub Walk(Optional ByVal distance As Integer = 0)
```

This does not provide you with a lot of flexibility, however, as the optional parameter or parameters must always be the last ones in the list. In addition, this merely enables you to pass or not pass the parameter. Suppose that you want to do something fancier, such as allow different data types or even entirely different lists of parameters.

Method overloading provides exactly those capabilities. By overloading methods, you can create several methods of the same name, with each one accepting a different set of parameters, or parameters of different data types.

As a simple example, instead of using the `Optional` keyword in the `Walk` method, you could use overloading. You keep the original `Walk` method, but you also add another `Walk` method that accepts a different parameter list. Change the code in the `Person` class back to the following (code file: `Person.vb`):

```
Public Sub Walk(ByVal Distance As Integer)
```

Now create another method with the same name but with a different parameter list (in this case, no parameters). Add this code to the class, without removing or changing the existing `Walk` method (code file: `Person.vb`):

```
Public Sub Walk()
   Walk(0)
End Sub
```

At this point, you have two `Walk` methods. The only way to tell them apart is by the list of parameters each accepts: the first requiring a single `Integer` parameter, the second having no parameter.

> **NOTE** *There is an* `Overloads` *keyword as well. This keyword is not needed for the simple overloading of methods described here, but it is required when combining overloading and inheritance, which is discussed in Chapter 4.*

You can call the `Walk` method either with or without a parameter, as shown in the following examples:

```
objPerson.Walk(42)
objPerson.Walk()
```

You can have any number of `Walk` methods in the class as long as each individual `Walk` method has a different method signature.

## Method Signatures

All methods have a signature, which is defined by the method name and the data types of its parameters:

```
Public Function CalculateValue() As Integer

End Sub
```

In this example, the signature is `f()`. The letter *f* is often used to indicate a method or function. It is appropriate here because you do not care about the name of the function; only its parameter list is important.

If you add a parameter to the method, then the signature is considered changed. For instance, you could change the method to accept a `Double`:

```
Public Function CalculateValue(ByVal value As Double) As Integer
```

In that case, the signature of the method is f(Double).

Notice that in Visual Basic the return value is not part of the signature. You cannot overload a Function routine by just having its return value's data type vary. It is the data types in the parameter list that must vary to utilize overloading.

Also note that the name of the parameter is totally immaterial; only the data type is important. This means that the following methods have identical signatures:

```
Public Sub DoWork(ByVal x As Integer, ByVal y As Integer)

Public Sub DoWork(ByVal value1 As Integer, ByVal value2 As Integer)
```

In both cases, the signature is f(Integer, Integer).

The data types of the parameters define the method signature, but whether the parameters are passed ByVal or ByRef does not. Changing a parameter from ByVal to ByRef will not change the method signature.

## Combining Overloading and Optional Parameters

Overloading is more flexible than using optional parameters, but optional parameters have the advantage that they can be used to provide default values, as well as make a parameter optional.

You can combine the two concepts: overloading a method and having one or more of those methods utilize optional parameters. Obviously, this sort of thing can become very confusing if overused, as you are employing two types of method "overloading" at the same time.

The Optional keyword causes a single method to effectively have two signatures. This means that a method declared as

```
Public Sub DoWork(ByVal x As Integer, Optional ByVal y As Integer = 0)
```

has two signatures at once: f(Integer, Integer) and f(Integer).

Because of this, when you use overloading along with optional parameters, the other overloaded methods cannot match either of these two signatures. However, as long as other methods do not match either signature, you can use overloading, as discussed earlier. For instance, you could implement methods with the signatures

```
Public Sub DoWork(ByVal x As Integer, Optional ByVal y As Integer = 0)
```
and

```
Public Sub DoWork(ByVal data As String)
```

because there are no conflicting method signatures. In fact, with these two methods, you have actually created three signatures:

1. f(Integer, Integer)
2. f(Integer)
3. f(String)

The IntelliSense built into the Visual Studio IDE will indicate that you have two overloaded methods, one of which has an optional parameter. This is different from creating three different overloaded methods to match these three signatures, in which case the IntelliSense would list three variations on the method, from which you could choose.

## Overloading Constructor Methods

In many cases, you may want the constructor to accept parameter values for initializing new objects, but also want to have the capability to create objects without providing those values. This is possible through method overloading, which is discussed later, or by using optional parameters.

Optional parameters on a constructor method follow the same rules as optional parameters for any other Sub routine: They must be the last parameters in the parameter list, and you must provide default values for the optional parameters.

For instance, you can change the Person class as shown here (code file: Person.vb):

```
Public Sub New(Optional ByVal PersonName As String = "", _
    Optional ByVal DOB As Date = #1/1/1900#)
  Name = PersonName
  BirthDate = DOB

  Phone("home") = "555-4321"
  Phone("work") = "555-8765"
End Sub
```

The preceding example changes both the Name and BirthDate parameters to be optional, and provides default values for both of them. Now you have the option to create a new Person object with or without the parameter values:

```
Dim myPerson As New Person("Bill", "1/1/1970")
```

or

```
Dim myPerson As New Person()
```

If you do not provide the parameter values, then the default values of an empty String and 1/1/1900 will be used, and the code will work just fine.

## Overloading the Constructor Method

You can combine the concept of a constructor method with method overloading to allow for different ways of creating instances of the class. This can be a very powerful combination, because it allows a great deal of flexibility in object creation.

You have already explored how to use optional parameters in the constructor. Now you will change the implementation in the Person class to make use of overloading instead. Change the existing New method as follows (code file: Person.vb):

```
Public Sub New(ByVal name As String, ByVal birthDate As Date)
    mName = name
    mBirthDate = birthDate
    Phone("home") = "555-1234"
    Phone("work") = "555-5678"
  End Sub
```

With this change, you require the two parameter values to be supplied. Now add that second implementation, as shown here:

```
Public Sub New()
   Phone("home") = "555-1234"
   Phone("work") = "555-5678"
End Sub
```

This second implementation accepts no parameters, meaning you can now create `Person` objects in two different ways — either with no parameters or by passing the name and birth date:

```
Dim myPerson As New Person()
```

or

```
Dim myPerson As New Person("Fred", "1/11/60")
```

This type of capability is very powerful because it enables you to define the various ways in which applications can create objects. In fact, the Visual Studio IDE considers this, so when you are typing the code to create an object, the IntelliSense tooltip displays the overloaded variations on the method, providing a level of automatic documentation for the class.

# Shared Methods, Variables, and Events

So far, all of the methods you have built or used have been instance methods, methods that require you to have an actual instance of the class before they can be called. These methods have used instance variables or member variables to do their work, which means that they have been working with a set of data that is unique to each individual object.

With Visual Basic, you can create variables and methods that belong to the class, rather than to any specific object. In other words, these variables and methods belong to all objects of a given class and are shared across all the instances of the class. When talking with C# developers you will hear this concept described as a static variable, since C# provides this same capability using a different keyword.

You can use the `Shared` keyword to indicate which variables and methods belong to the class, rather than to specific objects. For instance, you may be interested in knowing the total number of `Person` objects created as the application is running — kind of a statistical counter.

Warning in an ASP.NET or similar multithreaded application the use of `Shared` variables without code to ensure that updates to these values are single threaded will cause errors. Shared variables, as opposed to shared methods that are natively thread safe, should rarely be used.

## Shared Variables

Because regular variables are unique to each individual `Person` object, they do not enable you to easily track the total number of `Person` objects ever created. However, if you had a variable that had a common value across all instances of the `Person` class, you could use that as a counter. Add the following variable declaration to the `Person` class:

```
Private Shared mCounter As Integer
```

By using the `Shared` keyword, you are indicating that this variable's value should be shared across all `Person` objects within your application. This means that if one `Person` object makes the value 42, then all other `Person` objects will see the value as 42: It is a shared piece of data.

You can now use this variable within the code. For instance, you can add code to the constructor method, New, to increment the variable so that it acts as a counter — adding 1 each time a new Person object is created. Change the New methods as shown here (code file: Person.vb):

```
Public Sub New()
   Phone("home") = "555-1234"
   Phone("work") = "555-5678"
   mCounter += 1
End Sub

Public Sub New(ByVal name As String, ByVal birthDate As Date)
   mName = name
   mBirthDate = birthDate

   Phone("home") = "555-1234"
   Phone("work") = "555-5678"
   mCounter += 1
End Sub
```

The mCounter variable will now maintain a value indicating the total number of Person objects created during the life of the application. You may want to add a Property routine to allow access to this value by writing the following code (code file: MainWindow.xaml.vb):

```
Public ReadOnly Property PersonCount() As Integer
   Get
      Return mCounter
   End Get
End Property
```

Note that you are creating a regular property that returns the value of a shared variable, which is perfectly acceptable. As shown shortly, you could also create a shared property to return the value.

Now you could write code to use the class as follows (code file: MainWindow.xaml.vb):

```
Dim myPerson As Person
myPerson = New Person()
myPerson = New Person()
myPerson = New Person()

Messagebox.Show(myPerson.PersonCount)
```

The resulting display would show 3, because you've created three instances of the Person class. You would also need to decrement the counter after the objects are destroyed.

## Shared Methods

You can share not only variables across all instances of a class, but also methods. Whereas a regular method or property belongs to each specific object, a shared method or property is common across all instances of the class. There are a couple of ramifications to this approach.

First, because shared methods do not belong to any specific object, they can't access any instance variables from any objects. The only variables available for use within a shared method are shared variables, parameters passed into the method, or variables declared locally within the method itself. If you attempt to access an instance variable within a shared method, you'll get a compiler error.

In addition, because shared methods are actually part of the class, rather than any object, you can write code to call them directly from the class without having to create an instance of the class first.

For instance, a regular instance method is invoked from an object:

```
Dim myPerson As New Person()

myPerson.Walk(42)
```

However, a shared method can be invoked directly from the class itself without having to declare an instance of the class first:

```
Person.SharedMethod()
```

This saves the effort of creating an object just to invoke a method, and can be very appropriate for methods that act on shared variables, or methods that act only on values passed in via parameters. You can also invoke a shared method from an object, just like a regular method. Shared methods are flexible in that they can be called with or without creating an instance of the class first.

To create a shared method, you again use the Shared keyword. For instance, the PersonCount property created earlier could easily be changed to become a shared method instead (code file: MainWindow.xaml.vb):

```
Public Shared ReadOnly Property PersonCount() As Integer
   Get
      Return mCounter
   End Get
End Property
```

Because this property returns the value of a shared variable, it is perfectly acceptable for it to be implemented as a shared method. With this change, you can now determine how many Person objects have ever been created without having to actually create a Person object first:

```
Messagebox.Show(CStr(Person.PersonCount))
```

As another example, in the Person class you could create a method that compares the ages of two people. Add a shared method with the following code (code file: MainWindow.xaml.vb):

```
Public Shared Function CompareAge(ByVal person1 As Person, _
   ByVal person2 As Person) As Boolean

   Return person1.Age > person2.Age
End Function
```

This method simply accepts two parameters — each a Person — and returns true if the first is older than the second. Use of the Shared keyword indicates that this method doesn't require a specific instance of the Person class in order for you to use it.

Within this code, you are invoking the Age property on two separate objects, the objects passed as parameters to the method. It is important to recognize that you're not directly using any instance variables within the method; rather, you are accepting two objects as parameters, and invoking methods on those objects. To use this method, you can call it directly from the class:

```
If Person.CompareAge(myPerson1, myPerson2) Then
```

Alternately, you can also invoke it from any `Person` object:

```
Dim myPerson As New Person()

If myPerson.CompareAge(myPerson, myPerson2) Then
```

Either way, you're invoking the same shared method, and you'll get the same behavior, whether you call it from the class or a specific instance of the class.

## Shared Properties

As with other types of methods, you can also have shared property methods. Properties follow the same rules as regular methods. They can interact with shared variables but not member variables. They can also invoke other shared methods or properties, but cannot invoke instance methods without first creating an instance of the class. You can add a shared property to the `Person` class with the following code (code file: `Person.vb`):

```
Public Shared ReadOnly Property RetirementAge() As Integer
  Get
    Return 62
  End Get
End Property
```

This simply adds a property to the class that indicates the global retirement age for all people. To use this value, you can simply access it directly from the class:

```
Messagebox.Show(Person.RetirementAge)
```

Alternately, you can access it from any `Person` object:

```
Dim myPerson As New Person()

Messagebox.Show(myPerson.RetirementAge)
```

Either way, you are invoking the same shared property.

## Shared Events

As with other interface elements, events can also be marked as `Shared`. For instance, you could declare a shared event in the `Person` class:

```
Public Shared Event NewPerson()
```

Shared events can be raised from both instance methods and shared methods. Regular events cannot be raised by shared methods. Because shared events can be raised by regular methods, you can raise this one from the constructors in the `Person` class (code file: `Person.vb`):

```
Public Sub New()
  Phone("home") = "555-1234"
  Phone("work") = "555-5678"
  mCounter += 1
  RaiseEvent NewPerson()
End Sub

Public Sub New(ByVal PersonName As String, ByVal DOB As Date)
```

```
      Name = Name
      BirthDate = DOB

      Phone("home") = "555-1234"
      Phone("work") = "555-5678"
      mCounter += 1
      RaiseEvent NewPerson()
    End Sub
```

The interesting thing about receiving shared events is that you can get them from either an object, such as a normal event, or from the class itself. For instance, you can use the AddHandler method in the form's code to catch this event directly from the Person class.

First, add a method to the form to handle the event:

```
    Private Sub OnNewPerson()
      Messagebox.Show("new person " & Person.PersonCount)
    End Sub
```

Then, in the form's Load event, add a statement to link the event to this method (code file: MainWindow.xaml.vb):

```
    Private Sub Window_Loaded_1 (sender As System.Object, _
        e As RoutedEventArgs)

        AddHandler Person.NewPerson, AddressOf OnNewPerson

        If Microsoft.VisualBasic.Command = "nodisplay" Then
          AddHandler mPerson.Walked, AddressOf LogOnWalk
        Else
          AddHandler mPerson.Walked, AddressOf OnWalk
        End If
    End Sub
```

Notice that you are using the class, rather than any specific object in the AddHandler statement. You could use an object as well, treating this like a normal event, but this illustrates how a class itself can raise an event. When you run the application now, anytime a Person object is created you will see this event raised.

## Operator Overloading

Many basic data types, such as Integer and String, support the use of operators, including +, - , =, <>, and so forth. When you create a class, you are defining a new type, and sometimes it is appropriate for types to also support the use of operators.

In your class, you can write code to define how each of these operators works when applied to objects. What does it mean when two objects are added together? Or multiplied? Or compared? If you can define what these operations mean, you can write code to implement appropriate behaviors. This is called *operator overloading*, as you are overloading the meaning of specific operators.

Operator overloading is performed by using the Operator keyword, in much the same way that you create a Sub, Function, or Property method.

Most objects at least provide for some type of comparison, and so will often overload the comparison operators (=, <>, and maybe <, >, <=, and >=). You can do this in the Person class, for example, by adding the following code (code file: Person.vb):

```
Public Shared Operator =(ByVal person1 As Person, _
    ByVal person2 As Person) As Boolean

    Return person1.Name    person2.Name
End Operator

Public Shared Operator <>(ByVal person1 As Person, _
    ByVal person2 As Person) As Boolean

    Return person1.Name <> person2.Name
End Operator
```

Note that you overload both the = and <> operators. Many operators come in pairs, including the equality operator. If you overload =, then you must overload <> or a compiler error will result. Now that you have overloaded these operators, you can write code in MainWindow such as the following (code file: MainWindow.xaml.vb):

```
Private Sub CreatePeople()
    Dim p1 As New Person("Fred", #1/1/1960#)
    Dim p2 As New Person("Mary", #1/1/1980#)
    Dim p3 As Person = p1

    If p1 = p2 Then
        TextBox1.Text = "How?"
    End If
    If p1 = p3 Then
        TextBox1.Text = "Yes P3 and P1 are equal."
    End If
End Sub
```

Normally, it would be impossible to compare two objects using a simple comparison operator, but because you overloaded the operator, this becomes valid code. The result will display False and True.

Both the = and <> operators accept two parameters, so these are called *binary operators*. There are also *unary operators* that accept a single parameter. For instance, you might define the capability to convert a String value into a Person object by overloading the CType operator:

```
Public Shared Narrowing Operator CType(ByVal name As String) As Person
    Dim obj As New Person
    obj.Name = name
    Return obj
End Operator
```

To convert a String value to a Person, you assume that the value should be the Name property. You create a new object, set the Name property, and return the result. Because String is a broader, or less specific, type than Person, this is a *narrowing conversion*. Were you to do the reverse, convert a Person to a String, that would be a *widening conversion*:

```
Public Shared Widening Operator CType(ByVal person As Person) As String
    Return person.Name
End Operator
```

Few nonnumeric objects will overload most operators. It is difficult to imagine the result of adding, subtracting, or dividing two Customer objects against each other. Likewise, it is difficult to imagine performing bitwise comparisons between two `Invoice` objects. Table 3-5 lists the various operators that can be overloaded.

**TABLE 3-5:** Visual Basic Operators

| OPERATORS | DESCRIPTION |
| --- | --- |
| =, <> | Equality and inequality. These are binary operators to support the a = b and a <> b syntax. If you implement one, then you must implement both. |
| >, < | Greater than and less than. These are binary operators to support the a > b and a < b syntax. If you implement one, then you must implement both. |
| >=, <= | Greater than or equal to and less than or equal to. These are binary operators to support the a >= b and a <= b syntax. If you implement one, then you must implement both. |
| IsFalse, IsTrue | Boolean conversion. These are unary operators to support the `AndAlso` and `OrElse` statements. The `IsFalse` operator accepts a single object and returns `False` if the object can be resolved to a `False` value. The `IsTrue` operator accepts a single value and returns `True` if the object can be resolved to a `True` value. If you implement one, then you must implement both. |
| CType | Type conversion. This is a unary operator to support the `CType(a)` statement. The `CType` operator accepts a single object of another type and converts that object to the type of your class. This operator must be marked as either `Narrowing`, to indicate that the type is more specific than the original type, or `Widening`, to indicate that the type is broader than the original type. |
| +, - | Addition and subtraction. These operators can be unary or binary. The unary form exists to support the a += b and a -= b syntax, while the binary form exists to support a + b and a - b. |
| *, /, \, ^, Mod | Multiplication, division, exponent, and Mod. These are binary operators to support the a * b, a / b, a \ b, a ^ b, and a Mod b syntax. |
| & | Concatenation. This binary operator supports the a & b syntax. While this operator is typically associated with `String` manipulation, the & operator is not required to accept or return `String` values, so it can be used for any concatenation operation that is meaningful for your object type. |
| <<, >> | Bit shifting. These binary operators support the a << b and a >> b syntax. The second parameter of these operators must be a value of type `Integer`, which will be the integer value to be bit-shifted based on your object value. |
| And, Or, Xor | Logical comparison or bitwise operation. These binary operators support the a And b, a Or b, and a Xor b syntax. If the operators return Boolean results, then they are performing logical comparisons. If they return results of other data types, then they are performing bitwise operations. |
| Like | Pattern comparison. This binary operator supports the a `Like` b syntax. |

If an operator is meaningful for your data type, then you are strongly encouraged to overload that operator.

### Defining AndAlso and OrElse

Notice that neither the `AndAlso` nor the `OrElse` operators can be directly overloaded. This is because these operators use other operators behind the scenes to do their work. To overload `AndAlso` and `OrElse`, you need to overload a set of other operators, as shown in Table 3-6:

**TABLE 3-6:** Shortcut Boolean Operators

| ANDALSO | ORELSE |
| --- | --- |
| Overload the `And` operator to accept two parameters of your object's type and to return a result of your object's type. | Overload the `Or` operator to accept two parameters of your object's type and to return a result of your object's type. |
| Overload `IsFalse` for your object's type (meaning that you can return `True` or `False` by evaluating a single instance of your object). | Overload `IsTrue` for your object's type (meaning that you can return `True` or `False` by evaluating a single instance of your object). |

If these operators are overloaded in your class, then you can use `AndAlso` and `OrElse` to evaluate statements that involve instances of your class.

## Delegates

Sometimes it would be nice to be able to pass a procedure as a parameter to a method. The classic scenario is when building a generic sort routine, for which you need to provide not only the data to be sorted, but also a comparison routine appropriate for the specific data.

It is easy enough to write a sort routine that sorts `Person` objects by name, or to write a sort routine that sorts `SalesOrder` objects by sales date. However, if you want to write a sort routine that can sort any type of object based on arbitrary sort criteria, that gets pretty difficult. At the same time, because some sort routines can get very complex, it would be nice to reuse that code without having to copy and paste it for each different sort scenario.

By using *delegates*, you can create such a generic routine for sorting; and in so doing, you can see how delegates work and can be used to create many other types of generic routines. The concept of a delegate formalizes the process of declaring a routine to be called and calling that routine.

> **NOTE** *The underlying mechanism used by the .NET environment for callback methods is the delegate. Visual Basic uses delegates behind the scenes as it implements the* Event, RaiseEvent, WithEvents, *and* Handles *keywords.*

## Declaring a Delegate

In your code, you can declare what a delegate procedure must look like from an interface standpoint. This is done using the `Delegate` keyword. To see how this works, you will create a routine to sort any kind of data.

To do this, you will declare a delegate that defines a method signature for a method that compares the value of two objects and returns a Boolean indicating whether the first object has a larger value than the second object. You will then create a sort algorithm that uses this generic comparison method to sort data. Finally, you create an actual method that implements the comparison, and then you pass the method's address to the routine `Sort`.

Add a new module to the project by choosing Project ➪ Add Module. Name the module `Sort.vb`, click Add, and then add the following code (code file: `Sort.vb`):

```
Module Sort
    Public Delegate Function Compare(ByVal v1 As Object, ByVal v2 As Object) _
        As Boolean
End Module
```

This line of code does something interesting. It actually defines a method signature as a data type. This new data type is named `Compare`, and it can be used within the code to declare variables or parameters that are accepted by your methods. A variable or parameter declared using this data type could actually hold the address of a method that matches the defined method signature, and you can then invoke that method by using the variable.

Any method with the following signature can be viewed as being of type `Compare`:

```
f(Object, Object)
```

## Using the Delegate Data Type

You can write a routine that accepts the delegate data type as a parameter, meaning that anyone calling your routine must pass the address of a method that conforms to this interface. Add the following sort routine to the code module `Sort` (code file: `Sort.vb`):

```
Public Sub DoSort(ByVal theData() As Object, ByVal greaterThan As Compare)
    Dim outer As Integer
    Dim inner As Integer
    Dim temp As Object

    For outer = 0 To UBound(theData)
    For inner = outer + 1 To UBound(theData)
        If greaterThan.Invoke(theData(outer), theData(inner)) Then
         temp = theData(outer)
         theData(outer) = theData(inner)
         theData(inner) = temp
      End If
    Next
  Next
End Sub
```

The GreaterThan parameter is a variable that holds the address of a method matching the method signature defined by the Compare delegate. The address of any method with a matching signature can be passed as a parameter to your sort routine.

Note the use of the Invoke method, which is how a delegate is called from the code. In addition, note that the routine deals entirely with the generic System.Object data type, rather than with any specific type of data. The specific comparison of one object to another is left to the delegate routine that is passed in as a parameter.

## Implementing a Delegate Method

Now create the implementation of the delegate routine and call the Sort method. On a very basic level, all you need to do is create a method that has a matching method signature, add the following code to your Sort module:

```
Public Function PersonCompare(ByVal person1 As Object, _
   ByVal person2 As Object) As Boolean

End Function
```

The method signature of this method exactly matches what you defined by your delegate earlier:

```
Compare(Object, Object)
```

In both cases, you are defining two parameters of type Object.

Of course, there is more to it than simply creating the stub of a method. The method needs to return a value of True if its first parameter is greater than the second parameter. Otherwise, it should be written to deal with some specific type of data.

The Delegate statement defines a data type based on a specific method interface. To call a routine that expects a parameter of this new data type, it must pass the address of a method that conforms to the defined interface.

To conform to the interface, a method must have the same number of parameters with the same data types defined in your Delegate statement. In addition, the method must provide the same return type as defined. The actual name of the method does not matter; it is the number, order, and data type of the parameters and the return value that count.

To find the address of a specific method, you can use the AddressOf operator. This operator returns the address of any procedure or method, enabling you to pass that value as a parameter to any routine that expects a delegate as a parameter.

The Person class already has a shared method named CompareAge that generally does what you want. Unfortunately, it accepts parameters of type Person, rather than of type Object as required by the Compare delegate. You can use method overloading to solve this problem.

Create a second implementation of CompareAge that accepts parameters of type Object as required by the delegate, rather than of type Person as shown in the existing implementation (code file: Person.vb):

```
Public Shared Function CompareAge(ByVal person1 As Object, _
   ByVal person2 As Object) As Boolean
```

```
        Return CType(person1, Person).Age > CType(person2, Person).Age

    End Function
```

This method simply returns `True` if the first `Person` object's age is greater than the second. The routine accepts two `Object` parameters, rather than specific `Person` type parameters, so you have to use the `CType` method to access those objects as type `Person`. You accept the parameters as type `Object` because that is what is defined by the `Delegate` statement. You are matching its method signature:

```
    f(Object, Object)
```

Because this method's parameter data types and return value match the delegate, you can use it when calling the `Sort` routine. Place a button on the `MainWindow` form and write the following code behind that button (code file: `MainWindow.xaml.vb`):

```
    Private Sub CompareAge (ByVal sender As System.Object, _
        ByVal e As System.EventArgs)

      Dim myPeople(4) As Person

      myPeople(0) = New Person("Fred", #7/9/1960#)
      myPeople(1) = New Person("Mary", #1/21/1955#)
      myPeople(2) = New Person("Sarah", #2/1/1960#)
      myPeople(3) = New Person("George", #5/13/1970#)
      myPeople(4) = New Person("Andre", #10/1/1965#)

      DoSort(myPeople, AddressOf Person.CompareAge)
    End Sub
```

This code creates an array of `Person` objects and populates them. It then calls the `DoSort` routine from the module, passing the array as the first parameter, and the address of the shared `CompareAge` method as the second parameter. To display the contents of the sorted array in the application's window, you can add the following code (code file: `MainWindow.xaml.vb`):

```
    Dim myPerson As Person
    TextBox1.Text = ""
    For Each myPerson In myPeople
        TextBox1.Text = TextBox1.Text & myPerson.Name & " " & myPerson.Age & vbCrLf
    Next
```

When you run the application and click the button, the application window displays a list of the people sorted by age, as shown in Figure 3-14.

**FIGURE 3-14:** Sorting by age

What makes this so powerful is that you can change the comparison routine without changing the sort mechanism. Simply add another comparison routine to the `Person` class (code file: `Person.vb`):

```
Public Shared Function CompareName(ByVal person1 As Object, _
    ByVal person2 As Object) As Boolean

    Return CType(person1, Person).Name > CType(person2, Person).Name

End Function
```

Then, change the code behind the button on the form to use that alternate comparison routine (code file: `MainWindow.xaml.vb`):

```
Private Sub CompareName

    Dim myPeople(4) As Person

    myPeople(0) = New Person("Fred", #7/9/1960#)
    myPeople(1) = New Person("Mary", #1/21/1955#)
    myPeople(2) = New Person("Sarah", #2/1/1960#)
    myPeople(3) = New Person("George", #5/13/1970#)
    myPeople(4) = New Person("Andre", #10/1/1965#)

    DoSort(myPeople, AddressOf Person.CompareName)

    Dim myPerson As Person
    TextBox1.Text = ""
    For Each myPerson In myPeople
        TextBox1.Text = TextBox1.Text & myPerson.Name & " " &
            myPerson.Age & vbCrLf
    Next
End Sub
```

When you run this updated code, you will find that the array contains a set of data sorted by name, rather than age, as shown in Figure 3-15.

Simply by creating a new compare routine and passing it as a parameter, you can entirely change the way that the data is sorted. Better still, this sort routine can operate on any type of object, as long as you provide an appropriate delegate method that knows how to compare that type of object.

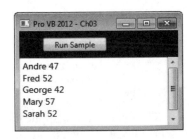

**FIGURE 3-15:** Sorting by name

## SUMMARY

Visual Basic offers a fully object-oriented language with all the capabilities you would expect. This chapter described the basic concepts behind classes and objects, as well as the separation of interface from implementation and data.

The chapter introduced the `System.Object` class and explained how this class is the base class for all classes in .NET. You were then introduced to concepts such as `Value` and `Reference` types as well as the implementation for primitive types. The chapter looked at most of the core primitive types available in Visual Basic and how to convert between types.

You have learned how to use the `Class` keyword to create classes, and how those classes can be instantiated into specific objects, each one an instance of the class. These objects have methods and properties that can be invoked by the client code, and can act on data within the object stored in member or instance variables.

You also explored some more advanced concepts, including method overloading, shared or static variables and methods, and the use of delegates and lambda expressions.

The next chapter continues the discussion of object syntax as you explore the concept of inheritance and all the syntax that enables inheritance within Visual Basic. You will also walk through the creation, implementation, and use of multiple interfaces — a powerful concept that enables objects to be used in different ways, depending on the interface chosen by the client application.

Also covered in the next chapter is a discussion of objects and object-oriented programming, applying all of this syntax. It explains the key object-oriented concepts of abstraction, encapsulation, polymorphism, and inheritance, and shows how they work together to provide a powerful way to design and implement applications.

# Custom Objects

**WROX.COM CODE DOWNLOADS FOR THIS CHAPTER**

The wrox.com code downloads for this chapter are found at www.wrox.com/remtitle .cgi?isbn=9781118314456 on the Download Code tab. The code is in the chapter 4 download and individually named according to the code filenames throughout the chapter.

Visual Basic is a fully object-oriented language. Chapter 3 covered the basics of creating classes and objects, including the creation of methods, properties, events, operators, and instance variables. You have seen the basic building blocks for abstraction, encapsulation, and polymorphism—concepts discussed in more detail at the end of this chapter. The final major techniques you need to understand are inheritance and the use of multiple interfaces.

Inheritance is the idea that you can create a class that reuses methods, properties, events, and variables from another class. You can create a class with some basic functionality, and then use that class as a base from which to create other, more detailed, classes. All these derived classes will have the same common functionality as that base class, along with new, enhanced, or even completely changed functionality.

This chapter covers the syntax that supports inheritance within Visual Basic. This includes creating the base classes from which other classes can be derived, as well as creating those derived classes.

Visual Basic also supports a related concept: multiple interfaces. As shown in Chapter 3, all objects have a native or default interface, which is defined by the public methods, properties, and events declared in the class. These additional interfaces define alternative ways in which your object can be accessed by providing clearly defined sets of methods, properties, and events. Like the native interface, these secondary interfaces define how the client code can interact with your object, essentially providing a "contract" that enables the client to know exactly what methods, properties, and events the object will provide. When you write code to interact with an object, you can choose which of the interfaces you want to use; basically, you are choosing how you want to view or interact with that object.

This chapter uses relatively basic code examples so that you can focus on the technical and syntactic issues surrounding inheritance and multiple interfaces. The last part of this chapter revisits these concepts using a more sophisticated set of code as you continue to explore object-oriented programming and how to apply inheritance and multiple interfaces in a practical manner.

Successfully applying Visual Basic's object-oriented capabilities requires an understanding of object-oriented programming. This chapter applies Visual Basic's object-oriented syntax, showing how it enables you to build object-oriented applications. It also describes in detail the four major object-oriented concepts: abstraction, encapsulation, polymorphism, and inheritance. By the end of this chapter, you will understand how to apply these concepts in your design and development efforts to create effective object-oriented applications.

# INHERITANCE

Inheritance is the concept that a new class can be based on an existing class, inheriting the interface and functionality from the original class. In Chapter 3, you explored the relationship between a class and an object, and saw that the class is essentially a template from which objects can be created. Inheritance is always through a single chain to the base `Object` class. While Visual Basic supports multiple interfaces, it does not support multiple inheritance.

While using objects is very powerful, a single object does not always provide all the capabilities you might like. In particular, in many cases a class only partially describes what you need for your object. You may have a class called `Person`, for instance, which has all the properties and methods that apply to all types of people, such as first name, last name, and birth date. While useful, this class probably does not have everything you need to describe a specific type of person, such as an employee or a customer. An employee would have a hire date and a salary, which are not included in `Person`, while a customer would have a credit rating, something neither the `Person` nor the `Employee` classes would need.

Without inheritance, you would probably end up replicating the code from the `Person` class in both the `Employee` and `Customer` classes so that they would have that same functionality as well as the ability to add new functionality of their own.

Inheritance makes it very easy to create classes for `Employee`, `Customer`, and so forth. You do not have to re-create that code for an employee to be a person; it automatically inherits any properties, methods, and events from the original `Person` class.

You can think of it this way: When you create an `Employee` class, which inherits from a `Person` class, you are effectively merging these two classes. If you then create an object based on the `Employee` class, then it has not only the interface (properties, methods, and events) and implementation from the `Employee` class, but also those from the `Person` class.

While an `Employee` object represents the merger between the `Employee` and `Person` classes, understand that the variables and code contained in each of those classes remain independent. Two perspectives are involved.

From the outside, the client code that interacts with the `Employee` object sees a single, unified object that represents the inheritance of the `Employee` and `Person` classes.

From the inside, the code in the `Employee` class and the code in the `Person` class are not totally intermixed. Variables and methods that are Private are only available within the class they were written. Variables and methods that are Public in one class can be called from the other class.

Variables and methods that are declared as Friend are available only between classes if both classes are in the same assembly. As discussed later in the chapter, there is also a Protected scope that is designed to work with inheritance, but, again, this provides a controlled way for one class to interact with the variables and methods in the other class.

Visual Studio 2012 includes a Class Designer tool that enables you to easily create diagrams of your classes and their relationships. The Class Designer diagrams are a derivative of a standard notation called the Unified Modeling Language (UML) that is typically used to diagram the relationships between classes, objects, and other object-oriented concepts. The Class Designer diagrams more accurately and completely model .NET classes, so that is the notation used in this chapter. The relationship between the `Person`, `Employee`, and `Customer` classes is illustrated in Figure 4-1.

Each box in this diagram represents a class; in this case, you have `Person`, `Employee`, and `Customer` classes. The line from `Employee` back up to `Person`, terminating in a triangle, indicates that `Employee` is derived from, or inherits from, `Person`. The same is true for the `Customer` class.

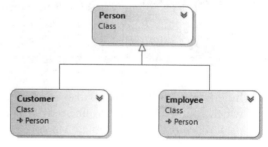

**FIGURE 4-1:** Person-Customer-Employee Class diagram

## When to Use Inheritance

Inheritance is one of the most powerful object-oriented features a language can support. At the same time, inheritance is one of the most dangerous and misused object-oriented features.

Properly used, inheritance enables you to increase the maintainability, readability, and reusability of your application by offering you a clear and concise way to reuse code, via both interface and implementation. Improperly used, inheritance creates applications that are very fragile, whereby a change to a class can cause the entire application to break or require changes.

Inheritance enables you to implement an is-a relationship. In other words, it enables you to implement a new class that "is a" more specific type of its base class. Properly used, inheritance enables you to create child classes that are actually the same as the base class.

For example, you know that a jet is an airplane. A jet is in part defined by its engine, though that is not its primary identity. Proper use of inheritance enables you to create an `Airplane` base class from which you can derive a `Jet` class. You would not subclass `Jet` from an `Engine` class, as jet isn't an engine—although it has an `Engine`.

This is the challenge. Inheritance is not just a mechanism for code reuse, but a mechanism to create classes that flow naturally from another class. If you use it anywhere you want code reuse, you will end up with a real mess on your hands. Using inheritance simply because you see a common interface during design isn't best practice. Instead if you just need a common set of methods and properties with a custom implementation for those methods and properties, you should use an `interface` definition. The creation of custom `interface` definitions is discussed later in this chapter.

> **NOTE** *The question you must ask when using inheritance is whether the child class is a more specific version of the base class. Does it pass the 'is-a' test?*

It's necessary to understand some basic terms associated with inheritance—and there are a lot of terms, partly because there are often several ways to say the same thing. The various terms are all used quite frequently and interchangeably.

> **NOTE** *Though this book attempts to use consistent terminology, be aware that in other books and articles, and online, all of these terms are used in various permutations.*

Inheritance, for instance, is also sometimes referred to as *generalization,* because the class from which you are inheriting your behavior is virtually always a more general form of your new class. A person is more general than an employee, for instance.

The inheritance relationship is also referred to as an *is-a* relationship. When you create a `Customer` class that inherits from a `Person` class, that customer is a person. The employee is a person as well. Thus, you have the is-a relationship. As shown later in the chapter, multiple interfaces can be used to implement something similar to the is-a relationship, the act-as relationship.

When you create a class using inheritance, it inherits behaviors and data from an existing class. That existing class is called the *base class*. It is also often referred to as a *superclass* or a *parent class*.

The class you create using inheritance is based on the parent class. It is called a *subclass*. Sometimes it is also called a *child class* or a *derived class*. In fact, the process of inheriting from a base class by a subclass is referred to as *deriving*. You are deriving a new class from the base class. This process is also called *subclassing*.

The way you use inheritance in the design of a framework is somewhat different from how you use inheritance in the design of an actual application. In this context, the word *framework* is being used to refer to a set of classes that provide base functionality that isn't specific to an application, but rather may be used across a number of applications within the organization, or perhaps even beyond the organization. The .NET Framework base class library is an example of a very broad framework you use when building your applications.

## Inheritance and Multiple Interfaces

While inheritance is powerful, it is really geared for implementing the is-a relationship. Sometimes you will have objects that need a common interface, even though they are not really a specific case of some base class that provides that interface. Often a custom `interface` is a better alternative than inheritance.

For starters, you can only inherit a single common interface. However, a class can implement multiple different interfaces. Multiple interfaces can be viewed as another way to implement the is-a relationship. However, it is often better to view inheritance as an is-a relationship and to view multiple interfaces as a way of implementing an act-as relationship.

When a class implements an abstract interface such as `IPrintableObject`, you are not really saying that your class is a printable object, you are saying that it can "act as" a printable object. An Employee is a Person, but at the same time it can act as a printable object. This is illustrated in Figure 4-2.

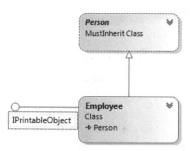

The drawback to this approach is that you have no inherited implementation when you use an abstract interface. While not as automatic or easy as inheritance, it is possible to reuse implementation code with a bit of extra work. But first you will look at implementing inheritance.

**FIGURE 4-2:** Class diagram showing inheritance and an interface

# Implementing Inheritance

To implement a class using inheritance, you start with an existing class from which you will derive your new subclass. This existing class, or base class, may be part of the .NET system class library framework, it may be part of some other application or .NET assembly, or you may create it as part of your application.

Once you have a base class, you can then implement one or more subclasses based on that base class. Each of your subclasses automatically inherits all of the methods, properties, and events of that base class—including the implementation behind each method, property, and event. Your subclass can also add new methods, properties, and events of its own, extending the original interface with new functionality. In addition, a subclass can replace the methods and properties of the base class with its own new implementation—effectively overriding the original behavior and replacing it with new behaviors.

Essentially, inheritance is a way of combining functionality from an existing class into your new subclass. Inheritance also defines rules for how these methods, properties, and events can be merged, including control over how they can be changed or replaced, and how the subclass can add new methods, properties, and events of its own. This is what you will learn in the following sections—what these rules are and what syntax you use in Visual Basic to make it all work.

## Creating a Base Class

Virtually any class you create can act as a base class from which other classes can be derived. In fact, unless you specifically indicate in the code that your class cannot be a base class, you can derive from it (you will come back to this later).

Create a new Windows Forms Application project in Visual Basic by selecting File ⇨ New Project and selecting Windows Forms Application. Then add a class to the project using the Project ⇨ Add Class menu option and name it `Person.vb`.

At this point, you technically have a base class, as it is possible to inherit from this class even though it doesn't do or contain anything. You can now add methods, properties, and events to this class. For instance, add the following code to the `Person.vb` class:

```
Public Class Person
   Public Property Name As String
   Public Property BirthDate As Date
End Class
```

## Creating a Subclass

To implement inheritance, you need to add a new class to your project. Use the Project ⇨ Add Class menu option and add a new class named `Employee.vb` as follows:

```
Public Class Employee
   Inherits Person
   Public Property HireDate As Date
   Public Property Salary As Double
End Class
```

This is a regular standalone class with no explicit inheritance. It can be represented by the class diagram shown in Figure 4-3. The diagram in Figure 4-3 also illustrates the fact that the `Employee` class is a subclass of `Person`.

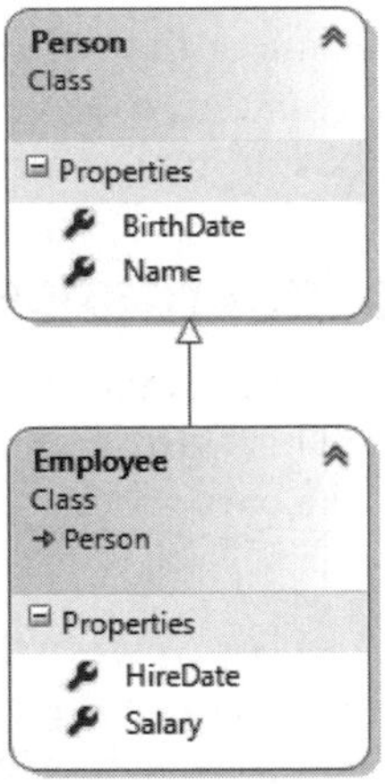

In this representation of the class as it is presented from Visual Studio, the top box represents the `Person` class. In the top section of this box is the name of the class and a specification that it is a class. The section below it contains a list of the properties exposed by the class, both marked as Public. If the class had methods or events, then they would be displayed in their own sections in the diagram.

**FIGURE 4-3:** Class diagram showing properties in parent and child classes

In the box below, you again see the `Employee` class name and properties. It turns out that behind the scenes, this class inherits some capabilities from `System.Object`. Chapter 3 made clear that every class in the entire .NET platform ultimately inherits from `System.Object` either implicitly or explicitly.

While having an `Employee` object with a hire date and salary is useful, it should also have `Name` and `BirthDate` properties, just as you implemented in the `Person` class. Without inheritance, you would probably just copy and paste the code from `Person` directly into the new `Employee` class, but with inheritance, you get to directly reuse the code from the `Person` class.

## The Inherits Keyword

The `Inherits` keyword indicates that a class should derive from an existing class, inheriting the interface and behavior from that class. You can inherit from almost any class in your project, from the .NET system class library, or from other assemblies. It is also possible to prevent inheritance, which is covered later in the chapter. When using the `Inherits` keyword to inherit from classes outside the current project, you need to either specify the namespace that contains that class or place an `Imports` statement at the top of the class to import that namespace for your use.

The line running from `Employee` back up to `Person` ends in an open triangle, which is the symbol for inheritance when using the Class Designer in Visual Studio. It is this line that indicates that the `Employee` class includes all the functionality, as well as the interface, of `Person`.

This means that an object created based on the `Employee` class has not only the methods `HireDate` and `Salary`, but also `Name` and `BirthDate`. To test this, bring up the designer for and add the controls shown in Table 4-1 to the form.

**TABLE 4-1:** List of TextBoxes and Buttons for Sample Code

| CONTROL TYPE | NAME PROPERTY VALUE | TEXT PROPERTY VALUE |
| --- | --- | --- |
| TextBox | TextBoxName | <blank> |
| TextBox | TextBoxDOB | <blank> |
| TextBox | TextBoxHireDate | <blank> |
| TextBox | TextBoxSalary | <blank> |
| button | ButtonOK | OK |

You should also add some labels to make the form readable. The Form Designer should now look something like Figure 4-4.

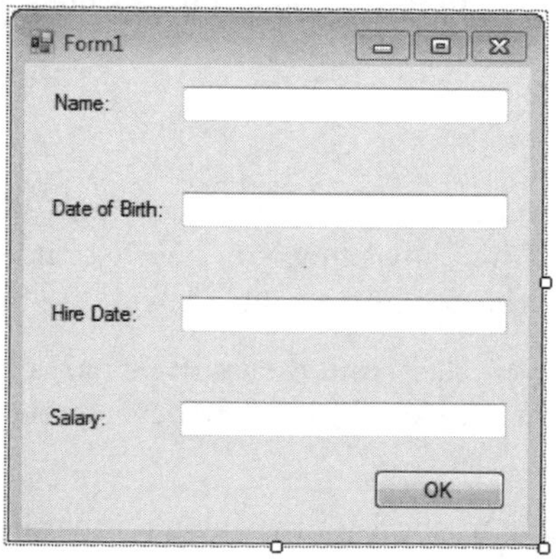

**FIGURE 4-4:** Demo app screen

Double-click the OK button to bring up the code window and enter the following into the `Form1.vb` code file:

```
Private Sub ButtonOK_Click(sender As Object, e As EventArgs) Handles ButtonOK.Click
    Dim emp As New Employee()
    With emp
        .Name = "Ben"
        .BirthDate = #1/1/1975#
        .HireDate = #1/1/2000#
        .Salary = 30000
        TextBoxName.Text = .Name
        TextBoxDOB.Text = Format(.BirthDate, "Short date")
        TextBoxHireDate.Text = Format(.HireDate, "Short date")
        TextBoxSalary.Text = Format(.Salary, "$0.00")
    End With
End Sub
```

> **NOTE** *The best Visual Basic practice is to use the* `With` *keyword.*

Even though `Employee` does not directly implement the `Name` or `BirthDate` methods, they are available for use through inheritance. When you run this application and click the button, your controls are populated with the values from the `Employee` object.

When the code in `Form1` invokes the `Name` property on the `Employee` object, the code from the `Person` class is executed, as the `Employee` class has no such property. However, when the `HireDate` property is invoked on the `Employee` object, the code from the `Employee` class is executed.

From the form's perspective, it doesn't matter whether a method is implemented in the `Employee` class or the `Person` class; they are all simply methods of the `Employee` object. In addition, because the code in these classes is merged to create the `Employee` object, there is no performance difference between calling a method implemented by the `Employee` class or calling a method implemented by the `Person` class.

## Overloading Methods

Although your `Employee` class automatically gains the `Name` and `BirthDate` methods through inheritance, it also has methods of its own—`HireDate` and `Salary`. This shows how you have extended the base `Person` interface by adding methods and properties to the `Employee` subclass.

You can add new properties, methods, and events to the `Employee` class, and they will be part of any object created based on `Employee`. This has no impact on the `Person` class whatsoever, only on the `Employee` class and `Employee` objects.

You can even extend the functionality of the base class by adding methods to the subclass that have the same name as methods or properties in the base class, as long as those methods or properties have different parameter lists. You are effectively overloading the existing methods from the base class. It is essentially the same thing as overloading regular methods, as discussed in Chapter 3.

For example, your Person class is currently providing your implementation for the Name property. Employees may have other names you also want to store, perhaps an informal name and a formal name in addition to their regular name. One way to accommodate this requirement is to change the Person class itself to include an overloaded Name property that supports this new functionality. However, you are really only trying to enhance the Employee class, not the more general Person class, so what you want is a way to add an overloaded method to the Employee class itself, even though you are overloading a method from its base class.

You can overload a method from a base class by using the Overloads keyword. The concept is the same as described in Chapter 3, but in this case an extra keyword is involved. To overload the Name property, for instance, you can add a new property to the Employee class. First, though, define an enumerated type using the Enum keyword. This Enum will list the different types of name you want to store. Add this Enum to the Employee.vb file, before the declaration of the class itself:

```
Public Enum NameTypes
   NickName = 1
   FullName = 2
End Enum
```

You can then add an overloaded Name property to the Employee class itself as follows:

```
Public Class Employee
   Inherits Person

   Public Property HireDate As Date
   Public Property Salary As Double
   Private mNames As New Generic.Dictionary(Of NameTypes, String)
   Public Overloads Property Name(ByVal type As NameTypes) As String
     Get
       Return mNames(type)
     End Get
     Set(ByVal value As String)
       If mNames.ContainsKey(type) Then
         mNames.Item(type) = value
       Else
         mNames.Add(type, value)
       End If
     End Set
   End Property
```

This Name property is actually a property array, which enables you to store multiple values via the same property. In this case, you are storing the values in a Generic.Dictionary(Of K, V) object, which is indexed by using the Enum value you just defined. Chapter 7 discusses generics in detail. For now, you can view this generic Dictionary just like any collection object that stores key/value data.

> **NOTE** *If you omit the* Overloads *keyword here, your new implementation of the* Name *method will shadow the original implementation. Shadowing is very different from overloading, and is covered later in the chapter.*

Though this method has the same name as the method in the base class, the fact that it accepts a different parameter list enables you to use overloading to implement it here. The original `Name` property, as implemented in the `Person` class, remains intact and valid, but now you have added a new variation with this second `Name` property, as shown in Figure 4-5.

**FIGURE 4-5:** Class diagram showing properties, fields and a custom enumeration

The diagram clearly indicates that the `Name` method in the `Person` class and the `Name` method in the `Employee` class both exist. If you hover over each `Name` property in the Class Designer, you will see a tooltip showing the method signatures, making it clear that each one has a different signature.

You can now change `Form1` to make use of this new version of the `Name` property. First, add a couple of new `TextBox` controls and associated labels. The `TextBox` controls should be named `TexboxFullName` and `TextBoxNickName`. Double-click the form's OK button to bring up the code window and overwrite the code with the following to work with the overloaded version of the `Name` property:

```
Private Sub ButtonOK_Click(sender As Object, e As EventArgs) Handles ButtonOK.Click
    Dim emp As New Employee()
    With emp
        .Name = "Ben"
        .Name(NameTypes.FullName) = "Benjamin Franklin"
        .Name(NameTypes.NickName) = "Benjie"
        .BirthDate = #1/1/1960#
        .HireDate = #1/1/1980#
        .Salary = 30000
        TextBoxName.Text = .Name
        TextBoxDOB.Text = Format(.BirthDate, "Short date")
        TextBoxHireDate.Text = Format(.HireDate, "Short date")
        TextBoxSalary.Text = Format(.Salary, "$0.00")
        TextBoxFullName.Text = .Name(NameTypes.FullName)
        TextBoxNickName.Text = .Name(NameTypes.NickName)
```

```
        End With
    End Sub
```

The code still interacts with the original `Name` property as implemented in the `Person` class, but you are now also invoking the overloaded version of the property implemented in the `Employee` class.

## The Overridable Keyword

So far, you have seen how to implement a base class and then use it to create a subclass. You also extended the interface by adding methods, and you explored how to use overloading to add methods that have the same name as methods in the base class but with different parameters.

However, sometimes you may want to not only extend the original functionality, but also actually change or entirely replace the functionality of the base class. Instead of leaving the existing functionality and just adding new methods or overloaded versions of those methods, you might want to override the existing functionality with your own.

You can do exactly that, if the base class allows it. When a base method is marked as overridable, then you can substitute your own implementation of a base class method—meaning your new implementation will be used instead of the original.

To do this the base class must be coded specifically to allow this to occur, by using the `Overridable` keyword. This is important, as you may not always want to allow a subclass to entirely change the behavior of the methods in your base class. However, if you do wish to allow the author of a subclass to replace your implementation, you can do so by adding the `Overridable` keyword to your method declaration.

Returning to the employee example, you may not like the implementation of the `BirthDate` method as it stands in the `Person` class. Suppose, for instance, that you can't employ anyone younger than 16 years of age, so any birth date within 16 years in the past is invalid for an employee.

To implement this business rule, you need to change the way the `BirthDate` property is implemented. While you could make this change directly in the `Person` class, that would not be ideal. It is perfectly acceptable to have a person under age 16, just not an employee.

Open the code window for the `Person` class and change the `BirthDate` property to include the `Overridable` keyword:

```
    Public Overridable Property BirthDate As Date
```

This change allows any class that inherits from `Person` to entirely replace the implementation of the `BirthDate` property with a new implementation.

If the subclass does not override this method, the method works just like a regular method and is still included as part of the subclass's interface. Putting the `Overridable` keyword on a method simply allows a subclass to override the method.

## The Overrides Keyword

In a subclass, you override a method by implementing a method with the same name and parameter list as the base class, and then you use the `Overrides` keyword to indicate that you are overriding that method.

This is different from overloading, because when you overload a method you are adding a new method with the same name but a different parameter list. When you override a method, you are actually replacing the original method with a new implementation.

Without the `Overrides` keyword, you will receive a compilation error when you implement a method with the same name as one from the base class. Open the code window for the `Employee` class and add a new `BirthDate` property as follows:

```
Private mBirthDate As Date
Public Overrides Property BirthDate() As Date
  Get
    Return mBirthDate
  End Get
  Set(ByVal value As Date)
    If DateDiff(DateInterval.Year, Value, Now) >= 16 Then
      mBirthDate = value
    Else
      Throw New ArgumentException( _
        "An employee must be at least 16 years old.")
    End If
  End Set
End Property
```

Because you are implementing your own version of the property, you have to declare a variable to store that value within the `Employee` class.

Notice how you have enhanced the functionality in the `Set` block. It now raises an error if the new birth-date value would cause the employee to be less than 16 years of age. With this code, you have now entirely replaced the original `BirthDate` implementation with a new one that enforces your business rule.

If you run your application and click the button on the form, then everything should work as it did before, because the birth date you are supplying conforms to your new business rule. Now change the code in your form to use an invalid birth date like "1/1/2012."

When you run the application (from within Visual Studio) and click the button, you receive an exception indicating that the birth date is invalid. This proves that you are now using the implementation of the `BirthDate` method from the `Employee` class, rather than the one from the `Person` class. Change the date value in the form back to a valid value so that your application runs properly.

## The MyBase Keyword

You have just seen how you can entirely replace the functionality of a method in the base class by overriding it in your subclass. However, this can be somewhat extreme; sometimes it's preferable to override methods so that you extend the base functionality, rather than replace it.

To do this, you need to override the method using the `Overrides` keyword as you just did, but within your new implementation you can still invoke the original implementation of the method.

To invoke methods from the base class, you can use the `MyBase` keyword. This keyword is available within any class, and it exposes all the methods of the base class for your use.

> **NOTE** *Even a base class such as* `Person` *is an implicit subclass of* `System.Object`, *so it can use* `MyBase` *to interact with its base class as well.*

This means that within the `BirthDate` implementation in `Employee`, you can invoke the `BirthDate` implementation in the base `Person` class. This is ideal, as it means that you can leverage any existing functionality provided by `Person` while still enforcing your Employee-specific business rules.

To do this, you modify the code in the `Employee` implementation of `BirthDate`. First, remove the declaration of `mBirthDate` from the `Employee` class. You won't need this variable any longer because the `Person` implementation will keep track of the value on your behalf. Then, change the `BirthDate` implementation in the `Employee` class as with the following:

```
Public Overrides Property BirthDate() As Date
  Get
    Return MyBase.BirthDate
  End Get

  Set(ByVal value As Date)
    If DateDiff(DateInterval.Year, Value, Now) >= 16 Then
      MyBase.BirthDate = value
    Else
      Throw New ArgumentException( _
        "An employee must be at least 16 years old.")
    End If
  End Set
End Property
```

Run your application, and you will see that it works just fine and returns the error, even though the `Employee` class no longer contains any code to actually keep track of the birth-date value. You have merged the `BirthDate` implementation from `Person` right into your enhanced implementation in `Employee`.

The `MyBase` keyword is covered in more detail later in the chapter.

## Virtual Methods

The `BirthDate` property is an example of a *virtual method*. Virtual methods are methods or properties in a base class that can be overridden by subclasses.

With a nonvirtual method, only one implementation matches any given method signature, so there's no ambiguity about which specific method implementation will be invoked. With virtual methods, however, there may be several implementations of the same method, with the same method signature, so you need to understand the rules that govern which specific implementation of that method will be called.

When working with virtual methods, keep in mind that the data type of the original object instance is used to determine the implementation of the method to call, rather than the type of the variable that refers to the object.

Looking at the code in your form, you are declaring an object variable of type `Employee`, and then creating an `Employee` object that you can reference via that object.

However, when you call the `BirthDate` property, you know that you are invoking the implementation contained in the `Employee` class, which makes sense because you know that you are using a variable of type `Employee` to refer to an object of type `Employee`.

Because your methods are virtual methods, you can experiment with a more interesting scenario. For instance, suppose that you change the code in your form to interact directly with an object of type `Person` instead of one of type `Employee` as follows (code file: `Form1.vb`):

```
Private Sub ButtonOK_Click(sender As Object, e As EventArgs) Handles
ButtonOK.Click
    Dim person As New Person()
    With person
        .Name = "Ben"
        .BirthDate = #1/1/1975#
        TextBoxName.Text = .Name
        TextBoxDOB.Text = Format(.BirthDate, "Short date")
    End With
End Sub
```

> **NOTE** *Note that the downloaded sample contains changes from later in this chapter; you can follow along on your own or review the final state.*

You can't call the methods implemented by the `Employee` class, because they do not exist as part of a `Person` object. However, you can see that the `Name` and `BirthDate` properties continue to function. When you run the application now, it will work just fine. You can even change the birth-date value to something that would be invalid for `Employee`, like "1/1/2012." It works just fine, because the `BirthDate` method you are invoking is the original version from the `Person` class.

Thus you have the ability to have either a variable and an object of type `Employee` or a variable and an object of type `Person`. However, because `Employee` is derived from `Person`, you can do something a bit more interesting. You can use a variable of type `Person` to hold a reference to an `Employee` object. For example, you can change the code in `Form1.vb` as follows:

```
Private Sub ButtonOK_Click(sender As Object, e As EventArgs) Handles
ButtonOK.Click
  Dim emp As Person
  emp = New Employee()
  With emp
    .Name = "Ben"
    .BirthDate = #1/1/1975#
    txtName.Text = .Name
    txtBirthDate.Text = Format(.BirthDate, "Short date")
  End With
End Sub
```

What you are doing now is declaring your variable to be of type `Person`, but the object itself is an instance of the `Employee` class. You have done something a bit complex here, as the data type of the variable is not the same as the data type of the object itself. Remember that a variable of a base-class type can always hold a reference to an object of any subclass.

> **NOTE** *This is why a variable of type* `System.Object` *can hold a reference to literally anything in the .NET Framework, because all classes are ultimately derived from* `System.Object`.

This technique is very useful when creating generic routines. It makes use of an object-oriented concept called *polymorphism*. This technique enables you to create a more general routine that populates your form for any object of type `Person`. Add the following code to `Form1.vb`:

```
Private Sub DisplayPerson(ByVal thePerson As Person)
    With thePerson
            TextBoxName.Text = .Name
            TextBoxDOB.Text = Format(.BirthDate, "Short date")
    End With
End Sub
```

Now you can change the code behind the button to make use of the generic `DisplayPerson` method:

```
Private Sub ButtonOK_Click(sender As Object, e As EventArgs) Handles
ButtonOK.Click
    Dim emp As Person
    emp = New Employee()

    With emp
      .Name = "Ben"
      .BirthDate = #1/1/2010#
    End With

    DisplayPerson(emp)
End Sub
```

The benefit here is that you can pass a `Person` object or an `Employee` object to `DisplayPerson`, and the routine will work the same either way.

When you run the application now, things get interesting. You will get an error when you attempt to set the `BirthDate` property because it breaks your 16-year-old business rule, which is implemented in the `Employee` class.

This clearly demonstrates the concept of a virtual method. It is the data type of the object, in this case `Employee`, that is important. The data type of the variable is not the deciding factor when choosing which implementation of an overridden method is invoked.

A base class can hold a reference to any subclass object, but it is the type of that specific object which determines the implementation of the method. Therefore, you can write generic routines that operate on many types of objects as long as they derive from the same base class. Before moving on, let's change the birth date to an acceptable year such as 1975.

## Overriding Overloaded Methods

Earlier, you wrote code in your `Employee` class to overload the `Name` method in the base `Person` class. This enabled you to keep the original `Name` functionality, but also extend it by adding another `Name` method that accepts a different parameter list.

You have also overridden the `BirthDate` method. The implementation in the `Employee` class replaced the implementation in the `Person` class. Overriding is a related but different concept from overloading. It is also possible to both overload and override a method at the same time.

In the earlier overloading example, you added a new `Name` property to the `Employee` class, while retaining the functionality present in the base `Person` class. You may decide that you not only want to have your second overloaded implementation of the `Name` method in the `Employee` class, but also want to replace the existing one by overriding the existing method provided by the `Person` class.

In particular, you may want to do this so that you can store the `Name` value in the `Hashtable` object along with your Formal and Informal names. Before you can override the `Name` method, you need to add the `Overridable` keyword to the base implementation in the `Person` class.

With that done, the `Name` method can now be overridden by any derived class. In the `Employee` class, you can now override the `Name` method, replacing the functionality provided by the `Person` class. However, before doing that you'll want to expand the `NameTypes` Enum and add a `Normal` entry with a value of 3.

Now you can add code to the `Employee` class to implement a new `Name` property. Note that you are using both the `Overrides` keyword (to indicate that you are overriding the `Name` method from the base class) and the `Overloads` keyword (to indicate that you are overloading this method in the subclass).

This new `Name` property merely delegates the call to the existing version of the `Name` property that handles the parameter-based names. To complete the linkage between this implementation of the `Name` property and the parameter-based version, you need to make one more change to that original overloaded version. Update the `Employee` class with the new property definition:

```
Public Overloads Property Name(ByVal type As NameTypes) As String
  Get
    Return mNames(Type)
  End Get
  Set(ByVal value As String)
    If mNames.ContainsKey(type) Then
      mNames.Item(type) = value
    Else
      mNames.Add(type, value)
    End If

    If type = NameTypes.Normal Then
      MyBase.Name = value
    End If
  End Set
End Property
```

This way, if the client code sets the `Name` property by providing the `Normal` index, you are still updating the name in the base class as well as in the `Dictionary` object maintained by the `Employee` class.

## Overriding Nonvirtual Methods—Shadowing

*Overloading* enables you to add new versions of existing methods as long as their parameter lists are different. *Overriding* enables your subclass to entirely replace the implementation of a base-class method with a new method that has the same method signature. As you just saw, you can even combine these concepts not only to replace the implementation of a method from the base class, but also to simultaneously overload that method with other implementations that have different method signatures.

However, anytime you override a method using the Overrides keyword, you are subject to the rules governing virtual methods—meaning that the base class must give you permission to override the method. If the base class does not use the Overridable keyword, then you can't override the method.

Sometimes, however, you may need to replace a method that is not marked as Overridable, and shadowing enables you to do just that. The Shadows keyword can be used to entirely change the nature of a method or other interface element from the base class.

However, shadowing should be done with great care, as it can seriously reduce the maintainability of your code. Normally, when you create an Employee object, you expect that it can act not only as an Employee but also as a Person, because Employee is a subclass of Person. However, with the Shadows keyword, you can radically alter the behavior of an Employee class so that it does not act like a Person. This sort of radical deviation from what is normally expected invites bugs and makes code hard to understand and maintain.

Shadowing methods is very dangerous and should be used as a last resort. It is primarily useful in cases for which you have a preexisting component, such as a Windows Forms control that was not designed for inheritance. If you absolutely *must* inherit from such a component, you may need to use shadowing to "rewrite" methods or properties. Despite the serious limits and dangers, it may be your only option.

> **NOTE** *Recall if you do not use the* Overridable *keyword when declaring a method, then it is nonvirtual.*

In the typical case, nonvirtual methods are easy to understand. They can't be overridden and replaced, so you know that there's only one method by that name, with that method signature. Therefore, when you invoke it, there is no ambiguity about which specific implementation will be called.

> **NOTE** *The* Shadows *keyword enables you to replace methods on the base class that the base-class designer didn't intend to be replaced.*

The designer of a base class is typically careful when marking a method as Overridable, ensuring that the base class continues to operate properly even when that method is replaced in a subclass.

Designers of base classes typically just assume that if they do not mark a method as Overridable, it will be called and not overridden. Thus, overriding a nonvirtual method by using the Shadows keyword can have unexpected and potentially dangerous side effects, as you are doing something that the base-class designer assumed would never happen.

If that isn't enough complexity, it turns out that shadowed methods follow different rules than virtual methods when they are invoked. That is, they do not act like regular overridden methods; instead, they follow a different set of rules to determine which specific implementation of the method will be invoked. The ability to call the child's implementation of a method that has been shadowed doesn't exist. Because the system isn't aware that the method could be overridden the base-class implementation is called.

To see how this works, add a new property to the base Person class using the following:

```
Public ReadOnly Property Age() As Integer
  Get
    Return CInt(DateDiff(DateInterval.Year, Now, BirthDate))
  End Get
End Property
```

Here you have added a new method called Age to the base class, and thus automatically to the subclass. This code has a bug, introduced intentionally for illustration. The DateDiff parameters are in the wrong order, so you will get negative age values from this routine. The bug was introduced to highlight the fact that sometimes you will find bugs in base classes that you didn't write (and which you can't fix because you don't have the source code).

The following example walks you through the use of the Shadows keyword to address a bug in your base class, acting under the assumption that for some reason you can't actually fix the code in the Person class. Note that you are not using the Overridable keyword on this method, so subclasses are prevented from overriding the method by using the Overrides keyword.

Before you shadow the method, you can see how it works as a regular nonvirtual method. First, you need to change your form to use this new value. Add a text box named TextBoxAge and a related label to the form. Next, change the Sub DisplayPerson to use the Age property. You will include the following code from to display the data on the form (code file: Form1.vb):

```
Private Sub DisplayPerson(ByVal thePerson As Person)
    With thePerson
        TextBoxName.Text = .Name
        TextBoxDOB.Text = Format(.BirthDate, "Short date")
        TextBoxAge.Text = .Age
    End With
End Sub
```

Run the application. The age field should appear in your display as expected, though with a negative value due to the bug you introduced. There's no magic or complexity here. This is basic programming with objects, and basic use of inheritance as described earlier in this chapter.

Of course, you don't want a bug in your code, but nor do you have access to the Person class, and the Person class does not allow you to override the Age method.

As a result you can shadow the Age method within the Employee class, replacing the implementation in the Person class, even though it is not marked as Overridable. Add the following code to the Employee class:

```
Public Shadows ReadOnly Property Age() As Integer
  Get
     Return CInt(DateDiff(DateInterval.Year, BirthDate, Now))
  End Get
End Property
```

Technically, the Shadows keyword is not required here. Shadowing is the default behavior when a subclass implements a method that matches the name and method signature of a method in the base class. However, it is better to include the keyword. This makes it clear that you shadowed the method intentionally.

Now you are declaring the variable to be of type Person, but you are creating an object that is of data type Employee. You did this earlier in the chapter when exploring the Overrides keyword, and in that case you discovered that the version of the method that was invoked was based on the data type of the object.

If you run the application now, you will see that the rules are different when the Shadows keyword is used. In this case, the implementation in the Person class is invoked, giving you the buggy negative value. When the implementation in the Employee class is ignored, you get the exact opposite behavior of what you got with Overrides.

This is a simple case, and can be corrected by updating the display back in the main method by casting to your base type as follows (code file: Form1.vb):

```
Private Sub ButtonOK_Click(sender As Object, e As EventArgs) Handles ButtonOK.Click
    Dim emp As Person
    emp = New Employee()
    With emp
        .Name = "Ben"
        .BirthDate = #1/1/1975#
    End With
    DisplayPerson(emp)
    TextBoxAge.Text = CType(emp, Employee).Age
End Sub
```

When you run the application you will see that the value of the age field is correct, as shown in Figure 4-6. This illustrates that you just ran the implementation of the Age property from the Employee class.

In most cases, the behavior you will want for your methods is accomplished by the Overrides keyword and virtual methods. However, in cases where the base-class designer does not allow you to override a method and you want to do it anyway, the Shadows keyword provides you with the needed functionality.

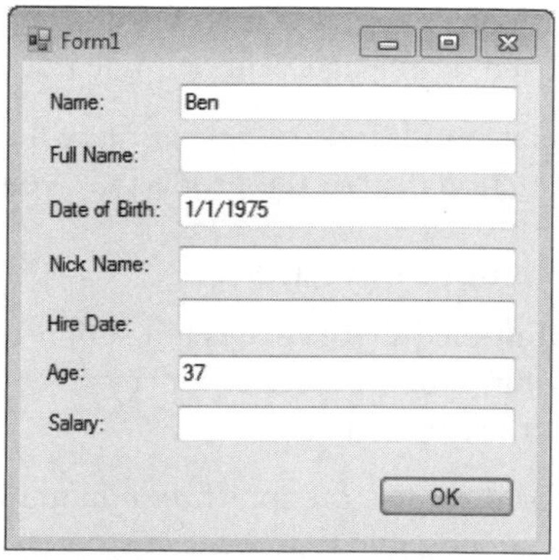

FIGURE 4-6: Displaying simple person info

## Shadowing Arbitrary Elements

The Shadows keyword can be used not only to override nonvirtual methods, but also to totally replace and change the nature of a base-class interface element. When you override a method, you are providing a replacement implementation of that method with the same name and method signature. Using the Shadows keyword, you can do more extreme things, such as change a method into an instance variable or change a property into a function.

However, this can be very dangerous, as any code written to use your objects will naturally assume that you implement all the same interface elements and behaviors as your base class, because that is the nature of inheritance. Any documentation or knowledge of the original interface is effectively invalidated because the original implementation is arbitrarily replaced.

> **NOTE** *By totally changing the nature of an interface element, you can cause a great deal of confusion for programmers who might interact with your class in the future.*

You can entirely change the nature of the Age property to see how you can replace an interface element from the base class. For example, you could change it from a read-only property to a read-write property. You could get even more extreme—change it to a Function or a Sub.

Remove the Age property from the Employee class and replace it with the following implementation (code file: Employee.vb):

```
Public Shadows Property Age() As Integer
  Get
    Return CInt(DateDiff(DateInterval.Year, BirthDate, Now))
  End Get
  Set(ByVal value As Integer)
    BirthDate = DateAdd(DateInterval.Year, -value, Now)
  End Set
End Property
```

With this change, the very nature of the Age method has changed. It is no longer a simple read-only property; now it is a read-write property that includes code to calculate an approximate birth date based on the age value supplied.

As it stands, your application will continue to run just fine because you are using only the read-only functionality of the property in your form.

## Multiple Inheritance

Multiple inheritance is not supported by either Visual Basic or the .NET platform itself. The idea behind multiple inheritance is that you can have a single subclass that inherits from two base classes at the same time.

For instance, an application might have a class for Customer and another class for Vendor. It is quite possible that some customers are also vendors, so you might want to combine the functionality of these two classes into a `CustomerVendor` class. This new class would be a combination of both `Customer` and `Vendor`, so it would be nice to inherit from both of them at once.

While this is a useful concept, multiple inheritance is complex. Numerous problems are associated with multiple inheritance, but the most obvious is the possibility of collisions of properties or methods from the base classes. Suppose that both `Customer` and `Vendor` have a `Name` property. `CustomerVendor` would need two `Name` properties, one for each base class. Yet it only makes sense to have one `Name` property on `CustomerVendor`, so to which base class does it link, and how will the system operate if it does not link to the other one?

These are complex issues with no easy answers. Within the object-oriented community, there is ongoing debate as to whether the advantages of code reuse outweigh the complexity that comes along for the ride.

Multiple inheritance isn't supported by the .NET Framework, so it is likewise not supported by Visual Basic, but you can use multiple interfaces to achieve an effect similar to multiple inheritance. This topic is addressed later in this chapter when discussing implementing multiple interfaces.

## Multilevel Inheritance

Unlike multiple inheritance, multilevel inheritance refers to the idea that your class can inherit methods and properties from not only its parent, but also from grandparent or further up the class hierarchy. Most of the examples discussed so far have illustrated how you can create a child class based on a single parent class. That is called *single-level inheritance*. In fact, inheritance can be many levels deep. These are sometimes referred to as *chains of inheritance*.

There is no hard-and-fast rule about how deep inheritance chains should go, but conventional wisdom and general experience with inheritance in other languages such as Smalltalk and C++ indicate that the deeper an inheritance chain becomes, the harder it is to maintain an application.

This happens for two reasons. First is the fragile base class or fragile superclass issue, discussed shortly. The second reason is that a deep inheritance hierarchy tends to seriously reduce the readability of your code by scattering the code for an object across many different classes, all of which are combined by the compiler to create your object.

One of the reasons for adopting object-oriented design and programming is to avoid so-called *spaghetti code*, whereby any bit of code you might look at does almost nothing useful but instead calls various other procedures and routines in other parts of your application. To determine what is going on with spaghetti code, you must trace through many routines and mentally piece together what it all means.

Object-oriented programming can help you avoid this problem. However, when you create deep inheritance hierarchies, you are often creating spaghetti code, because each level in the hierarchy not only extends the previous level's interface, but almost always also adds functionality.

Thus, when you look at a class, it may have very little code. To figure out what it does or how it behaves, you have to trace through the code in the previous four levels of classes, and you might not even have the code for some of those classes, as they might come from other applications or class libraries you have purchased.

On the one hand, you have the benefit of reusing code; but on the other hand, you have the draw-back that the code for one object is actually scattered through five different classes. Keep this in mind when designing systems with inheritance—use as few levels in the hierarchy as possible to provide the required functionality.

You have seen how a subclass derives from a base class with the Person and Employee classes, but nothing prevents the Employee subclass from being the base class for yet another class, a sub-subclass, so to speak. This is not at all uncommon. In the working example, you may have different kinds of employees, some who work in the office and others who travel.

To accommodate this, you may want OfficeEmployee and TravelingEmployee classes. Of course, these are both examples of an employee and should share the functionality already present in the Employee class. The Employee class already reuses the functionality from the Person class. Figure 4-7 illustrates how these classes will be related.

The Employee is a subclass of Person, and your two new classes are both subclasses of Employee. While both OfficeEmployee and TravelingEmployee are employees, and thus also people, they are each unique. An OfficeEmployee almost certainly has a cube or office number, while a TravelingEmployee could keep track of the number of miles traveled.

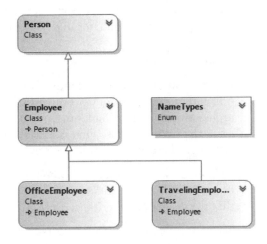

Add a new class to your project and name it OfficeEmployee. To make this class inherit from your existing Employee class, add the following code to the class:

```
Inherits Employee
```

With this change, the new class now has Name, BirthDate, Age, HireDate, and Salary methods. Notice that methods from both Employee and Person are inherited. A subclass gains all the methods, properties, and events of its base classes.

**FIGURE 4-7:** Multilevel inheritance hierarchy

You can now extend the interface and behavior of OfficeEmployee by adding a property to indicate which cube or office number the employee occupies, as follows (code file: Employee.vb):

```
Public Class OfficeEmployee
    Inherits Employee

    Public Property OfficeNumber() As String
End Class
```

To see how this works, you will enhance the form to display this value. Add a new TextBox control named TextBoxOffice and an associated label so that your form looks like the one shown in Figure 4-8. (Note Figure 4-8 also includes the data you'll see when the form is run.)

The following demonstrates how to change the code-behind for the button to use the new property (code file: Form1.vb).

```
Private Sub btnOK_Click(ByVal sender As System.Object, _
    Private Sub ButtonOK_Click(sender As Object, e As EventArgs)
        Handles ButtonOK.Click

    Dim emp = New OfficeEmployee()
    With emp
        .Name = "Ben"
        .BirthDate = #1/1/1975#
        .OfficeNumber = "NE Corner"
    End With
    DisplayPerson(emp)

    TextBoxAge.Text = CType(emp, Employee).Age

    If TypeOf emp Is OfficeEmployee Then
        TextBoxOffice.Text = CType(emp, OfficeEmployee).OfficeNumber
    End If
End Sub
```

**FIGURE 4-8:** Sample application display

You have changed the routine to declare and create an object of type OfficeEmployee—thus enabling you to make use of the new property, as well as all existing properties and methods from Employee and Person, as they've been "merged" into the OfficeEmployee class via inheritance. If you now run the application, the name, birth date, age, and office values are displayed in the form.

Inheritance like this can go many levels deep, with each level extending and changing the behaviors of the previous levels. In fact, there is no specific technical limit to the number of levels of inheritance you can implement in Visual Basic. But keep in mind that very deep inheritance chains are typically not recommended and are often viewed as a design flaw.

## The Fragile-Base-Class Problem

You have explored where it is appropriate to use inheritance and where it is not. You have also explored how you can use inheritance and multiple interfaces in conjunction to implement both is-a and act-as relationships simultaneously within your classes.

Earlier it was noted that while inheritance is an incredibly powerful and useful concept, it can also be very dangerous if used improperly. You have seen some of this danger in the discussion of the misapplication of the is-a relationship, and how you can use multiple interfaces to avoid those issues.

One of the most classic and common problems with inheritance is the fragile base-class problem. This problem is exacerbated when you have very deep inheritance hierarchies, but it exists even in a single level inheritance chain.

The issue you face is that a change in the base class always affects all child classes derived from that base class. This is a double-edged sword. On the one hand, you get the benefit of being able to change code in one location and have that change automatically cascade through all derived classes. On the other hand, a change in behavior can have unintended or unexpected consequences farther down the inheritance chain, which can make your application very fragile and hard to change or maintain.

## Interacting with the Base Class, Yourself, and Your Class

You have already seen how you can use the `MyBase` keyword to call methods on the base class from within a subclass. The `MyBase` keyword is one of three special keywords that enable you to interact with important object and class representations:

1. `MyBase`
2. `Me`
3. `MyClass`

### The MyBase Keyword

Earlier, you saw an example of this when you called back into the base class from an overridden method in the subclass. The `MyBase` keyword references only the immediate parent class, and it works like an object reference. This means that you can call methods on `MyBase` knowing that they are being called just as if you had a reference to an object of your parent class's data type.

> **NOTE** *There is no way to directly navigate up the inheritance chain beyond the immediate parent, so you can't directly access the implementation of a method in a base class if you are in a sub-subclass. Such behavior isn't a good idea anyway, which is why it isn't allowed.*

The `MyBase` keyword can be used to invoke or use any Public, Friend, or Protected element from the parent class. This includes all elements directly on the base class, and any elements the base class inherited from other classes higher in the inheritance chain.

You already used `MyBase` to call back into the base `Person` class as you implemented the overridden `Name` property in the `Employee` class.

> **NOTE** *Any code within a subclass can call any method on the base class by using the* MyBase *keyword.*

You can also use MyBase to call back into the base class implementation even if you have shadowed a method. The MyBase keyword enables you to merge the functionality of the base class into your subclass code as you deem fit.

## The Me Keyword

The Me keyword provides you with a reference to your current object instance. In some languages they have the concept of "this" object as the current instance. Typically, you do not need to use the Me keyword, because whenever you want to invoke a method within your current object, you can just call that method directly. Occasionally you may find it helpful to better screen your IntelliSense options when typing, but even then it doesn't need to remain in your code.

To see clearly how this works, add a new method to the Person class that returns the data of the Person class in the form of a String. Remember that all classes in the .NET Framework ultimately derive from System.Object, even if you do not explicitly indicate it with an Inherits statement.

This means that you can simply override the ToString method from the Object class within your Person class as follows:

```
Public Overrides Function ToString() As String
   Return Me.Name
End Function
```

This implementation returns the person's Name property as a result when ToString is called.

> **NOTE** *By default,* ToString *returns the class name of the class. Until now, if you called the* ToString *method on a* Person *object, you would get a result of* ProVB2012_Ch04.Person, *the fully qualified namespace and class name.*

Notice that the ToString method is calling another method within your same class—in this case, the Name method.

In most cases it is redundant because Me is the default for all method calls in a class, so typically the Me keyword is simply omitted to avoid the extra typing.

Earlier, you looked at virtual methods and how they work. Because either calling a method directly or calling it using the Me keyword invokes the method on the current object. Method calls within an object conform to the same rules as an external method call.

In other words, your ToString method may not actually end up calling the Name method in the Person class if that method was overridden by a class farther down the inheritance chain.

For example, the `Employee` class already overloads the `Name` property in your `Person` class. However, you can also override the version supplied by `Person` such that it always returns the informal version of the person's name, rather than the regular name. To make it more interesting you can override the `Name` property of the `OfficeEmployee` class as follows:

```
Public Overloads Overrides Property Name() As String
    Get
        Return MyBase.Name(NameTypes.NickName)
    End Get
    Set(ByVal value As String)
        MyBase.Name = value
    End Set
End Property
```

This new version of the `Name` method relies on the base class to actually store the value, but instead of returning the regular name on request, now you are always returning the nickname.

Before you can test this, you need to enhance the code in your form to actually provide a value for the informal name. Update the OK button code behind with the following (code file: `Form1.vb`):

```
Private Sub ButtonOK_Click(sender As Object, e As EventArgs) Handles ButtonOK.Click
    Dim emp = New OfficeEmployee()
    With emp
        .Name = "Ben"
        .Name(NameTypes.NickName) = "Benjie"
        .BirthDate = #1/1/1975#
        .OfficeNumber = "NE Corner"
    End With
    DisplayPerson(emp)

    TextBoxAge.Text = CType(emp, Employee).Age

    If TypeOf emp Is OfficeEmployee Then
        TextBoxOffice.Text = CType(emp, OfficeEmployee).OfficeNumber
    End If
End Sub

Private Sub DisplayPerson(ByVal thePerson As Person)
    With thePerson
        'TextBoxName.Text = .Name
        TextBoxName.Text = .ToString
        TextBoxDOB.Text = Format(.BirthDate, "Short date")
        TextBoxAge.Text = .Age
    End With
End Sub
```

When you run the application, the `Name` field displays the nickname. Even though the `ToString` method is implemented in the `Person` class, it is invoking the implementation of `Name` from the `OfficeEmployee` class. This is because method calls within a class follow the same rules for calling virtual methods as code outside a class, such as your code in the form. You will see this behavior with or without the `Me` keyword, as the default behavior for method calls is to implicitly call them via the current object.

Keep in mind that while methods called from within a class follow the same rules for virtual methods, this is not the case for shadowed methods.

> **NOTE** *Shadowing a method replaces all implementations from higher in the inheritance chain, regardless of their method signature or how they are called.*

Shadowed implementations in subclasses are ignored when calling the method from within a class higher in the inheritance chain. You will get this same behavior with or without the Me keyword.

The Me keyword exists primarily to enable you to pass a reference to the current object as a parameter to other objects or methods.

## The MyClass Keyword

As you have seen, when you use the Me keyword or call a method directly, your method call follows the rules for calling both virtual and nonvirtual methods.

While this behavior is often useful, sometimes you will want to ensure that you truly are running the specific implementation from your class; even if a subclass overrode your method, you still want to ensure that you are calling the version of the method that is directly in your class.

Maybe you decide that your ToString implementation in Person should always call the Name implementation that you write in the Person class, totally ignoring any overridden versions of Name in any subclasses.

This is where the MyClass keyword shines. This keyword is much like MyBase, in that it provides you with access to methods as though it were an object reference—in this case, a reference to an instance of the class that contains the code you are writing when using the MyClass keyword. This is true even when the instantiated object is an instance of a class derived from your class.

You have seen that a call to ToString from within Person actually invokes the implementation in Employee or OfficeEmployee if your object is an instance of either of those types.

You can force the use of the implementation in the current class through the use of MyClass. Change the ToString method in Person as follows:

```
Public Overrides Function ToString() As String
  Return MyClass.Name
End Function
```

You are now calling the Name method, but you are doing it using the MyClass keyword. When you run the application and click the button, the Name field in the form displays Ben rather than Benjie, proving that the implementation from Person was invoked even though the data type of the object itself is OfficeEmployee.

The ToString method is invoked from Person. Because you are using the MyClass keyword, the Name method is invoked directly from Person, explicitly defeating the default behavior you would normally expect.

# Constructors

As discussed in Chapter 3, you can provide a special constructor method, named New, on a class and it will be the first code run when an object is instantiated. You can also receive parameters via the constructor method, enabling the code that creates your object to pass data into the object during the creation process.

Constructor methods are affected by inheritance differently than regular methods.

## Simple Constructors

Constructors do not quite follow the same rules when it comes to inheritance.

To explore the differences, implement the following simple constructor method in the Person class:

```
Public Sub New()
   Debug.WriteLine("Person constructor")
End Sub
```

If you now run the application, you will see the text displayed in the Output window in the IDE. This occurs even though the code in your form is creating an object of type OfficeEmployee.

As you might expect, the New method from your base Person class is invoked as part of the construction process of the OfficeEmployee object—simple inheritance at work. However, interesting things occur if you implement a New method in the OfficeEmployee class itself using the the following:

```
Public Sub New()
   Debug.WriteLine("OfficeEmployee constructor")
End Sub
```

Notice that you are not using the Overrides keyword, nor did you mark the method in Person as Overridable. These keywords have no use in this context, and in fact will cause syntax errors if you attempt to use them on constructor methods.

When you run the application now, you might expect that only the implementation of New in OfficeEmployee would be invoked. That is what would occur with a normal overridden method. However, even though New doesn't specify overloading, when you run the application, both implementations are run, and both strings are output to the output window in the IDE.

Note that the implementation in the Person class ran first, followed by the implementation in the OfficeEmployee class. This occurs because when an object is created, all the constructors for the classes in the inheritance chain are invoked, starting with the base class and including all the subclasses one by one. In fact, if you implement a New method in the Employee class, you can see that it too is invoked.

## Constructors in More Depth

The rules governing constructors without parameters are pretty straightforward, but things get a bit more complex when you start adding parameters on your constructors.

To understand why, you need to consider how even your simple constructors are invoked. While you may see them as being invoked from the base class down through all subclasses to your final subclass, what is really happening is a bit different.

In particular, it is the subclass New method that is invoked first. However, Visual Basic automatically inserts a line of code into your routine at compile time.

For instance, in your OfficeEmployee class you have a constructor. Behind the scenes, Visual Basic inserts what is effectively a call to the constructor of your parent class on your behalf. You could do this manually by using the MyBase keyword with the following change:

```
Public Sub New()
   MyBase.New()
   Debug.WriteLine("OfficeEmployee constructor")
End Sub
```

This call must be the first line in your constructor. If you put any other code before this line, you will get a syntax error indicating that your code is invalid. Because the call is always required, and because it always must be the first line in any constructor, Visual Basic simply inserts it for you automatically.

Note that if you don't explicitly provide a constructor on a class by implementing a New method, Visual Basic creates one for you behind the scenes. The automatically created method simply has one line of code:

```
MyBase.New()
```

All classes have constructor methods, either created explicitly by you as you write a New method or created implicitly by Visual Basic as the class is compiled.

> **NOTE** *A constructor method is sometimes called a ctor, short for constructor. This term is often used by tools such as ILDASM or .NET Reflector.*

By always calling MyBase.New as the first line in every constructor, you are guaranteed that it is the implementation of New in your top-level base class that actually runs first. Every subclass invokes the parent class implementation all the way up the inheritance chain until only the base class remains. Then its code runs, followed by each individual subclass, as shown earlier.

## Constructors with Parameters

This works great when your constructors don't require parameters, but if your constructor does require a parameter, then it becomes impossible for Visual Basic to automatically make that call on your behalf. After all, how would Visual Basic know what values you want to pass as parameters?

To see how this works, change the New method in the Person class to require a Name parameter. You can use that parameter to initialize the object's Name property similar to what you see in the following:

```
Public Sub New(ByVal name As String)
   Me.Name = name
   Debug.WriteLine("Person constructor")
End Sub
```

Now your constructor requires a `String` parameter and uses it to initialize the `Name` property. You are using the `Me` keyword to make your code easier to read. Interestingly enough, the compiler actually understands and correctly compiles the following code:

```
Name = name
```

However, that is not at all clear to a developer reading the code. By prefixing the property name with the `Me` keyword, you make it clear that you are invoking a property on the object and providing it with the parameter value.

At this point, your application won't compile because there is an error in the `New` method of the `Employee` class. In particular, Visual Basic's attempt to automatically invoke the constructor on the `Person` class fails because it has no idea what data value to pass for this new name parameter. There are three ways you can address this error:

1. Make the name parameter `Optional`.

2. Overload the `New` method with another implementation that requires no parameter.

3. Manually provide the `Name` parameter value from within the `Employee` class.

If you make the `Name` parameter `Optional`, then you are indicating that the `New` method can be called with or without a parameter. Therefore, one viable option is to call the method with no parameters, so Visual Basic's default of calling it with no parameters works just fine.

If you overload the `New` method, then you can implement a second `New` method that doesn't accept any parameters, again allowing Visual Basic's default behavior to work as you have seen. Keep in mind that this solution invokes only the overloaded version of `New` with no parameter; the version that requires a parameter would not be invoked.

The final way you can fix the error is by simply providing a parameter value yourself from within the `New` method of the `Employee` class. Note that even though you have a constructor in the `OfficeEmployee` class, because `MyBase` always goes to the direct parent, which is the `Employee` class, you must add this to the `Employee` class. To do this, change the `Employee` class as follows (code file: `Person.vb`):

```
Public Sub New()
  MyBase.New("George")
  Debug.WriteLine("Employee constructor")
End Sub
```

Obviously, you probably do not want to hard-code a value in a constructor. However, this allows you to demonstrate calling the base-class constructor with a parameter. By explicitly calling the `New` method of the parent class, you are able to provide it with the required parameter value. At this point, your application will compile, and run.

## Constructors, Overloading, and Variable Initialization

What isn't clear from this code is that you have now introduced a condition that can lead to a very insidious bug. The constructor in the `Person` class is using the `Name` property. However, the `Name` property can be overridden by the `Employee` class, so that implementation will be run. In this case you're going to modify the implementation such that it stops using the property defined by `Person`. Instead you'll add the normal name to the local property of `Employee` as follows:

```
Public Overrides Property Name As String
    Get
        Return mNames(NameTypes.Normal)
    End Get
    Set(value As String)
        If mNames.ContainsKey(NameTypes.Normal) Then
            mNames.Item(NameTypes.Normal) = value
        Else
            mNames.Add(NameTypes.Normal, value)
        End If
    End Set
End Property
```

Unfortunately, this new implementation makes use of a `Dictionary` object, which isn't available yet! It turns out that any member variables declared in a class with the `New` statement, such as the `Dictionary` object in `Employee`, won't be initialized until after the constructor for that class has completed.

Because you are still in the constructor for `Person`, there's no way the constructor for `Employee` can be complete. To resolve this, you would need to change the implementation of the `Name` method to create the required `Dictionary` when called. Instead of presuming that the local field existed, your code would create it. This isn't a best practice in that none of this is necessary if your code simply continues to use the base class's storage for the default `Name` property.

The key is that your code can ensure that a `Dictionary` object is created in the `Employee` class code, even though its constructor hasn't yet run. For now you can comment out the `Override` of the `Name` property in the `Employee` class.

## Object Scope

You have seen how a subclass automatically gains all the Public methods and properties that compose the interface of the base class. This is also true of Friend methods and properties; they are inherited as well and are available only to other code in the same assembly as the subclass.

Private methods and properties are not exposed as part of the interface of the subclass, meaning that the code in the subclass cannot call those methods, nor can any code using your objects. These methods are available only to the code within the base class itself.

Sometimes you will want to create methods in your base class that can be called by a subclass, as well as the base class, but not by code outside of those classes. Basically, you want a hybrid between Public and Private access modifiers—methods that are private to the classes in the inheritance chain but usable by any subclasses that might be created within the chain. This functionality is provided by the Protected scope.

Protected methods are very similar to Private methods in that they are not available to any code that calls your objects. Instead, these methods are available to code within the base class and to code within any subclass. Table 4-2 lists the available scope options:

**TABLE 4-2:** Access Scope Keyword Definitions

| SCOPE | DESCRIPTION |
|---|---|
| Private | Only available to code within your class. |
| Protected | Available only to classes that inherit from your class. |
| Friend | Available to code within your project/component. |
| Protected Friend | Available to classes that inherit from your class, in any project. Also available to code within your project/component that doesn't inherit from your class. This is a combination of Protected and Friend. |
| Public | Available outside your class and project. |

To see how the Protected scope works, add an Identity field to the `Person` class as follows:

```
Protected Property Identity As String
```

This data field represents some arbitrary identification number or value assigned to a person. This might be a social security number, an employee number, or whatever is appropriate.

The interesting thing about this value is that it is not currently accessible outside your inheritance chain. For instance, if you try to use it from your code in the form, you will discover that there is no `Identity` property on your `Person`, `Employee`, or `OfficeEmployee` objects.

However, there is an `Identity` property now available inside your inheritance chain. The `Identity` property is available to the code in the `Person` class, just like any other method. Interestingly, even though `Identity` is not available to the code in your form, it is available to the code in the `Employee` and `OfficeEmployee` classes, because they are both subclasses of `Person`. `Employee` is directly a subclass, and `OfficeEmployee` is indirectly a subclass of `Person` because it is a subclass of `Employee`.

Thus, you can enhance your `Employee` class to implement an `EmployeeNumber` property by using the `Identity` property. To do this, add the following code to the `Employee` class:

```
Public Property EmployeeNumber() As Integer
  Get
    Return CInt(Identity)
  End Get
  Set(ByVal value As Integer)
    Identity = CStr(value)
  End Set
End Property
```

This new property exposes a numeric identity value for the employee, but it uses the internal `Identity` property to manage that value. You can override and shadow Protected elements just as you do with elements of any other scope.

Up to this point, you've focused on methods and properties and how they interact through inheritance. Inheritance, and, in particular, the Protected scope, also affects instance variables and how you work with them.

Though it is not recommended, you can declare variables in a class using Public scope. This makes the variable directly available to code both within and outside of your class, allowing any code that interacts with your objects to directly read or alter the value of that variable.

Variables can also have Friend scope, which likewise allows any code in your class or anywhere within your project to read or alter the value directly. This is also generally not recommended because it breaks encapsulation.

> **NOTE** *Rather than declare variables with Public or Friend scope, it is better to expose the value using a Property so that your implementation is private, and can be modified as needed without changing your public interface.*

Of course, you know that variables can be of Private scope, and this is typically the case. This makes the variables accessible only to the code within your class, and it is the most restrictive scope.

As with methods, however, you can also use the Protected scope when declaring variables. This makes the variable accessible to the code in your class and to the code in any class that derives from your class—all the way down the hierarchy chain.

Sometimes this is useful, because it enables you to provide and accept data to and from subclasses, but to act on that data from code in the base class. At the same time, exposing variables to subclasses is typically not ideal, and you should use Property methods with Protected scope for this instead, as they allow your base class to enforce any business rules that are appropriate for the value, rather than just hope that the author of the subclass provides only good values.

## Events and Inheritance

So far, you've looked at methods, properties, and variables in terms of inheritance—how they can be added, overridden, overloaded, and shadowed. In Visual Basic, events are also part of the interface of an object, and they are affected by inheritance as well.

### Inheriting Events

Chapter 3 introduced how to declare, raise, and receive events from objects. You can add such an event to the Person class by declaring it at the top of the class. Then, you can raise this event within the class anytime the person's name is changed as follows:

```
Public Event NameChanged(ByVal newName As String)
Private mName as String
Public Overridable Property Name As String
  Get
    Return mName
  End Get
  Set(ByVal value As String)
    mName = value
    RaiseEvent NameChanged(mName)
  End Set
End Property
```

At this point, you can modify `Form1` to handle this event. The nice thing about this is that your events are inherited automatically by subclasses—meaning your `Employee` and `OfficeEmployee` objects will also raise this event when they set the `Name` property of `Person`. Thus, you can change the code in your form to handle the event, even though you are working with an object of type `OfficeEmployee`.

One caveat you should keep in mind is that while a subclass exposes the events of its base class, the code in the subclass cannot raise the event. In other words, you cannot use the `RaiseEvent` method in `Employee` or `OfficeEmployee` to raise the `NameChanged` event. Only code directly in the `Person` class can raise the event.

Fortunately, there is a relatively easy way to get around this limitation. You can simply implement a `Protected` method in your base class that allows any derived class to raise the method. In the `Person` class, you can add a new event and protected method as follows:

```
Public Event PropertyChanged(PropName As String, NewValue As Object)
Protected Sub OnDataChanged(PropName As String, NewValue As Object)
    RaiseEvent PropertyChanged(PropName, NewValue)
End Sub
```

You can now use this method from within the `Employee` class as follows to indicate that `EmployeeNumber` has changed.

```
Public Property EmployeeNumber() As Integer
    Get
        Return CInt(Identity)
    End Get
    Set(ByVal value As Integer)
        Identity = CStr(value)
        OnDataChanged("EmployeeNumber", value)
    End Set
End Property
```

Note that the code in `Employee` is not raising the event, it is simply calling a Protected method in `Person`. The code in the `Person` class is actually raising the event, meaning everything will work as desired.

You can enhance the code in `Form1` to receive the event. First, create the following method to handle the event:

```
Private Sub OnDataChanged(ByVal PropertyName As String, ByVal NewValue As Object)
    MessageBox.Show("New " & PropertyName & ": " & NewValue.ToString())
End Sub
```

Then, link this handler to the event using the `AddHandler` method. Finally, ensure that you are changing and displaying the `EmployeeNumber` property as follows:

```
Private Sub ButtonOK_Click(sender As Object, e As EventArgs) Handles ButtonOK.Click
    Dim emp = New OfficeEmployee()

    AddHandler emp.PropertyChanged, AddressOf OnDataChanged

    With emp
        .Name = "Ben"
```

```
            .Name(NameTypes.NickName) = "Benjie"
            .BirthDate = #1/1/1975#
            .EmployeeNumber = 7
            .OfficeNumber = "NE Corner"
        End With
        DisplayPerson(emp)

        TextBoxAge.Text = CType(emp, Employee).Age

        If TypeOf emp Is OfficeEmployee Then
            TextBoxOffice.Text = CType(emp, OfficeEmployee).OfficeNumber
        End If
    End Sub
```

When you run the application and click the button now, you will get message boxes displaying the change to the `EmployeeNumber` property.

## Shared Methods

Chapter 3 explored shared methods and how they work: providing a set of methods that can be invoked directly from the class, rather than requiring that you create an actual object.

Shared methods are inherited just like instance methods and so are automatically available as methods on subclasses, just as they are on the base class. If you implement a shared method in a base class, you can call that method using any class derived from that base class.

Like regular methods, shared methods can be overloaded and shadowed. They cannot, however, be overridden. If you attempt to use the `Overridable` keyword when declaring a shared method, you will get a syntax error.

Shared methods can be overloaded using the `Overloads` keyword in the same manner as you overload an instance method. This means that your subclass can add new implementations of the shared method as long as the parameter list differs from the original implementation.

Shared methods can also be shadowed by a subclass. This allows you to do some very interesting things, including converting a shared method into an instance method or vice versa. You can even leave the method as shared but change the entire way it works and is declared. In short, just as with instance methods, you can use the `Shadows` keyword to entirely replace and change a shared method in a subclass.

## Creating an Abstract Base Class

So far, you have seen how to inherit from a class, how to overload and override methods, and how virtual methods work. In all of the examples so far, the parent classes have been useful in their own right and could be instantiated and do some meaningful work. Sometimes, however, you want to create a class such that it can only be used as a base class for inheritance.

### MustInherit Keyword

The current `Person` class is being used as a base class, but it can also be instantiated directly to create an object of type `Person`. Likewise, the `Employee` class is also being used as a base class for the `OfficeEmployee` class you created that derives from it.

If you want to make a class act only as a base class, you can use the MustInherit keyword, thereby preventing anyone from creating objects based directly on the class, and requiring them instead to create a subclass and then create objects based on that subclass.

This can be very useful when you are creating object models of real-world concepts and entities. The following snippet demonstrates how you should change Person to use the MustInherit keyword.

```
Public MustInherit Class Person
```

This has no effect on the code within Person or any of the classes that inherit from it, but it does mean that no code can instantiate objects directly from the Person class; instead, you can only create objects based on Employee or OfficeEmployee.

This does not prevent you from declaring variables of type Person; it merely prevents you from creating an object by using New Person. You can also continue to make use of Shared methods from the Person class without any difficulty.

## MustOverride Keyword

Another option you have is to create a method (Sub, Function, or Property) that must be overridden by a subclass. You might want to do this when you are creating a base class that provides some behaviors but relies on subclasses to also provide other behaviors in order to function properly. This is accomplished by using the MustOverride keyword on a method declaration.

If a class contains any methods marked with MustOverride, the class itself must also be declared with the MustInherit keyword or you will get a syntax error.

This makes sense. If you are requiring that a method be overridden in a subclass, it stands to reason that your class can't be directly instantiated; it must be subclassed to be useful.

You can see how this works by adding a LifeExpectancy method in Person that has no implementation and must be overridden by a subclass as follows:

```
Public MustOverride Function LifeExpectancy() As Integer
```

Notice that there is no End Function or any other code associated with the method. When using MustOverride, you cannot provide any implementation for the method in your class. Such a method is called an *abstract method* or *pure virtual function*, as it defines only the interface and no implementation.

Methods declared in this manner must be overridden in any subclass that inherits from your base class. If you do not override one of these methods, you will generate a syntax error in the subclass and it won't compile. You need to alter the Employee class to provide an implementation similar to the following:

```
Public Overrides Function LifeExpectancy() As Integer
   Return 90
End Function
```

Your application will compile and run at this point, because you are now overriding the LifeExpectancy method in Employee, so the required condition is met.

## Abstract Base Classes

You can combine these two concepts, using both `MustInherit` and `MustOverride`, to create something called an *abstract base class*, sometimes referred to as a *virtual class*. This is a class that provides no implementation, only the interface definitions from which a subclass can be created, as shown in the following example:

```
Public MustInherit Class AbstractBaseClass
  Public MustOverride Sub DoSomething()
  Public MustOverride Sub DoOtherStuff()
End Class
```

This technique can be very useful when creating frameworks or the high-level conceptual elements of a system. Any class that inherits `AbstractBaseClass` must implement both `DoSomething` and `DoOtherStuff`; otherwise, a syntax error will result.

In some ways, an abstract base class is comparable to defining an interface using the `Interface` keyword. The `Interface` keyword is discussed in detail later in this chapter. You could define the same interface shown in this example with the following code:

```
Public Interface IAbstractBaseClass
  Sub DoSomething()
  Sub DoOtherStuff()
End Interface
```

Any class that implements the `IAbstractBaseClass` interface must implement both `DoSomething` and `DoOtherStuff` or a syntax error will result, and in that regard this technique is similar to an abstract base class.

## Preventing Inheritance

If you want to prevent a class from being used as a base class, you can use the `NotInheritable` keyword. For instance, you can change your `OfficeEmployee` to prevent inheritance with the following keyword:

```
Public NotInheritable Class OfficeEmployee
```

At this point, it is no longer possible to inherit from this class to create a new class. Your `OfficeEmployee` class is now sealed, meaning it cannot be used as a base from which to create other classes.

If you attempt to inherit from `OfficeEmployee`, you will get a compile error indicating that it cannot be used as a base class. This has no effect on `Person` or `Employee`; you can continue to derive other classes from them.

Typically, you want to design your classes so that they can be subclassed, because that provides the greatest long-term flexibility in the overall design. Sometimes, however, you want to ensure that your class cannot be used as a base class, and the `NotInheritable` keyword addresses that issue.

# MULTIPLE INTERFACES

In Visual Basic, objects can have one or more interfaces. All objects have a primary, or native, interface, which is composed of any methods, properties, events, or member variables declared using the Public keyword. You can also have objects implement secondary interfaces in addition to their native interface by using the `Implements` keyword.

## Object Interfaces

The native interface on any class is composed of all the methods, properties, events, and even variables that are declared as anything other than Private. Though this is nothing new, do a quick review of what is included in the native interface to set the stage for discussing secondary interfaces. To include a method as part of your interface, you can simply declare a Public routine:

```
Public Sub AMethod()

End Sub
```

Notice that there is no code in this routine. Any code would be implementation and is not part of the interface. Only the declaration of the method is important when discussing interfaces. This can seem confusing at first, but it is an important distinction, as the separation of the interface from its implementation is at the very core of object-oriented programming and design.

Because this method is declared as Public, it is available to any code outside the class, including other applications that may make use of the assembly. If the method has a property, then you can declare it as part of the interface by using the `Property` keyword:

```
Public Property AProperty() As String

End Property
```

You can also declare events as part of the interface by using the `Event` keyword:

```
Public Event AnEvent()
```

Finally, you can include actual variables, or attributes, as part of the interface:

```
Public AnInteger As Integer
```

This is strongly discouraged, because it directly exposes the internal variables for use by code outside the class. Because the variable is directly accessible from other code, you give up any and all control over changing the implementation.

Rather than make any variable Public, you should always make use of a Property method to expose the value. That way, you can implement code to ensure that your internal variable is set only to valid values and that only the appropriate code has access to the value based on your application's logic.

Ultimately, the native (or primary) interface for any class is defined by looking at all the methods, properties, events, and variables that are declared as anything other than Private in scope. This includes any methods, properties, events, or variables that are inherited from a base class.

You are used to interacting with the default interface on most objects, so this should seem pretty straightforward. Consider this simple class:

```
Public Class TheClass
   Public Sub DoSomething()

   End Sub

   Public Sub DoSomethingElse()

   End Sub
End Class
```

This defines a class and, by extension, defines the native interface that is exposed by any objects you instantiate based on this class. The native interface defines two methods: DoSomething and DoSomethingElse. To make use of these methods, you simply call them:

```
Dim myObject As New TheClass()

myObject.DoSomething()

myObject.DoSomethingElse()
```

This is the same thing you did in Chapter 3 and so far in this chapter. However, you will now take a look at creating and using secondary interfaces, because they are a bit different.

## Abstract Interfaces

Sometimes it's helpful for an object to have more than one interface, thereby enabling you to interact with the object in different ways. You may have a group of objects that are not the same thing, but you want to be able to treat them as though they were the same. You want all these objects to act as the same thing, even though they are all different. Inheritance enables you to create subclasses that are specialized cases of the base class. For example, your Employee is a Person.

Next you may have a series of different objects in an application: product, customer, invoice, and so forth. Each of these would be a different class—so there's no natural inheritance relationship implied between these classes. At the same time, you may need to be able to generate a printed document for each type of object, so you would like to make them all act as a printable object.

To accomplish this, you can define an abstract interface that enables generating such a printed document. You can call it IPrintableObject.

> **NOTE** *By convention, this type of interface is typically prefixed with a capital "I" to indicate that it is a formal interface.*

Each of your application objects can choose to implement the IPrintableObject interface. Every object that implements this interface must include code to provide actual implementation of the interface, which is unlike inheritance, whereby the code from a base class is automatically reused.

By implementing this common interface, you can write a routine that accepts any object that implements the `IPrintableObject` interface and then print it—while remaining totally oblivious to the "real" data type of the object or methods its native interface might expose. Before you learn how to use an interface in this manner, you should walk through the process of actually defining an interface.

## Defining the Interface

You define a formal interface using the `Interface` keyword. This can be done in any code module in your project, but a good place to put this type of definition is in a standard module. An interface defines a set of methods (`Sub`, `Function`, or `Property`) and events that must be exposed by any class that chooses to implement the interface.

Add a module to the project using Project ➪ Add ➪ New Item... Within the Add New Item dialog select an Interface and name it `IprintableObject.vb`. Then, add the following code to the module, outside the Module code block itself:

```
Public Interface IPrintableObject

End Interface
```

Interfaces must be declared using either Public or Friend scope. Declaring a Private or Protected interface results in a syntax error. Within the Interface block of code, you can define the methods, properties, and events that make up your particular interface. Because the scope of the interface is defined by the `Interface` declaration itself, you can't specify scopes for individual methods and events; they are all scoped like the interface itself.

For instance, update `IPrintableObject` to look similar to the following. This won't be your final version of this interface, but this version will allow you to demonstrate another implementation feature of interfaces.

```
Public Interface IPrintableObject
    Function Label(ByVal index As Integer) As String
    Function Value(ByVal index As Integer) As String
    ReadOnly Property Count() As Integer
End Interface
```

This defines a new data type, somewhat like creating a class or structure, which you can use when declaring variables. For instance, you can now declare a variable of type `IPrintableObject`:

```
Private printable As IPrintableObject
```

You can also have your classes implement this interface, which requires each class to provide implementation code for each of the three methods defined on the interface.

Before you implement the interface in a class, it's a good idea to see how you can use the interface to write a generic routine that can print any object that implements `IPrintableObject`.

## Using the Interface

Interfaces define the methods and events (including parameters and data types) that an object is required to implement if you choose to support the interface. This means that, given just the interface definition, you can easily write code that can interact with any object that implements the interface, even though you do not know what the native data types of those objects will be.

To see how you can write such code, you can create a simple routine in your form that can display data to the output window in the IDE from any object that implements IPrintableObject. Bring up the code window for your form and add the following (code file: Form1.vb):

```
Public Sub PrintObject(obj As IPrintableObject)
  Dim index As Integer

  For index = 0 To obj.Count
    Debug.Write(obj.Label(index) & ": ")
    Debug.WriteLine(obj.Value(index))
  Next
End Sub
```

Notice that you are accepting a parameter of type IPrintableObject. This is how secondary interfaces are used, by treating an object of one type as though it were actually of the interface type. As long as the object passed to this method implements the IPrintableObject interface, your code will work fine.

Within the PrintObject routine, you are assuming that the object will implement three elements—Count, Label, and Value—as part of the IPrintableObject interface. Secondary interfaces can include methods, properties, and events, much like a default interface, but the interface itself is defined and implemented using some special syntax.

Now that you have a generic printing routine, you need a way to call it. Bring up the designer for Form1, add a button, and name it ButtonPrint. Double-click the button and put the following code within it (code file: Form1.vb):

```
Private Sub ButtonPrint_Click(sender As Object,
        e As EventArgs) Handles ButtonPrint.Click
    Dim obj As New Employee()
    obj.EmployeeNumber = 123
    obj.BirthDate = #1/1/1980#
    obj.HireDate = #1/1/1996#
    PrintObject(obj)
End Sub
```

This code simply initializes an Employee object and calls the PrintObject routine. Of course, this code produces runtime exceptions, because PrintObject is expecting a parameter that implements IPrintableObject, and Employee implements no such interface. Now you will move on and implement that interface in Employee so that you can see how it works.

## Implementing the Interface

Any class (other than an abstract base class) can implement an interface by using the Implements keyword. For instance, you can implement the IPrintableObject interface in Employee by adding the the following line:

```
Implements IPrintableObject
```

This causes the interface to be exposed by any object created as an instance of `Employee`. Adding this line of code and pressing Enter triggers the IDE to add skeleton methods for the interface to your class. All you need to do is provide implementations (write code) for the methods.

> **NOTE** *You can also use the* `AssemblyLoad` *method, which scans the directory containing your application's* `.exe` *file (and the global assembly cache) for any EXE or DLL containing the* `Objects` *assembly. When it finds the assembly, it loads it into memory, making it available for your use.*

Before actually implementing the interface, however, you can create an array to contain the labels for the data fields in order to return them via the `IPrintableObject` interface. Add the following code to the `Employee` class:

```
Private mLabels() As String = {"ID", "Age", "HireDate"}
```

To implement the interface, you need to create methods and properties with the same parameter and return data types as those defined in the interface. The actual name of each method or property does not matter because you are using the `Implements` keyword to link your internal method names to the external method names defined by the interface. As long as the method signatures match, you are all set.

This applies to scope as well. Although the interface and its methods and properties are publicly available, you do not have to declare your actual methods and properties as Public. In many cases, you can implement them as Private, so they do not become part of the native interface and are only exposed via the secondary interface.

However, if you do have a Public method with a method signature, you can use it to implement a method from the interface. This has the interesting side effect that this method provides implementation for both a method on the object's native interface and one on the secondary interface.

In this case, you will use a Private method, so it is only providing implementation for the `IPrintableObject` interface. Implement the `Label` method by adding the following code to `Employee`:

```
Private Function Label(ByVal index As Integer) As String _
    Implements IPrintableObject.Label

    Return mLabels(index)
End Function
```

This is just a regular Private method that returns a `String` value from the pre-initialized array. The interesting part is the `Implements` clause on the method declaration:

```
Implements IPrintableObject.Label
```

By using the `Implements` keyword in this fashion, you are indicating that this particular method is the implementation for the `Label` method on the `IPrintableObject` interface. The actual name of the private method could be anything. It is the use of the `Implements` clause that makes this work. The only requirement is that the parameter data types and the return value data type must match those defined by the `IPrintableObject` interface method.

This is very similar to using the `Handles` clause to indicate which method should handle an event. In fact, like the `Handles` clause, the `Implements` clause allows you to have a comma-separated list of interface methods implemented by this one function.

You can then finish implementing the `IPrintableObject` interface by adding the following code to `Employee`:

```
Private Function Value(ByVal index As Integer) As String _
    Implements IPrintableObject.Value

  Select Case index
    Case 0
      Return CStr(EmployeeNumber)
    Case 1
      Return CStr(Age)
    Case Else
      Return Format(HireDate, "Short date")
  End Select
End Function

Private ReadOnly Property Count() As Integer _
    Implements IPrintableObject.Count
  Get
    Return UBound(mLabels)
  End Get
End Property
```

You can now run this application and click the button. The output window in the IDE will display your results, showing the ID, age, and hire-date values as appropriate.

Any object could create a similar implementation behind the `IPrintableObject` interface, and the `PrintObject` routine in your form would continue to work, regardless of the native data type of the object itself.

## Reusing a Common Implementation

Secondary interfaces provide a guarantee that all objects implementing a given interface have exactly the same methods and events, including the same parameters.

The `Implements` clause links your actual implementation to a specific method on an interface. Sometimes, your method might be able to serve as the implementation for more than one method, either on the same interface or on different interfaces.

Add the following interface definition to your project (code file: `IValues.vb`):

```
Public Interface IValues
  Function GetValue(ByVal index As Integer) As String
End Interface
```

This interface defines just one method, `GetValue`. Notice that it defines a single `Integer` parameter and a return type of `String`, the same as the `Value` method from `IPrintableObject`. Even though the method name and parameter variable name do not match, what counts here is that the parameter and return value data types do match.

Now bring up the code window for `Employee`. You will have to implement this new interface in addition to the `IPrintableObject` interface as follows:

```
Implements IValues
```

You already have a method that returns values. Rather than reimplement that method, it would be nice to just link this new `GetValues` method to your existing method. You can easily do this because the `Implements` clause allows you to provide a comma-separated list of method names:

```
Private Function Value(ByVal index As Integer) As String _
    Implements IPrintableObject.Value, IValues.GetValue
```

This is very similar to the use of the `Handles` keyword, covered in Chapter 3. A single method within the class, regardless of scope or name, can be used to implement any number of methods as defined by other interfaces, as long as the data types of the parameters and return values all match.

You can combine implementation of abstract interfaces with inheritance. When you inherit from a class that implements an interface, your new subclass automatically gains the interface and implementation from the base class. If you specify that your base-class methods are overridable, then the subclass can override those methods. This not only overrides the base-class implementation for your native interface, but also overrides the implementation for the interface.

Combining the implementation of an interface in a base class with overridable methods can provide a very flexible object design.

## Implementing IPrintable

Now that you've looked academically at using an interface to provide a common way to define a printing interface, let's apply that to some actual printing logic. To do this will provide a somewhat reusable interface. First create another interface called `IPrintable`. Now add the following code to your new source file (code file: `IPrintable.vb`):

```
Public Interface IPrintable
  Sub Print()
  Sub PrintPreview()
  Sub RenderPage(ByVal sender As Object,
      ByVal ev As System.Drawing.Printing.PrintPageEventArgs)
End Interface
```

This interface ensures that any object implementing `IPrintable` will have `Print` and `PrintPreview` methods so you can invoke the appropriate type of printing. It also ensures that the object has a `RenderPage` method, which can be implemented by that object to render the object's data on the printed page.

At this point, you could simply implement all the code needed to handle printing directly within the `Employee` object. This isn't ideal, however, as some of the code will be common across any objects that want to implement `IPrintable`, and it would be nice to find a way to share that code.

To do this, you can create a new class, `ObjectPrinter`. This is a framework-style class in that it has nothing to do with any particular application, but can be used across any application in which `IPrintable` will be used.

Add a new class named `ObjectPrinter` to project. This class will contain all the code common to printing any object. It makes use of the built-in printing support provided by the .NET Framework class library.

Within the class you'll need two private fields. The first to define is a `PrintDocument` variable, which will hold the reference to your printer output. You will also declare a variable to hold a reference to the actual object you will be printing. Notice that the following code shows you are using the `IPrintable` interface data type for the `ObjectToPrint` variable (code file: `ObjectPrinter.vb`):

```
Public Class ObjectPrinter
    Private WithEvents document As System.Drawing.Printing.PrintDocument
    Private objectToPrint As IPrintable
End Class
```

Now you can create a routine to kick off the printing process for any object implementing `IPrintable`. The following code is totally generic; you will write it in the `ObjectPrinter` class so it can be reused across other classes.

```
Public Sub Print(ByVal obj As IPrintable)
    objectToPrint = obj
    document = New System.Drawing.Printing.PrintDocument()
    document.Print()
End Sub
```

Likewise, the following snippet shows how you can implement a method to show a print preview of your object. This code is also totally generic, so add it to the `ObjectPrinter` class for reuse. Note printing is a privileged operation, so if you see an issue when you run this code you may need to look at the permissions you are running under.

```
Public Sub PrintPreview(ByVal obj As IPrintable)
    Dim PPdlg As PrintPreviewDialog = New PrintPreviewDialog()
    objectToPrint = obj
    document = New PrintDocument()
    PPdlg.Document = document
    PPdlg.ShowDialog()
End Sub
```

Finally, you need to catch the `PrintPage` event that is automatically raised by the .NET printing mechanism. This event is raised by the `PrintDocument` object whenever the document determines that it needs data rendered onto a page. Typically, it is in this routine that you would put the code to draw text or graphics onto the page surface. However, because this is a generic framework class, you won't do that here; instead, delegate the call back into the actual application object that you want to print (code file: `ObjectPrinter.vb`):

```
Private Sub PrintPage(ByVal sender As Object,
    ByVal ev As System.Drawing.Printing.PrintPageEventArgs) _
    Handles document.PrintPage
    objectToPrint.RenderPage(sender, ev)
End Sub
```

This enables the application object itself to determine how its data should be rendered onto the output page. You do that by implementing the `IPrintable` interface on the `Employee` class.

By adding this interface, you require that your `Employee` class implement the `Print`, `PrintPreview`, and `RenderPage` methods. To avoid wasting paper as you test the code, make both the `Print` and `PrintPreview` methods the same. Both methods implement the print preview display, but that is sufficient for testing. Add the following code to the `Employee` class (code file: `ObjectPrinter.vb`):

```
Public Sub Print() Implements IPrintable.Print
    Dim printer As New ObjectPrinter()
    printer.PrintPreview(Me)
End Sub

Public Sub PrintPreview() Implements IPrintable.PrintPreview
    Dim printer As New ObjectPrinter()
    printer.PrintPreview(Me)
End Sub
```

Notice that you are using an `ObjectPrinter` object to handle the common details of doing a print preview. In fact, any class you ever create that implements `IPrintable` can have this exact same code to implement a print-preview function, relying on your common `ObjectPrinter` to take care of the details.

You also need to implement the `RenderPage` method, which is where you actually put your object's data onto the printed page (code file: `Employee.vb`):

```
Private Sub RenderPage(sender As Object,
                       ev As Printing.PrintPageEventArgs) _
                Implements IPrintable.RenderPage
    Dim printFont As New Font("Arial", 10)
    Dim lineHeight As Single = printFont.GetHeight(ev.Graphics)
    Dim leftMargin As Single = ev.MarginBounds.Left
    Dim yPos As Single = ev.MarginBounds.Top
    ev.Graphics.DrawString("ID: " & EmployeeNumber.ToString,
                        printFont, Brushes.Black,
                    leftMargin, yPos, New StringFormat())
    yPos += lineHeight
    ev.Graphics.DrawString("Name: " & Name,
                        printFont, Brushes.Black,
                    leftMargin, yPos, New StringFormat())
    ev.HasMorePages = False
End Sub
```

All of this code is unique to your object, which makes sense because you are rendering your specific data to be printed. However, you don't need to worry about the details of whether you are printing to paper or print preview; that is handled by your `ObjectPrinter` class, which in turn uses the .NET Framework. This enables you to focus on generating the output to the page within your application class.

By generalizing the printing code in `ObjectPrinter`, you have achieved a level of reuse that you can tap into via the `IPrintable` interface. Anytime you want to print a `Customer` object's data, you can have it act as an `IPrintableObject` and call its `Print` or `PrintPreview` method. To see this work, adjust the Print button handler for `Form1` with the following code:

```
Private Sub ButtonPrint_Click(sender As Object,
                              e As EventArgs) _
                    Handles ButtonPrint.Click
    Dim obj As New Employee()
    obj.EmployeeNumber = 123
```

```
        obj.BirthDate = #1/1/1980#
        obj.HireDate = #1/1/1996#
        'PrintObject(obj)
        CType(obj, IPrintable).PrintPreview()
    End Sub
```

This code creates a new `Employee` object and sets its `Name` property. You then use the `CType` method to access the object via its `IPrintableObject` interface to invoke the `PrintPreview` method.

When you run the application and click the button, you will get a print preview display showing the object's data as shown in Figure 4-9.

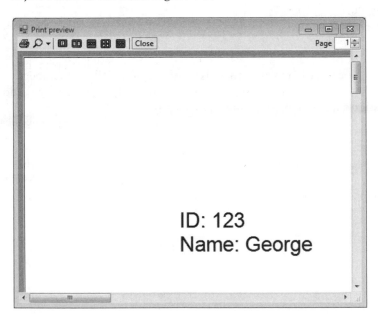

**FIGURE 4-9:** Print preview display from running sample project

## ABSTRACTION

Abstraction is the process by which you can think about specific properties or behaviors without thinking about a particular object that has those properties or behaviors. Abstraction is merely the ability of a language to create "black box" code, to take a concept and create an abstract representation of that concept within a program.

A `Customer` object, for example, is an abstract representation of a real-world customer. A `DataSet` object is an abstract representation of a set of data.

Abstraction enables you to recognize how things are similar and to ignore differences, to think in general terms and not in specifics. A `TextBox` control is an abstraction because you can place it on a form and then tailor it to your needs by setting properties. Visual Basic enables you to define abstractions using classes.

Any language that enables a developer to create a class from which objects can be instantiated meets this criterion, and Visual Basic is no exception. You can easily create a class to represent a customer, essentially providing an abstraction. You can then create instances of that class, whereby each object can have its own attributes, representing a specific customer.

In Visual Basic, you implement abstraction by creating a class using the `Class` keyword. To see this in action, right-click on your solution and select Add New Project. From the Add New Project dialogue select a Visual Basic Windows Forms Application project and name it "VB2012_ObjectDataSource." Once the project is open, add a new class to the project using the Project ⇨ Add Class menu option. Name the new class `Customer.vb`, and add the following code to make this class represent a real-world customer in an abstract sense (code file: `customer.vb`):

```
Public Class Customer
    Public Property ID As Guid
    Public Property Name As String
    Public Property Phone As String
End Class
```

You know that a real customer is a lot more complex than an ID, a name, and a phone number; but at the same time, you know that in an abstract sense, your customers really do have names and phone numbers, and that you assign them unique ID numbers to keep track of them.

You can then use this abstract representation of a customer from within your code by using data binding to link the object to a form. First, build the project by selecting Build ⇨ VB2012_ObjectDataSource. Then click the Data ⇨ Show Data Sources menu option to open the Data Sources window. Select the Add New Data Source link in the window to bring up the Data Source Configuration Wizard. Within the wizard, choose to add a new Object data source, click Next, and then select your Customer class, as shown in Figure 4-10.

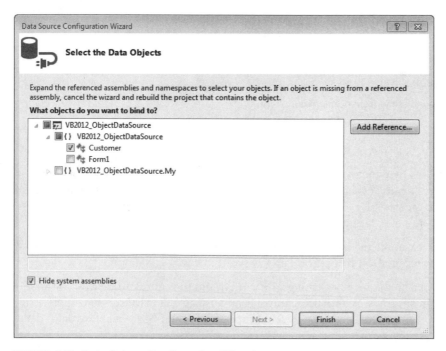

**FIGURE 4-10:** Data Source Configuration Wizard

Finish the wizard. The Customer class will be displayed as an available data source, as shown in Figure 4-11, when you are working in Design view for Form1.

Click on Customer in the Data Sources window. Customer should change its display to a combo box. Open the combo box and change the selection from DataGridView to Details. This way, you get a Details view of the object on your form. Open the designer for Form1 and drag the Customer class from the Data Sources window onto the form. The result in design view should look something like the dialog shown in Figure 4-12.

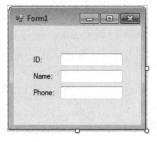

**FIGURE 4-11:** Data Sources Window in Visual Studio

**FIGURE 4-12:** Viewing the generated form in the designer

All you need to do now is add code to create an instance of the Customer class to act as a data source for the form. Double-click on the form to bring up its code window and add the following:

```
Public Class Form1
    Private Sub Form1_Load(sender As Object, e As EventArgs) _
                        Handles MyBase.Load
        Me.CustomerBindingSource.DataSource = New Customer()
    End Sub
End Class
```

You are using the ability of Windows Forms to data-bind to a property on an object. You'll learn more about data binding later. For now, it is enough to know that the controls on the form are automatically tied to the properties on your object.

Now you have a simple user interface (UI) that both displays and updates the data in your Customer object, with that object providing the UI developer with an abstract representation of the customer. When you run the application, you will see a display like the one shown in Figure 4-13.

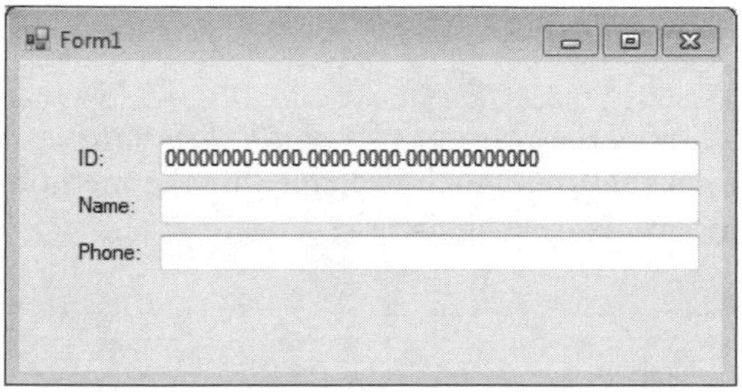

**FIGURE 4-13:** Running the sample code

# ENCAPSULATION

Perhaps the most important of the object-oriented concepts is that of encapsulation. Encapsulation is the idea that an object should totally separate its interface from its implementation. All the data and implementation code for an object should be entirely hidden behind its interface. This is the concept of an object as a black box.

The idea is that you can create an interface (by creating public methods in a class) and, as long as that interface remains consistent, the application can interact with your objects. This remains true even if you entirely rewrite the code within a given method. The interface is independent of the implementation.

Encapsulation enables you to hide the internal implementation details of a class. For example, the algorithm you use to find prime numbers might be proprietary. You can expose a simple API to the end user but hide all of the logic used in your algorithm by encapsulating it within your class.

This means that an object should completely contain any data it requires and should contain all the code required to manipulate that data. Programs should interact with an object through an interface, using the properties and methods of the object. Client code should never work directly with the data owned by the object.

Visual Basic classes hide their internal data and code, providing a well-established interface of properties and methods with the outside world. As was discussed during much of this chapter, you can change not only how a property or method is implemented but even where it is implemented within a class hierarchy. So long as you not changed the interface of the class, your working client program has no idea that you have switched from one implementation to the other.

The goal is to be able to totally change an implementation without any change of behavior visible to the client code. This is the essence of encapsulation.

# POLYMORPHISM

Polymorphism is often considered to be directly tied to inheritance. In reality, it is independent. Polymorphism in software engineering means that you can have two classes with different implementations or code, but with a common set of methods, properties, or events. You can then write a program that operates upon that interface and does not care about which type of object it operates at runtime.

## Method Signatures

To properly understand polymorphism, you need to explore the concept of a *method signature*, sometimes also called a *prototype*. All methods have a signature, which is defined by the method's name and the data types of its parameters. You might have code such as this:

```
Public Function CalculateValue() As Integer

End Sub
```

In this example, the signature is as follows:

```
f()
```

If you add a parameter to the method, the signature will change. For example, you could change the method to accept a `Double`:

```
Public Function CalculateValue(ByVal value As Double) As Integer
```

Then, the signature of the method is as follows:

```
f(Double)
```

Polymorphism merely says that you should be able to write client code that calls methods on an object, and as long as the object provides your methods with the method signatures you expect, it doesn't matter from which class the object was created. The following sections look at some examples of polymorphism within Visual Basic.

# Implementing Polymorphism

You can use several techniques to achieve polymorphic behavior:

- ➤ Inheritance
- ➤ Multiple interfaces
- ➤ Late binding
- ➤ Reflection

Much of this chapter has illustrated the concepts around using inheritance and multiple interfaces. These techniques are common implementations that help you achieve polymorphism. These methods provide the least performance penalty and can be easy to implement. Late binding enables you to implement "pure" polymorphism, although it comes with a slight performance cost. Additionally while it is deceptively easy to implement, it can introduce difficult-to-debug runtime issues.

Reflection enables you to use either late binding or multiple interfaces, but against objects created in a very dynamic way, even going so far as to dynamically load a DLL into your application at runtime so that you can use its classes. Reflection is neither performant nor easy to implement. Since inheritance and multiple interfaces have been discussed in detail, you will now start with a look at late binding.

## Polymorphism with Inheritance

Inheritance, discussed earlier in this chapter, can also be used to enable polymorphism. The idea is that a subclass can always be treated as though it were the data type of the parent class.

As described earlier, the `Person` class is an abstract base class, a class with no implementation of its own. The purpose of an abstract base class is to provide a common base from which other classes can be derived. Each of these child classes exhibits polymorphism because it can be treated using methods common to its parent—`Person`.

To implement polymorphism using inheritance, you do not need to use an abstract base class. Any base class that provides overridable methods (using either the `MustOverride` or `Overridable` keywords) will work fine, as all its subclasses are guaranteed to have that same set of methods as part of their interface, and yet the subclasses can provide custom implementation for those methods.

## Polymorphism Through Late Binding

Typically, when you interact with objects in Visual Basic, you are interacting with them through strongly typed variables. For example, in Form1 you interacted with the Person declaring and instance with the variable name emp. The emp variable is declared using a specific type—meaning that it is strongly typed or early bound.

You can also interact with objects that are late bound. Late binding means that your object variable has no specific data type, but rather is of type Object. To use late binding, you need to use the Option Strict Off directive at the top of your code file (or in the project's properties). This tells the Visual Basic compiler that you want to use late binding, so it will allow you to do this type of polymorphism.

By default, Option Strict is turned off in a new Visual Basic project. With Option Strict off, the Object data type is late bound and you will be able to attempt to call an arbitrary method, even though the Object data type does not implement those methods. Note Visual Basic isn't alone in leveraging late binding. C# has introduced this concept, which it originally didn't support, and it is leveraged heavily by all of the implementations of LINQ.

When late binding is enabled you get the same result as you did before, even if at compile time the environment was unsure if a class included a given method as part of its interface. The late-binding mechanism, behind the scenes, dynamically determines the real type of your object and invokes the appropriate method.

When you work with objects through late binding, neither the Visual Basic IDE nor the compiler is always certain at compile time if you are calling a valid method. It just assumes that you know what you are talking about and compiles the code.

At runtime, when the code is actually invoked, it attempts to dynamically call the method. If that is a valid method, then your code will work; otherwise, you will get an error.

Obviously, there is a level of danger when using late binding, as a simple typo can introduce errors that can be discovered only when the application is actually run. However, it also offers a lot of flexibility, as code that makes use of late binding can talk to any object from any class as long as those objects implement the methods you require.

There is a performance penalty for using late binding. The existence of each method is discovered dynamically at runtime, and that discovery takes time. Moreover, the mechanism used to invoke a method through late binding is not nearly as efficient as the mechanism used to call a method that is known at compile time.

## Polymorphism with Multiple Interfaces

Another way to implement polymorphism is to use multiple interfaces. This approach avoids late binding, meaning the IDE and compiler can check your code as you enter and compile it. Moreover, because the compiler has access to all the information about each method you call, your code runs much faster.

Visual Basic not only supports polymorphism through late binding, it also implements a stricter form of polymorphism through its support of multiple interfaces.

With multiple interfaces, you can treat all objects as equals by making them all implement a common data type or interface.

This approach has the benefit that it is strongly typed, meaning the IDE and compiler can help you find errors due to typos, because the names and data types of all methods and parameters are known at design time. It is also fast in terms of performance: Because the compiler knows about the methods, it can use optimized mechanisms for calling them, especially compared to the dynamic mechanisms used in late binding.

## Polymorphism through Reflection

You have learned how to use late binding to invoke a method on any arbitrary object as long as that object has a method matching the method signature you are trying to call. You have also walked through the use of multiple interfaces, which enables you to achieve polymorphism through a faster, early-bound technique. The challenge with these techniques is that late binding can be slow and hard to debug, and multiple interfaces can be somewhat rigid and inflexible.

Enter reflection. Reflection is a technology built into the .NET Framework that enables you to write code that interrogates an assembly to dynamically determine the classes and data types it contains. Using reflection, you can load the assembly into your process, create instances of those classes, and invoke their methods.

When you use late binding, Visual Basic makes use of the `System.Reflection` namespace behind the scenes on your behalf. The `System.Reflection` namespace can give you insight into classes by enabling to traverse information about an assembly or class.

You can choose to manually use reflection as well. However, this means that just as there is a performance impact for the Visual Basic runtime, there will be a performance impact in your own applications when using Reflection. More important, misused Reflection can have significant negative performance implications. Howerver, the presence of reflection gives you even more flexibility in terms of how you interact with objects.

While this section will introduce Reflection, fuller coverage of Reflection is handled in Chapter 17. With that in mind, suppose that the class you want to call is located in some other assembly on disk—an assembly you did not specifically reference from within your project when you compiled it. How can you dynamically find, load, and invoke such an assembly?

Reflection enables you to do this, assuming that the assembly is polymorphic. In other words, it has either an interface you expect or a set of methods you can invoke via late binding.

To see how reflection works with late binding, create a new class in a separate assembly (project) and use it from within the existing application. Add a new Class Library project to your solution. Name it "VB2012_Objects." It begins with a single class module that you can use as a starting point. Rename the default `Class1.vb` file to `External.vb` and change the code in that class to match this:

```
Public Class External
  Public Function Multiply(x As Double, y As Double) As Double
    Return x * y
  End Function
End Class
```

Now compile the assembly. Next, bring up the code window for `Form1`. Add an `Imports` statement at the top for the `System.Reflection` namespace:

```
Imports System.Reflection
```

Remember that because you are using late binding your project `ProVB2012_Ch04` must have `Option Strict Off`. Otherwise, late binding isn't available.

Add a button to `Form1` and label it Multiply. Rename the button as `ButtonMultiply` and implement an event handler for the `Click` event with the following code. Remember, you have to have imported the `System.Reflections` namespace for this to work (code file: `Customer.vb`):

```
Private Sub ButtonMultiply_Click(sender As Object,
  e As EventArgs) Handles ButtonMultiply.Click
        Dim obj As Object
        Dim dll As Assembly
        dll = Assembly.LoadFrom(
            "..\..\..\VB2012_Objects\bin\Debug\VB2012_Objects.dll")
        obj = dll.CreateInstance("VB2012_Objects.External")
        MessageBox.Show(obj.Multiply(10, 10))
End Sub
```

There is a lot going on here, so a step-by-step walk-through will be helpful. First, notice that you are reverting to late binding; your `obj` variable is declared as type `Object`. You will look at using reflection and multiple interfaces in a moment, but for now you will use late binding.

Next, you have declared a `dll` variable as type `Reflection.Assembly`. This variable will contain a reference to the `VB2012_Objects` assembly that you will be dynamically loading through your code. Note that you are not adding a reference to this assembly via Project ➪ Add Reference. You will dynamically access the assembly at runtime.

You then load the external assembly dynamically by using the `Assembly.LoadFrom` method:

```
dll = Assembly.LoadFrom(
            "..\..\..\VB2012_Objects\bin\Debug\VB2012_Objects.dll")
```

This causes the reflection library to load your assembly from a file on disk at the location you specify. Once the assembly is loaded into your process, you can use the `dll` variable to interact with it, including interrogating it to get a list of the classes it contains or to create instances of those classes.

> **NOTE** *You can also use the* `AssemblyLoad` *method, which scans the directory containing your application's* `.exe` *file (and the global assembly cache) for any EXE or DLL containing the* `Objects` *assembly. When it finds the assembly, it loads it into memory, making it available for your use.*

You can then use the `CreateInstance` method on the assembly itself to create objects based on any class in that assembly. In this case, you are creating an object based on the `External` class:

```
obj = dll.CreateInstance("VB2012_Objects.External")
```

Now you have an actual object to work with, so you can use late binding to invoke its `Multiply` method. At this point, your code is really no different from any late-binding method call, except that the assembly and object were created dynamically at runtime, rather than being referenced directly by your project. Note from a performance standpoint this can be an important difference. You should be able to run the application and have it dynamically invoke the assembly at runtime.

## Polymorphism via Reflection and Multiple Interfaces

You can also use both reflection and multiple interfaces together. You have seen how multiple interfaces enable you to have objects from different classes implement the same interface and thus be treated identically. You have also seen how reflection enables you to load an assembly and class dynamically at runtime.

You can combine these concepts by using an interface shared in common between your main application and your external assembly, using reflection to load that external assembly dynamically at runtime. Within this method there is no reason to have Option Strict disabled, as you will now be working with strongly typed method calls.

In fact this is the primary advantage of using interfaces with Reflection. By adding an interface definition that is shared across otherwise unrelated assemblies; it is possible to enforce strong typing with Reflection. Keep in mind that this does not change the performance characteristics of Reflection nor does it mean that the assembly you load will in fact have an object that hosts a given interface.

This technique is still very nice, as the code is strongly typed, providing all the coding benefits; but both the DLL and the object itself are loaded dynamically, providing a great deal of flexibility to your application. Note Reflection is covered in much more detail in Chapter 17.

## Polymorphism Summary

Polymorphism is a very important concept in object-oriented design and programming, and Visual Basic provides you with ample techniques through which it can be implemented.

Table 4-3 summarizes the different techniques covered and touches on key pros and cons. It also looks to provide some high-level guidelines about when to use each method of polymorphism. While most applications typically leverage some combination of inheritance and multiple interfaces, there are places for all of the polymorphic techniques listed. For example, LINQ is built around a late-bound implementation.

**TABLE 4-3:** Methods of Implementing Polymorphism.

| TECHNIQUE | PROS | CONS | GUIDELINES |
|---|---|---|---|
| Inheritance | Fast, easy to debug, full IntelliSense, inherits behaviors from base class. | Not totally dynamic or flexible, requires class author to inherit from common base class. | Use when you are creating objects that have an *is-a* relationship, i.e., when you have subclasses that are naturally of the same data type as a base class. Polymorphism through inheritance should occur because inheritance makes sense, not because you are attempting to merely achieve polymorphism. |
| Late binding | Flexible. | Can be difficult to debug, no IntelliSense. | Use to call arbitrary methods on literally any object, regardless of data type or interfaces. |
| Multiple interfaces | Fast, easy to debug, full IntelliSense. | Not totally dynamic or flexible, requires class author to implement formal interface. | Use when you are creating code that interacts with clearly defined methods that can be grouped together into a formal interface. |
| Reflection using late binding | Flexible, "pure" polymorphism, dynamically loads arbitrary assemblies from disk. | Slow, hard to debug, no IntelliSense. | Use to call arbitrary methods on objects when you do not know at design time which assemblies you will be using. |
| Reflection and multiple interfaces | Flexible, full IntelliSense, dynamically loads arbitrary assemblies from disk. | Slow, not totally dynamic or flexible, requires class author to implement formal interface. | Use when you are creating code that interacts with clearly defined methods that can be grouped together into a formal interface, but when you do not know at design time which assemblies you will be using. |

# SUMMARY

This chapter demonstrated how Visual Basic enables you to create and work with classes and objects. Visual Basic provides the building blocks for abstraction, encapsulation, polymorphism, and inheritance.

You have learned how to create both simple base classes as well as abstract base classes. You have also explored how you can define formal interfaces, a concept quite similar to an abstract base class in many ways.

You also walked through the process of subclassing, creating a new class that derives both interface and implementation from a base class. The subclass can be extended by adding new methods or altering the behavior of existing methods on the base class.

By the end of this chapter, you have seen how object-oriented programming flows from the four basic concepts of abstraction, encapsulation, polymorphism, and inheritance. The chapter provided basic information about each concept and demonstrated how to implement them using Visual Basic.

By properly applying object-oriented design and programming, you can create very large and complex applications that remain maintainable and readable over time. Nonetheless, these technologies are not a magic bullet. Improperly applied, they can create the same hard-to-maintain code that you might create using procedural or modular design techniques.

It is not possible to fully cover all aspects of object-oriented programming in a single chapter. Before launching into a full-blown object-oriented project, it is highly recommend that you look at other books specifically geared toward object-oriented design and programming.

In the next chapter you are going to explore some of the more advanced language concepts, like Lambdas, that have been introduced to Visual Basic.

# 5

# Advanced Language Constructs

**WHAT'S IN THIS CHAPTER?**

➤ Using and Understanding Lambda Expressions

➤ An Easy Way to Perform Tasks Asynchronously

➤ Working with Custom Iterators

**WROX.COM CODE DOWNLOADS FOR THIS CHAPTER**

The wrox.com code download for this chapter is found at www.wrox.com/remtitle .cgi?isbn=9781118314456 on the Download Code tab. The code is in the chapter 5 download and follows the single project sample application first discussed in Chapter 1, with some minor updates.

With any language, developers are typically provided with multiple ways to perform a given action. Some of these methods are easier and more efficient than others. One cause of this is simple growing pains. As a language evolves and grows, older ways of performing some functionality are replaced by more robust, efficient, and typically easier methodologies.

This is no different with Visual Basic 2012, which has many new features and improvements. Some of these come from its aforementioned growth as a language, while some can be attributed to its close relationship with C#. While C# may gain some new features and improvements first, Visual Basic is usually not far behind.

The focus of this chapter is to dive into several language features of Visual Basic that provide more advanced functionality. These features are deeply rooted into the framework and have very widespread uses, making them capable of fulfilling many needs. These features can be used to improve the overall appearance and flow of an application or decrease development time.

The first feature covered, Lambda Expressions, is not new to Visual Basic 2012 but deserves to be called out due to its many uses. A Lambda Expression is a specialized delegate that can be referred to as *inline function*. They are a core part of Language Integrated Query (LINQ), which is covered in depth in Chapters 8–10.

The second feature covered is brand-new to Visual Basic 2012 and one of the more exciting and anticipated for any developer who has had to work with asynchronous operations. The core to this feature is the new `Async` and `Await` keywords. While Chapter 19 dives into the gritty details of performing asynchronous operations on background threads and managing them, this chapter will tell you how much of that work can now be greatly simplified by using these two new keywords.

Finally, this chapter will conclude by covering another new feature of Visual Basic 2012 known as *Iterators*. C# has had iterators for a few versions now, and Visual Basic has finally caught up. They provide developers with a powerful and easy way to customize how iterated data is returned to the developer or user.

## PREPARING THE SAMPLE APPLICATION

Chapter 1 provided you with a Windows Presentation Foundation (WPF) application that serves as a base for most of the other chapters in this book. This chapter uses this base application, but you are going to make a few changes to it. These changes are specific to this chapter and should not be assumed to be valid in other chapters.

The first thing to change in the base application is the design of the main window: You need to change the layout grid to include a second column. Next you add a `ComboBox` to the form and put it in the first column using `Grid.Column="0"`. To ensure the combo box is correctly bound to the data on the back end, add the following properties and values:

➤ `ItemsSource = {Binding}`

➤ `DisplayMemberPath = "Name"`

➤ `SelectedValuePath = "Lambda"`

Now you need to ensure the `Button` that was in the original application is in the second column by using `Grid.Column="1"`. You can add a `Margin` to both controls to make them look a little better on the form. You should also name the new combo box *ExampleList* and the button *ExecuteButton*. Since the button's name changed, you will need to change the event handler name accordingly. Once these changes are complete your code should resemble the code in Listing 5-1.

**LISTING 5-1:** MainWIndow — MainWindow.xaml

```
<Window x:Class="MainWindow"
    xmlns="http://schemas.microsoft.com/winfx/2006/xaml/presentation"
    xmlns:x="http://schemas.microsoft.com/winfx/2006/xaml"
    Title="Pro VB 2012 Chapter 5" Height="400" Width="400">
    <Grid Background="Black">
        <Grid.ColumnDefinitions>
```

```xml
                    <ColumnDefinition Width="7*"/>
                    <ColumnDefinition Width="3*"/>
                </Grid.ColumnDefinitions>
                <Grid.RowDefinitions>
                    <RowDefinition Height="42"/>
                    <RowDefinition Height="139*"/>
                </Grid.RowDefinitions>
                <ComboBox Name="ExampleList" Grid.Column="0" Margin="5"
                        ItemsSource="{Binding}"
                        DisplayMemberPath="Name"
                        SelectedValuePath="Lambda" />
                <Button Name="ExecuteButton"
                        Content="Run Sample"
                        Margin="5"
                        Click="ExecuteButton_Click"
                        Grid.Column="1"/>
                <ScrollViewer  Margin="0,0,0,0" Grid.Row="1" Grid.ColumnSpan="2">
                    <TextBox Name="TextBoxResult" TextWrapping="Wrap" Text=""/>
                </ScrollViewer>
            </Grid>
        </Window>
```

The next step is to add the following code to the application.

```vb
        Private ReadOnly _examples As CollectionView

        Public Sub New()
            ' This call is required by the designer.
            InitializeComponent()

            ' Add any initialization after the InitializeComponent() call.
            Dim examplesList =
                {
                    New With {.Name = "To be continued", .Lambda = "To be continued"}
                }

            _examples = New CollectionView(examplesList)
        End Sub

        Public ReadOnly Property Examples As CollectionView
            Get
                Return _examples
            End Get
        End Property
```

The _examples field is used to hold a CollectionView of the collection created in the constructor. The Examples property provides read-only access to this field. Earlier, you bound this property to the ComboBox control on the user interface. This allows the data in the collection to be shown in the control.

At the moment, your examplesList collection is only stubbed out until you cover the first topic, Lambda Expressions. It is a collection of anonymous types where the anonymous type has a Name and Lambda property.

Your next step is to provide functionality for the button, which you accomplish by adding the following:

```
Private Sub ExecuteButton_Click(sender As Object, e As RoutedEventArgs)
    Dim ExampleMethod = TryCast(ExampleList.SelectedValue, Action)

    If ExampleMethod = Nothing Then
        TextBoxResult.Text = "Nothing to run"
        Return
    End If

    TextBoxResult.Text = String.Empty

    ExampleMethod.Invoke()
End Sub
```

In the example you built initially in Chapter 1, your button was called `Button`. Since we changed the button name to `Execute`, you will no longer need the `Button_Click_1` subroutine, in this version.

The detail on what this handler actually does will be covered later in this chapter. For now, you will finish setting up the application by handling the main window's `Loaded` event and binding the `Examples` property to the `ExampleList` control. The following event handler code should be added to the application:

```
Private Sub MainWindow_Loaded(sender As Object, e As RoutedEventArgs) _
    Handles Me.Loaded
    ExampleList.DataContext = Examples
End Sub
```

These changes and additions will prepare the application for use throughout this chapter. If you run the application, it will look like Figure 5-1. However, it won't actually do anything yet because you haven't added any examples. You have waited long enough—it is time to move on to the real purpose of this chapter!

**FIGURE 5-1:** Main Application

## LAMBDA EXPRESSIONS

In the simplest terms, a lambda expression is an anonymous method that is sometimes referred to as an inline method or function. While the name and general principle comes from Lambda calculus, lambda expressions were first introduced in version 3.5 of the .NET Framework. Language Integrated Query (LINQ), discussed in Chapters 8–10, was also first introduced in version 3.5 of the framework and would not function without lambda expressions.

An anonymous method is an unnamed method that is created inline, or inside of a method, rather than as a method block itself. They are typically used as delegates, which are discussed in Chapter 3. They behave just like any other method and can have both parameters and return values.

All code discussed in this section is related to the `MainWindow.xaml.vb` file.

## Creating a Lambda Expression Subroutine

As you already know, a subroutine is a method that has no return value. You create a lambda expression with no return value the same way you would a normal subroutine, but you either provide it as a delegate parameter or assign it to a variable.

```
Dim SayHello = Sub() TextBoxResult.Text = "Hello"
SayHello()
```

The lambda expression simply writes the word "Hello" to the text box on the main window. It is stored in the `SayHello` variable, and you can call it like you would any regular method.

If you debug the code and put the cursor over the `SayHello` variable, after that line has executed, you will see (as shown in Figure 5-2) that its type is *generated method*. This means that the compiler actually created a method for it and generated a name for it. You can see from the same figure that the name for this method is `Void_Lambda$_2`.

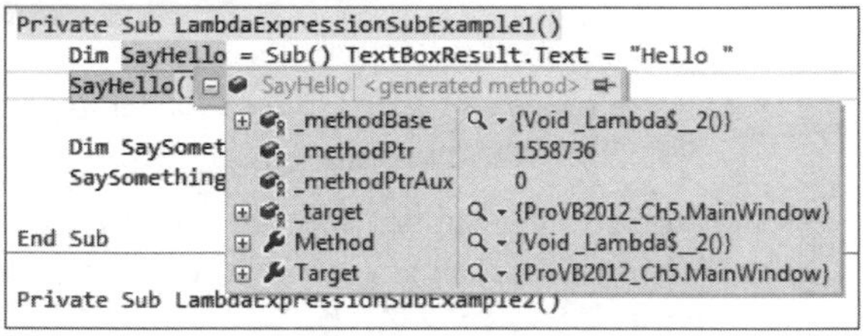

```
Private Sub LambdaExpressionSubExample1()
    Dim SayHello = Sub() TextBoxResult.Text = "Hello "
    SayHello()    SayHello  <generated method>
                       _methodBase      Q - {Void _Lambda$_2()}
    Dim SaySomet       _methodPtr       1558736
    SaySomething       _methodPtrAux    0
                       _target          Q - {ProVB2012_Ch5.MainWindow}
    End Sub            Method           Q - {Void _Lambda$_2()}
                       Target           Q - {ProVB2012_Ch5.MainWindow}
Private Sub LambdaExpressionSubExample2()
```

**FIGURE 5-2:** Subroutines example

Now you are going to update your sample application in order to test this out yourself. The first step is to add the following methods to the application:

```
Private Sub LambdaExpressionSubExample1()
    Dim SayHello = Sub() TextBoxResult.Text = "Hello"
    SayHello()

    Dim SaySomething = Sub(text) TextBoxResult.Text += text
    SaySomething("World")

End Sub

Private Sub LambdaExpressionSubExample2()

    Dim SayHelloWorld = Sub()
                            TextBoxResult.Text = "Hello"
                            TextBoxResult.Text += "World"
                            TextBoxResult.Text += "Again"
                        End Sub

    SayHelloWorld()

End Sub
```

The first example demonstrates using lambda expressions that are on a single line and that they can have zero or more parameters. The second example demonstrates how they can also support multiple lines.

Running the program now won't do anything, because you have not added these methods to the examples collection. You accomplish that by adding the boldfaced lines in the following snippet to the constructor:

```
Public Sub New()
    ' This call is required by the designer.
    InitializeComponent()

    ' Add any initialization after the InitializeComponent() call.
    Dim examplesList =
        {
            New With {.Name = "Lambda Expression - Subroutines 1", _
                        .Lambda = New Action(Sub() LambdaExpressionSubExample1())},
            New With {.Name = "Lambda Expression - Subroutines 2", _
                        .Lambda = New Action(Sub() LambdaExpressionSubExample2())}
        }

    _examples = New CollectionView(examplesList)
End Sub
```

When you run the application, the combo box will have the names you provided for your two examples. When the button is pressed, the selected method executes and the results are displayed in the text box.

This all works because of the Action specified for each example. Action(Of T) is a generic delegate. Chapter 7 covers the concept of *generics*, so you will not get into that here. The method has many definitions that allow for numerous generic-type parameters that correspond to parameters in the wrapped method. It has no return type, and the only parameter is the actual method to be wrapped. In the case of this example, you are wrapping a lambda expression which calls the appropriate method. Pressing the button retrieves this delegate and calls the Invoke method to execute it.

## Creating a Lambda Expression Function

As mentioned in the previous section, subroutines do not return a value. If you need to return a value from your lambda expression, you must define it as a function.

Update the sample application by adding the following methods:

```
Private Sub LambdaExpressionFunctionExample()
    Dim AreaOfCircle = Function(radius As Integer) As Double
                            ' Compute the area of a circle
                            Return Math.PI * Math.Pow(radius, 2)
                        End Function

    Dim Circumference = Function(radius As Integer)
                            ' Compute the circumference
                            Return Math.PI * (radius * 2)
```

```
              End Function

TextBoxResult.Text = "The area of a circle with a radius of 5 is " +
                     AreaOfCircle(5).ToString() + Environment.NewLine
TextBoxResult.Text += "The circumference of a circle with a radius of 5 is " +
                     Circumference(5).ToString()

    End Sub
```

This example shows you how to create lambda expressions that are capable of returning a method. As you might imagine, instead of using `Sub` you use `Function`. Both of the functions defined take a parameter and return a value, but only the first one specifies the data type of the return value. For the second function, the compiler will infer the return type.

Before you can actually test this example, you need to add it to the `examplesList` collection by appending the following to the collection initializer:

```
New With {.Name = "Lambda Expression - Functions", _
          .Lambda = New Action(Sub() LambdaExpressionFunctionExample())}
```

> **NOTE** *Since you are adding an item to a list of items, you will need to be sure to always separate the items with a comma. Where you place this comma depends on where you put the item. If you put the item at the top of your existing list, you will put a comma at the end. If you put the item at the bottom, you will add a comma to the end of the previous item. You will need to do this anytime you update this list.*

Once that is complete, you can run the application, select the *Lambda Expression - Functions* item from the list, and execute it by pressing the button. Your results should look similar to those in Figure 5-3.

# USING LAMBDA EXPRESSIONS

The previous section showed you how to create lambda expressions in their simplest forms. What are they for, though? It was mentioned earlier that they are delegates and can be used anywhere delegates are used, but what exactly does that mean? The purpose of this section is to answer those questions by showing you how they can be used in practical situations.

**FIGURE 5-3:** Functions example

# Handling Events with Lambdas

One of the most common places that you will find lambda expressions being used is as event handlers. Chapter 3 covers events and event handlers in detail, but a simple definition is that they are delegates that are called when a particular event is fired.

The typical approach for handling events is to create a method that represents the handler and providing the address of it in the AddHandler statement.

```
AddHandler timer.tick, AddressOf TimerTickHandler
Private Sub TimerTickHandler(ByVal sender As Object, ByVal e As EventArgs)
    ' Handle the event
End Sub
```

Lambda expressions allow you to do this without having to create the named handler method. To see this in action, add the following code to your sample application:

```
Private Sub LambdaExpressionAsEventHandler()
    Dim timer As DispatcherTimer =
        New DispatcherTimer(Windows.Threading.DispatcherPriority.Normal)

    timer.Interval = TimeSpan.FromSeconds(5)
    AddHandler timer.Tick, Sub(source, args)
                               timer.Stop()
                               TextBoxResult.Text = "The timer has elapsed at " +
                                   DateTime.Now.ToLongTimeString()
                           End Sub

    timer.Start()
    TextBoxResult.Text = "Timer started at " + DateTime.Now.ToLongTimeString()
End Sub
```

Be sure to add the following statement at the top of the code file in order to use the DispatcherTimer class:

```
Imports System.Windows.Threading
```

This example creates a dispatch timer, a timer that runs using the dispatcher. You configured with a five-second interval so the Tick event will fire five seconds after the timer is started.

You need to handle the Tick event, so you use the AddHandler statement specifying the name of the event and your handler. In this case, you use a lambda expression to provide the handler rather than specifically making a method and using the AddressOf operator. The handler stops the timer and updates the results text box. The timer is started by calling the Start method. The timer itself runs in the background, so the main thread continues to execute.

To actually run this example, you need to add it to the examplesList collection by appending the following to the collection initializer:

```
New With {.Name = "Lambda Expression - Event Handler", _
          .Lambda = New Action(Sub() LambdaExpressionAsEventHandler())}
```

Run the application and select the new entry in the drop-down list. It will execute when you press the button. The first thing you will see is the message "Timer started at" followed by the current time. The timer is running in the background, so you just need to wait five seconds, after which the result window will be updating to look like Figure 5-4.

**FIGURE 5-4:** Event Handler example

Using lambda expressions as event handlers works just like you may be used to, but it can make the task a little easier and make the code flow a little more natural. An added bonus with using lambda expressions is that you can use variables that are in the scope of the parent method within the expression itself. You did this in the example when you used the timer variable to stop the timer.

> **NOTE** *While lambda expressions are very powerful and useful, they can be abused. My personal experience has been that the contents of lambda expressions are short and concise. If you have a longer method, it most likely should be created as a method and called in the normal method. Also, try to constrain yourself on the amount of lambda expressions you use. You might be able to create an entire application from a single method that contains 50 lambda expressions, but it won't look very good or may not run very efficiently.*

## LINQ with Lambdas

Language Integrated Query (LINQ) allows you to create SQL-like queries against objects in code. You will not get into too much detail on what it is, since it is covered in great detail in Chapters 8 through 10, but certain points need to be understood in order for this to make the most sense.

LINQ queries typically rely on a set of *clauses*, such as Select and Where. These are key to supporting the SQL-like approach targeted by LINQ. What may not be obvious is that these *clauses* are just syntactic sugar that wraps extension methods of the IEnumerable(OF T) interface.

According to MSDN, the `Where` method (which corresponds to the `Where` clause) has the following declaration:

```
<ExtensionAttribute> _
Public Shared Function Where(Of TSource) ( _
        source As IEnumerable(Of TSource), _
        predicate As Func(Of TSource, Boolean) _
) As IEnumerable(Of TSource)
```

This is an extension method, so the first parameter is really the source collection that the method is being executed against. The second parameter is the one you are interested in. The `Action` delegate was mentioned in a previous section. `Func(Of T, TResult)` is also a delegate but differentiates itself from `Action` by allowing a return type, specified by the `TResult` parameter. As with the `Action` delegate, a lambda expression can be implicitly converted to a `Func` delegate.

All LINQ extension methods, and the clauses that wrap some of them, represent either an `Action(Of T)` or a `Func(Of T, TResult)`. This means lambda expressions can be used to provide additional functionality and support to queries.

To experiment with this, you need to update your application with the following:

```
Private Sub LambdaExpressionsWithLinq()

    Dim fireFlyCrew =
        {
            New With {.Name = "Malcolm Reynolds", .Age = 31},
            New With {.Name = "Zoe Washburne", .Age = 30},
            New With {.Name = "Hoban Washburne", .Age = 31},
            New With {.Name = "Inara Serra", .Age = 27},
            New With {.Name = "Jayne Cobb", .Age = 40},
            New With {.Name = "Kaylee Frye", .Age = 23},
            New With {.Name = "Simon Tam", .Age = 25},
            New With {.Name = "River Tam", .Age = 19},
            New With {.Name = "Shepherd Book", .Age = 52}
        }

    Dim minimumAge = fireFlyCrew.Min(Function(crewMember) crewMember.Age)
    Dim youngest = From crewMember In fireFlyCrew
                   Where crewMember.Age = minimumAge
                   Select crewMember.Name

    TextBoxResult.Text = "The youngest crew member is " + youngest.First +
                         Environment.NewLine

    Dim averageAge = fireFlyCrew.Average(Function(crewMember) crewMember.Age)
    TextBoxResult.Text += "The average age is " + averageAge.ToString

End Sub
```

The first thing this method does is create a collection of anonymous types that have a `Name` and `Age` property. Next, you determine the youngest age and save it in the `minimumAge` variable. To calculate the minimum age you use the `Min` extension method, which accepts a `Func(Of TSource, Integer)` delegate. You use a lambda expression here, which is called for every record in the collection and provided with an instance of the anonymous type. The body of the expression is used within the actual calculation for determining the minimum.

If you just called `Min()` without providing an expression, you would receive an exception. That is because your anonymous type is not of a type, such as an `Integer`, that the function knows how to calculate. You overcome this by providing the function what it needs to execute correctly.

The example uses the minimum value within a query in order to get the name of the youngest person. You then perform a similar action by using the `Average` extension method as an additional test.

As with all the examples in this chapter, you can't actually test it until you add it to the list. Do this by updating the `examplesList` field, in the constructor, with the following item:

```
New With {.Name = "Lambda Expression - LINQ", _
        .Lambda = New Action(Sub() LambdaExpressionsWithLinq())}
```

When this example is executed (by selecting the name from the list and pressing the button) you will be presented with the appropriate results as shown in Figure 5-5.

FIGURE 5-5: LINQ example

## ASYNC AND AWAIT

When writing an application, you may come across a situation where some method takes time to execute. This long-running task may cause your application to hang or a user interface to freeze until it completes. The reason for this is because it is executing synchronously, which means that it is running on the main thread and blocking that thread until the operation completes. For years, developers have worked at overcoming this by performing these *long-running tasks* asynchronously.

Many aspects of asynchronous programming are covered in detail in chapter 19, so this basic concept will be touched on here. Asynchronous programming involves performing long-running tasks, or those that would cause the main thread to pause, on another thread. This other thread would execute in the background, independent of the main thread, which would continue running unhindered. Since both threads are executing concurrently, they are considered asynchronous.

While this approach allows for a much more responsive application, it is somewhat more convoluted and difficult to follow in code and manage. The reason for this is because you are responsible for knowing when the background thread(s) is/are completed and for managing data and synchronicity across them.

The .NET framework has always supported asynchronous programming by providing asynchronous methods in classes where they make the most sense. This would typically be classes that included methods that access data such as reading files, making web calls, or performing communications over a socket.

Performing these actions asynchronously would require you to either handle events, that were fired once a given operation completed, or via *Begin* and *End* methods. In the later situation, you would call the appropriate **Begin** method (such as `Socket.BeginAccept`) to start the operation asynchronously. This method would require you to provide a callback, which would be executed once the method completed. Within this callback, you would call `Socket.EndAccept` to complete the operation.

As you can imagine, this can become very confusing and difficult to maintain. It also has the effect of breaking up the flow of your application, which can make it difficult to read and maintain. To help resolve some of these issues, Microsoft created `Async` and `Await`, first introduced as a CTP add-on to Visual Studio 2010, but now part of version 4.5 of the .NET framework.

As with the previous section, all examples in this section will update the `MainWindow.xaml.vb` file.

## The Core Concept

`Async` and `Await` are almost magical, which you will see when you first use them. `Async` is a method modifier that is used to identify a method as asynchronous. It can be used with a `Sub` or `Function`, if the return type is a `Task` or `Task(Of T)`. It also works with lambda expressions. It is as simple as just adding the modifier, like this:

```
Private Async Sub StartTimeConsumingTask()
    ' Some time-consuming task
End Sub
```

`Async` is only part of this equation, though. If you create the previous method, you will receive a compiler warning that states:

```
This async method lacks 'Await' operators and so will run synchronously.
Consider using the 'Await' operator to await non-blocking API calls, or
'Await Task.Run(...)' to do CPU-bound work on a background thread.
```

As Visual Studio was nice enough to tell everyone, you need to use `Await`. `Await` and `Async` are twins and work together at their assigned job of providing asynchronous magic. `Await` is a method operator usable with any function or lambda expression that returns a `Task(OF TResult)`. You would use `Await` for your long-running task or the task that you wish to execute asynchronously.

### An Example

In order for you to truly understand how this works, you are going to create a new example in your application. Start by adding the following:

```
Public Sub AsyncBasicExample()
    StartTimeConsumingTask()
    TextBoxResult.Text += "Main thread free for use while operation runs in" +
                          "background" + Environment.NewLine
End Sub
```

```
Private Async Sub StartTimeConsumingTask()
    TextBoxResult.Text += "Starting time-consuming task" + Environment.NewLine
    ExampleList.IsEnabled = False
    ExecuteButton.IsEnabled = False

    Await TimeConsumingTask()

    TextBoxResult.Text += "Time-consuming task completed" + Environment.NewLine
    ExampleList.IsEnabled = True
    ExecuteButton.IsEnabled = True
End Sub

Private Function TimeConsumingTask() As Task
    Return Task.Run(Sub() Thread.Sleep(10000))
End Function
```

Be sure to add the following statement at the top of the code file in order to use the `Thread` class:

```
Imports System.Threading
```

The `TimeConsumingTask` simply creates a `Task` and runs it. This task, a lambda expression delegate, simply sleeps for 10 seconds before ending. This serves as simulating a long-running task that runs in the background. Since `TimeConsumingTask` returns a `Task`, it is *awaitable*, which Visual Studio will tell you if you put the cursor over the method name.

The `StartTimeConsumingTask` method starts by adding some text to the result window and disabling the list box and button on the form. This portion of the method is currently running synchronously. Once the compiler hits the `Await` it starts running the `TimeConsumingMethod` in the background and immediately exits the method, returning to the line following the one that called it. This allows the main thread to continue running, which you will see when it writes a new value to the results textbox.

> **NOTE** *If an exception occurs within a method that has been* awaited, *the* Await *operator actually rethrows the exception so that you can catch it and deal with it appropriately.*

Once the task completes, control is returned to the method following the *awaited* method in the `StartTimeConsumingTask` method. Here you write text saying the task completed and reenable the UI controls that were previously disabled.

Now add the example to the list so you can actually run it:

```
New With {.Name = "Async and Await - The Basics", _
         .Lambda = New Action(Sub() AsyncBasicExample())}
```

Once you have completed that, you can run the application and execute the new example. Initially you will see that the UI controls become disabled and the results text box has the following:

```
Starting time-consuming task
Main thread free for use while operation runs in background
```

The second line proves that the main thread is not being blocked in any way. You can further prove it by dragging the window around for 10 seconds, while the background task is running. Once that task completes, the results textbox is updated as shown in Figure 5-6.

While this was a fairly basic example, you can clearly see the power you now have at your hands. Using Async and Await allowed you to very easily execute a task on the background, but it did it while maintaining the readability and maintainability of your code by preserving the flow.

## The Man Behind the Curtain

You are no doubt intrigued at this point, but you probably also have many questions related to how this all works. What is the compiler doing to make this all happen?

**FIGURE 5-6:** Basic Async/Await example

The best way to show you what is happening is to show you what happens if you don't use Async and Await. Figure 5-7 shows you what the IL, discussed in Chapter 2, looks like if you remove both keywords from the StartTimeConsumingTask method.

```
ProVB2012_Ch5.MainWindow::StartTimeConsumingTask : void()
Find  Find Next
.method private instance void  StartTimeConsumingTask() cil managed
{
  // Code size       132 (0x84)
  .maxstack  4
  .locals init (class [PresentationFramework]System.Windows.Controls.TextBox V_0)
  IL_0000:  nop
  IL_0001:  ldarg.0
  IL_0002:  callvirt    instance class [PresentationFramework]System.Windows.Controls.TextBo
  IL_0007:  stloc.0
  IL_0008:  ldloc.0
  IL_0009:  ldloc.0
  IL_000a:  callvirt    instance string [PresentationFramework]System.Windows.Controls.TextB
  IL_000f:  ldstr       "Starting time consuming task"
  IL_0014:  call        string [mscorlib]System.Environment::get_NewLine()
  IL_0019:  call        string [mscorlib]System.String::Concat(string,
                                                               string,
                                                               string)
  IL_001e:  callvirt    instance void [PresentationFramework]System.Windows.Controls.TextBox
  IL_0023:  nop
  IL_0024:  ldarg.0
  IL_0025:  callvirt    instance class [PresentationFramework]System.Windows.Controls.ComboB
  IL_002a:  ldc.i4.0
  IL_002b:  callvirt    instance void [PresentationCore]System.Windows.UIElement::set_IsEnab
  IL_0030:  nop
  IL_0031:  ldarg.0
  IL_0032:  callvirt    instance class [PresentationFramework]System.Windows.Controls.Button
  IL_0037:  ldc.i4.0
  IL_0038:  callvirt    instance void [PresentationCore]System.Windows.UIElement::set_IsEnab
  IL_003d:  nop
  IL_003e:  ldarg.0
  IL_003f:  callvirt    instance class [mscorlib]System.Threading.Tasks.Task ProVB2012_Ch5.M
  IL_0044:  pop
  IL_0045:  ldarg.0
  IL_0046:  callvirt    instance class [PresentationFramework]System.Windows.Controls.TextBo
  IL_004b:  stloc.0
  IL_004c:  ldloc.0
```

**FIGURE 5-7:** IL of StartTimeConsumingTask without Async/Await

Don't worry about understanding this gibberish right now—this is only for comparison purposes. Now look at Figure 5-8, which shows the same method with the `Async` and `Await` keywords restored to proper glory.

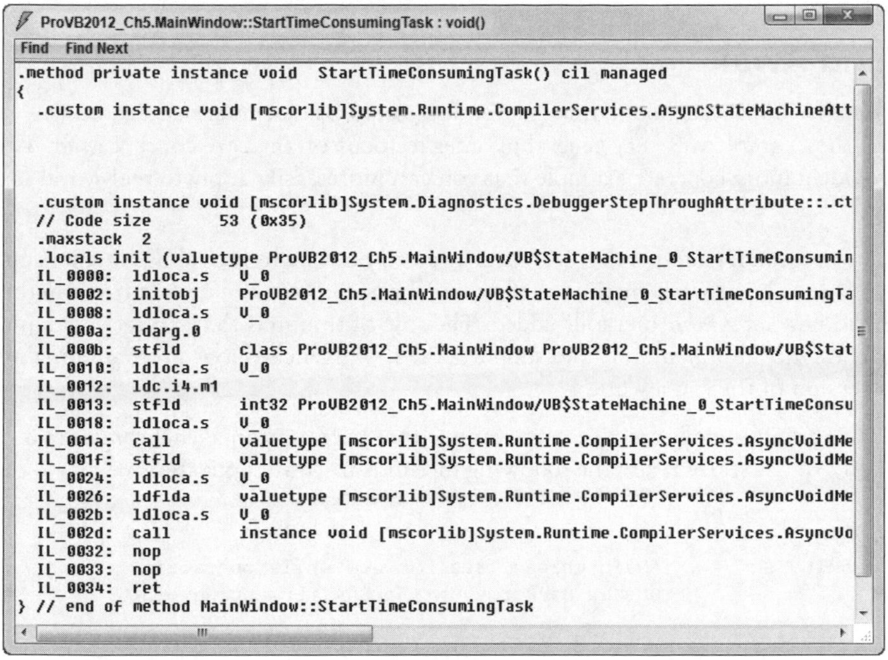

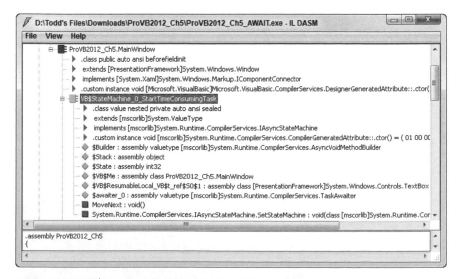

**FIGURE 5-8:** IL of StartTimeConsumingTask with Async/Await

The first thing you may notice is that the method is much shorter in this version. You may also notice the references to some object named `VB$StateMachine_0_StartTimeConsumingTask`. A closer look at this class is shown in Figure 5-9.

**FIGURE 5-9:** VB$StateMachine_0_StartTimeConsumingTask

This class is the secret behind `Async` and `Await`. The `Async` modifier told the compiler to create an anonymous class that represents the method. This class is a state machine that keeps track, using a stack, of the locations of each `Await` operator in order to allow execution to return. Most of this work is handled by the `MoveNext` method of the state machine.

## Using Async and Await

The previous section provided you enough information for you to be able to easily create asynchronous tasks, but the example was very general in order to focus on the core concept itself. This section aims to provide a more concrete example that you can more easily apply to real-world situations.

A very important thing to understand is that Microsoft wasted no time in providing internal support for `Async` and `Await`. Nearly any method that returned a `Task` has been updated, and many older classes have had new *awaitable* methods added. The rule of thumb is that if a method name ends with the word "Async" it is *awaitable* and supports the new asynchronous programming model introduced in this version of the framework.

The first thing you are going to do is create a new example that performs an asynchronous task using the old method. To get started, add the following methods to your application:

```
Public Sub OldAsyncExample()
    RetrieveSongData()
    TextBoxResult.Text += "**Main thread free for use while operation" +
                          "runs in background**" + Environment.NewLine
End Sub

Private Sub RetrieveSongData()
    Dim url As String = "http://lyrics.wikia.com/api.php?artist=Linkin" +
                        "Park&song=Lost in the echo&fmt=xml"

    TextBoxResult.Text += "Attempting to retrieve song lyrics" +
                          Environment.NewLine
    ExampleList.IsEnabled = False
    ExecuteButton.IsEnabled = False

    Using client As New WebClient
        AddHandler client.DownloadStringCompleted, _
            AddressOf DownloadStringCompletedHandler
        client.DownloadStringAsync(New Uri(url))
    End Using
End Sub

Private Sub DownloadStringCompletedHandler(sender As Object, _
            e As DownloadStringCompletedEventArgs)
    TextBoxResult.Text += e.Result
    TextBoxResult.Text += Environment.NewLine + "Completed retrieving song lyrics"
    ExampleList.IsEnabled = True
    ExecuteButton.IsEnabled = True
End Sub
```

Be sure to add the following statement at the top of the code file in order to use the `WebClient` class:

```
Imports System. Net
```

The `OldAsyncExample` method runs on the main thread and starts everything running. The `RetrieveSongData` method calls out to a freely usable rest service to retrieve song lyrics. You use the `WebClient.DownloadStringAsync` method to asynchronously get the results from calling the REST service. When the asynchronous operation has completed, it fires the `DownloadStringCompleted` event. You handle this event in order to provide the results and re-enable the UI controls.

Now add the following item to the examples lists:

```
New With {.Name = "Async and Await - Old Way", _
          .Lambda = New Action(Sub() OldAsyncExample())}
```

When the example is executed and completed, it will look like Figure 5-10.

**FIGURE 5-10:** Old methodology

This example executes asynchronously, and there is nothing wrong with it. The one main complaint to be made is that your code has been split, breaking the natural flow, in order to handle the completed event. You could alleviate this, to some extent, by using a lambda expression instead.

Since this section is on the new asynchronous programming model, you will create a new example that uses it. Start by updating your application with the following methods:

```
Public Sub AsyncAdvancedExample()
    RetrieveArtistDataAsync()
    TextBoxResult.Text += "**Main thread free for use while operation" +
                          "runs in background**" + Environment.NewLine
End Sub

Private Async Sub RetrieveArtistDataAsync()
```

```vbnet
        Dim url As String = "http://lyrics.wikia.com/api.php?artist=Linkin Park&fmt=xml"
        Using client As HttpClient = New HttpClient()
            TextBoxResult.Text += "Attempting to retrieve Linkin Park albums" +
                                Environment.NewLine
            ExampleList.IsEnabled = False
            ExecuteButton.IsEnabled = False

            Dim response As String = Await client.GetStringAsync(url)
            ProcessArtistData(response)

            TextBoxResult.Text += Environment.NewLine + "Completed retrieving albums"
            ExampleList.IsEnabled = True
            ExecuteButton.IsEnabled = True
        End Using
    End Sub
```

In order to use the `HttpClient` class you will need to add a reference to `System.Net.Http` to the project. To do this, just right-click on the name of your project (within *Solution Explorer*) and select *"Add Reference"* from the context menu. You will then need to add the following statement at the top of the code:

```vbnet
Imports System.Net
```

For starters, `RetrieveArtistDataAsync` uses the new `HttpClient` class. This class is a replacement for `WebClient` and fully supports `Async` and `Await`. The main difference between this method and `RetrieveSongData`, in the previous example, is that you use the new `GetStringAsync` method. This method runs on a background thread using `Task`, which it returns. Since it returns a `Task` it is *awaitable*.

Now add the following method, which is responsible for processing the data:

```vbnet
    Private Sub ProcessArtistData(rawXmlValue As String)
        TextBoxResult.Text += "Parsing album names from data" + Environment.NewLine

        Using sr As StringReader = New StringReader(rawXmlValue)
            Using reader As XmlReader = XmlReader.Create(sr)
                While reader.Read()
                    Select Case reader.NodeType
                        Case XmlNodeType.Element
                            Select Case reader.Name.ToLowerInvariant()
                                Case "album"
                                    TextBoxResult.Text += String.Format("{0}{1,-20}",
                                                        Environment.NewLine,
                                                        reader.ReadElementString)
                                Case "year"
                                    Dim value As String = reader.ReadElementString
                                    TextBoxResult.Text += " [" +
                                        IIf(Not (String.IsNullOrWhiteSpace(value)),
                                        value, "Not Listed") + "]"
                            End Select
                    End Select
                End While
            End Using
        End Using
```

```
    End Using

    TextBoxResult.Text += Environment.NewLine + "Complete Parsing album names"
End Sub
```

Since you make use of the StringReader and XmlReader classes, you will need to add the following import statements to your code:

```
Imports System.IO
Imports System.Xml
```

When the method runs, `ProcessArtistData` will not be called until after the `GetStringAsync` method completes. This method uses an `XmlReader` to parse the data and write it to the results text box.

> **NOTE** *You should be aware that the* `ProcessArtistData` *method runs synchronously. If the data processing was more intensive then it is in the example, it could potentially cause the main thread and the UI to block or freeze. However, you could resolve this issue by* awaiting *the* `XmlReader.ReadAsync` *method.*

To complete the updates, add the new example to the list:

```
New With {.Name = "Async and Await - Advanced", _
        .Lambda = New Action(Sub() AsyncAdvancedExample())}
```

With that updated, you can run the application and execute the new example. It will make a REST call to a service in order to retrieve album information. This operation executes on the background, allowing the application to continue running smoothly. Once the operation completes, control returns to the `RetrieveArtistDataAsync` method where the results are processed and displayed.

The final result is shown in Figure 5-11.

Since you used `Async` and `Await` in this scenario, you have retained control of the flow of the application and kept the appearance of the code clean and concise. There are no callbacks or event handlers visible. This new asynchronous programming model provides developers with a much-needed, and deserved, reprieve from the headache of traditional asynchronous development.

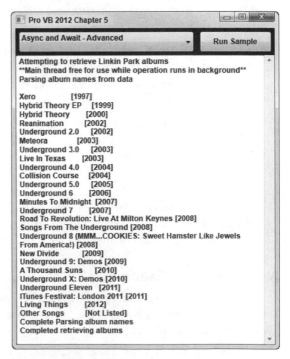

**FIGURE 5-11:** New methodology

# ITERATORS

*Iteration* refers to repeatedly performing some process. Therefore, an *iterator* is the component that allows this iteration to occur. In development terms, iterators provide a means to iterate over a collection. As discussed in Chapters 7 and 20, this is typically accomplished by using a `For Each` loop.

Most collections in the .NET framework implement the `IEnumerable` or `IEnumerable(Of T)` interface. This interface provides the `GetEnumerator` method which returns an `IEnumerator`, which performs the actual iteration for you. Again, all of this is covered in Chapters 7 and 19. The point here is that when you use a `For Each` loop and specify a collection, the compiler automatically calls the `GetEnumerator` method implemented by the class.

Providing custom or additional iterators required you to create customized classes that implemented `IEnumerator` or `IEnumerator(Of T)`. Creating enumerators required a little bit of work because you had to implement several methods that provide the iteration logic.

To help alleviate some of these issues and provide a more concise way to provide custom iterators or control the flow of your code, Microsoft created `Iterator` and `Yield`. The `Iterator` modifier and `Yield` operator were first introduced in the same CTP add-on that introduced `Async` and `Await`. They are now part of version 4.5 of the .NET framework.

## The Core Concept

It will quickly become apparent why Microsoft released both `Async`/`Await` and `Iterator`/`Yield` at the same time for both the Visual Studio 2010 update and the .NET 4.5 framework. They actually share much of the same code base and behave in a very similar fashion. `Iterator` is to `Async` as `Yield` is to `Await`.

The `Iterator` modifier can be applied to either a function or a `Get` accessor that returns an `IEnumerable`, `IEnumerbale(Of T)`, `IEnumerator`, or `IEnumerator(Of T)`. Once applied, it instructs the compile that the target is an iterator which allows a `For Each` operation to be performed against it.

Now you need some way to return the data back to the `For Each` loop that initially called it. This is accomplished using the `Yield` statement. The `Yield` operator is always followed by the data to be *yielded* and looks like this:

```
Yield "My Data"
```

Similar to how `Await` works, once the compiler hits the `Yield` statement, the *yielded* value is returned to the calling iterator loop. During the next iteration of the loop, control returns back to the iterator method at the line following the previous `Yield`.

### A Basic Iterator Example

In order to make the concepts discussed previously make more sense, you will create a new example that demonstrates them. Start by adding the following code to the application (code file: `MainWindow.xaml.vb`):

```
Public Sub IteratorBasicExample1()
    For Each value As String In HelloWorld()
```

```
            TextBoxResult.Text += value + " "
        Next
    End Sub

    Private Iterator Function HelloWorld() As IEnumerable(Of String)
        Yield "Hello"
        Yield "World"
    End Function
```

The `IteratorBasicExample1` method contains a `For Each` loop that iterators over the `HelloWorld` method. `For Each` can be used on this method, because it is marked with the `Iterator` modifier.

The `HelloWorld` contains only two `Yield` statements. The first yields the value "Hello" while the second yields "World." The way this works is that during the first iteration, "Hello" is returned back to the `IteratorBasicExample1` method and written to your text box. During the next iteration, `HelloWorld` is called again, but this time "World" is returned.

Behind the scenes, the compiler handles a method marked with `Iterator` in the same fashion that it handles one marked with `Async`. It creates an anonymous state machine class based on the method. Additional details on this were provided under the `Async` and `Await` section of this chapter.

As you should be accustomed to by now, you need to add the example to the list in order to run it. The line to add is:

```
New With {.Name = "Iterators - The Basics", _
            .Lambda = New Action(Sub() IteratorBasicExample1())}
```

Executing the application should provide you results similar to those in Figure 5-12.

**FIGURE 5-12:** Basic Iterator example

## An Advanced Iterator Example

The previous example touched only on the very basics. This example will go a little deeper into the same concepts and cover a few extra points. For this example, you will need the `Oceans` class.

Create this class now by creating a new class file and updating it with the following (code file: `Oceans.vb`):

```vb
Public Class Oceans
    Implements IEnumerable

    Dim oceans As List(Of String) = New List(Of String) From {"Pacific",
        "Atlantic", "Indian", "Southern", "Arctic"}
    Public ReadOnly Iterator Property WorldOceans As IEnumerable(Of String)
        Get
            For Each ocean In oceans
                Yield ocean
            Next
        End Get
    End Property

    Public Iterator Function GetEnumerator() As IEnumerator _
        Implements IEnumerable.GetEnumerator

        For Each ocean In oceans
            Yield ocean
        Next
    End Function
End Class
```

This class is a very simple class that just returns a list of oceans stored in an internal collection. The first iterator available is the `WorldOceans` property. The first new thing you will learn is that `Yield` statements work just fine inside a loop. The second is that `Get` accessors work as iterators in the same way as functions do.

The second iterator will be discussed in a moment; for now you need to add the following code to the main application (code file: `MainWindow.xaml.vb`):

```vb
Public Sub IteratorBasicExample2()
    Dim oceans As Oceans = New Oceans()

    TextBoxResult.Text = "Oceans from property:  " + Environment.NewLine
    For Each value As String In oceans.WorldOceans
        TextBoxResult.Text += value + " "
    Next
    TextBoxResult.Text += Environment.NewLine

    TextBoxResult.Text += "Oceans from GetEnumerator:  " + Environment.NewLine
    For Each value As String In oceans
        TextBoxResult.Text += value + " "
    Next
End Sub
```

Initially, an instance of your `Ocean` class is created. The next part of the code iterates over the `Ocean.WorldOceans` property, writing each returned value to the results text box.

In the second part of the method, you iterate over the object itself. You can do this because the object implements IEnumerable. As mentioned previously, the compiler will automatically call the GetEnumerator method in this situation.

Now look back at the GetEnumerator method that you created in the Ocean class. Since it is marked with the Iterator modifier, the compiler has been kind enough to implement all the underlying IEnumerator methods for you. This saves you the headache of having to do it

Again, you are just writing the returned values to the results text box. However, before you can run the example, you need to add this item to the exampleList collection:

```
New With {.Name = "Iterators - Oceans example", _
          .Lambda = New Action(Sub() IteratorBasicExample2())}
```

The final results of executing the example are shown in Figure 5-13.

**FIGURE 5-13:** Oceans example

## Using Iterators

The examples provided in the previous section may not seem very practical because they are focused on the core concepts themselves. They also did not touch on the most powerful feature of iterators, which is the ability to customize the iterator itself.

In order to really see this in action, you are going to create another example. Start by adding the following code to your application (code file: MainWindow.xaml.vb):

```
Private Iterator Function Primes(max As Integer) As IEnumerable(Of Long)
    Dim isPrime As Boolean = False
```

```
        For i As Integer = 2 To max
            isPrime = False

            ' We know 2 is a prime and we handle it now since
            ' we are going to rule out all other even numbers
            If i = 2 Then
                Yield i
                Continue For
            End If

            ' We don't care about even numbers (except 2)
            If i Mod 2 = 0 Then
                Continue For
            End If

            isPrime = True
            For j As Integer = 2 To CLng(Math.Sqrt(i))
                ' Check if current value is divisible by something
                ' other than 1 and itself
                If i Mod j = 0 Then
                    isPrime = False
                    Exit For
                End If
            Next

            If isPrime Then Yield i
        Next
    End Function
```

You marked the method with the `Iterator` modifier, so you know you can use `For Each` over it. You can also see several `Yield` statements. Basically, a `Yield` statement will be executed only if the value in question is a prime.

Without the use of iterators you would have had to perform the calculation and store each prime internal, returning a collection at the end. In this case you get each prime as it is discovered.

To use the new iterator, you need to add the following small method to the application (code file: `MainWindow.xaml.vb`):

```
    Public Sub IteratorAdvancedExample()
        For Each value As Long In Primes(100)
            TextBoxResult.Text += value.ToString() + Environment.NewLine
        Next
    End Sub
```

This method iterates over the results return by the `Primes` method. You provided the number `100` to the method, so all prime numbers between 2 and 100 will be returned.

Add the following item to the example list in order to be able to run it:

```
    New With {.Name = "Iterators - Primes example", _
            .Lambda = New Action(Sub() IteratorAdvancedExample())}
```

Running the application will product results similar to those seen in Figure 5-14.

**FIGURE 5-14:** Primes example

## SUMMARY

The purpose of this chapter was to provide you with additional weapons for your utility belt. It aimed to provide you additional insight into lambda expressions as well as the new asynchronous programming model and iterators.

You learned what lambda expressions are and how you can use them to provide cleaner and more efficient code. You also learned how they can be beneficial for use as event handlers and when working with LINQ.

The new and highly anticipated asynchronous programming model, lead by `Async` and `Await`, was also introduced. You experimented and explored how this new model could be used to quickly and easily develop asynchronous applications and cleaner code without the usual headache. Asynchronous programming no longer needs to be scary.

The chapter concluded by diving into iterators. While iterating over a collection is not new, you have now learned how iterators can allow you to make the process less cumbersome as well and more customizable.

You should have also learned how each of the topics covered by this chapter could easily reach into any of the other chapters and influence them in some manner. These features have endless uses, so feel free to experiment with them.

Anytime you write code you are inevitably going to be confronted with an error or some unforeseen results. The next chapter provides you information on how to appropriately handle errors and steps for debugging your application.

# Exception Handling and Debugging

- ➤ The general principles behind exception handling
- ➤ The Try...Catch...Finally structure for trapping exceptions
- ➤ How to send exceptions to other code using the Throw statement
- ➤ Obtaining information about an exception by using the exception object's methods and properties
- ➤ Event logging and simple tracing, and how you can use these methods to obtain feedback about how your program is working

## WROX.COM CODE DOWNLOADS FOR THIS CHAPTER

The wrox.com code downloads for this chapter are found at www.wrox.com/remtitle .cgi?isbn=9781118314456 on the Download Code tab. The code file name is MainWindow .xaml.vb and is located in the chapter 6 folder.

Production quality applications need to handle unexpected conditions. In .NET this is done with the structured exception syntax. When an unexpected condition arises .NET does not generate error codes. Instead when an unexpected condition occurs, the CLR creates a special object called an *exception*. This object contains properties and methods that describe the unexpected condition in detail and provide various items of useful information about what went wrong.

This chapter covers how structured exception handling works in Visual Basic. It discusses the common language runtime (CLR) exception handler in detail and illustrates some programming methods that are efficient when catching exceptions.

# SYSTEM.EXCEPTION

.NET generates an *exception object* any time an unexpected condition is encountered. This enables a comprehensive, consistent approach to handling such conditions in any type of .NET module.

An exception object is an instance of a class that derives from a class named `System.Exception`. A variety of subclasses of `System.Exception` are available for different circumstances. These subclasses allow condition-specific information about the exception to be exposed.

The base `Exception` class has properties that contain useful information about typical exceptions, as shown in Tables 6-1 and 6-2.

**TABLE 6-1:** Exception Class Properties

| PROPERTY | DESCRIPTION |
| --- | --- |
| HelpLink | A string indicating the link to help for this exception. |
| InnerException | Returns the exception object reference to an inner (nested) exception. |
| Message | A string that contains a description of the error, suitable for displaying to users. |
| Source | The name of the object that generated the error. |
| StackTrace | A read-only property. The stack trace is a list of the method calls at the point at which the exception was detected. That is, if MethodA called MethodB, and an exception occurred in MethodB, then the stack trace would contain both MethodA and MethodB. |
| TargetSite | A read-only string property that holds the method that threw the exception. |

**TABLE 6-2:** Exception Class Methods

| METHOD | DESCRIPTION |
| --- | --- |
| GetBaseException | Returns the first exception in the chain |
| ToString | Returns the error string, which might include as much information as the error message, the inner exceptions, and the stack trace, depending on the error |

There are many types of exception objects in the .NET Framework that derive from the base `Exception` class. Each is customized for a particular type of exception. For example, if a divide by zero is done in code, then an `OverflowException` is generated.

Special-purpose exception classes can be found in many namespaces. It is common for an exception class to reside in a namespace with the classes that typically generate the exception. For example, the `DataException` class is in `System.Data`, with the ADO.NET components that often generate a `DataException` instance.

In addition to the dozens of exception types available in the .NET Framework, you can create your own classes that inherit from `ApplicationException`. This allows you to add custom properties and methods for passing key data related to unexpected events within your application. Of course the next step is to understand how you will reference this class within your applications.

# HANDLING EXCEPTIONS

Structured exception handling is based around the idea that while exceptions should be used for unexpected conditions, they can be built within your application structure. Some older languages would allow for generic error handling that didn't exist within a defined set of boundaries. However, professional developers learned long ago that even unexpected conditions should be definable within your application structure.

To allow for this you may have what is known as a last-chance error handler at the topmost level of your application; however, most error handling is structured within individual modules. Within Visual Basic error handling depends on four keywords. Three of these are associated with properly identifying and handling exceptions, while the fourth is used when you wish to signal that an unexpected condition has occurred.

1. `Try`—Begins a section of code in which an exception might be generated from a code error. This section of code is often called a `Try` block. It is always used with one or more exception handlers.

2. `Catch`—Creates a standard exception handler for a type of exception. One or more `Catch` code blocks follow a `Try` block. Each `Catch` block must catch a different exception type. When an exception is encountered in the `Try` block, the first `Catch` block that matches that type of exception receives control. Can be omitted when a `Finally` block is used.

3. `Finally`—A handler that is always run as part of your structured exception handling. Contains code that runs when the `Try` block finishes normally, or when a `Catch` block receives control and then finishes. That is, the code in the `Finally` block always runs, regardless of whether an exception was detected. Typically, the `Finally` block is used to close or dispose of any resources, such as database connections, that might have been left unresolved by the code that had a problem.

4. `Throw`—Generates an exception. It can be done in a `Catch` block when an exception should be elevated to the calling method. Often exceptions become nexted. Can also be called in a routine that has itself detected an error, such as a bad argument passed in. For example, one common place to throw an exception is after a test on the arguments passed to a method or property. If a method discovers that an argument is missing or not valid and processing should not continue, an error can be thrown to the calling method.

The next section of the chapter covers the keywords in detail and includes code samples of the keywords in action. All the code in this section is included in the code download for this chapter.

## Try, Catch, and Finally

Now is a good time to build an example of some typical, simple structured exception-handling code in Visual Basic. In this case, the most likely source of an error will be a division by 0 error.

To keep from starting from scratch, you can take the sample WPF application from Chapter 1 and use it as a baseline framework. Similar to Chapter 1, individual modules (functions) can be created, which are then called from the default button handler. For the purposes of this chapter, the application will have the name ProVB_Ch06.

Start with the following code snippet, the iItems argument. If it has a value of zero, then this would lead to dividing by zero, which would generate an exception.

```
Private Function IntegerDivide(iItems As Integer, iTotal As Integer) As String
    Dim result As String
    ' Code that might throw an exception is wrapped in a Try block
    Try
        ' This will cause an exception to be thrown if iItems = 0
        result = iTotal \ iItems
    Catch ex As Exception
        ' If the calculation failed, you get here
        result = "Generic exception caught" & ex.Message
    End Try
    Return result
End Function
```

This code traps all exceptions using the generic type Exception, and doesn't include any Finally logic. Before running the program keep, in mind you'll be able to follow the sequence better if you place a breakpoint at the top of the IntegerDivide function and step through the lines. If you pass the value 0 in the first parameter you'll see you get a divide by zero exception. The message is returned.

The next code snippet illustrates a more complex example that handles the divide-by-zero exception explicitly. This code contains a separate Catch block for each type of handled exception. If an exception is generated, then .NET will progress through the Catch blocks looking for a matching exception type. This code helps illustrate that Catch blocks should be arranged with specific types first.

The IntegerDivide2 method also includes a Finally block. This block is always called and is meant to handle releasing key system resources like open files on the operating system, database connections, or other operating-system-level resources that are limited in availability.

```
Private Function IntegerDivide2(iItems As Integer, iTotal As Integer) As String
    Dim result As String
    ' Code that might throw an exception is wrapped in a Try block
    Try
        ' This will cause an exception to be thrown if iItems = 0
        result = iTotal \ iItems
    Catch ex As DivideByZeroException
        ' You'll get here with a DivideByZeroException in the Try block
        result = "Divide by zero exception caught: " & ex.Message
    Catch ex As Exception
        ' If the calculation failed, you get here
        result = "Generic exception caught: " & ex.Message
    Finally
        MessageBox.Show(
          "Always close file system handles and database connections.")
    End Try
    Return result
End Function
```

Keep in mind when you run this code that the event handler will display the message box prior to updating the main display.

# The Throw Keyword

Sometimes a `Catch` block isn't meant to fully handle an error. Some exceptions should be "sent back up the line" to the calling code. In some cases this allows the problem to be visible to the correct code to handle and possibly even log it. A `Throw` statement can be used to look for the next higher error handler without fully handling an error.

When used in a catch block the `Throw` statement ends execution of the exception handler—that is, no more code in the `Catch` block after the `Throw` statement is executed. However, `Throw` does not prevent code in the `Finally` block from running. That code still runs before the exception is kicked back to the calling routine.

Note when rethrowing an exception you have two alternatives, the first is to simply take the exception you've handled and literally throw it again. The second is to create a new exception, add your own information to that exception, and assign the original exception as an inner exception. In this way you can add additional information to the original exception to indicate where it was rethrown from.

`Throw` can also be used with exceptions that are created on the fly. For example, you might want your earlier function to generate an `ArgumentException`, as you can consider a value of `iItems` of zero to be an invalid value for that argument.

In such a case, a new exception must be instantiated. The constructor allows you to place your own custom message into the exception. The following code snippet illustrates all of the methods discussed related to throwing exceptions. This includes detecting and throwing your own exception as well as how to rethrow a previously occurring exception.

```
Private Function IntegerDivide3(iItems As Integer, iTotal As Integer) As String
    If iItems = 0 Then
        Dim argException = New _
            ArgumentException("Number of items cannot be zero")
        Throw argException
    End If
    Dim result As String
    ' Code that might throw an exception is wrapped in a Try block
    Try
        ' This will cause an exception to be thrown if iItems = 0
        result = iTotal \ iItems
    Catch ex As DivideByZeroException
        ' You'll get here with a DivideByZeroException in the Try block
        result = "Divide by zero exception caught: " & ex.Message
        Throw ex
    Catch ex As Exception
        ' If the calculation failed, you get here
        result = "Generic exception caught: " & ex.Message
        Dim myException = New Exception("IntegerDivide3: Generic Exception", ex)
        Throw myException
    Finally
        MessageBox.Show("Always close file system handles and database
```

```
connections.")
    End Try
    Return result
End Function
```

Error handling is particularly well suited to dealing with problems detected in property procedures. Property Set logic often includes a check to ensure that the property is about to be assigned a valid value. If not, then throwing a new ArgumentException (instead of assigning the property value) is a good way to inform the calling code about the problem.

## The Exit Try Statement

The Exit Try statement will, under a given circumstance, break out of the Try or Catch block and continue at the Finally block. In the following example, you exit a Catch block if the value of iItems is 0, because you know that your error was caused by that problem:

```
Private Function IntegerDivide4(iItems As Integer, iTotal As Integer) As String
    Dim result As String
    ' Code that might throw an exception is wrapped in a Try block
    Try
        ' This will cause an exception to be thrown if iItems = 0
        result = iTotal \ iItems
    Catch ex As DivideByZeroException
        ' You'll get here with a DivideByZeroException in the Try block
        result = "Divide by zero exception caught: " & ex.Message
        ' You'll get here with a DivideByZeroException in the Try block.
        If iItems = 0 Then
            Return 0
            Exit Try
        Else
            Throw ex
        End If
    Catch ex As Exception
        ' If the calculation failed, you get here
        result = "Generic exception caught: " & ex.Message
        Dim myException = New Exception("IntegerDivide3: Generic Exception",
                            ex)
        Throw myException

    Finally
        MessageBox.Show(
            "Always close file system handles and database connections.")
    End Try
    Return result
End Function
```

In your first Catch block, you have inserted an If block so that you can exit the block given a certain condition (in this case, if the overflow exception was caused because the value of iItems was 0). The Exit Try goes immediately to the Finally block and completes the processing there.

Now, if the overflow exception is caused by something other than division by zero, you'll get a message box displaying "Error not caused by iItems."

> **NOTE** *The best practice is to not have an exception you don't need. These examples have worked with a division-by-zero error, which can be avoided. Avoiding errors is always best practice.*

A Catch block can be empty. In that case, the exception is ignored. Also remember, exception handlers don't resume execution with the line after the line that generated the error. Once an error occurs, execution resumes either the Finally block or the line after the End Try if no Finally block exists.

Sometimes particular lines in a Try block may need special exception processing. Moreover, errors can occur within the Catch portion of the Try structures and cause further exceptions to be thrown. For both of these scenarios, nested Try structures are available.

When you need code to resume after a given line of code, or if you are doing something that may throw an error within a catch block, you'll want a nested structured error handler. As the name implies, because these handlers are structured it is possible to nest the structures within any other.

## Using Exception Properties

The preceding examples have all leveraged the Message property of the exception class. When reporting an error, either to a display such as a message box or to a log entry, describing an exception should provide as much information as possible concerning the problem.

### The Message Property

Because in most cases the output hasn't been the focus of the discussion on structured error handling, you haven't seen many screenshots of the output. Returning to the original example, which displayed an error message, you know that the display using the message property looks similar to what is seen in Figure 6-1.

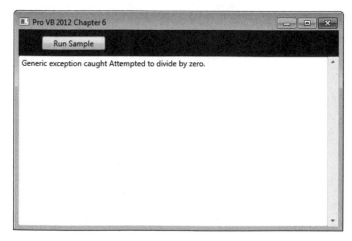

**FIGURE 6-1:** Displaying the message property

This is a reasonable error message that explains what happened without providing too much detail. While a professional would normally adjust the wording of this message, if this message was presented to a user it wouldn't cause too much of a problem.

On the other hand one of the most brutal ways to get information about an exception is to use the ToString method of the exception. Suppose that you modify the earlier example of IntegerDivide to change the displayed information about the exception, such as using ToString as follows:

```
Private Function IntegerDivide5(iItems As Integer, iTotal As Integer) As String
        Dim result As String
        ' Code that might throw an exception is wrapped in a Try block
        Try
            ' This will cause an exception to be thrown if iItems = 0
            result = iTotal \ iItems
        Catch ex As Exception
            ' If the calculation failed, you get here
            result = ex.ToString
        End Try
        Return result
End Function
```

The message shown in Figure 6-2 is helpful to a developer because it contains a lot of information, but it's not something you would typically want users to see. Instead, a user normally needs to see a short description of the problem. For the user, a message that looks like string in the Message property is appropriate. On the other hand, what the ToString method returns is, in fact, the concatenation of two properties: the message and the stack trace.

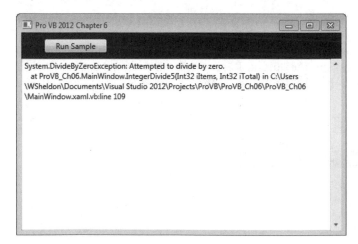

**FIGURE 6-2:** Displaying the default string property of an exception

## Source and StackTrace

The Source and StackTrace properties provide information regarding where an error occurred. This supplemental information can be useful. In the case of the Source property, the text returns the name of the assembly where the error occurred. You can test this by replacing the `ToString` method in `IntegerDivide5` with the `Source` property and rerunning the test.

The `StackTrace` is typically seen as more useful. This property not only returns information about the method where the error occurred, but returns information about the full set of methods used to reach the point where the error occurred. As noted, Figure 6-2 includes a sample of what is returned when you review this property.

## The InnerException

The `InnerException` property is used to store an exception trail. This comes in handy when multiple exceptions occur. It's quite common for an exception to occur that sets up circumstances whereby further exceptions are raised. As exceptions occur in a sequence, you can choose to stack them for later reference by use of the `InnerException` property of your `Exception` object. As each exception joins the stack, the previous `Exception` object becomes the inner exception in the stack.

For simplicity, we're going to copy the current `IntegerDivide5` method to create an inner exception handler in a new method `IntegerDivide6`. In this exception handler, when the divide by zero error occurs, create a new exception, passing the original exception as part of the constructor. Then in the outer exception handler, unwind your two exceptions displaying both messages.

The following code snippet illustrates the new method `IntegerDivide6`, and the results of running this new method are shown in Figure 6-3.

```
Private Function IntegerDivide6(iItems As Integer, iTotal As Integer) As String
    Dim result As String
    ' Code that might throw an exception is wrapped in a Try block
    Try
        Try
            ' This will cause an exception to be thrown if iItems = 0
            result = iTotal \ iItems
        Catch ex As Exception
            Dim myException = New Exception(
                            "IntegerDivide6: My Generic Exception",
                            ex)
            Throw myException
        End Try
        Return result
    Catch ex As Exception
        ' If the calculation failed, you get here
        result = "Outer Exception: " & ex.Message & vbCrLf
        result += "Inner Exception: " & ex.InnerException.Message
    End Try
    Return result
End Function
```

Figure 6-3 shows your custom message as the outer exception. Then the `InnerException` is referenced and the original error message, the divide-by-zero exception, is displayed.

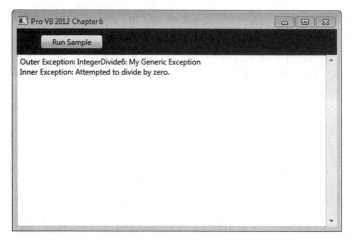

**FIGURE 6-3:** Displaying the inner and outer exception messages

## GetBaseException

The GetBaseException method comes in very handy when you are deep in a set of thrown exceptions. This method returns the originating exception by recursively examining the InnerException until it reaches an exception object that has a null InnerException property. That exception is normally the exception that started the chain of unanticipated events.

To illustrate this, modify the code in IntegerDivide6 and replace the original Outer and Inner exception messages with a single line of code as shown in the following code snippet:

```
'result = "Outer Exception: " & ex.Message & vbCrLf
'result += "Inner Exception: " & ex.InnerException.Message
result = "Base Exception: " & ex.GetBaseException.Message
```

As shown in Figure 6-4 the code traverses back to the original exception and displays only that message.

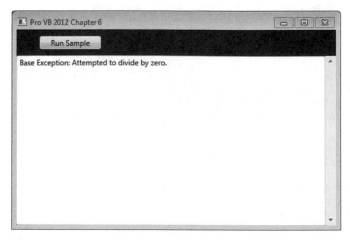

**FIGURE 6-4:** Displaying the innermost exception message

## HelpLink

The `HelpLink` property gets or sets the help link for a specific `Exception` object. It can be set to any string value, but it's typically set to a URL. If you create your own exception in code, you might want to set `HelpLink` to a URL (or a URN) describing the error in more detail. Then the code that catches the exception can go to that link. You could create and throw your own custom application exception with code like the following:

```
Dim ex As New ApplicationException("A short description of the problem")
ex.HelpLink = "http://mysite.com/somehtmlfile.htm"
Throw ex
```

When trapping an exception, the `HelpLink` can be used with something like `Process.Start` to start Internet Explorer using the help link to take the user directly to a help page, where they can see details about the problem.

# LOGGING ERRORS

Capturing error information is important for troubleshooting. Not only is it common for a user to forget details related to what error they received and how they got there, but if you've handled the error and replaced the default error message, the real error probably isn't even visible. Logging errors enables you to get the specific error message without re-creating the error or needing to provide details that are visible to an end user.

While error logging is very important, you only want to use it to trap specific levels of errors, because it carries overhead and can reduce the performance of your application. Your goal should be to log errors that are critical to your application's integrity—for instance, an error that would cause the data that the application is working with to become invalid.

There are three main approaches to error logging:

1. Write error information in a text file or flat file located in a strategic location.

2. Write error information to a central database.

3. Write error information to the system's Event Logs, which are available on all versions of Windows supported by the .NET Framework 4 or later. The .NET Framework includes a component that can be used to write to and read from the System, Application, and Security Logs on any given machine.

The type of logging you choose depends on the categories of errors you wish to trap and the types of machines on which you will run your application. If you choose to write to an Event Log, then you'll need to categorize the errors and write them in the appropriate log file. Resource-, hardware-, and system-level errors fit best into the System Event Log. Data-access errors fit best into the Application Event Log. Permission errors fit best into the Security Event Log.

## The Event Log

Three Windows Event Logs are commonly available: the System, Application, and Security Logs. Events in these logs can be viewed using the Event Viewer, which is accessed from the Control Panel.

Access Administrative Tools and then select the Event Viewer subsection to view events. Typically, your applications would use the Application Event Log.

Note that if you are creating a Windows RT application it is likely that your application will not have permission to write to the event log. Before you lament this fact, keep in mind that this is also true if you are working with an ASP.NET application. In both cases you will find that you are running in an account that does not have default permission to write to an event log.

Event logging, when available, can be found through the `EventLog` object. This object can both read and write to all of the available logs on a machine. The `EventLog` object is part of the `System.Diagnostics` namespace. This component allows adding and removing custom Event Logs, reading and writing to and from the standard Windows Event Logs, and creating customized Event Log entries.

Event Logs can become full, as they have a limited amount of space, so you only want to write critical information to your Event Logs. You can customize each of your system Event Log's properties by changing the log size and specifying how the system will handle events that occur when the log is full. You can configure the log to overwrite data when it is full or overwrite all events older than a given number of days. Remember that the Event Log that is written to is based on where the code is running from, so if there are many tiers, then you must locate the proper Event Log information to research the error further.

There are five types of Event Log entries you can make. These five types are divided into event-type entries and audit-type entries.

Event type entries are as follows:

➤ **Information**—Added when events such as a service starting or stopping occurs

➤ **Warning**—Occurs when a noncritical event happens that might cause future problems, such as disk space getting low

➤ **Error**—Should be logged when something occurs that prevents normal processing, such as a startup service not being able to start

Audit-type entries usually go into the Security Log and can be either of the following:

➤ **Audit Success**—For example, a success audit might be a successful login through an application to an SQL Server.

➤ **Audit Failure**—A failure audit might come in handy if a user doesn't have access to create an output file on a certain file system.

If you don't specify the type of Event Log entry, an information-type entry is generated.

Each entry in an Event Log has a `Source` property. This required property is a programmer-defined string that is assigned to an event to help categorize the events in a log. A new source must be defined prior to being used in an entry in an Event Log. The `SourceExists` method is used to determine whether a particular source already exists on the given computer. Use a string that is relevant to where the error originated, such as the component's name. Packaged software often uses the software name as the source in the Application Log. This helps group errors that occur by specific software package.

> **NOTE** *Certain security rights must be obtained in order to manipulate Event Logs. Application programs can access the event log based on the permissions under which the application is running. The ability to read and write to Event Logs is privileged.*

The following code snippet is a simple example of how to create and use an `EventLog` object to record errors that occur within your application. Note that it looks for a way to put messages into a custom event log, which typically would carry the application's name.

```
Sub LoggingExample1()
   Dim objLog As New EventLog()
   Dim objLogEntryType As EventLogEntryType
   Try
      Throw (New EntryPointNotFoundException())
   Catch objA As System.EntryPointNotFoundException
      If Not EventLog.SourceExists("VB2012") Then
         EventLog.CreateEventSource("VB2012", "System")
      End If
      objLog.Source = "Example"
      objLog.Log = "System"
      objLogEntryType = EventLogEntryType.Information
      objLog.WriteEntry("Error: " & objA.Message, objLogEntryType)
   End Try
End Sub
```

This code declares two variables: one to instantiate your log and one to hold your entry's type information. Note the code checks for the existence of a target log, and if not found creates it prior to attempting to log to it. If you attempt to write to a source that does not exist in a specific log, then you get an error.

After you have verified or created your source, you can set the `Source` property of the `EventLog` object, set the `Log` property to specify which log you want to write to, and set `EventLogEntryType` to `Information`. After you have set these three properties of the `EventLog` object, you can then write your entry. In this example, you concatenated the word `Error` with the actual exception's `Message` property to form the string to write to the log.

## Using the Trace and Debug Objects

As an alternative to the event log, you can write your debugging and error information to files. Trace files are also a good way to supplement your event logging if you want to track detailed information that would potentially fill the Event Log, or diagnosis of a problem requires analysis of a specific sequence of execution events. Just as important in an enterprise environment, you can arrange to either retrieve or email such files so that you can be notified when application issues occur.

This section will be leveraging the `Debug` and `Trace` shared objects that are available during your application's run time. Note that Windows applications and ASP.NET applications reference these objects in very different manners. This chapter will focus on using the `Trace` and `Debug` listeners.

The difference between the `Trace` and `Debug` objects relates to runtime availability. When you compile your application for debugging, both `Trace` and `Debug` object references are included in your executable. However, when you target your application for a release build, the compiler automatically omits any references to the `Debug` class. As a result you can create custom logging for use while developing your application, which is automatically removed when you are ready to deploy.

The `Debug` and `Trace` classes have the same methods and properties. For simplicity this chapter will simply refer to either the `Debug` or `Trace` class, even though in most cases the information provided is equally applicable to both the `Trace` and `Debug` classes.

The `Trace` class is interfaced with the `streamwriter` and other output objects by encapsulating them within listener objects. The job of any listener object is to collect, store, and send the stored output to text files, logs, and the Output window. In the example, you will use the `TextWriterTraceListener` class.

Trace listeners are output targets and can be a `TextWriter` or an `EventLog`, or can send output to the default Output window (which is `DefaultTraceListener`). The `TextWriterTraceListener` accommodates the `WriteLine` method of a `Debug` object by providing an output object that stores information to be flushed to the output stream, which you set up by the `StreamWriter` interface.

Table 6-3 lists some of the methods associated with the `Debug` object, which provides the output mechanism for the text file example to follow.

**TABLE 6-3:** Common Trace/Debug Object Methods

| METHOD | DESCRIPTION |
| --- | --- |
| `Assert` | Checks a condition and displays a message if `False` |
| `Close` | Executes a flush on the output buffer and closes all listeners |
| `Fail` | Emits an error message in the form of an Abort/Retry/Ignore message box |
| `Flush` | Flushes the output buffer and writes it to the listeners |
| `Write` | Writes bytes to the output buffer |
| `WriteLine` | Writes characters followed by a line terminator to the output buffer |
| `WriteIf` | Writes bytes to the output buffer if a specific condition is `True` |
| `WriteLineIf` | Writes characters followed by a line terminator to the output buffer if a specific condition is `True` |

The `TextWriterTraceListener` class is associated with a `StreamWriter` to output a trace file. In this case, a trace file is a text file, so you need to understand the concepts involved in writing to text files by setting up stream writers. The `StreamWriter` interface is handled through the `System.IO` namespace. It enables you to interface with the files in the file system on a given machine.

As you will see, the `StreamWriter` object opens an output path to a text file, and by binding the `StreamWriter` object to a listener object you can direct debug output to a text file. Table 6-4 lists some of the commonly used methods from the `StreamWriter` object.

**TABLE 6-4:** Common StreamWriter Methods

| METHOD | DESCRIPTION |
|---|---|
| Close | Closes the StreamWriter. |
| Flush | Flushes all content of the StreamWriter to the output file designated upon creation of the StreamWriter. |
| Write | Writes byte output to the stream. Optional parameters allow location designation in the stream (offset). |
| WriteLine | Writes characters followed by a line terminator to the current stream object. |

The following code snippet shows how you can open an existing file (called TraceResults.txt) for output and assign it to the Listeners object of the Trace object so that it can output your Trace.WriteLine statements.

```
Friend Shared LogPath As String = "TraceResults.txt"

Friend Shared Sub LogMessage(message As String)
    Dim id As Integer = Trace.Listeners.Add(New
                        TextWriterTraceListener(LogPath))
    Try
        Trace.WriteLine(Now.ToShortDateString & " @ " &
                        Now.ToShortTimeString & " , " & message)
        Trace.Listeners(id).Flush()

    Finally
        Trace.Listeners(id).Close()
        Trace.Listeners.RemoveAt(id)
    End Try
End Sub
```

Looking in detail at this code, you first see a declaration of a log path outside of the method. In a production environment, this is typically created as an application configuration setting. This allows for easy review and changes to the location of the resulting file. When no path but only a file name is used, the default behavior will create the file in the running application's default folder.

Next you see a Shared method declaration. The method is shared because there is nothing instance specific associated with it. It can live within a Module if you so desire. The key is it accepts a single parameter, which is the error message that needs to be logged.

The first step is to create a new TextWriterTraceListener and add it to the collection of listener currently associated with your Trace object. This collection can log errors to more than one listener, so if you wanted errors to also be reported to the event log, it is possible to just add multiple listeners. Note however, that because multiple listeners can be used, the final step in this method is to remove the listener which was just added.

Within the Try-Finally block that is then used to output the error, additional information that can be expanded to better classify the message time and/or location can be appended to the message. Once the output is written the buffer is flushed, the file handle is closed, and the Trace object is restored to the state it was in prior to calling this method.

Variations of this simple logging method can be used across multiple different production applications. Over the years the output recorded by such a simple function has proved invaluable in resolving "unexplained" application errors that occurred on remote client machines.

If you have been running the sample code this method was left uncommented specifically so that you could open the `TraceResults.txt` file and review all of your activity while testing the sample code that is part of this chapter.

## SUMMARY

This chapter reviewed the `Exception` object and the syntax available to work with exceptions. You have looked at the various properties of exceptions and learned how to use the exposed information. You have also seen how to promote exceptions to consuming code using the `Throw` statement.

The chapter also covered writing to Event Logs to capture information about generated exceptions. Event Logs require elevated permissions, and you should use Event Logs judiciously to avoid overloading them.

Regardless of how you capture errors, having information about exceptions captured for after-the-face analysis is an invaluable tool for diagnosis.

The chapter covered a simple technique for generating trace output for programs. By using the full capabilities for exception handling and error logging that are available in Visual Basic, you can make your applications more reliable, and diagnose problems faster when they do occur.

Now that you've covered the core elements of working in Visual Basic, you will shift to the data section. This section starts with memory data like arrays, lists, and dictionaries and then moves on to working with file and database storage.

# PART II
# Business Objects and Data Access

# 7

# Arrays, Collections, and Generics

## WHAT'S IN THIS CHAPTER?

➤ Working with arrays

➤ Iteration (looping)

➤ Working with collections

➤ Generics

➤ Nullable types

➤ Generic collections

➤ Generic methods

➤ Covariance and contravariance

## WROX.COM CODE DOWNLOADS FOR THIS CHAPTER

The wrox.com code downloads for this chapter are found at www.wrox.com/remtitle
.cgi?isbn=9781118314456 on the Download Code tab. The code is in the chapter 7 download and individually named according to the code filenames throughout the chapter.

In the beginning there were variables, and they were good. The idea that you map a location in
memory to a value was a key to tracking a value. However, most people want to work on data
as a set. Taking the concept of a variable holding a value, you've moved to the concept of a
variable that could reference an array of values. Arrays improved what developers could build,
but they weren't the end of the line.

Over time, certain patterns developed in how arrays were used. Instead of just collecting a
set of values, many have looked to use arrays to temporarily store values that were awaiting

processing, or to provide sorted collections. Each of these patterns started as a best practice for how to build and manipulate array data or to build custom structures that replicate arrays.

The computing world was very familiar with these concepts—for example, using a linked list to enable more flexibility regarding how data is sorted and retrieved. Patterns such as the stack (first in, last out) or queue (first in, first out) were in fact created as part of the original base Class Libraries. Referred to as *collections*, they provide a more robust and feature-rich way to manage sets of data than arrays can provide. These were common patterns prior to the introduction of .NET, and .NET provided an implementation for each of these collection types.

However, the common implementation of these collection classes relied on the `Object` base class. This caused two issues. The first, which is discussed in this chapter, is called *boxing*. Boxing wasn't a big deal on any given item in a collection, but it caused a slight performance hit; and as your collection grew, it had the potential to impact your application's performance. The second issue was that having collections based only on the type `Object` went against the best practice of having a strongly typed environment. As soon as you started loading items into a collection, you lost all type checking.

Solving the issues with collections based on the `Object` type is called *generics*. Originally introduced as part of .NET 2.0, generics provide a way to create collection classes that are type-safe. The type of value that will be stored in the collection is defined as part of the collection definition. Thus .NET has taken the type-safe but limited capabilities of arrays and combined them with the more powerful collection classes that were object-based to provide a set of collection classes which are type-safe.

This chapter looks at these three related ways to create sets of information. Starting with a discussion of arrays and the looping statements that process them, it next introduces collections and then moves to the use of generics, followed by a walk-through of the syntax for defining your own generic templates. Note that the sample code in this chapter is based on the ProVB2012 project created in Chapter 1. Rather than step through the creation of this project again, this chapter makes reference to it. A copy of all of the code is also available as part of the download for this book.

## ARRAYS

It is possible to declare any type as an array of that type. Because an array is a modifier of another type, the basic `Array` class is never explicitly declared for a variable's type. The `System.Array` class that serves as the base for all arrays is defined such that it cannot be created, but must be inherited. As a result, to create an `Integer` array, a set of parentheses is added to the declaration of the variable. These parentheses indicate that the system should create an array of the type specified. The parentheses used in the declaration may be empty or may contain the size of the array. An array can be defined as having a single dimension using a single index, or as having multiple dimensions by using multiple indices.

All arrays and collections in .NET start with an index of zero. However, the way an array is declared in Visual Basic varies slightly from other .NET languages such as C#. Back when the first .NET version of Visual Basic was announced, it was also announced that arrays would always begin at 0 and that they would be defined based on the number of elements in the array. In other words, Visual Basic would work the same way as the other initial .NET languages. However, in older versions of Visual Basic, it is possible to specify that an array should start at 1 by default. This meant that a lot of existing code didn't define arrays the same way.

To resolve this issue, the engineers at Microsoft decided on a compromise: All arrays in .NET begin at 0, but when an array is declared in Visual Basic, the index defines the upper limit of the array, not the number of elements. The challenge is to remember that all subscripts go from 0 to the upper bound, meaning that each array contains one more element than its upper bound.

The main result of this upper-limit declaration is that arrays defined in Visual Basic have one more entry by definition than those defined with other .NET languages. Note that it's still possible to declare an array in Visual Basic and reference it in C# or another .NET language. The following code examples illustrate five different ways to create arrays, beginning with a simple integer array as the basis for the comparison:

```
Dim arrMyIntArray1(20) as Integer
```

In the first case, the code defines an array of integers that spans from `arrMyIntArray1(0)` to `arrMyIntArray1(20)`. This is a 21-element array, because all arrays start at 0 and end with the value defined in the declaration as the upper bound.

Here is the second statement:

```
Dim arrMyIntArray2() as Integer = {1, 2, 3, 4}
```

The preceding statement creates an array with four elements numbered 0 through 3, containing the values 1 to 4.

In addition to creating arrays in one dimension it is possible to create arrays that account for multiple dimensions. Think of this as an array of arrays—where all of the contents are of the same type. Thus, in the third statement, you see an array of integers with two dimensions, a common representation of this is a grid:

```
Dim arrMyIntArray3(4,2) as Integer
```

The preceding declaration creates a multidimensional array containing five elements at the first level (or dimension). However, the second number 2 indicates that these five elements actually reference arrays of integers. In this case the second dimension for each of the first-level dimensions contains three elements. Visual Basic provides this syntax as shorthand for consistently accessing these contained arrays. Thus, for each of the items in the first dimensions, you can access a second set of elements each containing three integers.

The fourth statement which follows shows an alternative way of creating a multidimensional array:

```
Dim arrMyIntArray4( , ) as Integer = _
    { {1, 2, 3},{4, 5, 6}, {7, 8, 9},{10, 11, 12},{13, 14, 15} }
```

The literal array declaration creates a multidimensional array with five elements in the first dimension, each containing an array of three integers. The resulting array has 15 elements, but with the subscripts 0 to 4 at the first level and 0 to 2 for each second-level dimension. An excellent way to think of this is as a grid or a table with five rows and three columns. In theory you can have any number of dimensions; however, while having three dimensions isn't too difficult to conceptualize, increasing numbers of dimensions in your arrays can significantly increase complexity, and you should look for a design that limits the number of dimensions.

The fifth example demonstrates that it is possible to simply declare a variable and indicate that the variable is an array, without specifying the number of elements in the array:

```
Dim arrMyIntArray5() as Integer
```

Note that the preceding declaration is not multidimensional, it is a single-dimension array, just omitting the details for the number of elements defined. Similarly, if instead of creating arrMyIntArray5 with predefined values the goal had been to declare a two-dimensional array placeholder, the declaration would have included a comma: arrMyIntArray5(,). The usefulness of this empty declaration statement will become clearer as you look at various examples for using the preceding set of array declarations.

## Multidimensional Arrays

The definition of arrMyIntArray3 and arrMyIntArray4 are multidimensional arrays. In particular, the declaration of arrMyIntArray4 creates an array with 15 elements (five in the first dimension, each of which contains three integers) ranging from arrMyIntArray4(0,0) through arrMyIntArray4(2,1) to arrMyIntArray4(4,2). As with all elements of an array, when it is created without specific values, the value of each of these elements is created with the default value for that type. This case also demonstrates that the size of the different dimensions can vary. It is possible to nest deeper than two levels, but this should be done with care because such code is difficult to maintain.

For example, the value of arrMyIntArray4(0,1) is 2, while the value of arrMyIntArray4(3,2) is 12. The following code adds a method called SampleMD, which can be run from the ButtonTest_Click handler, and which returns the elements of this multidimensional array's contents (code file: form1.vb):

```
Private Sub SampleMD()
    Dim arrMyIntArray4(,) As Integer =
        {{1, 2, 3}, {4, 5, 6}, {7, 8, 9}, {10, 11, 12}, {13, 14, 15}}
    Dim intLoop1 As Integer
    Dim intLoop2 As Integer
    For intLoop1 = 0 To UBound(arrMyIntArray4)
        For intLoop2 = 0 To UBound(arrMyIntArray4, 2)
            TextBoxOutput.Text +=
                "{" & intLoop1 & ", " & intLoop2 & "} = " &
                arrMyIntArray4(intLoop1, intLoop2).ToString & vbCrLf
        Next
    Next
End Sub
```

When run in the Test window from Chapter 1, this results in the output shown in Figure 7-1. Note that Figure 7-1 is significantly simpler than what is in the code download. The code download includes additional samples, including an additional button which will be created later in this chapter. If you are working alongside the chapter with your own sample code, your result will be similar to what is seen in Figure 7-1.

## The UBound Function

Continuing to reference the arrays defined earlier, the declaration of arrMyIntArray2 actually defined an array that spans from arrMyIntArray2(0) to arrMyIntArray2(3). That's because when you declare an array by specifying the set of values, it still starts at 0. However, in this case you are not specifying the upper bound, but rather initializing the array with a set of values. If this set of values came from a database or other source, then the upper limit on the array might not be clear. To verify the upper bound of an array, a call can be made to the UBound function:

```
UBound(ArrMyIntArray2)
```

FIGURE 7-1: Sample output

The preceding line of code retrieves the upper bound of the first dimension of the array and returns 3. However, as noted in the preceding section, you can specify an array with several different dimensions. Thus, this old-style method of retrieving the upper bound carries the potential for an error of omission. The better way to retrieve the upper bound is to use the GetUpperBound method on your array instance. With this call, you need to tell the array which dimension's upper-bound value you want, as shown here (also returning 3):

```
ArrMyIntArray2.GetUpperBound(0)
```

This is the preferred method of obtaining an array's upper bound, because it explicitly indicates which upper bound is wanted when using multidimensional arrays, and it follows a more object-oriented approach to working with your array

The UBound function has a companion called LBound. The LBound function computes the lower bound for a given array. However, as all arrays and collections in Visual Basic are zero-based, it doesn't have much value anymore.

## The ReDim Statement

The following code considers the use of a declared but not instantiated array. Unlike an integer value, which has a default of 0, an array waits until a size is defined to allocate the memory it will use. The following example revisits the declaration of an array that has not yet been instantiated. If an attempt were made to assign a value to this array, it would trigger an exception.

```
Dim arrMyIntArray5() as Integer
' The commented statement below would compile but would cause a runtime exception.
'arrMyIntArray5(0) = 1
```

The solution to this is to use the `ReDim` keyword. Although `ReDim` was part of Visual Basic 6.0, it has changed slightly. The first change is that code must first `Dim` an instance of the variable; it is not acceptable to declare an array using the `ReDim` statement. The second change is that code cannot change the number of dimensions in an array. For example, an array with three dimensions cannot grow to an array of four dimensions, nor can it be reduced to only two dimensions.

To further extend the example code associated with arrays, consider the following, which manipulates some of the arrays previously declared:

```
Dim arrMyIntArray3(4,2) as Integer
Dim arrMyIntArray4( , ) as Integer =
    { {1, 2, 3},{4, 5, 6},{7, 8, 9},{10, 11, 12},{13, 14 , 15} }
ReDim arrMyIntArray5(2)
ReDim arrMyIntArray3(5,4)
ReDim Preserve arrMyIntArray4(UBound(arrMyIntArray4),1)
```

The `ReDim` of `arrMyIntArray5` instantiates the elements of the array so that values can be assigned to each element. The second statement redimensions the `arrMyIntArray3` variable defined earlier. Note that it is changing the size of both the first dimension and the second dimension. While it is not possible to change the number of dimensions in an array, you can resize any of an array's dimensions. This capability is required, as declarations such as `Dim arrMyIntArray6( , , ,) As Integer` are legal.

By the way, while it is possible to repeatedly `ReDim` a variable, for performance reasons this action should ideally be done only rarely, and never within a loop. If you intend to loop through a set of entries and add entries to an array, try to determine the number of entries you'll need before entering the loop, or at a minimum `ReDim` the size of your array in chunks to improve performance.

## The Preserve Keyword

The last item in the code snippet in the preceding section illustrates an additional keyword associated with redimensioning. The `Preserve` keyword indicates that the data stored in the array prior to redimensioning should be transferred to the newly created array. If this keyword is not used, then the data stored in an array is lost. Additionally, in the preceding example, the `ReDim` statement actually reduces the second dimension of the array. Although this is a perfectly legal statement, this means that even though you have specified preserving the data, the data values 3, 6, 9, 12, and 15 that were assigned in the original definition of this array will be discarded. These are lost because they were assigned in the highest index of the second array. Because `arrMyIntArray4(1,2)` is no longer valid, the value that resided at this location (6) has been lost.

Arrays continue to be very powerful in Visual Basic, but the basic `Array` class is just that, basic. It provides a powerful framework, but it does not provide a lot of other features that would enable more robust logic to be built into the array. To achieve more advanced features, such as sorting and dynamic allocation, the base `Array` class has been inherited by the classes that make up the `Collections` namespace.

## COLLECTIONS

The `Collections` namespace is part of the `System` namespace. It provides a series of classes that implement advanced array features. While the capability to make an a rray of existing types is powerful, sometimes more power is needed in the array itself. The capability to inherently sort or dynamically add dissimilar objects in an array is provided by the classes of the `Collections` namespace. This namespace contains a specialized set of objects that can be instantiated for additional features when working with a collection of similar objects. Table 7-1 defines several of the objects that are available as part of the `System.Collections` namespace.

**TABLE 7-1:** Collection Classes

| CLASS | DESCRIPTION |
| --- | --- |
| ArrayList | Implements an array whose size increases automatically as elements are added. |
| BitArray | Manages an array of Booleans that are stored as bit values. |
| Hashtable | Implements a collection of values organized by key. Sorting is done based on a hash of the key. |
| Queue | Implements a first in, first out collection. |
| SortedList | Implements a collection of values with associated keys. The values are sorted by key and are accessible by key or index. |
| Stack | Implements a last in, first out collection. |

Each of the objects listed focuses on storing a collection of objects. This means that in addition to the special capabilities each provides, it also provides one additional capability not available to objects created based on the `Array` class. Because every variable in .NET is based on the `Object` class, it is possible to have a collection that contains elements that are defined with different types. So a collection might contain an integer as its first item, a string as its second item, and a custom `Person` object as its third item. There is no guarantee of the type safety that is an implicit feature of an array.

Each of the preceding collection types stores an array of objects. All classes are of type `Object`, so a string could be stored in the same collection with an integer. It's possible within these collection classes for the actual objects being stored to be different types. Consider the following code example, which implements the `ArrayList` collection class within `Form1.vb`:

```
Private Sub SampleColl()
    Dim objMyArrList As New System.Collections.ArrayList()
    Dim objItem As Object
    Dim intLine As Integer = 1
    Dim strHello As String = "Hello"
    Dim objWorld As New System.Text.StringBuilder("World")

    ' Add an integer value to the array list.
    objMyArrList.Add(intLine)

    ' Add an instance of a string object
    objMyArrList.Add(strHello)

    ' Add a single character cast as a character.
    objMyArrList.Add(" "c)

    ' Add an object that isn't a primitive type.
```

```
        objMyArrList.Add(objWorld)

        ' To balance the string, insert a break between the line
        ' and the string "Hello", by inserting a string constant.
        objMyArrList.Insert(1, ". ")

        For Each objItem In objMyArrList
            ' Output the values on a single line.
            TextBoxOutput.Text += objItem.ToString()
        Next
        TextBoxOutput.Text += vbCrLf
        For Each objItem In objMyArrList
            ' Output the types, one per line.
            TextBoxOutput.Text += objItem.GetType.ToString() & vbCrLf
        Next
    End Sub
```

The collection classes, as this example shows, are versatile. The preceding code creates a new instance of an `ArrayList`, along with some related variables to support the demonstration. The code then shows four different types of variables being inserted into the same `ArrayList`. Next, the code inserts another value into the middle of the list. At no time has the size of the array been declared, nor has a redefinition of the array size been required. The output is shown in Figure 7-2.

**FIGURE 7-2:** Output shown when code is run

Visual Basic has additional classes available as part of the `System.Collections.Specialized` namespace. These classes tend to be oriented around a specific problem. For example, the `ListDictionary` class is designed to take advantage of the fact that although a hash table is very good at storing and retrieving a large number of items, it can be costly when it contains only a few items. Similarly, the `StringCollection` and `StringDictionary` classes are defined so that when working with strings, the time spent interpreting the type of object is reduced and overall performance is improved. Each class defined in this namespace represents a specialized implementation that has been optimized for handling special types of collections.

## Iterative Statements

The preceding examples have relied on the use of the `For...Next` statement, which has not yet been covered. Since you've now covered both arrays and collections, it's appropriate to introduce the primary commands for working with the elements contained in those variable types. Both the `For` loop and `While` loop share similar characteristics, and which should be used is often a matter of preference.

### For Each and For Next

The `For` structure in Visual Basic is the primary way of managing loops. It actually has two different formats. A standard `For Next` statement enables you to set a loop control variable that can be incremented by the `For` statement and custom exit criteria from your loop. Alternatively, if you are working with a collection in which the array items are not indexed numerically, then it is possible to use a `For Each` loop to automatically loop through all of the items in that collection. The following code shows a typical `For Next` loop that cycles through each of the items in an array:

```
For i As Integer = 0 To 10 Step 2
    arrMyIntArray1(i) = i
Next
```

The preceding example sets the value of every other array element to its index, starting with the first item, because like all .NET collections, the collection starts at 0. As a result, items 0, 2, 4, 6, 8, and 10 are set, but items 1, 3, 5, 7, and 9 are not explicitly defined, because the loop doesn't address those values. In the case of integers, they'll default to a value of 0 because an integer is a value type; however, if this were an array of strings or other reference types, then these array nodes would actually be undefined, that is, `Nothing`.

The `For Next` loop is most commonly set up to traverse an array, collection, or similar construct (for example, a data set). The control variable `i` in the preceding example must be numeric. The value can be incremented from a starting value to an ending value, which are `0` and `10`, respectively, in this example. Finally, it is possible to accept the default increment of 1; or, if desired, you can add a `Step` qualifier to your command and update the control value by a value other than 1. Note that setting the value of `Step` to `0` means that your loop will theoretically loop an infinite number of times. Best practices suggest your control value should be an integer greater than 0 and not a decimal or other floating-point number.

Visual Basic provides two additional commands that can be used within the `For` loop's block to enhance performance. The first is `Exit For`; and as you might expect, this statement causes the loop to end and not continue to the end of the processing. The other is `Continue`, which tells the loop that you are finished executing code with the current control value and that it should increment the value and reenter the loop for its next iteration:

```
For i = 1 To 100 Step 2
    If arrMyIntArray1.Count <= i Then Exit For
    If i = 5 Then Continue For
    arrMyIntArray1 (i) = i - 1
Next
```

Both the `Exit For` and `Continue` keywords were used in the preceding example. Note how each uses a format of the `If-Then` structure that places the command on the same line as the `If` statement so that no `End If` statement is required. This loop exits if the control value is larger than the number of rows defined for `arrMyIntArray1`.

Next, if the control variable `i` indicates you are looking at the sixth item in the array (index of five), then this row is to be ignored, but processing should continue within the loop. Keep in mind that even though the loop control variable starts at 1, the first element of the array is still at 0. The `Continue` statement indicates that the loop should return to the `For` statement and increment the associated control variable. Thus, the code does not process the next line for item six, where `i` equals `5`.

The preceding examples demonstrate that in most cases, because your loop is going to process a known collection, Visual Basic provides a command that encapsulates the management of the loop control variable. The `For Each` structure automates the counting process and enables you to quickly assign the current item from the collection so that you can act on it in your code. It is a common way to process all of the rows in a data set or most any other collection, and all of the loop control elements such as Continue and Exit are still available:

```
For Each item As Object In objMyArrList
    'Code A1
Next
```

## While, Do While, and Do Until

In addition to the For loop, Visual Basic includes the While and Do loops, with two different versions of the Do loop. The first is the Do While loop. With a Do While loop, your code starts by checking for a condition; and as long as that condition is true, it executes the code contained in the Do loop. Optionally, instead of starting the loop by checking the While condition, the code can enter the loop and then check the condition at the end of the loop. The Do Until loop is similar to the Do While loop:

```
Do While blnTrue = True
    'Code A1
Loop
```

The Do Until differs from the Do While only in that, by convention, the condition for a Do Until is placed after the code block, thus requiring the code in the Do block to execute once before the condition is checked. It bears repeating, however, that a Do Until block can place the Until condition with the Do statement or with the Loop statement. A Do While block can similarly have its condition at the end of the loop:

```
Do
    'Code A1
Loop Until (blnTrue = True)
```

In both cases, instead of basing the loop around an array of items or a fixed number of iterations, the loop is instead instructed to continue perpetually until a condition is met. A good use for these loops involves tasks that need to repeat for as long as your application is running. Similar to the For loop, there are Exit Do and Continue commands that end the loop or move to the next iteration, respectively. Note that parentheses are allowed but are not required for both the While and the Until conditional expression.

The other format for creating a loop is to omit the Do statement and just create a While loop. The While loop works similarly to the Do loop, with the following differences. The While loop's endpoint is an End While statement instead of a loop statement. Second, the condition must be at the start of the loop with the While statement, similar to the Do While. Finally, the While loop has an Exit While statement instead of Exit Do, although the behavior is the same. An example is shown here:

```
While blnTrue = True
    If blnFalse Then
        blnTrue = False
    End If
    If not blnTrue Then Exit While
    System.Threading.Thread.Sleep(500)
    blnFalse = True
End While
```

The `While` loop has more in common with the `For` loop, and in those situations where someone is familiar with another language such as C++ or C#, it is more likely to be used than the older `Do-Loop` syntax that is more specific to Visual Basic.

Finally, before leaving the discussion of looping, note the potential use of endless loops. Seemingly endless, or infinite, loops play a role in application development, so it's worthwhile to illustrate how you might use one. For example, if you were writing an e-mail program, you might want to check the user's mailbox on the server every 20 seconds. You could create a `Do While` or `Do Until` loop that contains the code to open a network connection and check the server for any new mail messages to download. You would continue this process until either the application was closed or you were unable to connect to the server. When the application was asked to close, the loop's `Exit` statement would execute, thus terminating the loop. Similarly, if the code were unable to connect to the server, it might exit the current loop, alert the user, and probably start a loop that would look for network connectivity on a regular basis.

> **WARNING** *One warning about endless loops: By default such loops consume endless processor resources. If you have a loop related to monitoring for a response you need to prevent this tight execution cycle. Always include a call to* `Thread.Sleep` *so that the loop only executes a single iteration within a given time frame to avoid consuming too much processor time.*

# Boxing

Normally, when a conversion (implicit or explicit) occurs, the original value is read from its current memory location, and then the new value is assigned. For example, to convert a `Short` to a `Long`, the system reads the two bytes of `Short` data and writes them to the appropriate bytes for the `Long` variable. However, under Visual Basic, if a value type needs to be managed as an object, then the system performs an intermediate step. This intermediate step involves taking the value on the stack and copying it as the referenced value of a new `object`, to the heap, a process referred to as *boxing*. In Chapter 3, in the section titled "Value and Reference Types," a distinction was made regarding how certain types were stored. As noted then, Value types are stored on the stack, while reference values are stored on the heap. As noted earlier, the `Object` class is implemented as a reference type, so the system needs to convert value types into reference types for them to be objects. This doesn't cause any problems or require any special programming, because boxing isn't something you declare or directly control, but it does affect performance.

If you're copying the data for a single value type, this is not a significant cost, but if you're processing an array that contains thousands of values, the time spent moving between a value type and a temporary reference type can be significant. Thus, if when reviewing code you find a scenario where a value is boxed, it may not be of significant concern. When it becomes something to address is if that boxing is called within a loop that is executed thousands or millions of times. When considering best practices, boxing is something to address when working with large collections and calls that are made repeatedly.

Fortunately, there are ways to limit the amount of boxing that occurs when using collections. One method that works well is to create a class based on the value type you need to work with. This might seem counterintuitive at first, because it costs more to create a class. The key is how often you reuse the data contained in the class. By repeatedly using the object to interact with other objects, you avoid creating a temporary boxed object.

Examples in two important areas will help illustrate boxing. The first involves the use of arrays. When an array is created, the portion of the class that tracks the element of the array is created as a reference object, but each element of the array is created directly. Thus, an array of integers consists of an `Array` object and a set of `Integer` value types. When you update one of the values with another integer value, no boxing is involved:

```
Dim arrInt(20) as Integer
Dim intMyValue as Integer = 1

arrInt(0) = 0
arrInt(1) = intMyValue
```

Neither of these assignments of an integer value into the integer array that was defined previously requires boxing. In each case, the array object identifies which value on the stack needs to be referenced, and the value is assigned to that value type. The point here is that just because you have referenced an object doesn't mean you are going to box a value. The boxing occurs only when the values being assigned are being transitioned from value types to reference types:

```
Dim strBldr as New System.Text.StringBuilder()
Dim mySortedList as New System.Collections.SortedList()
Dim count as Integer
For count = 1 to 100
    strBldr.Append(count)
    mySortedList.Add(count, count)
Next
```

The preceding snippet illustrates two separate calls to object interfaces. One call requires boxing of the value `intCount`, while the other does not. Nothing in the code indicates which call is which, but the `Append` method of `StringBuilder` has been overridden to include a version that accepts an integer, while the `Add` method of the `SortedList` collection expects two objects. Although the integer values can be recognized by the system as objects, doing so requires the runtime library to box these values so that they can be added to the sorted list.

When looking for boxing, the concern isn't that you are working with objects as part of an action, but that you are passing a value type to a parameter that expects an object, or you are taking an object and converting it to a value type. However, boxing does not occur when you call a method on a value type. There is no conversion to an object, so if you need to assign an integer to a string using the `ToString` method, there is no boxing of the integer value as part of the creation of the string. Conversely, you are explicitly creating a new string object, so the cost is similar.

## GENERICS

Generics refer to the technology built into the .NET Framework (introduced originally with the .NET Framework version 2.0) that enables you to define a template and then declare variables using that template. The template defines the operations that the new type can perform; and when you declare a variable based on the template, you are creating a new type. The benefit of generics over untyped collections or arrays is that a generic template makes it easier for collection types to be strongly typed. The introduction of covariance in .NET Framework 4 makes it easier to reuse the template code in different scenarios.

The primary motivation for adding generics to .NET was to enable the creation of strongly typed collection types. Because generic collection types are strongly typed, they are significantly faster than the previous inheritance-based collection model. Anywhere you presently use collection classes in your code, you should consider revising that code to use generic collection types instead.

Visual Basic 2012 allows not only the use of preexisting generics, but also the creation of your own generic templates. Because the technology to support generics was created primarily to build collection classes, it naturally follows that you might create a generic collection anytime you would otherwise build a normal collection class. More specifically, anytime you find yourself using the `Object` data type, you should instead consider using generics.

## Using Generics

There are many examples of generic templates in the .NET Base Class Library (BCL). Many of them can be found in the `System.Collections.Generic` namespace, but others are scattered through the BCL as appropriate. Many of the examples focus on generic collection types, but this is only because it is here that the performance gains, due to generics, are seen. In most cases, generics are used less for performance gains than for the strong typing benefits they provide. As noted earlier, anytime you use a collection data type, you should consider using the generic equivalent instead.

A generic is often written as something like `List(Of T)`. The type (or class) name in this case is `List`. The letter `T` is a placeholder, much like a parameter. It indicates where you must provide a specific type value to customize the generic. For instance, you might declare a variable using the `List(Of T)` generic:

```
Dim data As New List(Of Date)
```

In this case, you are specifying that the type parameter, `T`, is a `Date`. By providing this type, you are specifying that the list will contain only values of type `Date`. To make this clearer, let's contrast the new `List(Of T)` collection with the older `ArrayList` type.

When you work with an `ArrayList`, you are working with a type of collection that can store many types of values at the same time:

```
Dim data As New ArrayList()
data.Add("Hello")
data.Add(5)
data.Add(New Customer())
```

This `ArrayList` is loosely typed, internally always storing the values as type `Object`. This is very flexible but relatively slow because it is late bound. What this means is that when you determine something at runtime you are binding to that type. Of course, it offers the advantage of being able to store any data type, with the disadvantage that you have no control over what is actually stored in the collection.

The List(Of T) generic collection is quite different. It is not a type at all; it is just a template. A type is not created until you declare a variable using the template:

```
Dim data As New Generic.List(Of Integer)
data.Add(5)
data.Add(New Customer()) ' throws an exception
data.Add("Hello") ' throws an exception
```

When you declare a variable using the generic, you must provide the type of value that the new collection will hold. The result is that a new type is created—in this case, a collection that can hold only Integer values.

The important thing here is that this new collection type is strongly typed for Integer values. Not only does its external interface (its Item and Add methods, for instance) require Integer values, but its internal storage mechanism works only with type Integer. This means that it is not late bound like ArrayList, but rather is early bound. The net result is much higher performance, along with all the type-safety benefits of being strongly typed.

Generics are useful because they typically offer better performance than traditional collection classes. In some cases, they can also save you from writing code, as generic templates can provide code reuse, whereas traditional classes cannot. Finally, generics can sometimes provide better type safety compared to traditional classes, as a generic adapts to the specific type you require, whereas classes often must resort to working with a more general type such as Object.

Generics come in two forms: generic types and generic methods. For instance, List(Of T) is a generic type in that it is a template that defines a complete type or class. In contrast, some otherwise normal classes have single methods that are just method templates and that assume a specific type when they are called. You will look at both scenarios.

## Nullable Types

In addition to having the option to explicitly check for the DBNull value, Visual Basic 2005 introduced the capability to create a nullable value type. In the background, when this syntax is used, the system creates a reference type containing the same data that would be used by the value type. Your code can then check the value of the nullable type before attempting to set this into a value type variable. Nullable types are built using generics. Note that while the Visual Basic keyword for null is Nothing, it is common to discuss this type as supporting a null value even in Visual Basic.

For consistency let's take a look at how nullable types work. The key, of course, is that value types can't be set to null (aka Nothing). This is why nullable types aren't value types. The following statements show how to declare a nullable integer:

```
Dim intValue as Nullable(Of Integer)
Dim intValue2 as Integer?
```

Both intValue and intValue2 act like integer variables, but they aren't actually of type Integer. As noted, the syntax is based on generics, but essentially you have just declared an object of type Nullable and declared that this object will, in fact, hold integer data. Thus, both of the following assignment statements are valid:

```
intValue = 123
intValue = Nothing
```

However, at some point you are going to need to pass `intValue` to a method as a parameter, or set some property on an object that is looking for an object of type `Integer`. Because `intValue` is actually of type `Nullable`, it has the properties of a nullable object. The `Nullable` class has two properties of interest when you want to get the underlying value. The first is the property `value`. This represents the underlying value type associated with this object. In an ideal scenario, you would just use the `value` property of the `Nullable` object in order to assign to your actual value a type of integer and everything would work. If the `intValue.value` wasn't assigned, you would get the same value as if you had just declared a new `Integer` without assigning it a value which would be 0.

Unfortunately, that's not how the nullable type works. If the `intValue.value` property contains `Nothing` and you attempt to assign it, then it throws an exception. To avoid getting this exception, you always need to check the other property of the nullable type: `HasValue`. The `HasValue` property is a `Boolean` that indicates whether a value exists; if one does not, then you shouldn't reference the underlying value. The following code example shows how to safely use a nullable type:

```
Dim intValue as Nullable(Of Integer)
Dim intI as Integer
If intValue.HasValue Then
    intI = intValue.Value
End If
```

Of course, you could add an `Else` statement to the preceding and use either `Integer.MinValue` or `Integer.MaxValue` as an indicator that the original value was `Nothing`. The key point here is that nullable types enable you to easily work with nullable columns in your database, but you must still verify whether an actual value or null was returned.

# Generic Types

Now that you have a basic understanding of generics and how they compare to regular types, let's get into some more detail. To do this, you will make use of some other generic types provided in the .NET Framework. A generic type is a template that defines a complete class, structure, or interface. When you want to use such a generic, you declare a variable using the generic type, providing the real type (or types) to be used in creating the actual type of your variable.

## Basic Usage

First, consider the `Dictionary(Of K, T)` generic. This is much like the `List(Of T)` discussed earlier, but this generic requires that you define the types of both the key data and the values to be stored. When you declare a variable as `Dictionary(Of K, T)`, the new `Dictionary` type that is created accepts only keys of the one type and values of the other.

Add the following Sample Dictionary method to the `Form1.vb file` and call it from the `ButtonTest_Click` event handler:

```
Private Sub SampleDict()
    Dim data As New Generic.Dictionary(Of Integer, String)
    data.Add(5, "Bill")
    data.Add(1, "Johnathan")
    For Each item As KeyValuePair(Of Integer, String) In data
        TextBoxOutput.AppendText("Data: " & item.Key & ", " & _
                item.Value)
        TextBoxOutput.AppendText(Environment.NewLine)
```

```
        Next
        TextBoxOutput.AppendText(Environment.NewLine)

    End Sub
```

As you type, watch the IntelliSense information on the `Add` method. Notice how the `key` and `value` parameters are strongly typed based on the specific types provided in the declaration of the data variable. In the same code, you can create another type of `Dictionary` as follows:

```
    Private Sub SampleDict()
        Dim data As New Generic.Dictionary(Of Integer, String)
        Dim info As New Generic.Dictionary(Of Guid, Date)
        data.Add(5, "Bill")
        data.Add(1, "Johnathan")
        For Each item As KeyValuePair(Of Integer, String) In data
            TextBoxOutput.AppendText("Data: " & item.Key & ", " &
                item.Value)
            TextBoxOutput.AppendText(Environment.NewLine)
        Next
        TextBoxOutput.AppendText(Environment.NewLine)
        info.Add(Guid.NewGuid, Now)
        For Each item As KeyValuePair(Of Guid, Date) In info
            TextBoxOutput.AppendText("Info: " & item.Key.ToString &
                ", " & item.Value)
            TextBoxOutput.AppendText(Environment.NewLine)
        Next
        TextBoxOutput.AppendText(Environment.NewLine)

    End Sub
```

This code contains two completely different types. Both have the behaviors of a `Dictionary`, but they are not interchangeable because they have been created as different types.

Generic types may also be used as parameters and return types. For instance, adding the following `Function LoadData` method implements a generic return type:

```
    Private Function LoadData() As Generic.Dictionary(Of Integer, String)
      Dim data As New Generic.Dictionary(Of Integer, String)
      data.Add(5, "William")
      data.Add(1, "Johnathan")
      Return data
    End Function
```

Next, to call this method from the `ButtonTest_Click` event handler, add the following to the bottom of the `SampleDict` method:

```
    Dim results As Generic.Dictionary(Of Integer, String)
    results = LoadData()
    For Each item As KeyValuePair(Of Integer, String) In results
        TextBoxOutput.AppendText("Results: " & item.Key & ", " &
            item.Value)
        TextBoxOutput.AppendText(Environment.NewLine)
    Next
    TextBoxOutput.AppendText(Environment.NewLine)
```

The results of this method are displayed in Figure 7-3. Note that you will run this at a different time and will generate a new Globally Unique Identifier; thus your results will not exactly match what is shown.

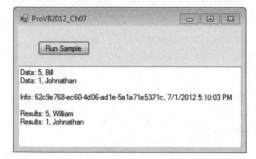

**FIGURE 7-3:** Display of output when running sample code

This works because both the return type of the function and the type of the data variable are exactly the same. Not only are they both `Generic.Dictionary` derivatives, they have exactly the same types in the declaration.

The same is true for parameters:

```
Private Sub DoWork(ByVal values As Generic.Dictionary(Of Integer, String))
   ' do work here
End Sub
```

Again, the parameter type is defined not only by the generic type, but also by the specific type values used to initialize the generic template.

## Inheritance

It is possible to inherit from a generic type as you define a new class. For instance, the .NET BCL defines the `System.ComponentModel.BindingList(Of T)` generic type. This type is used to create collections that can support data binding. You can use this as a base class to create your own strongly typed, data-bindable collection. Add new classes named `Customer` and `CustomerList` with the following:

➤   Class Customer (`Customer.vb`)

```
Public Class Customer
   Public Property Name() As String
End Class
```

➤   Class Customer List (`CustomerList.vb`)

```
Public Class CustomerList
   Inherits System.ComponentModel.BindingList(Of Customer)

   Private Sub CustomerList_AddingNew(ByVal sender As Object,
      ByVal e As System.ComponentModel.AddingNewEventArgs) Handles Me.AddingNew
      Dim cust As New Customer()
      cust.Name = "<new>"
    e.NewObject = cust
  End Sub
End Class
```

When you inherit from `BindingList(Of T)`, you must provide a specific type—in this case, `Customer`. This means that your new `CustomerList` class extends and can customize `BindingList(Of Customer)`. Here you are providing a default value for the `Name` property of any new `Customer` object added to the collection.

When you inherit from a generic type, you can employ all the normal concepts of inheritance, including overloading and overriding methods, extending the class by adding new methods, handling events, and so forth.

To see this in action, add a new `Button` control named `ButtonCustomer` to `Form1` and add a new form named `FormCustomerGrid` to the project. Add a `DataGridView` control to `FormCustomerGrid` and dock it by setting the Dock property to the Fill in the parent container option.

Next, double-click on the new button on `Form1` to generate a click event handler for the button. In the code-behind `ButtonCustomer_Click` event handler, add the following:

```
FormCustomerGrid.ShowDialog()
```

Next, customize the Form Customer Grid by adding the following behind `FormCustomerGrid`:

```
Public Class FormCustomerGrid
        Dim list As New CustomerList()
        Private Sub FormCustomerGrid_Load(ByVal sender As System.Object,
                        ByVal e As System.EventArgs) Handles MyBase.Load
            DataGridView1.DataSource = list
    End Sub
End Class
```

This code creates an instance of `CustomerList` and data-binds the list as the `DataSource` for the `DataGridView` control. When you run the program and click the button to open the `CustomerForm`, notice that the grid contains a newly added `Customer` object. As you interact with the grid, new `Customer` objects are automatically added, with a default name of `<new>`. An example is shown in Figure 7-4.

All this functionality of adding new objects and setting the default `Name` value occurs because `CustomerList` inherits from `BindingList(Of Customer)`.

**FIGURE 7-4:** Using a DataGridView control in a Windows Form

## Generic Methods

A generic method is a single method that is called not only with conventional parameters, but also with type information that defines the method. Generic methods are far less common than generic types. Due to the extra syntax required to call a generic method, they are also less readable than a normal method.

A generic method may exist in any class or module; it does not need to be contained within a generic type. The primary benefit of a generic method is avoiding the use of `CType` or `DirectCast` to convert parameters or return values between different types.

It is important to realize that the type conversion still occurs. Generics merely provide an alternative mechanism to use instead of CType or DirectCast.

Without generics, code often uses the Object type, such as:

```
Public Function AreEqual(ByVal a As Object, ByVal b As Object) As Boolean
    Return a.Equals(b)
End Function
```

The problem with this Object type code such as this is that a and b could be anything. There is no restriction here—nothing to ensure that they are even the same type. An alternative is to use generics, such as:

```
Public Function AreEqual(Of T)(ByVal a As T, ByVal b As T) As Boolean
    Return a.Equals(b)
End Function
```

Now a and b are forced to be the same type, and that type is specified when the method is invoked. In order to test these, create a new Sub method using the following:

```
Private Sub CheckEqual()
    Dim result As Boolean
    ' use normal method
    result = AreEqual(1, 2)
    result = AreEqual("one", "two")
    result = AreEqual(1, "two")
    ' use generic method
    result = AreEqual(Of Integer)(1, 2)
    result = AreEqual(Of String)("one", "two")
    'result = AreEqual(Of Integer)(1, "two")
End Sub
```

However, why not just declare the method as a Boolean? This code will probably cause some confusion. The first three method calls are invoking the normal AreEqual method. Notice that there is no problem asking the method to compare an Integer and a String.

The second set of calls looks very odd. At first glance, they look like nonsense to many people. This is because invoking a generic method means providing two sets of parameters to the method, rather than the normal one set of parameters.

The first set of parameters contain the type or types required to define the method. This is much like the list of types you must provide when declaring a variable using a generic class. In this case, you're specifying that the AreEqual method will be operating on parameters of type Integer.

The second set of parameters contains the conventional parameters that you'd normally supply to a method. What is special in this case is that the types of the parameters are being defined by the first set of parameters. In other words, in the first call, the type is specified to be Integer, so 1 and 2 are valid parameters. In the second call, the type is String, so "one" and "two" are valid. Notice that the third line is commented out. This is because 1 and "two" aren't the same type; with Option Strict On, the compiler will flag this as an error. With Option Strict Off, the runtime will attempt to convert the string at runtime and fail, so this code will not function correctly.

# CREATING GENERICS

Now that you have a good idea how to use preexisting generics in your code, let's take a look at how you can create generic templates. The primary reason to create a generic template instead of a class is to gain strong typing of your variables. Anytime you find yourself using the Object data type, or a base class from which multiple types inherit, you may want to consider using generics. By using generics, you can avoid the use of CType or DirectCast, thereby simplifying your code. If you can avoid using the Object data type, you will typically improve the performance of your code.

As discussed earlier, there are generic types and generic methods. A generic type is basically a class or structure that assumes specific type characteristics when a variable is declared using the generic. A generic method is a single method that assumes specific type characteristics, even though the method might be in an otherwise very conventional class, structure, or module.

## Generic Types

Recall that a generic type is a class, a structure, or an interface template. You can create such templates yourself to provide better performance, strong typing, and code reuse to the consumers of your types.

### Classes

A generic class template is created in the same way that you create a normal class, except that you require the consumer of your class to provide you with one or more types for use in your code. In other words, as the author of a generic template, you have access to the type parameters provided by the user of your generic.

For example, add a new class named SingleLinkedList to the project (code file: SingleLinkedList.vb):

```
Public Class SingleLinkedList(Of T)
End Class
```

In the declaration of the type, you specify the type parameters that will be required:

```
Public Class SingleLinkedList(Of T)
```

In this case, you are requiring just one type parameter. The name, T, can be any valid variable name. In other words, you could declare the type like this:

```
Public Class SingleLinkedList(Of ValueType)
```

Make this change to the code in your project.

> **NOTE** *By convention (carried over from C++ templates), the variable names for type parameters are single uppercase letters. This is somewhat cryptic, and you may want to use a more descriptive convention for variable naming.*

Whether you use the cryptic standard convention or more readable parameter names, the parameter is defined on the class definition. Within the class itself, you then use the type parameter anywhere that you would normally use a type (such as String or Integer).

To create a linked list, you need to define a `Node` class. This will be a nested class that lives within your public class:

```
Public Class SingleLinkedList(Of ValueType)
#Region " Node class "
  Private Class Node
    Private mValue As ValueType
    Public ReadOnly Property Value() As ValueType
      Get
            Return mValue
      End Get
    End Property
    Public Property NextNode() As Node

    Public Sub New(ByVal value As ValueType, ByVal newNode As Node)
        mValue = value
        NextNode = newNode
    End Sub
  End Class
#End Region
End Class
```

Notice how the `mValue` variable is declared as `ValueType`. This means that the actual type of `mValue` depends on the type supplied when an instance of `SingleLinkedList` is created.

Because `ValueType` is a type parameter on the class, you can use `ValueType` as a type anywhere in the code. As you write the class, you cannot tell what type `ValueType` will be. That information is provided by the user of your generic class. Later, when someone declares a variable using your generic type, that person will specify the type, like this:

```
Dim list As New SingleLinkedList(Of Double)
```

At this point, a specific instance of your generic class is created, and all cases of `ValueType` within your code are replaced by the Visual Basic compiler with `Double`. Essentially, this means that for this specific instance of `SingleLinkedList`, the `mValue` declaration ends up as follows:

```
Private mValue As Double
```

Of course, you never get to see this code, as it is dynamically generated by the .NET Framework's JIT compiler at runtime based on your generic template code.

The same is true for methods within the template. Your example contains a constructor method, which accepts a parameter of type `ValueType`. Remember that `ValueType` will be replaced by a specific type when a variable is declared using your generic.

So, what type is `ValueType` when you are writing the template itself? Because it can conceivably be any type when the template is used, `ValueType` is treated like the `Object` type as you create the generic template. This severely restricts what you can do with variables or parameters of `ValueType` within your generic code.

The `mValue` variable is of `ValueType`, which means it is basically of type `Object` for the purposes of your template code. Therefore, you can do assignments (as you do in the constructor code), and you can call any methods that are on the `System.Object` type:

➤     `Equals()`

➤     `GetHashCode()`

➤ GetType()

➤ ReferenceEquals()

➤ ToString()

No operations beyond these basics are available by default. Later in the chapter, you will learn about the concept of *constraints*, which enables you to restrict the types that can be specified for a type parameter. Constraints have the added benefit that they expand the operations you can perform on variables or parameters defined based on the type parameter.

However, this capability is enough to complete the SingleLinkedList class. Add the following after the End Class statement that closes the Node class:

```
Private mHead As Node
Default Public ReadOnly Property Item(ByVal index As Integer) As ValueType
  Get
    Dim current As Node = mHead
    For index = 1 To index
      current = current.NextNode
      If current Is Nothing Then
        Throw New Exception("Item not found in list")
      End If
    Next
    Return current.Value
  End Get
End Property
Public Sub Add(ByVal value As ValueType)
  mHead = New Node(value, mHead)
End Sub
Public Sub Remove(ByVal value As ValueType)
  Dim current As Node = mHead
  Dim previous As Node = Nothing
  While current IsNot Nothing
    If current.Value.Equals(value) Then
      If previous Is Nothing Then
        ' this was the head of the list
        mHead = current.NextNode
      Else
        previous.NextNode = current.NextNode
      End If
      Exit Sub
    End If
    previous = current
    current = current.NextNode
  End While
  'got to the end without finding the item.
  Throw New Exception("Item not found in list")
End Sub

Public ReadOnly Property Count() As Integer
  Get
    Dim result As Integer = 0
```

```
            Dim current As Node = mHead
            While current IsNot Nothing
                result += 1
                current = current.NextNode
            End While
            Return result
        End Get
    End Property
```

Notice that the `Item` property and the `Add` and `Remove` methods all use `ValueType` as either return types or parameter types. More important, note the use of the `Equals` method in the `Remove` method:

```
        If current.Value.Equals(value) Then
```

The reason why this compiles is because `Equals` is defined on `System.Object` and is therefore universally available. This code could not use the = operator because that is not universally available.

To try out the `SingleLinkedList` class, add the following, which can be called from the `ButtonTest_Click` method:

```
    Private Sub CustomList()
        Dim list As New SingleLinkedList(Of String)
        list.Add("Nikita")
        list.Add("Elena")
        list.Add("Benajmin")
        list.Add("William")
        list.Add("Abigail")
        list.Add("Johnathan")
        TextBoxOutput.Clear()
        TextBoxOutput.AppendText("Count: " & list.Count)
        TextBoxOutput.AppendText(Environment.NewLine)
        For index As Integer = 0 To list.Count - 1
            TextBoxOutput.AppendText("Item: " & list.Item(index))
            TextBoxOutput.AppendText(Environment.NewLine)
        Next
    End Sub
```

When you run the code, you will see a display similar to Figure 7-5.

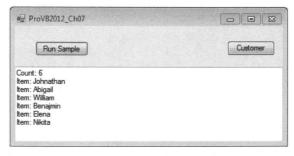

**FIGURE 7-5:** Output when running sample code

## Other Generic Class Features

Earlier in this chapter, you used the `Dictionary` generic, which specifies multiple type parameters. To declare a class with multiple type parameters, you use syntax such as the following (code file: `MyCoolType.vb`):

```
Public Class MyCoolType(Of T, V)
  Private mValue As T
  Private mData As V
  Public Sub New(ByVal value As T, ByVal data As V)
    mValue = value
    mData = data
  End Sub
End Class
```

In addition, it is possible to use regular types in combination with type parameters, as follows:

```
Public Class MyCoolType(Of T, V)
  Private mValue As T
  Private mData As V
  Private mActual As Double
  Public Sub New(ByVal value As T, ByVal data As V, ByVal actual As Double)
    mValue = value
    mData = data
    mActual = actual
  End Sub
End Class
```

Other than the fact that variables or parameters of types `T` or `V` must be treated as type `System .Object`, you can write virtually any code you choose. The code in a generic class is really no different from the code you'd write in a normal class.

This includes all the object-oriented capabilities of classes, including inheritance, overloading, overriding, events, methods, properties, and so forth. However, there are some limitations on overloading. In particular, when overloading methods with a type parameter, the compiler does not know what that specific type might be at runtime. Thus, you can only overload methods in ways in which the type parameter (which could be any type) does not lead to ambiguity.

For instance, adding the following two methods to `MyCoolType` before the .NET Framework 3.5 would have resulted in a compiler error:

```
Public Sub DoWork(ByVal data As Integer)
  ' do work here
End Sub
Public Sub DoWork(ByVal data As V)
  ' do work here
End Sub
```

Now this is possible due to the support for implicitly typed variables. During compilation in .NET, the compiler figures out what the data type of `v` should be. Next it replaces `v` with that type, which allows your code to compile correctly. This was not the case prior to .NET 3.5. Before this version of the .NET Framework, this kind of code would have resulted in a compiler error. It wasn't legal because the compiler didn't know whether `v` would be an `Integer` at runtime. If `v` were to end up defined as an `Integer`, then you'd have two identical method signatures in the same class.

## Classes and Inheritance

Not only can you create basic generic class templates, you can also combine the concept with inheritance. This can be as basic as having a generic template inherit from an existing class:

```
Public Class MyControls(Of T)
  Inherits Control
End Class
```

In this case, the MyControls generic class inherits from the Windows Forms Control class, thus gaining all the behaviors and interface elements of a Control.

Alternately, a conventional class can inherit from a generic template. Suppose that you have a simple generic template:

```
Public Class GenericBase(Of T)
End Class
```

It is quite practical to inherit from this generic class as you create other classes:

```
Public Class Subclass
  Inherits GenericBase(Of Integer)
End Class
```

Notice how the Inherits statement not only references GenericBase, but also provides a specific type for the type parameter of the generic type. Anytime you use a generic type, you must provide values for the type parameters, and this is no exception. This means that your new Subclass actually inherits from a specific instance of GenericBase, where T is of type Integer.

Finally, you can also have generic classes inherit from other generic classes. For instance, you can create a generic class that inherits from the GenericBase class:

```
Public Class GenericSubclass(Of T)
  Inherits GenericBase(Of Integer)
End Class
```

As with the previous example, this new class inherits from an instance of GenericBase, where T is of type Integer.

Things can get far more interesting. It turns out that you can use type parameters to specify the types for other type parameters. For instance, you could alter GenericSubclass like this:

```
Public Class GenericSubclass(Of V)
  Inherits GenericBase(Of V)
End Class
```

Notice that you're specifying that the type parameter for GenericBase is V—which is the type provided by the caller when declaring a variable of type GenericSubclass. Therefore, if a caller uses a declaration that creates an object as a GenericSubclass(Of String) then V is of type String. This means that the GenericSubclass is now inheriting from an instance of GenericBase, where its T parameter is also of type String. The point being that the type flows through from the subclass into the base class. If that is not complex enough, for those who just want a feel for how twisted this logic can become, consider the following class definition:

```
Public Class GenericSubclass(Of V)
  Inherits GenericBase(Of GenericSubclass(Of V))
End Class
```

In this case, the `GenericSubclass` is inheriting from `GenericBase`, where the `T` type in `GenericBase` is actually based on the declared instance of the `GenericSubclass` type. A caller can create such an instance with the simple declaration which follows:

```
Dim obj As GenericSubclass(Of Date)
```

In this case, the `GenericSubclass` type has a `V` of type `Date`. It also inherits from `GenericBase`, which has a `T` of type `GenericSubclass(Of Date)`.

Such complex relationships are typically not useful; in fact, they are often counterproductive, making code difficult to follow and debug. The point was that it is important to recognize how types flow through generic templates, especially when inheritance is involved.

## Structures

You can also define generic `Structure` types. The basic rules and concepts are the same as for defining generic classes, as shown here:

```
Public Structure MyCoolStructure(Of T)
   Public Value As T
End Structure
```

As with generic classes, the type parameter or parameters represent real types that are provided by the user of the `Structure` in actual code. Thus, anywhere you see a `T` in the structure, it will be replaced by a real type such as `String` or `Integer`.

Code can use the `Structure` in a manner similar to how a generic class is used:

```
Dim data As MyCoolStructure(Of Guid)
```

When the variable is declared, an instance of the `Structure` is created based on the type parameter provided. In this example, an instance of `MyCoolStructure` that holds `Guid` objects has been created.

## Interfaces

Finally, you can define generic interface types. Generic interfaces are a bit different from generic classes or structures, because they are implemented by other types when they are used. You can create a generic interface using the same syntax used for classes and structures:

```
Public Interface ICoolInterface(Of T)
   Sub DoWork(ByVal data As T)
   Function GetAnswer() As T
End Interface
```

Then the interface can be used within another type. For instance, you might implement the interface in a class:

```
Public Class ARegularClass
   Implements ICoolInterface(Of String)
   Public Sub DoWork(ByVal data As String) _
    Implements ICoolInterface(Of String).DoWork
   End Sub
   Public Function GetAnswer() As String _
```

```
        Implements ICoolInterface(Of String).GetAnswer
    End Function
End Class
```

Notice that you provide a real type for the type parameter in the `Implements` statement and `Implements` clauses on each method. In each case, you are specifying a specific instance of the `ICoolInterface` interface—one that deals with the `String` data type.

As with classes and structures, an interface can be declared with multiple type parameters. Those type parameter values can be used in place of any normal type (such as `String` or `Date`) in any `Sub`, `Function`, `Property`, or `Event` declaration.

## Generic Methods

You have already seen examples of methods declared using type parameters such as `T` or `V`. While these are examples of generic methods, they have been contained within a broader generic type such as a class, a structure, or an interface.

It is also possible to create generic methods within otherwise normal classes, structures, interfaces, or modules. In this case, the type parameter is not specified on the class, structure, or interface, but rather directly on the method itself.

For instance, you can declare a generic method to compare equality like this:

```
Public Module Comparisons
    Public Function AreEqual(Of T)(ByVal a As T, ByVal b As T) As Boolean
        Return a.Equals(b)
    End Function
End Module
```

In this case, the `AreEqual` method is contained within a module, though it could just as easily be contained in a class or a structure. Notice that the method accepts two sets of parameters. The first set of parameters is the type parameter—in this example, just `T`. The second set of parameters consists of the normal parameters that a method would accept. In this example, the normal parameters have their types defined by the type parameter, `T`.

As with generic classes, it is important to remember that the type parameter is treated as a `System` `.Object` type as you write the code in your generic method. This severely restricts what you can do with parameters or variables declared using the type parameters. Specifically, you can perform assignments and call the various methods common to all `System.Object` variables.

In a moment you will look at constraints, which enable you to restrict the types that can be assigned to the type parameters and expand the operations that can be performed on parameters and variables of those types.

As with generic types, a generic method can accept multiple type parameters:

```
Public Class Comparisons
    Public Function AreEqual(Of T, R)(ByVal a As Integer, ByVal b As T) As R
        ' implement code here
    End Function
End Class
```

In this example, the method is contained within a class, rather than a module. Notice that it accepts two type parameters, T and R. The return type is set to type R, whereas the second parameter is of type T. Also, look at the first parameter, which is a conventional type. This illustrates how you can mix conventional types and generic type parameters in the method parameter list and return types, and by extension within the body of the method code.

# Constraints

At this point, you have learned how to create and use generic types and methods, but there have been serious limitations on what you can do when creating generic type or method templates thus far. This is because the compiler treats any type parameters as the type System.Object within your template code. The result is that you can assign the values and call the various methods common to all System.Object instances, but you can do nothing else. In many cases, this is too restrictive to be useful.

Constraints offer a solution and at the same time provide a control mechanism. Constraints enable you to specify rules about the types that can be used at runtime to replace a type parameter. Using constraints, you can ensure that a type parameter is a Class or a Structure, or that it implements a certain interface or inherits from a certain base class.

Not only do constraints enable you to restrict the types available for use, but they also give the Visual Basic compiler valuable information. For example, if the compiler knows that a type parameter must always implement a given interface, then the compiler will allow you to call the methods on that interface within your template code.

## Type Constraints

The most common kind of constraint is a *type constraint*. A type constraint restricts a type parameter to be a subclass of a specific class or to implement a specific interface. This idea can be used to enhance the SingleLinkedList to sort items as they are added. Create a copy of the class called ComparableLinkedList, changing the declaration of the class itself to add the IComparable constraint:

```
Public Class SingleLinkedList(Of ValueType As IComparable)
```

With this change, ValueType is not only guaranteed to be equivalent to System.Object, it is also guaranteed to have all the methods defined on the IComparable interface.

This means that within the Add method you can make use of any methods in the IComparable interface (as well as those from System.Object). The result is that you can safely call the CompareTo method defined on the IComparable interface, because the compiler knows that any variable of type ValueType will implement IComparable. Update the original Add method with the following implementation (code file: ComparableLinkedList.vb):

```
Public Sub Add(ByVal value As ValueType)
  If mHead Is Nothing Then
    ' List was empty, just store the value.
    mHead = New Node(value, mHead)
  Else
    Dim current As Node = mHead
```

```
      Dim previous As Node = Nothing
      While current IsNot Nothing
        If current.Value.CompareTo(value) > 0 Then
          If previous Is Nothing Then
            ' this was the head of the list
            mHead = New Node(value, mHead)
          Else
            ' insert the node between previous and current
            previous.NextNode = New Node(value, current)
          End If
          Exit Sub
        End If
        previous = current
        current = current.NextNode
      End While
      ' you're at the end of the list, so add to end
      previous.NextNode = New Node(value, Nothing)
    End If
  End Sub
```

Note the call to the `CompareTo` method:

```
        If current.Value.CompareTo(value) > 0 Then
```

This is possible because of the `IComparable` constraint on `ValueType`. Run the project and test this modified code. The items should be displayed in sorted order, as shown in Figure 7-6.

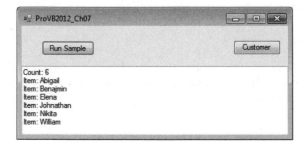

**FIGURE 7-6:** Sorted output shown when sample code runs

Not only can you constrain a type parameter to implement an interface, but you can also constrain it to be a specific type (class) or subclass of that type. For example, you could implement a generic method that works on any Windows Forms control:

```
    Public Shared Sub ChangeControl(Of C As Control)(ByVal control As C)
      control.Anchor = AnchorStyles.Top Or AnchorStyles.Left
    End Sub
```

The type parameter, `C`, is constrained to be of type `Control`. This restricts calling code to only specify this parameter as `Control` or a subclass of `Control`, such as `TextBox`.

Then the parameter to the method is specified to be of type `C`, which means that this method will work against any `Control` or subclass of `Control`. Because of the constraint, the compiler now knows that the variable will always be some type of `Control` object, so it allows you to use any methods, properties, or events exposed by the `Control` class as you write your code.

Finally, it is possible to constrain a type parameter to be of a specific generic type:

```
Public Class ListClass(Of T, V As Generic.List(Of T))
End Class
```

The preceding code specifies that the V type must be a List(Of T), whatever type T might be. A caller can use your class like this:

```
Dim list As ListClass(Of Integer, Generic.List(Of Integer))
```

Earlier in the chapter, in the discussion of how inheritance and generics interact, you saw that things can get quite complex. The same is true when you constrain type parameters based on generic types.

## Class and Structure Constraints

Another form of constraint enables you to be more general. Rather than enforce the requirement for a specific interface or class, you can specify that a type parameter must be either a reference type or a value type.

To specify that the type parameter must be a reference type, you use the Class constraint:

```
Public Class ReferenceOnly(Of T As Class)
End Class
```

This ensures that the type specified for T must be the type of an object. Any attempt to use a value type, such as Integer or Structure, results in a compiler error.

Likewise, you can specify that the type parameter must be a value type such as Integer or a Structure by using the Structure constraint:

```
Public Class ValueOnly(Of T As Structure)
End Class
```

In this case, the type specified for T must be a value type. Any attempt to use a reference type such as String, an interface, or a class results in a compiler error.

## New Constraints

Sometimes you want to write generic code that creates instances of the type specified by a type parameter. In order to know that you can actually create instances of a type, you need to know that the type has a default public constructor. You can determine this using the New constraint:

```
Public Class Factories(Of T As New)
  Public Function CreateT() As T
    Return New T
  End Function
End Class
```

The type parameter, T, is constrained so that it must have a public default constructor. Any attempt to specify a type for T that does not have such a constructor will result in a compile error.

Because you know that T will have a default constructor, you are able to create instances of the type, as shown in the CreateT method.

## Multiple Constraints

In many cases, you will need to specify multiple constraints on the same type parameter. For instance, you might want to require that a type be a reference type and have a public default constructor.

Essentially, you are providing an array of constraints, so you use the same syntax you use to initialize elements of an array:

```
Public Class Factories(Of T As {New, Class})
   Public Function CreateT() As T
      Return New T
   End Function
End Class
```

The constraint list can include two or more constraints, enabling you to specify a great deal of information about the types allowed for this type parameter.

Within your generic template code, the compiler is aware of all the constraints applied to your type parameters, so it allows you to use any methods, properties, and events specified by any of the constraints applied to the type.

# Generics and Late Binding

One of the primary limitations of generics is that variables and parameters declared based on a type parameter are treated as type System.Object inside your generic template code. While constraints offer a partial solution, expanding the type of those variables based on the constraints, you are still very restricted in what you can do with the variables.

One key example is the use of common operators. There is no constraint you can apply that tells the compiler that a type supports the + or – operators. This means that you cannot write generic code like this:

```
Public Function Add(Of T)(ByVal val1 As T, ByVal val2 As T) As T
   Return val1 + val2
End Function
```

This will generate a compiler error because there is no way for the compiler to verify that variables of type T (whatever that is at runtime) support the + operator. Because there is no constraint that you can apply to T to ensure that the + operator will be valid, there is no direct way to use operators on variables of a generic type.

One alternative is to use Visual Basic's native support for late binding to overcome the limitations shown here. Recall that late binding incurs substantial performance penalties, because a lot of work is done dynamically at runtime, rather than by the compiler when you build your project. It is also important to remember the risks that attend late binding—specifically, the code can fail at runtime in ways that early-bound code cannot. Nonetheless, given those caveats, late binding can be used to solve your immediate problem.

To enable late binding, be sure to add `Option Strict Off` at the top of the code file containing your generic template (or set the project property to change `Option Strict` projectwide from the project's properties). Then you can rewrite the `Add` function as follows:

```
Public Function Add(Of T)(ByVal value1 As T, ByVal value2 As T) As T
  Return CObj(value1) + CObj(value2)
End Function
```

By forcing the `value1` and `value2` variables to be explicitly treated as type `Object`, you are telling the compiler that it should use late-binding semantics. Combined with the `Option Strict Off` setting, the compiler assumes that you know what you are doing and it allows the use of the + operator even though its validity can't be confirmed.

The compiled code uses dynamic late binding to invoke the + operator at runtime. If that operator does turn out to be valid for whatever type `T` is at runtime, then this code will work great. In contrast, if the operator is not valid, then a runtime exception will be thrown.

## Covariance and Contravariance

As part of Visual Studio 2010, the concepts of covariance and contravariance were brought forward into generics. The basic ideas are related to concepts associated with polymorphism. In short, prior to Visual Studio 2010, if you attempted to take, for example, an instance of a generic that inherits from the base class `BindingList` and assign that instance to an instance of its base class, you would get an error. The ability to take a specialized or subclass and do a polymorphic assignment to its parent or base class describes covariance.

This topic can get complex, so before moving on to discuss contravariance, let's provide a very simple example of covariance in code. The following declares two classes, `Parent` and `ChildClass`, and shows covariance in action (code file: `CoVariance.vb`):

```
Public Class Parent(Of T)

End Class

Public Class ChildClass(Of T)
    Inherits Parent(Of T)

End Class

Public Class CoVariance
    Public Sub MainMethod()
        Dim cc As New ChildClass(Of String)
        Dim dad As Parent(Of String)
        'Show me the covariance
        dad = cc
    End Sub
End Class
```

You'll note that `ChildClass` inherits from `Parent`. The snippet continues with a method extracted from a calling application. It's called `MainMethod` and you see that the code creates an instance of `ChildClass` and declares an instance of `Parent`. Next it looks to assign the instance `cc` of

ChildClass to the instance dad of type Parent. It is this assignment which illustrates an example of covariance. There are, of course, dozens of different specializations that you could consider, but this provides the basis for all of those examples.

Note, if instead of declaring dad as being a Parent (Of String), the code had declared dad as a Parent (Of Integer), then the assignment of cc to dad would fail because dad would no longer be the correct Parent type. It is important to remember that the type assigned as part of the instantiation of a generic directly impacts the underlying class type of that generic's instance.

Contravariance refers to the ability to pass a derived type when a base type is called for. The reason these features are spoken of in a single topic is that they are both specializations of the variance concept. The difference is mainly an understanding that in the case of contravariance you are passing an instance of ChildClass when a Parent instance was expected. Unfortunately contravariance could be called contraintuitive. You are going to create a base method, and .NET will support its used by derived classes. To illustrate this concept, the following code creates two new classes (they are not generic classes), and then has another code snippet for a method that uses these new classes with generic methods to illustrate contravariance (code file: ContraVariance.vb):

```
Public Class Base

End Class

Public Class Derived
    Inherits Base

End Class

Public Class ContraVariance

    Private baseMethod As Action(Of Base) = Sub(param As Base)
                                               'Do something.
                                            End Sub
    Private derivedMethod As Action(Of Derived) = baseMethod

    Public Sub MainMethod()
        ' Show the contra-syntax
        Dim d As Derived = New Derived()
        derivedMethod(d)
        baseMethod(d)
    End Sub

End Class
```

As shown in the preceding example, you can have a method that expects an input parameter of type Base as its input parameter. In the past, this method would not accept a call with a parameter of type Derived, but with contravariance the method call will now accept a parameter of type Derived because this derived class will, by definition, support the same interface as the base class, just with additional capabilities that can be ignored. As a result, although at first glance it feels backward, you are in fact able to pass a generic that implements a derived class to a method which is expecting a generic that is defined using a base class.

## SUMMARY

This chapter took a look at the classes and language elements that target sets. You started with a look at arrays and the support for arrays within Visual Basic. The chapter then looked at collection classes. By default, these classes operate on the type `Object`, and it is this capability to handle any or all objects within their implementation that makes these classes both powerful and limited.

Following a quick review of the iterative language structures normally associated with these classes, the chapter moved on to looking at generics. Generics enable you to create class, structure, interface, and method templates. These templates gain specific types based on how they are declared or called at runtime. Generics provide you with another code reuse mechanism, along with procedural and object-oriented concepts.

Generics also enable you to change code that uses parameters or variables of type `Object` (or other general types) to use specific data types. This often leads to much better performance and increases the readability of your code.

Next you'll move into working with XML from Visual Basic. XML processing and generation are one of Visual Basic's strengths. As you'll see, while you may have an XML file with only a single entry, by its nature XML lends itself to creating collections of objects.

# 8

# Using XML with Visual Basic

**WHAT'S IN THIS CHAPTER?**

➤ The rationale behind XML

➤ How to serialize objects to XML (and vice versa)

➤ How to read and write XML

➤ How to use *LINQ to XML* to read and edit XML

➤ How to use XML literals within your code

**WROX.COM CODE DOWNLOADS FOR THIS CHAPTER**

The wrox.com code download for this chapter is found at www.wrox.com/remtitle .cgi?=isbn=9781118314456 on the Download Code tab. The code is in the chapter 8 download. The code for this chapter is a single solution with multiple projects. Each project represents a separate example.

This chapter describes how you can generate and manipulate *Extensible Markup Language* (*XML*) using Visual Basic 2012. The .NET Framework exposes many XML-specific namespaces that contain over 100 different classes. In addition, dozens of other classes support and implement XML-related technologies, such as those provided in ADO.NET, SQL Server, and BizTalk. Consequently, this chapter focuses on the general concepts and the most important classes.

The chapter is organized from older technologies and lower-level XML manipulation to the latest and greatest functionality. This is done because it is important you understand how XML is actually structured and manipulated in order for you to gain the most from it.

Visual Basic relies on the classes exposed in the following XML-related namespaces to transform, manipulate, and stream XML documents:

➤ System.Xml provides core support for a variety of XML standards, including DTD (Document Type Definition), namespace, DOM (Document Object Model), XDR (XML Data Reduced — an old version of the XML schema standard), XPath, XSLT (XML Transformation), and SOAP (formerly Simple Object Access Protocol; now the acronym doesn't stand for anything).

➤ System.Xml.Serialization provides the objects used to transform objects to and from XML documents or streams using serialization.

➤ System.Xml.Schema provides a set of objects that enable schemas to be loaded, created, and streamed. This support is achieved using a suite of objects that support in-memory manipulation of the entities that compose an XML schema.

➤ System.Xml.XPath provides a parser and evaluation engine for the XML Path language (XPath).

➤ System.Xml.Xsl provides the objects necessary when working with Extensible Stylesheet Language (XSL) and XSL Transformations (XSLT).

➤ System.Xml.Linq provides the support for querying XML using LINQ (also covered in chapter 9).

This chapter makes sense of this range of technologies by introducing some basic XML concepts and demonstrating how Visual Basic, in conjunction with the .NET Framework, can make use of XML.

At the end of this chapter, you will be able to generate, manipulate, and transform XML using Visual Basic.

## AN INTRODUCTION TO XML

XML is a tagged markup language similar to HTML. In fact, XML and HTML are distant cousins and have their roots in the Standard Generalized Markup Language (SGML). This means that XML leverages one of the most useful features of HTML—readability. However, XML differs from HTML in that XML represents data, whereas HTML is a mechanism for displaying data. The tags in XML describe the data, as shown in the following example:

```
<?xml version="1.0" encoding="utf-8" ?>
<Movies>
  <FilmOrder name="Grease" filmId="1" quantity="21"></FilmOrder>
  <FilmOrder name="Lawrence of Arabia" filmId="2" quantity="10"></FilmOrder>
  <FilmOrder name="Star Wars" filmId="3" quantity="12"></FilmOrder>
  <FilmOrder name="Shrek" filmId="4" quantity="14"></FilmOrder>
</Movies>
```

This XML document represents a store order for a collection of movies. The standard used to represent an order of films would be useful to movie rental firms, collectors, and others. This information can be shared using XML for the following reasons:

➤   The data tags in XML are self-describing.

➤   XML is an open standard and supported on most platforms today.

XML supports the parsing of data by applications not familiar with the contents of the XML document. XML documents can also be associated with a description (a schema) that informs an application about the structure of the data within the XML document.

At this stage, XML looks simple: it is just a human-readable way to exchange data in a universally accepted format. The essential points that you should understand about XML are as follows:

➤   XML data can be stored in a plain text file.

➤   A document is said to be well-formed if it adheres to the XML standard (see www.w3.org/standards/xml/ for more details on the XML standard).

➤   Tags are used to specify the contents of a document—for example, <FilmOrder>.

➤   XML elements (also called *nodes*) can be thought of as the objects within a document.

➤   Elements are the basic building blocks of the document. Each element contains both a start tag and an end tag; and a tag can be both a start tag and an end tag in one—for example, <FilmOrder/>. In this case, the tag specifies that there is no content (or inner text) to the element (there isn't a closing tag because none is required due to the lack of inner-text content). Such a tag is said to be *empty*.

➤   Data can be contained in the element (the element content) or within attributes contained in the element.

➤   XML is hierarchical. One document can contain multiple elements, which can themselves contain child elements, and so on. However, an XML document can have only one root element.

This last point means that the XML document hierarchy can be thought of as a tree containing nodes:

➤   The example document has a root node, <Movies>.

➤   The branches of the root node are elements of type <FilmOrder>.

➤   The leaves of the XML element, <FilmOrder>, are its attributes: name, quantity, and filmId.

Of course, you are interested in the practical use of XML by Visual Basic. A practical manipulation of the example XML is to display, for the staff of a movie supplier, a particular movie order. This would allow the supplier to fill the order and then save the information to a database. This chapter explains how you can perform such tasks using the functionality provided by the .NET Framework Class Library.

# XML SERIALIZATION

The simplest way to demonstrate Visual Basic's support for XML is to use it to serialize a class. The serialization of an object means that it is written out to a stream, such as a file or a socket. The reverse process can also be performed: an object can be deserialized by reading it from a stream and creating the XML from that stream. You may want to do this to save an object's data to a local file, or to transmit it across a network.

> **NOTE** *The type of serialization described in this chapter is XML serialization, whereby XML is used to represent a class in serialized form. You will see other forms of serialization in the WCF chapter (Chapter 11).*

To help you understand XML serialization, let's examine a class named `FilmOrder` in the `FilmOrder` project. This class could be used by a company for processing a movie order.

An instance of `FilmOrder` corresponding to each order could be serialized to XML and sent over a socket from a client's computer. We are talking about data in a proprietary form here: an instance of `FilmOrder` being converted into a generic form—XML—that can be universally understood.

The `System.Xml.Serialization` namespace contains classes and interfaces that support the serialization of objects to XML, and the deserialization of objects from XML. Objects are serialized to documents or streams using the `XmlSerializer` class.

# Serializing

Let's look at how you can use `XmlSerializer`. To make the sample simpler, you'll use a console application. This console application will use the class `FilmOrder` as follows (code file: `Main.vb`):

```vb
Public Class FilmOrder
  Public Name As String
  Public FilmId As Integer
  Public Quantity As Integer
  Public Sub New()
  End Sub
  Public Sub New(ByVal name As String, _
                 ByVal filmId As Integer, _
                 ByVal quantity As Integer)
    Me.Name = name
    Me.FilmId = filmId
    Me.Quantity = quantity
  End Sub
End Class
```

From there, you can move on to the module.

To make the `XmlSerializer` object accessible, you need to make reference to the `System.Xml` `.Serialization` namespace:

```
Imports System.Xml.Serialization
```

In the `Sub Main`, create an instance of `XmlSerializer`, specifying the type to be serialized, this case, the `FilmOrder` type:

```
Dim serialize As XmlSerializer = _
   New XmlSerializer(GetType(FilmOrder))
```

Next, you create an instance of the `FilmOrder` class, or whatever class it was that you provided the type for in the previous step. In a more complex application, you may have created this instance using data provided by the client, a database, or other source:

```
Dim MyFilmOrder As FilmOrder = _
   New FilmOrder("Grease", 101, 10)
```

> **NOTE** *It is important for you to know that serialization, and deserialization, use reflection. For that reason, the class being serialized* **must** *include a parameterless constructor. If it does not, attempting to serialize it will result in an exception.*

Call the `Serialize` method of the `XmlSerializer` instance specifying `Console.Out` as the output stream and the object to be serialized.

```
serialize.Serialize(Console.Out, MyFilmOrder)
Console.ReadLine()
```

Running the module, the following output is generated by the preceding code:

```
<?xml version="1.0" encoding="IBM437"?>
<FilmOrder xmlns:xsi="http://www.w3.org/2001/XMLSchema-instance"
        xmlns:xsd="http://www.w3.org/2001/XMLSchema">
  <Name>Grease</Name>
  <FilmId>101</FilmId>
  <Quantity>10</Quantity>
</FilmOrder>
```

This output demonstrates the default way in which the `Serialize` method serializes an object:

➤ Each object serialized is represented as an element with the same name as the class—in this case, `FilmOrder`.

➤ The individual data members of the class serialized are contained in elements named for each public data member—in this case, `Name`, `FilmId`, and `Quantity`.

Also generated are the following:

➤ The specific version of XML generated—in this case, 1.0

➤ The encoding used for the text—in this case, IBM437

➤ The schemas used to describe the serialized object—in this case, just the two schemas defined by the XML schema specification, www.w3.org/2001/XMLSchema-instance and www.w3.org/2001/XMLSchema

A schema can be associated with an XML document and describes the data it contains (name, type, scale, precision, length, and so on). Either the actual schema or a reference to where the schema is located can be contained in the XML document. In either case, an XML schema is a standard representation that can be used by all applications that consume XML. This means that applications can use the supplied schema to validate the contents of an XML document generated by the Serialize method of the XmlSerializer object.

The code snippet that demonstrated the Serialize method displayed the generated XML to the Console.Out stream. Clearly, you do not expect an application to use Console.Out when it would like to access a FilmOrder object in XML form. The point was to show how serialization can be performed in just two lines of code, one call to a constructor and one call to a method.

The Serialize method's first parameter is overridden so that it can serialize XML to a file, a Stream, a TextWriter, or an XmlWriter. When serializing to Stream, TextWriter, or XmlWriter, adding a third parameter to the Serialize method is permissible. This third parameter is of type XmlSerializerNamespaces and is used to specify a list of namespaces that qualify the names in the XML-generated document.

## Deserializing

Since serialization produces an XML document from an object, it stands to reason that deserialization would do the opposite. This is handled by the Deserialize method of XmlSerializer. This method is overridden and can deserialize XML presented as a Stream, a TextReader, or an XmlReader. The output of the various Deserialize methods is a generic Object, so you need to cast the resulting object to the correct data type.

The example that demonstrates how to deserialize an object can be found in the FilmOrderList project. This is just an updated version of the previous example. The first step is to look at the new FilmOrderList class. This class contains an array of film orders (actually an array of FilmOrder objects). FilmOrderList is defined as follows (code file: FileMorderList.vb):

```
Public Class FilmOrderList
    Public FilmOrders() As FilmOrder
    Public Sub New()
    End Sub
    Public Sub New(ByVal multiFilmOrders() As FilmOrder)
        Me.FilmOrders = multiFilmOrders
    End Sub
End Class
```

The FilmOrderList class contains a fairly complicated object, an array of FilmOrder objects. The underlying serialization and deserialization of this class is more complicated than that of a single instance of a class that contains several simple types, but the programming effort involved on your part is just as simple as before. This is one of the great ways in which the .NET Framework makes it easy for you to work with XML data, no matter how it is formed.

To work through an example of the deserialization process, first create a sample order stored as an XML file called `Filmorama.xml`:

```
<?xml version="1.0" encoding="utf-8" ?>
<FilmOrderList xmlns:xsi="http://www.w3.org/2001/XMLSchema-instance"
 xmlns:xsd="http://www.w3.org/2001/XMLSchema">
  <FilmOrders>
    <FilmOrder>
      <Name>Grease</Name>
      <FilmId>101</FilmId>
      <Quantity>10</Quantity>
    </FilmOrder>
    <FilmOrder>
      <Name>Lawrence of Arabia</Name>
      <FilmId>102</FilmId>
      <Quantity>10</Quantity>
    </FilmOrder>
    <FilmOrder>
      <Name>Star Wars</Name>
      <FilmId>103</FilmId>
      <Quantity>10</Quantity>
    </FilmOrder>
  </FilmOrders>
</FilmOrderList>
```

> **NOTE** *In order for this to run, you should either have the .xml file in the location of the executable or load the file using the full path of the file within the code example. To have the XML in the same directory as the executable, add the XML file to the project, and set the Copy to Output Directory to "Copy if newer."*

Once the XML file is in place, the next step is to change your console application so it will deserialize the contents of this file. First, ensure that your console application has made the proper namespace references:

```
Imports System.Xml
Imports System.Xml.Serialization
Imports System.IO
```

The code that actually performs the deserialization is found in the `Sub Main()` method (code file: `Main.vb`):

```
' Open file Filmorama.xml
Dim dehydrated As FileStream = _
   New FileStream("Filmorama.xml", FileMode.Open)
' Create an XmlSerializer instance to handle deserializing,
' FilmOrderList
```

```vb
Dim serialize As XmlSerializer = _
   New XmlSerializer(GetType(FilmOrderList))
' Create an object to contain the deserialized instance of the object.
Dim myFilmOrder As FilmOrderList = _
   New FilmOrderList
' Deserialize object
myFilmOrder = serialize.Deserialize(dehydrated)
```

This code demonstrates the deserialization of the `Filmorama.xml` file into a `FilmOrderList` instance. This is accomplished, mainly, by the call to the `Deserialize` method of the `XmlSerializer` class.

Once deserialized, the array of film orders can be displayed. The following code shows how this is accomplished (code file: `Main.vb`):

```vb
Dim SingleFilmOrder As FilmOrder
For Each SingleFilmOrder In myFilmOrder.FilmOrders
   Console.Out.WriteLine("{0}, {1}, {2}", _
      SingleFilmOrder.Name, _
      SingleFilmOrder.FilmId, _
      SingleFilmOrder.Quantity)
Next
Console.ReadLine()
```

Running the example will result in the following output:

```
Grease, 101, 10
Lawrence of Arabia, 102, 10
Star Wars, 103, 10
```

`XmlSerializer` also implements a `CanDeserialize` method. The prototype for this method is as follows:

```vb
Public Overridable Function CanDeserialize(ByVal xmlReader As XmlReader) _
   As Boolean
```

If `CanDeserialize` returns `True`, then the XML document specified by the `xmlReader` parameter can be deserialized. If the return value of this method is `False`, then the specified XML document cannot be deserialized. Using this method is usually preferable to attempting to deserialize and trapping any exceptions that may occur.

The `FromTypes` method of `XmlSerializer` facilitates the creation of arrays that contain `XmlSerializer` objects. This array of `XmlSerializer` objects can be used in turn to process arrays of the type to be serialized. The prototype for `FromTypes` is shown here:

```vb
Public Shared Function FromTypes(ByVal types() As Type) As XmlSerializer()
```

## Source Code Style Attributes

Thus far, you have seen attributes applied to a specific portion of an XML document. Visual Basic, as with most other languages, has its own flavor of attributes. These attributes refer to annotations to the source code that specify information, or *metadata*, that can be used by other applications without the need for the original source code. You will call such attributes *Source Code Style attributes*.

In the context of the `System.Xml.Serialization` namespace, Source Code Style attributes can be used to change the names of the elements generated for the data members of a class or to generate XML attributes instead of XML elements for the data members of a class. To demonstrate this, you will update the `FilmOrder` class using these attributes to change the outputted XML. This updated version is part of the new example found in the `FilmOrderAttributes` project.

In the previous section, you saw that serialization used the name of the property as the name of the element that is automatically generated. To rename this generated element, a Source Code Style attribute will be used. This Source Code Style attribute specifies that when `FilmOrder` is serialized, the name data member is represented as an XML element named `<Title>`. The actual Source Code Style attribute that specifies this is as follows:

```
<XmlElementAttribute("Title")>
Public Name As String
```

The updated `FilmOrder` also contains other Source Code Style attributes (code file: `FilmOrder.vb`):

```
Imports System.Xml.Serialization
Public Class FilmOrder
   <XmlElementAttribute("Title")> Public Name As String
   <XmlAttributeAttribute("ID")> Public FilmId As Integer
   <XmlAttributeAttribute("Qty")> Public Quantity As Integer
   Public Sub New()
   End Sub
   Public Sub New(ByVal name As String, _
                  ByVal filmId As Integer, _
                  ByVal quantity As Integer)
      Me.Name = name
      Me.FilmId = filmId
      Me.Quantity = quantity
   End Sub
End Class
```

The additional attributes that were added to the example class are:

➤ `<XmlAttributeAttribute("ID")>` specifies that `FilmId` is to be serialized as an XML attribute named `ID`.

➤ `<XmlAttributeAttribute("Qty")>` specifies that `Quantity` is to be serialized as an XML attribute named `Qty`.

Note that you needed to include the `System.Xml.Serialization` namespace to bring in the Source Code Style attributes used.

The following `Sub Main()` method for this project is no different from the ones previously shown (code file: `Main.vb`):

```
Dim serialize As XmlSerializer = _
    New XmlSerializer(GetType(FilmOrder))
Dim MyMovieOrder As FilmOrder = _
    New FilmOrder("Grease", 101, 10)
serialize.Serialize(Console.Out, MyMovieOrder)
Console.Readline()
```

The console output generated by this code reflects the Source Code Style attributes associated with the class:

```
<?xml version="1.0" encoding="IBM437"?>
<FilmOrder xmlns:xsi="http://www.w3.org/2001/XMLSchema-instance"
           xmlns:xsd="http://www.w3.org/2001/XMLSchema" ID="101" Qty="10">
  <Title>Grease</Title>
</FilmOrder>
```

Compare this to the earlier version that does not include the attributes.

The example only demonstrates the Source Code Style attributes XmlAttributeAttribute and XmlElementAttribute. Table 8-1 shows some additional attributes available.

**TABLE 8-1:** Additional Source Code Attributes Available

| ATTRIBUTE | DESCRIPTION |
| --- | --- |
| XmlArrayAttribute | Allows the name of an array element to be specified. |
| XmlArrayItemAttribute | Allows the name of an array's child elements to be specified. |
| XmlRoot | Denotes the root element. |
| XmlType | Used to specify the data type for an element.  This is used in XSD files, which are discussed later. |
| XmlIgnoreAttribute | Instructs the serializer to not serialize the current element or attribute. |
| XmlEnumAttribute | Controls how enumeration values are serialized. |

# SYSTEM.XML DOCUMENT SUPPORT

The System.Xml namespace implements a variety of objects that support standards-based XML processing. The XML-specific standards facilitated by this namespace include XML 1.0, Document Type Definition (DTD) support, XML namespaces, XML schemas, XPath, XQuery, XSLT, DOM Level 1 and DOM Level 2 (Core implementations), as well as SOAP 1.1, SOAP 1.2, SOAP Contract Language, and SOAP Discovery. The System.Xml namespace exposes over 30 separate classes in order to facilitate this level of the XML standard's compliance.

To generate and navigate XML documents, there are two styles of access:

**1.** Stream-based—System.Xml exposes a variety of classes that read XML from and write XML to a stream. This approach tends to be a fast way to consume or generate an XML document, because it represents a set of serial reads or writes. The limitation of this approach is that it does not view the XML data as a document composed of tangible entities, such as nodes, elements, and attributes. An example of where a stream could be used is when receiving XML documents from a socket or a file.

**2.** **Document Object Model (DOM)-based**—System.Xml exposes a set of objects that access XML documents as data. The data is accessed using entities from the XML document tree (nodes, elements, and attributes). This style of XML generation and navigation is flexible but may not yield the same performance as stream-based XML generation and navigation. This is because loading a document into the DOM loads the entire file into memory. DOM is an excellent technology for editing and manipulating documents. For example, the functionality exposed by DOM could simplify merging your checking, savings, and brokerage accounts.

## XML Stream-Style Parsers

Stream-based parsers read a block of XML in a forward-only manner, only keeping the current node in memory. When an XML document is parsed using a stream parser, the parser always points to the current node in the document. To provide you more insight into what these nodes are, look at the following small XML example and refer to Table 8-2, which provides the specifics.

```
<?xml version="1.0" encoding="utf-8"?>
<FilmOrder filmId="101">
  <Name>Grease</Name>
  <Quantity>10</Quantity>
</FilmOrder>
```

**TABLE 8-2:** Additional Source Code Attributes Available

| ELEMENT | NODE |
| --- | --- |
| XmlDeclaration | <?xml version="1.0" encoding="utf-8"?> |
| XmlAttribute | Version |
| XmlAttribute | Encoding |
| XmlElement | FilmOrder |
| XmlAttribute | FilmId |
| XmlElement | Name |
| XmlText | Grease |
| XmlEndElement | Name |
| XmlElement | Quantity |
| XmlText | 10 |
| XmlEndElement | Quantity |
| XmlWhitespace | Nothing |
| XmlEndElement | FilmOrder |

The following classes that access a stream of XML (read XML) and generate a stream of XML (write XML) are contained in the System.Xml namespace:

➤ XmlWriter—This abstract class specifies a noncached, forward-only stream that writes an XML document (data and schema).

➤ XmlReader—This abstract class specifies a noncached, forward-only stream that reads an XML document (data and schema).

The diagram of the classes associated with the XML stream-style parser refers to one other class, XslTransform. This class is found in the System.Xml.Xsl namespace and is not an XML stream-style parser. Rather, it is used in conjunction with XmlWriter and XmlReader. This class is covered in detail later.

The System.Xml namespace exposes a plethora of additional XML manipulation classes in addition to those shown in the architecture diagram. The classes shown in the diagram include the following:

➤ XmlResolver—This abstract class resolves an external XML resource using a Uniform Resource Identifier (URI). XmlUrlResolver is an implementation of an XmlResolver.

➤ XmlNameTable—This abstract class provides a fast means by which an XML parser can access element or attribute names.

## Writing an XML Stream

An XML document can be created programmatically in .NET. One way to perform this task is by writing the individual components of an XML document (schema, attributes, elements, and so on) to an XML stream. Using a unidirectional write-stream means that each element and its attributes must be written in order—the idea is that data is always written at the end of the stream. To accomplish this, you use a writable XML stream class (a class derived from XmlWriter). Such a class ensures that the XML document you generate correctly implements the W3C Extensible Markup Language (XML) 1.0 specification and the namespaces in the XML specification.

Why is this necessary when you have XML serialization? You need to be very careful here to separate interface from implementation. XML serialization works for a specific class, such as the FilmOrder class used in the earlier samples. This class is a proprietary implementation and not the format in which data is exchanged. For this one specific case, the XML document generated when FilmOrder is serialized just so happens to be the XML format used when placing an order for some movies. You can use Source Code Style attributes to help it conform to a standard XML representation of a film order summary, but the eventual structure is tied to that class.

In a different application, if the software used to manage an entire movie distribution business wants to generate movie orders, then it must generate a document of the appropriate form. The movie distribution management software achieves this using the XmlWriter object.

Before reviewing the subtleties of XmlWriter, note that this class exposes over 40 methods and properties. The example in this section provides an overview that touches on a subset of these methods and properties. This subset enables the generation of an XML document that corresponds to a movie order.

The example, located in the FilmOrdersWriter project, builds the module that generates the XML document corresponding to a movie order. It uses an instance of XmlWriter, called

`FilmOrdersWriter`, which is actually a file on disk. This means that the XML document generated is streamed to this file directly. Because the `FilmOrdersWriter` variable represents a file, you have to take a few actions against the file. For instance, you have to ensure the file is:

➤ **Created**—The instance of `XmlWriter`, `FilmOrdersWriter`, is created by using the `Create` method, as well as by assigning all the properties of this object by using the `XmlWriterSettings` object.

➤ **Opened**—The file the XML is streamed to, `FilmOrdersProgrammatic.xml`, is opened by passing the filename to the constructor associated with `XmlWriter`.

➤ **Generated**—The process of generating the XML document is described in detail at the end of this section.

➤ **Closed**—The file (the XML stream) is closed using the `Close` method of `XmlWriter` or by simply making use of the `Using` keyword, which ensures that the object is closed at the end of the `Using` statement.

Before you create the `XmlWriter` object, you first need to customize how the object operates by using the `XmlWriterSettings` object. This object, introduced in .NET 2.0, enables you to configure the behavior of the `XmlWriter` object before you instantiate it, as seen here:

```
Dim myXmlSettings As New XmlWriterSettings()
myXmlSettings.Indent = True
myXmlSettings.NewLineOnAttributes = True
```

You can specify a few settings for the `XmlWriterSettings` object that define how XML creation will be handled by the `XmlWriter` object.

Once the `XmlWriterSettings` object has been instantiated and assigned the values you deem necessary, the next steps are to invoke the `XmlWriter` object and make the association between the `XmlWriterSettings` object and the `XmlWriter` object.

The basic infrastructure for managing the file (the XML text stream) and applying the settings class is either

```
Dim FilmOrdersWriter As XmlWriter = _
    XmlWriter.Create("..\FilmOrdersProgrammatic.xml", myXmlSettings)
FilmOrdersWriter.Close()
```

or the following, if you are utilizing the `Using` keyword, which is the recommended approach:

```
Using FilmOrdersWriter As XmlWriter = _
    XmlWriter.Create("..\FilmOrdersProgrammatic.xml", myXmlSettings)
End Using
```

With the preliminaries completed, file created, and formatting configured, the process of writing the actual attributes and elements of your XML document can begin. The sequence of steps used to generate your XML document is as follows:

**1.** Write an XML comment using the `WriteComment` method. This comment describes from whence the concept for this XML document originated and generates the following code:

```
<!-- Same as generated by serializing, FilmOrder -->
```

2. Begin writing the XML element, `<FilmOrder>`, by calling the `WriteStartElement` method. You can only begin writing this element, because its attributes and child elements must be written before the element can be ended with a corresponding `</FilmOrder>`. The XML generated by the `WriteStartElement` method is as follows:

```
<FilmOrder>
```

3. Write the attributes associated with `<FilmOrder>` by calling the `WriteAttributeString` method twice, specifying a different attribute each time. The XML generated by calling the `WriteAttributeString` method twice adds to the `<FilmOrder>` XML element that is currently being written to the following:

```
<FilmOrder FilmId="101" Quantity="10">
```

4. Using the `WriteElementString` method, write the child XML element `<Title>`. The XML generated by calling this method is as follows:

```
<Title>Grease</Title>
```

5. Complete writing the `<FilmOrder>` parent XML element by calling the `WriteEndElement` method. The XML generated by calling this method is as follows:

```
</FilmOrder>
```

The complete code for accomplishing this is shown here (code file: `Main.vb`):

```vb
Imports System.Xml

Module Main
    Sub Main()
        Dim myXmlSettings As New XmlWriterSettings
        myXmlSettings.Indent = True
        myXmlSettings.NewLineOnAttributes = True
        Using FilmOrdersWriter As XmlWriter =
            XmlWriter.Create("FilmOrdersProgrammatic.xml", myXmlSettings)
            FilmOrdersWriter.WriteComment(" Same as generated " &
                "by serializing, FilmOrder ")
            FilmOrdersWriter.WriteStartElement("FilmOrder")
            FilmOrdersWriter.WriteAttributeString("FilmId", "101")
            FilmOrdersWriter.WriteAttributeString("Quantity", "10")
            FilmOrdersWriter.WriteElementString("Title", "Grease")
            FilmOrdersWriter.WriteEndElement() ' End  FilmOrder
        End Using
    End Sub
End Module
```

Once this is run, you will find the XML file `FilmOrdersProgrammatic.xml` created in the same folder as where the application was executed from, which is most likely the `bin` directory. The content of this file is as follows:

```xml
<?xml version="1.0" encoding="utf-8"?>
<!-- Same as generated by serializing, FilmOrder -->
<FilmOrder
  FilmId="101"
```

```
            Quantity="10">
            <Title>Grease</Title>
        </FilmOrder>
```

At a closer look, you should see that the XML document generated by this code is virtually identical to the one produced by the serialization example. Also, notice that in the previous XML document, the `<Title>` element is indented two characters and that each attribute is on a different line in the document. This formatting was achieved using the `XmlWriterSettings` class.

The sample application covers only a small portion of the methods and properties exposed by the XML stream-writing class, `XmlWriter`. Other methods implemented by this class manipulate the underlying file, such as the `Flush` method; and some methods allow XML text to be written directly to the stream, such as the `WriteRaw` method.

The `XmlWriter` class also exposes a variety of methods that write a specific type of XML data to the stream. These methods include `WriteBinHex`, `WriteCData`, `WriteString`, and `WriteWhiteSpace`.

You can now generate the same XML document in two different ways. You have used two different applications that took two different approaches to generating a document that represents a standardized movie order. The XML serialization approach uses the "shape" of the class to generate XML, whereas the `XmlWriter` allows you more flexibility in the output, at the expense of more effort.

However, there are even more ways to generate XML, depending on the circumstances. Using the previous scenario, you could receive a movie order from a store, and this order would have to be transformed from the XML format used by the supplier to your own order format.

## Reading an XML Stream

In .NET, XML documents can be read from a stream as well. Data is traversed in the stream in order (first XML element, second XML element, and so on). This traversal is very quick because the data is processed in one direction, and features such as write and move backward in the traversal are not supported. At any given instance, only data at the current position in the stream can be accessed.

Before exploring how an XML stream can be read, you need to understand why it should be read in the first place. Returning to your movie supplier example, imagine that the application managing the movie orders can generate a variety of XML documents corresponding to current orders, preorders, and returns. All the documents (current orders, preorders, and returns) can be extracted in stream form and processed by a report-generating application. This application prints the orders for a given day, the preorders that are going to be due, and the returns that are coming back to the supplier. The report-generating application processes the data by reading in and parsing a stream of XML.

One class that can be used to read and parse such an XML stream is `XmlReader`. The .NET Framework includes more specific XML readers, such as `XmlTextReader`, that are derived from the `XmlReader` class. `XmlTextReader` provides the functionality to read XML from a file, a stream, or another `XmlReader`. This example, found in the `FilmOrdersReader` project, uses an `XmlReader` to read an XML document contained in a file. Reading XML from a file and writing it to a file is not the norm when it comes to XML processing, but a file is the simplest way to access XML data. This simplified access enables you to focus on XML-specific issues.

The first step in accessing a stream of XML data is to create an instance of the object that will open the stream. This is accomplished with the following code (code file: `Main.vb`):

```
Dim myXmlSettings As New XmlReaderSettings()
Using readMovieInfo As XmlReader = XmlReader.Create(fileName, myXmlSettings)
```

This code creates a new `XmlReader`, called `readMovieInfo`, using the specified filename and `XmlReaderSettings` instance. As with the `XmlWriter`, the `XmlReader` also has a settings class. You will use this class a little later.

The basic mechanism for traversing each stream is to move from node to node using the `Read` method. Node types in XML include element and white space. Numerous other node types are defined, but this example focuses on traversing XML elements and the white space that is used to make the elements more readable (carriage returns, line feeds, and indentation spaces). Once the stream is positioned at a node, the `MoveToNextAttribute` method can be called to read each attribute contained in an element. The `MoveToNextAttribute` method only traverses attributes for nodes that contain attributes (nodes of type `element`). You accomplish this basic node and attribute traversal using the following code (code file: `Main.vb`):

```
While readMovieInfo.Read()
   ' Process node here.
   While readMovieInfo.MoveToNextAttribute()
      ' Process attribute here.
   End While
End While
```

This code, which reads the contents of the XML stream, does not utilize any knowledge of the stream's contents. However, a great many applications know exactly how the stream they are going to traverse is structured. Such applications can use `XmlReader` in a more deliberate manner and not simply traverse the stream without foreknowledge. This would mean you could use the `GetAttribute` method as well as the various `ReadContentAs` and `ReadElementContentAs` methods to retrieve the contents by name, rather than just walking through the XML.

Once the example stream has been read, it can be cleaned up using the `End Using` call:

```
End Using
```

The complete code for the method that reads the data is shown here (code file: `Main.vb`):

```
Private Sub ReadMovieXml(ByVal fileName As String)
   Dim myXmlSettings As New XmlReaderSettings()
   Using readMovieInfo As XmlReader = XmlReader.Create(fileName, _
      myXmlSettings)
      While readMovieInfo.Read()
         ' Process node here.
         ShowXmlNode(readMovieInfo)
         While readMovieInfo.MoveToNextAttribute()
            ' Process attribute here.
            ShowXmlNode(readMovieInfo)
         End While
      End While
   End Using
End Sub
```

The `ReadMovieXml` method takes a string parameter that specifies the name of the XML file to be read. For each node encountered after a call to the `Read` method, `ReadMovieXml` calls the `ShowXmlNode` subroutine. Similarly, for each attribute traversed, the `ShowXmlNode` subroutine is called. The code for the following ShowXmlNode method (code file: `Main.vb`):

```vb
Private Sub ShowXmlNode(ByVal reader As XmlReader)
    If reader.Depth > 0 Then
        For depthCount As Integer = 1 To reader.Depth
            Console.Write(" ")
        Next
    End If
    If reader.NodeType = XmlNodeType.Whitespace Then
        Console.Out.WriteLine("Type: {0} ", reader.NodeType)
    ElseIf reader.NodeType = XmlNodeType.Text Then
        Console.Out.WriteLine("Type: {0}, Value: {1} ", _
                              reader.NodeType, _
                              reader.Value)
    Else
        Console.Out.WriteLine("Name: {0}, Type: {1}, " & _
                              "AttributeCount: {2}, Value: {3} ", _
                              reader.Name, _
                              reader.NodeType, _
                              reader.AttributeCount, _
                              reader.Value)
    End If
End Sub
```

This subroutine breaks down each node into its subentities:

➤ **Depth**—This property of `XmlReader` determines the level at which a node resides in the XML document tree. To understand depth, consider the following XML document composed solely of elements:

```xml
<A>
    <B></B>
    <C>
        <D></D>
    </C>
</A>.
```

Element `<A>` is the root element, and when parsed would return a depth of 0. Elements `<B>` and `<C>` are contained in `<A>` and hence reflect a depth value of 1. Element `<D>` is contained in `<C>`. The `Depth` property value associated with `<D>` (depth of 2) should, therefore, be one more than the `Depth` property associated with `<C>` (depth of 1).

➤ **Type**—The type of each node is determined using the `NodeType` property of `XmlReader`. The node returned is of enumeration type, `XmlNodeType`. Permissible node types include `Attribute`, `Element`, and `Whitespace`. (Numerous other node types can also be returned, including CDATA, Comment, Document, Entity, and DocumentType.)

➤ **Name**—The name of each node is retrieved using the `Name` property of `XmlReader`. The name of the node could be an element name, such as `<FilmOrder>`, or an attribute name, such as `FilmId`.

➤ **Attribute Count**—The number of attributes associated with a node is retrieved using the `AttributeCount` property of `XmlReader NodeType`.

➤ **Value**—The value of a node is retrieved using the `Value` property of `XmlReader`. For example, the element node `<Title>` contains a value of `Grease`.

The subroutine `ShowXmlNode` is implemented as follows. Within the `ShowXmlNode` subroutine, each level of node depth adds two spaces to the output generated:

```
If reader.Depth > 0 Then
   For depthCount As Integer = 1 To reader.Depth
      Console.Write(" ")
   Next
End If
```

You add these spaces in order to create human-readable output (so you can easily determine the depth of each node displayed). For each type of node, `ShowXmlNode` displays the value of the `NodeType` property. The `ShowXmlNode` subroutine makes a distinction between nodes of type `Whitespace` and other types of nodes. The reason for this is simple: a node of type `Whitespace` does not contain a name or an attribute count. The value of such a node is any combination of white-space characters (space, tab, carriage return, and so on). Therefore, it doesn't make sense to display the properties if the `NodeType` is `XmlNodeType.WhiteSpace`. Nodes of type Text have no name associated with them, so for this type, subroutine `ShowXmlNode` displays only the properties `NodeType` and `Value`. For all other node types (including elements and attributes), the `Name`, `AttributeCount`, `Value`, and `NodeType` properties are displayed.

To finalize this module, add a `Sub Main` as follows:

```
Sub Main(ByVal args() As String)
   ReadMovieXml("MovieManage.xml")
End Sub
```

The `MovieManage.xml` file, used as input for the example, looks like this:

```
<?xml version="1.0" encoding="utf-8" ?>
<MovieOrderDump>
  <FilmOrderList>
    <multiFilmOrders>
      <FilmOrder filmId="101">
        <name>Grease</name>
        <quantity>10</quantity>
      </FilmOrder>
      <FilmOrder filmId="102">
        <name>Lawrence of Arabia</name>
        <quantity>10</quantity>
      </FilmOrder>
      <FilmOrder filmId="103">
        <name>Star Wars</name>
        <quantity>10</quantity>
      </FilmOrder>
    </multiFilmOrders>
  </FilmOrderList>
  <PreOrder>
    <FilmOrder filmId="104">
      <name>Shrek III - Shrek Becomes a Programmer</name>
      <quantity>10</quantity>
```

```
        </FilmOrder>
      </PreOrder>
      <Returns>
        <FilmOrder filmId="103">
          <name>Star Wars</name>
          <quantity>2</quantity>
        </FilmOrder>
      </Returns>
</MovieOrderDump>
```

Running this module produces the following output (a partial display, as it would be rather lengthy):

```
Name: xml, Type: XmlDeclaration, AttributeCount: 2, Value: version="1.0"
encoding="utf-8"
 Name: version, Type: Attribute, AttributeCount: 2, Value: 1.0
 Name: encoding, Type: Attribute, AttributeCount: 2, Value: utf-8
Type: Whitespace
Name: MovieOrderDump, Type: Element, AttributeCount: 0, Value:
Type: Whitespace
 Name: FilmOrderList, Type: Element, AttributeCount: 0, Value:
 Type: Whitespace
  Name: multiFilmOrders, Type: Element, AttributeCount: 0, Value:
  Type: Whitespace
   Name: FilmOrder, Type: Element, AttributeCount: 1, Value:
    Name: filmId, Type: Attribute, AttributeCount: 1, Value: 101
    Type: Whitespace
   Name: name, Type: Element, AttributeCount: 0, Value:
     Type: Text, Value: Grease
   Name: name, Type: EndElement, AttributeCount: 0, Value:
   Type: Whitespace
   Name: quantity, Type: Element, AttributeCount: 0, Value:
     Type: Text, Value: 10
   Name: quantity, Type: EndElement, AttributeCount: 0, Value:
   Type: Whitespace
  Name: FilmOrder, Type: EndElement, AttributeCount: 0, Value:
  Type: Whitespace
```

This example managed to use three methods and five properties of XmlReader. The output generated was informative but far from practical. XmlReader exposes over 50 methods and properties, which means that you have only scratched the surface of this highly versatile class. The remainder of this section looks at the XmlReaderSettings class, introduces a more realistic use of XmlReader, and demonstrates how the classes of System.Xml handle errors.

## The XmlReaderSettings Class

Just like the XmlWriter object, the XmlReader.Create method allows you to specify settings to be applied for instantiation of the object. This means that you can provide settings specifying how the XmlReader object behaves when it is reading whatever XML you might have for it. This includes settings for dealing with white space, schemas, and other common options. An example of using this settings class to modify the behavior of the XmlReader class is as follows:

```
Dim myXmlSettings As New XmlReaderSettings()
myXmlSettings.IgnoreWhitespace = True
```

```
myXmlSettings.IgnoreComments = True
Using readMovieInfo As XmlReader = XmlReader.Create(fileName, myXmlSettings)
    ' Use XmlReader object here.
End Using
```

In this case, the `XmlReader` object that is created ignores the white space that it encounters, as well as any of the XML comments. These settings, once established with the `XmlReaderSettings` object, are then associated with the `XmlReader` object through its `Create` method.

## Traversing XML Using XmlReader

In cases where the format of the XML is known, the `XmlReader` can be used to parse the document in a more deliberate manner rather than hitting every node. In the previous section, you implemented a class that serialized arrays of movie orders. The next example, found in the `FilmOrdersReader2` project, takes an XML document containing multiple XML documents of that type and traverses them. Each movie order is forwarded to the movie supplier via fax. The general process for traversing this document is outlined by the following pseudo code:

```
Read root element: <MovieOrderDump>
    Process each <FilmOrderList> element
        Read <multiFilmOrders> element
            Process each <FilmOrder>
                Send fax for each movie order here
```

The basic outline for the program's implementation is to open a file containing the XML document, parse, then traverse it from element to element as follows (code file: `Main.vb`):

```
Dim myXmlSettings As New XmlReaderSettings()
Using readMovieInfo As XmlReader = XmlReader.Create(fileName, myXmlSettings)
    readMovieInfo.Read()
    readMovieInfo.ReadStartElement("MovieOrderDump")
    Do While (True)
        '****************************************************
        '* Process FilmOrder elements here                *
        '****************************************************
    Loop
    readMovieInfo.ReadEndElement() '  </MovieOrderDump>
End Using
```

The preceding code opened the file using the constructor of `XmlReader`, and the `End Using` statement takes care of shutting everything down for you. The code also introduced two methods of the `XmlReader` class:

**1.** `ReadStartElement(String)`—This verifies that the current node in the stream is an element and that the element's name matches the string passed to `ReadStartElement`. If the verification is successful, then the stream is advanced to the next element.

**2.** `ReadEndElement()`—This verifies that the current element is an end tag; and if the verification is successful, then the stream is advanced to the next element.

The application knows that an element, `<MovieOrderDump>`, will be found at a specific point in the document. The `ReadStartElement` method verifies this foreknowledge of the document format. After all the elements contained in element `<MovieOrderDump>` have been traversed, the stream should point to the end tag `</MovieOrderDump>`. The `ReadEndElement` method verifies this.

The code that traverses each element of type `<FilmOrder>` similarly uses the `ReadStartElement` and `ReadEndElement` methods to indicate the start and end of the `<FilmOrder>` and `<multiFilmOrders>` elements. The code that ultimately parses the list of movie orders and then faxes the movie supplier (using the `FranticallyFaxTheMovieSupplier` subroutine) is as follows (code file: `Main.vb`):

```vb
Private Sub ReadMovieXml(ByVal fileName As String)
    Dim myXmlSettings As New XmlReaderSettings()
    Dim movieName As String
    Dim movieId As String
    Dim quantity As String

    Using readMovieInfo As XmlReader =
        XmlReader.Create(fileName, myXmlSettings)
        'position to first element
        readMovieInfo.Read()
        readMovieInfo.ReadStartElement("MovieOrderDump")
        Do While (True)
            readMovieInfo.ReadStartElement("FilmOrderList")
            readMovieInfo.ReadStartElement("multiFilmOrders")

            'for each order
            Do While (True)
                readMovieInfo.MoveToContent()
                movieId = readMovieInfo.GetAttribute("filmId")
                readMovieInfo.ReadStartElement("FilmOrder")

                movieName = readMovieInfo.ReadElementString()
                quantity = readMovieInfo.ReadElementString()
                readMovieInfo.ReadEndElement() ' clear </FilmOrder>

                FranticallyFaxTheMovieSupplier(movieName, movieId, quantity)

                ' Should read next FilmOrder node
                ' else quits
                readMovieInfo.Read()
                If ("FilmOrder" <> readMovieInfo.Name) Then
                    Exit Do
                End If
            Loop
            readMovieInfo.ReadEndElement() ' clear </multiFilmOrders>
            readMovieInfo.ReadEndElement() ' clear </FilmOrderList>
            ' Should read next FilmOrderList node
            ' else you quit
            readMovieInfo.Read() ' clear </MovieOrderDump>
            If ("FilmOrderList" <> readMovieInfo.Name) Then
                Exit Do
            End If
        Loop
        readMovieInfo.ReadEndElement() '  </MovieOrderDump>
    End Using
End Sub
```

The values are read from the XML file using the `ReadElementString` and `GetAttribute` methods. Notice that the call to `GetAttribute` is done before reading the `FilmOrder` element. This is because the `ReadStartElement` method advances the location for the next read to the next element in the XML file. The `MoveToContent` call before the call to `GetAttribute` ensures that the current read location is on the element, and not on white space.

While parsing the stream, it was known that an element named `name` existed and that this element contained the name of the movie. Rather than parse the start tag, get the value, and parse the end tag, it was easier to get the data using the `ReadElementString` method.

The intended output of this example is a fax, which is not implemented in order to focus on XML. The format of the document is still verified by `XmlReader` as it is parsed.

The `XmlReader` class also exposes properties that provide more insight into the data contained in the XML document and the state of parsing: `IsEmptyElement`, `EOF`, `HasAttributes`, and `IsStartElement`.

.NET CLR–compliant types are not 100 percent interchangeable with XML types. The .NET Framework includes methods in the `XmlReader` class to make the process of casting from one of these XML types to .NET types easier.

Using the `ReadElementContentAs` method, you can easily perform the necessary casting required, as seen here:

```
Dim username As String = _
    myXmlReader.ReadElementContentAs(GetType(String), Nothing)
Dim myDate As DateTime = _
    myXmlReader.ReadElementContentAs(GetType(DateTime), Nothing)
```

In addition to the general `ReadElementContentAs` method, there are specific `ReadElementContentAsX` methods for each of the common data types; and in addition to these methods, the raw XML associated with the document can also be retrieved, using `ReadInnerXml` and `ReadOuterXml`. Again, this only scratches the surface of the `XmlReader` class, a class quite rich in functionality.

## Handling Exceptions

XML is text and could easily be read using mundane methods such as `Read` and `ReadLine`. A key feature of each class that reads and traverses XML is inherent support for error detection and handling. To demonstrate this, consider the following malformed XML document found in the file named `Malformed.xml`, also included in the `FilmOrdersReader2` project:

```
<?xml version="1.0" encoding="IBM437" ?>
<FilmOrder FilmId="101", Qty="10">
   <Name>Grease</Name>
<FilmOrder>
```

This document may not immediately appear to be malformed. By wrapping a call to the method you developed (`ReadMovieXml`), you can see what type of exception is raised when `XmlReader` detects the malformed XML within this document as shown in `Sub Main()`. Comment out the line calling the `MovieManage.xml` file, and uncomment the line to try to open the `malformed.xml` file:

```
Try
    'ReadMovieXml("MovieManage.xml")
```

```
        ReadMovieXml("Malformed.xml")
    Catch xmlEx As XmlException
        Console.Error.WriteLine("XML Error: " + xmlEx.ToString())
    Catch ex As Exception
        Console.Error.WriteLine("Some other error: " + ex.ToString())
    End Try
```

The methods and properties exposed by the XmlReader class raise exceptions of type System. Xml.XmlException. In fact, every class in the System.Xml namespace raises exceptions of type XmlException. Although this is a discussion of errors using an instance of type XmlReader, the concepts reviewed apply to all errors generated by classes found in the System.Xml namespace. The XmlException extends the basic Exception to include more information about the location of the error within the XML file.

The error displayed when subroutine ReadMovieXML processes Malformed.xml is as follows:

```
XML Error: System.Xml.XmlException: The ',' character, hexadecimal value 0x2C,
    cannot begin a name. Line 2, position 49.
```

The preceding snippet indicates that a comma separates the attributes in element <FilmOrder FilmId="101", Qty="10">. This comma is invalid. Removing it and running the code again results in the following output:

```
XML Error: System.Xml.XmlException: This is an unexpected token. Expected
    'EndElement'. Line 5, position 27.
```

Again, you can recognize the precise error. In this case, you do not have an end element, </FilmOrder>, but you do have an opening element, <FilmOrder>.

The properties provided by the XmlException class (such as LineNumber, LinePosition, and Message) provide a useful level of precision when tracking down errors. The XmlReader class also exposes a level of precision with respect to the parsing of the XML document. This precision is exposed by the XmlReader through properties such as LineNumber and LinePosition.

## Document Object Model (DOM)

The Document Object Model (DOM) is a logical view of an XML file. Within the DOM, an XML document is contained in a class named XmlDocument. Each node within this document is accessible and managed using XmlNode. Nodes can also be accessed and managed using a class specifically designed to process a specific node's type (XmlElement, XmlAttribute, and so on). XML documents are extracted from XmlDocument using a variety of mechanisms exposed through such classes as XmlWriter, TextWriter, Stream, and a file (specified by a filename of type String). XML documents are consumed by an XmlDocument using a variety of load mechanisms exposed through the same classes.

A DOM-style parser differs from a stream-style parser with respect to movement. Using the DOM, the nodes can be traversed forward and backward; and nodes can be added to the document, removed from the document, and updated. However, this flexibility comes at a performance cost, since the entire document is read into memory. It is faster to read or write XML using a stream-style parser.

The DOM-specific classes exposed by `System.Xml` include the following:

➤ **XmlDocument**—Corresponds to an entire XML document. A document is loaded using the `Load` or `LoadXml` methods. The `Load` method loads the XML from a file (the filename specified as type `String`), `TextReader`, or `XmlReader`. A document can be loaded using `LoadXml` in conjunction with a string containing the XML document. The `Save` method is used to save XML documents. The methods exposed by `XmlDocument` reflect the intricate manipulation of an XML document. For example, the following creation methods are implemented by this class: `CreateAttribute`, `CreateCDataSection`, `CreateComment`, `CreateDocumentFragment`, `CreateDocumentType`, `CreateElement`, `CreateEntityReference`, `CreateNavigator`, `CreateNode`, `CreateProcessingInstruction`, `CreateSignificantWhitespace`, `CreateTextNode`, `CreateWhitespace`, and `CreateXmlDeclaration`. The elements contained in the document can be retrieved. Other methods support the retrieving, importing, cloning, loading, and writing of nodes.

➤ **XmlNode**—Corresponds to a node within the DOM tree. This is the base class for the other node type classes. A robust set of methods and properties is provided to create, delete, and replace nodes. The contents of a node can similarly be traversed in a variety of ways: `FirstChild`, `LastChild`, `NextSibling`, `ParentNode`, and `PreviousSibling`.

➤ **XmlElement**—Corresponds to an element within the DOM tree. The functionality exposed by this class contains a variety of methods used to manipulate an element's attributes.

➤ **XmlAttribute**—Corresponds to an attribute of an element (`XmlElement`) within the DOM tree. An attribute contains data and lists of subordinate data, so it is a less complicated object than an `XmlNode` or an `XmlElement`. An `XmlAttribute` can retrieve its owner document (property, `OwnerDocument`), retrieve its owner element (property, `OwnerElement`), retrieve its parent node (property, `ParentNode`), and retrieve its name (property, `Name`). The value of an `XmlAttribute` is available via a read-write property named `Value`. Given the diverse number of methods and properties exposed by `XmlDocument`, `XmlNode`, `XmlElement`, and `XmlAttribute` (and there are many more than those listed here), it's clear that any XML 1.0- or 1.1-compliant document can be generated and manipulated using these classes. In comparison to their XML stream counterparts, these classes offer more flexible movement within the XML document and through any editing of XML documents.

A similar comparison could be made between DOM and data serialized and deserialized using XML. Using serialization, the type of node (for example, attribute or element) and the node name are specified at compile time. There is no on-the-fly modification of the XML generated by the serialization process.

## DOM Traversing XML

The first DOM example, located in the `DomReading` project, loads an XML document into an `XmlDocument` object using a string that contains the actual XML document. The example over the next few pages simply traverses each XML element (`XmlNode`) in the document (`XmlDocument`) and displays the data to the console. The data associated with this example is contained in a variable, `rawData`, which is initialized as follows:

```
Dim rawData =
    <multiFilmOrders>
```

```
      <FilmOrder>
          <name>Grease</name>
          <filmId>101</filmId>
          <quantity>10</quantity>
      </FilmOrder>
      <FilmOrder>
          <name>Lawrence of Arabia</name>
          <filmId>102</filmId>
          <quantity>10</quantity>
      </FilmOrder>
   </multiFilmOrders>
```

The XML document in `rawData` is a portion of the XML hierarchy associated with a movie order. Notice the lack of quotation marks around the XML: this is an XML literal. XML literals allow you to insert a block of XML directly into your VB source code, and are covered a little later in this chapter. They can be written over a number of lines, and can be used wherever you might normally load an XML file.

The basic idea in processing this data is to traverse each `<FilmOrder>` element in order to display the data it contains. Each node corresponding to a `<FilmOrder>` element can be retrieved from your `XmlDocument` using the `GetElementsByTagName` method (specifying a tag name of `FilmOrder`). The `GetElementsByTagName` method returns a list of `XmlNode` objects in the form of a collection of type `XmlNodeList`. Using the `For Each` statement to construct this list, the `XmlNodeList` (`movieOrderNodes`) can be traversed as individual `XmlNode` elements (`movieOrderNode`). The general code for handling this is as follows:

```
Dim xmlDoc As New XmlDocument
Dim movieOrderNodes As XmlNodeList
Dim movieOrderNode As XmlNode
xmlDoc.LoadXml(rawData.ToString())
' Traverse each <FilmOrder>
movieOrderNodes = xmlDoc.GetElementsByTagName("FilmOrder")
For Each movieOrderNode In movieOrderNodes
    '*********************************************************
    ' Process <name>, <filmId> and <quantity> here
    '*********************************************************
Next
```

Each `XmlNode` can then have its contents displayed by traversing the children of this node using the `ChildNodes` method. This method returns an `XmlNodeList` (`baseDataNodes`) that can be traversed one `XmlNode` list element at a time, shown here (code file: `Main.vb`):

```
Dim baseDataNodes As XmlNodeList
Dim bFirstInRow As Boolean
baseDataNodes = movieOrderNode.ChildNodes
bFirstInRow = True
For Each baseDataNode As XmlNode In baseDataNodes
  If (bFirstInRow) Then
    bFirstInRow = False
  Else
    Console.Write(", ")
  End If
  Console.Write(baseDataNode.Name & ": " & baseDataNode.InnerText)
Next
Console.WriteLine()
```

The bulk of the preceding code retrieves the name of the node using the `Name` property and the `InnerText` property of the node. The `InnerText` property of each `XmlNode` retrieved contains the data associated with the XML elements (nodes) `<name>`, `<filmId>`, and `<quantity>`. The example displays the contents of the XML elements using `Console.Write`. The XML document is displayed to the console as follows:

```
name: Grease, quantity: 10
name: Lawrence of Arabia, quantity: 10
```

Other, more practical, methods for using this data could have been implemented, including the following:

> ➤ The contents could have been directed to an ASP.NET `Response` object, and the data retrieved could have been used to create an HTML table (`<table>` table, `<tr>` row, and `<td>` data) that would be written to the `Response` object.

> ➤ The data traversed could have been directed to a `ListBox` or `ComboBox` Windows Forms control. This would enable the data returned to be selected as part of a GUI application.

> ➤ The data could have been edited as part of your application's business rules. For example, you could have used the traversal to verify that the `<filmId>` matched the `<name>`. Something like this could be done if you wanted to validate the data entered into the XML document in any manner.

## Writing XML with the DOM

You can also use the DOM to create or edit XML documents. Creating new XML items is a two-step process, however. First, you use the containing document to create the new element, attribute, or comment (or other node type), and then you add that at the appropriate location in the document.

Just as there are a number of methods in the DOM for reading the XML, there are also methods for creating new nodes. The `XmlDocument` class has the basic `CreateNode` method, as well as specific methods for creating the different node types, such as `CreateElement`, `CreateAttribute`, `CreateComment`, and others. Once the node is created, you add it in place using the `AppendChild` method of `XmlNode` (or one of the children of `XmlNode`).

The example for this section is in the `DomWriting` project and will be used to demonstrate writing XML with the DOM. Most of the work in this sample will be done in two functions, so the `Main` method can remain simple, as shown here (code file: `Main.vb`):

```
Sub Main()

    Dim data As String
    Dim fileName As String = "filmorama.xml"
    data = GenerateXml(fileName)

    Console.WriteLine(data)
    Console.WriteLine("Press ENTER to continue")
    Console.ReadLine()

End Sub
```

The GenerateXml function creates the initial XmlDocument, and calls the CreateFilmOrder function multiple times to add a number of items to the structure. This creates a hierarchical XML document that can then be used elsewhere in your application. Typically, you would use the Save method to write the XML to a stream or document, but in this case it just retrieves the OuterXml (that is, the full XML document) to display (code file: Main.vb):

```vb
Private Function GenerateXml(ByVal fileName As String) As String
    Dim result As String
    Dim doc As New XmlDocument
    Dim elem As XmlElement

    'create root node
    Dim root As XmlElement = doc.CreateElement("FilmOrderList")
    doc.AppendChild(root)
    'this data would likely come from elsewhere
    For i As Integer = 1 To 5
        elem = CreateFilmOrder(doc, i)
        root.AppendChild(elem)
    Next
    result = doc.OuterXml
    Return result
End Function
```

The most common error made when writing an XML document using the DOM is to create the elements but forget to append them into the document. This step is done here with the AppendChild method, but other methods can be used, in particular InsertBefore, InsertAfter, PrependChild, and RemoveChild.

Creating the individual FilmOrder nodes uses a similar CreateElement/AppendChild strategy. In addition, attributes are created using the Append method of the Attributes collection for each XmlElement. The following shows the CreateFilOrder method (code file: Main.vb):

```vb
Private Function CreateFilmOrder(ByVal parent As XmlDocument, _
    ByVal count As Integer) As XmlElement
    Dim result As XmlElement
    Dim id As XmlAttribute
    Dim title As XmlElement
    Dim quantity As XmlElement

    result = parent.CreateElement("FilmOrder")
    id = parent.CreateAttribute("id")
    id.Value = 100 + count

    title = parent.CreateElement("title")
    title.InnerText = "Some title here"

    quantity = parent.CreateElement("quantity")
    quantity.InnerText = "10"

    result.Attributes.Append(id)
    result.AppendChild(title)
    result.AppendChild(quantity)
    Return result
End Function
```

This generates the following XML, although it will all be on one line in the output:

```
<FilmOrderList>
  <FilmOrder id="101">
    <title>Some title here</title>
    <quantity> 10 </quantity>
  </FilmOrder>
  <FilmOrder id="102">
    <title>Some title here</title>
    <quantity> 10 </quantity>
  </FilmOrder>
  <FilmOrder id="103">
    <title>Some title here</title>
    <quantity> 10 </quantity>
  </FilmOrder>
  <FilmOrder id="104">
    <title>Some title here</title>
    <quantity>10</quantity>
  </FilmOrder>
  <FilmOrder id="105">
    <title>Some title here</title>
    <quantity>10</quantity>
  </FilmOrder>
</FilmOrderList>
```

Once you get the hang of creating XML with the DOM (and forget to add the new nodes a few dozen times), it is quite a handy method for writing XML. If the XML you need to create can all be created at once, it is probably better to use the `XmlWriter` class instead. Writing XML with the DOM is best left for those situations when you need to either edit an existing XML document or move backward through the document as you are writing. In addition, because the DOM is an international standard, it means that code using the DOM is portable to other languages that also provide a DOM.

In addition to the `XmlWriter`, the `XElement` shown later in this chapter provides yet another method for reading and writing XML.

## LINQ TO XML

The previous sections of this chapter provided you with a general understanding of XML, how it is structured and how it can be accessed and manipulated using the .NET Framework. This section covers working with XML using newer features, specifically Language Integrated Query (LINQ), added in version 3.5 of the framework.

With the introduction of LINQ to the .NET Framework, the focus was on easy access to the data that you want to work with in your applications. One of the main data stores in the application space is XML, so it was really a no-brainer to create the LINQ to XML implementation. With the inclusion of `System.Xml.Linq`, you now have a series of capabilities that make the process of working with XML in your code much easier to achieve.

This chapter will only touch on how LINQ is used in relationship to XML. For the more basic description of LINQ and how it is used or works in a general sense, refer to chapter 9.

# LINQ Helper XML Objects

Even if the LINQ querying capability were not around, the new objects available to work with the XML are so good that they can even stand on their own outside LINQ. Within the new `System .Xml.Linq` namespace, you will find a series of new LINQ to XML helper objects that make working with an XML document in memory that much easier. The following sections describe the new objects that are available within this new namespace.

> **NOTE** *Many of the examples in this chapter use a file called* `Hamlet.xml`, *which you can find included in the file* `http://metalab.unc.edu/bosak/xml/eg/ shaks200.zip`. *At this link you'll find all of Shakespeare's plays as XML files.*

## XDocument

The `XDocument` class is a replacement of the `XmlDocument` object from the pre-LINQ world. While it does not comply with any international standards, the `XDocument` object is easier to work with when dealing with XML documents. It works with the other new objects in this space, such as the `XNamespace`, `XComment`, `XElement`, and `XAttribute` objects.

The `LinqRead` project provides an example that demonstrates the use of the `XDocument` class. This project is covered in more detail a little later. One of the more important members of the `XDocument` object is the `Load` method:

```
Dim xdoc As XDocument = XDocument.Load("C:\Hamlet.xml")
```

The preceding example loads the `Hamlet.xml` contents as an in-memory `XDocument` object. You can also pass a `TextReader` or an `XmlReader` object into the `Load` method. From here, you can programmatically work with the XML (code file: `Main.vb`):

```
Dim xdoc As XDocument = XDocument.Load("C:\Hamlet.xml")
Console.WriteLine(xdoc.Root.Name.ToString())
Console.WriteLine(xdoc.Root.HasAttributes.ToString())
```

This produces the following results:

```
PLAY
False
```

Another important member to be aware of is the `Save` method, which enables you to save to a physical disk location or to a `TextWriter` or an `XmlWriter` object:

```
Dim xdoc As XDocument = XDocument.Load("Hamlet.xml")
xdoc.Save("CopyOfHamlet.xml")
```

## XElement

Another common object that you will work with is the `XElement` object. With this object, you can easily create even single-element objects that are XML documents themselves, and even fragments of XML. For instance, here is an example of writing an XML element with a corresponding value:

```
Dim xe As XElement = New XElement("Company", "Wrox")
Console.WriteLine(xe.ToString())
```

When creating a new XElement object, you can define the name of the element as well as the value used in the element. In this case, the name of the element will be <Company>, while the value of the <Company> element will be Wrox. Running this in a console application, you will get the following result:

```
<Company>Wrox</Company>
```

The XElementWriting project provides an example that demonstrates how you can also create a more complete XML document using multiple XElement objects, as shown here (code file: Main.vb):

```vb
Imports System.Xml.Linq

Module Main

    Sub Main()

        Dim root As New XElement("Company",
                            New XAttribute("Type", "Publisher"),
                            New XElement("CompanyName", "Wrox"),
                            New XElement("CompanyAddress",
                                New XElement("Street", "111 River Street"),
                                New XElement("City", "Hoboken"),
                                New XElement("State", "NJ"),
                                New XElement("Country", "USA"),
                                New XElement("Zip", "07030-5774")))
        Console.WriteLine(root.ToString())
        Console.WriteLine("Press ENTER to exit")
        Console.ReadLine()
    End Sub

End Module
```

Running this application yields the results shown in Figure 8-1.

**FIGURE 8-1:** Output for the XElementWriting example

## XNamespace

The XNamespace is an object that represents an XML namespace, and it is easily applied to elements within your document. An example of this can be found in the XElementWritingNamespaces project. It is a variation of the previous example with only minor edits to include a namespace for the root element, as seen here:

```
Imports System.Xml.Linq

Module Main

    Sub Main()
        Dim ns as Xnamespace = "http://www.example.com/somenamespace"
        Dim root As New Xelement(ns + "Company",
                                 New XElement("CompanyName", "Wrox"),
                                 New XElement("CompanyAddress",
                                     New XElement("Street", "111 River Street"),
                                     New XElement("City", "Hoboken"),
                                     New XElement("State", "NJ"),
                                     New XElement("Country", "USA"),
                                     New XElement("Zip"; "07030-5774")))
        Console.WriteLine(root.ToString())
        Console.WriteLine("Press ENTER to exit")
        Console.ReadLine()
    End Sub

End Module
```

In this case, an `XNamespace` object is created by assigning it a value of `http://www.example.com/somenamespace`. From there, it is actually used in the root element `<Company>` with the instantiation of the `XElement` object:

```
Dim root As New XElement(ns + "Company",
```

This will produce the results shown in Figure 8-2.

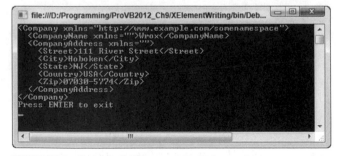

**FIGURE 8-2:** Output of `XElementWriting` using a namespace

Besides dealing with the root element, you can also apply namespaces to all your elements (code file: `Main.vb`):

```
Imports System.Xml.Linq

Module Main

    Sub Main()
```

```vb
        Dim ns1 As XNamespace = "http://www.example.com/ns/root"
        Dim ns2 As XNamespace = "http://www.example.com/ns/address"

        Dim root As New XElement(ns1 + "Company",
                                 New XElement(ns1 + "CompanyName", "Wrox"),
                                 New XElement(ns2 + "CompanyAddress",
                                     New XElement(ns2 + "Street",
                                                  "111 River Street"),
                                     New XElement(ns2 + "City", "Hoboken"),
                                     New XElement(ns2 + "State", "NJ"),
                                     New XElement(ns2 + "Country", "USA"),
                                     New XElement(ns2 + "Zip", "07030-5774")))
        Console.WriteLine(root.ToString())
        Console.WriteLine("Press ENTER to exit")
        Console.ReadLine()
    End Sub

    End Module
```

This produces the results shown in Figure 8-3.

**FIGURE 8-3:** Output for the `XElementWritingNamespaces` example

Since the namespace was applied to the `<CompanyAddress>`, all of its child elements (`<Street>`, `<City>`, `<State>`, `<Country>`, and `<Zip>`) also have this same namespace, since elements inherit the namespace of their parent.

## XAttribute

In addition to elements, another important aspect of XML is attributes, as mentioned earlier in this chapter. Adding and working with attributes is done through the use of the `XAttribute` object. The following example adds an attribute to the root `<Company>` node:

```vb
        Dim root As New XElement("Company",
                                 New XAttribute("Type", "Publisher"),
                                 New XElement("CompanyName", "Wrox"),
                                 New XElement("CompanyAddress",
                                     New XElement("Street", "111 River Street"),
                                     New XElement("City", "Hoboken"),
                                     New XElement("State", "NJ"),
                                     New XElement("Country", "USA"),
                                     New XElement("Zip", "07030-5774")))
```

Here, the attribute `MyAttribute` with a value of `MyAttributeValue` is added to the root element of the XML document, producing the results shown in Figure 8-4.

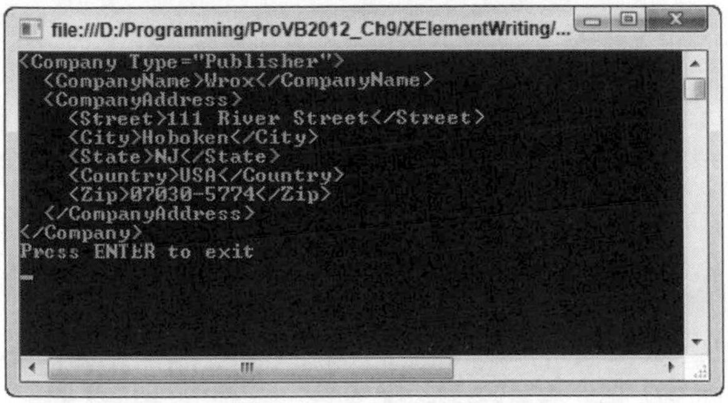

**FIGURE 8-4:** Output of `XElementWriting` with added attribute

# XML Literals

LINQ provides a great feature, called XML *literals*, that can be used to greatly simplify working with XML. Using *XML literals*, you can place XML directly in your code for working with the `XDocument` and `XElement` objects. This works due to the fact that the literal XML is converted directly to appropriate objects, such as `XElement` and `XAttribute`.

Earlier, in the `XElementWriting` example, the use of the `XElement` object was presented as follows:

```vb
Imports System.Xml.Linq

Module Main

    Sub Main()
        Dim root As New XElement("Company",
                                 New XElement("CompanyName", "Wrox"),
                                 New XElement("CompanyAddress",
                                     New XElement("Street", "111 River Street"),
                                     New XElement("City", "Hoboken"),
                                     New XElement("State", "NJ"),
                                     New XElement("Country", "USA"),
                                     New XElement("Zip", "07030-5774")))
        Console.WriteLine(root.ToString())
        Console.WriteLine("Press ENTER to exit")
        Console.ReadLine()
    End Sub

End Module
```

The `XmlLiterals` project instead uses XML literals to perform the same functionality, seen here (code file: `Main.vb`):

```vb
Module Main

    Sub Main()
        Dim root As XElement =
            <Company>
```

```
                <CompanyName>Wrox</CompanyName>
                <CompanyAddress>
                    <Street>111 River Street</Street>
                    <City>Hoboken</City>
                    <State>NJ</State>
                    <Country>USA</Country>
                    <Zip>07030-5774</Zip>
                </CompanyAddress>
            </Company>
        Console.WriteLine(root.ToString())
        Console.WriteLine("Press ENTER to exit")
        Console.ReadLine()
    End Sub

End Module
```

This enables you to place the XML directly in the code. The best part about this is the IDE support for XML literals. Visual Studio 2012 has IntelliSense and excellent color-coding for the XML that you place in your code file. As Figure 8-5 shows, there is no difference in the output between this example and the previous one, which didn't use XML literals.

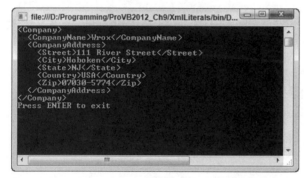

**FIGURE 8-5:** Output of `XElementWriting` using XML literals

You can also use inline variables in the XML document. For instance, if you wanted to declare the value of the `<CompanyName>` element outside the XML literal, then you could use a construct similar to the following:

```
Module Module1
    Sub Main()
        Dim companyName As String = "Wrox"
        Dim xe As XElement = _
            <Company>
            <CompanyName><%= companyName %></CompanyName>
                <CompanyAddress>
                <Street>111 River Street</Street>
                <City>Hoboken</City>
                <State>NJ</State>
                <Country>USA</Country>
                <Zip>07030-5774</Zip>
            </CompanyAddress>
```

```
        </Company>
        Console.WriteLine(xe.ToString())
        Console.ReadLine()
    End Sub
End Module
```

In this case, the `<CompanyName>` element is assigned a value of `Wrox` from the `companyName` variable, using the syntax `<%= companyName %>`.

# Querying XML Documents

As mentioned in the beginning of this section, and in other chapters, LINQ stands for Language Integrated Query. The primary purpose for its existence is to provide a streamlined approach to querying data.

Now that you can get your XML documents into an `XDocument` object and work with the various parts of this document, you can also use LINQ to XML to query your XML documents and work with the results.

## Static XML Documents

The functionality provided by LINQ makes querying a static XML document take almost no work at all. The following example, from the `LinqRead` project, makes use of the `hamlet.xml` file. The example demonstrates querying for all the players (actors) who appear in a play. Each of these players is defined in the XML document with the `<PERSONA>` element (code file: `Main.vb`):

```
Module Main
    Sub Main()
        Dim xdoc As XDocument = XDocument.Load("C:\hamlet.xml")
        Dim query = From people In xdoc.Descendants("PERSONA") _
                    Select people.Value
        Console.WriteLine("{0} Players Found", query.Count())
        Console.WriteLine()
        For Each item In query
            Console.WriteLine(item)
        Next
        Console.WriteLine("Press ENTER to exit")
        Console.ReadLine()
    End Sub
End Module
```

In this case, an `XDocument` object loads a physical XML file (`hamlet.xml`) and then performs a LINQ query over the contents of the document:

```
Dim query = From people In xdoc.Descendants("PERSONA") _
            Select people.Value
```

The `people` object is a representation of all the `<PERSONA>` elements found in the document. Then the `Select` statement gets at the values of these elements. From there, a `Console.WriteLine` method is used to write out a count of all the players found, using `query.Count`. Next, each of the items is written to the screen in a `For Each` loop. The results you should see are presented here:

```
26 Players Found
CLAUDIUS, king of Denmark.
```

```
HAMLET, son to the late, and nephew to the present king.
POLONIUS, lord chamberlain.
HORATIO, friend to Hamlet.
LAERTES, son to Polonius.
LUCIANUS, nephew to the king.
VOLTIMAND
CORNELIUS
ROSENCRANTZ
GUILDENSTERN
OSRIC
A Gentleman.
A Priest.
MARCELLUS
BERNARDO
FRANCISCO, a soldier.
REYNALDO, servant to Polonius.
Players.
Two Clowns, grave-diggers.
FORTINBRAS, prince of Norway.
A Captain.
English Ambassadors.
GERTRUDE, queen of Denmark, and mother to Hamlet.
OPHELIA, daughter to Polonius.
Lords, Ladies, Officers, Soldiers, Sailors, Messengers, and other Attendants.
Ghost of Hamlet's Father.
```

## Dynamic XML Documents

Numerous dynamic XML documents can be found on the Internet these days. Blog feeds, pod-cast feeds, and more provide XML documents by sending a request to a specific URL endpoint. These feeds can be viewed either in the browser, through an RSS aggregator, or as pure XML. The LinqReadDynamic project includes an example to demonstrate reading and querying an RSS feed. The code to do this is (code file: Main.vb):

```
Module Module1
    Sub Main()
        Dim xdoc As XDocument = _
                       XDocument.Load("http://weblogs.asp.net/mainfeed.aspx")
        Dim query = From rssFeed In xdoc.Descendants("channel") _
                Select Title = rssFeed.Element("title").Value, _
                    Description = rssFeed.Element("description").Value, _
                    Link = rssFeed.Element("link").Value
        For Each item In query
            Console.WriteLine("TITLE: " + item.Title)
            Console.WriteLine("DESCRIPTION: " + item.Description)
            Console.WriteLine("LINK: " + item.Link)
        Next
        Console.WriteLine()
        Dim queryPosts = From myPosts In xdoc.Descendants("item") _
                Select Title = myPosts.Element("title").Value, _
                    Published = _
                       DateTime.Parse(myPosts.Element("pubDate").Value), _
                    Description = myPosts.Element("description").Value, _
                    Url = myPosts.Element("link").Value
        For Each item In queryPosts
```

```
                        Console.WriteLine(item.Title)
              Next
              Console.WriteLine("Press ENTER to exit")
              Console.ReadLine()
         End Sub
    End Module
```

Here, the `Load` method of the `XDocument` object points to a URL where the XML is retrieved. The first query pulls out all the main subelements of the `<channel>` element in the feed and creates new objects called `Title`, `Description`, and `Link` to get at the values of these subelements.

From there, a `For Each` statement is run to iterate through all the items found in this query. The second query works through all the `<item>` elements and the various subelements it contains (these are all the blog entries found in the blog). Though a lot of the items found are rolled up into properties, in the `For Each` loop, only the `Title` property is used. You will see results similar to that shown in Figure 8-6.

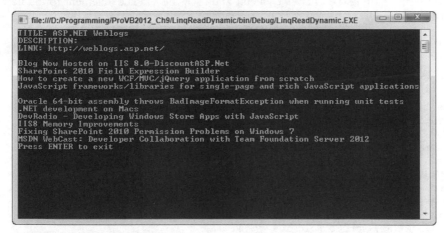

**FIGURE 8-6:** Output for the `LinqReadDynamic` example

# Reading and Writing XML Documents

If you have been working with the XML document `hamlet.xml`, you probably noticed that it is quite large. You've seen how you can query into the XML document in a couple of ways, and now this section takes a look at reading and writing to the XML document.

## Reading from an XML Document

Earlier you saw just how easy it is to query into an XML document using the LINQ query statements, as shown here:

```
Dim query = From people In xdoc.Descendants("PERSONA") _
            Select people.Value
```

This query returns all the players found in the document. Using the `Element` method of the `XDocument` object, you can also get at specific values of the XML document you are working with.

For instance, continuing to work with the `hamlet.xml` document, the following XML fragment shows you how the title is represented:

```
<?xml version="1.0"?>
<PLAY>
    <TITLE>The Tragedy of Hamlet, Prince of Denmark</TITLE>
    <!-- XML removed for clarity -->
</PLAY>
```

As you can see, the `<TITLE>` element is a nested element of the `<PLAY>` element. You can easily get at the title by using the following bit of code:

```
Dim xdoc As XDocument = XDocument.Load("hamlet.xml")
Console.WriteLine(xdoc.Element("PLAY").Element("TITLE").Value)
```

This bit of code writes out the title "The Tragedy of Hamlet, Prince of Denmark" to the console screen. In the code, you were able to work down the hierarchy of the XML document by using two `Element` method calls—first calling the `<PLAY>` element, and then the `<TITLE>` element found nested within the `<PLAY>` element.

Continuing with the `hamlet.xml` document, you can view a long list of players who are defined with the use of the `<PERSONA>` element:

```
<?xml version="1.0"?>
<PLAY>
    <TITLE>The Tragedy of Hamlet, Prince of Denmark</TITLE>
    <!-- XML removed for clarity -->
    <PERSONAE>
        <TITLE>Dramatis Personae</TITLE>
        <PERSONA>CLAUDIUS, king of Denmark. </PERSONA>
        <PERSONA>HAMLET, son to the late,
         and nephew to the present king.</PERSONA>
        <PERSONA>POLONIUS, lord chamberlain. </PERSONA>
        <PERSONA>HORATIO, friend to Hamlet.</PERSONA>
        <PERSONA>LAERTES, son to Polonius.</PERSONA>
        <PERSONA>LUCIANUS, nephew to the king.</PERSONA>
        <!-- XML removed for clarity -->
    </PERSONAE>
</PLAY>
```

Using that, review the following bit of the code's use of this XML:

```
Dim xdoc As XDocument = XDocument.Load("hamlet.xml")
Console.WriteLine( _
    xdoc.Element("PLAY").Element("PERSONAE").Element("PERSONA").Value)
```

This piece of code starts at `<PLAY>`, works down to the `<PERSONAE>` element, and then makes use of the `<PERSONA>` element. However, using this you will get the following result:

```
CLAUDIUS, king of Denmark
```

Although there is a collection of `<PERSONA>` elements, you are dealing only with the first one that is encountered using the `Element().Value` call.

## Writing to an XML Document

In addition to reading from an XML document, you can also write to the document just as easily. The LinqWrite project demonstrates this by providing an example that allows you to change the name of the first player of the hamlet file. The code to accomplish this is (code file: Main.vb):

```
Module Module1
    Sub Main()
        Dim xdoc As XDocument = XDocument.Load("hamlet.xml")
        xdoc.Element("PLAY").Element("PERSONAE"). _
            Element("PERSONA").SetValue("Foo deBar, King of Denmark")
        Console.WriteLine(xdoc.Element("PLAY"). _
            Element("PERSONAE").Element("PERSONA").Value)
        Console.ReadLine()
    End Sub
End Module
```

In this case, the first instance of the <PERSONA> element is overwritten with the value of Foo deBar, King of Denmark using the SetValue method of the Element object. After the SetValue is called and the value is applied to the XML document, the value is then retrieved using the same approach as before. Running this bit of code, you can indeed see that the value of the first <PERSONA> element has been changed.

Another way to change the document is shown in the LinqAddElement project. This example creates the elements you want as XElement objects and then adds them to the document, shown here (code file: Main.vb):

```
Module Module1
    Sub Main()
        Dim xdoc As XDocument = XDocument.Load("hamlet.xml")
        Dim xe As XElement = New XElement("PERSONA", _
                "Foo deBar, King of Denmark")
        xdoc.Element("PLAY").Element("PERSONAE").Add(xe)
        Dim query = From people In xdoc.Descendants("PERSONA") _
                Select people.Value
        Console.WriteLine("{0} Players Found", query.Count())
        Console.WriteLine()
        For Each item In query
            Console.WriteLine(item)
        Next
        Console.ReadLine()
    End Sub
End Module
```

In this case, an XElement document called xe is created. The construction of xe gives you the following XML output:

```
<PERSONA>Foo deBar, King of Denmark</PERSONA>
```

Then, using the Element().Add method from the XDocument object, you are able to add the created element:

```
xdoc.Element("PLAY").Element("PERSONAE").Add(xe)
```

Next, querying all the players, you will now find that instead of 26, as before, you now have 27, with the new one at the bottom of the list. Besides `Add`, you can also use `AddFirst`, which does just that—adds the player to the beginning of the list instead of the end, which is the default.

## XSL TRANSFORMATIONS

Now that you know all about creating and manipulating XML it is time to introduce Extensible Stylesheet Language Translations, or XSLT. XSLT is used to transform XML documents into another format altogether. One popular use of XSLT is to transform XML into HTML so that XML documents can be presented visually. The idea is to use an alternate language (XSLT) to transform the XML, rather than rewrite the source code, SQL commands, or some other mechanism used to generate XML.

Conceptually, XSLT is straightforward. A file (an `.xsl` file) describes the changes (transformations) that will be applied to a particular XML file. Once this is completed, an XSLT processor is provided with the source XML file and the XSLT file, and performs the transformation. The `System.Xml .Xsl.XslTransform` class is such an XSLT processor. Another processor you will find (introduced in the .NET Framework 2.0) is the `XsltCommand` object found at `SystemXml.Query.XsltCommand`. This section looks at using both of these processors.

You can also find some features in Visual Studio that deal with XSLT. The IDE supports items such as XSLT data breakpoints and XSLT debugging. Additionally, XSLT style sheets can be compiled into assemblies even more easily with the command-line style sheet compiler, `XSLTC.exe`.

The XSLT file is itself an XML document. Dozens of XSLT commands can be used in writing an XSLT file. The first example explores the following XSLT elements (commands):

➤ `stylesheet`—This element indicates the start of the style sheet (XSL) in the XSLT file.

➤ `template`—This element denotes a reusable template for producing specific output. This output is generated using a specific node type within the source document under a specific context. For example, the text `<xsl: template match="/">` selects all root nodes ("/") for the specific transform template. The template is applied whenever the match occurs in the source document.

➤ `for-each`—This element applies the same template to each node in the specified set. Recall the example class (`FilmOrderList`) that could be serialized. This class contained an array of movie orders. Given the XML document generated when a `FilmOrderList` is serialized, each movie order serialized could be processed using

   `<xsl:for-each select = "FilmOrderList/multiFilmOrders/FilmOrder">`.

➤ `value-of`—This element retrieves the value of the specified node and inserts it into the document in text form. For example, `<xsl:value-of select="name" />` would take the value of the XML element `<name>` and insert it into the transformed document.

You can use XSLT to convert an XML document to generate a report that is viewed by the manager of the movie supplier. This report is in HTML form so that it can be viewed via the Web. The XSLT elements you previously reviewed (`stylesheet`, `template`, and `for-each`) are the only XSLT elements required to transform the XML document (in which data is stored) into an HTML file (data that can be displayed).

The example for this section relates to the Transformation project. This project includes the following XSLT file (code file: DisplayOrders.xslt):

```xml
<?xml version="1.0" encoding="UTF-8" ?>
<xsl:stylesheet xmlns:xsl="http://www.w3.org/1999/XSL/Transform" version="1.0">
  <xsl:template match="/">
    <html>
      <head><title>What people are ordering</title>
      </head>
      <body>
        <table border="1">
          <tr>
            <th>
              Film Name
            </th>
            <th>
              Film ID
            </th>
            <th>
              Quantity
            </th>
          </tr>
          <xsl:for-each select=
            "//FilmOrder">
            <tr>
              <td>
                <xsl:value-of select="Title" />
              </td>
              <td>
                <xsl:value-of select="@id" />
              </td>
              <td>
                <xsl:value-of select="Quantity" />
              </td>
            </tr>
          </xsl:for-each>
        </table>
      </body>
    </html>
  </xsl:template>
</xsl:stylesheet>
```

In the preceding XSLT file, the XSLT elements are marked in bold. These elements perform operations on the source XML file, Filmorama.xml, containing a serialized FilmOrderList object, and generate the appropriate HTML file.

Your generated file contains a table (marked by the table tag, <table>) that contains a set of rows (each row marked by a table row tag, <tr>). The columns of the table are contained in table data tags, <td>. The XSLT element, for-each, is used to traverse each <FilmOrder> element, producing a separate row for each.

In this case, a shorthand for the location of the `FilmOrder` element was used: `//FilmOrder` returns all `FilmOrder` elements, regardless of their depth in the XML file. Alternately, you could have specified the full path using `FilmOrderList/FilmOrders/FilmOrder` here.

The individual columns of data are generated using the `value-of` XSLT element, in order to query the elements contained within each `<FilmOrder>` element (`<Title>`, `<id>`, and `<Quantity>`).

The code in `Sub Main()` to create a displayable XML file using the `XslCompiledTransform` object is as follows (code file: `Main.vb`):

```
Dim xslt As New XslCompiledTransform
Dim outputFile As String = "output.html"

xslt.Load("displayorders.xslt")
xslt.Transform("filmorama.xml", outputFile)

Process.Start(outputFile)
```

This consists of only five lines of code, with the bulk of the coding taking place in the XSLT file. The previous code snippet created an instance of a `System.Xml.Xsl.XslCompiledTransform` object named `xslt`. The `Load` method of this class is used to load the XSLT file you previously reviewed, `DisplayOrders.xslt`. The `Transform` method takes a source XML file as the first parameter, which in this case was a file containing a serialized `FilmOrderList` object. The second parameter is the destination file created by the transform, `Output .html`. The `Start` method of the `Process` class is used to display the HTML file in the system default browser. This method launches a process that is best suited for displaying the file provided. Basically, the extension of the file dictates which application will be used to display the file. On a typical Windows machine, the program used to display this file is Internet Explorer, as shown in Figure 8-7.

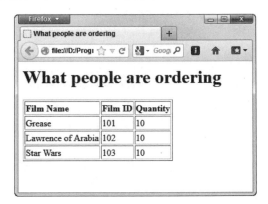

**FIGURE 8-7:** Output for the `Transformation` example

> **NOTE** *Don't confuse displaying this HTML file with ASP.NET. Displaying an HTML file in this manner takes place on a single machine without the involvement of a Web server.*

As demonstrated, the backbone of the `System.Xml.Xsl` namespace is the `XslCompiledTransform` class. This class uses XSLT files to transform XML documents. `XslCompiledTransform` exposes the following methods and properties:

➤ **XmlResolver**—This get/set property is used to specify a class (abstract base class, `XmlResolver`) that is used to handle external references (import and include elements within the style sheet). These external references are encountered when a document is transformed (the method, `Transform`, is executed). The `System.Xml` namespace contains a class, `XmlUrlResolver`, which is derived from `XmlResolver`. The `XmlUrlResolver` class resolves the external resource based on a URI.

➤ **Load**—This overloaded method loads an XSLT style sheet to be used in transforming XML documents. It is permissible to specify the XSLT style sheet as a parameter of type `XPathNavigator`, filename of an XSLT file (specified as parameter type `String`), `XmlReader`, or `IXPathNavigable`. For each type of XSLT supported, an overloaded member is provided that enables an `XmlResolver` to also be specified. For example, it is possible to call `Load(String, XsltSettings, XmlResolver)`, where `String` corresponds to a filename, `XsltSettings` is an object that contains settings to affect the transformation, and `XmlResolver` is an object that handles references in the style sheet of type `xsl:import` and `xsl:include`. It would also be permissible to pass in a value of `Nothing` for the third parameter of the `Load` method (so that no `XmlResolver` would be specified).

➤ **Transform**—This overloaded method transforms a specified XML document using the previously specified XSLT style sheet. The location where the transformed XML is to be output is specified as a parameter to this method. The first parameter of each overloaded method is the XML document to be transformed. The most straightforward variant of the `Transform` method is `Transform(String, String)`. In this case, a file containing an XML document is specified as the first parameter, and a filename that receives the transformed XML document is specified as the second. This is exactly how the first XSLT example utilized the `Transform` method:

```
myXslTransform.Transform("FilmOrders.xml", destFileName)
```

The first parameter to the `Transform` method can also be specified as `IXPathNavigable` or `XmlReader`. The XML output can be sent to an object of type `Stream`, `TextWriter`, or `XmlWriter`. In addition, a parameter containing an object of type `XsltArgumentList` can be specified. An `XsltArgumentList` object contains a list of arguments that are used as input to the transform. These may be used within the XSLT file to affect the output.

## XSLT Transforming between XML Standards

The first example used four XSLT elements to transform an XML file into an HTML file. Such an example has merit, but it doesn't demonstrate an important use of XSLT: transforming XML from one standard into another standard. This may involve renaming elements/attributes, excluding elements/attributes, changing data types, altering the node hierarchy, and representing elements as attributes, and vice versa.

Returning to the example, a case of differing XML standards could easily affect your software that automates movie orders coming into a supplier. Imagine that the software, including its XML representation of a movie order, is so successful that you sell 100,000 copies. However, just as you are celebrating, a consortium of the largest movie supplier chains announces that they are no longer accepting faxed orders and that they are introducing their own standard for the exchange of movie orders between movie sellers and buyers.

Rather than panic, you simply ship an upgrade that includes an XSLT file. This upgrade (a bit of extra code plus the XSLT file) transforms your XML representation of a movie order into the XML representation dictated by the consortium of movie suppliers. Using an XSLT file enables you to ship the upgrade immediately. If the consortium of movie suppliers revises their XML representation, then you are not obliged to change your source code. Instead, you can simply ship the upgraded XSLT file that ensures each movie order document is compliant.

This new example can be found in the `Transformation2` project. This project includes the `MovieOrdersOriginal.xml` file, which is no different than the `Filmorama.xml` file used in the previous example. This document represents the original source file.

The project also includes the `ConvertLegacyToNewStandard.xslt` file. This file is the XSLT transform that is responsible for transforming the source file into the new format as follows (code file: `ConvertLegacyToNewStandard.xslt`):

```
<?xml version="1.0" encoding="UTF-8" ?>
<xsl:stylesheet
  xmlns:xsl="http://www.w3.org/1999/XSL/Transform"
  version="1.0">
  <xsl:template match="FilmOrders">
    <xsl:element name="DvdOrders">
      <xsl:attribute name="Count">
        <xsl:value-of select="count(FilmOrder)"/>
      </xsl:attribute>
      <xsl:for-each select="FilmOrder">
        <xsl:element name="DvdOrder">
          <xsl:attribute name="HowMuch">
            <xsl:value-of select="Quantity"/>
          </xsl:attribute>
          <xsl:attribute name="FilmOrderNumber">
            <xsl:value-of select="@id"/>
          </xsl:attribute>
        </xsl:element>
      </xsl:for-each>
    </xsl:element>
  </xsl:template>
</xsl:stylesheet>
```

In the previous snippet of XSLT, the following XSLT elements are used to facilitate the transformation:

➤ `<xsl:template match="FilmOrders">`—All operations in this template XSLT element take place on the original document's `FilmOrders` node.

➤ `<xsl:element name="DvdOrders">`—The element corresponding to the source document's `FilmOrders` element will be called `DvdOrders` in the destination document.

➤ `<xsl:attribute name="Count">`—An attribute named `Count` will be created in the element `<DvdOrders>`.

➤ `<xsl:value-of select="Quantity">`—Retrieve the value of the source document's `<Quantity>` element and place it in the destination document. This instance of XSLT element `value-of` provides the value associated with the attribute `HowMuch`.

➤ `<xsl:for-each select="FilmOrder">`—Iterate over all `<FilmOrder>` elements.

Several new XSLT terms have crept into your vocabulary: element, attribute, and for-each. Using the element node in an XSLT places an element in the destination XML document, while an attribute node places an attribute in the destination XML document. The for-each element iterates over all of the specified elements in the document.

Now that you have and understand the XSLT, here is the code to perform the actual transform (code file: Main.vb):

```vb
Dim xslt As New XslCompiledTransform
Dim outputFile As String = "MovieOrdersModified.xml"

xslt.Load("ConvertLegacyToNewStandard.xslt")
xslt.Transform("MovieOrdersOriginal.xml", outputFile)
```

Those lines of code accomplish the following:

➤ Create an XslCompiledTransform object

➤ Use the Load method to load an XSLT file (ConvertLegacyToNewStandard.xslt)

➤ Use the Transform method to transform a source XML file (MovieOrdersOriginal.xml) into a destination XML file (MovieOrdersModified.xml)

Recall that the input XML document (MovieOrdersOriginal.xml) does not match the format required by your consortium of movie supplier chains. The content of this source XML file is as follows:

```xml
<?xml version="1.0" encoding="utf-8" ?>
<FilmOrderList>
    <FilmOrders>
        <FilmOrder>
            <name>Grease</name>
            <filmId>101</filmId>
            <quantity>10</quantity>
        </FilmOrder>
        ...
    </FilmOrders>
</FilmOrderList>
```

The format exhibited in the preceding XML document does not match the format of the consortium of movie supplier chains. To be accepted by the collective of suppliers, you must transform the document as follows:

➤ Remove element <FilmOrderList>.

➤ Rename element <FilmOrders> to <DvdOrders>.

➤ Add a Count attribute to <DvdOrders>.

➤ Rename element <FilmOrder> to <DvdOrder>.

➤ Remove element <name>, since the film's name is not to be contained in the document.

➤ Rename element <quantity> to HowMuch and make HowMuch an attribute of <DvdOrder>.

➤ Rename element `<filmId>` to `FilmOrderNumber` and make `FilmOrderNumber` an attribute of `<DvdOrder>`.

➤ Displays attribute `HowMuch` before attribute `FilmOrderNumber`.

Many of the steps performed by the transform could have been achieved using an alternative technology. For example, you could have used Source Code Style attributes with your serialization to generate the correct XML attribute and XML element name. Had you known in advance that a consortium of suppliers was going to develop a standard, you could have written your classes to be serialized based on the standard. The point is that you did not know, and now one standard (your legacy standard) has to be converted into a newly adopted standard of the movie suppliers' consortium. The worst thing you could do would be to change your working code and then force all users working with the application to upgrade. It is vastly simpler to add an extra transformation step to address the new standard.

The file produced by this example looks like this (code file: `MovieOrdersModified.xml`):

```
<?xml version="1.0" encoding="UTF-8"?>
<DvdOrders count="3">
  <DvdOrder FilmOrderNumber="101" HowMuch="10"/>
  <DvdOrder FilmOrderNumber="102" HowMuch="5"/>
  <DvdOrder FilmOrderNumber="103" HowMuch="25"/>
</DvdOrders>
```

The preceding example spans several pages but contains just a few lines of code. This demonstrates that there is more to XML than learning how to use it in Visual Basic and the .NET Framework. Among other things, you also need a good understanding of XSLT, XPath, and XQuery. For more details on these standards, see Professional XML from Wrox.

## Other Classes and Interfaces in System.Xml.Xsl

You just took a good look at XSLT and the `System.Xml.Xsl` namespace, but there is a lot more to it than that. Other classes and interfaces exposed by the `System.Xml.Xsl` namespace include the following:

➤ `IXsltContextFunction`—This interface accesses at run time a given function defined in the XSLT style sheet.

➤ `IXsltContextVariable`—This interface accesses at run time a given variable defined in the XSLT style sheet.

➤ `XsltArgumentList`—This class contains a list of arguments. These arguments are XSLT parameters or XSLT extension objects. The `XsltArgumentList` object is used in conjunction with the `Transform` method of `XslTransform`. Arguments enable you to use a single XSLT transformation for multiple uses, changing the parameters of the transformation as needed.

➤ `XsltContext`—This class contains the state of the XSLT processor. This context information enables XPath expressions to have their various components resolved (functions, parameters, and namespaces).

➤ `XsltException`, `XsltCompileException`—These classes contain the information pertaining to an exception raised while transforming data. `XsltCompileException` is derived from `XsltException` and is thrown by the `Load` method.

# XML IN ASP.NET

Most Microsoft-focused Web developers have usually concentrated on either Microsoft SQL Server or Microsoft Access for their data storage needs. Today, however, a large amount of data is stored in XML format, so considerable inroads have been made in improving Microsoft's core Web technology to work easily with this format.

## The XmlDataSource Server Control

ASP.NET contains a series of data source controls designed to bridge the gap between your data stores, such as XML, and the data-bound controls at your disposal. These data controls not only enable you to retrieve data from various data stores, they also enable you to easily manipulate the data (using paging, sorting, editing, and filtering) before the data is bound to an ASP.NET server control.

With XML being as important as it is, a specific data source control is available in ASP.NET just for retrieving and working with XML data: `XmlDataSource`. This control enables you to connect to your XML data and use this data with any of the ASP.NET data-bound controls. Just like the `SqlDataSource` and the `ObjectDataSource` controls, the `XmlDataSource` control enables you to not only retrieve data, but also insert, delete, and update data items. With increasing numbers of users turning to XML data formats, such as Web services, RSS feeds, and more, this control is a valuable resource for your Web applications.

To show the `XmlDataSource` control in action, first create a simple XML file and include this file in your application. The following code, from the `XmlWeb` project, reflects a simple XML file of Impressionist painters (code file: `painters.xml`):

```xml
<?xml version="1.0" encoding="utf-8" ?>
<Artists>
  <Painter name="Claude Monet">
    <Painting>
      <Title>Water Lilies</Title>
      <Year>1906</Year>
    </Painting>
  </Painter>
  <Painter name="Edgar Degas">
    <Painting>
      <Title>Blue Dancers</Title>
      <Year>1899</Year>
    </Painting>
  </Painter>
  <Painter name="Vincent Van Gogh">
    <Painting>
```

```
        <Title>The Starry Night</Title>
        <Year>1889</Year>
      </Painting>
    </Painter>
  </Artists>
```

Now that the `Painters.xml` file is in place, the next step is to use an ASP.NET `DataList` control and connect this `DataList` control to an `<asp:XmlDataSource>` control, as shown here (code file: `Default.aspx`):

```
<%@ Page Language="vb" AutoEventWireup="false"
    CodeBehind="Default.aspx.vb" Inherits="XmlWeb._Default" %>

<!DOCTYPE html PUBLIC "-//W3C//DTD XHTML 1.0 Transitional//EN"
"http://www.w3.org/TR/xhtml1/DTD/xhtml1-transitional.dtd">
<html xmlns="http://www.w3.org/1999/xhtml">
<head runat="server">
    <title>Using XmlDataSource</title>
</head>
<body>
    <form id="form1" runat="server">
    <div>
        <asp:DataList ID="PainterList" runat="server"
            DataSourceID="PainterData">
            <ItemTemplate>
                <p>
                    <b>
                        <%# XPath("@name") %></b><br />
                    <i>
                        <%# XPath("Painting/Title") %></i><br />
                    <%# XPath("Painting/Year") %></p>
            </ItemTemplate>
        </asp:DataList>
        <asp:XmlDataSource ID="PainterData" runat="server"
            DataFile="~/Painters.xml" XPath="Artists/Painter" />
    </div>
    </form>
</body>
</html>
```

This is a simple example, but it shows you the power and ease of using the `XmlDataSource` control. Pay attention to two properties in this example. The first is the `DataFile` property. This property points to the location of the XML file. Because the file resides in the root directory of the Web application, it is simply `~/Painters.xml`. The next property included in the `XmlDataSource` control is the `XPath` attribute. The `XmlDataSource` control uses XPath for the filtering of XML data. In this case, the `XmlDataSource` control is taking everything within the `<Painter>` set of elements. The value `Artists/Painter` means that the `XmlDataSource` control navigates to the `<Artists>` element and then to the `<Painter>` element within the specified XML file.

The `DataList` control next must specify the `DataSourceID` as the `XmlDataSource` control. In the `<ItemTemplate>` section of the `DataList` control, you can retrieve specific values from the XML file by using XPath commands. The XPath commands filter the data from the XML file. The first value retrieved is an element attribute (name) contained in the `<Painter>` element. When you retrieve an attribute of an element, you preface the name of the attribute with an @ symbol. In this case, you simply specify @name to get the painter's name. The next two XPath commands go deeper into the XML file, getting the specific painting and the year of the painting. Remember to separate nodes with a /. When run in the browser, this code produces the results shown in Figure 8-8.

Besides working from static XML files such as the `Painters.xml` file, the `XmlDataSource` file can work from dynamic, URL-accessible XML files. One popular XML format pervasive on the Internet today is *blogs*, or *weblogs*. Blogs can be viewed either in the browser (see Figure 8-9), through an RSS aggregator, or just as pure XML.

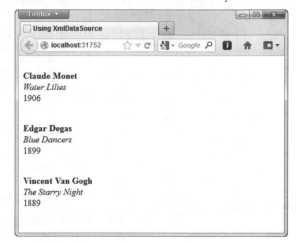

**FIGURE 8-8:** Output for the `XmlWeb` example

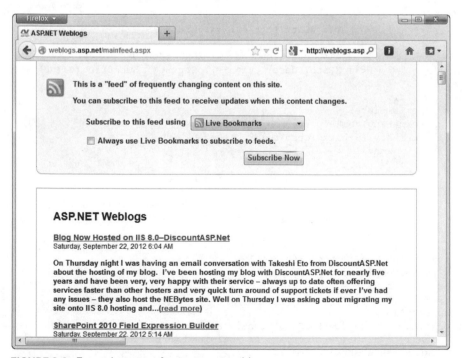

**FIGURE 8-9:** Example output from asp.net weblog

Now that you know the location of the XML from the blog, you can use this XML with the
XmlDataSource control and display some of the results in a DataList control. The code for this
example, from the ViewRss project, is shown here (code file: Default.aspx):

```
<%@ Page Language="vb" AutoEventWireup="false"
    CodeBehind="Default.aspx.vb" Inherits="ViewingRss._Default" %>

<!DOCTYPE html PUBLIC "-//W3C//DTD XHTML 1.0 Transitional//EN"
    "http://www.w3.org/TR/xhtml1/DTD/xhtml1-transitional.dtd">
<html xmlns="http://www.w3.org/1999/xhtml">
<head runat="server">
    <title>Viewing RSS</title>
</head>
<body>
    <form id="form1" runat="server">
    <div>
        <asp:DataList ID="RssList" runat="server"
            DataSourceID="RssData">
            <HeaderTemplate>
                <table border="1" cellpadding="3">
            </HeaderTemplate>
            <ItemTemplate>
                <tr>
                    <td>
                        <b>
                            <%# XPath("title") %></b><br />
                        <i>
                            <%# "published on " + XPath("pubDate") %></i><br />
                        <%# XPath("description").ToString().Substring(0,100) %>
                    </td>
                </tr>
            </ItemTemplate>
            <AlternatingItemTemplate>
                <tr style="background-color: #e0e0e0;">
                    <td>
                        <b>
                            <%# XPath("title") %></b><br />
                        <i>
                            <%# "published on " + XPath("pubDate") %></i><br />
                        <%# XPath("description").ToString().Substring(0,100) %>
                    </td>
                </tr>
            </AlternatingItemTemplate>
            <FooterTemplate>
                </table>
            </FooterTemplate>
        </asp:DataList>
        <asp:XmlDataSource ID="RssData" runat="server"
            DataFile="http://weblogs.asp.net/mainfeed.aspx"
            XPath="rss/channel/item" />
    </div>
    </form>
</body>
</html>
```

This example shows that the `DataFile` points to a URL where the XML is retrieved. The `XPath` property filters out all the `<item>` elements from the RSS feed. The `DataList` control creates an HTML table and pulls out specific data elements from the RSS feed, such as the `<title>`, `<pubDate>`, and `<description>` elements. To make things a little more visible, only the first 100 characters of each post are displayed.

Running this page in the browser results in something similar to what is shown in Figure 8-10.

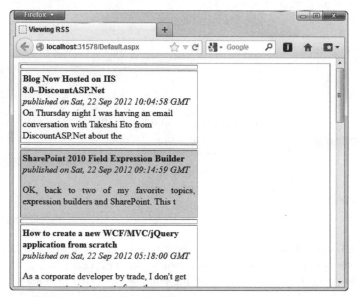

**FIGURE 8-10:** Output for the `Transformation` example

This approach also works with XML Web Services, even those for which you can pass in parameters using `HTTP-GET`. You just set up the `DataFile` value in the following manner:

```
DataFile="http://www.someserver.com/GetWeather.asmx/ZipWeather?zipcode=63301"
```

## The XmlDataSource Control's Namespace Problem

One big issue with using the `XmlDataSource` control is that when using the XPath capabilities of the control, it is unable to understand namespace-qualified XML. The `XmlDataSource` control chokes on any XML data that contains namespaces, so it is important to yank out any prefixes and namespaces contained in the XML.

To make this a bit easier, the `XmlDataSource` control includes the `TransformFile` attribute. This attribute takes your XSLT transform file, which can be applied to the XML pulled from the `XmlDataSource` control. That means you can use an XSLT file, which will transform your XML in such a way that the prefixes and namespaces are completely removed from the overall XML document. An example of this XSLT document is illustrated here:

```
<?xml version="1.0" encoding="UTF-8"?>
<xsl:stylesheet version="1.0"
```

```
  xmlns:xsl="http://www.w3.org/1999/XSL/Transform">
    <xsl:output method="xml" version="1.0" encoding="UTF-8" indent="yes"/>
    <xsl:template match="*">
        <!-- Remove any prefixes -->
        <xsl:element name="{local-name()}">
            <!-- Work through attributes -->
            <xsl:for-each select="@*">
                <!-- Remove any attribute prefixes -->
                <xsl:attribute name="{local-name()}">
                    <xsl:value-of select="."/>
                </xsl:attribute>
            </xsl:for-each>
        <xsl:apply-templates/>
        </xsl:element>
    </xsl:template>
</xsl:stylesheet>
```

Now, with this XSLT document in place within your application, you can use the `XmlDataSource` control to pull XML data and strip that data of any prefixes and namespaces:

```
<asp:XmlDataSource ID="XmlDataSource1" runat="server"
 DataFile="NamespaceFilled.xml" TransformFile="~/RemoveNamespace.xsl"
 XPath="ItemLookupResponse/Items/Item"></asp:XmlDataSource>
```

## The Xml Server Control

Since the very beginning of ASP.NET, there has always been a server control called the `Xml` server control. This control performs the simple operation of XSLT transformation upon an XML document. The control is easy to use: all you do is point to the XML file you wish to transform using the `DocumentSource` attribute, and the XSLT transform file using the `TransformSource` attribute. The `XmlControl` project contains an example to demonstrate this.

To see this in action, use the `Painters.xml` file shown earlier. Create your XSLT transform file, as shown in the following example (code file: `painters.xslt`):

```
<?xml version="1.0" encoding="utf-8"?>
<xsl:stylesheet version="1.0"
    xmlns:xsl="http://www.w3.org/1999/XSL/Transform">
  <xsl:template match="/">
      <html>
      <body>
        <h3>List of Painters &amp; Paintings</h3>
        <table border="1">
          <tr bgcolor="LightGrey">
            <th>Name</th>
            <th>Painting</th>
            <th>Year</th>
          </tr>
          <xsl:apply-templates select="//Painter"/>
        </table>
      </body>
    </html>
  </xsl:template>
```

```
    <xsl:template match="Painter">
      <tr>
        <td>
          <xsl:value-of select="@name"/>
        </td>
        <td>
          <xsl:value-of select="Painting/Title"/>
        </td>
        <td>
          <xsl:value-of select="Painting/Year"/>
        </td>
      </tr>
    </xsl:template>
  </xsl:stylesheet>
```

With the XML document and the XSLT document in place, the final step is to combine the two using the Xml server control provided by ASP.NET (code file: Default.aspx):

```
<%@ Page Language="vb" AutoEventWireup="false"
    CodeBehind="Default.aspx.vb" Inherits="XmlControl._Default" %>

<!DOCTYPE html PUBLIC "-//W3C//DTD XHTML 1.0 Transitional//EN"
    "http://www.w3.org/TR/xhtml1/DTD/xhtml1-transitional.dtd">

<html xmlns="http://www.w3.org/1999/xhtml" >
<head runat="server">
    <title>Using the Xml Control</title>
</head>
<body>
    <form id="form1" runat="server">
    <div>
        <asp:Xml ID="PainterView" runat="server"
            DocumentSource="~/Painters.xml"
            TransformSource="~/painters.xslt" />
    </div>
    </form>
</body>
</html>
```

The result is shown in Figure 8-11.

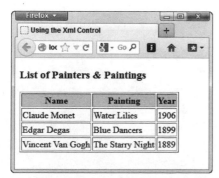

**FIGURE 8-11:** Output for the XmlControl example

## SUMMARY

The beauty of XML is that it isolates data representation from data display. Technologies such as HTML contain data that is tightly bound to its display format. XML does not suffer this limitation, and at the same time it has the readability of HTML. Accordingly, the XML facilities available to a Visual Basic application are vast, and a large number of XML-related features, classes, and interfaces are exposed by the .NET Framework.

This chapter showed you how to use `System.Xml.Serialization.XmlSerializer` to serialize classes. Source Code Style attributes were introduced in conjunction with serialization. This style of attributes enables the customization of the XML serialized to be extended to the source code associated with a class. What is important to remember about the direction of serialization classes is that a required change in the XML format becomes a change in the underlying source code. Developers should resist the temptation to rewrite serialized classes in order to conform to some new XML data standard (such as the example movie order format endorsed by the consortium of movie rental establishments). Technologies such as XSLT, exposed via the `System.Xml.Query` namespace, should be examined first as alternatives. This chapter demonstrated how to use XSLT style sheets to transform XML data using the classes found in the `System.Xml.Query` namespace.

The most useful classes and interfaces in the `System.Xml` namespace were reviewed, including those that support document-style XML access: `XmlDocument`, `XmlNode`, `XmlElement`, and `XmlAttribute`. The `System.Xml` namespace also contains classes and interfaces that support stream-style XML access: `XmlReader` and `XmlWriter`.

This chapter also described how to use LINQ to XML and some of the options available to you in reading from and writing to XML files and XML sources, whether the source is static or dynamic. Next, you were also introduced to the LINQ to XML helper objects `XDocument`, `XElement`, `XNamespace`, `XAttribute`, and `XComment`. These outstanding new objects make working with XML easier than ever before. Finally, you looked at how to use XML with ASP.NET. While you can use the `XmlReader` and `XmlDocument` (and related) classes with ASP.NET, there are included controls to make working with XML easier.

As you learned from reviewing this chapter, XML serves as a powerful method for storing and transferring data. You also learned that Language Integrated Query (LINQ) provides a strong framework for easily working with and manipulating this data and the XML structure itself. In the next chapter you will learn how to perform similar actions using LINQ with data stored in databases and accessible via ADO.NET.

# ADO.NET and LINQ

## WROX.COM CODE DOWNLOADS FOR THIS CHAPTER

The wrox.com code downloads for this chapter are found at `www.wrox.com/remtitle` `.cgi?isbn=9781118314456` on the Download Code tab. The code is in the chapter 9 download and individually named according to the code file names throughout the chapter.

ADO.NET 1.x was the successor to ActiveX Data Objects 2.6 (ADO). The goal of ADO. NET 1.x was to enable developers to easily create distributed, data-sharing applications in the .NET Framework. The goals of ADO.NET today are to improve the performance of existing features in ADO.NET 1.x, to provide easier use, and to add new features without breaking backward compatibility.

> **NOTE** *Throughout this chapter, when ADO.NET is mentioned without a version number after it (that is, 1.x, 2.0, 3.5, 4 or 4.5), the statement applies to all versions of ADO.NET.*

ADO.NET 1.x was built upon industry standards such as XML and XSD, and it provided a data-access interface to communicate with data sources such as SQL Server and Oracle. ADO

.NET 4.5 continues to build upon these concepts, while increasing performance. Applications can use ADO.NET to connect to these data sources and retrieve, manipulate, and update data. ADO.NET 4.5 does not break any compatibility with ADO.NET 2.0 or 1.x; it only adds to the stack of functionality.

In solutions that require disconnected or remote access to data, ADO.NET uses XML to exchange data between programs or with Web pages. Any component that can read XML can make use of ADO.NET components. A receiving component does not even have to be an ADO.NET component if a transmitting ADO.NET component packages and delivers a data set in an XML format. Transmitting information in XML-formatted data sets enables programmers to easily separate the data processing and user interface components of a data-sharing application onto separate servers. This can greatly improve both the performance and the maintainability of systems that support many users.

For distributed applications, ADO.NET 1.x proved that the use of XML data sets provided performance advantages relative to the COM marshaling used to transmit disconnected data sets in ADO. Because transmission of data sets occurred through XML streams in a simple text-based standard accepted throughout the industry, receiving components did not require any of the architectural restrictions required by COM. XML data sets used in ADO.NET 1.x also avoided the processing cost of converting values in the `Fields` collection of a `Recordset` object to data types recognized by COM. Virtually any two components from different systems can share XML data sets, provided that they both use the same XML schema for formatting the data set. This continues to be true in ADO.NET 4.5, but the story gets better. The XML integration in ADO.NET today is even stronger, and extensive work was done to improve the performance of the `DataSet` object, particularly in the areas of serialization and memory usage.

ADO.NET also supports the scalability required by Web-based data-sharing applications. Web applications must often serve hundreds, or even thousands, of users. By default, ADO.NET does not retain lengthy database locks or active connections that monopolize limited resources. This enables the number of users to grow with only a small increase in the demands made on the resources of a system.

One of the issues some developers experience when working with ADO.NET and various databases is that you need to leverage at least two languages: Visual Basic and the version of SQL used by the database. To reduce this separation, Microsoft developed LINQ (Language Integrated Query). With LINQ, you can include the query within your Visual Basic code, and the query you add to your code is translated into the specific query language of the data store. One of the most common uses for LINQ is in working with databases (you will also see LINQ used in querying XML in Chapter 8) in its form as a "better" SQL.

The use of LINQ and SQL Server leads to one point of confusion: While LINQ can be used to query any database (or set of objects, XML, or other LINQ provider), there is also a specific technology known as LINQ to SQL. This is an SQL Server–specific query tool that uses LINQ as its query mechanism.

In this chapter, you will see that ADO.NET is a very extensive and flexible API for accessing many types of data, and because ADO.NET 4.5 represents an incremental change to the previous versions of ADO.NET, all previous ADO.NET knowledge already learned can be leveraged. In fact, to get the most out of this chapter, you should be fairly familiar with earlier versions of ADO.NET and the entire .NET Framework.

This chapter demonstrates how to use the ADO.NET object model in order to build flexible, fast, and scalable data-access objects and applications. Specifically, it covers the following:

➤ The ADO.NET architecture

➤ Some of the specific features offered in ADO.NET, `DataSet` performance improvements, and asynchronous processing

➤ Working with the common provider model

## ADO.NET ARCHITECTURE

The main design goals of ADO.NET are:

➤ Customer-driven features that are still backwardly compatible with ADO.NET 1.x

➤ Improving performance on your data-store calls

➤ Providing more power for power users

➤ Taking advantage of SQL Server–specific features

ADO.NET addresses a couple of the most common data-access strategies used for applications today. When classic ADO was developed, many applications could be connected to the data store almost indefinitely. Today, with the explosion of the Internet as the means of data communication, a new data technology is required to make data accessible and updateable in a disconnected architecture.

The first of these common data-access scenarios is one in which a user must locate a collection of data and iterate through this data just a single time. This is a popular scenario for Web pages. When a request for data from a Web page that you have created is received, you can simply fill a table with data from a data store. In this case, you go to the data store, grab the data that you want, send the data across the wire, and then populate the table. In this scenario, the goal is to get the data in place as fast as possible.

The second way to work with data in this disconnected architecture is to grab a collection of data and use this data separately from the data store itself. This could be on the server or even on the client. Even though the data is disconnected, you want the capability to keep the data (with all of its tables and relations in place) on the client side. Classic ADO data was represented by a single table that you could iterate through; but ADO.NET can be a reflection of the data store itself, with tables, columns, rows, and relations all in place. When you are done with the client-side copy of the data, you can persist the changes that you made in the local copy of data directly back into the data store. The technology that gives you this capability is the `DataSet` class, which is covered shortly.

Although classic ADO was geared for a two-tiered environment (client-server), ADO.NET addresses a multitiered environment. ADO.NET is easy to work with because it has a unified programming model. This unified programming model makes working with data on the server similar to working with data on the client. Because the models are the same, you find yourself more productive when working with ADO.NET. This productivity increases even more when you use some of the more recent tools such as LINQ to SQL or Entity Framework.

## BASIC ADO.NET FEATURES

This chapter begins with a quick look at the basics of ADO.NET and then provides an overview of ADO.NET capabilities, namespaces, and classes. It also reviews how to work with the `Connection`, `Command`, `DataAdapter`, `DataSet`, and `DataReader` classes. Later chapters will cover some of the more recently added ADO.NET features.

## Common ADO.NET Tasks

Before jumping into the depths of ADO.NET, step back and make sure that you understand some of the common tasks you might perform programmatically within ADO.NET. This section looks at the process of selecting, inserting, updating, and deleting data.

> **NOTE** *For all of the data-access examples in this chapter, you need the Adventure Works database titled AdventureWorks2012 Data File (SQL Server 2008) or AdventureWorksDW2012 Data File (SQL Server 2012). As of this writing, you can find this link at* `http://msftdbprodsamples.codeplex.com/releases/view/55330`*. You can then attach this database to your SQL Server 2012 Express instance using SQL Server Management Studio. This chapter was written using the SQL Server 2008 database file.*

In addition, stored procedure SQL files required for the sample code can be found with the code download for this chapter.

### Selecting Data

After the connection to the data source is open and ready to use, you probably want to read the data from it. If you do not want to manipulate the data but simply read it or transfer it from one spot to another, use the `DataReader` class (or one of the classes that inherit from `DataReader` for each database type).

The following example retrieves a list of vendor names from the database (code file: DataReaderExample). (You may need to update the connection string to match the location of the AdventureWorks database on your computer.)

```
Imports System.Data.SqlClient

Module Main
  Sub Main()
    Dim connection As SqlConnection
    Dim command As SqlCommand

    Console.WriteLine("Loading records...")
```

```
    'update to match the location of AdventureWorks on your computer
    Dim cmdString As String = "Select Name from [Purchasing].[Vendor]"
    connection = New SqlConnection("Data Source=.\SQLEXPRESS;" +
                                   "Initial Catalog=AdventureWorks;" +
                                   "Integrated Security=True")
    command = New SqlCommand(cmdString, connection)
    connection.Open()

    Dim reader As SqlDataReader
    reader = command.ExecuteReader(CommandBehavior.CloseConnection)

    While reader.Read()
      Console.WriteLine(reader("Name").ToString())
    End While

    Console.WriteLine("Press ENTER to exit")
    Console.ReadLine()

  End Sub
End Module
```

In this example, you create an instance of both the SqlConnection and the SqlCommand classes. Then, before you open the connection, you simply pass the SqlCommand class an SQL statement selecting specific data from the database. After your connection is opened (based upon the commands passed in), you create a DataReader. To read the data from the database, you iterate through the data with the DataReader by using the reader.Read method. Each time you call the Read method, the current position of the reader is set to point to the next line returned by the SQL statement. Once the position moves to the end, the Read method returns false, exiting the loop. In the sample application, this data is displayed in the console window.

## Inserting Data

When working with data, you often insert the data into the data source, in this case an SQL Server database. The following shows you how to do this (code file: DataInsertExample) :

```
Imports System.Data.SqlClient

Module Main
  Sub Main()
    Dim connection As SqlConnection
    Dim command As SqlCommand

    Console.WriteLine("Inserting data...")

    connection = New SqlConnection("Data Source=.\SQLEXPRESS;" +
                                   "Initial Catalog=AdventureWorks;" +
                                   "Integrated Security=True")

    Dim insert As String = "Insert [Purchasing].[Vendor]([AccountNumber]," +
                "[Name],[CreditRating],[PreferredVendorStatus]," +
                "[ActiveFlag],[PurchasingWebServiceURL],[ModifiedDate])" +
                "Values ('ACME10000', 'Acme Supply', 1, 1, 1, " +
                "'http://acmesupply.com', '10/10/2012')"
```

```
      command = New SqlCommand(insert, connection)
      connection.Open()
      command.ExecuteNonQuery()

      Console.WriteLine("Loading data...")

      'Confirm we have it inserted
      Dim query As String = "SELECT [Name] FROM [Purchasing].[Vendor] " +
                            "WHERE Name='Acme Supply'"
      command = New SqlCommand(query, connection)

      Dim reader As SqlDataReader
      reader = command.ExecuteReader(CommandBehavior.CloseConnection)

      While reader.Read()
        Console.WriteLine(reader("Name").ToString())
      End While

      Console.WriteLine("Press ENTER to exit")
      Console.ReadLine()
    End Sub
  End Module
```

Inserting data into SQL is pretty straightforward and simple. Using the SQL command string, you insert specific values for specific columns. The actual insertion is initiated using the `ExecuteNonQuery` command. This executes a command on the data when you don't want anything in return. If you were expecting data back from the insert, you could use `ExecuteScalar` (if a single value—such as the inserted record ID—is returned) or `ExecuteReader` (if data—such as the complete inserted record—is returned).

## Updating Data

In addition to inserting new records into a database, you frequently need to update existing rows of data in a table. The following changes revision numbers of documents (code file: DataUpdateExample):

```
    Imports System.Data.SqlClient

    Module Main
      Sub Main()
        Dim records As Integer
        records = ChangeDocumentRevision(1, 2)
        Console.WriteLine("{0} records affected", records)
        Console.WriteLine("Press ENTER to exit.")
        Console.ReadLine()
      End Sub

      Public Function ChangeDocumentRevision(ByVal oldRevison As Integer,
                                             ByVal newRevision As Integer) As Integer
        Dim command As SqlCommand
        Dim connection As SqlConnection
        Dim result As Integer
```

```
        Dim updateQuery As String =
                    String.Format("UPDATE [Production].[Document] SET " +
                                    "[Revision]={0} where [Revision]={1}",
                                    newRevision, oldRevison)

        connection = New SqlConnection("Data Source=.\SQLEXPRESS;" +
                                    "Initial Catalog=AdventureWorks;" +
                                    "Integrated Security=True")
        connection.Open()

        'Display the record before updating
        DisplayData(connection, "before")

        Console.WriteLine("Updating data...")

        command = New SqlCommand(updateQuery, connection)
        result = command.ExecuteNonQuery()

        'Display the record after updating
        DisplayData(connection, "after")

        Return result
    End Function

    Private Sub DisplayData(ByVal connection As SqlConnection,
                            ByVal direction As String)
        Dim query As String = "SELECT [Title], [Revision] FROM " +
                            "[Production].[Document] ORDER BY [Title]"
        Dim command As New SqlCommand(query, connection)

        Console.WriteLine("Displaying data ({0})", direction)
        Dim reader As SqlDataReader = command.ExecuteReader

        While reader.Read
            Console.WriteLine("Document: {0}  Rev. {1}",
                            reader.GetString(0),
                            reader.GetString(1))

        End While

        reader.Close()
    End Sub
End Module
```

This update function changes the revision number for the `Production.Document` from 1 to 2. This is done with the SQL command string. The great thing about these update capabilities is that you can capture the number of records that were updated by assigning the result of the `ExecuteNonQuery` command to the `records` variable. The total number of affected records is then returned by the function.

## Deleting Data

Along with reading, inserting, and updating data, you sometimes need to delete data from the data source. Deleting data is a simple process of using the SQL command string and then the

`ExecuteNonQuery` command as you did in the update example. The following bit of code illustrates this (code file: DataDeleteExample):

```
Imports System.Data.SqlClient

Module Main
  Sub Main()
    Dim deletes As Integer
    deletes = ClearDatabaseLog(DateTime.Now())
    Console.WriteLine("{0} records deleted", deletes)
    Console.WriteLine("Press ENTER to exit.")
    Console.ReadLine()
  End Sub

  Public Function ClearDatabaseLog(ByVal queryDate As DateTime) As Integer
    Dim result As Integer
    Dim command As SqlCommand
    Dim connection As SqlConnection
    Dim deleteQuery As String = String.Format("DELETE [DatabaseLog] " +
                                        "WHERE [PostTime] < '{0}'" +
                                        queryDate)

    connection = New SqlConnection("Data Source=.\SQLEXPRESS;" +
                               "Initial Catalog=AdventureWorks;" +
                               "Integrated Security=True")
    connection.Open()

    command = New SqlCommand(deleteQuery, connection)

    DisplayData(connection, "before")

    Console.WriteLine("Deleting data...")
    result = command.ExecuteNonQuery()

    DisplayData(connection, "after")

    connection.Close()

    Return result
  End Function

  Private Sub DisplayData(ByVal conn As SqlConnection,
                    ByVal direction As String)
    Dim query As String = "SELECT count(*) FROM [DatabaseLog]"
    Dim command As New SqlCommand(query, conn)

    Dim count As Integer = CType(command.ExecuteScalar(), Integer)
    Console.WriteLine("Number of log records {0}: {1}", direction, count)
  End Sub
End Module
```

You can assign the `ExecuteNonQuery` command to an `Integer` variable (just as you did for the update function) to return the number of records deleted in order to verify that the records are deleted.

# Basic ADO.NET Namespaces and Classes

The core ADO.NET namespaces are shown in Table 9-1. In addition to these namespaces, each new data provider will have its own namespace. For example, the Oracle .NET data provider adds a namespace of `System.Data.OracleClient` (for the Microsoft-built Oracle data provider).

**TABLE 9-1:** Core ADO.NET Namespaces

| NAMESPACE | DESCRIPTION |
|---|---|
| System.Data | This namespace is the core of ADO.NET. It contains classes used by all data providers. Its classes represent tables, columns, rows, and the `DataSet` class. It also contains several useful interfaces, such as `IDbCommand`, `IDbConnection`, and `IDbDataAdapter`. These interfaces are used by all managed providers, enabling them to plug into the core of ADO.NET. |
| System.Data.Common | This namespace defines common classes that are used as base classes for data providers. All data providers share these classes. Two examples are `DbConnection` and `DbDataAdapter`. |
| System.Data.OleDb | This namespace defines classes that work with OLE-DB data sources using the .NET OLE DB data provider. It contains classes such as `OleDbConnection` and `OleDbCommand`. |
| System.Data.Odbc | This namespace defines classes that work with the ODBC data sources using the .NET ODBC data provider. It contains classes such as `OdbcConnection` and `OdbcCommand`. |
| System.Data.SqlClient | This namespace defines a data provider for the SQL Server 7.0 or later database. It contains classes such as `SqlConnection` and `SqlCommand`. |
| System.Data.SqlTypes | This namespace defines classes that represent specific data types for the SQL Server database. |
| System.Data.Linq | This namespace provides support for connecting, querying, and editing databases using LINQ (Language Integrated Query). |
| System.Data.Services | This namespace provides support for ADO.NET Data Services, a server-side method of providing data using a REST-like syntax. It is covered in Chapter 12. |
| System.Data.EntityClient | This namespace provides support for the Entity Framework for working with data. It is covered in Chapter 11. |

ADO.NET has three distinct types of classes commonly referred to as:

1. **Disconnected**—These provide the basic structure for the ADO.NET Framework. A good example of this type of class is the `DataTable` class. The objects created from these disconnected class types are capable of storing data without any dependency on a specific data provider.

2. **Shared**—These form the base classes for data providers and are shared among all data providers.

3. **Data providers**—These are meant to work with different kinds of data sources. They are used to perform all data-management operations on specific databases. The `SqlClient` data provider, for example, works only with the SQL Server database.

A *data provider* contains `Connection`, `Command`, `DataAdapter`, and `DataReader` objects. Typically, in programming ADO.NET, you first create the `Connection` object and provide it with the necessary information, such as the connection string. You then create a `Command` object and provide it with the details of the SQL command that is to be executed. This command can be an inline SQL text command, a stored procedure, or direct table access. You can also provide parameters to these commands if needed.

After you create the `Connection` and the `Command` objects, you must decide whether the command returns a result set. If the command doesn't return a result set, then you can simply execute the command by calling one of its several `Execute` methods. Conversely, if the command returns a result set, you must decide whether you want to retain the result set for future use without maintaining the connection to the database. If you want to retain the result set but not the connection, then you must create a `DataAdapter` object and use it to fill a `DataSet` or a `DataTable` object. These objects are capable of maintaining their information in a disconnected mode. However, if you don't want to retain the result set, but rather simply process the command in a swift fashion, then you can use the `Command` object to create a `DataReader` object. The `DataReader` object needs a live connection to the database, and it works as a forward-only, read-only cursor.

## ADO.NET Components

To better support the disconnected model as defined above, the ADO.NET components separate data access from data manipulation. This is accomplished via two main components: the `DataSet` and the .NET data provider. Figure 9-1 illustrates the concept of separating data access from data manipulation.

The `DataSet` is the core component of the disconnected architecture of ADO.NET. It is explicitly designed for data access independent of any data source. As a result, it can be used with multiple and differing data sources, with XML data, or even to manage data local to an application such as an in-memory data cache. The `DataSet` contains a collection of one or more `DataTable` objects made up of rows and columns of data, as well as primary key, foreign key, constraint, and relation information about the data in the `DataTable` objects. It is basically an in-memory database, but what sets it apart is that it doesn't care whether its data is obtained from a database, an XML file, a combination of the two, or somewhere else. You can apply inserts, updates, and deletes to the `DataSet` and then push the changes back to the data source, no matter where the data source lives! This chapter offers an in-depth look at the `DataSet` object family.

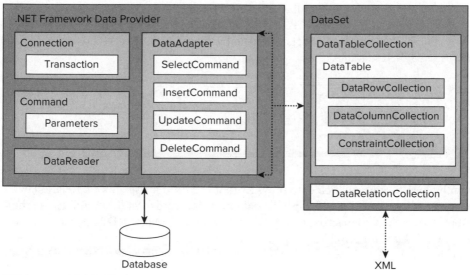

**FIGURE 9-1:** ADO.NET Data Provider & Dataset

The other core element of the ADO.NET architecture is the .NET data provider, whose components are designed for data manipulation (as opposed to data access with the DataSet). These components are listed in Table 9-2.

**TABLE 9-2:** .NET Data Provider Components

| OBJECT | ACTIVITY |
|---|---|
| Connection | Provides connectivity to a data source |
| Command | Enables access to database commands to return and modify data, run stored procedures, and send or retrieve parameter information |
| DataReader | Provides a high-performance, read-only stream of data from the data source |
| DataAdapter | Provides the bridge between the DataSet object and the data source |

The DataAdapter uses Command objects to execute SQL commands at the data source, both to load the DataSet with data and to reconcile changes made to the data in the DataSet with the data source. You will take a closer look at this later in the detailed discussion of the DataAdapter object.

> **NOTE** *.NET data providers can be written for any data source, though this is a topic beyond the scope of this chapter.*

The .NET Framework 4.5 ships with a number of .NET data providers, including ones for accessing SQL Server and Oracle databases, as well as more generic data providers, such as the ODBC and OLE DB data providers. Other data providers are available for just about every other database out there, for example, a MySQL database.

> **NOTE** *Do not confuse the OLE DB .NET data provider with generic OLE DB providers. The OLE DB .NET data provider connects to specific OLE DB providers to access each data source.*

The rule of thumb when deciding which data provider to use is to first use a .NET Relational Database Management System (RDBMS)–specific data provider if it is available, and to use the .NET OLE DB provider when connecting to any other data source. (Most RDBMS vendors are now producing their own .NET data providers in order to encourage .NET developers to use their databases.) Finally, if no OLE DB provider is available, try ODBC access using the .NET ODBC data provider.

For example, if you were writing an application that uses SQL Server, then you would want to use the SQL Server .NET data provider. The .NET OLE DB provider is used to access any data source exposed through OLE DB, such as Microsoft Access. You will be taking a closer look at these later.

# .NET DATA PROVIDERS

.NET data providers are used for connecting to a RDBMS-specific database (such as SQL Server or Oracle), executing commands, and retrieving results. Those results are either processed directly (via a `DataReader`) or placed in an ADO.NET `DataSet` (via a `DataAdapter`) in order to be exposed to the user in an ad hoc manner, combined with data from multiple sources, or passed around between tiers. .NET data providers are designed to be lightweight, to create a minimal layer between the data source and the .NET programmer's code, and to increase performance while not sacrificing any functionality.

## Connection Object

To connect to a specific data source, you use a data connection object. To connect to Microsoft SQL Server 7.0 or later, you need to use the `SqlConnection` object of the SQL Server .NET data provider. You need to use the `OleDbConnection` object of the OLE DB .NET data provider to connect to an OLE DB data source, or the OLE DB provider for SQL Server (SQLOLEDB) to connect to versions of Microsoft SQL Server earlier than 7.0.

### Connection String Format — OleDbConnection

For the OLE DB .NET data provider, the connection string format is the same as the connection string format used in ADO, with the following exceptions:

➤ The `Provider` keyword is required.

➤ The `URL`, `Remote Provider`, and `Remote Server` keywords are not supported.

Here is an example `OleDbConnection` connection string connecting to an Access database:

```
Provider=Microsoft.Jet.OLEDB.4.0;Data Source=
"C:\Program Files\Microsoft Expression\Web 2\WebDesigner\1033\FPNWIND.MDB";
```

### Connection-String Format — SqlConnection

The SQL Server .NET data provider supports a connection-string format that is similar to the OLE DB (ADO) connection-string format. The only thing that you need to omit, obviously, is the provider name-value pair, as you know you are using the SQL Server .NET data provider. Here is an example of an `SqlConnection` connection string:

```
Data Source=(local);Initial Catalog=AdventureWorks;Integrated Security=SSPI;
```

Alternately, you can use a connection-string format that is more specific to SQL Server. This sample would connect to the same database as the previous one:

```
Server=(local);Database=AdventureWorks;Trusted Connection=true;
```

# Command Object

After establishing a connection, you can execute commands and return results from a data source (such as SQL Server) using a `Command` object. A `Command` object can be created using the `Command` constructor, or by calling the `CreateCommand` method of the `Connection` object. When creating a `Command` object using the `Command` constructor, you need to specify an SQL statement to execute at the data source, and a `Connection` object. The `Command` object's SQL statement can be queried and modified using the `CommandText` property. The following code is an example of executing a SELECT command and returning a `DataReader` object:

```
'Build the SQL and Connection strings.
Dim query As String = "SELECT * FROM ErrorLog"
Dim connectionString As String = "Data Source=.\SQLEXPRESS;" +
                                  "Initial Catalog=AdventureWorks;" +
                                  "Integrated Security=True"

'Initialize the SqlCommand with the SQL and Connection strings.
Dim command As SqlCommand = New SqlCommand(query,
                                    New SqlConnection(connectionString))
'Open the connection.
command.Connection.Open()

'Execute the query, return a SqlDataReader object.
'CommandBehavior.CloseConnection flags the
'DataReader to automatically close the DB connection
'when it is closed.
Dim dataReader As SqlDataReader =
  command.ExecuteReader(CommandBehavior.CloseConnection)
```

The `CommandText` property of the `Command` object executes all SQL statements in addition to the standard SELECT, UPDATE, INSERT, and DELETE statements. For example, you could create tables, foreign keys, primary keys, and so on, by executing the applicable SQL from the `Command` object.

The `Command` object exposes several `Execute` methods to perform the intended action. When returning results as a stream of data, `ExecuteReader` is used to return a `DataReader` object. `ExecuteScalar` is used to return a singleton value. `ExecuteNonQuery` is used to execute commands that do not return rows, which usually includes stored procedures that have output parameters and/or return values. (You will learn about stored procedures later in this chapter.) Finally, the `ExecuteXmlReader` returns an XmlReader, which can be used to read a block of XML returned from the database. (You will see how this is used in the XML chapter.)

When using a `DataAdapter` with a `DataSet`, Command objects are used to return and modify data at the data source through the `DataAdapter` object's `SelectCommand`, `InsertCommand`, `UpdateCommand`, and `DeleteCommand` properties.

The `InsertCommand`, `UpdateCommand`, and `DeleteCommand` properties must be set before the `Update` method is called. You will take a closer look at this when you look at the `DataAdapter` object.

## Using Stored Procedures with Command Objects

The motivation for using stored procedures is simple. Imagine you have the following SQL query:

```
SELECT Name FROM [Purchasing].[Vendor] WHERE [CreditRating] = 1
```

If you pass that to SQL Server using `ExecuteReader` on `SqlCommand` (or any execute method, for that matter), SQL Server has to compile the code before it can run it, in much the same way that VB.NET applications have to be compiled before they can be executed. This compilation takes up SQL Server's time, so it is easy to deduce that if you can reduce the amount of compilation that SQL Server has to do, database performance should increase. (Compare the speed of execution of a compiled application against interpreted code.)

That's what stored procedures are all about: you create a procedure, store it in the database, and because the procedure is recognized and understood ahead of time, it can be compiled ahead of time and ready for use in your application.

One other benefit of using stored procedures in your code is that it is generally safer. When using SQL without stored procedures, there is always the temptation to build the SQL statement by concatenating strings. With this, there is the danger—particularly if some of those strings are user generated—that the resulting SQL is invalid or malicious; for example, if you had a text box where a user could type in search criteria, that you then concatenated into a query, using code such as:

```
Dim query As String = "SELECT Name FROM [Purchasing].[Vendor] WHERE " +
                      "[NAME] LIKE '%" + query + "%'"
```

This looks innocent enough, but you could get into trouble very quickly if the user entered something like:

```
Acme;delete * from systables;
```

Using stored procedures can help prevent an attack like this from happening.

Stored procedures are very easy to use, but the code to access them is sometimes a little verbose. The next section demonstrates some code that can make accessing stored procedures a bit more straightforward, but to make things clearer, you'll start by building a simple application that demonstrates how to create and call a stored procedure.

## Creating a Stored Procedure

To create a stored procedure, you can either use the tools in Visual Studio .NET or you can use the tools in SQL Server's Enterprise Manager if you are using SQL Server 2000, or in SQL Server Management Studio if you are using SQL Server 2005–2012. (Technically, you can use a third-party tool or just create the stored procedure in a good, old-fashioned SQL script.)

This example builds a stored procedure that returns columns from the Sales.CreditCard database for a given ID. The SQL to do this looks like the following:

```
SELECT
  CardType, CardNumber, ExpMonth, ExpYear
FROM
  Sales.CreditCard
WHERE
  (CreditCardID = whatever author ID you want)
```

The "whatever author ID you want" part is important. When using stored procedures, you typically have to be able to provide parameters into the stored procedure and use them from within code. This is not a book about SQL Server, so this example focuses only on the principle involved. You can find many resources on the Web about building stored procedures (they have been around a very long time, and they are most definitely not a .NET-specific feature).

Variables in SQL Server are prefixed by the @ symbol, so if you have a variable called CreditCardId, then your SQL will look like this:

```
SELECT
  CardType, CardNumber, ExpMonth, ExpYear
FROM
  Sales.CreditCard
WHERE
  (CreditCardID = @CreditCardId)
```

In Visual Studio, stored procedures can be accessed using the Server Explorer. Simply add a new data connection (or use an existing data connection), and then drill down into the Stored Procedures folder in the management tree.

To create a new stored procedure, just right-click the Stored Procedures folder in the Server Explorer and select Add New Stored Procedure to invoke the editor window.

A stored procedure can be either a single SQL statement or a complex set of statements. T-SQL supports branches, loops, and other variable declarations, which can make for some pretty complex stored procedure code. However, your stored procedure is just a single line of SQL. You need to declare the parameter that you want to pass in (@CreditCardId) and the name of the procedure: Sales.CreditCards_GetById. Here's code for the stored procedure:

```
CREATE PROCEDURE Sales.CreditCards_GetById
  @CreditCardId tinyint
AS
BEGIN
  SELECT
```

```
    CardType, CardNumber, ExpMonth, ExpYear
  FROM
    Sales.CreditCard
  WHERE
    (CreditCardID = @CreditCardId)
END
GO
```

Click the Save icon to save the stored procedure in the database. You are now able to access this stored procedure from code.

## Calling the Stored Procedure

Calling the stored procedure is just a matter of creating an `SqlConnection` object to connect to the database, and an `SqlCommand` object to run the stored procedure.

Now you have to decide what you want to return by calling the stored procedure. In this case, you return an instance of the `SqlDataReader` object. Pass in the ID of the record in the `@CreditCardId` parameter by adding a new `SQLParameter` (code file: StoredProcedureExample):

```
Imports System.Data.SqlClient

Module Main

  Sub Main()
    'Build the SQL and Connection strings.
    Dim storedProcedure As String = "Sales.CreditCards_GetById"
    Dim connectionString As String = "Data Source=.\SQLEXPRESS;" +
                               "Initial Catalog=AdventureWorks;" +
                               "Integrated Security=True"

    'Initialize the SqlCommand with the SQL and Connection strings.
    Dim command As SqlCommand = New SqlCommand(storedProcedure,
                                      New SqlConnection(connectionString))

    command.CommandType = CommandType.StoredProcedure

    'Add the @CreditCardId parameter information to the command
    command.Parameters.Add(New SqlParameter("@CreditCardId", 1)

    'Open the connection.
    command.Connection.Open()

    Dim reader As SqlDataReader = command.ExecuteReader

    While reader.Read
      Console.WriteLine(reader.GetString(0) + "|" + reader.GetString(1) + "|" +
                        reader.GetByte(2).ToString + "|" +
                        reader.GetInt16(3).ToString)
    End While

    reader.Close()

    Console.ReadLine()
  End Sub

End Module
```

Notice that in the `SqlCommand`'s constructor call, you have factored out creating a connection to the database into a separate helper method. This is used later in other code examples in your form.

Accessing a stored procedure is more verbose (but not more difficult) than accessing a normal SQL statement through the methods discussed thus far. The approach is as follows:

**1.** Create an `SqlCommand` object.

**2.** Configure it to access a stored procedure by setting the `CommandType` property.

**3.** Add parameters that exactly match those in the stored procedure itself.

**4.** Execute the stored procedure using one of the `SqlCommand` object's `ExecuteX` methods.

The benefit to using stored procedures is that it prevents SQL injection attacks, they are precompiled, and it's easy to add security so that only certain roles has access to it.

## DataReader Object

You can use the `DataReader` to retrieve a read-only, forward-only stream of data from the database. Using the `DataReader` can increase application performance and reduce system overhead because only one buffered row at a time is ever in memory. With the `DataReader` object, you are getting as close to the raw data as possible in ADO.NET; you do not have to go through the overhead of populating a `DataSet` object, which sometimes may be expensive if the `DataSet` contains a lot of data. The disadvantage of using a `DataReader` object is that it requires an open database connection and increases network activity.

After creating an instance of the `Command` object, a `DataReader` is created by calling the `ExecuteReader` method of the `Command` object. Here is an example of creating a `DataReader` and iterating through it to print out its values to the screen (code file: DataReaderExample):

```vb
Imports System.Data.SqlClient

Module Main

  Sub Main()
    Dim connection As SqlConnection
    Dim command As SqlCommand

    Console.WriteLine("Loading records...")

    'Update to match the location of AdventureWorks on your computer
    Dim cmdString As String = "Select Name from [Purchasing].[Vendor]"
    connection = New SqlConnection("Data Source=.\SQLEXPRESS;" +
                                   "Initial Catalog=AdventureWorks;" +
                                   "Integrated Security=True")
    command = New SqlCommand(cmdString, connection)
    connection.Open()

    Dim reader As SqlDataReader
    reader = command.ExecuteReader(CommandBehavior.CloseConnection)

    While reader.Read()
      Console.WriteLine(reader("Name").ToString())
    End While
```

```
        reader.Close()

        Console.WriteLine("Press ENTER to exit")
        Console.ReadLine()

    End Sub

End Module
```

This code snippet uses the `SqlCommand` object to execute the query via the `ExecuteReader` method. This method returns a populated `SqlDataReader` object, which you loop through and then print out the vendor names. The main difference between this code and looping through the rows of a `DataTable` is that you have to stay connected while you loop through the data in the `DataReader` object; this is because the `DataReader` reads in only a small stream of data at a time to conserve memory space.

> **NOTE** *At this point, an obvious design question is whether to use the* `DataReader` *or the* `DataSet`. *The answer depends upon performance and how you will use the data. If you want high performance and you only need to access the data you are retrieving once, then the* `DataReader` *is the way to go. If you need access to the same data multiple times, or if you need to model a complex relationship in memory, or if you need to use the data when not connected to the database, then the* `DataSet` *is the way to go. As always, test each option thoroughly before deciding which one is the best.*

The `Read` method of the `DataReader` object is used to obtain a row from the results of the query. Each column of the returned row may be accessed by passing the name or ordinal reference of the column to the `DataReader`; or, for best performance, the `DataReader` provides a series of methods that enable you to access column values in their native data types (`GetDateTime`, `GetDouble`, `GetGuid`, `GetInt32`, and so on). Using the typed accessor methods when the underlying data type is known reduces the amount of type conversion required (converting from type `Object`) when retrieving the column value.

The `DataReader` provides a nonbuffered stream of data that enables procedural logic to efficiently process results from a data source sequentially. The `DataReader` is a good choice when retrieving large amounts of data; only one row of data is loaded in memory at a time. You should always call the `Close` method when you are through using the `DataReader` object, as well as close the `DataReader` object's database connection; otherwise, the connection will be open until the garbage collector gets around to collecting the object. Alternately, use the `Using` statement to automatically close the database connection at the end of the `Using` clause.

Note how you use the `CommandBehavior.CloseConnection` enumeration value on the `SqlDataReader.ExecuteReader` method. This tells the `SqlCommand` object to automatically close the database connection when the `SqlDataReader.Close` method is called.

> **NOTE** *If your command contains output parameters or return values, they will not be available until the* DataReader *is closed.*

## Executing Commands Asynchronously

In ADO.NET, additional support enables Command objects to execute their commands asynchronously, which can result in a huge perceived performance gain in many applications, especially in WPF applications. This can come in very handy, especially if you ever have to execute a long-running SQL statement. This section examines how this functionality enables you to add asynchronous processing to enhance the responsiveness of an application.

The SqlCommand object provides three different asynchronous call options: BeginExecuteReader, BeginExecuteNonQuery, and BeginExecuteXmlReader. Each of these methods has a corresponding "end" method — that is, EndExecuteReader, EndExecuteNonQuery, and EndExecuteXmlReader. Now that you are familiar with the DataReader object, you'll now look at an example using the BeginExecuteReader method to execute a long-running query.

In the AsyncExample project, a button and an associated Click event handler have been added to the form that will initiate the asynchronous call to get a DataReader instance (code file: AsyncExample):

```
Private Sub LoadDataAsycButton_Click(sender As Object,
                                     e As EventArgs) Handles
                                     LoadDataAsycButton.Click

    Dim connection As SqlConnection
    Dim command As SqlCommand

    'update to match the location of AdventureWorks on your computer
    Dim cmdString As String = "Long_Running_Procedure"
    connection = New SqlConnection("Data Source=.\SQLEXPRESS;" +
                                   "Initial Catalog=AdventureWorks;" +
                                   "Integrated Security=True; " +
                                   "Asynchronous Processing=true;")
    command = New SqlCommand(cmdString, connection)

    'Set the command type to stored procedure
    command.CommandType = CommandType.StoredProcedure
    connection.Open()

    'Make the asynchronous call to the database
    command.BeginExecuteReader(AddressOf Me.AsyncCallback, command,
                               CommandBehavior.CloseConnection)
End Sub
```

First, and this is very important, you append the statement "Asynchronous Processing=true" to your Connection object's connection string. This must be set in order for ADO.NET to make asynchronous calls to SQL Server.

After getting the connection set, you then build an `SqlCommand` object and initialize it to be able to execute the `Long_Running_Procedure` stored procedure. This procedure simulates a long-running query by using the SQL Server `WAITFOR DELAY` statement to create a 20-second delay before it executes the `HumanResources.Employees_Get` stored procedure. As you can probably guess, the `HumanResources.Employees_Get` stored procedure simply selects all of the employees from the `HumanResources.Employees` table. The delay is added simply to demonstrate that while this stored procedure is executing, you can perform other tasks in your Windows Forms application. Here is the SQL code for the stored procedures:

```
CREATE PROCEDURE HumanResources.Employees_Get
AS
BEGIN
    SELECT * From [HumanResources].[Employee]
END
GO

CREATE PROCEDURE Long_Running_Procedure
AS
SET NOCOUNT ON
WAITFOR DELAY '00:00:20'
EXEC HumanResources.Employees_Get
GO
```

The last line of code in the Button's `Click` event handler is the call to `BeginExecuteReader`. In this call, the first thing you are passing in is a delegate method (`Me.AsyncCallback`) for the `System.AsyncCallback` delegate type. This is how the .NET Framework calls you back once the method is finished running asynchronously. You then pass in your initialized `SqlCommand` object so that it can be executed, as well as the `CommandBehavior` value for the `DataReader`. In this case, you pass in the `CommandBehavior.CloseConnection` value so that the connection to the database will be closed once the `DataReader` has been closed. You will look at the `DataReader` in more detail in the next section.

Now that you have initiated the asynchronous call, and have defined a callback for your asynchronous call, you'll now look at the actual method that is being called back, the `AsyncCallback` method (code file: AsyncExample):

```
Private Sub AsyncCallback(ByVal ar As IAsyncResult)
    'Get the command that was passed from the AsyncState of the IAsyncResult.
    Dim command As SqlCommand = CType(ar.AsyncState, SqlCommand)

    'Get the reader from the IAsyncResult.
    Dim reader As SqlDataReader = command.EndExecuteReader(ar)

    'Get a table from the reader.
    Dim table As DataTable = New DataTable()
    table.Load(reader)

    'Call the BindGrid method on the Windows main thread,
    'passing in the table.
    Me.Invoke(New BindGridDelegate(AddressOf Me.BindGrid), New Object() {table})

    reader.Close()

End Sub
```

The first line of the code is simply retrieving the `SqlCommand` object from the `AsyncState` property of the `IAsyncResult` that was passed in. Remember that when you called `BeginExecuteReader` earlier, you passed in your `SqlCommand` object. You need it so that you can call the `EndExecuteReader` method on the next line. This method gives you your `SqlDataReader`. On the next line, you then transform the `SqlDataReader` into a `DataTable` (covered later when the `DataSet` is discussed).

The last line of this method is probably the most important. If you tried to just take your `DataTable` and bind it to the grid, it would not work, because right now you are executing on a thread other than the main Windows thread. The helper method named `BindGrid` can do the data binding, but it must be called only in the context of the Windows main thread. To bring the data back to the main Windows thread, it must be marshaled via the `Invoke` method of the `Form` object. Invoke takes two arguments: the delegate of the method you want to call and (optionally) any parameters for that method. In this case, you define a delegate for the `BindGrid` method, called `BindGridDelegate`. Here is the delegate declaration:

```
Private Delegate Sub BindGridDelegate(ByVal table As DataTable)
```

Notice how the signature is exactly the same as the `BindGrid` method shown here:

```
Private Sub BindGrid(ByVal table As DataTable)
   'Clear the grid.
   Me.MainDataGridView.DataSource = Nothing

   'Bind the grid to the DataTable.
   Me.MainDataGridView.DataSource = table
End Sub
```

Here is another look at the call to the form's `Invoke` method:

```
Me.Invoke(New BindGridDelegate(AddressOf Me.BindGrid),
          New Object() {table})
```

You pass in a new instance of the `BindGridDelegate` delegate and initialize it with a pointer to the `BindGrid` method. As a result, the .NET worker thread that was executing your query can now safely join up with the main Windows thread.

## DataAdapter Objects

Each .NET data provider included with the .NET Framework has a `DataAdapter` object. A `DataAdapter` is used to retrieve data from a data source and populate `DataTable` objects and constraints within a `DataSet`. The `DataAdapter` also resolves changes made to the `DataSet` back to the data source. The `DataAdapter` uses the `Connection` object of the .NET data provider to connect to a data source, and `Command` objects to retrieve data from, and resolve changes to, the data source from a `DataSet` object.

This differs from the `DataReader`, in that the `DataReader` uses the `Connection` object to access the data directly, without having to use a `DataAdapter`. The `DataAdapter` essentially decouples the `DataSet` object from the actual source of the data, whereas the `DataReader` is tightly bound to the data in a read-only fashion.

The `SelectCommand` property of the `DataAdapter` is a `Command` object that retrieves data from the data source. A nice, convenient way to set the `DataAdapter`'s `SelectCommand` property is to pass in a Command object in the DataAdapter's constructor. The InsertCommand, UpdateCommand, and DeleteCommand properties of the DataAdapter are Command objects that manage updates to the data in the data source according to modifications made to the data in the DataSet. The Fill method of the DataAdapter is used to populate a DataSet with the results of the SelectCommand of the DataAdapter. It also adds or refreshes rows in the DataSet to match those in the data source. The following example code demonstrates how to fill a DataSet object with information from the HumanResources.Employee table (code file: DataAdapterExample):

```vb
Imports System.Data.SqlClient

Module Main
  Sub Main()
    Dim connection As SqlConnection

    Console.WriteLine("Loading records...")

    'Update to match the location of AdventureWorks on your computer
    Dim cmdString As String = "SELECT * From [HumanResources].[Employee]"
    connection = New SqlConnection("Data Source=.\SQLEXPRESS;" +
                                   "Initial Catalog=AdventureWorks;" +
                                   "Integrated Security=True")

    'Initialize the SqlDataAdapter with the SQL
    'and Connection strings, and then use the
    'SqlDataAdapter to fill the DataSet with data.
    Dim adapter As New SqlDataAdapter(cmdString, connection)
    Dim employees As New DataSet
    adapter.Fill(employees)

    'Iterate through the DataSet's table.
    For Each row As DataRow In employees.Tables(0).Rows
      Console.WriteLine(row("LoginID").ToString)
    Next

    Console.WriteLine("Press ENTER to get DataSet xml")
    Console.ReadLine()

    'Print the DataSet's XML.
    Console.WriteLine(employees.GetXml())

    Console.WriteLine("Press ENTER to exit")
    Console.ReadLine()
  End Sub
End Module
```

Note how you use the constructor of the SqlDataAdapter to pass in and set the SelectCommand, as well as pass in the connection string in lieu of an SqlCommand object that already has an initialized Connection property. You then just call the SqlDataAdapter object's Fill method and pass in an initialized DataSet object. If the DataSet object is not initialized, then the Fill method raises an exception (System.ArgumentNullException).

Ever since ADO.NET 2.0, a significant performance improvement was made in the way that the DataAdapter updates the database. In ADO.NET 1.x, the DataAdapter's Update method would loop through each row of every `DataTable` object in the `DataSet` and subsequently make a trip to the database for each row being updated. In ADO.NET 2.0, batch update support was added to the `DataAdapter`. This means that when the `Update` method is called, the `DataAdapter` batches all of the updates from the `DataSet` in one trip to the database.

Now take a look at a more advanced example. Here, you use a `DataAdapter` to insert, update, and delete data from a `DataTable` back to the database (code file: DataAdapterAdvancedExample):

```vb
Private Sub BatchUpdateButton_Click(sender As Object,
                                    e As EventArgs)
                                    Handles BatchUpdateButton.Click
    'Build insert, update, and delete commands.
    'Build the parameter values.
    Dim updateParams() As String = {"@DocumentID", "@FileName", "@FileExtension",
                                     "@Revision", "@ChangeNumber", "@Status",
                                     "@ModifiedDate"}
    Dim insertParams() As String = {"@Title", "@FileName", "@FileExtension",
                                     "@Revision", "@ChangeNumber", "@Status",
                                     "@ModifiedDate"}
```

The preceding code begins by initializing a string array of parameter names to pass into the `BuildSqlCommand` helper method:

```vb
    'Insert command.
    Dim insertCommand As SqlCommand =
        BuildSqlCommand("[Production].[uspInsertDocument]",
                        insertParams)
```

Next, you pass the name of the stored procedure to execute and the parameters for the stored procedure to the `BuildSqlCommand` helper method. This method returns an initialized instance of the `SqlCommand` class. Here is the `BuildSqlCommand` helper method:

```vb
    Private Function BuildSqlCommand(ByVal storedProcedureName As String,
                                     ByVal parameterNames() As String) As SqlCommand
        Dim connection As SqlConnection
        Dim command As SqlCommand

        connection = New SqlConnection("Data Source=.\SQLEXPRESS;" +
                                       "Initial Catalog=AdventureWorks;" +
                                       "Integrated Security=True; " +
                                       "Asynchronous Processing=true;")

        command = New SqlCommand(storedProcedureName, connection)

        'Set the command type to stored procedure.
        command.CommandType = CommandType.StoredProcedure

        'Build the parameters for the command.
        'See if any parameter names were passed in.
        If Not parameterNames Is Nothing Then
          ' Iterate through the parameters.
          Dim parameter As SqlParameter = Nothing
          For Each parameterName As String In parameterNames
            ' Create a new SqlParameter.
            parameter = New SqlParameter()
```

```
            parameter.ParameterName = parameterName

            ' Map the parameter to a column name in the DataTable/DataSet.
            parameter.SourceColumn = parameterName.Substring(1)

            ' Add the parameter to the command.
            command.Parameters.Add(parameter)
        Next
    End If
    Return command
End Function
```

This method first initializes an `SqlCommand` class and passes in the name of a stored procedure. The next step is to set the command type of the `SqlCommand` to a stored procedure. This is important because ADO.NET uses this to optimize how the stored procedure is called on the database server. You then check whether any parameter names have been passed (via the `parameterNames` string array); if so, you iterate through them. While iterating through the parameter names, you build up `SqlParameter` objects and add them to the `SqlCommand`'s collection of parameters.

The most important step in building up the `SqlParameter` object is setting its `SourceColumn` property. This is what the `DataAdapter` later uses to map the parameter name to the name of the column in the `DataTable` when its `Update` method is called. An example of such a mapping is associating the `@DocumentID` parameter name with the `DocumentID` column name. As shown in the code, the mapping assumes that the stored procedure parameters all have exactly the same names as the columns, except for the mandatory @ character in front of the parameter. That's why when assigning the `SqlParameter`'s `SourceColumn` property value, you use the `Substring` method to strip off the @ character to ensure that it maps correctly.

You then call the `BuildSqlCommand` method two more times to build your update and delete `SqlCommand` objects:

```
'Update command.
Dim updateCommand As SqlCommand =
    BuildSqlCommand("[Production].[uspUpdateDocument]",
                    updateParams)

'Delete command.
Dim deleteCommand As SqlCommand =
    BuildSqlCommand("[Production].[uspDeleteDocument]",
                    New String() {"@DocumentID"})
```

Now that the `SqlCommand` objects have been created, the next step is to create an `SqlDataAdapter` object. Once the `SqlDataAdapter` is created, you set its `InsertCommand`, `UpdateCommand`, and `DeleteCommand` properties with the respective `SqlCommand` objects that you just built:

```
'Create an adapter.
Dim adapter As New SqlDataAdapter()

'Associate the commands with the adapter.
adapter.InsertCommand = insertCommand
adapter.UpdateCommand = updateCommand
adapter.DeleteCommand = deleteCommand
```

The next step is to get a `DataTable` instance of the Production.Document table from the database:

```vb.net
Dim command As SqlCommand
Dim connection As SqlConnection

connection = New SqlConnection("Data Source=.\SQLEXPRESS;" +
                               "Initial Catalog=AdventureWorks;" +
                               "Integrated Security=True; " +
                               "Asynchronous Processing=true;")
command = New SqlCommand(cmdString, connection)

connection.Open()

'Get the Documents reader.
Dim reader As SqlDataReader
reader = command.ExecuteReader(CommandBehavior.Default)


'Load a DataTable from the reader.
Dim table As DataTable = New DataTable()
table.Load(reader)
```

Once you have your `DataTable` filled with data, you begin modifying it so you can test the new batch update capability of the `DataAdapter`. The first change to make is an insert in the `DataTable`. In order to add a row, you first call the `DataTable`'s `NewRow` method to give you a `DataRow` initialized with the same columns as your `DataTable`:

```vb.net
'Add a new document to the DataTable.
Dim row As DataRow = table.NewRow()
```

Once that is done, you can set the column values of the `DataRow`:

```vb.net
row("Title") = "Test Document " + New Random().Next(100, 999).ToString
row("FileName") =
        My.Computer.FileSystem.CombinePath(Environment.GetFolderPath(
        Environment.SpecialFolder.MyDocuments), "TestFile" +
        New Random().Next(10000, 99999).ToString)
row("FileExtension") = ".docx"
row("Revision") = New Random().Next(0, 999).ToString
row("ChangeNumber") = New Random().Next(1, 999).ToString
row("Status") = 1
row("ModifiedDate") = DateTime.Now.ToString
table.Rows.Add(row)
```

Then you call the `Add` method of the `DataTable`'s `DataRowCollection` property and pass in the newly populated `DataRow` object:

```vb.net
table.Rows.Add(row)
```

Now that there is a new row in the `DataTable`, the next test is to update one of its rows:

```vb.net
'Change revison number in the DataTable.
table.Rows(0)("Revision") = Integer.Parse(table.Rows(0)("Revision")) + 1
```

Finally, you delete a row from the `DataTable`. In this case, it is the second-to-last row in the `DataTable`:

```vb.net
'Delete the second to last document from the table
table.Rows(table.Rows.Count - 2).Delete()
```

Now that you have performed an insert, update, and delete action on your `DataTable`, it is time to send the changes back to the database. You do this by calling the `DataAdapter`'s `Update` method and passing in either a `DataSet` or a `DataTable`. Note that you are calling the `GetChanges` method of the `DataTable`; this is important, because you only want to send the changes to the `DataAdapter`:

```
'Send only the changes in the DataTable to the database for updating.
adapter.Update(table.GetChanges())
```

To prove that the update worked, you get back a new `DataTable` from the server using the same technique as before, and then bind it to the grid with your helper method to view the changes that were made:

```
'Get the new changes back from the server to show that the update worked.
reader = command.ExecuteReader(CommandBehavior.CloseConnection)

'Load a DataTable from the reader.
table.Load(reader)

'Bind the grid to the new table data.
BindGrid(table)
End Sub
```

## SQL Server .NET Data Provider

The SQL Server .NET data provider uses Tabular Data Stream (TDS) to communicate with the SQL Server. This offers a great performance increase, as TDS is SQL Server's native communication protocol that can be up to 70 percent faster than the OLE DB .NET data provider.

> **NOTE** *This is very important, as going through the OLE DB or ODBC layers means that the CLR has to marshal (convert) all of the COM data types to .NET CLR data types each time data is accessed from a data source. When using the SQL Server .NET data provider, everything runs within the .NET CLR, and the TDS protocol is faster than the other network protocols previously used for SQL Server.*

To use this provider, you need to include the `System.Data.SqlClient` namespace in your application. Note that it works only for SQL Server 7.0 and later. Use the SQL Server .NET data provider anytime you are connecting to an SQL Server 7.0 and later database server. The SQL Server .NET data provider requires the installation of MDAC 2.6 or later.

## OLE DB .NET Data Provider

The OLE DB .NET data provider uses native OLE DB through COM interop to enable data access. The OLE DB .NET data provider supports both manual and automatic transactions. For automatic transactions, the OLE DB .NET data provider automatically enlists in a transaction and obtains transaction details from Windows 2000 Component Services. The OLE DB .NET data provider does not support OLE DB 2.5 interfaces. OLE DB providers that require support for OLE DB 2.5 interfaces will not function properly with the OLE DB .NET data provider. This includes the Microsoft OLE DB provider for Exchange and the Microsoft OLE DB provider for Internet Publishing. The OLE DB .NET data provider requires the installation of MDAC 2.6 or later. To use this provider, you need to include the `System.Data.OleDb` namespace in your application.

## THE DATASET COMPONENT

The `DataSet` is central to supporting disconnected, distributed data scenarios with ADO.NET. The `DataSet` is a memory-resident representation of data that provides a consistent relational programming model regardless of the data source. The `DataSet` represents a complete set of data, including related tables, constraints, and relationships among the tables; basically, it's like having a small relational database residing in memory.

> **NOTE** *Because the `DataSet` contains a lot of metadata, you need to be careful about how much data you try to stuff into it, as it consumes memory.*

The methods and objects in a `DataSet` are consistent with those in the relational database model. The `DataSet` can also persist and reload its contents as XML, and its schema as XSD. It is completely disconnected from any database connections, so it is totally up to you to fill it with whatever data you need in memory.

Ever since ADO.NET 2.0, several new features have been added to the `DataSet` and the `DataTable` classes, as well as enhancements to existing features. The features covered in this section are:

➤ The binary serialization format option

➤ Additions to make the `DataTable` more of a standalone object

➤ The capability to expose `DataSet` and `DataTable` data as a stream (`DataReader`), and to load stream data into a `DataSet` or `DataTable`

## DataTableCollection

An ADO.NET `DataSet` contains a collection of zero or more tables represented by `DataTable` objects. The `DataTableCollection` contains all of the `DataTable` objects in a `DataSet`.

A `DataTable` is defined in the `System.Data` namespace and represents a single table of memory-resident data. It contains a collection of columns represented by the `DataColumnCollection`, which defines the schema and rows of the table. It also contains a collection of rows represented by the `DataRowCollection`, which contains the data in the table. Along with the current state, a `DataRow` retains its original state and tracks changes that occur to the data.

## DataRelationCollection

A `DataSet` contains relationships in its `DataRelationCollection` object. A relationship (represented by the `DataRelation` object) associates rows in one `DataTable` with rows in another `DataTable`. The relationships in the `DataSet` can have constraints, which are represented by

`UniqueConstraint` and `ForeignKeyConstraint` objects. It is analogous to a `JOIN` path that might exist between the primary and foreign key columns in a relational database. A `DataRelation` identifies matching columns in two tables of a `DataSet`.

Relationships enable you to see what links information within one table to another. The essential elements of a `DataRelation` are the name of the relationship, the two tables being related, and the related columns in each table. Relationships can be built with more than one column per table, with an array of `DataColumn` objects for the key columns. When a relationship is added to the `DataRelationCollection`, it may optionally add `ForeignKeyConstraints` that disallow any changes that would invalidate the relationship. Relationships are also an important tool in maintaining valid data, not just a tool for seeing links.

## ExtendedProperties

The `DataSet` (as well as the `DataTable` and `DataColumn`) has an `ExtendedProperties` property. `ExtendedProperties` is a `PropertyCollection` in which a user can place customized information, such as the `SELECT` statement that is used to generate the result set, or a date/time stamp indicating when the data was generated. Because the `ExtendedProperties` contains customized information, this is a good place to store extra user-defined data about the `DataSet` (or `DataTable` or `DataColumn`), such as a time when the data should be refreshed. The `ExtendedProperties` collection is persisted with the schema information for the `DataSet` (as well as `DataTable` and `DataColumn`). The following code example adds an expiration property to a `DataSet` (code file: DataSetExtendedPropertiesExample):

```
'Build the SQL and Connection strings.
Dim cmdString As String = "SELECT * FROM [Sales].[SalesOrderHeader]"
Dim connection As SqlConnection
Dim command As SqlCommand

connection = New SqlConnection("Data Source=.\SQLEXPRESS;" +
                               "Initial Catalog=AdventureWorks;" +
                               "Integrated Security=True; " +
                               "Asynchronous Processing=true;")

command = New SqlCommand(cmdString, connection)

'Initialize the SqlDataAdapter with the SQL
'and Connection strings, and then use the
'SqlDataAdapter to fill the DataSet with data.
Dim adapter As SqlDataAdapter =New SqlDataAdapter(cmdString, connection)
Dim salesOrders As New DataSet
adapter.Fill(salesOrders)

'Add an extended property called "expiration."
'Set its value to the current date/time + 1 hour.
salesOrders.ExtendedProperties.Add("expiration",
                              DateAdd(DateInterval.Hour, 1, Now))
MessageBox.Show(salesOrders.ExtendedProperties("expiration").ToString,
              "Sales Orders Expiration")
```

This code begins by filling a `DataSet` with the Sales.SalesOrderHeader table. It then adds a new extended property, called `expiration`, and sets its value to the current date and time plus one hour.

You then simply read it back. As you can see, it is very easy to add extended properties to DataSet objects. The same pattern also applies to DataTable and DataColumn objects.

## Creating and Using DataSet Objects

The ADO.NET DataSet is a memory-resident representation of the data that provides a consistent relational programming model, regardless of the source of the data it contains. A DataSet represents a complete set of data, including the tables that contain, order, and constrain the data, as well as the relationships between the tables. The advantage to using a DataSet is that the data it contains can come from multiple sources, and it is fairly easy to get the data from multiple sources into the DataSet. In addition, you can define your own constraints between the DataTables in a DataSet.

There are several methods for working with a DataSet, and they can be applied independently or in combination:

➤ Programmatically create DataTables, DataRelations, and constraints within the DataSet and populate them with data.

➤ Populate the DataSet or a DataTable from an existing RDBMS using a DataAdapter.

➤ Load and persist a DataSet or DataTable using XML.

➤ Load a DataSet from an XSD schema file.

➤ Load a DataSet or a DataTable from a DataReader.

Here is a typical usage scenario for a DataSet object:

**1.** A client makes a request to a Web service.

**2.** Based on this request, the Web service populates a DataSet from a database using a DataAdapter and returns the DataSet to the client.

**3.** The client then views the data and makes modifications.

**4.** When finished viewing and modifying the data, the client passes the modified DataSet back to the Web service, which again uses a DataAdapter to reconcile the changes in the returned DataSet with the original data in the database.

**5.** The Web service may then return a DataSet that reflects the current values in the database, but this is not recommended as mentioned earlier in this chapter.

**6.** Optionally, the client can then use the DataSet class's Merge method to merge the returned DataSet with the client's existing copy of the DataSet; the Merge method will accept successful changes and mark with an error any changes that failed.

The design of the ADO.NET DataSet makes this scenario fairly easy to implement. Because the DataSet is stateless, it can be safely passed between the server and the client without tying up server resources such as database connections. Although the DataSet is transmitted as XML, Web services and ADO.NET automatically transform the XML representation of the data to and from a DataSet, creating a rich, yet simplified, programming model.

In addition, because the DataSet is transmitted as an XML stream, non-ADO.NET clients can consume the same Web service consumed by ADO.NET clients. Similarly, ADO.NET clients can interact easily with non-ADO.NET Web services by sending any client `DataSet` to a Web service as XML and by consuming any XML returned as a `DataSet` from the Web service. However, note the size of the data; if your `DataSet` contains a large number of rows, it will eat up a lot of bandwidth (code file: DataSetLoadingExample):

```
'Build the SQL and Connection strings.
Dim cmdString As String = "SELECT * FROM [Sales].[SalesOrderHeader]"
Dim connection As SqlConnection
Dim command As SqlCommand

connection = New SqlConnection("Data Source=.\SQLEXPRESS;" +
                              "Initial Catalog=AdventureWorks;" +
                              "Integrated Security=True; " +
                              "Asynchronous Processing=true;")

command = New SqlCommand(cmdString, connection)

'Initialize the SqlDataAdapter with the SQL
'and Connection strings, and then use the
'SqlDataAdapter to fill the DataSet with data.
Dim adapter As SqlDataAdapter = New SqlDataAdapter(cmdString, connection)
Dim salesOrders As New DataSet
adapter.Fill(salesOrders)

'Add an extended property called "expiration."
mainGrid.DataSource = salesOrders.Tables(0)
```

## ADO.NET DataTable Objects

A `DataSet` is made up of a collection of tables, relationships, and constraints. In ADO.NET, `DataTable` objects are used to represent the tables in a `DataSet`. A `DataTable` represents one table of in-memory relational data. The data is local to the .NET application in which it resides, but it can be populated from a data source such as SQL Server using a `DataAdapter`.

The `DataTable` class is a member of the `System.Data` namespace within the .NET Framework Class Library. You can create and use a `DataTable` independently or as a member of a `DataSet`, and `DataTable` objects can be used by other .NET Framework objects, including the `DataView`. You access the collection of tables in a `DataSet` through the `DataSet` object's `Tables` property.

The schema, or structure, of a table is represented by columns and constraints. You define the schema of a `DataTable` using `DataColumn` objects as well as `ForeignKeyConstraint` and `UniqueConstraint` objects. The columns in a table can map to columns in a data source, contain calculated values from expressions, automatically increment their values, or contain primary key values.

If you populate a `DataTable` from a database, it inherits the constraints from the database, so you don't have to do all of that work manually. A `DataTable` must also have rows in which to contain and order the data. The `DataRow` class represents the actual data contained in the table. You use the `DataRow` and its properties and methods to retrieve, evaluate, and manipulate the data in a table. As you access and change the data within a row, the `DataRow` object maintains both its current and original state.

You can create parent-child relationships between tables within a database, such as SQL Server, using one or more related columns in the tables. You create a relationship between DataTable objects using a DataRelation, which can then be used to return a row's related child or parent rows.

# Advanced ADO.NET Features of the DataSet and DataTable Objects

One of the main complaints developers had about ADO.NET 1.x was related to the performance of the DataSet and its DataTable children — in particular, when they contained a large amount of data. The performance hit comes in two different ways. The first way is the time it takes to actually load a DataSet with a lot of data. As the number of rows in a DataTable increases, the time to load a new row increases almost proportionally to the number of rows. The second way is when the large DataSet is serialized and remoted. A key feature of the DataSet is the fact that it automatically knows how to serialize itself, especially when you want to pass it between application tiers. Unfortunately, the serialization is quite verbose and takes up a lot of memory and network bandwidth. Both of these performance problems have been addressed since ADO.NET 2.0.

## Indexing

The first improvement made since ADO.NET 2.0 to the DataSet family was a complete rewrite of the indexing engine for the DataTable, which now scales much better for large DataSets. The addition of the new indexing engine results in faster basic inserts, updates, and deletes, which also means faster Fill and Merge operations. Just as in relational database design, if you are dealing with large DataSets, then it pays big dividends if you first add unique keys and foreign keys to your DataTable. Even better, you don't have to change any of your code at all to take advantage of this new feature.

## Serialization

The second improvement made to the DataSet family was adding new options to the way the DataSet and DataTable are serialized. The main complaint about retrieving DataSet objects from Web services and remoting calls was that they were way too verbose and took up too much network bandwidth. In ADO.NET 1.x, the DataSet serializes as XML, even when using the binary formatter. Using ADO.NET, you can also specify true binary serialization by setting the newly added RemotingFormat property to SerializationFormat.Binary, rather than (the default) SerializationFormat.XML. In the DataSetLoadingExample project of the Examples solution, a Button (serializeButton_Click) has been added to the Form and its associated Click event handler that demonstrates how to serialize a DataTable in binary format (DataSetLoadingExample):

```
Dim table As DataTable = salesOrders.Tables(0)

' Save the table in a binary format
Dim filename As String = Path.Combine(FileIO.SpecialDirectories.MyDocuments,
                                       "SalesOrders.dat")

Using fs As New FileStream(filename, FileMode.Create)
  salesOrders.RemotingFormat = SerializationFormat.Binary
```

```
        Dim format As New BinaryFormatter
        format.Serialize(fs, table)
    End Using

    'Tell the user what happened
    MessageBox.Show(String.Format("Successfully serialized the DataTable to {0}",
                            filename))
```

This code takes advantage of the Using statement for Visual Basic to wrap up creating and disposing of a FileStream instance that will hold your serialized DataTable data. The next step is to set the DataTable's RemotingFormat property to the SerializationFormat.Binary enumeration value. Once that is done, you simply create a new BinaryFormatter instance, and then call its Serialize method to serialize your DataTable into the FileStream instance. You then finish by showing users a message box indicating that the data has been serialized.

## DataReader Integration

Another nice feature of the DataSet and DataTable classes is the capability to both read from and write out to a stream of data in the form of a DataReader. You will first take a look at how you can load a DataTable from a DataReader. To demonstrate this, a Button (loadFromDataReaderButton) has been added to the project (DataSetLoadingExample):

```
    Dim reader As SqlDataReader
    reader = command.ExecuteReader()

    'Load the DataTable from the reader.
    Dim table As New DataTable("SalesOrderHeader")
    table.Load(reader)

    'Close the reader.
    reader.Close()

    'Load Grid
    mainGrid.DataSource = table
```

This method begins by first creating an instance of a DataTable and initializing it with the table name. Once the new DataTable has been initialized, you call the new Load method and pass in the SqlDataReader that was passed into the method via the reader argument. This is where the DataTable takes the DataReader and populates the DataTable instance with the column names and data from the DataReader. The next step is to close the DataReader, as it is no longer needed; and finally, DataTable is loaded into the grid control.

## DataTable Independence

One of the most convenient capabilities in ADO.NET is the inclusion of several methods from the DataSet class in the DataTable class. The DataTable is now much more versatile and useful than it was in the early ADO.NET days. The DataTable now supports all of the same read and write methods for XML as the DataSet — specifically, the ReadXml, ReadXmlSchema, WriteXml, and WriteXmlSchema methods.

The Merge method of the DataSet has now been added to the DataTable as well; and in addition to the existing functionality of the DataSet class, some of the new features of the DataSet class have been added to the `DataTable` class — namely, the `RemotingFormat` property, the `Load` method, and the `GetDataReader` method.

## WORKING WITH THE COMMON PROVIDER MODEL

In ADO.NET 1.x, you could code to either the provider-specific classes, such as `SqlConnection`, or the generic interfaces, such as `IDbConnection`. If there was a possibility that the database you were programming against would change during your project, or if you were creating a commercial package intended to support customers with different databases, then you had to use the generic interfaces. You cannot call a constructor on an interface, so most generic programs included code that accomplished the task of obtaining the original `IDbConnection` by means of their own factory method, such as a `GetConnection` method that would return a provider-specific instance of the `IDbConnection` interface.

ADO.NET today has a more elegant solution for getting the provider-specific connection. Each data provider registers a `ProviderFactory` class and a provider string in the .NET `machine.config` file. A base `ProviderFactory` class (`DbProviderFactory`) and a `System.Data.Common.ProviderFactories` class can return a `DataTable` of information (via the `GetFactoryClasses` method) about different data providers registered in `machine.config`, and can return the correct `ProviderFactory` given the provider string (called `ProviderInvariantName`) or by using a `DataRow` from this `DataTable`. Instead of writing your own framework to build connections based on the name of the provider, ADO.NET now makes it much more straightforward, flexible, and easy to solve this problem.

Now take a look at an example of using the common provider model to connect to the database and display some rows from the Employees table. The code shown below is broken down into six steps. The first step is to get the provider factory object based on a configuration value of the provider's invariant name (code file: ProviderExample):

```
Private Sub loadDataButton_Click(sender As Object,
                                 e As EventArgs)
                                 Handles loadDataButton.Click
    'Create the provider factory from config value.
    Dim factory As DbProviderFactory = DbProviderFactories.GetFactory(
                                 My.Settings.ProviderName)
```

You are able to get the factory via the `DbProviderFactories` object's `GetFactory` method and pass in the string name of the provider invariant stored in project Settings. Here is the entry in the `app.config` file:

```
<setting name="ProviderName" serializeAs="String">
    <value>System.Data.SqlClient</value>
</setting>
```

In this case, you are using the SQL Server data provider. Once you have the factory object, the next step is to use it to create a connection:

```
'Create the connection from the factory.
Dim connection As DbConnection = factory.CreateConnection()

'Get the connection string from config.
```

```
connection.ConnectionString = My.Settings.DatabaseConnection
```

The connection is created by calling the `DbProviderFactory`'s `CreateConnection` method. In this case, the factory is returning an `SqlConnection`, because you chose to use the `System.Data.SqlClient` provider invariant. To keep your code generic, you will not be directly programming against any of the classes in the `System.Data.SqlClient` namespace. Note how the connection class you declare is a `DbConnection` class, which is part of the `System.Data` namespace.

The next step is to create a `Command` object so you can retrieve the data from the Employees table:

```
'Create the command from the connection.
Dim command As DbCommand = connection.CreateCommand()
command.CommandType = CommandType.StoredProcedure
command.CommandText = "HumanResources.Employees_Get"
```

You begin by declaring a generic `DbCommand` class variable and then using the `DbConnection`'s `CreateCommand` method to create the `DbCommand` instance. Once you have done that, you set the command type to `StoredProcedure` and then set the stored procedure name.

This example uses a `DbDataAdapter` to fill a `DataTable` with the employees' data. Here is how you create and initialize the `DbDataAdapter`:

```
'Create the adapter from the factory.
Dim adapter As DbDataAdapter = factory.CreateDataAdapter()
adapter.SelectCommand = command
```

Just as you did when you created your `DbConnection` instance, you use the factory to create your `DbDataAdapter`. After creating it, you then set the `SelectCommand` property's value to the instance of the previously initialized `DbCommand` instance.

After finishing these steps, the next step is to create a `DataTable` and fill it using the `DataAdapter`:

```
'Create a new DataTable.
Dim employees As New DataTable
adapter.Fill(employees)
```

The final step is to bind the table to the form's grid:

```
'Populate the grid with the data.
BindGrid(employees)
End Sub
```

You already looked at the `BindGrid` helper method in the asynchronous example earlier. In this example, you are simply reusing this generic method again:

```
Private Sub BindGrid(ByVal table As DataTable)
  'Clear the grid.
  Me.MainDataGridView.DataSource = Nothing

  'Bind the grid to the DataTable.
  Me.MainDataGridView.DataSource = table
End Sub
```

The main point to take away from this example is that you were able to easily write database-agnostic code with just a few short lines. ADO.NET 1.x required a lot of lines of code to create this functionality; you had to write your own abstract factory classes and factory methods in order to create instances of the generic database interfaces, such as `IDbConnection`, `IDbCommand`, and so on.

# CONNECTION POOLING IN ADO.NET

Pooling connections can significantly enhance the performance and scalability of your application. Both the SQL Client .NET data provider and the OLE DB .NET data provider automatically pool connections using Windows Component Services and OLE DB session pooling, respectively. The only requirement is that you must use the exact same connection string each time if you want a pooled connection.

ADO.NET now enhances the connection pooling functionality offered in ADO.NET 1.x by enabling you to close all of the connections currently kept alive by the particular managed provider that you are using. You can clear a specific connection pool by using the shared `SqlConnection.ClearPool` method or clear all of the connection pools in an application domain by using the shared `SqlConnection.ClearPools` method. Both the SQL Server and Oracle managed providers implement this functionality.

# TRANSACTIONS AND SYSTEM.TRANSACTIONS

While you can do simple transaction support with ADO.NET, Visual Basic includes a set of classes specifically designed for working with transactions: the `System.Transactions` namespace. As the name implies, these classes allow you to define and work with transactions in your code.

You may well be wondering at this point why you need two methods of working with transactions. The classes of `System.Transaction`, particularly the `Transaction` class itself, abstract the code from the resource managers participating in the transaction. Transactions in ADO.NET are specific to each database you may access. There is no unified method of creating a transaction, nor is there a standard way of sharing a database transaction across multiple databases or other transaction supporters. The `Transaction` class provides for these limitations, and can coordinate multiple resource managers itself.

The classes of `System.Transaction` also provide the means to create your own resource managers. These resource managers may then participate in transactions. At first, you may balk at this prospect, wondering how you could write something that manages all the details of a transactional data store. Aren't the details enormous? Fortunately, the classes make it easy to enlist in a transaction and report on your results.

## Creating Transactions

`System.Transaction` supports two means of working with transactions: *implicit* and *explicit*. With implicit transactions, you define a boundary for the transaction. Any resource managers you use within this boundary become part of the transaction. That is, if you have defined a boundary and then call a database such as SQL Server, the actions performed on the database are part of the transaction. If the code reaches the boundary without incident, then the transaction is committed.

If an exception occurs during this implicit transaction, then the transaction is rolled back. Explicit transactions, as you may have guessed, mean that you explicitly commit or roll back the transaction as needed.

Using the implicit model can greatly simplify the code involved in a transaction. The following code demonstrates inserting a record using the insert command seen previously using an implicit transaction (code file: DataAdapterAdvancedExample):

```
Using ts As New TransactionScope
   Try
      'Add a new document to the DataTable.
      Dim row As DataRow = table.NewRow()
      row("Title") = "Test Document " + New Random().Next(100, 999).ToString
      row("FileName") = My.Computer.FileSystem.CombinePath(
                        Environment.GetFolderPath(
                        Environment.SpecialFolder.MyDocuments), "TestFile" +
                        New Random().Next(10000, 99999).ToString)
      row("FileExtension") = ".docx"
      row("Revision") = New Random().Next(0, 999).ToString
      row("ChangeNumber") = New Random().Next(1, 999).ToString
      row("Status") = 1
      row("ModifiedDate") = DateTime.Now.ToString
      table.Rows.Add(row)

      'Send only the changes in the DataTable to the database for updating.
      adapter.Update(table.GetChanges())

      'Complete the transaction
      ts.Complete()
   Catch ex As Exception
      MessageBox.Show(ex.Message)
   Finally
      connection.Close()
   End Try
End Using
```

The Using clause wraps the inserts within an implicit transaction. All resource managers that recognize transactions participate in this transaction. The Using clause guarantees that the TransactionScope object is disposed of when the transaction is complete. The TransactionScope Complete method completes the transaction and saves the row to the database.

Using explicit transactions requires a bit more code but provides greater control over the transaction. You can use either the Transaction class or the CommittableTransaction class to wrap transactions in this model. CommittableTransaction is a child class of Transaction, and adds the capability to commit a transaction, as the name implies.

Using a CommittableTransaction in the above scenario changes it as follows:

```
Using ct As New CommittableTransaction
   Try
      'Add a new document to the DataTable.
      Dim row As DataRow = table.NewRow()
      row("Title") = "Test Document " + New Random().Next(100, 999).ToString
      row("FileName") = My.Computer.FileSystem.CombinePath(
```

```
                            Environment.GetFolderPath(\
                            Environment.SpecialFolder.MyDocuments),
                            "TestFile" + New Random().Next(10000, 99999).ToString)
        row("FileExtension") = ".docx"
        row("Revision") = New Random().Next(0, 999).ToString
        row("ChangeNumber") = New Random().Next(1, 999).ToString
        row("Status") = 1
        row("ModifiedDate") = DateTime.Now.ToString
        table.Rows.Add(row)

        'Send only the changes in the DataTable to the database for updating.
        adapter.Update(table.GetChanges())

        'Complete the transaction
        ct.Commit()
    Catch ex As Exception
        ct.Rollback()
        MessageBox.Show(ex.Message, "Error - Data Rolled Back")
    Finally
        connection.Close()
    End Try
End Using
```

Notice that the transaction must now be explicitly committed or rolled back. You could also pass the transaction variable to other methods to vote on the transaction. If you do this, you can enlist other transaction containers using the EnlistTransaction method (or EnlistDistributedTransaction if the transaction will span multiple computers). Once it is a part of the transaction, it can then use the transaction methods to commit or roll back each part of the transaction.

Using the TransactionScope and Transaction classes can greatly decrease the amount of effort involved in creating and working with transactions in your applications. Generally, using implicit transactions using TransactionScope is easier and less error prone, and should be your first choice.

## Creating Resource Managers

In addition to using the classes in System.Transactions for managing transactions, you can also use them to define your own resource managers. These resource managers can then participate in transactions with databases, MSDTC, message queues, and more. There are three basic steps to defining a resource manager:

1. Create an enlistment class. This class is used to track the resource manager's participation in the transaction. That is, this is the class that will vote on whether the transaction should complete or be rolled back. This class should implement the IEnlistmentNotification interface.

2. Enlist the new enlistment class in the transaction. There are two main ways the class may participate in the transaction: EnlistDurable or EnlistVolatile. You use EnlistDurable if your resource manager stores data permanently, such as in a file or database. EnlistVolatile is used if your resource manager stores its information in memory or in some other nonrecoverable location.

**3.** Implement the methods of the IEnlistmentNotification interface to react to the states of the transaction. The IEnlistmentNotification interface provides four methods: Prepare, Commit, Rollback, and InDoubt. Commit and Rollback are self-explanatory, used at these two phases of the transaction. Prepare is called before Commit, to determine whether it is possible to commit the transaction. Finally, InDoubt is called if the transaction is questionable. This can happen if the transaction coordinator has lost track of one of the resource managers.

Why would you define your own resource managers, rather than simply use an existing one such as SQL Server? You might need to store data in another database that does not directly participate in transactions. Alternately, you may want to enable a normally nontransactional component with transactional behavior. For example, the cache in ASP.NET doesn't support the addition of items using transactions. You could create a resource manager that wraps the ASP.NET cache and adds support for commit and rollback of entries. This might be part of a system in which you want to use the cache as an in-memory data store. While this would work without the transactions, adding transactional support would ensure that if the database write fails for any reason, then the entry could be rolled back out of the cache.

## SUMMARY

This chapter looked at ADO.NET and some of its more advanced features. You have seen and used the main objects in ADO.NET that you need to quickly get up and running in order to build data-access into your .NET applications. You took a fairly in-depth look at the DataSet and DataTable classes, as these are the core classes of ADO.NET.

This chapter also looked at stored procedures, including how to create them in SQL Server and how to access them from your code. Finally, you looked at wrapping calls to the database in a transaction to allow them to be rolled back if necessary.

# 10

# Data Access with the Entity Framework

**WHAT'S IN THIS CHAPTER?**

➤ What is Object-Relational Mapping?

➤ What is the Entity Framework?

➤ How the Entity Framework works with databases

➤ Using the Entity Framework to edit data

**WROX.COM CODE DOWNLOADS FOR THIS CHAPTER**

The wrox.com code downloads for this chapter are found at www.wrox.com/remtitle .cgi?isbn=9781118314456 on the Download Code tab. The code discussed throughout this chapter is contained in the EFSimpleExample project.

In the past, Microsoft has been known to change the recommended data access strategy relatively frequently. For example, Data Access Objects (DAO) was released in the Visual Basic 3.0 time frame, followed by RDO (Remote Data Objects) as an option in the Visual Basic 4 days, and ADO (Active Database Objects) with Visual Basic 6. Of course, all of these were COM libraries, so it was no surprise when they were superseded by ADO.NET when the .NET Framework shipped. There have been remarkably few changes to ADO.NET since then.

The Entity Framework (EF) does not replace ADO.NET. You can continue to use ADO.NET without fear of it going away, even as a recommended data access tool. The Entity Framework simply provides a different — richer and more flexible — model for working with data sources.

Beyond simply being a set of classes you use to access your data, Entity Framework enables you to work naturally with the data using the classes you have designed, while saving the data to the underlying database schema. The Entity Framework provides the mapping necessary to convert the data structures, variable types, and relationships between the Visual Basic data you work with in your applications to the SQL Server, Oracle, or other database. It offers a means of working with your database more easily and more naturally than with ADO.NET, without requiring you to manually build your own data access layer.

Compared to LINQ to SQL, Entity Framework provides most of the same functionality for rapidly accessing your data. Where it differs is that Entity Framework provides a great deal of functionality not provided by LINQ to SQL, such as the ability to use databases other than SQL Server, and the ability to use client-side classes that don't directly map to database tables.

## OBJECT-RELATIONAL MAPPING

While ADO.NET allows a certain degree of abstraction between databases, at its heart it mirrors the database structure. You use a database `Connection` object that accesses a command that either returns data in the form of a `DataReader` or populates a `DataSet`. You work with stored procedures or the database tables to maintain your database. However, as many developers discover, the data types used in the various databases are not the same, and they definitely do not match the data types you use in your Visual Basic applications. This can lead to errors in your application, such as when a database `NULL` is passed to a Visual Basic type. In addition, some of the interactions may be clumsy, such as when saving the contents of an object to the database, where you may need to map properties to the data in one or more database rows or tables.

To solve this object-to-database mismatch, a number of strategies have been developed. Many developers struggle with this process manually, handwriting a data access layer to convert between .NET and SQL. Another common strategy — and one requiring less work — is to use tools known as Object-Relational Mapping (ORM) tools. These tools either manually or automatically map the data types used in a database to those used by the client program, and vice versa. The best of these enable the actual structure of the database to be hidden from the client program, providing a more natural interaction between the program and the database. In the .NET world, the oldest and most used is nHibernate, itself a port of the Hibernate library developed first for Java development. However, there are many other ORMs, including SubSonic, LightSpeed, OpenAccess, and now Microsoft's Entity Framework. Even LINQ to SQL could be viewed as an ORM, in that it converts between Visual Basic types and SQL types.

While still a relatively young framework, the Entity Framework provides many of the capabilities available in the older, more mature frameworks. This includes the capability to split an object across multiple tables, map multiple objects to the same table, perform "lazy loading" (a performance optimization whereby an object is not loaded into memory until it is actually accessed), and much more. In addition, Microsoft is likely to continue to improve it over time, so it is definitely a strong competitor in the ORM space.

## ENTITY FRAMEWORK ARCHITECTURE

Figure 10-1 shows the architecture used within the Entity Framework. As you can see from the diagram, the Entity Framework is composed of a number of logical layers. The lowest layer is related to the actual data access, and involves the familiar ADO.NET data providers. The Entity Framework is not an entirely new method of retrieving data, but is an extension of your existing knowledge of ADO.NET. The additional layers are intended to make your development experience easier and more flexible. At the data layer, Entity Framework does not differ from ADO.NET or LINQ to SQL, as it deals with the tables directly.

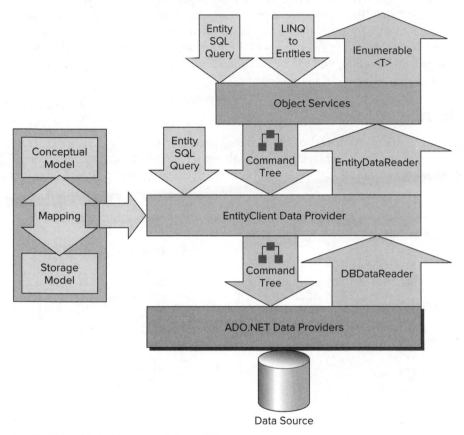

**FIGURE 10-1:** Entity Framework Layer Diagram

Above the actual data access layer is the storage layer. This is basically a representation of the structure of the database, using XML syntax. It includes any of the tables you've added to your model, as well as the relationships between them.

Above the storage layer is the mapping layer. This serves as a means of translating between the storage layer below and the conceptual layer above. You can think of it as a relatively thin layer, responsible for mapping the fields of the database tables to the appropriate properties of the classes used by your application.Next is the conceptual layer. This is the layer that provides the entities of your model, providing you with the classes you will work with in your applications — either the classes generated by the Entity Framework designer or your own classes, as you'll see later.

Finally, there is the object services layer. This serves to provide LINQ and Entity Query Language (Entity SQL) syntax over your conceptual model.

When you see a diagram like the one shown in Figure 10-1, your first instinct may be to worry about the performance penalties that these additional layers cause to your application. Of course, every mapping, abstraction, or communication adds to the query and/or update time; this is to be expected. However, the decision to use Entity Framework should not be entirely based on whether it is faster or slower than classic ADO.NET. Rather, it should depend on a combination of "Is it fast enough for my needs?" and "How much more productive does it make me?" Because Entity Framework uses the core ADO.NET objects, there is no way it can be faster than, or even as fast as, using those classes themselves. However, working with Entity Framework can be a much more natural development process, meaning you can be much more productive in creating — and, more important, maintaining — your data access code.

## Conceptual Model

Your Entity Framework applications deal directly with the conceptual models you either generate or create. To see how these are constructed, create a simple console application (EFSimpleExample) and add an ADO.NET Entity Data Model to the application by selecting Project ➪ Add New Item (see Figure 10-2).

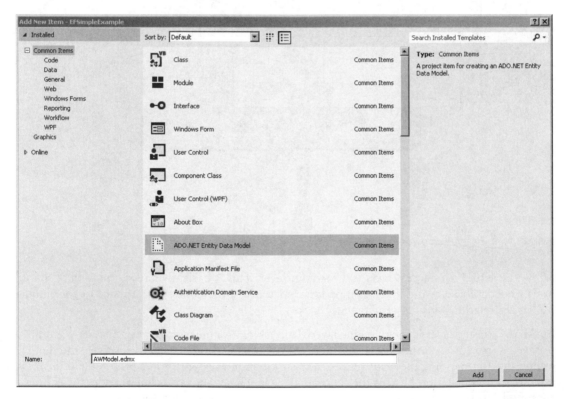

**FIGURE 10-2:** Add ADO.NET Entity Data Model

When you add an Entity Framework model to your application, it starts a wizard to generate the classes. The first step is to decide if you will generate your classes initially from a database or from a blank slate. For now, select to generate the classes from the database (see Figure 10-3). Select the `AdventureWorks` database.

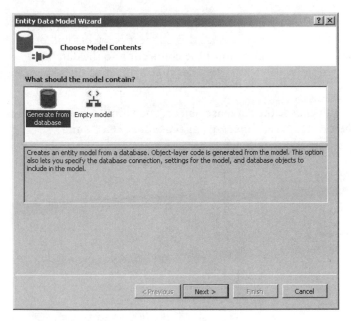

**FIGURE 10-3:** Generate Model from Database

The connection string generated at this stage (see Figure 10-4) can look a little foreboding to anyone used to the simpler SQL Server or Access connection strings.

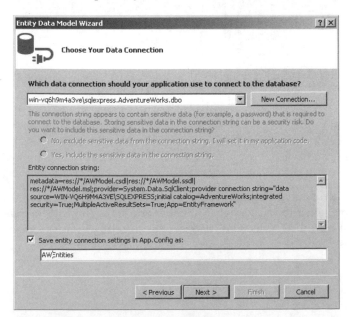

**FIGURE 10-4:** Choose Data Connection

```
metadata=res://*/AWModel.csdl|res://*/AWModel.ssdl|res://*/AWModel.msl;
provider=System.Data.SqlClient;provider connection
string="data source=WIN-VQ6H9M4A3VE\SQLEXPRESS;
initial catalog=AdventureWorks;integrated security=True;
MultipleActiveResultSets=True;App=EntityFramework"
```

Ignoring the first few sections, you can see the "normal" connection string contained within this connection. The reason it has the additional sections is because this connection string will be used by all three layers (storage, conceptual, and mapping), not just the connection to the database. The three additional parts of the connection string identify the files that will define the structure of each layer.

Next, just as with LINQ to SQL, you can choose the database objects you would like to include in your model. For now, just select the CreditCard, Customer, SalesOrderDetail, and SalesOrderHeader tables (see Figure 10-5) and click Finish.

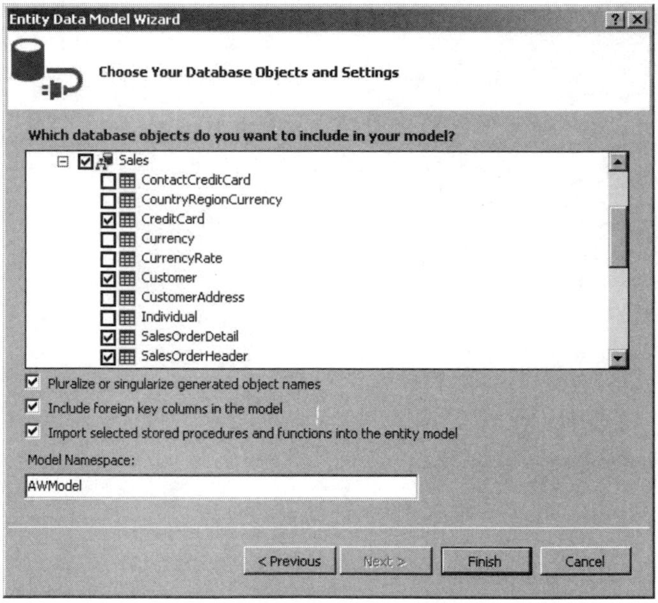

**FIGURE 10-5:** Choose Database Objects

Figure 10-6 shows the resulting model in Visual Studio. Notice that it includes the relationships between the three tables in the model in addition to creating properties that represent the columns in the database.

Finally, the wizard has created a number of *navigation properties* that represent the foreign key relationships. You can explore your model within this designer window or use the Model Browser pane that opens in Visual Studio (see Figure 10-7) which you can view by selecting View ➪ Other Windows ➪ Entity Data Model Browser.

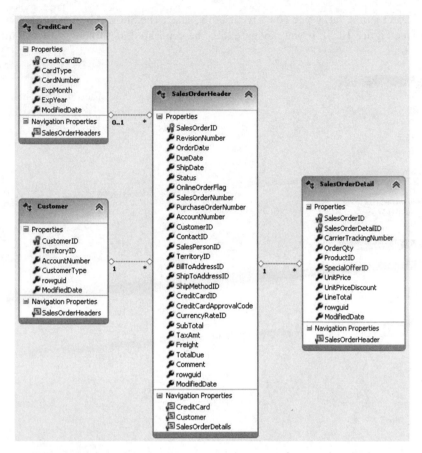

**FIGURE 10-6:** New Data Model

**FIGURE 10-7:** Model Browser

Build the application but don't run it yet. Once you have it built, select the Show All Files option in the Solution Explorer (see Figure 10-8). If you navigate into the generated `obj` folder, you will find the three generated XML files.

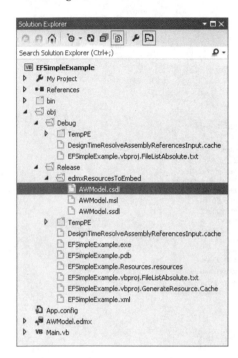

**FIGURE 10-8:** Generate XML Files

The following code shows a portion of the CSDL file, which is the conceptual model:

```
<?xml version="1.0" encoding="utf-8"?>
<Schema Namespace="AWModel" Alias="Self" p1:UseStrongSpatialTypes="false"
  xmlns:annotation="http://schemas.microsoft.com/ado/2009/02/edm/annotation"
  xmlns:p1="http://schemas.microsoft.com/ado/2009/02/edm/annotation"
  xmlns="http://schemas.microsoft.com/ado/2009/11/edm">
  <EntityContainer Name="AWEntities" p1:LazyLoadingEnabled="true">
    <EntitySet Name="CreditCards" EntityType="AWModel.CreditCard" />
    <EntitySet Name="Customers" EntityType="AWModel.Customer" />
    <EntitySet Name="SalesOrderDetails" EntityType="AWModel.SalesOrderDetail" />
    <EntitySet Name="SalesOrderHeaders" EntityType="AWModel.SalesOrderHeader" />
    <AssociationSet Name="FK_SalesOrderHeader_CreditCard_CreditCardID"
      Association="AWModel.FK_SalesOrderHeader_CreditCard_CreditCardID">
      <End Role="CreditCard" EntitySet="CreditCards" />
      <End Role="SalesOrderHeader" EntitySet="SalesOrderHeaders" />
    </AssociationSet>
    <AssociationSet Name="FK_SalesOrderHeader_Customer_CustomerID"
      Association="AWModel.FK_SalesOrderHeader_Customer_CustomerID">
      <End Role="Customer" EntitySet="Customers" />
      <End Role="SalesOrderHeader" EntitySet="SalesOrderHeaders" />
    </AssociationSet>
```

```
    <AssociationSet Name="FK_SalesOrderDetail_SalesOrderHeader_SalesOrderID"
      Association="AWModel.FK_SalesOrderDetail_SalesOrderHeader_SalesOrderID">
      <End Role="SalesOrderHeader" EntitySet="SalesOrderHeaders" />
      <End Role="SalesOrderDetail" EntitySet="SalesOrderDetails" />
    </AssociationSet>
  </EntityContainer>
  <EntityType Name="CreditCard">
    <Key>
      <PropertyRef Name="CreditCardID" />
    </Key>
    <Property Name="CreditCardID" Type="Int32" Nullable="false"
      p1:StoreGeneratedPattern="Identity" />
    <Property Name="CardType" Type="String" Nullable="false" MaxLength="50"
      Unicode="true" FixedLength="false" />
    <Property Name="CardNumber" Type="String" Nullable="false" MaxLength="25"
      Unicode="true" FixedLength="false" />
    <Property Name="ExpMonth" Type="Byte" Nullable="false" />
    <Property Name="ExpYear" Type="Int16" Nullable="false" />
    <Property Name="ModifiedDate" Type="DateTime" Nullable="false" Precision="3" />
    <NavigationProperty Name="SalesOrderHeaders"
      Relationship="AWModel.FK_SalesOrderHeader_CreditCard_CreditCardID"
      FromRole="CreditCard" ToRole="SalesOrderHeader" />
  </EntityType>
  ...
```

This snippet shows some of the main terms you will see repeatedly throughout your work with the Entity Framework. The `EntityType` defines one of your objects — in this case, the `CreditCard` class. The collection of credit cards is defined as an `EntitySet`. There are `AssociationSets` that define the relationships between the various `EntityTypes`. Finally, there is an `EntityContainer` that groups everything. One point to notice is that each of the Property elements in the XML file has a Type attribute. This attribute uses Visual Basic data types, rather than database-specific types. This XML file will be updated as you change your conceptual model.

If you look at one of the generated types in the Class View window (see Figure 10-9), you will see that it inherits from `EntityObject`. The `EntityObject` class in turn inherits from `StructuralObject` and implements three interfaces (`IEntityWithChangeTracker`, `IEntityWithKey` and `IEntityWithRelationships`). The names of these three interfaces give you some idea of what the generated classes are capable of:

1. They are able to identify one another via one or more key properties.

2. They are aware of changes to their properties; therefore, you will be able to identify changed objects and/or properties without requiring a trip back to the database.

3. They track their relationship to one or more other `EntityObjects`.

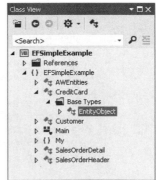

**FIGURE 10-9:** Class View

## Storage Model

The storage model XML initially looks similar to the conceptual model XML (see the generated `AWModel.ssdl` file in the Solution Explorer View):

```xml
<?xml version="1.0" encoding="utf-8"?>
<Schema Namespace="AWModel.Store" Alias="Self" Provider="System.Data.SqlClient"
  ProviderManifestToken="2008"
  xmlns:store="http://schemas.microsoft.com/ado/2007/12/edm/
  EntityStoreSchemaGenerator"
  xmlns="http://schemas.microsoft.com/ado/2009/11/edm/ssdl">
  <EntityContainer Name="AWModelStoreContainer">
    <EntitySet Name="CreditCard" EntityType="AWModel.Store.CreditCard"
      store:Type="Tables" Schema="Sales" />
    <EntitySet Name="Customer" EntityType="AWModel.Store.Customer"
      store:Type="Tables" Schema="Sales" />
    <EntitySet Name="SalesOrderDetail" EntityType="AWModel.Store.SalesOrderDetail"
      store:Type="Tables" Schema="Sales" />
    <EntitySet Name="SalesOrderHeader" EntityType="AWModel.Store.SalesOrderHeader"
      store:Type="Tables" Schema="Sales" />
    <AssociationSet Name="FK_SalesOrderDetail_SalesOrderHeader_SalesOrderID"
                    Association="AWModel.Store.
                    FK_SalesOrderDetail_SalesOrderHeader_SalesOrderID">
      <End Role="SalesOrderHeader" EntitySet="SalesOrderHeader" />
      <End Role="SalesOrderDetail" EntitySet="SalesOrderDetail" />
    </AssociationSet>
    <AssociationSet Name="FK_SalesOrderHeader_CreditCard_CreditCardID"
      Association="AWModel.Store.FK_SalesOrderHeader_CreditCard_CreditCardID">
      <End Role="CreditCard" EntitySet="CreditCard" />
      <End Role="SalesOrderHeader" EntitySet="SalesOrderHeader" />
    </AssociationSet>
    <AssociationSet Name="FK_SalesOrderHeader_Customer_CustomerID"
      Association="AWModel.Store.FK_SalesOrderHeader_Customer_CustomerID">
      <End Role="Customer" EntitySet="Customer" />
      <End Role="SalesOrderHeader" EntitySet="SalesOrderHeader" />
    </AssociationSet>
  </EntityContainer>
  <EntityType Name="CreditCard">
    <Key>
      <PropertyRef Name="CreditCardID" />
    </Key>
    <Property Name="CreditCardID" Type="int" Nullable="false"
      StoreGeneratedPattern="Identity" />
    <Property Name="CardType" Type="nvarchar" Nullable="false" MaxLength="50" />
    <Property Name="CardNumber" Type="nvarchar" Nullable="false" MaxLength="25" />
    <Property Name="ExpMonth" Type="tinyint" Nullable="false" />
    <Property Name="ExpYear" Type="smallint" Nullable="false" />
    <Property Name="ModifiedDate" Type="datetime" Nullable="false" />
  </EntityType>
  ...
```

One major difference between this file and the earlier conceptual model is that the types in the storage model are SQL Server data types. In addition, unlike the conceptual model file, this file will not change as you update your Entity Framework model, as it is tied to the database structure.

## Mapping Model

Finally, you have the third XML file, the mapping schema language (MSL) file:

```xml
<?xml version="1.0" encoding="utf-8"?>
<Mapping Space="C-S" xmlns="http://schemas.microsoft.com/ado/2009/11/mapping/cs">
  <EntityContainerMapping StorageEntityContainer="AWModelStoreContainer"
      CdmEntityContainer="AWEntities">
    <EntitySetMapping Name="CreditCards">
      <EntityTypeMapping TypeName="AWModel.CreditCard">
        <MappingFragment StoreEntitySet="CreditCard">
          <ScalarProperty Name="CreditCardID" ColumnName="CreditCardID" />
          <ScalarProperty Name="CardType" ColumnName="CardType" />
          <ScalarProperty Name="CardNumber" ColumnName="CardNumber" />
          <ScalarProperty Name="ExpMonth" ColumnName="ExpMonth" />
          <ScalarProperty Name="ExpYear" ColumnName="ExpYear" />
          <ScalarProperty Name="ModifiedDate" ColumnName="ModifiedDate" />
        </MappingFragment>
      </EntityTypeMapping>
    </EntitySetMapping>
    ...
```

This may seem like a great deal of overhead, as it appears to map properties of the classes to the identical fields of tables. However, as you customize the conceptual model, the mapping model will change to reflect the new structure. As the Entity Framework supports mapping a single object to multiple tables, or vice versa, this mapping model increases in importance, and is the core benefit of using a framework such as Entity Framework.

## LINQ to Entities

Just as there is LINQ to SQL, LINQ to XML, and LINQ to objects, there is also LINQ syntax for working with Entity Framework models. The syntax is very similar to that used by LINQ to SQL, in that a context object is used as your access point to the exposed classes. You first create an instance of that context object and then use it to access the entities in your model. The following shows a LINQ query to retrieve customers in territory 1:

```vb
Sub Main()

  Dim ctx As New AWEntities

  Dim customers = From
                  c In ctx.Customers
                Where
                  c.TerritoryID = 1
                Order By
                  c.AccountNumber
                Select
                  c

  For Each c In customers.ToList
    Console.WriteLine("# {0} Last Updated: {1}", c.AccountNumber, c.ModifiedDate)
  Next

  Console.ReadLine()

End Sub
```

Here, the new context object (`AWEntities`) is defined within the routine, but you are more likely to create it once and use it throughout your application. The remainder of the query defines a restriction and a sort, and returns all the properties.

## The ObjectContext

As you have seen from the preceding query, you use a context object as the root of all your queries. This context is the logical equivalent of the `Connection` object in ADO.NET, but it does much more. The context object is a class that inherits from `ObjectContext`. In addition to providing access to the database, the `ObjectContext` is also responsible for allowing you to retrieve metadata about the entities within your model and helping the objects track their changes.

Once you have made changes to one or more objects tracked by an object context, you can apply those changes back to the database using the `ObjectContext`. The `SaveChanges` method submits the changes you have made to the database. It iterates over all the added, updated, and deleted objects and submits these changes, and returns the number of records updated.

At this point, the objects do not know that they have been saved, so you must set them back to their unchanged state. There are two ways you can do this. First, you can call the `SaveChanges` method with a single `Boolean` parameter set to `SaveOptions.AcceptAllChangesAfterSave`. This automatically updates the changed objects. Alternately, you can call the `AcceptAllChanges` method of the `ObjectContext`. This also iterates through all the successful updates, resetting the change tracking. The following code shows these steps while adding and updating credit cards in the database:

```
Sub AddCreditCard()

    Dim ctx As New AWEntities

    ''Add New Credit Card
    Dim newCC = CreditCard.CreateCreditCard(
        0, "Visa", "12345678901234567890012123",
        10, 2015, DateTime.Now)

    ctx.CreditCards.AddObject(newCC)

    ''Edit Credit Card
    Dim editCC = (From
                    cc In ctx.CreditCards
                  Where
                      cc.CardNumber = "33335500655096"
                  Select
                      cc
                 ).Single

    editCC.ExpMonth = 12
    editCC.ModifiedDate = DateTime.Now

    ''Save Changes
    Dim changeCount =
            ctx.SaveChanges(Objects.SaveOptions.AcceptAllChangesAfterSave)

    Console.WriteLine("{0} records changed.", changeCount)

    Console.WriteLine("Credit card state: {0} Date updated: {1}",
            editCC.EntityState.ToString(), editCC.ModifiedDate.ToString)
```

```
        Console.ReadLine()

    End Sub
```

The output of this routine should be as follows:

```
2 records changed.
Credit card state: Unchanged Date updated: 7/15/2012 10:19:08 AM
```

The update process operates within a single transaction, so if any of the changes fail, the entire `SaveChanges` will fail.

# MAPPING OBJECTS TO ENTITIES

Once you have completed the Entity Data Model wizard, you have a basic Entity Framework model that enables you to query your database. However, you have definitely not seen all the benefits of using the Entity Framework. Exploring these benefits involves improving the conceptual model to better map to the desired structure.

## Simple Mapping

The mapping created above left you with a very thin layer over the database. Each of the generated properties were identical to the field names, and the field names in the AdventureWorks database are not exactly "friendly." Changing these to create more "Visual Basic–like" property names is a simple matter.

Select the sales order detail table in the model and open the Mapping Details pane of Visual Studio. If it is closed, you can open it by selecting View ⇨ Other Windows ⇨ Entity Data Model Mapping Details.

As shown in the Mapping Details pane in Figure 10-10, the `SalesOrderDetail` object maps to the `SalesOrderDetail` table, and each property maps to the field with the same name. By changing the `Name` property for each field in the Properties pane, you can create a mapping that better explains what some of the fields represent (for example SalesOrder.SalesOrderId to SalesOrder.ID).

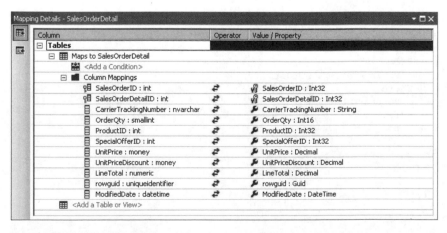

**FIGURE 10-10:** Entity Mapping

In addition, once you've changed the mapping, the code used to access the types reflects the new mapping (see Figure 10-11):

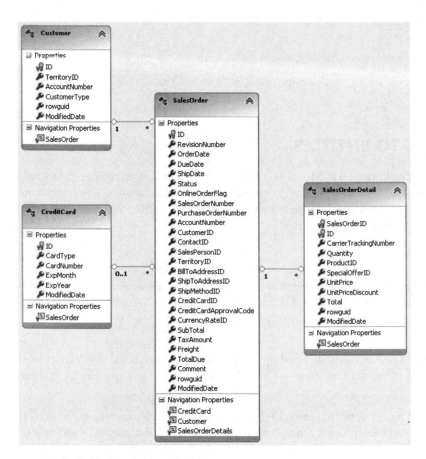

**FIGURE 10-11:** Updated Entity Model

```
Sub DisplaySalesOrders()
  Dim ctx As New AWEntities

  Dim orders = From
               so In ctx.SalesOrders
             Where
               so.Status = 5
             Select
               so

  For Each order In orders.ToList
```

```
            Console.WriteLine("#{0} Ordered On: {1}",
                            order.SalesOrderNumber,
                            order.OrderDate.ToString)
        Next

        Console.WriteLine("{0} orders", orders.Count.ToString)
    End Sub
```

Recall that the Entity Framework model included a number of navigation properties that represented the relationships between the defined classes, such as the SalesOrder property on the Customer and CreditCard classes. These navigation properties — as their name implies — enable you to navigate between the classes in your queries. For example, you can query and return the sales orders that have a status of 5 with the following query:

```
    Sub DisplaySalesOrdersInfo()
        Dim ctx As New AWEntities

        Dim orders = From
                    so In ctx.SalesOrders
                 Where
                    so.Status = 5
                 Select New With
                    {
                        .SalesOrderNumber = so.SalesOrderNumber,
                        .CreditCardNumber = so.CreditCard.CardNumber,
                        .AccountNumber = so.Customer.AccountNumber
                    }

        For Each order In orders.ToList
            Console.WriteLine("#{0} CreditCard: {1} Account:{2}",
                            order.SalesOrderNumber,
                            order.CreditCardNumber,
                            order.AccountNumber)
        Next

        Console.WriteLine("{0} orders", orders.Count.ToString)
    End Sub
```

This query demonstrates the use of projections in a LINQ query. Rather than return the data that is queried, a new object is created using the Select New With {} syntax. This enables you to define a new object to be returned as a result of the query. Each of the properties in the new object are defined by including them in the braces, starting with a dot. In the preceding query, the new object will have three properties: SalesOrderNumber, CreditCardNumber, and AccountNumber, and the values of these properties come from the results of the query. This returned object is an anonymous object. That is, it does not have a usable name within the system (if you look at it in the debugger, it will have a name that has been generated by the compiler). Still, the returned object can be used normally. Because it is a collection, you can iterate over the collection using a For Each loop to display the list (see Figure 10-12).

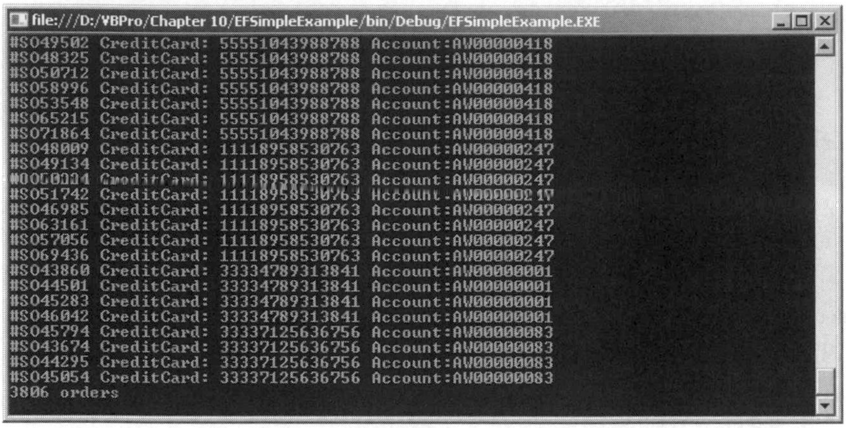

**FIGURE 10-12:** Credit Card Information

## Using a Single Table for Multiple Objects

Within your application design, you may have one or more classes that inherit from another. For example, you might have a SalesOrder base class, with online orders that inherit from them. The SalesOrder base class has the standard SalesOrderNumber, OrderDate, and other properties. The OnlineSalesOrder child class might add a property for ShipDate. These types of designs are traditionally very difficult to map to a database. If you were to save this structure to a database, you would have a couple of options. One, you might include all the properties, and add a property to identify the type of the resulting object, as shown in Figure 10-13.

In this table, the OnlineOrderFlag field is true if the order was made online, and false if not. The identifier will indicate if the order was made online or not. Figure 10-14 shows the desired conceptual model (see the AWModel in the EFSimpleExample project).

**FIGURE 10-13:** OnlineOrderFlag Properties

In this model, OnlineSalesOrder inherits from SalesOrder. Notice that the OnlineOrderFlag field is not on the model, and the OnlineSalesOrder has unique properties.

To create this structure, you use the Mapping Details pane of Visual Studio. After you have generated a model based on the SalesOrderHeader table (refer to Figure 10-14), add a new entity that will represent an OnlineSalesOrder. Remove the Id property that is created by default and create a new property called ShipDate. Set the Type property to DateTime. Select the Inheritance item from the Toolbox, and drag an inheritance from OnlineSalesOrder to SalesOrder.

Once the basic model is done, you're ready to add the mapping. Select the SalesOrder entity and delete the ShipDate property by right-clicking on them and selecting Delete. This will remove the mapping of the property to the SalesOrder object.

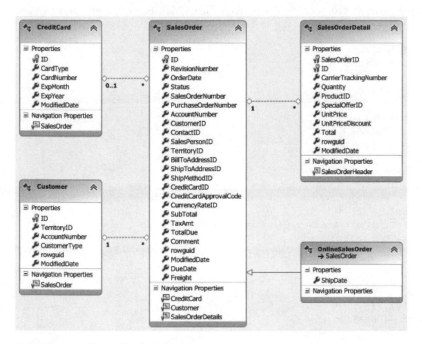

**FIGURE 10-14:** Entity Model Inheritance

Select the OnlineSalesOrder entity. Select the SalesOrderHeader table under the Tables collection. Map the ShipDate field to the ShipDate property. Notice that above the field mapping is a Condition mapping. This is how you will distinguish sales orders from online sales orders. Select the OnlineOrderFlag field, and set the Condition's value to true (see Figure 10-15).

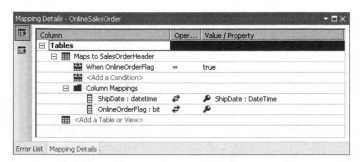

**FIGURE 10-15:** SalesOrderHeader Condition for OnlineOrderFlag

Do a similar mapping for the `SalesOrder` entity, but set the Condition to select the `OnlineOrderFlag=false` records. You should now be able to validate the model by right-clicking the designer and selecting Validate.

You can now work with the table as you would expect from the model. For example, you can create a new `OnlineSalesOrder` with the following code:

```
Sub CreateOnlineSalesOrder()
  Dim ctx As New AWEntities

  Dim order As New OnlineSalesOrder
  With order
    .RevisionNumber = 1
    .OrderDate = DateTime.Now
    .DueDate = DateTime.Now
    .Status = 5
    .SalesOrderNumber = "1234567890"
    .CustomerID = 1
    .ContactID = 1
    .BillToAddressID = 1
    .ShipDate=DateTime.Now.Add(New TimeSpan(2,0,0,0))
    .ShipToAddressID = 1
    .SubTotal = 100
    .ShipMethodID = 1
    .TaxAmt = 7.25
    .Freight = 0
    .TotalDue = 107.25
    .ModifiedDate = DateTime.Now
  End With

  ctx.SalesOrders.AddObject(order)

  ctx.SaveChanges(Objects.SaveOptions.AcceptAllChangesAfterSave)

  Console.WriteLine("Online sales order created.")

End Sub
```

Here, you create a new sales order, assign some values to the properties, and save. Notice that you do not directly set the `OnlineSalesFlag` field. Instead, it is set based on whether you create either a `SalesOrder` or an `OnlineSalesOrder`. Figure 10-16 shows the newly added record in the `SalesOrder` table.

| | SalesOrderID | RevisionNumber | OrderDate | DueDate | ShipDate | Status | OnlineOrderFlag | SalesOrderNum... |
|---|---|---|---|---|---|---|---|---|
| | 75117 | 1 | 2004-07-31 00:... | 2004-08-12 00:... | 2004-08-07 00:... | 5 | True | SO75117 |
| | 75118 | 1 | 2004-07-31 00:... | 2004-08-12 00:... | 2004-08-07 00:... | 5 | True | SO75118 |
| | 75119 | 1 | 2004-07-31 00:... | 2004-08-12 00:... | 2004-08-07 00:... | 5 | True | SO75119 |
| | 75120 | 1 | 2004-07-31 00:... | 2004-08-12 00:... | 2004-08-07 00:... | 5 | True | SO75120 |
| | 75121 | 1 | 2004-07-31 00:... | 2004-08-12 00:... | 2004-08-07 00:... | 5 | True | SO75121 |
| | 75122 | 1 | 2004-07-31 00:... | 2004-08-12 00:... | 2004-08-07 00:... | 5 | True | SO75122 |
| | 75123 | 1 | 2004-07-31 00:... | 2004-08-12 00:... | 2004-08-07 00:... | 5 | True | SO75123 |
| ▶ | 75126 | 1 | 2012-07-18 19:... | 2012-07-18 19:... | 2012-07-20 19:... | 5 | True | SO75126 |
| ✱ | NULL | NULL | NULL | NULL | NULL | NULL | NULL | NULL |

**FIGURE 10-16:** OnlineSalesOrder Data

Selecting records when using these types of models can be slightly confusing the first few times, as you will find that the context does not have an `OnlineSalesOrder` collection on them. If you look at the properties for these entities, it makes more sense; you will see that the `EntitySetName` property is `SalesOrder` (how they were defined in the `EntitySetName` for the `SalesOrder` collection). Therefore, you still query them as sales order, but you add an additional qualifier to the query to select for the desired child class:

```
Sub DisplayOnlineSalesOrders()
  Dim ctx As New AWEntities

  Dim orders = From
               so In ctx.SalesOrders.OfType(Of OnlineSalesOrder)()
             Where
               so.Status = 5
             Order By
               so.OrderDate
             Select New With
               {
                 .SalesOrderNumber = so.SalesOrderNumber,
                 .CreditCardNumber = so.CreditCard.CardNumber,
                 .AccountNumber = so.Customer.AccountNumber
               }

  For Each order In orders.ToList
    Console.WriteLine("#{0} CreditCard: {1} Account:{2}",
                 order.SalesOrderNumber,
                 order.CreditCardNumber,
                 order.AccountNumber)
  Next

  Console.WriteLine("{0} orders", orders.Count.ToString)
End Sub
```

In this code, the `OfType(Of OnlineSalesOrder)` clause defines the type you are retrieving. The `OfType` clause limits the returned records to just those with the correct value in the Condition mappings you created.

## Updating the Model

Eventually, you will have to make changes to your model, due to changes to the database or new requirements for your model. You can add new tables, change the data types of columns easily with the Entity Framework designer. You can update your model by right-clicking on the designer and selecting Update Model from Database. This will start up the Update Wizard (see Figure 10-17).

This dialog has three tabs, depending on what you'd like to update from your database. The Add and Delete tabs enable you to identify database items you'd like to add or delete from your model (tables, views or stored procedures, and function). The Refresh tab enables you to identify structures that may have changed in the database. The wizard will update the corresponding entities in your model.

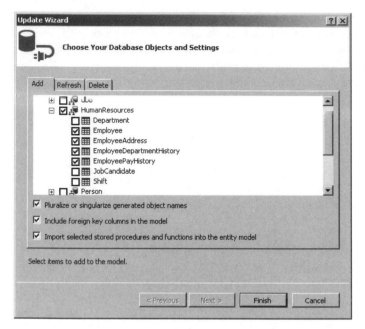

**FIGURE 10-17:** Data Model Update Wizard

> **NOTE** *If you get an error saving the changes to the database, it may be because Visual Studio is configured to not allow changes that require re-creating tables. To enable this functionality, go to the Visual Studio options dialog Tools ⇨ Options ⇨ Designers ⇨ Table and Database Designers and uncheck the property Prevent saving changes that require table re-creation.*

## SUMMARY

Using an Object-Relational Mapping (ORM) tool like the Entity Framework greatly simplifies the creation of a database application. The Entity Framework manages many of the details of converting your logical application model into the physical database model, automatically mapping data types between Visual Basic and T-SQL. It provides the ease of use of LINQ to SQL while giving you the flexibility to work with the entities as designed, rather than being constrained to what is possible with T-SQL.

This chapter looked at how you can connect to a database using Entity Framework. One of the benefits of the Entity Framework is that the model you use to work with your data does not have to exactly match the tables in your database. As you saw, the Entity Framework does this through the creation of three XML files to manage the mapping between the two.

In addition, you saw how the Entity Framework greatly simplifies editing the database. The amount of code required to update a database "by hand" using ADO.NET (i.e., using `DataReader` and/ or `DataSet`) is much larger than the amount you need to write when working with the Entity Framework.

This chapter showed only the features of Entity Framework that you are most likely to use for quick, simple models. There are many more features, like code first and the new `DbContext` object, just to name a few. To learn on more of what you can do with the Entity Framework visit the Entity Framework site by going to `http://msdn.microsoft.com/en-us/data/ef.aspx`. Also check out the `http://channel9.msdn.com` website for a wealth of videos of Entity Framework examples.

# 11

# Services (XML/WCF)

**WROX.COM CODE DOWNLOADS FOR THIS CHAPTER**

The wrox.com code downloads for this chapter are found at www.wrox.com/remtitle .cgi?isbn=9781118314456 on the Download Code tab. The code is in the chapter 11 download and individually named according to the code filenames throughout the chapter.

Over the years there has been an ongoing effort to make communication between distributed components as easy as communication between components and objects within a single executable.

WCF is a framework for building services. Originally introduced as part of the .NET 3.5 enhancements, WCF combines support for several different protocols. Microsoft wanted to provide its developers with a framework that would offer the fastest means to getting a service solution in place, while remaining somewhat agnostic of the underlying transport protocol.

Using the WCF, you can take advantage of a variety of powerful protocols under the covers—everything from binary to basic XML Web Services can be supported with the same implementation. WCF is the successor to a series of different distributed communication technologies.

## WEB SERVICES

A Web service is a means of exposing application logic or data via standard protocols such as XML or SOAP (Simple Object Access Protocol). A Web service comprises one or more function endpoints, packaged together for use in a common framework throughout a network. Web services provide access to information through standard Internet protocols, such as HTTP/HTTPS. A Web Services Description Language (WSDL) contract is used to detail the input and output requirements for calling the interface. Consumers of the Web service can learn about the structure of the data the Web service provides, as well as all the details about how to actually consume this data, from the WSDL. A WSDL provides a detailed description of the remote interface offered from the Web service.

This simple concept provides for a very wide variety of potential uses by developers of Internet and intranet applications alike. Today, the Web services model is often the heart of the next generation of systems architecture because it is all of the following:

➤ **Architecturally neutral**—Web services do not depend on a proprietary wire format, schema description, or discovery standard.

➤ **Ubiquitous**—Any service that supports the associated Web service standards can support the service.

➤ **Simple**—Creating Web services is quick and easy. The data schema is human readable. Any programming language can participate.

➤ **Interoperable**—Because the Web services all conform to the same standards, and use common communication protocols, they are not concerned about the technology of the application calling them.

In basic terms, a Web service is an interface with an XML document describing all of the methods and properties available for use by the caller. Any body of code written in just about any programming language can be described with this XML document, and any application that understands XML (or SOAP) over the assigned protocol (such as HTTP) can access the object. That's because the parameters you type after the function name are passed via XML to the Web service, and because SOAP is an open standard.

Web services are remarkably easy to deploy. The power of Web services comes from the use of the WSDL contract. In addition, Web services are inherently cross-platform, even when created with Microsoft products. The standard XML schemas are part of the WSDL specification.

The key is that even though this protocol may not be as efficient or fast as some of the binary protocols of the past, its implementation-agnostic contracts make it more useful. Given that you can create a communication protocol that is either available for use by 50% of users and which runs superfast versus one that is available to 100% of users and runs fast, the tendency will be to adopt the solution with greater reach. Thus, Web services became the interoperability baseline for service communication.

For this reason, they best represent where the Internet is heading—toward an architecturally neutral collection of devices, rather than millions of PCs surfing the World Wide Web. Encapsulating code so that you can simply and easily enable cell phones to use your logic is a major boon to developers, even if they do not realize it yet.

## How This All Fits Together

Microsoft's support for Web services really took off with the introduction of .NET. However, support was available to have Web services run on older operating systems like Windows NT4 SP6, with the SOAP Toolkit installed.

The .NET Framework encapsulated the Web service protocol into objects. This was great initially, but as noted earlier, over time it was generally agreed that not every communication needed to be put up as a HTTP/HTTPS-based service. WCF was the result of Microsoft taking a look at the common concepts from all of the preceding communication technologies and seeking a unified solution.

While Web services remain one of the most common underlying implementations for WCF services, the reality is that they are now a subset of what you can do with WCF. Things like the WS-* protocols become configuration settings; similarly, you can have a single interface that supports multiple different communication protocols. Thus, the same service that is used with a client that supports a binary transfer protocol like Remoting can communicate via HTTP protocol for a client that doesn't support those binary protocols.

WCF is now an integrated part of the service-oriented architecture strategy. Historically, the starting place on MSDN for Web Services was `http://msdn.microsoft.com/webservices`, but that link was retired. Now for WCF in .NET 4.5, you'll want to start at: `http://msdn.microsoft.com/dd456779.aspx`. It's not that Web services have gone away or become less important, it's simply that Web services are a subset of the complete WCF communication framework.

The goal of WCF is to provide a loosely coupled, ubiquitous, universal information exchange format. Toward that end, SOAP is not the only mechanism for communicating with WCF services.

## What Makes a WCF Service

A WCF service consists of three parts:

1. The service
2. One or more endpoints
3. An environment in which to host the service

A service is a class that is written in (or in the case of Interop, wrapped by) one of the .NET-compliant languages. The class can contain one or more methods that are exposed through the WCF service. A service can have one or more endpoints, which are used to communicate through the service to the client.

Endpoints themselves are also made up of three parts. These parts are usually defined by Microsoft as the "ABC" of WCF. Each letter of WCF means something in particular in the WCF model. Similarly,

➤ "A" is for address

➤ "B" is for binding

➤ "C" is for contract

Basically, you can think of this as follows: "A" is the *where*, "B" is the *how*, and "C" is the *what*. Finally, a hosting environment is where the service is contained. This constitutes an application domain and process. All three of these elements (the service, the endpoints, and the hosting environment) together create a WCF service offering, as depicted in Figure 11-1.

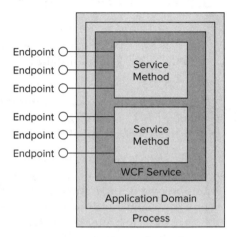

The core idea is that when you want to create an enterprise architecture supporting multiple different applications, the most appropriate protocol will vary depending on how a service is currently being used. Having a unified strategy that allows you, as a developer, to specify a given endpoint and how that endpoint communicates means that the same underlying implementation can power multiple different endpoints. Thus, questions of security and performance can be viewed on a per-connection basis. This enables an organization to create a service-oriented architecture (SOA).

**FIGURE 11-1:** Logical diagram of the implementation layers of a service

## THE LARGER MOVE TO SOA

Looking at what WCF provides, you will find that it is supporting of a larger move that organizations are making to the much-discussed SOA. Keep in mind that an SOA is a message-based service architecture that is vendor-agnostic. This means you have the capability to distribute messages across a system, and the messages are interoperable with other systems that would otherwise be considered incompatible with the provider system.

Looking back, you can see the gradual progression to the service-oriented architecture model. In the 1980s, the revolutions arrived amid the paradigm of everything being an object. When object-oriented programming came on the scene, it was enthusiastically accepted as the proper means to represent entities within a programming model. The 1990s took that one step further, and the component-oriented model was born. This enabled objects to be encapsulated in a tightly coupled manner. It was only recently that the industry turned to a service-oriented architecture, once developers and architects needed to distribute components to other points in an organization, to their partners, or to their customers. This distribution system needed to have the means to transfer messages between machines that were generally incompatible with one another. In addition, the messages had to include the capability to express the metadata about how a system should handle a message.

If you ask 10 people what an SOA is, you'll probably get 11 different answers, but there are some common principles that are considered to be the foundation of a service-oriented architecture:

➤ **Boundaries are explicit**—Any data store, logic, or entity uses an interface to expose its data or capabilities. The interface provides the means to hide the behaviors within the service, and the interface front end enables you to change this behavior as required without affecting downstream consumers.

➤ **Services are autonomous**—All the services are updated or versioned independently of one another. This means that you don't upgrade a system in its entirety; instead, each component of these systems is an individual entity within itself and can move forward without waiting for other components to progress forward. Note that with this type of model, once you publish an interface, that interface must remain unchanged. Interface changes require new interfaces (versioned, of course).

➤ **Services are based upon contracts**—All services developed require a contract regarding what is needed to consume items from the interface (usually done through a WSDL document).

➤ **Schemas are used to define the data formats**—Along with a contract, schemas are required to define the items passed in as parameters or delivered through the service (using XSD schemas).

➤ **Service compatibility that is based upon policy**—The final principle enables services to define policies (decided at runtime) that are required to consume the service. These policies are usually expressed through WS-Policy. A policy provides consumers with an understanding of what is actually required to consume a service.

If your own organization is considering establishing an SOA, the WCF is a framework that works on these principles and makes it relatively simple to implement. The next section looks at what the WCF offers. Then you can dive into building your first WCF service.

As stated, the Windows Communication Foundation is a means to build distributed applications in a Microsoft environment. Though the distributed application is built upon that environment, this does not mean that the consumers are required to be Microsoft clients; nor is any Microsoft component or technology necessary to accomplish the task of consumption. Conversely, building WCF services means you are also building services that abide by the principles set forth in the aforementioned SOA discussion, and that these services are vendor-agnostic—that is, they can be consumed by almost anyone. WCF is part of the .NET Framework and is available to applications targeting .NET 3.0 or later.

## Capabilities of WCF

WCF provides you with the capability to build all kinds of distributed applications. You can build Web services just as you could previously in earlier .NET Framework releases. This means that your services will support SOAP, and therefore will be compatible with older .NET technologies, older Microsoft technologies, and even non-Microsoft technologies (such as any Java-based consumers).

WCF is not limited to pure SOAP over a wire; you can also work with an InfoSet, and create a binary representation of your SOAP message that can then be sent along your choice of protocol.

This is for folks who are concerned about the performance of their services and have traditionally turned to .NET remoting for this binary-based distribution system.

The WCF framework can also work with a message through its life cycle, meaning that WCF can deal with transactions. Along with distributed transactions, WCF can deal with the queuing of messages, and it allows for the intermittent connected nature that an application or process might experience across the web. Of course, what WCF truly provides is a framework to communicate with tools that support many of these capabilities. It's not that WCF provides a message store and forward capability so much as it supports the protocols used in message store and forward.

When you need to get messages from one point to another, the WCF is the big gun in your arsenal to get the job accomplished. For instance, many developers might consider using WCF primarily to communicate ASP.NET Web Service–like messages (SOAP) from one disparate system to another, but you can use WCF for much more than this. For instance, WCF can be used to communicate messages to components contained on the same machine on which the WCF service is running.

This means you can use WCF to communicate with components contained in different processes on the same machine. For example, the same service might be called by a WPF application using a binary format within your organization, while the same service may expose an endpoint hosted on a web server and accessible over the Web via HTTP and SOAP. You use WCF to communicate with components on the same machine or on another machine—even accepting calls from a client that is not a Microsoft-based machine.

## Contracts and Metadata

Probably the biggest and most exciting part of the WCF model is that it enables you to develop a service once and then expose that service via multiple endpoints (even endpoints on entirely different protocols) via simple configuration changes. These changes start with the interface definition. As part of creating a service you'll be able to define an interface, and that interface has two top-level contracts.

From an implementation standpoint a contract is an attribute that is associated with either an interface or a class definition. The `<Service Contract>` is used as part of an interface definition. That interface will expose a series of `<OperationContract>` method definitions, which describe what services this service provides.

A Service Contract with at least one operation is required in order to have a service. Without this minimum definition there isn't anything to call. The methods within the `ServiceContract` interface are attributed with the `<OperationContract>` to define the various interfaces.

Optionally, if your service is going to accept data types other than primitive types, it needs to provide metadata to define these data types. A `<DataContract>` attribute can be associated with one or more classes to define these custom data structures. An interface does not need to expose any custom data structures, but if it does, it needs to determine which properties of the class to include in the interface. Each property to be exposed is associated with a `<DataMember>` attribute to identify it as part of the `DataContract`.

## Working with the WS-* Protocols

WCF understands and can work with the full set of WS-* specifications, and these specifications can be enabled to create messages that meet defined ways of dealing with security, reliability, and transactions. A few of these protocols and an understanding of how messages are managed are important enough to take a closer look at their implementation details.

Messages, as defined by the Messaging layer, rely on SOAP (sent as open text or in a binary format). The advanced WS-* specifications make heavy use of the SOAP header, enabling messages to be self-contained and not have any real reliance on the transport protocol to provide items such as security, reliability, or any other capability beyond the simple transmission of the message itself. *Message Transmission Optimization Mechanism (MTOM)* is a capability to replace *Direct Internet Message Encapsulation (DIME)* as a means to transmit binary objects along with a SOAP message. An example binary object would be a JPEG image that you want to expose through a WCF service.

The security implementation in WCF enables you to work with WS-Security. Before WS-Security came along, the initial lack of a security model in Web services kept many companies from massively adopting them companywide and moving to a service-oriented architecture. WS-Security addresses the main areas that are required to keep messages secure—credential exchange, message integrity, and message confidentiality.

To do this WS-Security supports implementing security at two levels. The first is at the message level. WS-Security enables entities to provide and validate credentials within the messages that are exchanged. Alternatively WS-Security also enables transport level security. This form of security focuses on establishing credentials based on the transport protocol, for example, using HTTPS to securely transmit data.

With message-level security WS-Security enables two entities to exchange their security credentials from within the message itself (actually, from the SOAP header of the message). The great thing about WS-Security is that it doesn't require a specific type of credential set to be used. Instead, it allows any type of credentials to be used. In addition, it is possible to send messages through multiple routers. In effect, this allows your solution to bounce messages from here to there before they reach their final destination while ensuring that the messages are not tampered with in transport. As messages move from one SOAP router to another, these SOAP nodes can make additions to or subtractions from the messages. If such SOAP nodes were to get into the hands of malicious parties, the integrity of the messages could be compromised. This is where WS-Security comes into play.

The other area in which WS-Security helps is when you need to have WS-Security encrypt all or part of your SOAP messages. When your messages are zipping across the virtual world, there is a chance that they might be intercepted and opened for viewing by parties who should not be looking at their contents. That's why it is often beneficial to scramble the contents of the message. When it reaches the intended receiver, the application can then use your encryption key and unscramble the message to read the contents.

WS-SecureConversation works to establish a connection that enables entities to exchange multiple messages and maintain their established security arrangements. WS-Trust, conversely, works in conjunction with WS-Security and allows for the issuance of security tokens and a way in which entities can exchange these tokens. This specification also deals with establishing trust relationships between two entities.

WS-ReliableMessaging allows for reliable end-to-end communications of messages to ensure that they are delivered.

The Transactions section allows for the use of WS-Coordination and WS-AtomicTransaction. WS-Coordination is there for the purpose of addressing the description of the relationships that multiple services have to one another. As a company starts developing a multitude of services within its enterprise, it realizes that many of the services developed have a relationship with one another, and that's where WS-Coordination comes into play. This specification is meant to be expanded by other specifications that will further define particular coordination types.

WS-AtomicTransaction uses WS-Coordination and WS-Security to allow for the definition of a service transaction process. An atomic transaction is a way of creating a transaction process that works on an all-or-nothing basis. These are meant to be short-lived transactions, so when you use them you are locking data resources and holding onto physical resources such as connections, threads, and memory.

The main point of this discussion is to emphasize the slew of WS-* specifications at your disposal. Even better, when working with WCF you really don't have to be aware that these specifications are even there—you can access the capabilities these specifications offer through programmatic or declarative programming.

# BUILDING A WCF SERVICE

Building a WCF service is not hard to accomplish. Using Visual Studio 2012, you'll see the WCF new project templates shown in Figure 11-2. One word of warning, however—in order to host a WCF service you'll need Administrator rights. Before attempting to replicate all of the steps in the sample, make sure you've started Visual Studio using the 'Run as Administrator' option from the context menu.

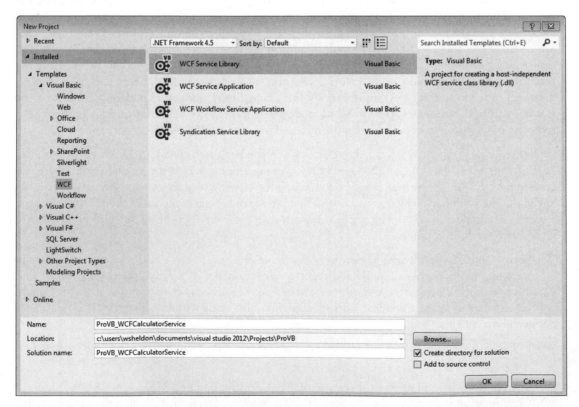

**FIGURE 11-2:** New WCF project templates

When you build a WCF project in this manner, the idea is that you build a traditional class library that is compiled down to a DLL that can then be added to another project. The separation of code and use of multiple projects is a powerful tool for managing complexity on larger projects. That said, though, you can also just as easily build a WCF service directly in your .NET project, whether that is a console application or a Windows Forms application.

This example will first create a new WCF service in a Service Library. It then demonstrates how to host the WCF service inside a console application. Start by creating a new Service Library with the name ProVB_WCFCalculatorLibrary.

Once you have created your new library project, Visual Studio will look similar to what is shown in Figure 11-3.

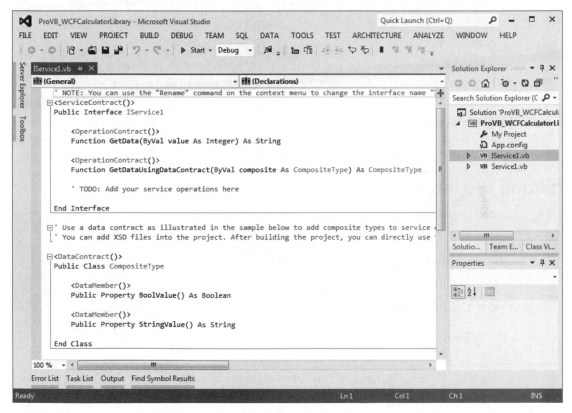

**FIGURE 11-3:** WCF project template interface definition

This example first demonstrates how to build the WCF service. It then demonstrates how to build a console application that will host this service, and finally demonstrates how to leverage Visual Studio 2010 to test this service.

## Creating the Interface

To create your service, you need a service contract, which is the interface of the service. This consists of all the methods exposed, as well as the input and output parameters that are required to invoke the methods. To accomplish this task, rename the file `IService1.vb` to `ICalculator.vb`. Then replace the contents of the generated file with the code presented in Listing 11-1.

**LISTING 11-1:** Service Interface Definition—ICalculator.vb

```
<ServiceContract()>
Public Interface ICalculator
    <OperationContract()>
    Function Add(ByVal a As Integer, ByVal b As Integer) As Integer
    <OperationContract()>
    Function Subtract(ByVal a As Integer, ByVal b As Integer) As Integer
    <OperationContract()>
    Function Multiply(ByVal a As Integer, ByVal b As Integer) As Integer
    <OperationContract()>
    Function Divide(ByVal a As Integer, ByVal b As Integer) As Integer
End Interface
```

This is pretty much the normal interface definition you would expect, but with a couple of new attributes included. The `<ServiceContract()>` attribute is used to define the class or interface as the service class, and it needs to precede the opening declaration of the class or interface.

Within the interface, four methods are defined. Each of these methods is going to be exposed through the WCF service as part of the service contract, so they all require that the `<OperationContract()>` attribute be applied to them.

## Utilizing the Interface

The next step is to create a class that implements the interface. Not only is the new class implementing the interface defined, it is also implementing the service contract. From Solution Explorer, right-click on the generated `Service1.vb` file and rename this file as `Calculator.vb`. Next, replace the code in this file with the code shown in Listing 11-2.

**LISTING 11-2:** Calculator Implementation—Calculator.vb

```
Public Class Calculator
    Implements ICalculator
    Public Function Add(ByVal a As Integer,
                        ByVal b As Integer) As Integer _
                    Implements ICalculator.Add
        Return (a + b)
    End Function
    Public Function Subtract(ByVal a As Integer,
                             ByVal b As Integer) As Integer _
                        Implements ICalculator.Subtract
        Return (a - b)
    End Function
    Public Function Multiply(ByVal a As Integer,
                             ByVal b As Integer) As Integer _
                        Implements ICalculator.Multiply
        Return (a * b)
    End Function
    Public Function Divide(ByVal a As Integer,
```

```
                              ByVal b As Integer) As Integer _
                        Implements ICalculator.Divide
            Return (a / b)
        End Function
    End Class
```

From these new additions, you can see that nothing is done differently with the `Calculator` class than what you might do otherwise. It is a simple class that implements the `ICalculator` interface and provides implementations of the `Add`, `Subtract`, `Multiply`, and `Divide` methods.

With the interface and the class available, you now have your WCF service built and ready to go. The next step is to get the service hosted. This is a simple service. One of the simplicities of the service is that it exposes only simple types, rather than a complex type. This enables you to build only a service contract and not have to deal with construction of a data contract. Constructing data contracts is presented later in this chapter.

## Hosting the WCF Service in a Console Application

The next step is to take the service just developed and host it in some type of application process. You have many available hosting options, including the following:

➤ Console applications

➤ Windows Forms applications

➤ Windows Presentation Foundation applications

➤ Managed Windows Services

➤ Internet Information Services (IIS) 5.1

➤ Internet Information Services (IIS) 6.0

➤ Internet Information Services (IIS) 7.0 and the Windows Activation Service (WAS)

As stated earlier, this example hosts the service in a simple console application. There are a couple of ways to activate hosting—either through the direct coding of the hosting behaviors or through declarative programming (usually done via the configuration file).

For this example, the console application will define the host through coding the behaviors of the host environment directly. As mentioned at the start of this sample, in order to host a WCF service this way, you need to have started Visual Studio with the Run as Administrator menu link. If you are not running as administrator, you will get a permissions error when the console application attempts to start.

Using the File menu in Visual Studio, select Add ➪ New Project to add a new Console Application to your solution. Name the new console application ProVB_ServiceHost. After creating the new project, right-click the project name in Solution Explorer and set this project to be the startup project.

Next, right-click the project and select Add Reference. You need to add two references for this console application to act as a service host. The first is available from the Solution ➪ Projects tab, Add a reference to the ProVB_WCFCalculatorLibrary. After adding this reference, open the dialog a second time and switch to the Assemblies ➪ Framework tab. Scroll down and select `System.ServiceModel.dll`, as shown in Figure 11-4.

You are now ready to start making changes to the code. The code shown in Listing 11-3 implements the console application:

```vb
Imports System.ServiceModel
Imports System.ServiceModel.Description

Module Module1
    Sub Main()
        Using svcHost As New ServiceHost( _
                GetType(ProVB_WCFCalculatorLibrary.Calculator))
            Dim netBind As New NetTcpBinding(SecurityMode.None)
            svcHost.AddServiceEndpoint( _
                GetType(ProVB_WCFCalculatorLibrary.ICalculator),
                netBind,
                New Uri("net.tcp://localhost:8080/Calculator/"))
            Dim smb As New ServiceMetadataBehavior()
            smb.HttpGetEnabled = True
            smb.HttpGetUrl = New Uri("http://localhost:8000/Calculator")
            svcHost.Description.Behaviors.Add(smb)
            svcHost.Open()
            Console.WriteLine("Press <Enter> to close and end the Service Host")
            Console.ReadLine()
        End Using
    End Sub
End Module
```

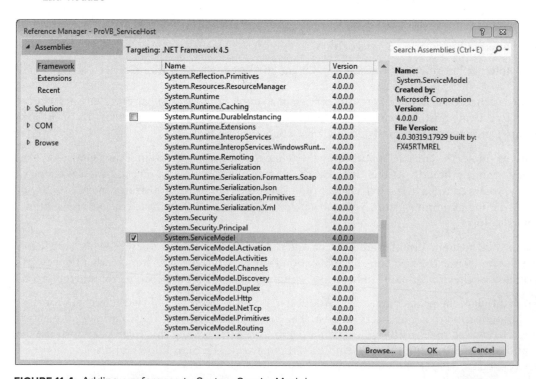

**FIGURE 11-4:** Adding a reference to System.ServiceModel

A couple of things are going on in this file. First, in order to gain access to work with any of the WCF framework pieces, you need a reference to the `System.ServiceModel` and the `System.ServiceModel.Description` namespaces in the file. The `System.ServiceModel` gives you access to defining things such as the endpoints that you need to create, while the `System.ServiceModel.Description` namespace reference gives you access to defining things such as the WSDL file.

Remember that creating endpoints uses the ABC model (address, binding, and contract). The address part here is `net.tcp://localhost:8080/Calculator`. The binding is a TCP binding—`NetTcpBinding`—while the contract part is the `ICalculator` interface.

Many different bindings are available to you when coding WCF services. Here, this example makes use of the `NetTcpBinding`. The full list of available bindings is as follows:

➤ `System.ServiceModel.BasicHttpBinding`

➤ `System.ServiceModel.Channels.CustomBinding`

➤ `System.ServiceModel.MsmqBindingBase`

➤ `System.ServiceModel.NetNamedPipeBinding`

➤ `System.ServiceModel.NetPeerTcpBinding`

➤ `System.ServiceModel.NetTcpBinding`

➤ `System.ServiceModel.WebHTTPBinding`

➤ `System.ServiceModel.WSDualHttpBinding`

➤ `System.ServiceModel.WSHttpBindingBase`

Clearly, several bindings are available. In the preceding example, the `NetTcpBinding` class is the transport pipe being used. This means that the service being built will be delivered over TCP. At this point your development environment should look similar to what is shown in Figure 11-5. However, before running the new console, let's look at the various commands it will use to host your custom service.

In the first step of the example, for the console-application code, a `ServiceHost` object is established:

```
Using svcHost As New ServiceHost( _
            GetType(ProVB_WCFCalculatorLibrary.Calculator))
```

By working with the `Using` keyword, when the `End Using` statement is encountered, the `ServiceHost` object is destroyed. In the creation of the host, the `Calculator` type is assigned. From there, the endpoint is established. In this case, a `NetTcpBinding` object is created with a security setting of `None` through the command `SecurityMode.None`:

```
Dim netBind = New NetTcpBinding(SecurityMode.None)
```

This means that no security is applied to the message. The other options include `Message`, `Transport`, and `TransportWithMessageCredential`. The `Message` option signifies that the security credentials will be included in the message (in the SOAP header, for instance), whereas the `Transport` option indicates that the transport protocol provides the security implementation. The last option, `TransportWithMessageCredential`, means that the message contains some security credentials along with the transport protocol security provided by the transport protocol.

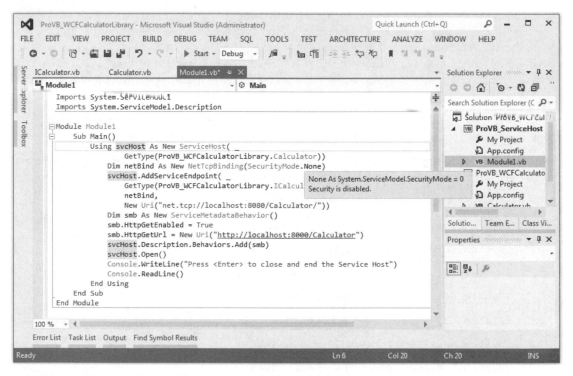

**FIGURE 11-5:** Editing the SecurityMode property in Visual Studio

Once the `NetTcpBinding` object is in place, the next step is to finalize the endpoint creation. This is done through the use of the `ServiceHost` object's `AddServiceEndpoint` method:

```
svcHost.AddServiceEndpoint( _
    GetType(ProVB_WCFCalculatorLibrary.ICalculator),
    netBind,
    New Uri("net.tcp://localhost:8080/Calculator/"))
```

From this, you can see that the entire ABC statement is used in the creation of the endpoint, although not necessarily in ABC order; in fact, the first item defined is actually the "C"—the contract. This is done through the `GetType(ICalculator)` setting. The "B" is next (the binding) with the reference to the `NetTcpBinding` object. Then, finally, the "A" is defined through an instantiation of a `Uri` object pointing to `net.tcp://localhost:8080/Calcuator/`.

The next step is a process to bring forth the WSDL document so that it can be viewed by the developer consuming this service:

```
Dim smb As New ServiceMetadataBehavior()
smb.HttpGetEnabled = True
smb.HttpGetUrl = New Uri("http://localhost:8000/calculator")
serviceHost.Description.Behaviors.Add(smb)
```

This bit of code is the reason why the `System.ServiceModel.Description` namespace is imported into the file at the beginning. Here, a `ServiceMetadataBehavior` object is created, the object's

HttpGetEnabled property is set to True, and the HttpGetUrl property is provided an address of http://localhost:8000/calculator. The documents can be located anywhere you like.

After the ServiceMetadataBehavior object is created as you wish, the next step is to associate this object with the ServiceHost through the serviceHost.Description.Behaviors.Add method.

After all of these items are defined, you need only open the ServiceHost for business, using the serviceHost.Open method. The console application is kept alive through the use of a Console.ReadLine method call, which waits for the end user to press the Enter key before shutting down the application. You want the Console.ReadLine command there because you want to keep the host open.

Compiling and running this application produces the results illustrated in Figure 11-6. Note that you may initially get a firewall warning when you run this application, but you'll want to allow access for this application to communicate (at least locally) through your local firewall. Additionally, if you didn't start Visual Studio with Administrator rights as noted at the beginning of this step, you'll get a runtime error related to permissions.

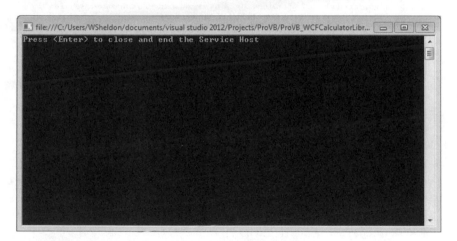

**FIGURE 11-6:** Running ProVB_ServiceHost to host the service

Keep in mind that your service is available only for as long as that console window is open and active; when you close the console you are stopping the listener for your new service. Also note that you aren't running the service within the Visual Studio's built-in tools. To do so you would need to edit the app.config file in the ProVB_WCFCalculatorLibrary project to properly reference your ICalculator interface.

## Reviewing the WSDL Document

The preceding console-application code provides an instantiation of the ServiceMetadataBehavior object and defines a Uri object for it as well. You can simply type in that address to get at the WSDL file for the service you just built. Therefore, calling http://localhost:8000/calculator from your browser provides the WSDL file shown in Figure 11-7.

**FIGURE 11-7:** Looking at the WSDL in Internet Explorer

With this WSDL file, you can now consume the service it defines through TCP. Note the following element at the bottom of the document:

```
<wsdl:service name="Calculator">
   <wsdl:port name="NetTcpBinding_ICalculator"
    binding="tns:NetTcpBinding_ICalculator">
      <soap12:address location="net.tcp://localhost:8080/Calculator/" />
      <wsa10:EndpointReference>
         <wsa10:Address>net.tcp://localhost:8080/Calculator/</wsa10:Address>
      </wsa10:EndpointReference>
   </wsdl:port>
</wsdl:service>
```

This element in the XML document indicates that in order to consume the service, the end user needs to use SOAP 1.2 over TCP. This is presented through the use of the `<soap12:address>` element in the document. The `<wsa10:EndpointReference>` is a WS-Addressing endpoint definition.

Using this simple WSDL document, you can now build a consumer that makes use of this interface. Just as important, you have created not only a service that meets the standards for a Web service, but also a custom host that is communicating via standard protocols.

# BUILDING A WCF CONSUMER

Now that a TCP service is out there, which you built using the WCF framework, the next step is to build a consumer application that uses the simple Calculator service. The consumer sends its request via TCP using SOAP. Using TCP means that the consumption can actually occur with a binary encoding of the SOAP message on the wire, substantially decreasing the size of the payload being transmitted.

This section describes how to consume this service. You have two options at this point: You can open a second instance of Visual Studio and create a new WPF Application project to reference your service or you can add a new WPF Application project to your current solution. For simplicity, this example uses the latter.

The only difference in terms of what is needed occurs as part of adding a reference to the service. If you create your application in a new solution, then in order to add the reference you'll need to have a copy of the service running. To that end, after you add a new project to your current called ProVB_WCFCalculatorClient you can start the add reference process by adding a reference to the service project in the shared solution.

## Adding a Service Reference

Right-click on the project name in the Solution Explorer and select Add Service Reference from the dialogue. After selecting Add Service Reference, you are presented with the dialogue shown in Figure 11-8. The selections you make within this dialogue, and to some extent what you'll get at the other end, depends on how you've approached creating your project. You'll start with what you need to do if you have your client in a separate solution.

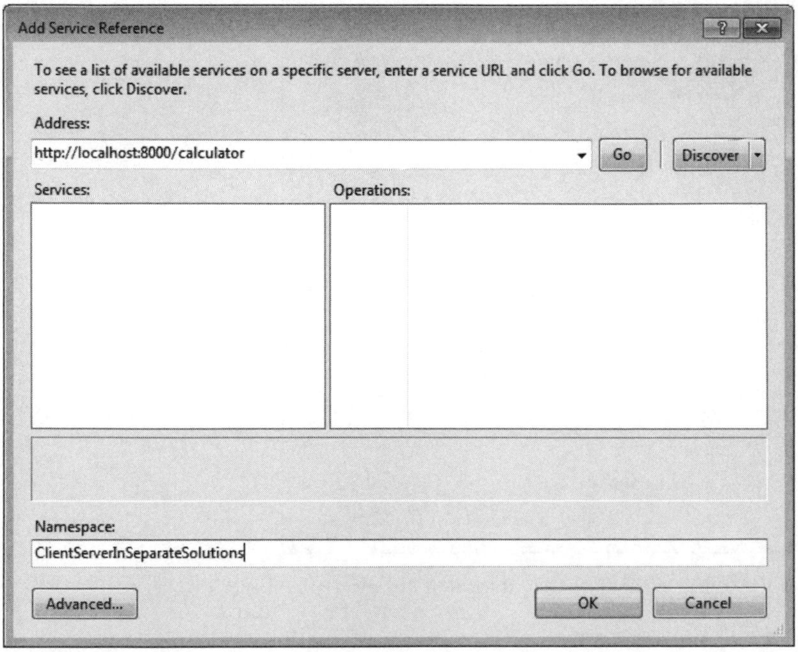

**FIGURE 11-8:** Adding a reference to the service while it is running in your custom console application

The Add Service Reference dialog asks you for two things: the Service URI (basically a pointer to the WSDL file) and the name you want to give to the reference. The name you provide the reference is the name that will be used for the instantiated object that enables you to interact with the service.

Referring to Figure 11-8, you can see that the name provided for the Address text box is `http://localhost:8000/calculator`. Remember that this is the location you defined earlier when you built the service. This URI was defined in code directly in the service:

```
Dim smb As New ServiceMetadataBehavior()
smb.HttpGetEnabled = True
smb.HttpGetUrl = New Uri("http://localhost:8000/calculator")
serviceHost.Description.Behaviors.Add(smb)
```

Manually entering that URL is the difference between having your client in a separate solution and what you are about to do for a client in the same solution. Since in this case you are working with a service within the same solution, you are going to use the Discover button. The Discover button has a single option: Services in Solution. Using this button will trigger Visual Studio to look at the current solution, locate any services, and dynamically create a host for that service.

This is a great feature of Visual Studio, as it recognizes and supports the developer who needs to implement and test a WCF Service. Instead of needing that production URL, which you would need to track, it will simply create a runtime reference. Figure 11-9 illustrates the Add Service Reference dialog after having located the local service using the Discover button.

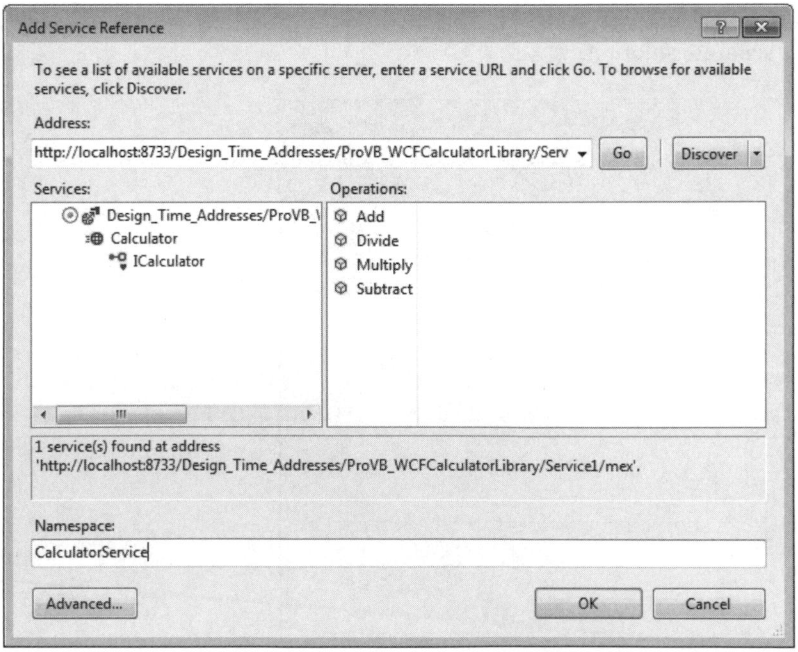

**FIGURE 11-9:** Adding a reference to the WCF service in the same solution

> **NOTE** *The port shown in Figure 11-9 was randomly generated by Visual Studio. Running this code locally, you can expect to see a different port generated.*

Notice that by expanding the top-level Calculator node within the Services pane in Figure 11-9, a single interface is exposed, and selecting that interface populates the available operations in the Operations pane.

Rename the service reference to `CalculatorService` from `ServiceReference1` (refer to Figure 11-9). Press the OK button in the Add Service Reference dialog.

Finally, a quick best practices note concerning the address. For this example and as a tester, you will of course have a generated or test URI. When the application is ready to deploy, you want this URI to reflect production. The best practice is to have a custom configuration setting in your `app.config` (or `web.config`) file that is updated with the production URI. This application setting is read at run-time, and then after the service reference is created, its `uri` property is updated with the correct value from the application configuration file.

## Reviewing the Reference

You've now added a Service References folder to your project, which contains the proxy details for your Calculator service. This proxy is a collection of files, as shown in Figure 11-10. Note that you'll need to show all the files in order to see the files shown in Figure 11-10.

Digging down into these files, you will find `Reference.svcmap` and `Reference.vb`. The other important addition to note is the `System.ServiceModel` reference, made for you in the References folder.

Looking at the `Reference.svcmap` file, shown in Listing 11-4, you see that it is a simple XML file that provides information about where the WSDL file is located, as well as the location of the service (referenced through the `configuration.svcinfo` file):

---

**LISTING 11-4:** Service Mapping—Reference.svcmap

```xml
<?xml version="1.0" encoding="utf-8"?>
<ReferenceGroup xmlns:xsi=http://www.w3.org/2001/XMLSchema-instance
    xmlns:xsd="http://www.w3.org/2001/XMLSchema"
    ID="d5ec45e4-5a67-4609-840b-e332497cfb00"
    xmlns="urn:schemas-microsoft-com:xml-wcfservicemap">
  <ClientOptions>
    <GenerateAsynchronousMethods>false</GenerateAsynchronousMethods>
    <GenerateTaskBasedAsynchronousMethod>true</GenerateTaskBasedAsynchronousMethod>
    <EnableDataBinding>true</EnableDataBinding>
    <ExcludedTypes />
    <ImportXmlTypes>false</ImportXmlTypes>
    <GenerateInternalTypes>false</GenerateInternalTypes>
    <GenerateMessageContracts>false</GenerateMessageContracts>
    <NamespaceMappings />
    <CollectionMappings />
```

*continues*

LISTING 11-4 *(continued)*

```
    <GenerateSerializableTypes>true</GenerateSerializableTypes>
    <Serializer>Auto</Serializer>
    <UseSerializerForFaults>true</UseSerializerForFaults>
    <ReferenceAllAssemblies>true</ReferenceAllAssemblies>
    <ReferencedAssemblies />
    <ReferencedDataContractTypes />
    <ServiceContractMappings />
  </ClientOptions>
  <MetadataSources>
    <MetadataSource Address="http://localhost:8733/Design_Time_Addresses/
ProVB_WCFCalculatorLibrary/Service1/mex"
          Protocol="mex" SourceId="1" />
  </MetadataSources>
  <Metadata>
    <MetadataFile FileName="service.wsdl"
     MetadataType="Wsdl" ID="b37c05b8-9185-433b-8138-c1ee6fff00e4" SourceId="1"
SourceUrl="http://localhost:8733/Design_Time_Addresses/
ProVB_WCFCalculatorLibrary/Service1/mex" />
    <MetadataFile FileName="service.xsd"
     MetadataType="Schema" ID="4558c7db-7585-4726-9b85-f8bdfc066c9c" SourceId="1"
SourceUrl="http://localhost:8733/Design_Time_Addresses/
ProVB_WCFCalculatorLibrary/Service1/mex" />
    <MetadataFile FileName="service1.xsd" MetadataType="Schema"
     ID="c532cecc-b644-4883-88b0-81ff697b608c" SourceId="1"
SourceUrl="http://localhost:8733/Design_Time_Addresses/
ProVB_WCFCalculatorLibrary/Service1/mex" />
  </Metadata>
  <Extensions>
    <ExtensionFile FileName="configuration91.svcinfo"
                   Name="configuration91.svcinfo" />
    <ExtensionFile FileName="configuration.svcinfo"
                   Name="configuration.svcinfo" />
  </Extensions>
</ReferenceGroup>
```

Note that due to the length of many of the embedded strings, the preceding snippet has additional carriage returns embedded that are not part of the original file.

This file provides the capability to later update the reference to the service if needed, due to a change in the service interface. You can see this capability by right-clicking on the CalculatorService reference; an Update Service Reference option appears in the provided menu.

The other file in the reference collection of files, the Reference.vb file, is your proxy to interact with the service. The Reference.vb file, not shown, defines the four methods and the class CalculatorClient, which contains the method stubs to call the Calculator service built earlier in the chapter.

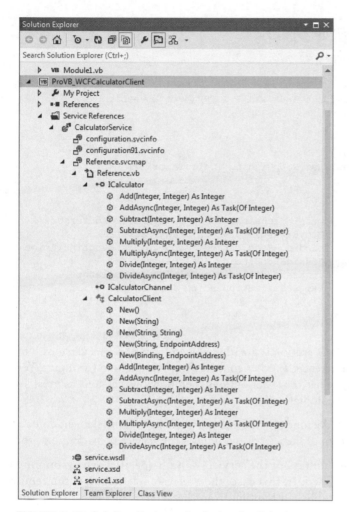

**FIGURE 11-10:** Solution Explorer displaying the Calculator service methods

# Configuration File Changes

Another addition to your project is the `app.config` file. After the service reference is made, the `app.config` file contains several new configuration settings. These configuration settings were automatically added by the Visual Studio WCF extensions. The new `app.config` file is presented in Listing 11-5:

---

**LISTING 11-5: Configuration—App.config**

```xml
<?xml version="1.0" encoding="utf-8" ?>
<configuration>
    <startup>
        <supportedRuntime version="v4.0" sku=".NETFramework,Version=v4.5" />
    </startup>
    <system.serviceModel>
        <bindings>
            <basicHttpBinding>
                <binding name="BasicHttpBinding_ICalculator" />
            </basicHttpBinding>
        </bindings>
        <client>
            <endpoint address= "http://localhost:8733/Design_Time_Addresses/
                                ProVB_WCFCalculatorLibrary/Service1/"
                                binding="basicHttpBinding" bindingConfiguration=
                                "BasicHttpBinding_ICalculator"
                                contract="CalculatorService.ICalculator"
                                name="BasicHttpBinding_ICalculator" />
        </client>
    </system.serviceModel>
</configuration>
```

The information in the `basicHttpBinding` section is greatly reduced from previous versions. Note that if you right-click on your service reference, another context menu option is to Configure Your Service Reference. The resulting dialogue has far fewer options then previous versions as most settings are now handled under the covers automatically.

The other key node in the configuration document is the `<client>` element. This element contains a child element called `<endpoint>` that defines the *where* and *how* of the service consumption process.

The `<endpoint>` element provides the address of the service—and it specifies which binding of the available WCF bindings should be used. In this case, the `BasicHttpBinding` is the required binding. Although you are using an established binding from the WCF framework, from the client side you can customize how this binding behaves. As noted, the settings that define the behavior of the binding are specified using the `bindingConfiguration` attribute of the `<endpoint>` element. In this case, the value provided to the `bindingConfiguration` attribute is `BasicHttpBinding_ICalculator`, which is a reference to the `<binding>` element contained within the `<basicHttpBinding>` element.

Note one important distinction here. If instead of using the built-in Visual Studio test engine to test your service declaration, you bound to the custom client, you would find that this configuration file would be subtly different. Instead of having a `basicHttpBinding`, you would have a `netTCP` binding. This binding would have different setting defaults and, more important, indicate a different transport protocol for your requests. If you play with these two different bindings, you'll find that the binary format used by `netTCP` responds much more quickly than the `basicHttpBinding` that Visual Studio has generated for you.

As demonstrated, the Visual Studio 2012 capabilities for WCF make the consumption of these services fairly trivial. The next step is to code the Windows Forms project to test the consumption of the service interface.

# Writing the Consumption Code

The code to consume the interface is quite minimal. End users will merely select the radio button of the operation they want to perform. The default radio button selected is Add. The user places a number in each of the two text boxes provided and clicks the Calculate button to call the service to perform the designated operation on the provided numbers.

To accomplish this, add two text boxes, four radio buttons, one button, and one label to your window. The display (for labeling the controls) should look similar to what is shown in Figure 11-11. Next, you want to create two event handlers; the first is on `Form Load` to prepopulate the text boxes with default numbers (to speed testing), and the second is an event handler for the button you've labeled Calculate.

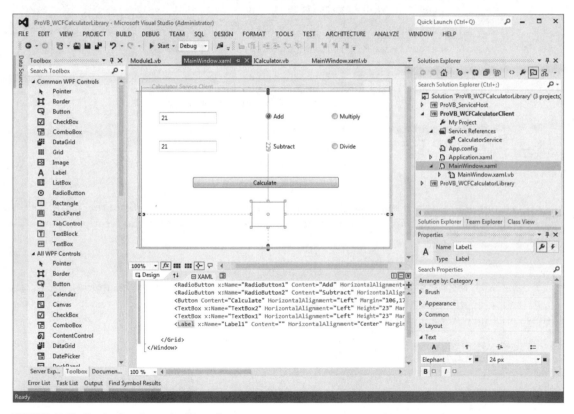

**FIGURE 11-11:** Designing the calculator client

Clicking the Calculate button will create an instance of the service and then open a connection and make the appropriate call. In a production environment, you might keep a static instance of the service available in your application so you could create it once instead of for each event. Similarly, you'll want to follow the best practice mentioned earlier of assigning the URI at runtime based on an application setting.

To implement a call to the service add a button handler for the button labeled Calculate. Also note that you'll need to name each of the radio buttons and the text boxes used in the client. The button doesn't need a name. A copy of the code is shown in listing 11-6:

**LISTING 11-6:** Calculate Event Handler—MainWindow.xaml.vb

```
Class MainWindow

    Private Sub Button_Click_1(sender As Object, e As RoutedEventArgs)
        Dim result As Integer
        Dim ws As New CalculatorService.CalculatorClient()
        ws.Open()
        If RadioButton1.IsChecked = True Then
            result = ws.Add(Integer.Parse(TextBox1.Text),
                        Integer.Parse(TextBox2.Text))
        ElseIf RadioButton2.IsChecked = True Then
            result = ws.Subtract(Integer.Parse(TextBox1.Text),
                            Integer.Parse(TextBox2.Text))
        ElseIf RadioButton3.IsChecked = True Then
            result = ws.Multiply(Integer.Parse(TextBox1.Text),
                            Integer.Parse(TextBox2.Text))
        ElseIf RadioButton4.IsChecked = True Then
            result = ws.Divide(Integer.Parse(TextBox1.Text),
                            Integer.Parse(TextBox2.Text))
        End If
        ws.Close()
        Label1.Content = result.ToString()


    End Sub
End Class
```

This is quite similar to the steps taken when working with Web references from the XML Web Services world. First is an instantiation of the proxy class, as shown with the creation of the svc object:

```
Dim ws As New CalculatorService.CalculatorClient()
```

Working with the ws object now, the IntelliSense options provide you with the appropriate Add, Subtract, Multiply, and Divide methods. Running this application provides results similar to those presented in Figure 11-12.

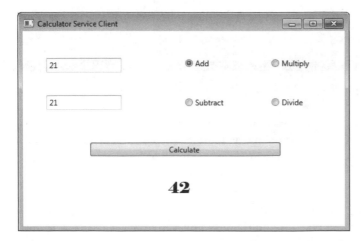

**FIGURE 11-12:** Displaying the results of the service call in the client

In this case, the Add method is invoked from the service when the form's Calculate button is pressed.

Another best practice is to get a tool such as Fiddler2 to track communication with your service. (www.fiddler2.com/fiddler2/) This free tool enables you to view messages sent across a HTTP/HTTPS connection.

Note that while this tool will work if you've used Visual Studio to configure your testing to be transported via HTTP, if you've relied on the custom client, you'll find that the requests are instead sent as binary data over TCP and are not available to Fiddler2.

Using a binding to the custom client means the requests and responses are sent over TCP as binary, dramatically decreasing the size of the payload for large messages. This is something that .NET Remoting was used for prior to the release of the WCF framework.

This concludes the short tutorial demonstrating how to build a single service that can support two different endpoints. Visual Studio 2012 can generate one such endpoint, which is based on the same XML and open standards as a traditional Web service. The other you built manually into your command-line application to support the TCP protocol and binary data transfer. Depending on how you map that service to your client, you can consume the service as either an XML-based data transfer or a binary data transfer that can map directly into your .NET Windows Forms application.

## WORKING WITH DATA CONTRACTS

In the preceding sample WCF service, the data contract depended upon simple types or primitive data types. A .NET type of Integer was exposed, which in turn was mapped to an XSD type of int. You might not have noticed the input and output types actually defined in the WSDL document that was provided via the WCF-generated one, but they are there. These types are exposed through an imported .xsd document (a dynamic document). This bit of the WSDL document is presented here:

```xml
<wsdl:types>
    <xsd:schema targetNamespace="http://tempuri.org/Imports">
    <xsd:import schemaLocation="http://localhost:8000/calculator?xsd=xsd0"
     namespace="http://tempuri.org/" />
    <xsd:import schemaLocation="http://localhost:8000/calculator?xsd=xsd1"
     namespace="http://schemas.microsoft.com/2003/10/Serialization/" />
    </xsd:schema>
</wsdl:types>
```

Typing in the XSD location of http://localhost:8000/calculator?xsd=xsd0 gives you the input and output parameters of the service. For instance, looking at the definition of the Add method, you will see the following bit of XML:

```xml
<xs:element name="Add">
    <xs:complexType>
        <xs:sequence>
            <xs:element minOccurs="0" name="a" type="xs:int" />
            <xs:element minOccurs="0" name="b" type="xs:int" />
        </xs:sequence>
    </xs:complexType>
</xs:element>
<xs:element name="AddResponse">
    <xs:complexType>
```

```
        <xs:sequence>
            <xs:element minOccurs="0" name="AddResult" type="xs:int" />
        </xs:sequence>
    </xs:complexType>
</xs:element>
```

This XML code indicates that there are two required input parameters (a and b) that are of type int; in return, the consumer gets an element called <AddResult>, which contains a value of type int.

As a builder of this WCF service, you didn't have to build the data contract, mainly because this service uses simple types. When using complex types, you have to create a data contract in addition to your service contract.

For an example of working with data contracts, you can create a new WCF service called ProVB_WCFWithDataContract (you will again host the services with a Console Application). As with the other samples this solution is available as part of the online code download. In this case, you will need to define a class that implements the data contract.

Like the service contract, which makes use of the <ServiceContract()> and the <OperationContract()> attributes, the data contract uses the <DataContract()> and <DataMember()> attributes.

The full WCF interface definition located in IHelloCustomer.vb is shown in Listing 11-7:

**LISTING 11-7: Contract Definitions—IHelloCustomer.vb**

```
<ServiceContract()> _
Public Interface IHelloCustomer
    <OperationContract()> _
    Function HelloFirstName(ByVal cust As Customer) As String
    <OperationContract()> _
    Function HelloFullName(ByVal cust As Customer) As String
End Interface

<DataContract()> _
Public Class Customer
    <DataMember()> _
    Public FirstName As String
    <DataMember()> _
    Public LastName As String
End Class
```

Similarly, the project contains the file HelloCustomer.vb, which contains the implementation class as shown in Listing 11-8:

**LISTING 11-8: Service Implementation—HelloCustomer.vb**

```
Public Class HelloCustomer
    Implements IHelloCustomer
```

```
        Public Function HelloFirstName(ByVal cust As Customer) As String _
           Implements IHelloCustomer.HelloFirstName
              Return "Hello " & cust.FirstName
        End Function
        Public Function HelloFullName(ByVal cust As Customer) As String _
           Implements IHelloCustomer.HelloFullName
              Return "Hello " & cust.FirstName & " " & cust.LastName
        End Function
     End Class
```

This class, the `Customer` class, has two members: `FirstName` and `LastName`. Both of these properties are of type `String`. You specify a class as a data contract as part of the interface definition through the use of the `<DataContract()>` attribute:

```
<DataContract()> _
Public Class Customer
     ' Code removed for clarity
End Class
```

Now, any of the properties contained in the class are also part of the data contract through the use of the `<DataMember()>` attribute:

```
<DataContract()> _
Public Class Customer
     <DataMember()> _
     Public FirstName As String
     <DataMember()> _
     Public LastName As String
End Class
```

Finally, the `Customer` object is used in the interface, as well as the class that implements the `IHelloCustomer` interface.

## NAMESPACES

Note that the services built in the chapter have no defined namespaces. If you looked at the WSDL files that were produced, you would see that the namespace provided is `http://tempuri.org`. Obviously, you do not want to go live with this default namespace. Instead, you need to define your own namespace.

To accomplish this task, the interface's `<ServiceContract()>` attribute enables you to set the namespace:

```
<ServiceContract(Namespace:="http://www.Wrox.com/ns/")> _
Public Interface IHelloCustomer
     <OperationContract()> _
     Function HelloFirstName(ByVal cust As Customer) As String
     <OperationContract()> _
     Function HelloFullName(ByVal cust As Customer) As String
End Interface
```

Here, the `<ServiceContract()>` attribute uses the `Namespace` property to provide a namespace.

## Building the Host

Next create a service host, using the same steps as before: Create a new Console Application project to act as the WCF service host. Name the new project **ProVB_WCFWithDataContractHost** and change the Module1.vb file so that it becomes the host of the WCF service you just built. Keep in mind that you'll need to add the appropriate project reference and System.ServiceModel references to the code. Once that is complete, the updated code will look similar to Listing 11-9:

> **LISTING 11-9:** Service Host Implementation—ProVB_WCFWithDataContractHost\Module1.vb

```
Imports System.ServiceModel
Imports System.ServiceModel.Description

Module Module1
    Sub Main()
        Using svcHost =
            New ServiceHost(GetType(ProVB_WCFWithDataContract.HelloCustomer))
                Dim netBind = New NetTcpBinding(SecurityMode.None)
        svcHost.AddServiceEndpoint(GetType(ProVB_WCFWithDataContract.IHelloCustomer),
                        netBind,
                        New Uri("net.tcp://localhost:8080/HelloCustomer/"))
            Dim smb = New ServiceMetadataBehavior()
            smb.HttpGetEnabled = True
            smb.HttpGetUrl = New Uri("http://localhost:8000/HelloCustomer")
            svcHost.Description.Behaviors.Add(smb)
            svcHost.Open()
            Console.WriteLine("Press the <ENTER> key to close the host.")
            Console.ReadLine()
        End Using
    End Sub
End Module
```

This host uses the IHelloCustomer interface and builds an endpoint at net.tcp://localhost:8080/HelloCustomer. This time, however, you'll have this running when you map your interface so you can see an example of the TCP binding. Build your solution and show all files in the Solution Explorer for your host project. You can then see the bin folder for your project, which contains the Debug folder. Right-click the Debug folder and from the context menu select Open Folder in Windows Explorer.

This should give you a view similar to what is shown in Figure 11-13. Right-click on ProVB_WCFWithDataContractHost and run your application as Administrator (you may be prompted to resolve a firewall issue and to confirm that you want to elevate the privileges of this process) to start your WCF host outside of Visual Studio. By starting this application outside of Visual Studio, you can directly reference the TCP-based binding you created as part of your host console from the Add Service Reference dialogue. Just leave this running in the background as you continue this example.

## Building the Consumer

Now that the service is running and in place, the next step is to build the consumer. To begin, add a new Console Application project to your Service Library solution called **ProVB_HelloWorldConsumer**. Right-click on the project and select Add Service Reference from the options provided. In short you are going to create another copy of the service host created in the previous example.

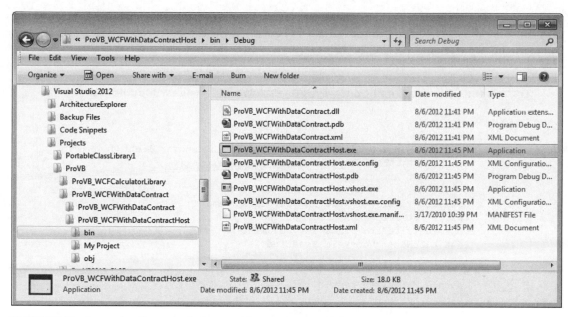

**FIGURE 11-13:** Accessing the compiled assembly to test run as Administrator

From the Add Service Reference dialog, target your custom service host by entering `http://localhost:8000/HelloCustomer` as the service URI. Then simply rename the default `ServiceReference1` with the name `HelloCustomerService` as shown in Figure 11-14.

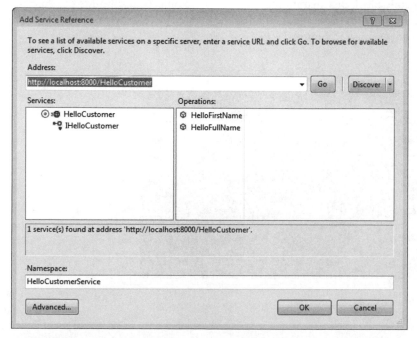

**FIGURE 11-14:** Add a service reference to your running service

This will add the changes to the references and the app.config file just as before, enabling you to consume the service. You can use the steps to create the service host from the first sample, but update the connections to reference the new service, as shown in Listing 11-10.

LISTING 11-10: Service Client Code—ProVB_HelloWorldConsumer\Module1.vb

```vb
Module Module1
    Sub Main()
        Dim svc As New HelloCustomerService.HelloCustomerClient()
        Dim cust As New HelloCustomerService.Customer()
        Dim result As String
        svc.Open()
        Console.WriteLine("What is your first name?")
        cust.FirstName = Console.ReadLine()
        Console.WriteLine("What is your last name?")
        cust.LastName = Console.ReadLine()
        result = svc.HelloFullName(cust)
        svc.Close()
        Console.WriteLine(result)
        Console.ReadLine()
    End Sub
End Module
```

As a consumer, once you make the reference, the service reference doesn't just provide a HelloCustomerClient object; you will also find the Customer object that was defined through the service's data contract.

Therefore, the preceding code block just instantiates both of these objects and builds the Customer object before it is passed into the HelloFullName method provided by the service. Running this bit of code will return the results shown in Figure 11-15.

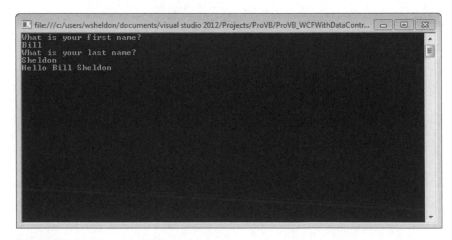

FIGURE 11-15: Consuming the service

## Looking at WSDL and the Schema for HelloCustomerService

After you made the reference to the HelloCustomer service, it was possible for you to review the WSDL in your new reference. With the Solution Explorer showing all files, you'll see the `HelloCustomer1.wsdl` within your solution. You can open this file to look at the WSDL, where you will find the following XSD imports:

```
<wsdl:types>
  <xsd:schema targetNamespace="http://www.Wrox.com/ns/Imports">
    <xsd:import schemaLocation="http://localhost:8000/HelloCustomer?xsd=xsd0"
    namespace="http://www.Wrox.com/ns/" />
    <xsd:import schemaLocation="http://localhost:8000/HelloCustomer?xsd=xsd1"
     namespace="http://schemas.microsoft.com/2003/10/Serialization/" />
    <xsd:import schemaLocation="http://localhost:8000/HelloCustomer?xsd=xsd2"
     namespace="http://schemas.datacontract.org/2004/07/
     ProVB_WCFWithDataContract" />
  </xsd:schema>
</wsdl:types>
```

`http://localhost:8000/HelloCustomer?xsd=xsd2` provides the details about your `Customer` object. The code from the file `HelloCustomer2.xsd`, which is part of your reference definition, is shown here:

```
<?xml version="1.0" encoding="utf-8"?>
<xs:schema
  xmlns:tns="http://schemas.datacontract.org/2004/07/ProVB_WCFWithDataContract"
  elementFormDefault="qualified"
  targetNamespace=
          "http://schemas.datacontract.org/2004/07/ProVB_WCFWithDataContract"
  xmlns:xs="http://www.w3.org/2001/XMLSchema">
  <xs:complexType name="Customer">
    <xs:sequence>
      <xs:element minOccurs="0" name="FirstName" nillable="true"
                                      type="xs:string" />
      <xs:element minOccurs="0" name="LastName" nillable="true"
                                      type="xs:string" />
    </xs:sequence>
  </xs:complexType>
  <xs:element name="Customer" nillable="true" type="tns:Customer" />
</xs:schema>
```

This is an XSD description of the `Customer` object. Making a reference to the WSDL that includes the XSD description of the `Customer` object causes the auto-generated proxy class (located in the file `Reference.vb`) to create the following class as part of the proxy (this code follows the `Namespace` declaration in the downloadable sample):

```
<System.Diagnostics.DebuggerStepThroughAttribute(),  _
System.CodeDom.Compiler.GeneratedCodeAttribute("System.Runtime.Serialization" _
, "4.0.0.0"),  _
    System.Runtime.Serialization.DataContractAttribute(Name:="Customer", _
    [Namespace]:= _
    "http://schemas.datacontract.org/2004/07/ProVB_WCFWithDataContract"),  _
```

```
        System.SerializableAttribute()> _
    Partial Public Class Customer
        Inherits Object
        Implements System.Runtime.Serialization.IExtensibleDataObject,
                System.ComponentModel.INotifyPropertyChanged
        <System.NonSerializedAttribute()> _
        Private extensionDataField As _
                    System.Runtime.Serialization.ExtensionDataObject


        <System.Runtime.Serialization.OptionalFieldAttribute()> _
        Private FirstNameField As String


        <System.Runtime.Serialization.OptionalFieldAttribute()> _
        Private LastNameField As String


        <Global.System.ComponentModel.BrowsableAttribute(false)> _
        Public Property ExtensionData() As _
        System.Runtime.Serialization.ExtensionDataObject _
    Implements System.Runtime.Serialization.IExtensibleDataObject.ExtensionData
            Get
                Return Me.extensionDataField
            End Get
            Set
                Me.extensionDataField = value
            End Set
        End Property


        <System.Runtime.Serialization.DataMemberAttribute()> _
        Public Property FirstName() As String
            Get
                Return Me.FirstNameField
            End Get
            Set
                If (Object.ReferenceEquals(Me.FirstNameField, value) <> _
                                                    true) Then
                    Me.FirstNameField = value
                    Me.RaisePropertyChanged("FirstName")
                End If
            End Set
        End Property


        <System.Runtime.Serialization.DataMemberAttribute()> _
        Public Property LastName() As String
            Get
                Return Me.LastNameField
            End Get
            Set
                If (Object.ReferenceEquals(Me.LastNameField, value) <> _
                                                    true) Then
                    Me.LastNameField = value
                    Me.RaisePropertyChanged("LastName")
                End If
            End Set
        End Property
```

As you can see, Visual Studio and WCF provide the tools you need to define and share complex data types across a distributed system. Combined with the other powerful features supported by WCF, you have the tools to build robust, enterprise-quality distributed solutions.

## SUMMARY

This chapter looked at one of the more outstanding capabilities provided to the Visual Basic world. Visual Studio 2012 and .NET are a great combination for building advanced services that take your application to a distributed level.

Though not exhaustive, this chapter broadly outlined the basics of the WCF framework. As you begin to dig more deeply into the technology, you will find strong and extensible capabilities.

From here you will transition to creating custom user interfaces. While we've placed simple applications user interfaces in many of the samples, you have now covered enough of what is needed to work behind complex user interfaces. The next block of chapters moves away from looking at business or application tier code and focuses firmly on the user interface.

# PART III
# Specialized Topics and Libraries

# 12

# XAML Essentials

**WROX.COM CODE DOWNLOADS FOR THIS CHAPTER**

The wrox.com code downloads for this chapter are found at www.wrox.com/remtitle .cgi?isbn=9781118314456 on the Download Code tab. The code is in the chapter 12 download and individually named according to the names throughout the chapter.

XAML has become a mainstream way of creating user interfaces in Visual Studio. There are currently three different user interface technology platforms which use the XAML markup language: Windows Presentation Foundation (WPF), Silverlight, and Window 8 / WinRT.

These platforms vary in many details. Visual elements in one platform may not be available in another. For example, WPF and Silverlight libraries contain a DataGrid element, but the WinRT libraries do not have such an element.

However, many basic concepts are the same in all three platforms. These include layout and composition of user interfaces, working with data, and styling. This chapter will cover those aspects of XAML that all three platforms have in common.

The examples shown in the chapter will work in all three platforms, though occasionally minor changes may be needed for a particular platform. The code downloads for this chapter will contain the examples done in each platform.

This chapter is aimed at those who have little or no experience with XAML. It can be helpful for developers just getting started in XAML, regardless of the XAML platform they will be using.

Readers who have created production-level applications in WPF or Silverlight, and wish to apply XAML for Windows 8 applications, may proceed directly to Chapter 13 on XAML in Windows 8.

One caution is in order. It's not possible to cover everything you'll need to know about XAML is two chapters, regardless of the platform you will be using. Entire books have been written about XAML. If you need to go past the basics presented in these two chapters, you should choose a book that targets the platform you will be using.

## FEATURES SHARED BY ALL XAML PLATFORMS

The XAML markup language is a variant of XML, and basic XAML syntax is the same for all three XAML platforms. The objects used in the XAML may vary; each platform has its own libraries, which may contain objects not available in other XAML platforms. But the syntax used to declare the objects used in a user interface are the same for all three.

The three platforms also share the way visual elements are sized and arranged. This is known as the *layout system*. The layout system is part of the way visual elements and other objects are composed into a complete user interface. This aspect of XAML is usually called the *composition model*, and it is also the same in all three platforms.

User interfaces normally work with data, and need a way to expose data values in the interface. XAML has a sophisticated data binding subsystem for this purpose, and its fundamental features work the same in all three platforms.

To present lists of data items to users, XAML allows a user interface developer to create a *data template* that determines what the user will see for a particular item. This is one of the most powerful capabilities of XAML, and again works fundamentally the same in all three platforms.

Finally, XAML includes ways to customize and refine user interfaces via styles and control templates. Styles are a standard way of setting a family of properties for visual elements, and while the properties affected may change with the three platforms, the way styles are used to set property values are the same. Similarly, control templates control the visual appearance of controls, and while details vary, all three platforms use control templates in a conceptually similar fashion.

## THE XAML MARKUP LANGUAGE

XAML stands for eXtensible Application Markup Language. It's pronounced "xammel," rhyming with "camel."

Most of the XAML in your applications will be produced by visual designers. However, it is sometimes necessary to edit XAML directly, and you also need to understand the role that XAML plays in your application. Consequently, in this chapter, XAML will be presented as bare markup language, with no reference to the visual designers. Chapter 13 will introduce the visual designer specifically for Window 8 XAML applications.

XAML is XML with a certain schema. You can edit it with any text editor, as long as you produce valid XAML. But like all XML, it's tedious to edit, which is why you'll want to use visual designers whenever possible.

There's nothing magical about XAML. Anything that's possible in XAML is also possible in code, though the XAML is often more compact and easier to understand.

Strictly speaking, XAML isn't just for user interfaces. Windows Workflow uses XAML to describe workflows, for example. However, for simplicity in this book, XAML will be discussed solely as a user interface technology.

## A Sample Page of XAML

A page of XAML describes a set of instances of .NET classes. It includes property settings for those classes, and how the classes are grouped together. The grouping takes the form of a logical tree. There is a root element, which contains other elements. Those elements may then contain sub-elements, and so on.

Here's an example to illustrate the idea. This is real, valid XAML, though for a very simple and pointless user interface (code file: `FirstExample.xaml`):

```
<UserControl x:Class="SampleUC"
    xmlns="http://schemas.microsoft.com/winfx/2006/xaml/presentation"
    xmlns:x="http://schemas.microsoft.com/winfx/2006/xaml"
    Height="300" Width="300" >
    <Border BorderThickness="4" BorderBrush="Blue">
        <StackPanel>
            <Button Margin="5">I'm a button</Button>
            <Image Margin="5" Source="http://billyhollis.com/TextureWavy.jpg" />
            <TextBox Margin="5">Text for editing</TextBox>
        </StackPanel>
    </Border>
</UserControl>
```

The first line tells us that the root element you are using is a `UserControl`. Almost any XAML element can be a root element, but normally the root is a container for holding other elements. `Page`, `Window`, and `UserControl` are common root elements.

The declaration of the `UserControl` element includes several XML attributes. Some of them are simple property settings, such as the `Height` and `Width` of the `UserControl`. Others are more complex, and declare XML namespaces. These namespaces refer to the assemblies that contain the elements references in the rest of the XAML page. At first, you won't have to worry about these, because the designers will be inserting and managing them for you. The previous page, in fact, was generated by the Visual Studio designer.

This chapter assumes that you have a minimal understanding of XML, at least to the point of understanding the difference between an XML element and an XML attribute, and what an XML namespace is. If that's not true for you, then you should gain some exposure to XML basics before working with XAML.

After the `UserControl` element's declaration, the next element is a `Border`. This visual element illustrates a basic principle about XAML. Each visual element normally has a narrow functionality set. The `Border` element only knows how to draw a border. It doesn't know how to scroll, for example; a different element is needed for that, called `ScrollViewer`.

The `Border` also doesn't know how to arrange other elements. In fact, it can have only a single child. However, that child can be a type of container that does know how to arrange multiple elements. In this case, the `Border` contains a `StackPanel`.

The `StackPanel` can be a container for other elements such as buttons and text boxes. `StackPanel`'s narrow responsibility is just to stack its child elements. (By default, the stacking is vertical.) `StackPanel` doesn't have any capability, for example, to draw a border around itself. It must depend on a `Border` element for that.

The subelements of the `StackPanel` declare the visual elements that will be stacked inside the `StackPanel`. In our example, there are three: a `Button`, an `Image`, and a `TextBox`.

If you place the previous XAML in an application, you can get a visual surface based on it, which would look something like Figure 12-1.

**FIGURE 12-1:** The sample page of XAML, rendered in Windows 8 (left) and WPF in Windows 7 (right)

As the screens in Figure 12-1 indicate, there are some significant differences in the way XAML is rendered on the different platforms. Sometimes defaults are different, as you see in the different default backgrounds. Varying defaults may even affect sizing, as seen in the differing `Button` elements. In Windows 8 XAML, the `Button` is left aligned by default, but it is stretched by default in WPF.

## Code-Behind and Naming of Elements

XAML describes object instances, and sometimes those objects generate events which must be handled. Suppose, for example, the `Button` defined in the XAML you saw earlier needs to cause some code to run when the `Button` is clicked.

Visual Studio allows you to enter such code by double-clicking the Button in the visual designer. XAML also allows hookup of event handler via an XAML attribute. Here is a line of XAML from the earlier example, with the addition of an event handler for the button.

```
<Button Margin="5" Click="Button_Click"> >I'm a button</Button>
```

The code in a code-behind module must have some way to identity a XAML element before it can work with that element. That identification is usually done with a `Name` property, just as it is in other designers.

Naming an element in XAML is not required unless you want to reference the element in code. In the first example of XAML discussed previously, none of the elements had a name.

You can name most elements in XAML using a `Name` attribute, which sets the `Name` property on the element. All routine controls and containers have a `Name` property.

Some elements do not have a name property. XAML provides a special way to reference those elements in code: the `x:Name` attribute. `x:Name` works just like the `Name` property for the purposes of referring to an element in code, but it is available for any element, whether or not it has a `Name` property.

## Getting Our Terminology Straight

In most user interface technologies, the word *control* is used generically to refer to just about anything you might place on a visual design surface. In XAML, the word *control* has a more restrictive meaning. A control in XAML is a visual element that is designed with user input in mind. A `TextBox`, for example, clearly fits that meaning. A `StackPanel` does not.

Containers such as `StackPanels` are generically referred to as panels rather than controls. Controls and panels do not exhaust the possibilities; the `Border` element shown in the earlier example is in a category called decorators.

The generic word for a XAML visual object is an element. That's reflected in the base classes for visual elements, which have names like `UIElement` and `FrameworkElement`. Panels, controls, and decorators, then, are all different categories of elements.

## The UIElement and FrameworkElement Classes

The `UIElement` base class for visual XAML elements implements functionality needed by all elements, such as input via the keyboard, mouse, touch, and stylus. The `FrameworkElement` base class inherits from `UIElement` and adds layout capabilities, data binding, and styling. For routine application development, you will not need to know anything more about these classes.

You will use the `FrameworkElement` type on occasion. For example, the children of a panel are a collection of `FrameworkElement` instances. To loop through such a collection, you'll need an index variable of type `FrameworkElement`.

## Commonly Used Elements

All XAML platforms support some commonly used elements. Two panels are always available: `StackPanel` and `Grid`. Several standard controls are included in all three, including `Button`,

TextBox, Image, Slider, CheckBox, and RadioButton. TextBlock is available in all three platforms for display of text. Border and ScrollViewer are used on all three platforms for drawing borders and scrolling text.

There are other elements that are included in all three platforms, but each platform also has specific elements that other platforms do not have. You'll look at several of the elements specific to Windows 8 in the next chapter.

## Property Setting: Attribute Syntax vs. Element Syntax

As mentioned in the very first description of XAML, visual elements can have properties set via XML attributes. Here's another example:

```
<StackPanel Width="150" Background="Blue">
```

There is sometimes more going on with such a property setting than meets the eye. Setting the Width property to 150 units is straightforward. However, setting the Background property in this case requires more work under the covers. The setting of "Blue" is transformed by the XAML parser into an element called a SolidColorBrush. That element has a property that holds a color, and the color is set to blue.

There is another way to set a property value besides using an attribute. It's done using a specially constructed XML element. Here is another XAML example, and it yields exactly the same results as the one immediately previous one:

```
<StackPanel Width="150">
    <StackPanel.Background>Blue</StackPanel.Background>
```

In this case the property value of Blue is between two element tags, one starting and one ending. The element tag is constructed from the class name and the property name.

All properties can be set this way. Normally, attributes are used because the XAML is more concise and easier to read. However, sometimes the alternative element-based syntax is needed because an attribute value cannot be used for the desired property value.

For example, the Background property can be set to other types of brushes. (The "Brushes" section to come covers basics on brushes.) One example is a linear gradient brush.

There is no simple string to set the Background to a linear gradient brush. It requires several lines of XAML to do it. Element-based syntax creates a "hole" in the XAML, so to speak, that provides a place to put such additional XAML. Let's see what the previous example of setting the Background property looks like when it is set to a linear gradient brush:

```
<StackPanel Width="150">
    <StackPanel.Background>
        <LinearGradientBrush EndPoint="1,0.5" StartPoint="0,0.5">
            <GradientStop Color="Black" Offset="0" />
            <GradientStop Color="White" Offset="1" />
        </LinearGradientBrush>
    </StackPanel.Background>
```

Don't worry at this point about the detailed syntax of LinearGradientBrush; the visual designers usually write that XAML for you. The point is that the XAML is complex enough that it can't be placed in an attribute. Element-based syntax is a necessity to set the value of the `Background` property to a `LinearGradientBrush`.

You must become comfortable switching between attribute-based and element-based syntax in XAML as necessary. In many cases, what begins as a simple attribute-based property must later be changes to a more complex value that requires element-based syntax.

## Referencing Additional Namespaces in XAML

As mentioned earlier, the capability to reference a namespace with "xmlns" is a part of the XML standard. You can think of these namespace definitions as similar in concept to specifying an `Imports` statement in Visual Basic or a using statement in C#.

The first example only showed two namespaces:

```
<UserControl x:Class="SampleUC"
    xmlns="http://schemas.microsoft.com/winfx/2006/xaml/presentation"
    xmlns:x="http://schemas.microsoft.com/winfx/2006/xaml"
```

The first namespace is the default XML namespace, and it contains elements that can be used without a prefix, such as `<Button>`. The second namespace includes some helper objects; the `x:Name` attribute discussed previously is from that namespace.

Only one default namespace can exist per XML page. All other namespaces defined in the XML page must have an identifier. The second namespace has such an identifier.

You can add your own namespace definitions to a XAML page to reference other classes. There are several situations in which you might need to do this. If you are using third-party controls, for example, those controls will be in their own namespace, and that namespace will need to be referenced in any XAML page that uses the controls. If you drag third-party controls out of the toolbox, the visual designer may insert additional namespace references into the XAML page for you, but if you are hand-coding those controls into the XAML, you may have to specify the namespace references manually.

If you write your own classes that are used in XAML, you will also need to add a namespace reference to your XAML pages to use those classes. You'll see an example later in this chapter: value converters, which translate property values during the binding process.

Namespace references in XAML don't have to use the URI tag approach. The `xmlns` definition can directly reference the assembly by name.

The different XAML platforms have slightly different syntax for such namespace references. If your local project assembly were named `MyXAMLApp`, in WPF or Silverlight, declaring a namespace for the local assembly would be done like this:

```
xmlns:local="clr-namespace:MyXAMLApp "
```

In Windows 8 XAML, the syntax is slightly different:

```
xmlns:local="using:MyXAMLApp "
```

The XAML editor in Visual Studio offers a drop-down to help you create your namespace declarations, so you don't need to memorize this syntax.

## THE LAYOUT SYSTEM

The previous XAML example indicates an interesting aspect of XAML interfaces. The XAML didn't set the width of the `Border`, the `StackPanel`, the `Button`, the `Image`, or the `TextBox`. Only the `UserControl`'s width was declared. Everything else automatically sized itself, based on the width of its container.

You can create XAML interfaces in which all sizes and positions are explicitly declared, just like you can in older technologies such as Windows Forms. For most applications, that is most assuredly not recommended. You'll take maximum advantage of XAML by using its built-in features for sizing and positioning visual elements. Used properly, these features can allow your application to run at varying resolutions and sizes. (Wouldn't it be nice to stop those arguments about whether to support 800×600 or 1024×768 or 1280×1024?)

## Measurement Units

To explicitly set size and position of units in XAML, a special type of unit is used. It can be thought of as a "virtual pixel." That is, under default conditions (default desktop dots per inch, for example), one unit will correspond to one pixel. But there are some important differences.

First, the properties holding the units are not integers, as would be common with older pixel-based technologies. The properties are of type `Double`. This allows applications to have a finer grain, which is important if an element is zoomed, for example.

Second, changing factors such as desktop dpi or the browser zoom factor for Silverlight applications will cause the units to change in size accordingly. If the WPF desktop dpi changes from the default of 96 to 120, then a unit becomes 1.25 pixels in width instead of a single pixel in width.

## Panels

If you've done ASP.NET development, you're probably comfortable with the idea that you place your visual elements in a container that does the final arrangement. XAML takes that concept and adds many more options for controlling the final layout result.

If you've concentrated on Windows Forms development, you're probably accustomed to the idea that you should position all of your visual elements precisely, using properties for Left and Top. In that case, you'll need to adjust to a different technique. You must learn to do layout with a combination of explicit positioning and various kinds of automatic layout.

### Different Panels for Different Purposes

In XAML, you can choose from several different panels to contain your visual elements, each performing a different type of layout. Combining and nesting these panels gives even more flexibility.

That means you can't just pick one type of panel and stick with it. Instead, you need to learn what each panel can do and often use the principle of composition to choose the combination of panels that will give you the particular user interface layout that you want.

First, let's discuss some characteristics shared by all panels. Then you'll briefly review three commonly used panels that all three XAML platforms share: `StackPanel`, `Grid`, and `Canvas`.

## The Panel Class

All panels in XAML descend from a class named `Panel`. Since `Panel` is an abstract class, it can't be directly instantiated. It just serves as the base class for all panels, encompassing those included in various XAML libraries and those developed by third parties.

As you saw in our simple example, a panel such as `StackPanel` can contain multiple child elements. Those elements are placed in the panel's `Children` collection. The elements in the `Children` collection must descend from the `FrameworkElement` class.

In code, you can add elements to a panel by using the `Add` method of the `Children` collection, the same way that you would add elements to any other collection. For routine development, you won't need to do that very often. You'll likely be creating interfaces either by doing drag-and-drop in a visual designer, or by typing XAML directly.

When a panel's XAML definition contains other nested visual elements, those visual elements are added to the panel's `Children` collection automatically. You saw that in our first XAML example, which is reproduced here (code file: `FirstExample.xaml`):

```
<UserControl x:Class="SampleUC"
    xmlns="http://schemas.microsoft.com/winfx/2006/xaml/presentation"
    xmlns:x="http://schemas.microsoft.com/winfx/2006/xaml"
    Height="300" Width="300" >
    <Border BorderThickness="4" BorderBrush="Blue">
        <StackPanel>
            <Button Margin="5">I'm a button</Button>
            <Image Margin="5" Source="http://billyhollis.com/TextureWavy.jpg" />
            <TextBox Margin="5">Text for editing</TextBox>
        </StackPanel>
    </Border>
</UserControl>
```

The `Button`, `Image`, and `TextBox` element definitions are inside the definition for `StackPanel`. When the XAML is compiled into a running program, those elements become children of the `StackPanel`.

The order of the elements in the `Children` collection is important. The previous example illustrates this. The final rendered `UserControl` showed the elements stacked in the order in which they were added to the panel.

## StackPanel

You've seen the basic behavior of `StackPanel`. It stacks elements vertically by default, making space for each element.

`StackPanel` can also stack elements horizontally by changing the `Orientation` property to `Horizontal`.

## Attached Properties

To discuss the `Grid` panel, first you need to understand a XAML concept called *attached properties*. These are used to allow the XAML definition of a child element to also contain information the parent panel needs to know about the child.

Attached properties are used for a wide variety of other purposes, too. Some of those will be covered later, but many of them are beyond the scope of this book.

Attached properties have the following form in XAML:

```
<Button FontSize=20 Grid.Column="2" Grid.Row=3>Cancel</Button>
```

Contrast the first two attributes after the `Button` tag. The `FontSize` attribute sets a property value on this instance of the `Button`. However, the `Grid.Column` attribute does not set a property on the `Button`. It sets an *attached property* value on the `Grid` class. The XAML parser automatically handles this difference, handing the value of "2" over to the `Grid` class to store for the `Button` instance.

## Setting Attached Properties in Code

It's occasionally necessary to set attached properties in code. That brings up an interesting twist. The attached property isn't really a property at all; it's a set of shared methods on the class that implements the attached property.

For every attached property, there is a `Get` method on the implementing class and a `Set` method. The methods have a standard naming convention. The `Get` method for `Column` must be named `GetColumn`, for example, and the `Set` method for `Column` is similarly required to be `SetColumn`.

These `Get` and `Set` methods for an attached property take an argument to specify the control to which the property value is "attached." For example, to get the current value of the `Grid.Column` setting for `Button1`, you might use a line of code like this:

```
Dim d As Integer = Grid.GetColumn(Button1)
```

The `Set` method needs one more argument. It contains the property value that is being set. To set the `Grid.Column` attached property on a button named `Button1` to a value of 3, the following code would be used:

```
Grid.SetColumn(Button1, 3)
```

## Grid

The most flexible panel for most XAML applications is the `Grid`. The `Grid` is so flexible and useful that the Visual Studio XAML visual designers use it as the default layout container for a new `Window`, `Page`, or `UserControl`.

For many developers, "grid" is synonymous with "data grid." That association does not apply in XAML. The `Grid` panel in XAML is not a data grid in any sense.

The `Grid` panel allocates its space to cells. Those cells are the intersections of rows and columns. Typically, the first thing you do for a `Grid` is to define the rows and columns of the `Grid`.

The rows do not need to be the same height, and the columns do not need to be the same width. They can be, of course.

A `Grid` has a property called `ColumnDefinitions`, which contains a collection of `ColumnDefinition` elements, each of which is the definition for one column. Similarly there is a `RowDefinitions` property for `RowDefinition` elements. Naturally, you can create these collections in XAML. Here is simple XAML showing `ColumnDefinitions` and `RowDefinitions` for a `Grid`, in this case defining three columns and two rows:

```
<Grid.ColumnDefinitions>
    <ColumnDefinition />
    <ColumnDefinition />
    <ColumnDefinition />
</Grid.ColumnDefinitions>

<Grid.RowDefinitions>
    <RowDefinition />
    <RowDefinition />
</Grid.RowDefinitions>
```

## Sizing Grid Rows and Columns

The previous simple example has no sizing information for the rows or columns. Before presenting the XAML for sizing rows and columns, the sizing options need to be explained. First you'll look at sizing columns, and then you'll relook at the discussion for rows, because they both use the same sizing concepts.

Columns in a `Grid` can be a *fixed width*, a *proportional width*, or an *automatic size*. These settings can be mixed and matched as needed for different columns in the `Grid`:

➤ **Fixed width** works just as you would expect. The width of a column can be set to a specific number of units.

➤ **Automatic width** means that the column is sized to the largest element contained in a cell of that column. If the column does not contain any elements, it has zero width.

➤ **Proportional width** relates the width of a column to the width of other columns. After fixed width columns and automatically sized columns have been sized, any remaining width is divided among proportional width columns.

The amount each proportional column gets depends on a number associated with that column. All the numbers are added up for the proportional width columns to give a sum. Then each column's width is calculated by dividing that column's number by the sum, and multiplying times the available width for all the proportional columns.

Math always sounds complex when expressed in words, so let's look at an example. Suppose you have three proportional width columns, and the numbers for them are 1, 4, and 5. Then the sum of the numbers for all columns is 10. Column one gets 1/10 of the available width, column two gets 4/10 (or two-fifths), and column three gets 5/10 (or a half). If the amount of width left in the `Grid` for proportional columns were 200 units, column one would be 20 units wide, column two would be 80 units, and column three would be 100 units.

The XAML for all three sizing options is straightforward. The `ColumnDefinition`'s `Width` property is used. For a fixed size, `Width` is set to number of units desired. For automatic size, `Width` is set to `Auto`. For a proportional size, `Width` is set to a number with an asterisk at the end.

The following XAML example contains a set of column definitions showing each sizing option. The first column has a fixed width of 60. The second column has an automatic width. The third and fourth columns receive 40% and 60%, respectively, of the remaining width of the `Grid`.

```
<Grid.ColumnDefinitions>
    <ColumnDefinition Width="60" />
```

```
            <ColumnDefinition Width ="Auto"/>
            <ColumnDefinition Width ="4*" />
            <ColumnDefinition Width ="6*" />
        </Grid.ColumnDefinitions>
```

If you create a `Grid` with only one row and the columns as defined in the previous XAML, and then place buttons in each cell of the Grid, the result will look much like Figure 12-2. That example is rendered in Windows 8 XAML on the left and in WPF XAML on the right. The width of the first column is 60 unconditionally, while the width of the second column is based on the width of the button placed in it. The third and fourth columns share what's left, in a ratio of 2 to 3.

 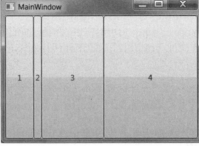

**FIGURE 12-2:** A Grid with four columns defined by the XAML example shown earlier, and with four buttons included to show the sizes and locations of the columns

Notice how narrow the second column is. The content of the button, namely the numeral "2," is quite narrow, and the button automatically sizes to that narrow width. The `Grid` column then sizes itself to contain that `Button` element. You'll see much more in the `Sizing` and `Layout` section later in the chapter.

If you do this example in Windows 8, you'll need to tell the `Button` elements to stretch horizontally and vertically using the `HorizontalAlignment` and `VerticalAlignment` properties. The default for `Button` in WPF is to stretch, but the default for Windows 8 XAML is not to stretch.

The numbers on the last two columns could have been "6*" and "9*," or "100*" and "150*," or any other numbers with a ratio of 2 to 3, and the end result on the screen would be exactly the same. For proportional widths, it doesn't matter what the numbers are. It only matters what fractional portion a column's number makes up of the sum for proportional columns.

The exact same sizing options are available for rows. The only difference is that you use the `Height` property of a `RowDefinition` in place of the `Width` property of a `ColumnDefinition`. To avoid boredom, this won't go through a virtually identical example for rows.

The Visual Studio visual designer contains various ways to define columns and rows. One way is to use special editors. You can get to those editors in the Properties window for the `Grid`. The entry in the Properties window for `ColumnDefinitions` has a button on the right with an ellipsis. Clicking that button brings up the `ColumnDefinitions` editor, which gives you precise control over all the different properties of each `ColumnDefinition`. The `ColumnDefinition` editor is shown in Figure 12-3, with four columns as discussed in the earlier example. There is a similar editor for `RowDefinitions`.

**FIGURE 12-3:** The ColumnDefinition editor in Visual Studio 2012. It is accessed by pressing the button next to the ColumnDefinitions property in the Properties window

## Placing Elements in a Grid

To specify the column and row for an element, you use the Grid.Column and Grid.Row attached properties. The numbering for rows and columns is zero-based, just like all collections in .NET. To place a Button in the second row and third column of a Grid, the Button would be defined inside a Grid with a line of XAML like this:

```
<Button Grid.Row="1" Grid.Column="2">Button text</Button>
```

The default for Grid.Row and Grid.Column are zero. Elements that don't set a row or column end up in the top left cell of the Grid.

You can place multiple elements in the same Grid cell. Those elements, if their areas intersect, are layered on top of one another. Elements later in the Children collection, which means further down in the XAML definition, are rendered on top of earlier elements in the Children collection.

## Spanning Columns and Rows

By default, an element is placed in a single cell of a Grid. However, an element can begin in the cell assigned by Grid.Column and Grid.Row, and then span additional rows and/or columns.

The attached properties `Grid.ColumnSpan` and `Grid.RowSpan` determine the number of columns and rows an element spans. Their default is, of course, 1. You can set either or both for an element. Setting only `Grid.ColumnSpan` restricts an element to a single row, but extends the element into extra columns. Similarly, setting only `Grid.RowSpan` extends through multiple rows in the same column. Setting both causes an element to span a rectangular block of cells.

To see `Grid.Column`, `Grid.Row`, `Grid.ColumnSpan`, and `Grid.RowSpan` in action, let's look at an example. The following XAML defines a `Grid` with several `Buttons`, using varying rows, columns, and spans. Figure 12-4 shows what that `Grid` would look like in design view in Visual Studio for a WPF project. The design view is shown so that you can see the blue lines that define rows and columns, and how buttons span the rows and columns based on their settings in XAML (code file: GridWithButtons.xaml):

```
<Grid>
    <Grid.RowDefinitions>
        <RowDefinition Height="50*" />
        <RowDefinition Height="20*" />
        <RowDefinition Height="30*" />
    </Grid.RowDefinitions>
    <Grid.ColumnDefinitions>
        <ColumnDefinition Width="20*" />
        <ColumnDefinition Width="20*" />
        <ColumnDefinition Width="45*" />
        <ColumnDefinition Width="15*" />
    </Grid.ColumnDefinitions>
    <Button>1 cell</Button>
    <Button Grid.Column="1" Grid.RowSpan="2">2 cells</Button>
    <Button Grid.Row="2" Grid.ColumnSpan="2">2 cells</Button>
    <Button Grid.Column="2" Grid.ColumnSpan="2" Grid.RowSpan="2">4 cells</Button>
    <Button Grid.Column="3" Grid.Row="2">1 cell</Button>
</Grid>
```

## Canvas

The `Canvas` panel is perhaps the easiest panel to understand. It is placed it at the end of the panel discussion, though, because it should be used sparingly in XAML interfaces.

If you're a Windows Forms developer, you will probably feel an affinity for the `Canvas` panel. It positions children in almost exactly the way as a `Form` in Windows Forms. That may tempt you to rely on the `Canvas` so that you can avoid understanding the complexity of the other panels.

You should resist that temptation. While the `Canvas` certainly has valid uses, it should not normally be the dominant element on a XAML user interface. If it is, the interface will not possess many of the best characteristics of a XAML interface. It won't automatically adjust children to fit different aspect ratios, for example. This would be a particularly major drawback for Windows 8 XAML applications.

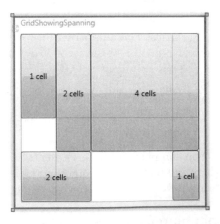

**FIGURE 12-4:** A design view of a Grid, showing elements positioned in various cells and some elements spanning multiple cells. This example is rendered in WPF on Windows 7

However, Canvas is a good choice for several application scenarios. Here are a few examples:

➤ Graphing and charting surfaces

➤ Animation of positions of elements

➤ Surfaces that allow users to move elements around

➤ Positioning elements in certain types of control

## Positioning Child Elements on a Canvas

Children are positioned on a Canvas with the attached properties Canvas.Top and Canvas.Left. These correspond to the Top and Left properties of Windows Forms controls in the way they are used for positioning. The two properties position the upper left corner of an element; Canvas.Top determines the distance down from the top of the Canvas, and Canvas.Left determines the distance over from the left side.

WPF also has Canvas.Bottom and Canvas.Right attached properties, but since Silverlight and Windows 7 lack them, they are not discussed in this chapter.

## Nesting Panels

It is common to nest panels to gain more flexible control over layout. For example, you might want a stack of buttons in a Grid cell. That is achieved by making a StackPanel a child element of a Grid, and then placing the buttons you want as children of the StackPanel. Here is a XAML example (code file: GridContainingStackPanel.xaml):

```
<Grid>
    <Grid.RowDefinitions>
        <RowDefinition />
        <RowDefinition />
    </Grid.RowDefinitions>
    <Grid.ColumnDefinitions>
        <ColumnDefinition />
        <ColumnDefinition />
        <ColumnDefinition />
    </Grid.ColumnDefinitions>
    <StackPanel Grid.Column="2" Grid.Row="1" >
        <Button Margin="4">Save</Button>
        <Button Margin="4">Cancel</Button>
    </StackPanel>
</Grid>
```

As another example, you could put a Canvas in a cell of a Grid to gain pixel-by-pixel positioning just inside that cell.

# Sizing and Layout of Elements

One of the primary goals of XAML is allowing creation of interfaces that scale themselves to the space they are given. With widely varying resolutions, plus the fact that an application window can be in a wide range of sizes, many different factors affect the final rendered size and position of a XAML element. Windows 8 introduces some new complexities in the form of "snapped" application windows.

This section presents an overview of the major factors that affect sizing and layout of XAML elements. It doesn't try to tell you everything there is to know about the subject—just enough to handle the common cases you will run into during application programming.

Don't be surprised if you have to read this section a couple of times to sort out all of the factors involved in sizing and layout. It's a complex subject, but a necessary one to understand if you're going to design anything beyond very simple interfaces in XAML.

## What Is Layout?

In XAML, layout means sizing and arranging the children of a panel. This is a complicated, recursive process. Since panels may contain other panels as children, sizing and positioning must be done at several "levels" before a complete Window or Page can be rendered. The process starts in the root element, and goes down through the tree of child elements. At each level, there is interaction between child elements and their parent to decide on size and position.

If you don't understand some of the mechanisms used for this process, you'll constantly be producing XAML interfaces that don't act the way you expect.

## First Step: Measuring the Child Elements

Measurement is the process of determining the size that an element wants to be when it is rendered. That size is usually called the desired size, and in fact elements have a property named DesiredSize. It may or may not be the actual rendered size; that depends on several other factors, including whether the height and width values are hard-coded, and what the container holding the element wants to do with the element.

The base FrameworkElement class contains several properties that furnish information to the measurement process, including:

➤ Height and Width

➤ MinHeight, MaxHeight, MinWidth, and MaxWidth

➤ Margin

## Using Height and Width Properties

Height and Width work exactly as you would expect. They hard-code the size of an element, just as they do in other user interface technologies. If an element with hard-coded size is placed in a panel, the panel will respect that size and will not change it, even if there's not enough room to show the element and the element must be clipped.

Since these two properties work in a way you'll find familiar, at first you may be tempted to bypass the whole process of understanding XAML's complex sizing process, and just set the sizes you want. For most XAML applications, that's a mistake. It requires giving up much of the flexibility of XAML to respond to different conditions. You should be conservative in using explicit settings for Height and Width; do it only if automatic sizing doesn't fit your needs.

One common place to explicitly set Height and Width is on the root element of your interface. For example, when you create a new WPF Window in Visual Studio, it will have Height and Width explicitly set to default values.

## Applying Minimum and Maximum Values

The next level of control over size is to set a range of values for the height and width of an element. The four properties MinHeight, MaxHeight, MinWidth, and MaxWidth contain the range settings. This discussion is presented in terms of width, but the exact same discussion applies to height.

If MinWidth is set for an element, it won't be sized less than that amount. If a MaxWidth is set, the element won't be made wider than that amount.

Within that range, an element will be sized based on other factors, including the space available within the element's container and the size of child elements (if any).

## Applying a Margin

For the purposes of fitting an element within its container, the element's Margin setting must also be taken into account. The container will have a certain size available for the element; that size must then be reduced by any Margin on the element. If an element has a Margin, room is always made for it, even if that means truncating the control.

Margin can be set uniformly around an element, or Margin can be different for all four sides. Consider a Button with the following XAML definition:

```
<Button Margin="5,10,0,-10">Save</Button>
```

This instructs the layout engine to place 5 units of margin on the left side, 10 units on the top, and no margin on the right side. It also includes a negative margin for the bottom of the Button, which allows the Button to flow outside its normal area by 10 units on the bottom.

## Second Step: Arranging the Child Elements in a Panel

After the measurement phase, an element has either an explicit size or a desired size, and possibly a Margin that must be included. Using that information, the parent panel then arranges each child element inside a space in the panel allocated for the element. For example, for a Grid, the allocated space includes the cell or group of cells determined by the elements Grid.Row, Grid.Column, Grid .Rowspan, and Grid.Columnspan properties.

Arrangement includes placement of the element in the space available, and may include additional adjustments to the size. Any necessary adjustments are made independently for width and height.

The arrangement process depends on several factors:

➤ The type of panel involved

➤ The sizing results from the measurement phase

➤ The values of the HorizontalAlignment and VerticalAlignment properties for an element

Each of these factors can have many different possibilities. The number of combinations of factors is consequently quite large. To explain the process, let's simplify it a bit and leave out some of the less common cases. While the resulting explanation isn't complete, it should be enough for you to understand what happens for most of the situations you are likely to encounter as you begin developing XAML interfaces.

Because height and width are sized and arranged independently, the discussion is focused on an explanation on height. The exact same principles apply to width, with changes for the names of the properties involved.

## Desired or Required Height vs. Available Height

During the arrangement phase, the final rendered height for an element must be decided. The first factor to consider is whether the element's explicit or desired height will fit in the space allocated for the element. In proper Goldilocks fashion, the allocated height in the panel might be too big, too small, or just right.

If the allocated height happens to be just what the element wants for a height, then the process is finished. That's the height that's used, and the element exactly fills the allocated space from top to bottom.

If the allocated height is too small, then the element must be sized bigger than the allocated height. In that case, the visual part of the element is a truncated portion of the element. How the truncation is done depends on the vertical positioning of the element, which you'll take up later.

If the allocated height is bigger than the element needs, then the actual height of the element depends on whether the height was explicitly set. For an explicit height, that's the height used for rendering. For a desired height, the actual rendered height depends on the value of the `VerticalAlignment` property. That property is also used for vertical positioning of the element.

## Vertical Positioning and the VerticalAlignment Property

The `VerticalAlignment` property has four possible values: `Top`, `Center`, `Bottom`, or `Stretch`. `Stretch` is the default.

The vertical positioning of an element depends on this setting. `Top`, `Center`, and `Bottom` position the edges of the control. The `Stretch` setting causes more complex decision making, so the other settings will be considered first.

As you would probably expect, if you set your element with a `VerticalAlignment` of `Top`, the top edge of the element will be at the top of the allocated space. That's true whether the element is too tall or too short for its space. If the element is too tall for its space, then the top of the element is at the top of the space and the element is truncated at the bottom. If the element is too short for its space, then the element is positioned at the top of the space and any space that's left over is simply unused by the element. Figure 12-5 shows the visual effect of both cases. Examples are shown in Figure 12-5 of height set

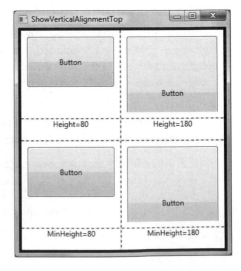

**FIGURE 12-5:** Four Buttons with VerticalAlignment of Top and a Margin of 10, all contained in a Grid

both with the Height property and the MinHeight property, and as you can see, the results are the same for a VerticalAlignment of Top.

The left Buttons are too short for their allocated space. The right Buttons are too tall for their allocated height, so they are truncated. A Border decorator around the Grid is used for clarity, and the Grid has ShowGridLines set to True to let you see the Grid's cells.

Similarly, a VerticalAlignment of Bottom places the bottom edge at the bottom of the allocation space, and clips or leaves empty space at the top, as necessary. A VerticalAlignment of Center places the center of the control at the center of the allocated space, and clips or leaves empty space at both top and bottom.

If VerticalAlignment is set to Stretch, and the height is too big, then the result is the same as if VerticalAlignment has been set to Top. If VerticalAlignment is set to Stretch, and the height is smaller than the allocated height, then the result depends on whether the height was explicitly set or just a desired height. For a desired height, the element will be stretched to fill the entire vertical space available to it.

For height that is explicitly set but shorter than the allocated height, the effect is the same as if VerticalAlignment had been set to Center. The element gets its required height and is centered vertically in the allocated space, leaving extra space at the top and bottom.

There are a lot of combinations, and it's hard to keep them straight at first. However, most XAML developers find that predicting the effects of sizing and alignment becomes second nature after a while.

The process for arriving at a final width is conceptually identical to the one for height. Of course, the properties used are different. The property used for final position is named HorizontalAlignment instead of VerticalAlignment, and it has values of Left, Center, Right, and Stretch. However, if you understand the discussion on height, you should have no problem mapping the concepts to width.

## Arrangement in a StackPanel

The arrangement phase is somewhat different in a StackPanel. If a StackPanel's Orientation property is at the default of Vertical, then a StackPanel will only stretch elements horizontally. Even if VerticalAlignment for an element is set to Stretch, the element won't be stretched vertically beyond its desired or hard-coded size.

This makes complete sense, because the StackPanel expects other elements to possible be stacked underneath a child, so it would not be appropriate to stretch a child arbitrarily.

However, a vertical StackPanel will stretch horizontally if the HorizontalAlignment is set to Stretch. If the HorizontalAlignment is set to anything else, the element will not be stretched. It will remain at its desired or hard-coded width, and positioned according the HorizontalAlignment, much as an element in a Grid cell would be positioned horizontally.

If the StackPanel's Orientation is set to Horizontal, then the vertical and horizontal dimensions merely swap the way they work in the above description.

## CONTROLS AND CONTENT

Earlier in this chapter, a control was defined as an element that is intended for user input. All XAML elements can respond to mouse and keyboard events, but elements such as the Grid do not, by default, do anything with those events. Controls possess functionality to process events and respond to them in some way.

The base Control class implements a lot of functionality needed by all controls, including:

- ➤ Font properties for sizing and formatting of text
- ➤ Properties for a background, foreground, and border
- ➤ The TabIndex property to control the tab order
- ➤ The capability to use a *template* to radically alter the appearance of a control

Most developers will have no issues in using these properties, so detailed descriptions are not necessary. This chapter does include a section on Brushes, which is relevant for setting Foreground and Background properties. Also, a section on control templates is included toward the end of the chapter to describe how to alter the fundamental appearance of a control.

## Content Controls

Some controls in XAML descend from a base class named ContentControl, and have a property named Content. It is of type Object. You can set the Content property to any .NET object, and XAML will attempt to render it.

The Content property can be set explicitly, or by placing something between the tags of a ContentControl. Both of these are shown in this XAML example:

```
<Button Content="Save" />
<Button>
    Cancel
</Button>
```

These two ways of expressing a Button are equivalent. In either case, the Content property is set to a string.

Even though the Content property can be set to any object, from the standpoint of rendering content, objects fall into only two categories: objects that descend from the FrameworkElement class and objects that don't.

For general objects that do not descend from FrameworkElement, their rendering is simple. XAML calls the ToString method of the object, and uses the result as string-based content. XAML automatically creates a simple, lightweight text container called a TextBlock to hold and render the string.

That's the type of rendering used in all of the Button examples shown in the chapter up to this point. Since String is just another .NET type, XAML can call the ToString method (which just returns the string!) and places that in a XAML TextBlock created for the purpose.

For objects that do descend from UIElement, XAML already knows how to render them. They all have rendering behavior built in.

# Implications of the Content Model

The concept of `Content` for controls is a game changer in terms of designing user interfaces. In older technologies, what you could place in controls such as buttons and tooltips was very restricted. In XAML, it's very open. You can set the `Content` property of `Button` to a `Grid`, for example, and then put whatever you like inside the `Grid`.

For example, if you need to put both an `Image` and a string in a XAML button, all you need do is construct appropriate content (code file: `ButtonWithContent.xaml`):

```
<Button Margin="5">
    <Grid>
        <Grid.ColumnDefinitions>
            <ColumnDefinition Width="Auto" />
            <ColumnDefinition />
        </Grid.ColumnDefinitions>
        <Image MaxHeight="60"
            Source="http://billyhollis.com/SkewedBooks.png" />
        <TextBlock Grid.Column="1" TextWrapping="Wrap"
                Margin="3" Text="Order Books" />
    </Grid>
</Button>
```

This would yield a `Button` with the interior rendered exactly the way you specified. Figure 12-6 shows this XAML rendered in both WPF and Windows 8. The `Button` on the left is rendered in Windows 8 XAML, and the `Button` on the right is rendered in WPF on Windows 7, both using exactly the same XAML.

**FIGURE 12-6:** A Button with its interior determined by content featuring an Image and some text inside a Grid panel

Notice that you have complete control over how the image and text are arranged. In older technologies, some `Button` controls had minimal capability to display images and text, but control was always limited to a few choices.

The difference in XAML is based on the composition model. In older technologies, a `Button` control was totally responsible for its own internal layout. In essence, the `Button` had a layout engine built into it. It wasn't really practical to make that layout engine very flexible.

In XAML, the `Button` *does not have any layout capability built in*. It delegates layout to other XAML elements that specialize in layout. That means the entire spectrum of layout flexibility from the panels and related elements in XAML can be used inside a `Button` or other `ContentControl`. A `Button` can look like anything you like. Such capabilities as playing video inside a `Button` are possible and easy to construct (though you probably will not need particular capability in a typical business application).

Another example that illustrates the implications of the `Content` concept is XAML is the `ScrollViewer`. This element is responsible for scrolling on all three XAML platforms. `ScrollViewer` is a `ContentControl`, with the ability to scroll its content. That means you can make anything scrollable by placing it as content inside a `ScrollViewer`.

You can change our earlier example of XAML to allow scrolling of the `StackPanel` and its children very simply (code file: `ScrollingStackPanel.xaml`):

```
<UserControl x:Class="SampleUC"
    xmlns="http://schemas.microsoft.com/winfx/2006/xaml/presentation"
    xmlns:x="http://schemas.microsoft.com/winfx/2006/xaml"
    Height="300" Width="300" >
    <Border BorderThickness="4" BorderBrush="Blue">
        <ScrollViewer>
            <StackPanel>
                <Button Margin="5">I'm a button</Button>
                <Image Margin="5"
                Source="http://billyhollis.com/TextureWavy.jpg"
                 />
                <TextBox Margin="5">Text for editing</TextBox>
            </StackPanel>
        </ScrollViewer>
    </Border>
</UserControl>
```

## Brushes

Controls and other elements have properties such as `Foreground`, `Background`, `Fill`, `Stroke`, and `BorderBrush` to control how the elements are rendered. These properties are all of type `Brush`. In earlier technologies, you might expect properties like these to be of type `Color`, but the `Brush` type is more general and adds flexibility.

### Expressing Colors in XAML

There are colors in XAML, of course. One type of `Brush` is a `SolidColorBrush`, and a `Color` is used to specify the solid color to be used.

Colors can be expressed in XAML in several ways. Each XAML platform has a set of named colors, accessible in code through the `Colors` class. The list is longer in some XAML platforms than others, but every XAML platform has the common colors you would expect, such as `Red`, `Blue`, `Yellow`, and so on.

Using a named color, the XAML for defining a background of solid green in a `Border` element looks like this:

```
<Border Background="Green"></Border>
```

The is parsed by the XAML engine to mean "create a `SolidColorBrush` using the named color `Green` and assign it to the `Background` of the `Border`."

Colors can also be specified by HTML-like RGB values. The `Border` could have a grayish-cyan color set with this XAML:

```
<Border Background="#20A79E"></Border>
```

However, even though the XAML parser understands such colors, the visual designers will never insert RGB color values this way. Instead, the designers will insert colors with 4 hex pairs instead of 3, like this:

```
<Border Background="#FF20A79E"></Border>
```

The extra hex pair is inserted before the hex pairs for the red, green, and blue channels. That beginning hex pair (FF in the previous XAML) specifies the *alpha channel*, which controls the translucency of the color. Translucency ranges from FF (fully opaque) to 00 (fully transparent).

## Layering Translucent Elements

In addition to getting translucency via the alpha channel, elements have an `Opacity` property. It ranges from 1 (full opaque) to 0 (fully transparent). It is of type `Double`, so it can take very fine grained values in between those two.

If elements are layered, and have translucent colors and/or translucency from their `Opacity` setting, the rendering engine will resolve all the layers for each pixel it paints. You may wish to experiment with translucent colors and the `Opacity` property to see some of the effects you can produce.

## LinearGradientBrush and RadialGradientBrush

Because `Foreground`, `Background`, etc. are of type `Brush`, they can accept any value that is descended from that base type. Besides `SolidColorBrush`, there is one other brush type that is available for all three XAML platforms: `LinearGradientBrush`. Each individual XAML platform then has additional brushes. WPF has `RadialGradientBrush`, `ImageBrush`, and `VisualBrush`, Silverlight has `RadialGradientBrush`, `ImageBrush`, and `VideoBrush`, and Windows 8 XAML has `TileBrush`.

`LinearGradientBrush` can accept more than one color. It has a collection of `GradientStop` objects, and each `GradientStop` has a color. `LinearGradientBrush` then blends colors in a linear interpolation during rendering.

You don't really need to know the syntax of `LinearGradientBrush` in detail at this point. The visual designers do a good job of letting you create a `LinearGradientBrush`. The following is a typical `LinearGradientBrush` in XAML. Figure 12-7 shows the result of using it to fill a `Rectangle`.

**FIGURE 12-7:** A Rectangle filled with a LinearGradientBrush that is Black in the upper left corner and White in the lower right

```
<LinearGradientBrush EndPoint="1,1" StartPoint="0,0">
    <GradientStop Color="Black" Offset="0" />
    <GradientStop Color="White" Offset="1" />
</LinearGradientBrush>
```

The `StartPoint` and `EndPoint` properties of the `LinearGradientBrush` are relative to the element's bounding box. Thus, a `StartPoint` of "0,0" is the upper left corner of the element, and an `EndPoint` of "1,1" is the lower right corner. Any fractional values can be used for these properties, including values that get outside the bounding box.

The gradient stops are then positioned along a line drawn from the `StartPoint` to the `EndPoint`. The `Offset` property of the `GradientStop` determines its position along that line. Offset of "0" means the `StartPoint`, and an Offset of "1" means the `EndPoint`. `Offset` values may be anywhere in between, and a single `LinearGradientBrush` may have any number of `GradientStops` with differing `Offset` properties.

## Importance of Gradients

You might think gradient brushes are frivolous, but used judiciously, they can dramatically improve the look of your application. Instead of the monochrome battleship gray that you might have used in the past, gradients can impart a natural feel to an application. After all, the real world does not contain much monochrome. Users are primed to consider monochrome as artificial, and gradients as natural.

The key is to create subtle gradients that are almost unnoticed by the user. Many developers start by using garish gradients that stand out. That is rarely a good use of that capability.

# RESOURCES IN XAML

Efficient developers like to create capabilities once, and then reuse them as necessary. The usual object-oriented techniques for reuse are available in XAML, because the .NET Framework provides them. But XAML also includes a special capability to create constructs for reuse, in the form of XAML resources.

If you are an experienced .NET developer, the term *resources* may already be familiar to you. .NET supports resources for capabilities such as localization. Resource files in .NET normally have the extension .resx. **However, that's a completely separate concept from XAML resources.** This section has nothing to do with .resx files, localization, or any of the subjects you might normally associate with .NET resources.

In XAML, the term *resources* has a different meaning. XAML resources are objects that are declared once and then available for use in several places. Resources are usually declared in XAML, but as with all other XAML objects, they can also be created in code. In this chapter, you will work exclusively with XAML resources created in XAML.

## The Resources Property

XAML elements have a property named Resources, and it holds a dictionary of objects called a ResourceDictionary. Any type of object can go in the dictionary.

Because it's a dictionary, every item in a ResourceDictionary needs a key. This key is normally supplied with another helper capability in the x: namespace, which is the x:Key attribute.

To see the syntax, suppose our UserControl in the original example needed to have a linear gradient brush that would be used for multiple elements. Syntax to declare such a brush in the UserControl's resources dictionary looks like this:

```
<UserControl.Resources>
    <LinearGradientBrush x:Key="ReusableBrush"
                         EndPoint="1,0.5" StartPoint="0,0.5">
        <GradientStop Color="Blue" Offset="0" />
        <GradientStop Color="Turquoise" Offset="1" />
    </LinearGradientBrush>
</UserControl.Resources>
```

This brush can then be applied to any property that takes a brush, for any element in the UserControl. The syntax for applying the brush to a Button's Foreground property looks like this:

```
<Button Margin="5" Click="Button_Click"
        Foreground="{StaticResource ReusableBrush}">
    I'm a button
</Button>
```

When a property is set to a resource, the resource can be located on that element, its parent, or any ancestor of the element in the tree. For resources that need to be shared among all visual surfaces in an application, there is a Resources property for the Application object. The Application object is declared in a XAML file named Application.xaml in WPF, or App.xaml in Silverlight or WinRT.

## More about Resource Dictionaries

Beginning XAML developers often do not realize that the largest portion of XAML in a typical application is located in various resource dictionaries. Styles and control templates, covered later in this chapter, are normally placed in resource dictionaries.

A ResourceDictionary can hold any type of object, and reusable nonvisual objects are also often placed there. You'll see an example in the next section on data binding when we discuss value converters.

In addition to being places in the Resources property, as in the previous UserControl example, ResourceDictionary collections can also be placed in their own dedicated XAML files for sharing among multiple applications. The syntax for that is beyond the scope of this chapter, but examples of that syntax are found in the help files for the ResourceDictionary class.

## Scope of a Resource

As mentioned, a resource is located by going up the tree through parents of the current element. As soon a resource matching a resource key is found, the search stops.

That means that it's possible to "override" resources. If you have a resource named "StandardForegroundBrush" at the application level, it can be used throughout the application. But suppose in a single UserControl, another resource is defined in the UserControl's Resources property with the same name of "StandardForegroundBrush." Elements in that UserControl use the local version of the resource.

Elements in other parts of the application will not encounter that resource in their search for "StandardForegroundBrush," so they will use the one at the application level instead.

## DATA BINDING

Most business applications deal extensively with data. As a developer, you have a constant need to expose data in a user interface.

You can do that in a brute-force fashion by writing a lot of code to move data between user interface elements and data containers. However, such code is repetitive, bug-prone, tedious to write, and difficult to maintain.

Recognizing the problems with that approach, user interface technologies often offer an alternative called *data binding*, which automates much of the process of moving data into user interface elements. You're probably familiar with data binding from such earlier user interface technologies

XAML includes a data binding subsystem, and it's one of the most advanced and powerful of any user interface technology stack. If you have been skeptical of data binding in other technologies, you should put that doubt aside and fully embrace data binding in XAML. It's a necessity for developing anything more than trivial programs.

## Data Binding: Fundamental Concepts

At its most fundamental, data binding is an association between a property on one object and a property on a different object. The value in one of the properties is used to automatically update the value in the other property.

Suppose a data object of type `Book` had a property named `Title`. You can set up a binding in XAML so that the value in that property was automatically moved into the `Text` property of a `TextBox` named `TitleTextBox`.

To get some terminology straight, in this case the `Title` property of the `Book` object was the source of the data, and the `Text` property of `TitleTextBox` was the target. That distinction is important; several data binding capabilities require you to understand it. Typically, the source is where the data comes from, and the target is something in a user interface to expose the data to the user. Figure 12-8 diagrams the objects used in this example, and applies this new terminology to them.

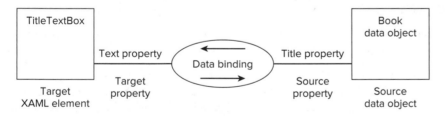

**FIGURE 12-8:** The Book object on the right contains the source property, named Title. The TitleTextBox object contains the target property, which is the Text property

For XAML data binding, the target property is always a property on a XAML object. The source property might be on a XAML object, too, or it might be on some other .NET object, such as a `Book` object created in code.

The target property of a data binding must be a special type of property called a *dependency property*. Almost all the properties you would ever likely use as the target of a binding are dependency properties, so this isn't normally a concern. However, if you advance to writing your own elements that need bindable target properties, you'll need to learn more about dependency properties. Creating objects with dependency properties is an advanced XAML topic, and is not covered in this book.

# The Binding Class and Binding Expressions

The ellipse in the middle of the diagram in Figure 12-8 represents the activities needed to transfer property values back and forth between the target element and the source data object. Those activities are carried out by an instance of the `Binding` class.

The `Binding` class has properties to configure the binding. The two most commonly used properties are the `Path` property, which specifies the source property for the binding, and the `Mode`, which determines which ways the property values can flow.

Binding objects are most commonly defined in XAML with a binding expression, which is a special type of markup expression.

## What Is a Markup Expression?

A *markup expression* is a XAML construct that allows definition of a fairly complex object instance in a single string. The string is delimited by braces, and the first word inside the leading brace indicates the type of markup expression.

You have already seen one simple markup expression. The syntax for assigning a property to a resource is a markup expression:

```
Foreground="{StaticResource ReusableBrush}"
```

The `StaticResource` type of markup expression tells the XAML parser to go look for a resource with the name that is included in the expression.

## What Is a Binding Expression?

The specific type of markup expression used to define a data binding is usually called a *binding expression*. The result of a binding expression is an instance of the `Binding` class, with appropriate property values set on the instance.

Here is a simple binding expression that will bind the `Text` property of a `TextBox` to a `Title` property of a data object:

```
<TextBox Text="{Binding Title}" />
```

This is actually a shortcut version of a slightly longer binding expression, which is:

```
<TextBox Text="{Binding Path=Title}" />
```

In this binding expression, it's more explicit that the `Path` property of the `Binding` object is being set to point to a `Title` property. If necessary, additional properties can be set for the `Binding` object, with each property setting in the binding expression separated by a comma. This example sets both the data property and another property called `Mode`:

```
<TextBox Text="{Binding Path=Title, Mode=TwoWay}" />
```

The `Mode` property specifies whether data is transferred only from the data object to the visual element (`Mode=OneWay`) or if data is transferred both ways between the data object and visual element (`Mode=TwoWay`). Depending on the XAML platform other values for `Mode` are also possible. Note that a `OneWay` binding is essentially read-only—changes to the visual element based on user input are *not* transferred back to the data object.

The default for the Mode property varies depending on the XAML platform. For Silverlight and Windows 8, the default mode is always OneWay. For WPF, the default is more complicated; if you need details, consult the Mode property in the WPF documentation.

Other properties that are commonly set in binding expressions are the ElementName property, which allows the data source to be another element instead of a normal data object, and Converter, which specifies an object for converting the data during the binding process. Both are discussed in the next section.

## DataContext

The previous examples assume there is a data source object (in our case with a Title property), but the binding expression contains nothing to identify the data source. How, then, does a binding on a XAML element find its data source? That is done with an element property called DataContext.

If no data source is specified in a binding, then the Binding object uses an object specified by the DataContext property as its data source. However, it's not necessary to set DataContext for every element that has a binding. DataContext can be set on a container, and elements inside the container are able to use that DataContext.

To be a bit more precise, DataContext is an *inherited property*. Elements that don't have a setting for the property inherit the setting from something further up the tree of elements in the user interface.

Normally, DataContext is set at the root level (for a UserControl or Page), or for a panel on a visual surface (such as Grid or StackPanel). DataContext can be set for individual elements such as TextBox elements, but it's rarely appropriate to do that.

## Data Bindings between XAML Elements

As mentioned earlier, the target of a data binding is always a XAML element. The default data source is specified by the DataContext property.

However, there are other possibilities for the data source. One of them is to let the source be another XAML element.

If the source is also a XAML element, you can specify that element as part of the binding. To do that, you use the aptly named ElementName property of the binding. ElementName can be set to any XAML element in your XAML page that has a name.

Binding between XAML elements can provide more interactivity in your interface designs. Here is an example to illustrate. Suppose you would like to have a user interface with a CheckBox to indicate if a patient smokes, and a TextBox to find out how many cigarettes a day the patient smokes. Good interactive design would suggest that the TextBox needs to be enabled only when the CheckBox is checked.

Let's assume the CheckBox is named PatientSmokesCheckBox, and the TextBox is named Number-OfCigarettesTextBox. You can create that behavior described previously by binding the IsEnabled property of the TextBox to the IsChecked property of the CheckBox. The binding would be set up on the TextBox, and would look like this:

```
<TextBox IsEnabled="{Binding ElementName=PatientSmokesCheckBox, Path=IsChecked}"...
```

If you include such a binding, checking the CheckBox will cause the TextBox to be enabled and thus available to the user. Unchecking the CheckBox will disable the TextBox.

In previous user interface technologies, you could only make such an association in code, by handling an event on the CheckBox and subsequently setting the TextBox to be enabled or disabled. In XAML, you can do it declaratively, allowing faster development and less chance of a bug.

Here's another example: Suppose you have a button that sits on top of content the reader might need to see. You may wish to allow the user to make the button translucent, so that the content underneath can be seen. In XAML, you can accomplish that by setting a binding between a value on a slider control and the Opacity property of the Button. The following XAML snippet contains an example. You can try it out by creating a new XAML application in Visual Studio for any of the three platforms, and including the XAML snippet:

```
<StackPanel>
    <TextBlock >The button can become translucent</TextBlock>
    <Slider Name="OpacitySlider"  Value="1" Maximum="1"
            Minimum="0.1" LargeChange="0.1" SmallChange="0.01" />
    <Button Opacity="{Binding Path=Value, ElementName=OpacitySlider}"
            Name="Button1" Width="75">
        Slide the bar to make me translucent
    </Button>
</StackPanel>
```

Notice that the Slider restricts its value to be between 0.1 to 1. That's because the Opacity property is in the range from 0 to 1, with 0 being completely transparent. With the lowest value set to 0.1, the Button cannot completely disappear.

The binding expression on the Button is:

```
Opacity="{Binding Path=Value, ElementName=OpacitySlider}"
```

This sets the Opacity property of the button to the Value property of the OpacitySlider control, with no code or event handling required. If you create the example, you can see this in action. As you move the slider, the Button will become translucent to match the slider's Value setting.

## Other Ways to Specify a Data Source

There are two additional properties of a binding that can specify the source object; the Source property and the RelativeSource property.

The Source property names an object already defined in XAML as the source object. It differs from ElementName because the source object need not be a XAML element. It can be any .NET object that can be defined in XAML.

Most commonly, the Source property is set to an object that is defined in XAML as a XAML resource. That can lead to a fairly complex binding expression. Here's an example of the syntax:

```
<UserControl.Resources>
    <local:Settings x:Key="MySettings" MaxPages="50" />
</UserControl.Resources>
<Grid>
    <TextBlock Text="{Binding Source={StaticResource MySettings},
```

```
        Path=MaxPages}" />
        </Grid>
```

The `Source` property is set with another markup expression inside the binding expression. That inner markup expression indicates that the data source is the `Settings` object declared as a resource.

The `RelativeSource` property points to an object indirectly, by using the bound element as a starting point of the reference. The object can point to itself, so that one of its properties is bound to another.

The `RelativeSource` property can also point to the parent of the bound object, or to some other ancestor. This capability is most often used in data templates and control templates. You won't be showing any examples of that usage in this chapter.

## Property Change Notification

Binding objects always know when properties change in XAML elements. That capability is part of the dependency property system.

However, binding objects also need to know when data source objects change. That's no problem if they are elements, that is, if `ElementName` or `RelativeSource` is used to specify the data source. However, for normal data objects, an additional capability is needed called property change notification, which means that the object raises an event when a property changes.

Data objects that you create do not have property change notification unless you build it into the classes for those data objects. If you leave it out, changing the value of a source property in code will not typically cause the XAML element that is bound to the property to be updated.

To give property change notification capability to your data objects, you must implement an interface called `INotifyPropertyChanged`. This interface predates XAML, so many data object frameworks will have this interface in place on the data objects they create.

## Data Conversion during Binding

Sometimes the value in a data object can't be used directly to set an element property. For example, a phone number might be represented in a data object as nine consecutive digits, but you would prefer it to be placed in a `TextBox` as a formatted phone number with parentheses and dashes. When an edited phone number is transferred back to the data object, the formatting needs to be stripped out.

Direct binding also might not work if the data types of the source and target properties don't match. For example, suppose you had a `TextBox` that was bound to the quantity on hand of an item. A negative quantity means the item is on backorder. You might want the background of that `TextBox` to be different for items on backorder.

That means the `Background` property for the `TextBox` needs to be bound to a `Quantity` property on a data object. However, the `Quantity` is probably an integer property, and `Background` is a `Brush`. So it's necessary to peek at the value in `Quantity` and return an appropriate `Brush` to paint the background of the `TextBox`.

To handle such binding cases in XAML, you must create a type of object called a *value converter*. This object is responsible for any necessary conversion of values in either binding direction. It can convert between two properties of the same type, as in the phone number scenario, or between two properties of different types. The binding between a Quantity (of type Integer) and a Background (of type Brush) would be an example of a binding between two different data types. An example of such a value converter is presented in the section "Example: A Quantity-to-Brush converter."

## The IValueConverter Interface

A value converter is a .NET class that implements the IValueConverter interface. In WPF and Silverlight, this interface is in the System.Windows.Data namespace. In Windows 8 / WinRT, the interface is in Windows.UI.Xaml.Data.

The IValueConverter interface contains two methods. The Convert method takes the value in the source property (usually a property of a data object) and creates the value that should be placed in the target property (usually a property of some XAML element). The ConvertBack method does the reverse; it takes the value in the target XAML element and changes it as necessary to place it back in the source.

Note that the ConvertBack method isn't needed if the binding is one-way, because it will never be called. It still must be implemented in the class to satisfy the interface, but it can just return a null value.

The method signature for Convert and ConvertBack are slightly different in value converters for Windows 8 XAML. That means you can't simply copy value converter code used in WPF or Silverlight straight to Windows 8. You will need to make minor changes to the argument lists in the Convert and ConvertBack methods.

## Example: A Quantity-to-Brush Converter

To create a value converter example for the Quantity to Brush conversion discussed earlier, three parts are needed. First, you need a data object with a Quantity property. Second, you need a value converter that peeks at a quantity value and returns a Brush. Finally, you need a data binding that applies the converter for a particular TextBox.

The complete, running example is available in the code downloads for this chapter, in all three XAML platforms. This walkthrough shows the parts needed and how they look in XAML or code.

For the data object, you will use a very simple Book class. This class is just to demonstrate the concept; it lacks even property change notification, and is not intended to show what a production data object would be like.

```
Public Class Book
    Public Property Title As String
    Public Property Author As String
    Public Property Quantity As String
End Class
```

Our XAML will need an instance of this class declared as a DataContext for our UserControl:

```
<UserControl.DataContext>
    <local:Book Title="Ender's Game"
            Author="Orson Scott Card"
```

```
                        Quantity="-5" />
    </UserControl.DataContext>
```

The value converter, which takes in a quantity value and outputs a corresponding `Brush`, looks like the following code (code file: `QuantityToBrushConverter.vb`):

```vb
Public Class QuantityToBrushConverter
    Implements IValueConverter

    Public Property PositiveBrush As Brush = New SolidColorBrush(Colors.White)
    Public Property NegativeBrush As Brush = New SolidColorBrush(Colors.Yellow)

    Public Function Convert(value As Object, …
        If CInt(value) < 0 Then
            Return NegativeBrush
        Else
            Return PositiveBrush
        End If
    End Function

    Public Function ConvertBack(value As Object, …
        Return Nothing
    End Function
End Class
```

Ellipses are used in the argument list for `Convert` and `ConvertBack`, because those lists vary a bit between platforms. The complete example in the code download contains complete code for each platform.

To be used in a binding, an instance of this value converter can be declared as a resource:

```xml
<UserControl.Resources>
        <local:QuantityToBrushConverter x:Key="QuantityToBrushConverter1" />
</UserControl.Resources>
```

Then a `TextBox` can be created in XAML to allow editing of the quantity value, and display a different background depending on whether the quantity is positive or negative:

```xml
<TextBox Name="QuantityTextBox" Text="{Binding Path=Quantity, Mode=TwoWay}"
        Background="{Binding Path=Quantity, Converter={StaticResource
    QuantityToBrushConverter1}}" />
```

The code downloads show all these parts in action, with a few minor variations between platforms. The downloads also include property change notification, so that when the user changes the quantity, if needed, the background of the `TextBox` also changes when the user leaves the `TextBox`.

The XAML parser only knows about classes after a build in Visual Studio. Sometimes when you attempt to enter XAML, such as the value converter example for converting a quantity to a brush, you'll get an error in the XAML that claims the element is unrecognized. This is usually because you have not done a build on the assembly containing the newly created value converter. Until the build is done, the XAML parser doesn't know the value converter class exists.

## Another Example: Collapsing Unneeded Elements

Because value converters are such an important part of the XAML developer's toolbox, let's quickly look at one more example to stretch your mind a bit.

Sometimes there are elements on a screen that are not always needed. A typical example is the second address line in a mailing-label style address. If the second address line is an empty string, then the element holding that line (typically a `TextBlock`) is unnecessary or even annoying.

A better user experience is gained if the `TextBlock` simply disappears if it's empty. That is done by binding its `Visibility` property to the string. The `Visibility` property type can take values of `Visible` or `Collapsed`. (WPF has an additional value of Hidden.)

It's easy to write a value converter that deals with that situation. It peeks at a string value to see if it's a null value or an empty string. If so, it returns a `Visibility` value of `Collapsed`. If the string has a length greater than zero, it returns a `Visibility` value of `Visible`. Here is such a value converter in code (code file: `AutoCollapse.vb`):

```vb
Imports System
Imports System.Windows
Imports System.Windows.Data

Public Class AutoCollapse
    Implements IValueConverter

    Public Function Convert(ByVal value As Object, …
        If value Is Nothing OrElse value.ToString.Length = 0 Then
            Return Visibility.Collapsed
        Else
            Return Visibility.Visible
        End If
    End Function

    Public Function ConvertBack(ByVal value As Object, …
        Return Nothing
    End Function
End Class
```

## Dealing with Binding Failures

Data bindings which fail do not cause an exception. Instead, the binding simply doesn't do anything, and program execution continues. This is by design, because data binding is used internally for concepts such as control templates in XAML, and a missing or malformed control template that only affects cosmetics should not cause a program to crash.

You can get information on a binding failure in the Output window in Visual Studio. This capability is important because a binding can fail for a number of reasons. For example, if you specify a property on the source data object that does not exist on that object, the binding cannot succeed, and the message in the Output window will include information about the property that was not found.

There are quite a number of other reasons a binding might fail. If a binding is attempted between properties of different types, and no value converter is available to convert the types, the binding will fail.

While the silent failure of data binding makes sense overall, it introduces the possibility of bugs in your XAML programs that you won't notice without looking very closely indeed. Take special care when crafting your bindings, and try to check each one individually in your running program if you can. And check your Output window a lot during development.

## Complex Binding Paths

In some cases, a binding needs to specify a more complex source than a simple property off of the source object. For example, suppose our earlier `Customer` class also had a `Contact` property, and the `Contact` property itself was an object representing information about a person, such as name, phone number, and title. This scenario can be represented graphically in Figure 12-9.

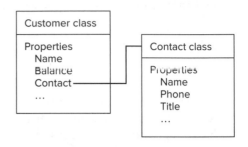

**FIGURE 12-9:** A class diagram of a Customer class and a Contact class, with a property on the Customer class that holds a Contact instance

Now suppose our user interface for a customer also needs to show the name and phone number of the `Contact` for that customer. The following XAML defines two `TextBlock` elements that include bindings to that information:

```
<TextBlock Text="{Binding Path=Contact.Name}" . . . />
<TextBlock Text="{Binding Path=Contact.Phone}" . . . />
```

In this case, the `Path` setting for the binding is not a simple property. It is, in effect, a property of a property. The `Path` of a `Binding` can be set using dot syntax to chain together the required references to get to the final property value needed.

This example only went two levels deep on the path. A `Path` setting can have any number of levels.

One of the most common reasons to use a multilevel path for a binding is working with a property that is a date. Suppose you have a date property called `DatePublished`, and you want to bind to the month or year of the date. You would need binding paths that looks something like the following:

```
<TextBlock Text ="{Binding Path=DatePublished.Month}" . . . />
<TextBlock Text ="{Binding Path=DatePublished.Year}" . . . />
```

## Working with Data Bindings in Code

So far, all the data bindings you've seen have been set up in XAML. Data binding can also be set up and managed in code. The objects that handle the binding process, including the `Binding` object and various helper objects such as value converters, can be instantiated and managed in code just as any other .NET object can be.

You should create your data bindings declaratively in XAML most of the time, but there are situations where that is impractical or impossible. For example, if you are creating highly dynamic user interfaces, the information needed to set up the binding might not be known until runtime. Since XAML is static and completely set when the program starts, any such dynamic management of bindings must be in code.

Creating a data binding in code is not difficult, though the syntax is more complex than the equivalent XAML. You must instantiate the binding, set its properties, and finally tie the binding to the appropriate property. Here is a code sample that creates a binding of a `Text` property on a `TextBox` to a `Balance` property:

```
Dim b As New Binding
b.Path = New PropertyPath("Balance")
BalanceTextBox.SetBinding(TextBox.TextProperty, b)
```

The `Path` property of the binding can't just be set to a string. The `Path` property is of type `PropertyPath`, so it must be set to a `PropertyPath` instance. When declaring a binding in XAML, the `PropertyPath` instance is created automatically via a `TypeConverter`, but you must create it yourself if you create the binding in code.

To tie the binding to the target property, the `SetBinding` method of the XAML element is used. The identifier for the property is `Shared`/`Static` member of the class for the element. That is, to refer to the `Text` property of `BalanceTextBox`, you use `TextBox.TextProperty`.

You may set as many properties on the binding in code as you need. The same properties available in XAML (`Mode`, `ElementName`, etc.) are all available in code.

# DATA TEMPLATES AND ITEMCONTROLS

Most business applications contain lists of data items. In earlier user interface technologies, these items were often displayed in a data grid, with each item in a separate row. Other controls used to show lists included list boxes and combo boxes.

These controls didn't have a lot of flexibility on what to show to the user. A Windows Forms `ListBox`, for example, was restricted to showing a single string for each item. HTML interfaces did a little better, but sophisticated HTML coding was needed for all but the simplest lists.

Displaying lists of data items to the user is an area in which XAML absolutely shines. The developer has exquisite control over what the user will see, and even has capabilities for vary what the user sees depending on various aspects of the data, the role of the user, or many other factors.

The controls in XAML that are designed to work with lists of data items all descend from a base class called `ItemControl`, and they are often referred to collectively as `ItemControls`. `ItemControls` can be bound to a list of data items, so that each item in the list is displayed in the control.

However, `ItemControls` need a way to declare the aspects of the data that will be shown to the user, and how that information will be laid out. That's the function of a *data template*.

This section will cover the basics of `ItemControls` and data templates. For simplicity, most of the content in this section will work with the `ListBox` control. However, the concepts shown apply to all `ItemControls`, though in some cases there are minor variations in details of implementation.

`ListBox` is the most commonly used `ItemControl` in many WPF and Silverlight applications. It is not quite as prominent in Windows 8, though it still works there. In Windows 8, it is more common to use the `ListView` control, which has some difference in how items are arranged and scrolled. However, as mentioned, the concepts are the same, and learning data templates and associated concepts in the context of a `ListBox` will produce expertise that can immediately be applied with `ListView` and other `ItemControls`.

# Setting the Stage with Some Sample Data

If you're going to review lists of data items, you'll need a sample list to serve a tangible example. Here is how you will get a list of data items for our examples.

First you'll need a class for our data objects, such as a Customer data item. A simple version, without property change notification, looks like this (code file: Customer.vb):

```
Public Class Customer

    Public Property Name As String
    Public Property Balance As Integer
    Public Property Active As Boolean
    Public Property ContactName As String
    Public Property Phone As String
    Public Property Logo As String

End Class
```

To declare a collection of these Customer objects in XAML, it's helpful to have another simple class named Customers, which looks like this (code file: Customers.vb):

```
Public Class Customers
    Inherits List(Of Customer)

End Class
```

You also need some sample data objects based on these classes. For simplicity, those objects will be declared in XAML. A resource named CustomerList will contain five Customer data items, inside a Customers list. Here is the XAML for declaring that list as a resource, assuming a local namespace has been declared in our XAML page (code file: CustomerList.xaml):

```
<UserControl.Resources>
    <local:Customers x:Key="CustomerList">
        <local:Customer Name="BigBux, Inc." Balance="100"
                    Active="True" ContactName="Sherlock Holmes"
                    Phone="223-555-1234"
                    Logo="http://billyhollis.com/Logos/BigBuxLogo.png" />
        <local:Customer Name="SmallPotatoes, Ltd." Balance="-300"
                    Active="False" ContactName="Oliver Twist"
                    Phone="212-555-1234"
                    Logo="http://billyhollis.com/Logos/SmallPotatoesLogo.png"/>
        <local:Customer Name="Medium Enterprises, Inc." Balance="2000"
                    Active="True" ContactName="Elizabeth Bennet"
                    Phone="313-555-1234"
                    Logo=http://billyhollis.com/Logos/MediumEnterprisesLogo.png
                    />
        <local:Customer Name="Globe Theatre" Balance="-200"
                    Active="False" ContactName="Romeo Montague"
                    Phone="515-555-1234"
                    Logo="http://billyhollis.com/Logos/GlobeTheatreLogo.png"/>
        <local:Customer Name="Global Traders" Balance="-300"
                    Active="True" ContactName="Silas Marner"
                    Phone="616-555-1234"
```

```
                      Logo="http://billyhollis.com/Logos/GlobalTradersLogo.png"/>
        </local:Customers>
    </UserControl.Resources>
```

The `Logo` property for these items contains a URL, which points to images on a web server. As such, if you are not connected to the Internet as you are trying out these concepts, you will not see the actual images.

All the examples from this point will assume that this list of data items is available in the page where the example XAML is placed.

The generic collection type `List(of T)` is fine for static, read-only lists. However, if the list will have items added or removed while the list is used in a `ListBox`, a better choice for the collection type is the `ObservableCollection(of T)`.

## ItemControls

You've almost certainly used controls such as list boxes, combo boxes, and the like in other user interface technologies. However, XAML takes a radically different approach to such controls, and thereby gives you a lot of power and flexibility you don't have in other technologies. While some of the basic functionality of those controls will feel familiar, the way the controls display items is radically changed.

You may think that just providing more display flexibility is a nice change, but not a radical one. Not so. The capabilities of XAML `ItemsControls` drive changes in best practices for user interface design. Hopefully some of the examples in this chapter will demonstrate that to you convincingly.

The next section begins by covering the `ListBox` in detail. It's a typical and commonly used `ItemsControl`. Once you've seen what it can do, you'll learn about the other `ItemControls`.

## The XAML ListBox

Superficially, the XAML `ListBox` resembles the `Listbox` in older technologies. It contains a collection of items, and it displays something for each item. This main difference is that the XAML `ListBox` has dramatically more flexibility in how the item is displayed.

You can certainly use the traditional display of a simple string for each item, and you'll see how to do that first. But that's just the start. In essence, you can display an item in a `ListBox` using any of the layout capabilities of XAML.

The foundation for that capability is that a `ListBox` always holds a collection of `ListBoxItem` instances. `ListBoxItem` is a `ContentControl`, which means it can have content inside as complex as you like.

It's possible to merely construct `ListBoxItem` instances manually in XAML. Here is a short example (code file: `RandomListBoxItems.xaml`):

```
<ListBox>
    <ListBoxItem>
        I'm a list box item
    </ListBoxItem>
</ListBox>
```

```
<ListBoxItem>
    <StackPanel Orientation="Horizontal">
        <Ellipse Fill="Gray" Height="30" Width="60" />
        <TextBlock Text="Me, too" />
    </StackPanel>
</ListBoxItem>
</ListBox>
```

However, this capability is rarely used. Instead, the `ListBox` is bound to a list of data items, and a `ListBoxItem` must be automatically created for each data item in the list.

The `ListBox` has an `ItemsSource` property to bind a list of items to the `ListBox`. That property can be set to anything that implements the .NET `IEnumerable` interface, and that includes arrays and most types of collections.

For example, suppose you have a `UserControl`, and the resources block for the `Control` contains our list of `Customers`, as shown in the XAML featured previously. You can bind the list to a `ListBox` in the `UserControl` by setting the `ItemsSource` property of the `ListBox` to the resource. Here's a XAML snippet that does that:

```
<ListBox ItemsSource="{StaticResource CustomerList}" . . . />
```

If you create such a `ListBox` and bind the list of customers to it using the previous XAML in WPF, the result will look something like Figure 12-10.

Windows Forms developers have seen this problem before. Since the `ListBox` does not know how the render the item, each item is displayed by calling the `ToString` method of the item and showing the returned value. If the `ToString` method is not overridden in a class, it returns the name of the type for an object. Since the items in the bound list are `Customer` objects, you get the result in Figure 12-10.

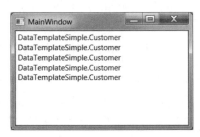

**FIGURE 12-10:** A ListBox showing a list of Customer objects, without a data template or DisplayMemberPath set. This example is rendered in WPF on Windows 7

The solution will also be familiar to Windows Forms developers. The `ListBox` has a property to specify where the item's string comes from. The property is named `DisplayMemberPath`, and you set it to a property or property path on your data object. If you set `DisplayMemberPath` in the Visual Studio Properties window to "Name," then the `ListBox` will look more like Figure 12-11.

However, `DisplayMemberPath` is rarely used in XAML production applications nearly as often as it is in Windows Forms. There's nothing wrong with it; it's just that there are better options in XAML. Once you see these options, you'll understand why they're better.

**FIGURE 12-11:** The same ListBox as in Figure 12-10, with DisplayMemberPath set to show the customer's name. This example is rendered in WPF on Windows 7

# Data Templates

Instead of just displaying a simple string for each item, you can supply a `ListBox` with a template that describes how you want the item laid out. Then the `ListBox` can use the template whenever it needs to display an item. That kind of template is called a data template.

You can think of a data template as a pattern for each item in the `ListBox`. It specifies the controls that will be shown, how they are laid out, and where each control gets its information through data binding. Then, when an item needs to be rendered, the pattern is used to create a XAML element to display the item.

A data template in XAML is an instance of the `DataTemplate` element, and contains a tree of elements, just as a `Window` or `Page` does. Usually, that tree of elements is defined in XAML. A `DataTemplate` instance normally has a root container, such as a `Border`, `Grid`, or `StackPanel`, to hold other controls. That panel can then contain XAML controls such as `TextBlocks` and `Images`. All of the features you've seen previously for laying out controls in panels are also available in a data template.

Using data binding, the controls in a data template can display any information that comes from a data object. The data object is the actual item in the `ListBox`; the data template is just the pattern used to transform the item into a visual representation.

The `ListBox` has an `ItemTemplate` property that is used to set the desired data template for the `ListBox`. The data type of the property is `DataTemplate`. You can create such a `DataTemplate` right in the XAML definition for a `ListBox`.

Here is an example of a `ListBox` with a simple data template for display of records in our list of customers (code file: `ListBoxWithTemplate.xaml`):

```
<ListBox ItemsSource="{StaticResource CustomerList}"
        Name="CustomerListBox" HorizontalContentAlignment="Stretch">
    <ListBox.ItemTemplate>
        <DataTemplate>
            <Border Margin="3" Padding="3" BorderBrush="Blue"
                    BorderThickness="2" CornerRadius="4">
                <StackPanel>
                    <TextBlock Text="{Binding Name}" />
                    <TextBlock Text="{Binding ContactName}" />
                    <TextBlock Text="{Binding Phone}" />
                </StackPanel>
            </Border>
        </DataTemplate>
    </ListBox.ItemTemplate>
</ListBox>
```

Notice that the `DisplayMemberPath` setting discussed earlier is not present. You cannot include both a data template and a `DisplayMemberPath` setting in the same `ListBox` at the same time.

The `ItemTemplate` property is set to a `DataTemplate` instance. The `DataTemplate` instance contains a `Border` as the root element, which will cause each item in the `ListBox` to have a border around it. Inside the `Border` is a `StackPanel` which contains three `TextBlocks`. Each `TextBlock` is data bound to a different property of a `Customer` object.

Figure 12-12 shows the output of such a program in Windows 8, and Figure 12-13 shows the output of the same XAML in WPF/Windows 7. The two `ListBox` results are quite similar, with the main differences being the lack of window chrome in Windows 8, and a different default font.

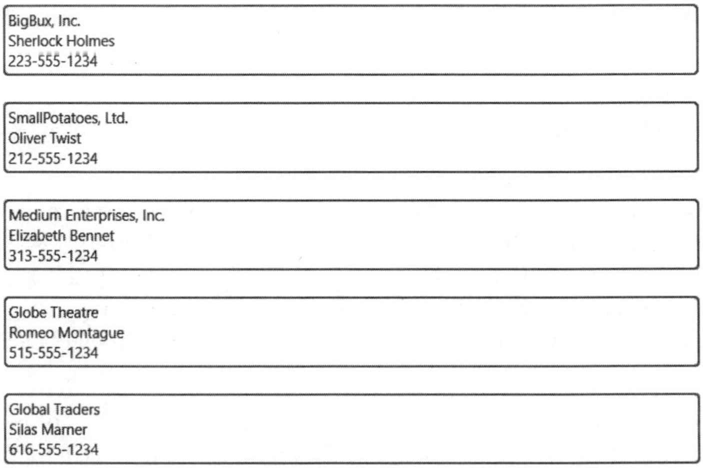

BigBux, Inc.
Sherlock Holmes
223-555-1234
SmallPotatoes, Ltd.
Oliver Twist
212-555-1234
Medium Enterprises, Inc.
Elizabeth Bennet
313-555-1234
Globe Theatre
Romeo Montague
515-555-1234
Global Traders
Silas Marner
616-555-1234

**FIGURE 12-12:** A ListBox with a simple data template for Customer objects, rendered in Windows 8 XAML

There is one other subtlety to note. The items are all the same width. That is done in WPF by setting the `HorizontalContentAlignment` property of the `ListBox` to `Stretch`. However, in Silverlight and Windows 8, a different technique is needed, involving a property of the `ListBox` called `ItemContainerStyle`. That syntax will be shown later in this chapter, after discussing `Styles`.

This is an interesting advance over list boxes in ASP.NET and Windows Forms, even with a very simple data template. However, a data template can have a layout as complex as you wish. You can set various properties, such as fonts and colors, for the various controls in the template. Or you could use a `Grid` instead of a `StackPanel` and gain more control over positioning of the controls used in the data template.

MainWindow
BigBux, Inc.
Sherlock Holmes
223-555-1234
SmallPotatoes, Ltd.
Oliver Twist
212-555-1234
Medium Enterprises, Inc.
Elizabeth Bennet
313-555-1234
Globe Theatre
Romeo Montague
515-555-1234
Global Traders
Silas Marner
616-555-1234

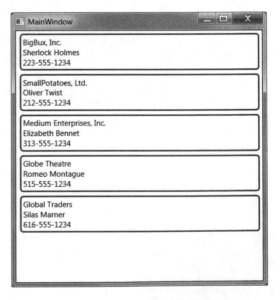

**FIGURE 12-13:** A ListBox with a simple data template for Customer objects, rendered in WPF on Windows 7

Let's look at a somewhat more interesting data template. The `Customer` object has a property for a logo. It's a string property that points to a file

name. Loading an Image at the bottom of the StackPanel wouldn't look very nice, and there's all that lovely room on the right side of the item that is currently unused. Let's fix the data template to use a Grid as the root element, and set up the Grid to place the Image on the right (code file: CustomerDataTemplate.xaml):

```xaml
<DataTemplate>
    <Border Margin="3" Padding="3" BorderBrush="Blue"
            BorderThickness="2" CornerRadius="4">
        <Grid>
            <Grid.ColumnDefinitions>
                <ColumnDefinition />
                <ColumnDefinition Width="100" />
                <ColumnDefinition Width="15" />
            </Grid.ColumnDefinitions>
            <StackPanel>
                <TextBlock Text="{Binding Name}" />
                <TextBlock Text="{Binding ContactName}" />
                <TextBlock Text="{Binding Phone}" />
            </StackPanel>
            <Image Height="50" Grid.Column="1"  Source="{Binding Logo}" />
        </Grid>
    </Border>
</DataTemplate>
```

Now the ListBox will look more like Figure 12-14 when rendered in Windows 8, and like Figure 12-15 when rendered in WPF/Windows 7.

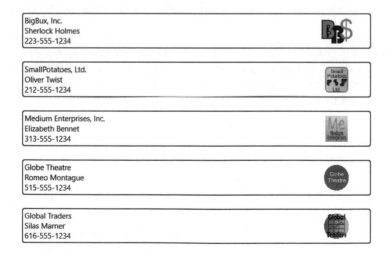

**FIGURE 12-14:** A ListBox with a data template for Customer objects, including an Image control for the logo, rendered in Windows 8 XAML

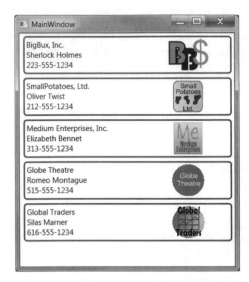

**FIGURE 12-15:** A ListBox with a data template for Customer objects, including an Image control for the logo, rendered in WPF on Windows 7

## Data Binding in Data Templates

In the previous section on Data Binding, you discussed several data binding capabilities, such as value conversion. The bindings in a data template are just regular bindings, and can take advantage of any of those capabilities.

For example, suppose you wanted some visual signal in an item to reflect the customer's balance. For example, the background of an item could be changed if the customer had a negative balance. In this case, the Background property of the Border element would be bound to the Balance property of the Customer, with a value converter that could peek at the Balance and return an appropriate Brush. That value converter would be very similar to the QuantityToBrushConverter example covered earlier.

Items in ListBox elements are also a good place to use RelativeSource bindings. Suppose, for example, you wished to have only the logo image appear if the customer was selected. The ListBoxItem class has an IsSelected property, which is Boolean. However, to use a parent ListBoxItem as a data source, the binding must be able to locate it.

That's one of the functions of a RelativeSource binding. In this case, you don't know the name of the ListBoxItem, but you do know where it is—namely, up the tree from the items in the data template. You'll see the syntax to apply a RelativeSource binding, which locates the ListBoxItem, in just a moment. First, though, there's one other concern you need to address.

The IsSelected property is a Boolean, but the Visibility property of the Image is of type Visibility. As you saw earlier, that property type can take values of Visible or Collapsed. (WPF has an additional value of Hidden.) To bind a Boolean property to a Visibility property, a value converter is needed.

In WPF, that value converter is built in, and is called, naturally enough, `BooleanToVisibilityConverter`. Silverlight and Windows 8 XAML lack that built-in converter, but it's quite easy to write one. It looks like this (code file: `BooleanToVisibilityConverter.vb`):

```vb
Public Class BooleanToVisibilityConverter
    Implements IValueConverter

    Public Function Convert(value As Object, …
        If CBool(value) Then
            Return Visibility.Visible
        Else
            Return Visibility.Collapsed
        End If
    End Function

    Public Function ConvertBack(value As Object, …
        If CType(value, Visibility) = Visibility.Visible Then
            Return True
        Else
            Return False
        End If
    End Function
End Class
```

Again, ellipses are used to deal with the differing method signatures in Windows 8 XAML vs. WPF and Silverlight.

You can create an instance of this converter as a resource, giving it a key of "B2VConverter":

```xml
<local:BooleanToVisibilityConverter x:Key="B2VConverter" />
```

Then you can create the `RelativeSource` binding you need to make the logo visible only for a selected `Customer`, but changing the `Image` element in the earlier `DataTemplate` to look like this:

```xml
<Image Height="50" Grid.Column="1"  Source="{Binding Logo}"
Visibility="{Binding RelativeSource={RelativeSource FindAncestor,
AncestorType=ListBoxItem, AncestorLevel=1}, Path=IsSelected,
Converter={StaticResource B2VConverter}}" />
```

The result rendered in WPF would look like Figure 12-16, with only the selected item showing the logo.

## Switching between Data Templates

Designing user interfaces can be frustrating, because you usually have a wide range of users. What works best for one type of user might not work well for another type. One of XAML's strengths is to give more options for dealing with that challenge.

You have seen two different data templates for the `Customer` object, one that includes the logo and a simpler one that does not. Neither of these templates is particular well designed; they're intended simply to demonstrate the syntax of data templates. However, let's pretend that they're both worthy templates for different situations. Some users like the richer template with the logo, while others prefer the simpler template.

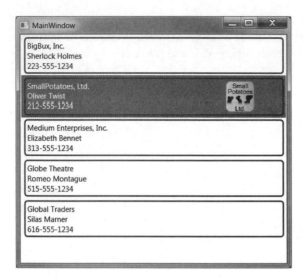

**FIGURE 12-16:** A ListBox with a data template for Customer objects, including an Image control for the logo. It is rendered in WPF on Windows 7

You can provide users a means to switch between the two templates. Each template is just an object instance of a `DataTemplate` class. The `ListBox` has an `ItemTemplate` property that points to the currently used data template. While our examples set the `ItemTemplate` property in XAML, there's nothing stopping us from setting it in code.

However, you need to be able to locate data templates to use them in code. If you know what resource dictionary the data templates are defined in, that's easy.

Let's run through an example that does all this.

First, you'll need to place both our data templates in the `Resources` property of the `UserControl`. The XAML for that is exactly the same as the earlier XAML for our two data templates, except that each template needs an `x:Key`. The template with the logo will get the key "`TemplateWithLogo`" and the other one will get "`TemplateWithoutLogo`." Here are those resource declarations (code file: `TwoDataTemplates.xaml`):

```
<DataTemplate x:Key="TemplateWithLogo">
    <Border Margin="3" Padding="3" BorderBrush="Blue"
    BorderThickness="2" CornerRadius="4">
        <Grid>
            <Grid.ColumnDefinitions>
                <ColumnDefinition />
                <ColumnDefinition Width="100" />
                <ColumnDefinition Width="15" />
            </Grid.ColumnDefinitions>
            <StackPanel>
                <TextBlock Text="{Binding Name}" />
                <TextBlock Text="{Binding ContactName}" />
                <TextBlock Text="{Binding Phone}" />
```

```
                </StackPanel>
                <Image Height="50" Grid.Column="1"  Source="{Binding Logo}"/>
            </Grid>
        </Border>
    </DataTemplate>

    <DataTemplate x:Key="TemplateWithoutLogo">
        <Border Margin="3" Padding="3" BorderBrush="Blue"
                BorderThickness="2" CornerRadius="4">
            <StackPanel>
                <TextBlock Text="{Binding Name}" />
                <TextBlock Text="{Binding ContactName}" />
                <TextBlock Text="{Binding Phone}" />
            </StackPanel>
        </Border>
    </DataTemplate>
```

To arrange switching between the templates, you could use two `Button` elements, a `CheckBox`, a `ComboBox`, or various other possibilities for user interaction. To keep our example simple, let's assume it's a `CheckBox`. One of the templates will be used when the `CheckBox` is checked and the other when it is unchecked.

The declaration for the `CheckBox` would look something like this:

```
<CheckBox VerticalAlignment="Bottom"
          IsChecked="True"
          Checked="CheckBox_Checked"
          Unchecked="CheckBox_Checked"
          Content="Use template with logo" />
```

The event handler referenced in this XAML, plus a helper routine, would look something like this (code file: `SwitchDataTemplates.vb`):

```
Private Sub CheckBox_Checked(sender As System.Object, e As
                            System.Windows.RoutedEventArgs)
    If CType(sender, CheckBox).IsChecked Then
        CustomerListBox.ItemTemplate = GetDataTemplate("TemplateWithLogo")
    Else
        CustomerListBox.ItemTemplate = GetDataTemplate("TemplateWithoutLogo")
    End If
End Sub

Private Function GetDataTemplate(sName As String) As DataTemplate
    If Me.Resources.Contains(sName) Then
        Return CType(Me.Resources.Item(sName), DataTemplate)
    Else
        Return Nothing
    End If
End Function
```

This code could stand some hardening, but it demonstrates the concept. As soon as the `CheckBox` is checked or unchecked, the appropriate template is located in the resources collection, and applied to the `ItemTemplate` property of `CustomerListBox`.

## Changing Layout of ListBox Items with ItemsPanel

Befitting the philosophy of XAML, a ListBox doesn't really know how to stack up items. It only stacks items by default because it contains a variant of a StackPanel inside. The special StackPanel used by a ListBox is called a VirtualizingStackPanel, and has special rendering logic for long lists.

The default VirtualizingStackPanel can be replaced. For example, if you would like the items in your ListBox to stack horizontally instead of vertically, you can change the panel used for stacking to a StackPanel with Orientation set to Horizontal.

The panel used to arrange items is set with the ItemsPanel property of the ListBox. Here is a ListBox with the ItemsPanel property modified to use a horizontal StackPanel:

```
<ListBox.ItemsPanel>
    <ItemsPanelTemplate>
        <StackPanel Orientation="Horizontal" />
    </ItemsPanelTemplate>
</ListBox.ItemsPanel>
```

Any available panel can be used as a layout panel for a ListBox, though some of them require additional work to get items properly positioned. The code download for this chapter includes a ListBox in WPF that uses a Canvas as a layout panel.

## Additional ItemControls

As mentioned at the start of this section, the ListBox was used to discuss concepts that apply to all ItemControls. Each XAML platform has other ItemControls, and all of them use DataTemplates for determining layout of their items.

Examples of other ItemControls on the various XAML platforms include ComboBox, TreeView, ListView, ContextMenu, and DataGrid. If you understand how data templates work, you should have no difficulty in applying that understanding to any of these controls.

# STYLES

Developers of business applications might be a bit wary of becoming an expert in styling. Windows Forms had no such capability, and web applications often have specialists that do the styling.

However, styles in XAML are quite a bit more flexible than styles in earlier technologies, and address functionality that's not strictly cosmetic. That means developers need to understand styles, too.

## What Is a Style?

At the most basic level, a Style in XAML is simply a way to set several property values for an element at one time. In syntactical terms, a Style is a collection of Setter objects, and each Setter object knows how to set a particular property to a particular value.

Here is a simple `Style` for a `Button` element (code file: `SimpleStyle.xaml`):

```
<Style x:Key="ButtonStyle" TargetType="Button">
    <Setter Property="Margin" Value="4" />
    <Setter Property="FontSize" Value="22"/>
    <Setter Property="FontStyle" Value="Italic" />
    <Setter Property="Foreground" >
        <Setter.Value>
            <LinearGradientBrush
                EndPoint="0.8,0.8"
                StartPoint="0.2,0.2">
                <GradientStop Color="DarkBlue" Offset="0"/>
                <GradientStop Color="ForestGreen" Offset="1"/>
            </LinearGradientBrush>
        </Setter.Value>
    </Setter>
</Style>
```

In this case, the `Style` is declared as a resource, and so has an `x:Key` attribute. That's the common case. There are a few scenarios where a `Style` is not used as a resource, and in fact you will see one a bit further on. However, normally the power of a `Style` is to apply it widely through much or all of an application, and as a resource it gains that kind of accessibility.

The `Style` also has a `TargetType`. There are limited scenarios in which this property of a `Style` does not need to be declared, but the common case is to declare a `TargetType`, and all the `Style` examples in this chapter will do so.

The `Style` then contains a collection of `Setter` objects. The first `Setter` object sets the `Margin` style to a `Value` of 4.

Many `Setter` objects will set simple values, but sometimes the value needed can't be expressed in a simple string. This is another case where element-based syntax is necessary to set the property. The `Setter` for the `Foreground` property shows an example. The `Foreground` is set to a linear gradient brush, and that requires additional lines of XAML between the `<Setter.Value>` and `</Setter.Value>` element tags.

To apply this style to an individual `Button`, the `Style` property of the `Button` should point to the `Style` resource. Here's an example:

```
<Button Content="Press me"
        Style="{StaticResource ButtonStyle}" />
```

## Determining the Scope of a Style

In the discussion on Resources, it was noted that an individual resource is visible to all the elements further down in the element tree from the resource's location. When a `Style` is defined as a resource, the same principle applies. An individual element can use only a style that is defined for itself or one of its ancestors.

That means a `Style` can be replaced at any level in the application, simply by defining a style at that level with the same resource key. It's common to place a default `Style` at the application level, and then replace that style in individual XAML pages if that page requires a different `Style`.

## Implicit Styles

As you saw previously, an element can apply a Style by setting the element's Style property to a resource. It's also possible to put a Style directly in a property for an element, without using a resource, and the following section on ItemContainerStyle has an example.

However, the real power of XAML styling is founded on the ability for styles to be automatically applied to elements. That type of Style is called an *implicit* Style. It's quite simple to create an implicit Style. Just put the Style in the resources area, the same as you saw earlier, but *leave off the* x:Key *attribute*.

You might expect that to cause a syntax error, since every resource in a resource dictionary must have a key. The reason it works is that the XAML parser has a special consideration for styles. If no key is present, the XAML parser creates a key out of the TargetType.

This allows the rendering engine to check for an implicit style for any type of visual element. If one is found anywhere in the ancestor tree, that style is applied automatically to the element.

If an implicit style exists for an element, but the Style property is set to a different Style manually, the locally declared value of the Style property takes precedence. That means the implicit style can be overridden for individual elements as necessary.

## BasedOn Styles

It's not uncommon to have a "standard" style for an element type, and also need to have some minor variations on it. While it's possible to simply copy the whole standard Style object to another Style and make changes, it's better for maintenance if the Style with minor variations can "inherit" from the standard style.

That is done in XAML with the BasedOn property. The BasedOn property for a Style can point to a Style resource already defined. That immediately makes all the Setter objects in the base Style available. The new Style can then add new Setter objects, or replace Setter objects in the base style with different Setter objects in the new style.

Here is an example of a Style that is based on the ButtonStyle resource created earlier (code file: BasedOnStyle.xaml):

```
<Style x:Key="ExtraStuff" TargetType="Button"
       BasedOn="{StaticResource ButtonStyle}">
    <Setter Property="FontSize" Value="14"/>
    <Setter Property="FontWeight" Value="Bold" />
</Style>
```

This Style replaces the original FontSize of 22 with a new FontSize of 14, and adds a Setter that sets FontWeight to Bold.

## ItemContainerStyle

The previous examples show Styles as resources. That's the most common use of Styles by far. However, there are a few scenarios where it is desirable to place a Style directly in the definition of an element. The one you will likely encounter first is setting the ItemContainerStyle of a ListBox.

In the data template examples, something must tell the item to stretch to the full width of the ListBox. Otherwise, the ListBoxItem elements will be of different widths, and the overall list of items will look ragged. Figure 12-17 shows such a ListBox.

In WPF, this is easy to remedy. Just set the HorizontalContentAlignment of the ListBox to Stretch. However, for Silverlight and Windows 8 XAML, that technique will not work.

The difficulty in this situation is that the ListBoxItem elements that need to be stretched are not created until runtime. Therefore, there is no place in XAML to set the HorizontalContentAlignment for them.

This is just one example of a scenario in which it's desirable to affect the ListBoxItems that will be created at runtime. To provide that capability, the ListBox includes a property named ItemContainerStyle. That property holds a Style with any number of Setter objects, and the Style is automatically applied to all ListBoxItem elements that are created at runtime.

**FIGURE 12-17:** A ListBox in which the items are ragged

The ItemContainerStyle that will make ListBoxItem elements stretched looks like this:

```
<ListBox.ItemContainerStyle>
    <Style TargetType="ListBoxItem">
        <Setter Property="HorizontalContentAlignment" Value="Stretch" />
    </Style>
</ListBox.ItemContainerStyle>
```

## CONTROL TEMPLATES

A Style can set just about any property of an element. The examples in the Style section show rather prosaic properties affecting fonts and such. However, a Style for a ListBox could set the ItemTemplate property to a particular DataTemplate, which has more dramatic effects.

For controls, a Style can also set a very important property named Template. That property points to a *control template*, which determines the visualization of the control.

## "Lookless" Controls

In XAML, the behavior of a control, that is, how it responds to user actions in code, is completely separate from the way the control is rendered. In fact, the code for a control normally doesn't contain any information about how the control is rendered at all. The control's rendering is specified by a control template.

Control authors include a default control template in controls. That way, when the control is placed in a XAML page, a default rendering is in place, and the control can be seen and used.

However, that rendering is just the default. The control template can be changed. The new template can make the control look radically different, using any of the visual elements available in XAML.

## Reskinning a CheckBox

Suppose you want a CheckBox to control whether a microphone is turned on or off. You could just drag over a CheckBox and be done with it, and from a functional perspective, that would work. However, usability would be significantly enhanced if you could make the CheckBox indicate its function visually.

You can do that with a control template. Let's create a CheckBox with a control template that will make the CheckBox look like a microphone. Figure 12-18 shows our reskinned CheckBox, in both unchecked and checked states. On the left is the unchecked state. On the right is the checked state. The top of the microphone is maroon in the checked state. The rendering is the same on Windows 8 and WPF if the background is the same.

**FIGURE 12-18:** A CheckBox reskinned with a control template to look like a microphone

Here is the XAML for the CheckBox (code file: MicrophoneCheckBox.xaml):

```
<CheckBox IsChecked="True" Height="120" Width="40">
    <CheckBox.Template>
        <ControlTemplate TargetType="CheckBox">
            <Grid>
                <Grid.RowDefinitions>
                    <RowDefinition />
                    <RowDefinition />
                    <RowDefinition />
                </Grid.RowDefinitions>
                <Grid >
                    <Grid.RowDefinitions>
                        <RowDefinition />
                        <RowDefinition />
                    </Grid.RowDefinitions>
                    <Ellipse Grid.RowSpan="2" Fill="Gray" />
                    <Ellipse Grid.RowSpan="2" Fill="Maroon"
                            Visibility="{Binding RelativeSource={RelativeSource
                            TemplatedParent}, Path=IsChecked,
                            Converter={StaticResource B2VConverter}}" />

                    <Rectangle Grid.Row="1" Fill="Gray" />

                </Grid>
                <Rectangle Grid.Row="1" Fill="Black" />
                <Grid Grid.Row="2" >
                    <Grid.RowDefinitions>
                        <RowDefinition />
                        <RowDefinition />
                    </Grid.RowDefinitions>
                    <Grid.ColumnDefinitions >
```

```
                <ColumnDefinition />
                <ColumnDefinition />
                <ColumnDefinition />
            </Grid.ColumnDefinitions>
            <Rectangle Grid.Column="1" Fill="Black" />
            <Rectangle Grid.Row="1" Grid.ColumnSpan="3" Fill="Black" />
        </Grid>
      </Grid>
    </ControlTemplate>
  </CheckBox.Template>
</CheckBox>
```

This XAML may look a bit complex at first, but you have seen all the techniques it uses in this chapter. The root of the control template is a `Grid` with three rows. In the first row, another `Grid` contains two circles and a rectangle.

One of the circles is `Maroon`, and its visibility is tied to the control's `IsChecked` property by a data binding. That binding requires a converter for changing a `Boolean` to a `Visibility` value, and you saw such a converter in the section on data templates. When the `CheckBox` is clicked, the `IsSelected` property changes, and the binding ties that change to a change in the visibility of the `Maroon` circle.

In the second row, another rectangle extends the "microphone" down a bit further. Then, in the third row, a `Grid` with some `Rectangle` elements draw a "base" for the "microphone."

This control template works equally well in Windows 8, and it can be resized. The interior elements will change size proportionally, because the control template is based on `Grid` elements with proportional rows.

## Creating Control Templates

It is beyond the scope of this chapter to get into several other concepts and techniques commonly used for control templates. The main area that's being left out is the use of visual states to change the control's appearance under various circumstances. XAML contains a `VisualStateManager` for that capability. The preferred tool for working with the `VisualStateManager` is Expression Blend.

## SUMMARY

This chapter has covered the most important concepts and capabilities needed by a beginning XAML developer. However, there is still much to know to take complete advantage of what XAML can do.

Chapter 13 goes into more detail on using XAML in Windows 8. If your preferred platform for XAML will be Windows 8, that chapter should be your next step.

If you will be doing WPF or Silverlight development, then you will need to turn to other resources to go more in-depth on XAML. Some of the topics that you should learn next include:

➤  Additional panels: `WrapPanel`, `Canvas`

➤  Additional controls: `TabControl`, `DataGrid`, `TreeView`, etc.

➤   Transforms

➤   Animation

➤   `VisualStateManager`

➤   Using the visual designers in Visual Studio and Expression Blend

Later, you may need to cover some advanced concepts. If you will be writing XAML frameworks, for example, you will need to be quite familiar with the dependency property system, attached properties, and other internal aspects of XAML.

# 13

# Creating XAML Applications for Windows 8

**WHAT'S IN THIS CHAPTER?**

➤ Differences in Windows 8 XAML from earlier XAML platforms

➤ UX and UI conventions in Windows 8

➤ New elements and new features in Windows 8 XAML

➤ The Visual Studio 2012 designer for XAML

➤ Application templates in Visual Studio 2012 for XAML apps

➤ Implementing Live Tiles

➤ Implementing contracts to work with Windows 8 charms

## WROX.COM CODE DOWNLOADS FOR THIS CHAPTER

The wrox.com code downloads for this chapter are found at `www.wrox.com/remtitle` `.cgi?isbn=9781118314456` on the Download Code tab. The code is in the chapter 13 download and individually named according to the names throughout the chapter.

In chapter 12, you looked at XAML in a general way. That chapter covered capabilities and syntax that work exactly the name, except for minor details, on all three XAML platforms: WPF, Silverlight, and Windows 8 / WinRT. This chapter looks more deeply at XAML in the Windows 8 environment. The objective of the chapter is to build on general XAML expertise so that it can be applied to the creation of Windows 8 apps.

This chapter is aimed at those who have already absorbed enough about XAML to at least write simple applications on earlier XAML platforms. Chapter 12 was designed to assist those who have not yet used XAML in production on earlier platforms by presenting foundational

XAML concepts. This chapter assumes that, at a minimum, the reader is familiar with all the concepts presented in Chapter 12.

For the benefit of those with more extensive experience in XAML, you'll begin by looking at a few significant ways in which Windows 8 XAML differs from that on earlier platforms. This section isn't intended to be comprehensive. Rather, it highlights differences that you are likely to encounter early in your attempts to create Windows 8 apps.

Then, you'll take up some of the user interface and user experience conventions you are expected to satisfy in Windows 8 apps. Some of these are advisory, but a number of them are required to place your app in the Windows Store for deployment. Chapter 20 covers how to use the Windows Store, including how to check your application to see if it satisfies necessary conventions.

Windows 8 contains a number of new visual elements, and some of them are designed to fit well within Windows 8 conventions. The chapter includes an overview of the most important of these new elements. You'll also need to look at several elements that existed in earlier XAML platforms, but have some special usage or significance in Windows 8 XAML, such as Frame and Popup.

The chapter also includes some discussion of the visual designer for XAML in Visual Studio 2012, particularly the associated Properties window, primarily to highlight differences from previous versions of Visual Studio.

Then, you'll get an overview of how to use the application templates for Windows 8 XAML apps offered by Visual Studio 2012. These templates are much more extensive than equivalents in earlier XAML platforms, and learning to use them is correspondingly harder.

Finally, you'll look at how your app fits into Windows 8 overall, including having your application expose an ActiveTile, and implementing a contract for search functionality.

# HOW XAML DIFFERS IN WINDOWS 8

If you have experience with previous versions of XAML, you need to know about some key differences in Windows 8 XAML from previous versions. There are missing elements, some of which simply don't have an analog in Windows 8, and others which have a functional replacement.

## Missing Elements

Some of your old friends from those platforms are not present in Windows 8. Some were left out because they are not easy to fit into a touch-optimized experience. Because this is a version 1.0 product, some desirable features didn't make it into the released product simply because of lack of time.

The differences are too extensive to present a comprehensive list, but here are the panels and controls you are most likely to miss:

- ➤ TreeView
- ➤ DataGrid
- ➤ TabControl
- ➤ Expander

➤ `DatePicker` and `MonthCalendar`

➤ `DockPanel`

➤ `WrapPanel`

➤ `UniformGrid`

Except for `WrapPanel`, these missing elements have no replacement element that supplies near-equivalent functionality. The user interaction patterns for `TreeView`, `DataGrid`, and `TabControl` are not easy to translate to a touch-first mode, so analogs were not attempted in the first version of Windows 8 XAML. `DockPanel` and `UniformGrid` are lesser used panels, and that's probably why they didn't make the cut.

`Expander`, `DatePicker`, and `MonthCalendar` are missing as well. With `Expander`, it is an open question of whether it fits the Windows 8 UI conventions. However, it's clear that line-of-business apps need date controls, so you'll probably see those in a future version. For the present, the lack of date controls is one of the most compelling reasons to obtain a package of third-party controls. Some of them do have date controls, and writing one yourself would certainly be tedious.

For layout panels, the most important omission is the `WrapPanel`. However, two replacement panels with somewhat similar functionality are available—`WrapGrid` and its cousin `VariableSizedWrapGrid`. They are more restrictive than `WrapPanel`, however, because they can only be used inside `ItemControls`. You will see `VariableSizedWrapGrid` used in an example later in the chapter.

## Old Elements Replaced by Functional Equivalents in Windows 8

There are several other missing elements that have replacements with similar functionality, but adapted for the Windows 8 environment:

➤ **ContextMenu**—replaced by `PopupMenu`.

➤ **MessageBox**—replaced by `MessageDialog`.

➤ **Common dialogs**—replaced by "pickers"; for example, the `OpenFileDialog` is replaced by `FilePicker`.

➤ **RichTextBox**—replaced by `RichEditBox`.

Pickers are discussed in the section below on new Windows 8 elements, and the example for a picker shows the `MessageDialog` in use.

## Syntax Differences

The last chapter mentioned that there are variations between Windows 8 XAML and previous versions in both XAML syntax and certain APIs. In case you skipped that chapter because you have XAML experience, the two examples mentioned in that chapter were the way XAML namespaces were declared (with "using" instead of "clr-namespace"), and the different method signature for the `IValueConverter` interface. If you're experienced with WPF or Silverlight, you will find a number of other minor API differences as you attempt to apply familiar capabilities.

## Using Page as the Root Visual Element

In WPF, the most commonly used root visual elements are `Window` and `UserControl`. `Window` (or its subclass `NavigationWindow`) is almost always used as the entry point for an application. Silverlight applications more commonly use `UserControl` as the root visual element, though `Window` is available for some out-of-browser scenarios.

In Windows 8, by contrast, the most common root visual elements are `Page` and other classes that inherit from `Page`. As you'll see, the standard application templates in Visual Studio offer a subclass of `Page` called `LayoutAwarePage` that you will likely use a lot. It adds more functionality to `Page` for scenarios such as snapped views.

`UserControl` is still used a lot in Windows 8, but not as a root class that takes over the whole screen. Typically, a `UserControl` is used for sections of screens that need to contain a reusable arrangement of elements, such a `UserControl` to hold all the fields to enter an address.

## WINDOWS 8 UI CONVENTIONS

It's possible to develop Windows 8 apps on a non-touch machine. However, if you are going to design and build apps that function smoothly in a touch environment, you should become familiar with Windows 8 as a user. It's a good idea to acquire a touch-based Windows 8 machine, and use it regularly for a few weeks. Gestures such as swipes and tap/hold need to become second nature to you.

If you've been using a touch-based smartphone or tablet with a different OS, you'll be familiar with some touch conventions. However, Windows 8 has its own conventions for touch, and you'll need to be fluent with them.

You particularly need to understand how Windows presents its main visual elements. Some elements are managed by the operating system, and your application will need to interact with them. Other elements have a standard location, but vary by application, and you will need to create our own version.

When a Windows 8 style application is running, there are three main elements that can be brought into view with swipes from the sides of the screen: a charms bar (sometimes referred to as the start bar), an app bar, and a navigation bar. Figure 13-1 shows all three of these elements in a screen shot of Internet Explorer, with the browser content removed for clarity. Each of them is brought into view by swiping from their respective side: right for charms, bottom for app bar, and top for navigation bar. If your app has both an app bar and a nav bar, bringing either one of them into view will cause the other one to also come into view.

The start bar is managed by the operating system. However, your application does interact with it in several key ways.

The Search charm at the top of the start bar is the new way Windows 8 handles search. It yields the sort of search results you would expect from previous versions of Windows, such as programs that match a search string. For the first time, though, Windows 8 search allows custom apps to contribute search results.

Your app also has the ability to share information with other apps via the Share charm. Interacting with the Windows 8 operating system via the Search and Share charms is done by implementing a contract in your app. You'll see how to do that later in the chapter. Your application can also participate with the Settings charm to put up app-specific settings.

**FIGURE 13-1:** The major elements that swipe in from the sides of a Windows 8 app are charms (on the right), the app bar (from the bottom), and the navigation bar (from the top).

Charms are always present; they're part of the OS. The other two bars are optional parts of your application. You get to choose whether your app will have an app bar, a navigation bar, or both. Windows controls when they appear, but you are responsible for all the functionality on them.

An app bar contains app-specific operations. In Internet Explorer's app bar, shown in Figure 13-1, the app bar contains the address bar for entering a URL, and buttons such as Refresh (the arrowed circle) and Favorites (the pushpin).

For your own applications, common examples of app bar functionality would be an Add operation to add a new record to a list, or a Save operation to save changes. A typical line of business apps will usually have an app bar.

The nav bar is intended for use as a navigator inside an application. You can see a typical use of the nav bar in Internet Explorer, as shown in Figure 13-1. The Windows 8 style version of Internet Explorer does not explicitly show browser tabs. The equivalent functionality is displayed in the nav bar, which shows open browser pages and allows the user to choose the active one, or to request a new tab via the button containing a plus sign. Your app might need a similar navigation pattern if it keeps more than one record open at a time.

App bars and nav bars are both implemented in your code with the AppBar element, and you'll see how to do that when you look at the new elements you'll be using routinely in Windows 8 apps. However, before you look at those elements, it's helpful for you to know some of the guidelines to which you must adhere when designing and developing Windows 8 apps.

## UI/UX GUIDELINES

Becoming familiar with all the guidelines for Windows 8 users is an essential part of being a Windows 8 developer. If you violate certain conventions, your application cannot even be deployed via the Window Store.

Learning these guidelines and conventions will take you a while. You can find a launch page for the complete set of guidelines at `http://bit.ly/Win8UXGuidelines`. You should study those carefully.

To set the stage, though, here are a few of the most important concepts, particularly ones that are probably at significant variance from the applications you have written before.

## Interaction between Your App and the Windows 8 OS

The earlier discussion of charms, app bar, and nav bar are part of the standard way apps are supposed to interact with the OS. So are contracts for Search and Share.

There are a number of other conventions in this general area of OS interaction. For example, your application should not have a Close button, or any equivalent functionality. A standard gesture is available to close an app. It can be done with either touch or mouse; while an app is open, start at the top of the screen, and drag toward the middle until you see the app shrink and center on the screen. Then continue dragging to the bottom, and the app will be closed.

## Chromeless Apps

Windows 8 apps are "chromeless." That simply means none of the border cosmetics in earlier versions of Windows are present. Windows 8 apps have no sizable borders, no title bar, and none of the buttons you associate with the title bar. The OS expects the user to focus most of the time on one application, and thus it is optimized to show one application on a clean surface.

The screens in an app are commonly called views. In older technologies, it was common for views to have buttons for operations such as Save. Views in Windows 8 apps should not have such buttons on the main view, because it's easy for them to be activated inadvertently during a touch operation. The app bar is the preferred location for any such buttons needed by your app, because it comes into view only when the user does the proper gesture to request it.

## Snapped Views

Multiple apps are shown only via a "snapped" view, with a limit of two apps at a time. In a snapped view, one app gets a reduced slice of the screen that is 320 pixels wide. This view can be on either side of the screen. The rest of the screen, which is significantly bigger, hosts the other app. An example screen with a snapped view is shown in Figure 13-2.

Windows 8 furnishes a mouse or touch gesture to make an app snapped. It's similar to the close gesture just discussed. With an app open in full screen, drag from the middle top until the app shrinks and centers in the screen. Then, instead of dragging to the bottom as you do with a close, drag to either side to make the app snap to that side.

To pass certification for placement in the Windows Store, your app is required to support a snapped view. It is up to you to design an appropriate view for when your app is snapped. In the case of the

Music player shown in Figure 13-2, the designer decided to show a sparse vertical view of the music being played, with some minimal controls. Some applications merely place status information in the snapped view.

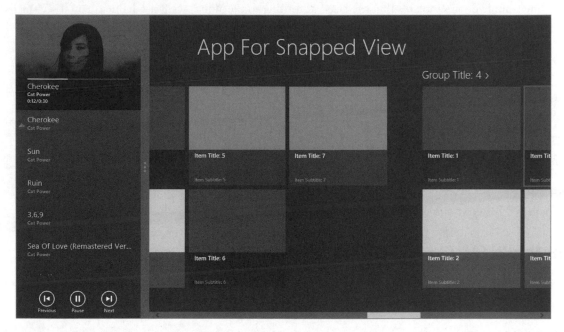

**FIGURE 13-2:** Only two apps can share the Windows 8 screen at a time. One app is in a "snapped view" which is 320 pixels wide. The other app takes up the remaining screen space.

## Typeface and Font Guidelines

Windows 8 has a standard set of typefaces you are supposed to use in your apps. The most commonly used typeface is Segoe, an elegant sans serif typeface. It's nicer than the typical fonts such as Arial that many applications use today, and there's no reason to change it for line-of-business applications.

If you application has a lot of content to be read and/or edited, you are expected to take advantage of two other standard typefaces. For parts of an application where the user would be reading and editing, such a detailed product description or an email message, you should use Calibri. For apps that are primarily intended for reading, such as a newsreader app, content should be in Cambria.

The Windows 8 UX guidelines include recommendations about using particular font sizes and weights. You should become familiar with those and use them unless you have a very good reason not to do so.

## Sizing and Layout of Visual Elements in an App

In earlier XAML platforms, you were on your own to decide sizing of elements. For apps in Windows XAML, however, you need to try to be consistent with the conventions for screen layout in Windows 8 apps.

Most sizing of items, such as data items in a list, should be based on the "grid system," in which blocks of 20×20 pixels for the basis for a number of larger sizes. Spacer areas are often 10 pixels wide or high. The built-in application templates can give you a push in that direction. They include some sample data templates that are sized according to the Windows 8 guidelines. You'll see the list of templates and sizes in the section on Windows 8 Application Templates below.

You also need to provide appropriately sized header areas and margins. These can vary to suit the type of touch navigation that is being used.

The UX guidelines give precise details and recommendations, but you'll look at one typical case. Suppose you wanted a view with a list of items on the left side of the screen, and you intended the list to scroll vertically. Such a view might provide a header area that was 100 pixels high, and provide a margin on the left of 120 pixels. In fact, you will use those numbers in the first ListView example later in the chapter, because it does vertical scrolling.

The topics above only furnish a starting point for user experience guidelines. You should invest time to become familiar with the entire set. Remember, some of the user experience guidelines are required for your app to be certified in the Windows Store, which is discussed in Chapter 20.

# NEW VISUAL ELEMENTS IN WINDOWS 8

Windows 8 includes quite a number of new elements. In this section, you'll look at the new elements you are most likely to need early in your Windows 8 app development.

## AppBar

Earlier, you learned how Windows 8 allows an app bar to slide into your application from the bottom, and a nav bar to slide in from the top. By convention, these bars hold user actions and navigation options, as discussed in the UI conventions earlier.

Both of these visual elements are constructed from the same XAML element: the AppBar. This same element can be used in two different places.

You also learned how the root visual element for parts of your app will usually be the Page control or one of its subclasses. Page has two properties for specifying app bars: Page.BottomAppBar for the app bar, and Page.TopAppBar for the nav bar.

Both of these properties take an AppBar element. AppBar is just a container. You can think of it as a content control. The AppBar class just provides a surface to show when the user makes the proper gestures. All of the appearance and functionality inside the AppBar is up to you.

### Constructing a Bottom App Bar

An app bar can have any elements on it. For simple app bars, the recommended arrangement of elements features two sets of buttons, one on the left side of the app bar, and one on the right. The left side is for operations or actions specific to an item currently shown in the view. The right side is for operations that apply to the application as a whole. Figure 13-3 shows an app bar with such an arrangement.

One XAML layout that will give you such an arrangement is to make the root element inside the app bar a Grid with two equal columns. Place a horizontal StackPanel in each column of the Grid, with the one in the first column aligned to the left, and the one in the second column aligned to the right. Then put appropriate buttons in each `StackPanel`.

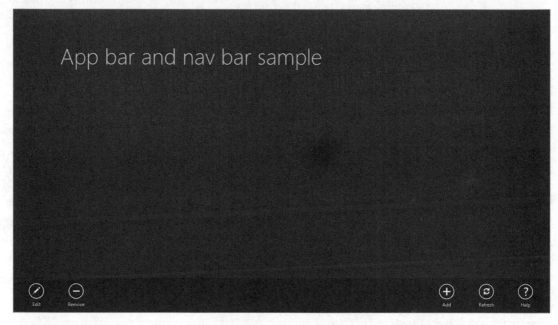

**FIGURE 13-3:** An app bar appears on a swipe from the bottom of the screen. Item-specific buttons should be on the left, and general app action buttons on the right.

The XAML for the app bar shown in Figure 13-3 follows this pattern, and looks like this (code file: `BottomAppBar.xaml`):

```
<Page.BottomAppBar>
    <AppBar>
        <Grid>
            <Grid.ColumnDefinitions>
                <ColumnDefinition />
                <ColumnDefinition />
            </Grid.ColumnDefinitions>
            <!--StackPanel on the left for item-specific buttons-->
            <StackPanel Orientation="Horizontal"
                    HorizontalAlignment="Left">
                <Button Name="AppBarEditButton"
                        Style="{StaticResource EditAppBarButtonStyle}"
                    />
                <Button Name="AppBarDeleteButton"
                        Style="{StaticResource RemoveAppBarButtonStyle}"
                />
            </StackPanel>
            <!--StackPanel on the right for general app buttons-->
            <StackPanel Orientation="Horizontal" Grid.Column="1"
                    HorizontalAlignment="Right">
                <Button Name="AppBarAddButton"
                    Style="{StaticResource AddAppBarButtonStyle}"
                        />
```

```
                  <Button Name="AppBarRefreshButton"
                          Style="{StaticResource RefreshAppBarButtonStyle}"
                  />
                  <Button Name="AppBarHelpButton"
                          Style="{StaticResource HelpAppBarButtonStyle}"
                          />
              </StackPanel>
          </Grid>
      </AppBar>
  </Page.BottomAppBar>
```

Notice that the buttons in the app bar are all created using styles. Even the icon inside each button is part of the style.

It isn't necessary for you to write the styles needed for common app bar buttons. A set of 62 styles is available to you in a XAML file called StandardStyles.xaml. However, they are commented out in the file, because it doesn't make sense to load all of them if they are not needed. So you must uncomment the ones you need. For the sample, all the styles referred to in the XAML snippet above were uncommented.

App bars can contain a lot more than buttons, and can be as complex as needed for your app. They don't have a specific size either—an app bar will be automatically sized to hold whatever is placed in it. All the layout techniques covered in Chapter 12 are at your disposal to create a richer app bar, and you can place any elements you need in the app bar.

## Constructing a Top Nav Bar

The process for creating a nav bar is the same as that for creating an app bar, except that you use the Page.TopAppBar property instead of Page.BottomAppBar. However, where typical app bars often generally look the same, there is no consistent layout for a nav bar.

A common use of a nav bar is to allow the user to navigate to open items. In this case, some kind of ItemControl is often used to hold the available items in a horizontal orientation. Here is an example, with some fudged-up items for demonstration. This example uses a ListView to hold several items, and the ListView control will be covered in detail later in this section (code file: TopAppBar.xaml):

```
<Page.TopAppBar>
    <AppBar>
        <StackPanel Orientation="Horizontal" Height="250">
            <ListView Margin="20">
                <ListView.ItemsPanel>
                    <ItemsPanelTemplate>
                        <VirtualizingStackPanel Orientation="Horizontal" />
                    </ItemsPanelTemplate>
                </ListView.ItemsPanel>
                <ListViewItem>
                    <Border Width="120" Height="160"
                            BorderBrush="LightGray"
                            Background="DarkGray" BorderThickness="3">
                        <TextBlock Margin="4" FontSize="20"
                                   Text="An active item"
                                   TextWrapping="Wrap" />
```

```
                    </Border>
                </ListViewItem>
                <ListViewItem>
                    <Border Width="120" Height="160"
                            BorderBrush="LightGray"
                            Background="DarkGray" BorderThickness="3">
                        <TextBlock Margin="4" FontSize="20"
                                   Text="The second active item"
                                   TextWrapping="Wrap" />
                    </Border>
                </ListViewItem>
                <ListViewItem>
                    <Border Width="120" Height="160"
                            BorderBrush="LightGray"
                            Background="DarkGray"  BorderThickness="3">
                        <TextBlock Margin="4" FontSize="20"
                                   Text="Another active item"
                                   TextWrapping="Wrap" />
                    </Border>
                </ListViewItem>
                <ListViewItem>
                    <Border Width="120" Height="160"
                            BorderBrush="LightGray"
                            Background="DarkGray" BorderThickness="3">
                        <TextBlock Margin="4" FontSize="20"
                                   Text="Yet another active item"
                                   TextWrapping="Wrap" />
                    </Border>
                </ListViewItem>
                <ListViewItem>
                    <Border Width="120" Height="160"
                            BorderBrush="LightGray"
                            Background="DarkGray" BorderThickness="3">
                        <TextBlock Margin="4" FontSize="20"
                                   Text="The last active item"
                                   TextWrapping="Wrap" />
                    </Border>
                </ListViewItem>
            </ListView>
            <Button Margin="20" Content="A button for something" FontSize="20" />
        </StackPanel>
    </AppBar>
</Page.TopAppBar>
```

The resulting nav bar is shown in Figure 13-4, with the second item selected by the user. Note that since the app now has both an app bar and nav bar, both are shown when the top nav bar is brought into view.

## ListView, GridView, and FlipView Controls

In earlier XAML platforms, the ListBox was a commonly used control to show lists of data items. The ListBox is one of a general category of XAML controls called ItemControls. As seen in Chapter 12, ItemControls have an ItemsSource property to point to the list of data items to be displayed, and an `ItemTemplate` property to point to a data template used to format individual items for display.

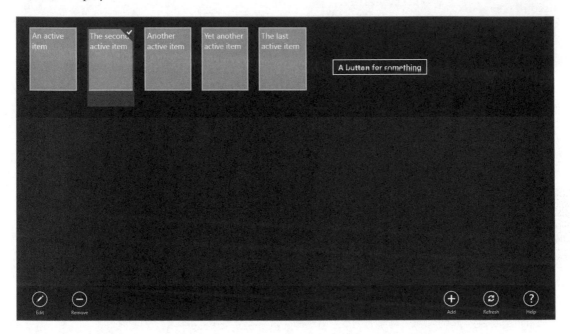

**FIGURE 13-4:** A nav bar appears on a swipe from the top of the screen. The app bar (bottom) also appears when the nav bar is called into view.

In Windows 8, `ListBox` is used less, and its niche is occupied by two other `ItemControls`: `GridView` and `ListView`. `ListView` is very much like a `ListBox`, but has some added capabilities. `GridView` offers a different arrangement of the displayed items. Let's look at `ListView` and `GridView` individually, with visual examples to show how they work. These examples will also be used to show some of the conventions and styles you'll typically use in a Windows 8 app.

`FlipView` is another `ItemsControl` that is new to Windows 8. As an `ItemsControl`, it shares a fair amount of syntax with `ListView` and `GridView`, but the navigation between items is completely new. `FlipView` allows one item at a time to take over the entire control, and supports touch and mouse gestures to "flip" between the data items.

## Sample Data for Examples of ItemControls

Before you can look at the new `ItemControls` in Windows 8 XAML, there's a bit of prep work required. Seeing these `ItemControls` in operation requires sample data, so you need to construct it.

The sample data is constructed by first creating data object classes, and then declaring some instances of those classes in XAML.

## About Data Models

There are a wide variety of ways to access and package data in Visual Basic. This chapter will not go into detail about that; Chapters 9, 10, and 11 discuss some of the details.

Since this chapter is not primarily about data, the data models used in examples are about as simple as it is possible to make them. The overall schema is an expansion of the Customer record model used in Chapter 12. It adds contact records, and each Customer includes a collection of contacts.

The classes used will include:

➤ Customer—a data object for a single customer

➤ Customers—a collection of Customer data objects

➤ Contact—a data object for a single contact record

➤ Contacts—a collection of Contact data objects

These models are simpler than the sample data models used in the application templates in Windows 8 XAML. Those models add additional features to support a code organization pattern that some developers like to use in their data models, which is called Model-View-ViewModel, commonly abbreviated MVVM. Since MVVM isn't required to do Windows 8 apps, and since there are many resources that go into intricate detail on MVVM, it is not discussed further in this chapter.

## Technical Notes for the Customer/Contact Sample Data Model

The classes for Customer and Contact records, and their respective collection classes, must satisfy a couple of important capabilities to work well in Windows 8 XAML. The data records (Customer and Contact) must have property change notification. That simply means they implement an interface called INotifyPropertyChanged. That allows properties to raise an event called PropertyChanged, which is monitored by the data binding system so that bindings are updated when properties are changed. Your implementation of INotifyPropertyChanged will be minimal, because best practices for data classes are beyond the scope of this chapter.

The collection classes must be of a type that has events when items are added to or removed from the collection. The class used for that will be familiar to experienced XAML developers. It is a generic collection class called ObservableCollection(of T).

The code for the data model is included in the code download for the chapter. However, for reference, the code listings are included here as well.

Here are code listings for the Contact and Contacts classes (code file: ContactClasses.vb):

```
Public Class Contact
    Implements INotifyPropertyChanged

    Private _ContactName As String
    Public Property ContactName() As String
        Get
            Return _ContactName
        End Get
        Set(ByVal value As String)
            If _ContactName <> value Then
                _ContactName = value
                NotifyPropertyChanged("ContactName")
            End If
        End Set
    End Property
```

```vb
        Private _Phone As String
        Public Property Phone() As String
            Get
                Return _Phone
            End Get
            Set(ByVal value As String)
                If _Phone <> value Then
                  _Phone = value
                  NotifyPropertyChanged("Phone")
                End If
            End Set
        End Property

        Public Event PropertyChanged(ByVal sender As Object,
                ByVal e As System.ComponentModel.PropertyChangedEventArgs)
                Implements
                System.ComponentModel.INotifyPropertyChanged.PropertyChanged

        Private Sub NotifyPropertyChanged(ByVal PropertyName As String)
            Dim eNew As New PropertyChangedEventArgs(PropertyName)
            RaiseEvent PropertyChanged(Me, eNew)
        End Sub

    End Class


    Public Class Contacts
        Inherits ObservableCollection(Of Contact)

    End Class
```

Here are code listings for the `Customer` and `Customers` classes (code file: `CustomerClasses.vb`):

```vb
    Public Class Customer
        Implements INotifyPropertyChanged

        Public Sub New()
            _Contacts = New Contacts
        End Sub

        Private _CustomerName As String
        Public Property CustomerName() As String
            Get
                Return _CustomerName
            End Get
            Set(ByVal value As String)
                If _CustomerName <> value Then
                  _CustomerName = value
                  NotifyPropertyChanged("Name")
                End If
            End Set
        End Property

        Public Event PropertyChanged(ByVal sender As Object,
            ByVal e As System.ComponentModel.PropertyChangedEventArgs)
```

```vb
        Implements System.ComponentModel.INotifyPropertyChanged.PropertyChanged

Private Sub NotifyPropertyChanged(ByVal PropertyName As String)
    Dim eNew As New PropertyChangedEventArgs(PropertyName)
    RaiseEvent PropertyChanged(Me, eNew)
End Sub

Private _Active As Boolean
Public Property Active() As Boolean
    Get
        Return _Active
    End Get
    Set(ByVal value As Boolean)
        If _Active <> value Then
            _Active = value
            NotifyPropertyChanged("Active")
        End If
    End Set
End Property

Private _Contacts As Contacts
Public Property Contacts() As Contacts
    Get
        Return _Contacts
    End Get
    Set(ByVal value As Contacts)
        If _Contacts IsNot value Then
            _Contacts = value
            NotifyPropertyChanged("ContactName")
        End If
    End Set
End Property

Private _Phone As String
Public Property Phone() As String
    Get
        Return _Phone
    End Get
    Set(ByVal value As String)
        If _Phone <> value Then
            _Phone = value
            NotifyPropertyChanged("Phone")
        End If
    End Set
End Property

Private _Logo As String
Public Property Logo() As String
    Get
        Return _Logo
    End Get
    Set(ByVal value As String)
        If _Logo <> value Then
            _Logo = value
            NotifyPropertyChanged("Logo")
```

```
            End If
        End Set
    End Property

End Class


Public Class Customers
    Inherits ObservableCollection(Of Customer)

End Class
```

Finally, here is the XAML that is used to declare a set of five customer objects, each with a `Contacts` collection. This resource, named `CustomerList`, is then used as the `ItemsSource` for various `ItemControls` in the examples (code file: `SampleCustomerList.xaml`):

```xml
<local:Customers x:Key="CustomerList">
    <local:Customer CustomerName="BigBux, Inc."
                    Active="True"
                    Phone="223-555-1234"
                    Logo="http://billyhollis.com/Logos/BigBuxLogo.png" >
        <local:Customer.Contacts>
            <local:Contact ContactName="Sherlock Holmes" Phone="212-555-1234" />
            <local:Contact ContactName="John Watson" Phone="212-555-3456" />
            <local:Contact ContactName="Mycroft Holmes" Phone="212-555-6789" />
        </local:Customer.Contacts>
    </local:Customer>
    <local:Customer CustomerName="SmallPotatoes, Ltd."
                    Active="False"
                    Phone="212-555-1234"
                    Logo="http://billyhollis.com/Logos/SmallPotatoesLogo.png">
        <local:Customer.Contacts>
            <local:Contact ContactName="Oliver Twist" Phone="414-555-1234" />
        </local:Customer.Contacts>

    </local:Customer>
    <local:Customer CustomerName="Medium Enterprises, Inc."
                    Active="True"
                    Phone="313-555-1234"
                    Logo="http://billyhollis.com/Logos/MediumEnterprisesLogo.png" >
        <local:Customer.Contacts>
            <local:Contact ContactName="Elizabeth Bennet" Phone="313-555-1234" />
            <local:Contact ContactName="John Darcy" Phone="313-555-3456" />
            <local:Contact ContactName="Charlotte Lucas" Phone="313-555-6789" />
        </local:Customer.Contacts>

    </local:Customer>
    <local:Customer CustomerName="Globe Theatre"
                    Active="False"
                    Phone="515-555-1234"
                    Logo="http://billyhollis.com/Logos/GlobeTheatreLogo.png">
        <local:Customer.Contacts>
            <local:Contact ContactName="Romeo Montague" Phone="505-555-1234" />
            <local:Contact ContactName="Othello Jones" Phone="505-555-3456" />
            <local:Contact ContactName="Juliet Capulet" Phone="505-555-6789" />
        </local:Customer.Contacts>
```

```
        </local:Customer>
        <local:Customer CustomerName="Global Traders"
                Active="True"
                Phone="616-555-1234"
                Logo="http://billyhollis.com/Logos/GlobalTradersLogo.png">
            <local:Customer.Contacts>
                <local:Contact ContactName="Silas Marner" Phone="707-555-1234" />
            </local:Customer.Contacts>

        </local:Customer>
    </local:Customers>
```

For all the examples in this section, you should assume that the four classes above are part of the project, and that the XAML declaring CustomerList has been placed in the Resources section of App.xaml.

## ListView

ListView is so similar to ListBox that in many cases you can easily change your old ListBox XAML to use a ListView instead. Unless you're doing something fancy with the ListBox, you can just change the tag from ListBox to ListView, and the XAML will work.

The main advantage of ListView over ListBox is that is has better touch functionality, and works more transparently with standard Windows 8 gestures. For example, if you are swiping through a list (which is often called panning), then when you raise your finger the list shows inertia. It continues moving while it decelerates to a stop. This generates a more natural interaction pattern, because that's the way things act in the real world.

Using the sample customer data defined earlier, let's look at the XAML for a ListView example, including a data template that will format Customer data records. To construct the example, just create a new Blank App and replace the Grid element in MainPage with the following XAML (code file:CustomerDataTemplate.xaml):

```
<Page.Resources>
    <DataTemplate x:Key="Standard250x250ItemTemplate">
        <Grid HorizontalAlignment="Left" Width="250" Height="250"
                Background="{StaticResource
ListViewItemPlaceholderBackgroundThemeBrush}">

            <StackPanel Margin="4" VerticalAlignment="Top"
                    Background="{StaticResource
ListViewItemOverlayBackgroundThemeBrush}">
                <TextBlock LineHeight="28" FontSize="24"
                            Text="{Binding CustomerName}"
                    Foreground="{StaticResource
ListViewItemOverlayForegroundThemeBrush}"

                        Style="{StaticResource TitleTextStyle}" Margin="15,0,15,0"/>
                <TextBlock LineHeight="24" FontSize="18" Text="{Binding Phone}"
                    Foreground="{StaticResource
ListViewItemOverlayForegroundThemeBrush}"

                        Style="{StaticResource TitleTextStyle}" Margin="15,0,15,0"/>
```

```
                    <Image Source="{Binding Logo}" MaxWidth="120"
                            HorizontalAlignment="Center" Margin="20"/>
                </StackPanel>
            </Grid>
        </DataTemplate>



    </Page.Resources>

    <Grid Background="{StaticResource ApplicationPageBackgroundThemeBrush}">
        <Grid.RowDefinitions>
            <RowDefinition Height="140"/>
            <RowDefinition Height="*"/>
        </Grid.RowDefinitions>
        <TextBlock x:Name="pageTitle" Grid.Column="1" Text="ListView Example"
                    Margin="120,0,0,0" Style="{StaticResource PageHeaderTextStyle}"/>
        <ListView Grid.Row="1" Margin="120,0,0,0"
                    ItemTemplate="{StaticResource Standard250x250ItemTemplate}"
                    ItemsSource="{StaticResource CustomerList}" />
    </Grid>
```

The data template is one of the standard sizes used in Windows 8, and the resource name indicates that. In fact, it was created by copying the resource of the same name out of `StandardStyles.xaml`.

Notice that the layout of the `Page` containing the `ListView` satisfies simple Windows 8 conventions. The top header area, which often contains the application name, is 140 pixels high, and both the header area and the `ListView` have a left margin of 120 pixels. For vertically scrolling content, the bottom margin is often zero, and the `ListView` does vertical scrolling by default (though it has an `ItemsPanel` property to change that, just as a `ListBox` does).

If this XAML is placed in a Blank App project that has your earlier `Customer`/`Contact` data model incorporated, then the running application will look like Figure 13-5.

Just as the items in a `ListBox` are `ListBoxItem` instances, the items in a `ListView` are `ListViewItem` instances. These can be created manually instead of being manufactured from data, as the example in Figure 13-4 above showed. This is rarely used for line-of-business applications.

## GridView

`GridView` is very similar to `ListView` with the following exceptions:

➤  The default arrangement of data items is wrapped, similar to a `WrapPanel` in earlier XAML platforms.

➤  The default scrolling of items is horizontal instead of vertical.

➤  The items in a `GridView` are `GridViewItem` instances.

The syntax is so similar that if you simply change the `ListView` tag to a `GridView` tag in the XAML shown above, it will work fine, and you'll get a running program that looks like Figure 13-6.

Like `ListView`, `GridView` is nicely optimized for touch interaction. In fact, both `ListView` and `GridView` inherit from a class named `ListViewBase`, where much of that touch interaction functionality is implemented.

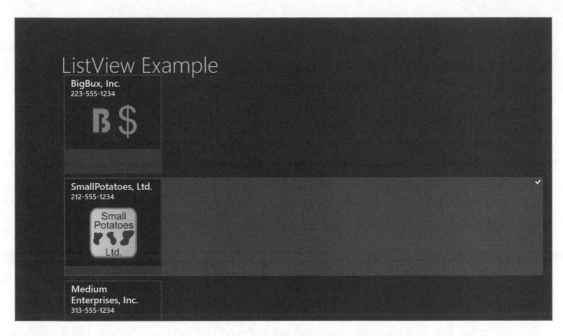

**FIGURE 13-5:** A ListView provides a touch-friendly, vertically scrolling list of data items. The second item has been selected by the user.

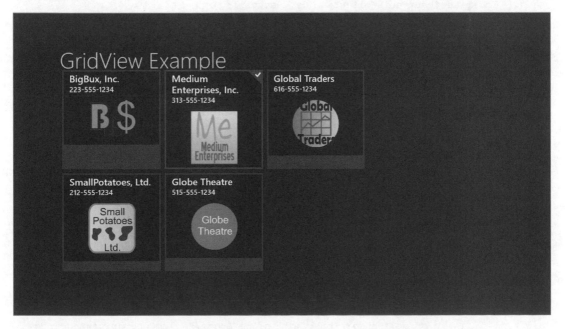

**FIGURE 13-6:** A GridView provides a touch-friendly, horizontally scrolling list of data items, wrapped into columns. The third item has been selected by the user.

## Grouping in ListView and GridView

Some data models include data items grouped by some factor, usually a property value. For example, `Customer` data items might be grouped by the state in which the customer is located, or by whether or not the `Customer` is active.

If you are familiar with XAML in WPF, you may know about grouping in the `ListBox` control, using a `CollectionViewSource` to obtain a collection view, and then altering its `GroupDescriptions` property. Grouping is also available in the `ListView` and `GridView` controls in Windows 8, and the grouping still involves a `CollectionViewSource`. However, the underlying mechanisms are different. Windows 8 grouping depends on a data model that implement groups, instead of having groups automatically created via a `CollectionView`.

To see grouping in action in a `GridView`, you'll need to do some changes to your default data model. The `CustomerGroups` class will serve as the container of your groups of customer objects, and it will hold a collection of instances of the `Customers` class.

You've already seen the `Customers` class, and how it holds a collection of `Customer` objects. However, it does need one additional property to describe the particular group of `Customers` in an instance. That simply means that the following line needs to be added to the `Customers` class:

```
Public Property GroupName As String
```

Here is the rather simple code for the `CustomerGroups` class that holds a collection of instances of `Customers` collections:

```
Public Class CustomerGroups
    Inherits ObservableCollection(Of Customers)

End Class
```

With these data classes in place, you change the way your sample data is declared to create a sample data source holding groups of customers instead of just customer objects. Here is that XAML, which is placed in the `App.xaml` resources area (code file: `GroupedCustomers.xaml`):

```
<local:CustomerGroups x:Key="GroupedCustomers">
    <local:Customers GroupName="Active Customers">
        <local:Customer CustomerName="BigBux, Inc."
                Active="True" Special="True"
                Phone="223-555-1234"
                Logo=" http://billyhollis.com/Logos/BigBuxLogo.png" >
            <local:Customer.Contacts>
                <local:Contact ContactName="Sherlock Holmes"
                            Phone="212-555-1234" />
                <local:Contact ContactName="John Watson" Phone="212-555-3456" />
                <local:Contact ContactName="Mycroft Holmes" Phone="212-555-6789" />
            </local:Customer.Contacts>
        </local:Customer>
        <local:Customer CustomerName="Medium Enterprises, Inc."
                Active="True"
                Phone="313-555-1234"
                Logo=" http://billyhollis.com/Logos/MediumEnterprisesLogo.png" >
            <local:Customer.Contacts>
                <local:Contact ContactName="Elizabeth Bennet"
                            Phone="313-555-1234" />
                <local:Contact ContactName="John Darcy" Phone="313-555-3456" />
```

```
                <local:Contact ContactName="Charlotte Lucas"
                                Phone="313-555-6789" />
            </local:Customer.Contacts>

        </local:Customer>
        <local:Customer CustomerName="Global Traders"
            Active="True"
            Phone="616-555-1234"
            Logo=" http://billyhollis.com/Logos/GlobalTradersLogo.png">
            <local:Customer.Contacts>
                <local:Contact ContactName="Silas Marner" Phone="707-555-1234" />
            </local:Customer.Contacts>

        </local:Customer>
    </local:Customers>

    <local:Customers GroupName="Inactive Customers">
        <local:Customer CustomerName="SmallPotatoes, Ltd."
                Active="False"
                Phone="212-555-1234"
                Logo=" http://billyhollis.com/Logos/SmallPotatoesLogo.png">
            <local:Customer.Contacts>
                <local:Contact ContactName="Oliver Twist" Phone="414-555-1234" />
            </local:Customer.Contacts>

        </local:Customer>
        <local:Customer CustomerName="Globe Theatre"
                Active="False"
                Phone="515-555-1234"
                Logo=" http://billyhollis.com/Logos/GlobeTheatreLogo.png">
            <local:Customer.Contacts>
                <local:Contact ContactName="Romeo Montague" Phone="505-555-1234" />
                <local:Contact ContactName="Othello Jones" Phone="505-555-3456" />
                <local:Contact ContactName="Juliet Capulet" Phone="505-555-6789" />
            </local:Customer.Contacts>

        </local:Customer>
    </local:Customers>


</local:CustomerGroups>
```

With this sample data, a `CollectionViewSource` can be declared to use in your `GridView`. It is declared in the `Resources` for the `Page`, and looks like this:

```
<CollectionViewSource x:Key="GroupedCustomersSource"
                Source="{StaticResource GroupedCustomers}"
                IsSourceGrouped="True"  />
```

To make the `GridView` display groups, two changes are essential. First, the `ItemsSource` must be changed to become the `CollectionViewSource` that holds the groups instead of being a simple list of customers. Second, the `GridView` must have a `GroupStyle` defined, so that the `GridView` knows how to display the head for groups and, optionally, how data items in groups will be arranged. Taking all that into account, the `GridView` XAML definition needs to look something like this (code file: `GridViewExample.xaml`):

```
<GridView Margin="120,133,0,7" Name="MainGridView"
                ItemsSource="{Binding Source={StaticResource
```

```
GroupedCustomersSource}}"
                        ItemTemplate="{StaticResource Standard250x250ItemTemplate}"
                        Grid.RowSpan="2" >
        <GridView.GroupStyle>
            <GroupStyle>
                <GroupStyle.HeaderTemplate>
                    <DataTemplate>
                        <TextBlock Text="{Binding GroupName}"
                                   Style="{StaticResource SubheaderTextStyle}"
                                   Margin="5,15" />
                    </DataTemplate>
                </GroupStyle.HeaderTemplate>
                <GroupStyle.Panel>
                    <ItemsPanelTemplate>
                        <VariableSizedWrapGrid Orientation="Vertical"
Margin="0,0,80,0"/>
                    </ItemsPanelTemplate>
                </GroupStyle.Panel>
            </GroupStyle>
        </GridView.GroupStyle>

</GridView>
```

If you make these changes to the earlier GridView example and run the program, you'll get a sample screen that looks something like Figure 13-7.

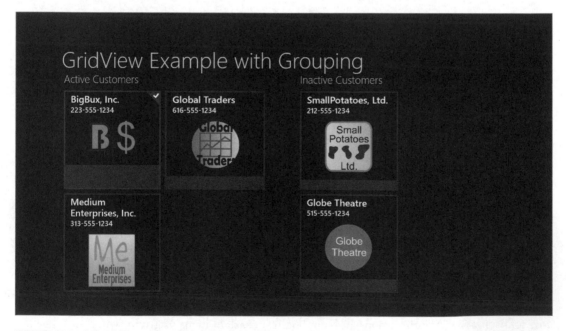

**FIGURE 13-7:** A GridView with grouped customer items

The amount of work involved to create a data model for a grouped data source is not trivial, but if your users need to look at data in groups, GridView and ListView can easily show them. In many cases, you will find it easier to use LINQ in code to produce your groups.

## FlipView

`FlipView` is another touch-optimized `ItemControl`. However, while the XAML `FlipView` strongly resembles that for `ListView` or `GridView`, its navigation/interaction pattern is quite distinct from other `ItemControls`.

Like all `ItemControls`, `FlipView` includes a collection of items in a list. The item type is `FlipViewItem`.

However, unlike all the other `ItemControls` you've likely seen, `FlipView` only shows one item at a time. The entire area of the `FlipView` is available to show a data item. The `FlipView` then offers gestures to move between items, which is sometimes called "flipping."

The touch gesture to flip between items is a horizontal swipe. A swipe to the left brings up the next item, while a swipe to the right goes back to the previous item in the list.

To allow equivalent interaction with a mouse, when a mouse moves over a `FlipView`, navigation buttons fade in on the sides to provide a place to click and navigate. A button is present only if navigation is possible in that direction. That is, when you are on the last item in the list, the button on the right does not appear. Likewise, the left button is absent in you are on the first item in the list.

If you would like the items to be a "ring" in which navigating from the last item loops back to the first item, then set the `TabNavigation` property to "Cycle." If you are familiar with Windows Phone development, you may have used the `Panorama` control. A `FlipView` with `TabNavigation` set to `Cycle` provides similar functionality, though the small part of the next record that shows on the right side in the `Panorama` is not present.

In the first `ListView` XAML example, if the tags are changed to a `FlipView`, then you'll see a screen similar to Figure 13-8. Since the data template wasn't changed, the single data item shown is much smaller than the screen, and isn't centered. In a real app, you'll rarely use a `FlipView` unless you need room for a larger data item, and centering the item is almost always appropriate.

Touch gestures and mouse gestures are active for navigation at this point. If you move the mouse over the `FlipView`, the navigation buttons will show, as in Figure 13-9.

Figure 13-9 shows that the navigation buttons are inside the `FlipView`, and will be on top of a data item if necessary. In many cases, when using a `FlipView`, you will want the `FlipView` control to be as wide as the whole view, and set up the data template to be centered and to allow space on the sides for the navigation buttons to appear.

## DataTemplateSelector

In Chapter 12, data templates were discussed in detail. In all those examples, an `ItemsControl` used a data template by setting the `ItemTemplate` property to a data template.

WPF developers may be familiar with a different way to determine the data templates used in an `ItemsControl`—a data template selector. This is an object that inherits from the `DataTemplateSelector` class, and contains logic to examine each data item and decide which template should be used to render that item.

`GridView`, `ListView`, and `FlipView` can all use a data template selector in Windows 8. The way the class is constructed is slightly different from WPF. Instead of overriding the `SelectTemplate` method, as in WPF, the `SelectTemplateCore` method is overridden instead.

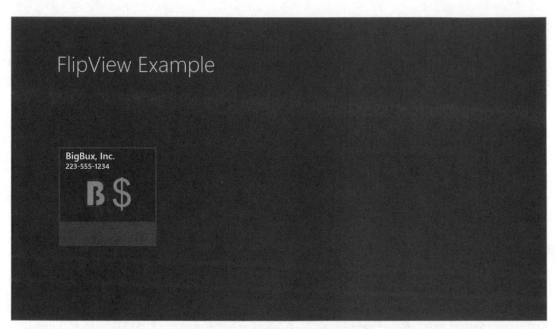

**FIGURE 13-8:** A FlipView showing the first record in your sample data

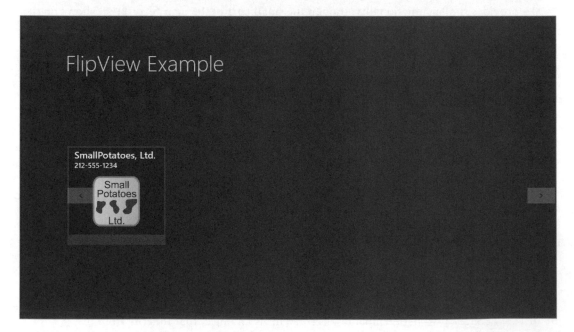

**FIGURE 13-9:** A FlipView showing the second record in your sample data, after a mouse has been moved over it. Note the navigation buttons to the left and right.

The class for a data template selector usually has some properties to hold the templates that are being used to render various data items. In your example below, you will construct a

CustomerDataTemplateSelector, and give it properties for ActiveCustomerTemplate and InactiveCustomerTemplate.

Typically, an instance of the DataTemplateSelector is created in a project as a resource, and the ItemTemplateSelector of a GridView, ListView, or FlipView is set to that resource. For an example, you'll modify the earlier GridView example to add the data template selector.

The code download for the chapter includes that example. The data template selector is a class named CustomerDataTemplateSelector. Here is the code for that class (code file: CustomerDataTemplateSelector.vb):

```
Public Class CustomerDataTemplateSelector
    Inherits Controls.DataTemplateSelector

    Public Property ActiveCustomerTemplate As DataTemplate
    Public Property InactiveCustomerTemplate As DataTemplate

    Protected Overrides Function SelectTemplateCore(item As Object,
                                            container As
                                            DependencyObject)
                                            As DataTemplate

        Dim c As Customer
        c = CType(item, Customer)
        If c.Active Then
            Return ActiveCustomerTemplate
        Else
            Return InactiveCustomerTemplate
        End If

    End Function

End Class
```

As you can see, in the example, the data template used is determined by the Active property of the customer record.

Then a new data template was added to the resources collection, using the key InactiveCustomerTemplate. The XAML is similar to the data template used earlier in the ListView example, except that the Image control is removed and text elements get a gray foreground (code file: InactiveCustomerTemplate.xaml):

```
<DataTemplate x:Key="InactiveCustomerTemplate">
    <Grid HorizontalAlignment="Left" Width="250" Height="250"
        Background="{StaticResource
ListViewItemPlaceholderBackgroundThemeBrush}">

        <StackPanel Margin="4" VerticalAlignment="Top"
            Background="{StaticResource
ListViewItemOverlayBackgroundThemeBrush}">
            <TextBlock LineHeight="28" FontSize="24"
                Text="{Binding CustomerName}"
                Foreground="Gray"
                Style="{StaticResource TitleTextStyle}"
```

```
                          Margin="15,0,15,0"/>
            <TextBlock LineHeight="24" FontSize="18"
                       Text="{Binding Phone}"
                       Foreground="Gray"
                       Style="{StaticResource TitleTextStyle}"
                       Margin="15,0,15,0"/>
            <TextBlock LineHeight="28" FontSize="24"
                       Text="Inactive" FontStyle="Italic"
                       Foreground="Gray"
                       Style="{StaticResource TitleTextStyle}"
                       Margin="15,20,15,20"/>
        </StackPanel>
    </Grid>
</DataTemplate>
```

Then an instance of the `CustomerDataTemplateSelector` was added to the resource collection, with a key of `MyCustomerTemplateSelector`:

```
<local:CustomerDataTemplateSelector x:Key="MyCustomerTemplateSelector"
        ActiveCustomerTemplate="{StaticResource Standard250x250ItemTemplate}"
        InactiveCustomerTemplate="{StaticResource InactiveCustomerTemplate}" />
```

Notice how the templates to be used are assigned to the `ActiveCustomerTemplate` and `InactiveCustomerTemplate` properties, based on the resources that are already in the XAML.

The final step is to change the `GridView` XAML to remove the ItemTemplate property setting, and set the `ItemTemplateSelector` property to the `MyCustomerTemplateSelector` resource:

```
<GridView Grid.Row="1" Margin="120,0,0,0"
        ItemTemplateSelector="{StaticResource MyCustomerTemplateSelector}"
        ItemsSource="{StaticResource CustomerList}" />
```

The resulting program will yield a screen much like Figure 13-10.

## Pickers

In earlier versions of XAML, as well as other UI technologies such as Windows Forms, getting access to the file system was done via a set of common dialogues. The classes were actually thin wrappers over parts of the Windows API, with the wrappers serving to make the dialogues object-oriented.

In Windows 8, the native API is object-oriented. Therefore no wrappers are needed. Accessing the file system dialogues means calling the corresponding API objects. Instead of being called common dialogues, they are called pickers.

Since these are native API objects, they don't reside in any of the XAML related namespaces. Pickers and their associated helper classes are in the `Windows.Storage.Pickers` namespace.

The calling conventions are also different. Windows 8 apps are required to do just about everything asynchronously, which lets apps be suspended, hibernated, switched out, etc., more easily. So whereas common dialogues are modal, pickers are required to be asynchronous.

Chapter 5 discussed asynchronous syntax for Visual Basic, and you'll need that syntax to work with pickers. Here is an example routine that could be place behind a button to access the `FolderPicker`, which is the object used to choose a folder object and returns an object of type `StorageFolder` (code file: `FolderPickerExample.vb`):

```
Private Async Sub Button_Click_1(sender As Object, e As RoutedEventArgs)
    Dim fp As New Windows.Storage.Pickers.FolderPicker
    fp.SuggestedStartLocation =
          Windows.Storage.Pickers.PickerLocationId.DocumentsLibrary
    fp.FileTypeFilter.Add(".docx")

    Dim PickedFolder As Windows.Storage.StorageFolder
    PickedFolder = Await fp.PickSingleFolderAsync
    If PickedFolder Is Nothing Then
        ' User did not choose a folder
    Else
        ' PickedFolder contains the folder chosen by the user
        Dim md As New MessageDialog("The user chose " & PickedFolder.DisplayName)
        Await md.ShowAsync()

    End If

End Sub
```

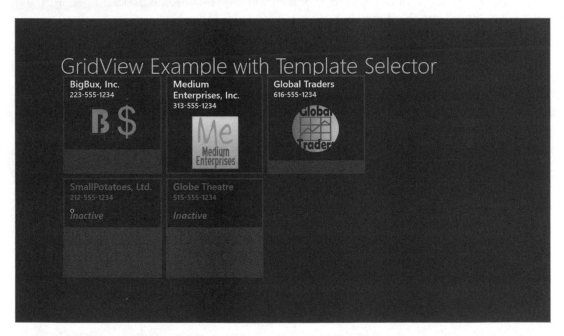

**FIGURE 13-10:** The earlier GridView example has been modified to use a data template selector. Inactive customers are rendered in a different template from active customers.

Notice that the click event handler is declared with the `Async` keyword, and that the `Await` keyword is used before the `FolderPicker` method call, which is `PickSingleFolderAsync`. The `MessageDialog` showing the result is also used asynchronously.

## ProgressRing

Previous XAML platforms has a `ProgressBar` control to indicate progress on an operation. Windows 8 has such an element, but it also has a complementary `ProgressRing` control.

When you use `ProgressBar`, you are responsible for giving it periodic updates as to the completion percentage. With `ProgressRing`, that's not necessary. It just continually displays an animation indicating that an operation is ongoing. No progress value is involved.

All you do to make a `ProgressRing` active is to set the `IsActive` property to `True`. The `ProgressRing` will show and animate until `IsActive` is changed to `False`. It's common to do this in code, but for simplicity, the example below will bind `IsActive` to another control, which is a `ToggleSwitch`.

Since the example for `ProgressRing` uses `ToggleSwitch`, let's cover that first and then look at the XAML example for both of them.

## ToggleSwitch

In earlier XAML platforms, `CheckBox` was the usual way to indicate a true/false selection. In Windows 8 XAML, `CheckBox` is still present, but should be used much more sparingly. If the user needs to turn settings on or off, or turn on actions, the `ToggleSwitch` is preferred because it is designed to fit well into the Windows 8 UI standards.

`CheckBox` uses the `IsChecked` property to expose a true/false or on/off status. The corresponding property for `ToggleSwitch` is named `IsOn`, which also exposes a `Boolean`.

`CheckBox` is a `ContentControl`, and simply displays a single piece of static content. `ToggleSwitch` is not a `ContentControl`. Instead, it has three properties that allow content:

1. **OnContent**—the content shown when `IsOn` is `True`.

2. **OffContent**—the content shown when `IsOn` is `False`.

3. **Header**—content to tell the user what the `ToggleSwitch` is for. This content displays above the `ToggleSwitch` by default.

Let's look at an example in which a `ToggleSwitch` is used to turn a `ProgressRing` on and off:

```
<Grid Background="{StaticResource ApplicationPageBackgroundThemeBrush}">
    <StackPanel Orientation="Horizontal">
        <ToggleSwitch   Name="ProgressToggleSwitch" FontSize="28"
                        Header="ToggleSwitch and ProgressRing Example"
                        OffContent="Idle" OnContent="Working" />
        <ProgressRing Height="60" Width="60"
                      Foreground="Aquamarine"
                      IsActive="{Binding ElementName=ProgressToggleSwitch,
Path=IsOn}"/>
    </StackPanel>

</Grid>
```

This XAML can be placed in a new Blank App, and when the `ToggleSwitch` is turned out, the screen will look like Figure 13-11.

## Other New Elements

There are several other new controls and elements, but in this brief introduction to Windows 8 XAML, you can't cover them all. Most of them are straightforward, and should be easy to learn when you need them. Here are some of the more notable new controls and elements that you will be omitting:

➤ **WebView**—used to show HTML content

➤ **RichTextBlock**—displays rich content, including embedded images and other advanced layout

➤ **RichEditBox**—displays rich content, including embedded images and other advanced layout, and allows the user to edit the content

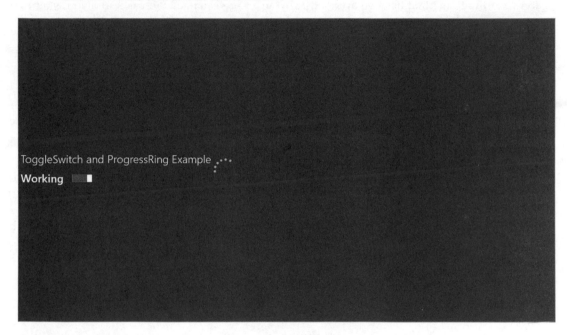

**FIGURE 13-11:** The ToggleSwitch on the left controls the ProgressRing, which animates the dots in a circle.

## Old Elements with New Usage

In general, Windows 8 XAML does a pretty good job of keeping down confusion between XAML platforms. You've seen that it has a number of its own elements that are optimized to Windows 8 purposes, such as `RichEditBox`. Since it has a different name from the `RichTextBox` control in earlier XAML platforms, it's much less likely for you to get their functionality mixed up.

However, there are two elements that have exactly the same name in Windows 8, but have some critical differences you should know about. They are `Frame` and `Popup`.

### Frame

The `Frame` control existed in WPF and Silverlight versions of XAML, but it had different capabilities in each. The Silverlight version of Frame, for example, had integration with the browser's address bar.

The Frame in Windows 8 has its own differences. For that reason, Chapter 12 didn't discuss the `Frame`. Here are the basics of the `Frame` in Windows 8 XAML.

The `Frame` is used most often as a host for a `Page`, or more rarely, a `UserControl` element. `Frame` has a `Navigate` method to place a `Page` in the `Frame`. Note that this is different from the `NavigateURI` used in Silverlight's `Frame`. Instead of using a URI for navigation, in Windows 8 XAML, most navigation is done by navigating to a new instance of a type.

You can place a `Frame` in a XAML surface, and use it as a host for part of your view. `Frame` is also commonly used as the root `ContentControl` for an entire application, with the `Navigate` method of the `Frame` used to transfer application control to entirely different views.

`Frame`'s `Navigate` method has two overloads. If your `Frame` is named `MyFrame`, and you want to navigate it to a new view of type `CustomerPage`, then the two overloads look like this:

```
MyFrame.Navigate(CustomerPage)

MyFrame.Navigate(CustomerPage, ParameterObject)
```

In the second overload, `ParameterObject` can be an object of any type. Normally, you would construct such an object that held the information which needed to be transferred to the new instance of the `CustomerPage`.

The reason `Page` is most often used as the navigation target is that `Page` has an `OnNavigatedTo` method that is fired when the `Page` is activated by navigation. The parameter object in the second overload above is available in the arguments for that method. The most common pattern, then, is to look at the parameter object, and take whatever steps are appropriate to configure the target `Page`. For example, the parameter object might include a database ID, and the ID could be used to set the `DataContext` for the `Page`.

You will examples of `Frame` usage, including the `Navigate` method, in the section below on the standard application templates used by Visual Studio to produce a new application.

## PopUp

The `PopUp` element is familiar to most XAML developers. It provides a surface that is guaranteed to float on top of a view. Some internal controls, such as `ComboBox`, use `PopUp` internally. In the case of `ComboBox`, the items that appear when the `ComboBox` is opened are on a `PopUp` element.

In Windows 8, the `PopUp` is used for similar purposes as earlier versions of XAML, but it has some missing capabilities compared to earlier versions. In particular, whereas the WPF and Silverlight `PopUp` elements know how to position themselves relative to another element on a page, the Windows 8 `PopUp` does not. It has `HorizontalOffset` and `VerticalOffset` properties to position the `PopUp` on the entire visual surface, but it is your responsibility to calculate those offsets and configure the `PopUp` before showing it.

As with older versions of `PopUp`, the interior of the `PopUp` is determined by setting the `Child` property of the `PopUp`. It's common for the `Child` to be set to a `Grid`, `UserControl`, or other container, and that becomes the design surface for the visuals that will display in the `PopUp`.

After a `PopUp` is configured, it is brought into view by setting the `IsOpen` property to `True`. Then, when it's finished, `IsOpen` should be set to `False`. Usually various touch and mouse events are detected to indicate that the user is no longer interested in the PopUp, and then the PopUp is closed in the code for those events.

## CHANGES TO THE VISUAL DESIGNER IN VISUAL STUDIO 2012

The visual designer for Visual Studio 2012 is fundamentally similar to the designers for XAML in earlier versions, with one major exception: The Properties window has been totally replaced. Otherwise, though there are numerous cosmetic differences, the operation of the drag-and-drop visual designer and the associated XAML editor are fundamentally similar. That means, unfortunately, that dragging elements from the toolbox to your XAML surface still isn't very helpful; more often than not you are better off editing XAML directly to get the layout you need.

The new Properties window is a significant improvement, however. It shares many features with Expression Blend, and thus offers a better experience at configuring many property values. Here are some of the improvements.

### Better Resource Selector

The Resource selector has been improved for all properties. The glyph that brings up a menu of Advanced Property options for setting a property is similar to the one in Visual Studio 2010, but it has now been moved to the right side of the property value. It is shown circled in Figure 13-12. Figure 13-13 then shows the menu that results from pressing the glyph, with a submenu of system resources.

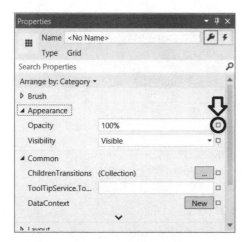

**FIGURE 13-12:** The glyph that calls up advanced settings for a property has been moved to the far right in Visual Studio 2012.

It's also easier to choose resources to associate with a property of type Brush. The Brush editor, which automatically appears in the Properties windows for properties that take a Brush such as Background, Foreground, and Fill, now has easier access to available Brush resources. At the top of the `Brush` editor, where the brush type is selected, a new option appears at the far right to get a tab showing all the available `Brush` resources.

**FIGURE 13-13:** The advanced settings menu has several options for working with resources. The Local Resource and System Resource options now have a scrollable list of resources.

## Common vs. Advanced Property Categories

Each category of properties is now divided into Common and Advanced properties. Common properties are those the Visual Studio team decided that you are likely to set frequently. Advanced properties are expected to be set less frequently, and are available by pressing the down arrow at the bottom of the category.

As in Expression Blend, if you search for a property by name, it appears in the Properties window regardless of whether it is in the Common or Advanced group for its category. Unlike past versions of Expression Blend, the Properties window in Visual Studio 2012 retains the ability to sort properties alphabetically.

## Transform Properties

You can now set `Transform` properties in the Visual Studio 2012 Properties window. The two properties in the `Transform` category are `RenderTransform` and `Projection`. Even though Chapter 12 did not include coverage of transforms and projections, most experienced XAML developers will be familiar with them.

Visual Studio 2010 had no ability to set `RenderTransform` or `Projection` property values in the Properties window, and developers were forced to either use Expression Blend or fall back on hand-coded XAML. Now the Expression Blend property editor for those properties is available in Visual Studio. Figure 13-14 shows a `RenderTransform` being set with a rotation angle of 15 degrees.

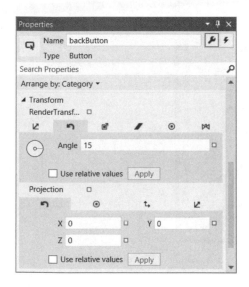

**FIGURE 13-14:** The Properties window now includes the ability to set Transform properties such as RenderTransform. Here, a rotation angle of 15 degrees is being set.

## Animation

One of the more difficult aspects of developing in earlier XAML platforms was working with animation. While those platforms had very rich animation support, using it required a high level of expertise.

Windows 8 shares the rich animation support supported by earlier versions, but it adds an entry point that makes commonly used animations very accessible. A set of animations called `ThemeTransitions` are available merely by adding them to the Transitions property for an element, or the `ChildTransitions` property for a panel.

To use a `ThemeTransition`, in the Properties window, locate the `Transitions` property and click the button with the ellipsis on the right. You will see a dialogue similar to Figure 13-15.

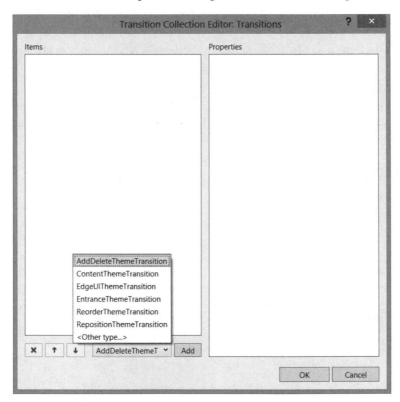

**FIGURE 13-15:** Setting transitions in the Visual Studio 2012 Properties window. The drop-down of available transitions is shown open.

To add a transition animation, first select the kind of transition you want to work with by picking an option in the drop-down on the bottom right. This drop-down has been opened in Figure 13-15. For example, suppose you choose `EntranceThemeTransition`. You can then add animation for that transition by pressing the Add button.

At that point the dialogue will look like Figure 13-16. Notice that the transition has several properties you can use to tweak the animation. In this case, you can specify the amount of horizontal and vertical animation applied to the animation when it appears.

If you add such a transition to an element, when the element is added to the UI, or when the element changes in visibility from `Collapsed` to `Visible`, the transition will be animated. The code download for the chapter includes a sample program that animates a rectangle when it appears.

**FIGURE 13-16:** The transitions editor with an EntranceThemeTransition added

## APPLICATION TEMPLATES IN VISUAL STUDIO 2012

For earlier XAML platforms, the projects in Visual Studio to create a XAML applications are very simple. A `Window` or `UserControl` is created, along with a XAML file for the `Application` object, named `App.xaml` in Silverlight and `Application.xaml` in WPF.

The standard templates for WPF and Silverlight applications place nothing in the `Window` or `UserControl` except a root layout `Grid`. No starting resources of any kind are included. It is up to the developer to supply styling, brushes, and so forth.

If Silverlight has RIA Services installed, an alternate template is available for a Navigation Application. This template places quite a bit more items into the project, and has some minimal navigation functionality right away.

The application templates for Windows 8 start with same approach as the Navigation Application and then take it further. All three templates, including the Blank App template, include a library of styles in a XAML file called `StandardStyles.xaml`. It is placed in a folder named Common.

The other templates, Grid App and Split App, also include multiple pages, with controls already on them. Sample data is included, and navigation logic is built in to allow selection of data items to navigate to new pages.

Using the Grid App or Split App template, you immediately have an application that satisfies basic Windows 8 conventions. However, this also makes for a rather complex starting point for your application. You'll need to study these templates to understand how they work in order to adapt tem to your own purposes.

## Split App

The Split App template is simpler than the Grid App template, and serves as a good starting point in your Windows 8 app development. It is a Windows 8 version of a master/detail navigation pattern.

To create an application with the Split App template, just start a new Project in Visual Studio 2012 and select the Split App template. As mentioned, the app will immediately have some minimal functionality, with sample data to create screens.

The starting screen for a Split App is shown in Figure 13-17. The items can be scrolled vertically with swipes or a mouse.

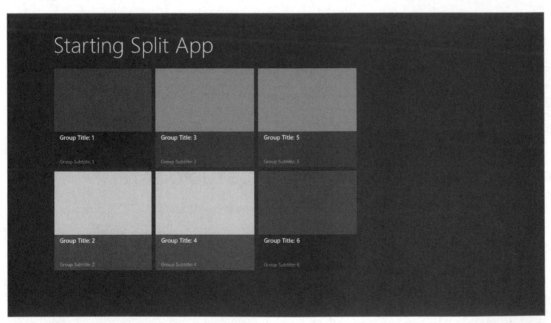

**FIGURE 13-17:** The starting screen for a Split App

## Grid App

The Grid App template has more complex navigation built in than the Split App template. If you create an application with the Grid App template, the starting screen for your application will look like Figure 13-19.

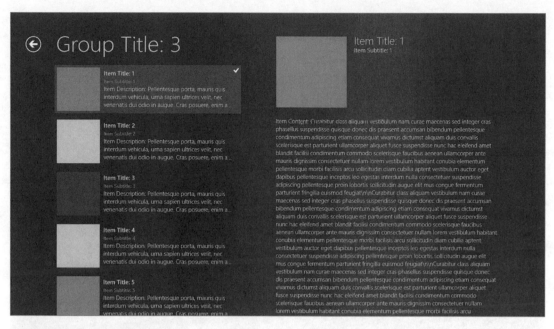

**FIGURE 13-18:** The screen for a group of items in an application created with the Split App template. Selecting an item in the ListView on the left brings up the item on the left.

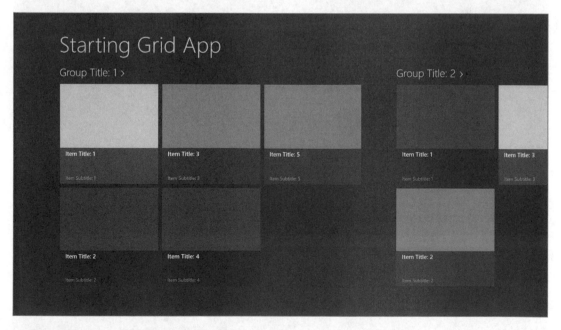

**FIGURE 13-19:** The starting screen for a Grid App

From this point, the user can touch or click on one of the group names (such as "Group Title 1"), or select one of the items in a group. If the user selects a group name, the resulting screen looks like Figure 13-20. Selecting an item brings up the screen in Figure 13-21.

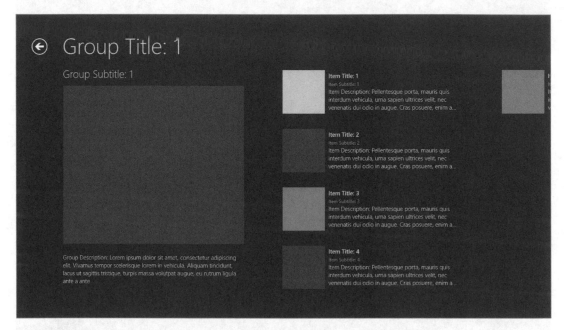

**FIGURE 13-20:** The Group screen in an application created with the Grid App template

**FIGURE 13-21:** The screen for an individual item in an application created with the Grid App template

## Layout Aware Pages

All the pages placed in a new application by the Grid App and Split App templates are layout aware. That means they know how to respond when the app is transitioned to a snapped view, or between portrait orientation and landscape orientation.

It's still your responsibility to determine what the page does for those orientations. Only very simple default behavior is included in a layout aware page.

You can also use layout aware pages in an app created with the Blank App template. There are six item types in the Add Item dialog that are layout aware pages. Figure 13-22 shows the Add Item dialogue with a bracket around these six page types.

If you add one of these page types to a Blank App, in addition to getting a new item for the layout aware page, several new items are also added to the Common folder.

## Items in the Common Folder

The Common folder is created by all Windows 8 XAML application templates, but in a Blank App, it only holds StandardStyles.xaml. In Split App and Grid App, it holds several additional items. As just mentioned, these additional items are added to Common folder for a blank app if a layout aware page is added to the project. Let's take a look at the contents of the Common folder for a project containing a layout aware page.

There are two base classes in the Common folder, BindableBase and LayoutAwarePage. BindableBase is used as the base class for the sample data models, and it implements INotifyPropertyChanged to provide property change notification. You can use it as a base class for your own data models if you like.

LayoutAwarePage is used as the base class for all the layout aware pages, and it includes functionality to help with navigation and to help application pages work better with Windows 8. For example, LayoutAwarePage has events for switching to a snapped view, or switching between portrait and landscape orientations. When you add new Page items to your project, it's a good idea to base most of them on LayoutAwarePage instead of the standard Page element.

The Common folder also contains several useful helper classes. One is a helper object for app suspension, called SuspensionManager.vb. Two commonly used value converters are present, BooleanToVisibilityConverter and BooleanNegationConverter. These converters provide functionality needed in the majority of XAML apps; in fact, WPF included BooleanToVisibilityConverter is its framework libraries. These converters are not part of the framework libraries. They are just source code in the application templates. Still, at least you don't have to write them.

## StandardStyles.xaml

As mentioned earlier, the Common folder includes a set of resources in StandardStyles.xaml. You'll probably use those resources a lot, and in fact some were used in earlier examples in this chapter. Most of the resources are Style definitions, hence the name of the item.

`StandardStyles.xaml` is loaded into the application in the `App.xaml Resources` collection. That means that all styles in `StandardStyles.xaml` are available throughout your application.

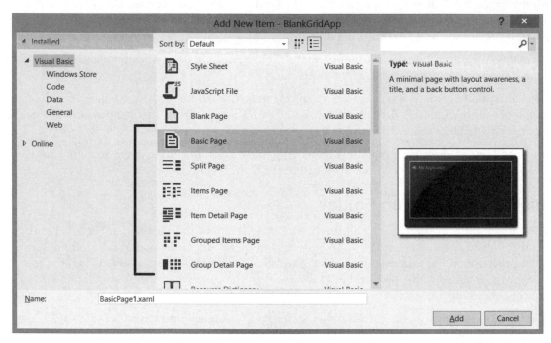

**FIGURE 13-22:** The Add New Item dialog in Visual Studio 2012, with a bracket showing the item types that are layout aware pages.

`StandardStyles.xaml` has almost 2,000 lines of resources. However, as discussed in the section above on app bars, `StandardStyles.xaml` contains dozens of styles for app bar buttons, all commented out. You should be aware of the styles for app bar buttons in `StandardStyles.xaml`, and uncomment the ones you need.

Except for uncommenting app bar button styles, it's a good idea to avoid major changes in `StandardStyles.xaml` until you become very familiar with the application templates and how these styles are used. If you decide you want your own version of one of these styles in a page, you can copy the `Style` from `StandardStyles.xaml` into the `Resources` collection for that page, and make the changes there. As discussed in Chapter 12, local resources with the same name override resources at a higher level in the application.

## Online Documentation for Grid App and Split App Templates

The Grid App and Split App templates include a link to online documentation for the template. It is located at the top of the code-behind module for `App.xaml`. Other pages in the template also have links at the top, which goes straight to the documentation for that particular page.

The documentation is reasonably extensive, and is likely to be refined over time, so it is not reproduced here. If you want to use these templates, you'll need to study that documentation in depth.

# IMPLEMENTING A LIVE TILE

By now, you should be familiar with the Windows 8 start menu, which features tiles for installed programs. There are two sizes of tiles, a square tile, and a wide tile. The wide tile is a landscape-oriented rectangle that is the size of two square tiles.

Some tiles update their content via logic in the associated app. These are called live tiles. Typically, the new content animates into place.

Live tiles have two basic purposes:

1. Place important information in front of the user without the user needing to open up an application

2. Induce the user to open an application by providing some teaser information

For line-of-business applications, the second purpose will rarely be needed. But if you are creating a app aimed at consumers, it might be relevant.

Use caution when designing live tiles. When a live tile changes its content too often, the associated animation can be distracting and irritating to the users. Used judiciously, however, live tiles can be a nice addition to an app.

Live tiles are templates with XML files. That makes the process of updating a live tile somewhat tedious. You need to manipulate an XMLDocument and its nodes to fill in the updated content for a live tile.

Several starting point templates are available, and you can see the list in an enumeration of type TileTemplateImage. You can build your own XML document for a tile template up from scratch if you like, as long as you get all the nodes right. However using the built-in templates and just manipulating nodes is usually easier and more reliable.

Here is a brief code snippet that updates a live tile to place an image in the tile. The template type is TileSquareImage (code file: LiveTileUpdate.vb):

```
Dim TileXML As XmlDocument =
    TileUpdateManager.GetTemplateContent(TileTemplateType.TileSquareImage)

Dim XMLNodes As XmlNodeList = TileXML.GetElementsByTagName("image")
XMLNodes(0).InnerText = "http://localhost/BigBuxInc.png"
Dim s As String = XMLNodes(0).InnerText
TileUpdateManager.CreateTileUpdaterForApplication().Update(New
    TileNotification(TileXML))
```

Notice that the starting point is to obtain an XML document with the proper nodes. From there, the necessary logic varies. The XML document might have several nodes that need to be updated. For this one, I'm only updating the image node to provide a URL for an image.

The image supplied was hardcoded in this code for simplicity. In production, typically the values placed in the XML nodes are dependent on data.

If you app allows wide tiles, which apps do by default, then you will probably want your tile update logic to update both kinds of styles. That requires combining XML nodes from different templates.

# IMPLEMENTING CONTRACTS

Early in the chapter, we discussed interaction with charms on the start bar. Those interactions are handled in your app by implementing the appropriate *contracts*. There are several contracts your app can implement, with Search and Share being the most important.

Saying that a contract is "implemented" sounds like implementing an abstract interface, but in fact many contracts are implemented merely by taking two steps:

**1.** Declare that the app will work with the control by changing the `Package.appmanifest` item in the project.

**2.** Handling an event at the application level to find out when the user selected the charm associated with the contract.

Let's step through a very simple case for working with the Search charm. This is by no means a full search implementation; it just shows the minimum code to detect when a Search has been requested and then do something in the UI.

First, start a new app with the Blank App template, and name it `SearchContractExample`.

To declare support for the Search contract, open the `Package.appmanifest` item in the project and go to the Declarations tab. It has a drop-down for the various declarations, and the Search contract is in the list. Figure 13-23 shows the Declarations page, with the list of available declarations dropped down.

To declare support for a Search contract, just select Search in the list and then press the Add button. Some properties will come up on the right side in case you want your app to delegate the searching to another app. To do searching within your app, you can ignore those properties.

Then you need to handle the associated event for searching at the application level. In the code behind for `App.xaml`, place the following sub (code file: `SearchContract.vb`):

```
Protected Overrides Sub OnSearchActivated(args As SearchActivatedEventArgs)

    ' Carry out search operations here
    ' and display results somewhere in the app.
    ' You might use LINQ or other techniques to find records
    ' that match args.QueryText.

    ' In this demo version, I'm just passing the search
    ' query string to the main page of the app.

    Dim pg As MainPage
    pg = CType(CType(Window.Current.Content, Frame).Content, MainPage)

    ' Search query text is available in args.QueryText
    pg.DisplaySearchResults(args.QueryText)

End Sub
```

Finally, place a `TextBlock` somewhere in `MainPage.xaml` with the `Name` set to `SearchResultsTextBox`. Then place the `DisplaySearchResults` method referenced above in the code-behind for `MainPage.xaml`:

```
Public Sub DisplaySearchResults(sQueryString As String)
    SearchResultsTextBox.Text = "Search activated with query string " &
sQueryString
End Sub
```

**FIGURE 13-23:** The Package.appmanifest Declarations page, showing the drop-down of declarations. The Search contract declaration is selected in the drop-down.

This is enough to show that the search operation is active in the app. Run the app, swipe the charms bar into place, and select the Search charm. Put in a search query string, and press the search button. You should see the TextBlock update with the search query string you entered.

How you actually carry out the search operation in your application is up to you. Typically, you would either carry out a database query, or use LINQ to query against data you have already fetched.

Updating views directly from the App.xaml code behind is not a good practice in general. This example is just to show you the basics. If you intend to handle searching, a good pattern for your code is to have a property on your data model or viewmodel that holds search results. Then you can bind an appropriate element to that property. That way, the App.xaml does not need to know where the search results are displayed. It needs only to update the model.

## SUMMARY

This chapter has provided a brief introduction to some of the most important concepts in creating Windows 8 XAML apps. It's only intended to get you started. If you find yourself working on complex Windows 8 apps, you may wish to find a more comprehensive resource.In the next chapter, the focus shifts from XAML-based user interfaces to HTML interfaces created with ASP.NET.

# 14

# Applications with ASP.NET, MVC, JavaScript, and HTML

**WROX.COM CODE DOWNLOADS FOR THIS CHAPTER**

The wrox.com code downloads for this chapter are found at www.wrox.com/remtitle .cgi?isbn=9781118314456 on the Download Code tab. The code is in the chapter 14 download and individually named according to the code file names listed throughout the chapter.

ASP.NET is a Web application framework (built on top of the .NET framework) that enables you to build powerful, secure, and dynamic applications in a highly productive environment. Over their 10-year lifetime, ASP.NET and the associated Visual Studio tools have changed quite a bit to keep up with the evolution of technologies and practices around Web development. Major additions to the framework like the provider model, ASP.NET AJAX, ASP.NET MVC, the Web API, ASP.NET Web Pages, and the Razor view engine have enabled Web developers on the Microsoft platform to build applications that meet the needs and expectations of today's consumer. However the addition of these technologies presents a bit of problem: you need to understand each well enough to decide if and when you should use them.

The goal of this chapter is to introduce you to different frameworks and technologies available within ASP.NET and Visual Studio and to provide you with enough information to enable you to decide which you'd like to explore further

# VISUAL STUDIO SUPPORT FOR ASP.NET

Visual Studio 2012 offers a wide range of features to assist you in building applications: IntelliSense, code snippets, integrated debugging, CSS style support, and the ability to target multiple versions of the .NET framework are a few examples. When working with ASP.NET you'll see that many of these productivity features also apply when working with inline code, client-side JavaScript code, XML, and HTML markup.

## Web Site and Web Application Projects

Visual Studio gives you two models for ASP.NET projects:

1. Web site projects

2. Web application projects

The Web application project model is very similar to other project types. The structure is based on a project file (.vbproj), and all VB code in the project compiles into a single assembly. To deploy it you copy the assembly along with markup and static content files to the server. You can create a new Web application project by selecting File ➪ New ➪ Project from the main menu in Visual Studio.

The Website project model was added with Visual Studio 2005. This model is designed to be very lightweight and familiar to Web developers and designers coming to Visual Studio from other tools. It uses a folder structure to define the contents of a project, enabling you to open a website just by pointing Visual Studio at a folder or a virtual directory. The default deployment model uses dynamic compilation whereby VB source files are deployed along with markup and other content files. Alternately, the project can be precompiled, which creates an assembly per folder or an assembly per page, depending on the settings passed to the compiler. You can create a new website by selecting File ➪ New ➪ Web Site from the main menu in Visual Studio.

## Web Server Options

ASP.NET gives you three options to host your Web projects:

1. ASP.NET Development Server

2. IIS Express

3. IIS

IIS Express is the default for Web application projects, and the ASP.NET Development Server is the default for Website projects. IIS Express and the ASP.NET Development Server are lightweight and convenient but both only allow you to run and test pages locally.

The mechanism used to select which server will be used depends on the project type. For Website projects, you can choose in the New Web Site dialog by selecting an option from the Web Location drop-down. Selecting File System will use the development server, while selecting HTTP will use IIS.

For Web application projects, you can select which server to use after the project has been created. This is done through the Web tab of the project properties. You can even switch back and forth, enabling you to do most of your development with the IIS Express but switching to IIS when you want to test in an environment closer to production.

## SERVER-SIDE DEVELOPMENT

ASP.NET offers three main server-side development models for building Web applications:

1. Web Forms
2. ASP.NET MVC (or just MVC for short)
3. Web Pages

Web Forms was the original Web development model in .NET and is now in version 4.5. MVC was first released in March 2009 and is now in version 4. Web Pages (and the associated Razor view engine) was first released in January 2011 and is now in version 2.

## Web Forms

The goal of Web Forms is to make the Web development experience as close to the Windows Forms (or Classic VB) development experience as possible. You build pages by dragging and dropping controls on a design surface, you set properties of those controls though the Properties window, and you add event handlers by double-clicking the controls. This gives separation between the code generated by the designer and the code you write.

Following the premise that the most effective way to learn a new technology is to use it, you'll now walk through a sample application of the core features of Web Forms. You can follow along with the instructions below or you can examine the project included with the code downloads for the book.

Open Visual Studio and select File ➪ New ➪ Project. In the New Project dialog, select the ASP.NET Web Forms Application template, set the Name to WebFormsDemo, and click the OK button (see Figure 14-1).

The project created by the template is a working Web application containing several sample pages. The project is designed to be a starting point you can use for your custom applications, and that is exactly how you will use it. Run the application by pressing the F5 key to see how it looks (see Figure 14-2).

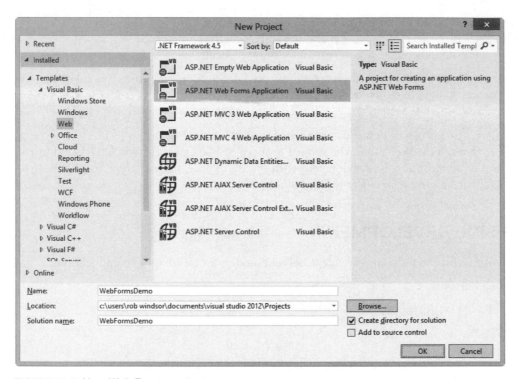

**FIGURE 14-1:** New Web Forms project

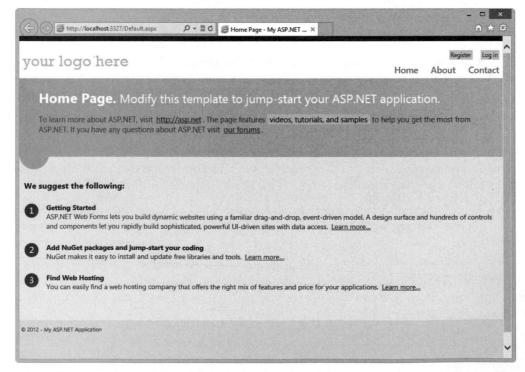

**FIGURE 14-2:** Default page of sample site generated by the project template

## Pages

Web Forms applications are made up of one or more pages. Pages are also known as Web Forms because they are designed to emulate a form in a Windows Forms application. Pages consist of a combination of markup and code. The code can use the classic ASP style and be placed inline in the same file as your markup, but the more common approach is to use a code-behind file. The idea of using the code-behind model is to separate the business logic and presentation into their own files. This makes it easier to work with your pages, especially if you are working in a team environment where visual designers work on the UI of the page and coders work on the business logic that sits behind the presentation pieces.

Add a page to the sample project by right-clicking on the project and select Add ⇨ New Item. In the Add New Item dialog, select the Web Form template, set the Name to ServerControls.aspx, and click the Add button (see Figure 14-3).

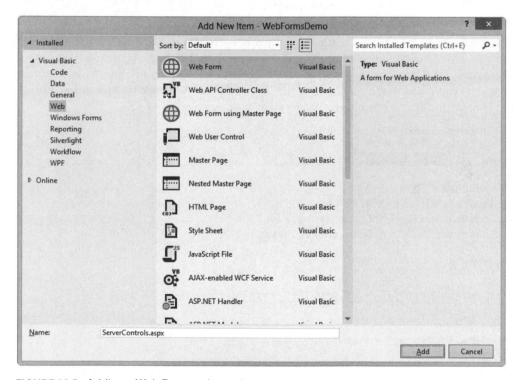

**FIGURE 14-3:** Adding a Web Form to the project

A new item will be added in the Solution Explorer to represent your page, but three files were actually created: ServerControls.aspx, which contains the markup; ServerControls.aspx.designer.vb, which contains code generated by Visual Studio as you work with the markup (you will very rarely have to look at or edit this file); and ServerControls.aspx.vb, which contains the VB code-behind for the page.

To see the code-behind, right-click on ServerControls.aspx in the Solution Explorer and select View Code. At the top of the file you will find the declaration of the ServerControls class. Note that this class inherits from System.Web.UI.Page, which is the base class for pages in Web Forms (see Figure 14-4).

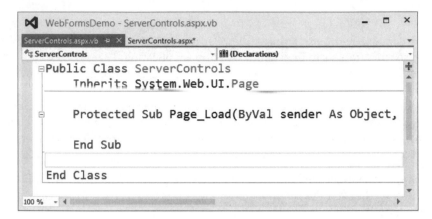

**FIGURE 14-4:** Code-behind for the ServerControls page

Now switch back to the markup. If the file is not already open, you can open it by right-clicking on ServerControls.aspx in the Solution Explorer and selecting View Markup. At the top of the markup you will find a `<% Page %>` directive. It is the `CodeBehind` and `Inherits` attributes of this directive that link the markup file with the code-behind file. In this file you will also find the `Form` control which will contain the other controls you place on the page (see Figure 14-5).

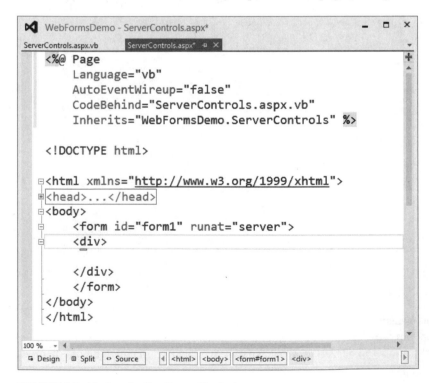

**FIGURE 14-5:** Markup for the ServerControls page

## Server Controls

Server controls are logical elements that represent user interface and behavior when rendered on a page. You add the control to the page and configure its properties, and ASP.NET determines the appropriate HTML tags (and quite often JavaScript) to send to the browser to implement desired functionality. The control can be something simple like a button, or something complex like a grid that supports sorting and filtering.

To use drag-and-drop to add controls to your page, click the Design or Split tab at the bottom of the design area in the IDE. When either of these views is active, you can drag and drop controls from the Toolbox onto the design surface, or you can place the cursor in the location where you want the control to appear and then double-click the control.

You also can work directly in the markup. Because many developers prefer this, it is the default view of a page. Hand-coding your pages may seem to be a slower approach than simply dragging and dropping controls onto a design surface, but it isn't as slow as you might think. Many of the same productivity features available when editing Visual Basic code, such as IntelliSense and Code Snippets, are also available when editing page markup. Also, like Design view, the Source view enables you to drag and drop controls from the Toolbox into the markup itself.

Whether you are in Design view or Source view, you can highlight a control to edit its properties in the Properties window. Changing the properties will change the appearance or behavior of the high-lighted control. Because all controls inherit from a specific base class (`WebControl`), you can high-light multiple controls at the same time and change the base properties of all the controls at once by holding down the Ctrl key as you make your control selections.

On the `ServerControls.aspx` page you want to add a `DropDownList` and set the ID to FruitDropDown; add a `Button` and set the ID to SubmitButton and Text to Submit; and add a `Label` and set the ID to ResultLabel. Also set the title of the page by setting the value of the `<title>` element in the markup to Server Control Example.

Use the techniques described in this section to add these controls and set their properties so that the page looks like Figure 14-6.

If you chose to add the markup using the code editor instead of the designer, the contents of the page should look something like this (code file: `ServerControls-Step01.aspx`):

```
<html xmlns="http://www.w3.org/1999/xhtml">
<head runat="server">
    <title>Server Control Example</title>
</head>
<body>
    <form id="form1" runat="server">
    <div>
        <asp:DropDownList ID="FruitDropDown" runat="server">
        </asp:DropDownList>
        <br />
        <br />
        <asp:Button ID="SubmitButton" runat="server" Text="Button" />
        <br />
        <br />
        <asp:Label ID="ResultLabel" runat="server" Text="Label"></asp:Label>
```

```
        </div>
        </form>
    </body>
    </html>
```

At this point you could view the page by selecting ServerControls.aspx in the Solution Explorer and pressing F5, but there won't be any data or behavior. You'll add those next using page and control events.

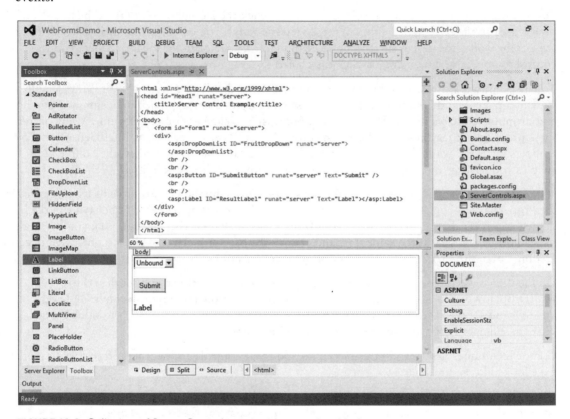

**FIGURE 14-6:** Split view of ServerControls.aspx with controls added

## Page Events

You will often want to handle the events raised as the page is being generated. This enables you to tailor the generation of the page to suit your needs.

Here is a list of the commonly used events in the page life cycle. Additional events are possible, but those are primarily used by developers creating custom server controls.

➤    PreInit

➤    Init

➤ InitComplete

➤ PreLoad

➤ Load

➤ LoadComplete

➤ PreRender

➤ SaveStateComplete

➤ Unload

Of these, the most frequently used is the Load event, which is generally used to initialize the properties of the page and its child controls. You'll use the Load event to add some data into the dropdown.

Right-click on the `ServerControls.aspx` file and select View Code to open the Code view of the page. Notice that the shell for the method that handles the Load event (`Page_Load`) is already there. Inside this method, write the code to populate the choices in the drop-down by adding the names of a few of your favorite fruits into the `Items` collection of the FruitDropDown control. Also, the ResultLabel shouldn't show any text when the page is first loaded, so set its `Text` property to an empty string (code file: `ServerControls-Step02.aspx.vb`).

```
Protected Sub Page_Load(ByVal sender As Object, _
    ByVal e As System.EventArgs) Handles Me.Load
    FruitDropDown.Items.Add("Apple")
    FruitDropDown.Items.Add("Banana")
    FruitDropDown.Items.Add("Grape")
    FruitDropDown.Items.Add("Orange")
    ResultLabel.Text = String.Empty
End Sub
```

Next, you need to add the code to handle the event raised when the SubmitButton is clicked.

## Control Events

ASP.NET Web Forms uses an event-driven model similar to that used with Windows Forms. The key difference between ASP.NET Web Forms events and those of Windows Forms is what happens when an event occurs. The objects that make up a Windows Form exist as long as the form exists; thus, they maintain state across user interactions. Because of the stateless model of the Web, the objects that make up the page (in the sample project that means the page, the drop-down, the button, and the label) only live long enough to generate the markup for that page. Once a request is complete and the final markup has been sent to the client browser, the objects that comprise the page are orphaned, and they await garbage collection.

Since the original objects are no longer available, new objects will need to be created for the event code to run. Therefore, when a user interaction triggers a server-side event, a request is sent to the server that includes information about the event; the page and the control objects are created on the server; the internal state of these objects is set using information passed in the request; the event handler executes; and an updated version of the page is sent back to the client browser. This process is called a *postback*.

How do you hook up these events for server controls? Again, the model is similar to that seen in Windows Forms. You can double-click a control in the Design view to add the handler for the default event for that control, you can use Event view in the Properties window (see Figure 14-7), or you can use the drop-downs at the top of the Code Editor (see Figure 14-8).

Add the event handler for the Click event of the SubmitButton. In the event handler, show the value the user selected from the FruitDropDown in the ResultLabel (code file: ServerControls-Step02.aspx.vb).

**FIGURE 14-7:** Adding an event handler using the Properties window

```vb
Private Sub SubmitButton_Click(sender As Object, e As EventArgs) _
    Handles SubmitButton.Click
    ResultLabel.Text = "You selected: " & FruitDropDown.Text
End Sub
```

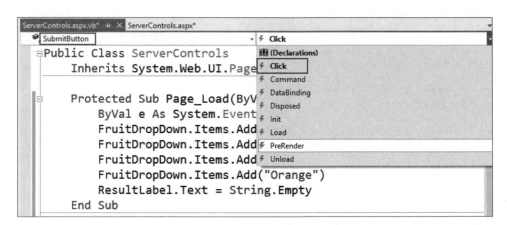

**FIGURE 14-8:** Adding an event handler using the drop-downs in the code editor

Figure 14-9 shows the page after a fruit has been selected and the Submit button has been clicked.

The sample application seems to work correctly, but if you inspect the items in the FruitDropDown after clicking the SubmitButton at least once, you'll notice that the options appear multiple times (see Figure 14-10).

It seems that the values in the control are being persisted across page requests, and that the code in the Page_Load event handler is

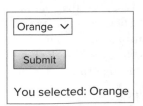

**FIGURE 14-9:** Running page after the Submit button has been clicked

adding to the existing items instead of populating the Items collection from scratch. It turns out that this is exactly what is happening through a mechanism known as *ViewState*.

## ViewState

As previously mentioned, the `Page` object and each of its child controls are constructed on each request. The ASP.NET team needed a way to persist some of the properties of the controls across postbacks to maintain the illusion that pages were living across requests. What they came up with is a somewhat ingenious trick called ViewState.

The properties that need to be persisted across calls are packaged up and encoded and then placed in a hidden field within the page. When a postback occurs, these values are unpackaged and placed into the properties of the newly created server controls. The ViewState for a page will look something like this:

**FIGURE 14-10:** Contents of the drop-down after the Submit button has been pressed twice

```
<input type="hidden" name="__VIEWSTATE" id="__VIEWSTATE"
value="/wEPDwUKMjAxNDUzMTQ4NA9kFgICAw9kFgQCEQ8QZA8WAYCAQICFg
MQBQhOZXcgWW9yawUITmV3IFlvcmtnEAUKQ2FsaWZvcm5pYYUKQ2FsaWZvcm5
pYWcQBQdGbG9yaWRhBQdGbG9yaWRhZ2RkAhUPDxYCHgRUZXh0ZWRkZFU1smgJ
JtYR8JfiZ/9yASSM5EIp" />
```

ViewState can be turned off at the page or the control level via the `EnableViewState` property. The ASP.NET team has gone to great lengths to keep the size of ViewState as small as possible but it still needs to be monitored and managed. Unchecked, ViewState can get large enough to affect the load times of your pages.

With these facts in mind, a simple adjustment is all that is required to address the issue with the sample project. In the `Page_Load` event handler, you need to check if the current request is a postback. If it is, the items will be populated automatically from the ViewState; otherwise, you need to execute your code as follows to get the items into the control (code file: `ServerControls-Step03.aspx.vb`):

```
Protected Sub Page_Load(ByVal sender As Object, ByVal e As System.EventArgs) _
    Handles Me.Load
    If Not IsPostBack Then
        FruitDropDown.Items.Add("Apple")
        FruitDropDown.Items.Add("Banana")
        FruitDropDown.Items.Add("Grape")
        FruitDropDown.Items.Add("Orange")
        ResultLabel.Text = String.Empty
    End If
End Sub
```

Now, no matter how many times you click the button, the list will have the proper number of items.

## Master and Content Pages

Many Web applications are built so that each page of the application has a similar look and feel; and there may be common page elements such as a header, navigation sections, advertisements, footers, and more. Most people prefer uniformity in their applications in order to give end users a consistent experience across pages.

Web Forms includes a feature called master pages that enable you to create a template (or a set of templates) that define the common elements for a set of pages. Once a master page is created, you can then create a content page that defines the content specific to a single page. The content page and the master page are associated by attributes in the Page directive so ASP.NET can combine the two files into a single web page to display in a browser (see Figure 14-11).

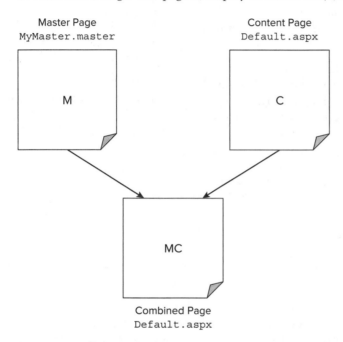

**FIGURE 14-11:** Relationship between master and content pages

A master page contains one or more ContentPlaceHolder controls that will be "filled in" by the associated content pages. The master page included in your project (Site.Master) contains three of these placeholders (see Figure 14-12).

You'll create a content page using this master page. Right-click on the project in the Solution Explorer and select Add ⇨ New Item. In the Add New Item dialog select the Web Form using Master Page template, setting the Name to Products.aspx, and click the Add button (see Figure 14-13).

You will then be presented with the Select a Master Page dialog. Your project has only one master page (Site.Master); select it and click the OK button (see Figure 14-14).

```
<%@ Master
    Language="VB" AutoEventWireup="true"
    CodeBehind="Site.master.vb"
    Inherits="WebFormsDemo.SiteMaster" %>

<!DOCTYPE html>
<html lang="en">
<head runat="server">
    <meta charset="utf-8" />
    <title><%: Page.Title %> - My ASP.NET Application</title>
    <asp:PlaceHolder>...</asp:PlaceHolder>
    <webopt:BundleReference runat="server" Path="~/Content/css" />
    <link href="~/favicon.ico" rel="shortcut icon" type="image/x-icon" />
    <meta name="viewport" content="width=device-width" />
    <asp:ContentPlaceHolder runat="server" ID="HeadContent" />
</head>
<body>
    <form runat="server">
    <asp:ScriptManager>...</asp:ScriptManager>
    <header>...</header>
    <div id="body">
        <asp:ContentPlaceHolder runat="server" ID="FeaturedContent" />
        <section class="content-wrapper main-content clear-fix">
            <asp:ContentPlaceHolder runat="server" ID="MainContent" />
        </section>
    </div>
    <footer>...</footer>
    </form>
</body>
</html>
```

**FIGURE 14-12:** ContentPlaceHolder controls in the master page

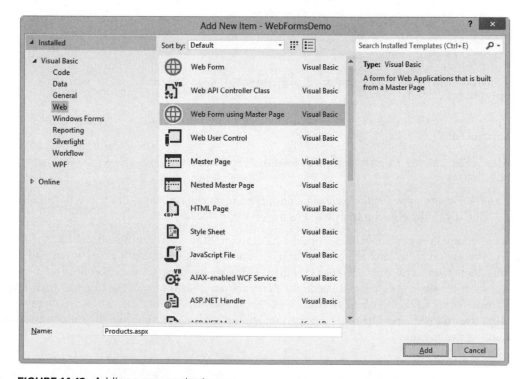

**FIGURE 14-13:** Adding a new content page

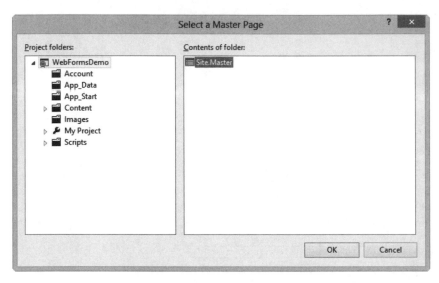

**FIGURE 14-14:** Selecting the master page

Visual Studio will examine the selected master page and generate a content page with one `Content` control for each of the `ContentPlaceHolder` controls in the master. The content controls are linked to the placeholder in the master by the `ContentPlaceHolderID` attribute. Visual Studio will also add a `MasterPageFile` attribute to the Page directive that links the content page to the master page.

```
<%@ Page Title="" Language="vb" AutoEventWireup="false"
    MasterPageFile="~/Site.Master"
    CodeBehind="Products.aspx.vb"
    Inherits="WebFormsDemo.Products" %>

<asp:Content ID="Content1" ContentPlaceHolderID="HeadContent" runat="server">
</asp:Content>

<asp:Content ID="Content2" ContentPlaceHolderID="FeaturedContent" runat="server">
</asp:Content>

<asp:Content ID="Content3" ContentPlaceHolderID="MainContent" runat="server">
</asp:Content>
```

Now go into the Design view for the page. The designer shows the full page, but you will only be able to add controls to the content areas (see Figure 14-15).

In this page, you are going to show data from the Northwind SQL Server sample database. Specifically, you are going to have the user select a category of products from a drop-down and show the products for the selected category in a grid. Using the designer or the markup, add a `DropDownList` and a `GridView` control inside the main content. Set the `ID` of the `DropDownList` to CategoryDropDown and the `ID` of the `GridView` to ProductsGrid. Also set the `Title` attribute of the Page directive to Products. The resulting markup should look something like the following (code file: `Products-Step01.aspx`).

```
<%@ Page Title="Products" Language="vb" AutoEventWireup="false"
    MasterPageFile="~/Site.Master"
    CodeBehind="Products.aspx.vb"
    Inherits="WebFormsDemo.Products" %>

<asp:Content ID="Content1" ContentPlaceHolderID="HeadContent" runat="server">
</asp:Content>

<asp:Content ID="Content2" ContentPlaceHolderID="FeaturedContent" runat="server">
</asp:Content>

<asp:Content ID="Content3" ContentPlaceHolderID="MainContent" runat="server">
    Category:
      
    <asp:DropDownList ID="CategoryDropDown" runat="server"></asp:DropDownList>
    <br />
    <br />
    <asp:GridView ID="ProductsGrid" runat="server"></asp:GridView>
</asp:Content>
```

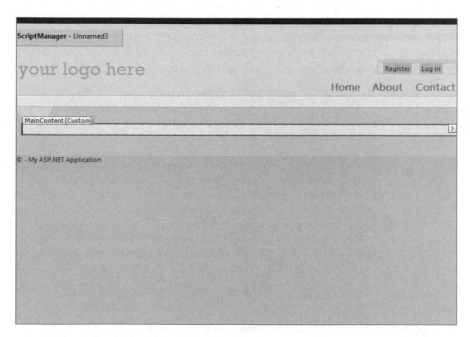

**FIGURE 14-15:** Content page in Design view

## Simple Data Binding

ASP.NET provides a number of server controls that you can use to display and interact with data on a page. These controls have sophisticated two-way data-binding, enabling you to attach to the data by setting a few properties. In addition to the standard controls such as the TextBox, ListBox, and CheckBox, there are more complex controls such as the GridView, FormView, and ListView.

> **WARNING** *For all of the data-access examples in this chapter you will need the Northwind sample database. The install script (instnwnd.sql) is included in the downloadable code in the Northwind.Services solution. It is also available for download from Microsoft. Do a search for "Northwind and pubs Sample Databases for SQL Server 2000." This should take you to* www.microsoft.com/en-us/download/details.aspx?id=23654 *Even though the download page indicates the databases are for SQL Server 2000, they will work with newer versions of the product. Also note that the database connection strings used in this chapter assume you are using a local SQL Server Express instance named SqlExpress. If you are not you will need to change the connection strings used in the applications accordingly. For more information on configuring connection strings see Chapter 9, "ADO.NET and LINQ."*

Data access is covered in other chapters in this book, so you will use a pre-created project to interact with the Northwind database. The project, which is included in the downloadable code for the course, is called Northwind.Services and the assembly it produces is called Northwind.Services.dll. Add a reference to this assembly by right-clicking on the WebFormsDemo project and selecting Add Reference. In the Reference Manager dialog, click the Browse button (at the bottom), navigate to the Northwind.Services.dll, click the Add button, and click the OK button.

This discussion doesn't go into great detail of how the Northwind.Service code works, but you will get enough information to use it effectively. The service exposes data transfer objects for categories (`CategoryDto`) and products (`ProductDto`). Note the properties of the `ProductDto` have been attributed with some validation information. These attributes will come into play later in the chapter.

The following code snippets show the declarations of the properties exposed by the data transfer objects (code files: `Northwind.Services.CategoryDto.vb` and `Northwind.Services.ProductDto.vb`):

### CATEGORYDTO

```
Public Class CategoryDto
    Public Property CategoryID As Integer
    Public Property CategoryName As String
End Class
```

### PRODUCTDTO

```
Imports System.ComponentModel.DataAnnotations

Public Class ProductDto
    Public Property ProductID As Integer
    <Required(), StringLength(40)>
    Public Property ProductName As String
    <StringLength(20)>
    Public Property QuantityPerUnit As String
    <DataType(DataType.Currency)>
    Public Property UnitPrice As Decimal?
    <Range(0, Short.MaxValue)>
    Public Property UnitsInStock As Short?
```

```
            <Range(0, Short.MaxValue)>
            Public Property UnitsOnOrder As Short?
            Public Property CategoryID As Integer
            Public Property CategoryName As String
      End Class
```

You retrieve and send the data transfer objects using methods of two classes. Not surprisingly, one for categories (`CategoryService`) and one for products (`ProductsService`). The category service has one method that enables us to get the list of categories. The products service has four methods: one to get all the products, one to get the products for a given category, one to get a single product by ID, and one to update a product.

The following code snippets show the signatures of the methods exposed by the services (code files: `Northwind.Services.CategoryService.vb` and `Northwind.Services.ProductService.vb`):

### CATEGORYSERVICE

```
      Public Class CategoryService
            Public Function GetCategoryList() As IEnumerable(Of CategoryDto)
            End Function
      End Class
```

### PRODUCTSERVICE

```
      Public Class ProductService

            Public Function GetProducts() As IEnumerable(Of ProductDto)
            End Function

            Public Function GetProducts(categoryID As Integer) As
                  IEnumerable(Of ProductDto)
            End Function

            Public Function GetProducts(categoryName As String) As
                  IEnumerable(Of ProductDto)
            End Function

            Public Function GetProduct(productID As Integer) As ProductDto
            End Function

            Public Sub UpdateProduct(ByVal productDto As ProductDto)
            End Sub

      End Class
```

With the reference to Northwind.Services assembly added you can now modify the code-behind for your page to populate the controls. Server controls that support data binding have a `DataSource` property and a `DataBind` method. You set the `DataSource` property to an object containing the data you wish to use in the control and then you call the `DataBind` method. Modify the code-behind for the Products.aspx page to look like the following code snippet. Don't forget to add the Imports statement at the top to avoid syntax errors (code file: `Products-Step02.aspx.vb`):

```
Imports Northwind.Services

Public Class Products
    Inherits System.Web.UI.Page

    Protected Sub Page_Load(ByVal sender As Object, _
        ByVal e As System.EventArgs) Handles Mc.Load
        If Not IsPostBack Then
            Dim service As New CategoryService()
            CategoryDropDown.DataSource = service.GetCategoryList()
            CategoryDropDown.DataBind()
        End If

        ShowProducts()
    End Sub

    Protected Sub CategoryDropDown_SelectedIndexChanged(sender As Object, _
        e As EventArgs) Handles CategoryDropDown.SelectedIndexChanged
        ShowProducts()
    End Sub

    Private Sub ShowProducts()
        Dim service As New ProductService()
        Dim categoryID = CInt(CategoryDropDown.SelectedValue)
        ProductsGrid.DataSource = service.GetProducts(categoryID)
        ProductsGrid.DataBind()
    End Sub

End Class
```

Most controls will have additional properties (beyond `DataSource`) you need to set to indicate how the data should be displayed in and retrieved from the control. These properties can be set in the code-behind or in the markup. You'll set them in the markup.

You are binding a collection of `CategoryDto` objects to the CategoryDropDown. You need to indicate which property of the data transfer object should be shown in the drop-down and which property should be returned as the selected value. You can do this by setting the `DataTextField` and `DataValueField` properties to CategoryName and CategoryID consecutively. You also need to set the `AutoPostBack` property to true so that the `SelectedIndexChanged` event will fire when the user selects an item.

You are binding a collection of `ProductDto` objects to the ProductsGridView. Instead of using the default rendering of the grid you will explicitly define the columns you want and how they should look. You do this by setting the `AutoGenerateColumns` property to false and then defining the columns you want using Field controls. If you are using the designer, you can configure the fields by clicking the ellipses button in the Columns property of the Properties Window and using the Fields designer (see Figure 14-16).

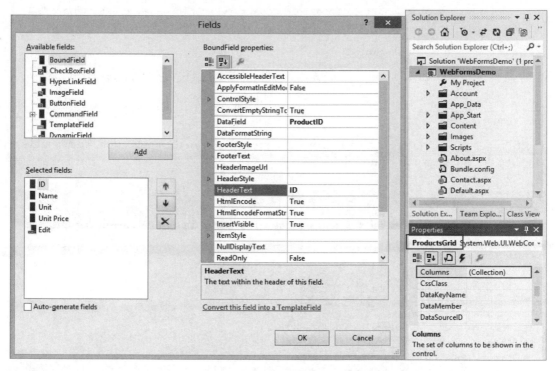

**FIGURE 14-16:** Adding columns to the Products grid using the Fields designer

Note that the last column in the grid uses a `HyperLinkField` to create a link to a page where you can edit the selected item. You'll create this page in the next section.

Whether you use the designer or add it by hand, the markup to implement the tasks described above will look something like this (code file: `Products-Step02.aspx`):

```
<asp:Content ID="Content3" ContentPlaceHolderID="MainContent" runat="server">
    Category:
      
    <asp:DropDownList
        ID="CategoryDropDown"
        AutoPostBack="true"
        DataTextField="CategoryName"
        DataValueField="CategoryID"
        runat="server">
    </asp:DropDownList>
    <br />
    <br />
    <asp:GridView
        ID="ProductsGrid"
        AutoGenerateColumns="false"
        runat="server">
        <Columns>
            <asp:BoundField DataField="ProductID" HeaderText="ID" />
            <asp:BoundField DataField="ProductName" HeaderText="Name" />
```

```
        <asp:BoundField DataField="QuantityPerUnit" HeaderText="Unit" />
        <asp:BoundField DataField="UnitPrice" HeaderText="Unit Price" />
        <asp:HyperLinkField
            Text="Edit"
            DataNavigateUrlFields="ProductID"
            DataNavigateUrlFormatString="ProductDetails.aspx?id={0}" />
    </Columns>
  </asp:GridView>
</asp:Content>
```

Select Products.aspx in the Solution Explorer and press F5 to run the application. You should see a page like the one shown in Figure 14-17.

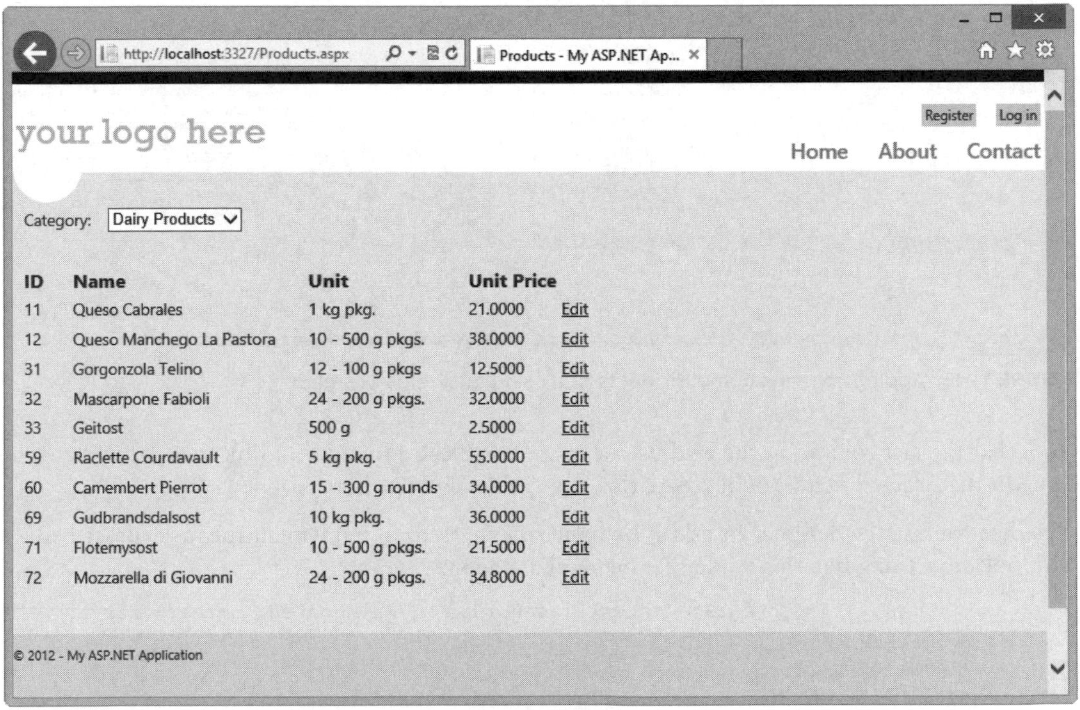

**FIGURE 14-17:** Running site showing a list of dairy products

## Data Source Controls

In the previous section you bound data directly to the server controls (the drop-down and the grid). As an alternative you could have bound the data to a data source control and then set that control as the data source for the server controls. The advantage to this technique is that the data source controls provide additional functionality you won't get when binding data directly to server controls. Table 14-1 presents several data source controls included in ASP.NET.

**TABLE 14-1:** DataSource Controls

| CONTROL | DESCRIPTION |
| --- | --- |
| SqlDataSource | Enables you to work with any SQL-based database, such as Microsoft SQL Server or Oracle |
| ObjectDataSource | Enables you to work with custom business objects |
| LinqDataSource | Enables you to use LINQ to query everything from in-memory collections to databases |
| EntityDataSource | Enables you to work with an Entity Data Model |
| XmlDataSource | Enables you to work with the information from an XML source (e.g., a file or an RSS feed) |
| SiteMapDataSource | Enables you to work with the hierarchical data represented in the site map file (.sitemap) |

You could use these data source controls in your application (in fact that's exactly what you did in previous editions of this book) but instead you are going to use a new data-binding technology known as *model binding.*

## Model Binding

Model binding, which first appeared in MVC, not only simplifies data access code, it significantly reduces the amount of code you need to write. To use model binding you write methods in the code-behind for a page and then attach those methods to controls by setting the appropriate properties. The controls will then call the methods when they need to get data or when data needs to be updated.

You'll use model binding to create a page that will enable us to edit a product. Right-click on the project in the Solution Explorer and select Add ➪ New Item. In the Add New Item dialog select the Web Form using Master Page template, setting the Name to ProductDetails.aspx, and click the Add button. You will then be presented with the Select a Master Page dialog. Select Site.Master and click the OK button.

Set the `Title` attribute of the Page directive to Product Details and then add a `FormView` control to the main content of the page. The properties of the `FormView` control that enable model binding are `ItemType`, `SelectMethod`, and `UpdateMethod`. `ItemType` tells the `FormView` the type of objects it will be displaying/editing. This enables strongly typed data-binding within templates. The `SelectMethod` and `UpdateMethod` properties indicate the names of the methods that should be called to retrieve or update a product. You will implement these methods in the code-behind of the page later in this section. You also need to define the form that will be used to edit a product. You do this inside the `EditItemTemplate` of the `FormView` control.

A `TextBox` control will be added for each of the editable properties of the product. Inside the binding expression used to set the `Text` property of each of these controls, you choose a property of the `BindItem` object. This is strongly typed to `ProductDto` because you set the `ItemType` of the `FormView` to that value.

You also need a `HiddenField` to store the value of the ProductID of the item you are editing and a `Button` the user can click to initiate the save process.

To implement the user interface described above, add the following markup to the main content of the Product Details page (code file: `ProductDetails-Step01.aspx`):

```
<asp:Content ID="Content3" ContentPlaceHolderID="MainContent" runat="server">
    <asp:FormView
        ID="ProductFormView"
        DefaultMode="Edit"
        ItemType="Northwind.Services.ProductDto"
        SelectMethod="GetProduct"
        UpdateMethod="UpdateProduct"
        runat="server">
        <EditItemTemplate>
            <div>
                <h2>
                    Product ID: <%# Item.ProductID%>
                </h2>
            </div>
            <asp:HiddenField
                ID="IDHidden"
                Value='<%# BindItem.ProductID %>'
                runat="server" />
            <table>
                <tr>
                    <td>Name</td>
                    <td>
                        <asp:TextBox
                            ID="NameTextBox"
                            Text='<%# BindItem.ProductName%>'
                            runat="server" />
                    </td>
                </tr>
                <tr>
                    <td>Quantity per Unit</td>
                    <td>
                        <asp:TextBox
                            ID="UnitTextBox"
                            Text='<%# BindItem.QuantityPerUnit%>'
                            runat="server" />
                    </td>
                </tr>
                <tr>
                    <td>Unit Price</td>
                    <td>
                        <asp:TextBox
                            ID="PriceTextBox"
                            Text='<%# BindItem.UnitPrice%>'
                            runat="server" />
                    </td>
                </tr>
```

```
            <tr>
                <td>Units in Stock</td>
                <td>
                    <asp:TextBox
                        ID="UnitsInStockTextBox"
                        Text='<%# BindItem.UnitsInStock %>'
                        runat="server" />
                </td>
            </tr>
            <tr>
                <td>Units on Order</td>
                <td>
                    <asp:TextBox
                        ID="UnitsOnOrderTextBox"
                        Text='<%# BindItem.UnitsOnOrder %>'
                        runat="server" />
                </td>
            </tr>
        </table>
        <br />
        <asp:Button
            ID="SaveButton"
            CommandName="Update"
            Text="Save"
            runat="server" />
    </EditItemTemplate>
  </asp:FormView>
</asp:Content>
```

When you are done the design view of the page should look like Figure 14-18.

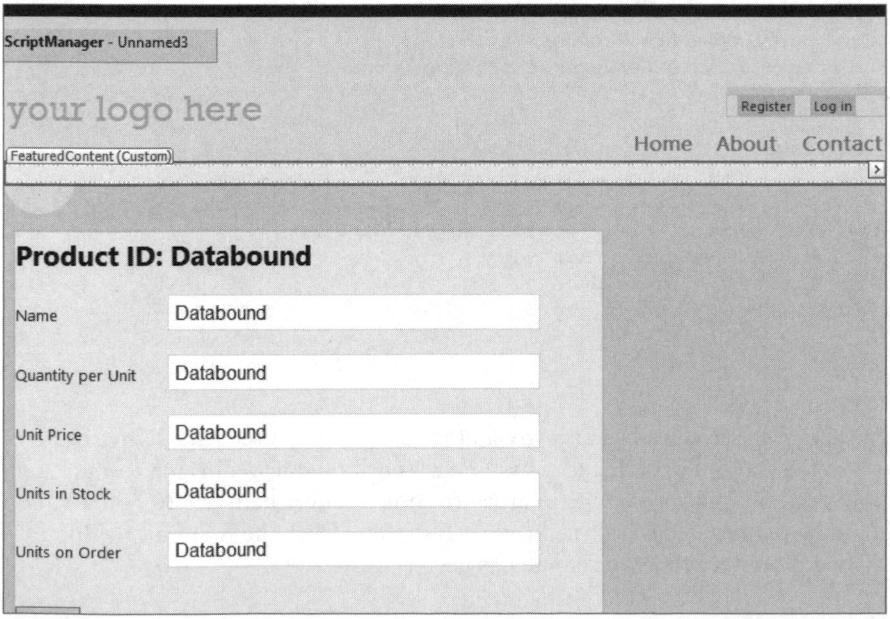

FIGURE 14-18: Design view of the Product Details page

Now you need to add the code-behind for the page. The ID of the product you will be editing in the form is passed to us in the query string (e.g., `ProductDetails.aspx?id=6`). You use this value as a parameter to the `GetProduct` method using the `<QueryString>` attribute. Notice the type of the parameter is nullable as there is no guarantee that the query string will contain a value for `"id"`. In the body of the method you'll check to see if the `productID` parameter has a value. If it does you'll get and return the associated product; if it doesn't you'll return `Nothing`. The model binding system will take the return value and populate the controls on the page.

When the user clicks the Save button, the model binding system will call `UpdateProduct` passing the edited instance of the `ProductDto` as a parameter. You just need to save it.

Update the code-behind for the Product Details page with the following code to implement the functionality described above (code file: `ProductDetails-Step01.aspx.vb`):

```
Imports Northwind.Services
Imports System.Web.ModelBinding

Public Class ProductDetails
    Inherits System.Web.UI.Page

    Protected Sub Page_Load(ByVal sender As Object, _
        ByVal e As System.EventArgs) Handles Me.Load

    End Sub

    Public Function GetProduct( _
        <QueryString("id")> ByVal productID As Integer?) _
        As ProductDto
        Dim result As ProductDto = Nothing

        If (productID.HasValue) Then
            Dim service As New ProductService()
            result = service.GetProduct(productID.Value)
        End If

        Return result
    End Function

    Public Sub UpdateProduct(ByVal product As ProductDto)
        Dim service As New ProductService()
        service.UpdateProduct(product)
        Server.Transfer("Products.aspx")
    End Sub

End Class
```

In the Solution Explorer, select ProductsDetails.aspx and press F5 to open the page. Once the browser is open, add `?id=43` to the end of the URL and press Enter. You should be redirected to the Product Details page for Ipoh Coffee. Change the Units in Stock to some number between 20 and 50 and then click Save. You should be redirected back to the Product List page. Click the Edit link for Ipoh Coffee one more time, and you should see that the change has been persisted.

## Validation

To try one more update, add a breakpoint on the line that calls the UpdateProduct method on the service object inside the page's UpdateProduct method. Then in the Solution Explorer, select ProductsDetails.aspx and press F5 to open the page. Once the browser is open, add ?id=43 to the end of the URL and press Enter. You should be redirected to the Product Details page for Ipoh Coffee. Change the Units in Stock to 100000 and then click Save. The breakpoint should be hit and Visual Studio should get focus. Now open the data tip for the product parameter and you should see that value is 0 (see Figure 14-19). This happened because the value 100000 was too large to fit in the UnitsInStock property and, instead of throwing an exception, the process that created the product object just put the default value for a Short.

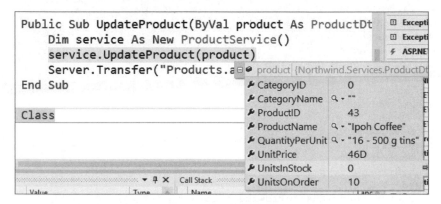

**FIGURE 14-19:** Debugging the Product Details page

Now you'll modify the UpdateProduct method to check for validation errors and to only persist the updates if there are none. To do this you'll use a couple features of the model binding system. First you'll change the parameter to the UpdateProduct method from a ProductDto object to the ProductID. You'll then retrieve the existing product from the data-access layer and attempt to push the changes the user has made into it using TryUpdateModel.

Recall that the properties in the ProductDto type have been attributed with validation information. The model binding system will check if the data the user has entered is invalid and, if so, it will record the validation errors in the ModelState property. You can then check ModelState's IsValid property to determine if you should push the users changes back to the data-access layer. Replace the existing implementation of the UpdateProduct method with the following (code file: ProductDetails-Step02.aspx.vb):

```vb
Public Sub UpdateProduct(ByVal productID As Integer)
    Dim service As New ProductService()
    Dim product = service.GetProduct(productID)

    TryUpdateModel(product)

    If (ModelState.IsValid) Then
```

```
            service.UpdateProduct(product)
            Server.Transfer("Products.aspx")
        End If
    End Sub
```

In the page markup you need to set the `DataKeyNames` property of the `FormView` so the model binding system will know which property to pass as a parameter to the `UpdateMethod`. You'll also add
a `ValidationSummary` control which will show a summary of any errors that have been recorded in
the `ModelState`. In the following code snippet, the markup you need to add is shown in bold (code
file: `ProductDetails-Step02.aspx`):

```
<asp:FormView
    ID="ProductFormView"
    DefaultMode="Edit"
    DataKeyNames="ProductID"
    ItemType="Northwind.Services.ProductDto"
    SelectMethod="GetProduct"
    UpdateMethod="UpdateProduct"
    runat="server">
    <EditItemTemplate>
        <!-- Removed for brevity -->
    </EditItemTemplate>
</asp:FormView>
<asp:ValidationSummary
    ID="ValidationSummary1"
    ShowModelStateErrors="true"
    ForeColor="Red"
    HeaderText="Please check the following errors:"
    runat="server" />
```

Run the application and get to the Product Details page for Ipoh Coffee (ID 43). Enter some invalid
values and click the Save button. You should see a result similar to the one shown in Figure 14-20.

## Web Pages and Razor

If you were to cover the ASP.NET development models in chronological order, MVC would be next.
But you are going to look at Web Pages before MVC because it will allow us to examine the very
important topic of the *Razor View Engine*.

In the summer of 2010, Scott Guthrie announced on his blog (`http: weblogs.asp.net/scottgu/
archive/2010/07/06/introducing-webmatrix.aspx` and `http: weblogs.asp.net/scottgu/
archive/2010/07/02/introducing-razor.aspx`) that Microsoft was working on a new Web
development tool named WebMatrix and a new view engine named Razor. The goals of WebMatrix
and Razor were to provide a simple, easy-to-learn development experience for those new to Web
development and for those coming from languages like PHP. The use of the term *Web Pages* to
describe Web development using Razor came later on.

In this book you'll examine Web development with Web Pages and Razor using Visual Studio. For
more information on WebMatrix, check out *Beginning ASP.NET Web Pages with WebMatrix* by
Mike Brind and Imar Spaanjaars (Wiley, 2011).

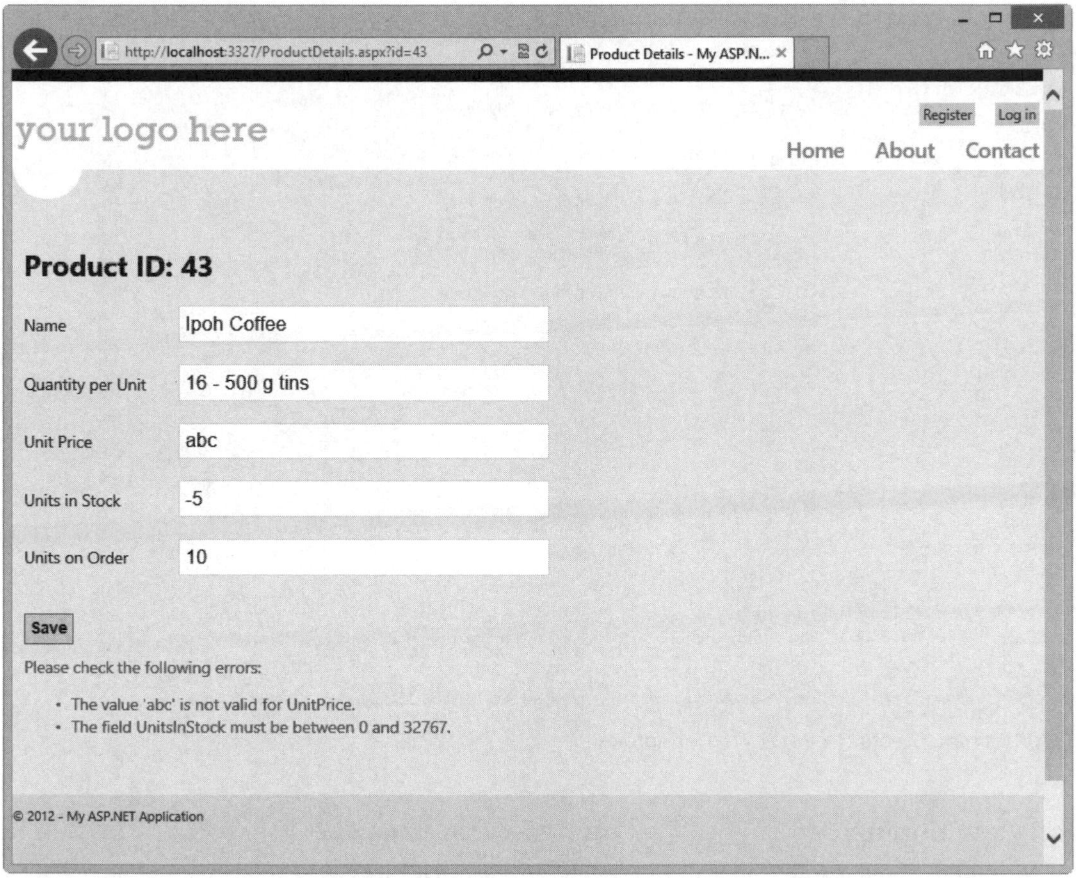

**FIGURE 14-20:** Product Details page showing validation errors

There are no Web Application Project templates for Web Pages, so you'll create a Web Site Project instead. Open Visual Studio and select File ➪ New ➪ Web Site. In the New Web Site dialog, select the ASP.NET Web Site (Razor v2) template, set the name of the folder that will contain the website to WebPagesDemo, and click the OK button (see Figure 14-21).

The project template generates a working website, one very similar to the one generated by the Web Forms project template. Run the application and take a brief look around (see Figure 14-22).

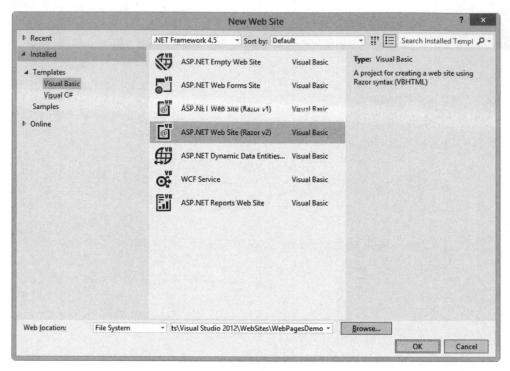

**FIGURE 14-21:** Creating a Razor Web Site project

## Razor View Engine

In addition to being simple and easy to learn, Razor was designed to be compact and fluid. This is important because there is no code-behind in a Razor page. The code and markup all go in the same file and are quite often combined together.

Now compare what it's like to write markup combined with code in a Web Forms (ASPX) and a Razor (VBHTML) page. Open the WebFormsDemo project you created in the last section and add a new content page named Simple.aspx (recall that you create a content page using the Web Form using Master Page item template). In the placeholder for the main content add the following code (code file: Simple.aspx):

```
<asp:Content ID="Content3" ContentPlaceHolderID="MainContent" runat="server">
    <% For size = 18 To 30 Step 2%>
        <div style="font-size:<%= size %>px">Hello, World</div>
    <% Next%>
</asp:Content>
```

The `<% %>` symbols, sometimes referred to as "bee stings," surround any managed code embedded inside the page markup. When you run the application you should see a page similar to the one shown in Figure 14-23.

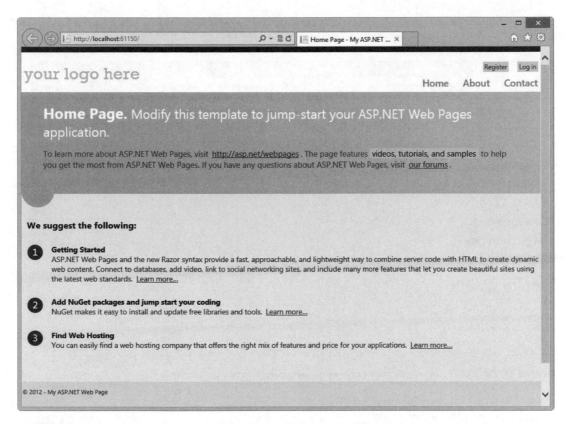

**FIGURE 14-22:** Default page of sample site generated by the project template

Now you'll come back to the WebPagesDemo project and do something similar. In the Solution Explorer, right-click on the project and select Add ➪ Add New Item. In the Add New Item dialog select the Content Page (Razor v2) template, set the Name to Simple.vbhtml, and click the Add button. Then add this code (code file: Simple.vbhtml):

```
@Code
    PageData("Title") = "Simple Page"
    Layout = "~/_SiteLayout.vbhtml"
End Code

<div>
    @For size = 18 To 30 Step 2
        @<div style="font-size:@(size)px">Hello, World</div>
    Next
</div>
```

Don't worry about the values being set in the @Code section (you'll look at what's happening there in a moment). The important code is inside the <div> tag. This code does the same thing as the code you added to the ASPX page, but it's much cleaner and easy to read. When you run the application you should see a page similar to the one shown in Figure 14-24.

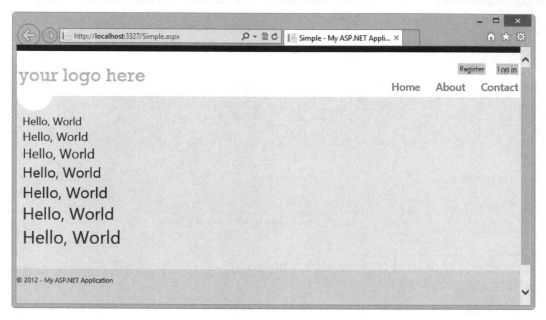

**FIGURE 14-23:** Web Form with mixed code and markup running in the browser

**FIGURE 14-24:** Razor page with mixed code and markup running in the browser

## Layout Pages

In Web Forms you used master pages to define the overall layout of the site and content pages to define the content of individual pages. Web Pages have a similar concept with a somewhat simplified implementation. Instead of a master page you have a layout page. The name of this page should start with an underscore as the Web Pages infrastructure will not allow users to navigate to pages named this way.

The layout page included in the project template is named _SiteLayout.vbhtml. The interesting markup is contained inside the body div tag. Here you have two place holders for content marked by @RenderSection and @RenderBody. (code file: _SiteLayout.vbhtml)

```
<div id="body">
    @RenderSection("featured", required:=false)
    <section class="content-wrapper main-content clear-fix">
        @RenderBody()
    </section>
</div>
```

One of the content pages included in the project template is Default.vbhtml. This content page is linked to the layout page by the Layout property. Each @Section section defines the content for the corresponding @RenderSection in the layout page—in this case it's the featured section. Note that this section has been marked as optional so it did not have to be defined. Finally you have markup outside a @Section section. This content corresponds to the @RenderBody in the layout page (code file: Default.vbhtml):

```
@Code
    Layout = "~/_SiteLayout.vbhtml"
    PageData("Title") = "Home Page"
End Code
@Section featured
    <section class="featured">
        <!-- Removed for brevity -->
    </section>
End Section
<h3>
    We suggest the following:</h3>
<ol class="round">
    <!-- Removed for brevity -->
</ol>
```

## Database Access

Software architecture best practices indicate that you should separate applications into logical layers: user interface, business logic, data access, and data storage. The Web Forms application you just built only implemented the user interface; you didn't have any business logic to speak of, so you did not implement that layer; you used the pre-created Northwind.Services assembly for data access; and you used SQL Server Express for data storage. There are many benefits to using this kind of logical architecture, but to do so adds some complexity to the application development process.

As mentioned earlier, Web Pages and Razor are designed to be simple, easy to learn, and easy to use. To achieve these goals the general development practice is to build self-contained pages where all the data access, business logic, and user interface needed for a page is included in the page itself. You'll follow this practice while building this Web Pages application.

To be able to connect to a database you need to add a database connection string to the `Web.config` file. Open this file and add the `<add>` element inside the `<connectionStrings>` element shown in bold (code file: `Web.config`):

```
<connectionStrings>
  <add name="StarterSite"
    connectionString="Data Source=|DataDirectory|\StarterSite.sdf" ... />
  <add name="Northwind"
    connectionString="Data Source=localhost\sqlexpress;
      Initial Catalog=Northwind;Integrated Security=True"
    providerName="System.Data.SqlClient" />
</connectionStrings>
```

With the connection string configured you'll now add a page that shows data from the Categories table. Add a new Razor content page named CategoryList.vbhtml and set the page title and layout page to "Category List" and "~/_SiteLayout.vbhtml" respectively (code file: `CategoryList-Step01.vbhtml`).

```
@Code
    PageData("Title") = "Category List"
    Layout = "~/_SiteLayout.vbhtml"
End Code
```

Now add the following code to open a connection to the Northwind database and retrieve the `CategoryID` and `CategoryName` for each of the rows in the Category table. You can do this inside the existing `@Code` section or you can add the code inside a new `@Code` section. Notice the very simple syntax used to perform these operations. The call to the `Query` method returns an `IEnumerable(Of Object)`, where each object in the collection has properties representing the values of the columns returned from the query. These properties are late-bound so they will not appear in Intellisense (code file: `CategoryList-Step01.vbhtml`).

```
@Code
    Dim db = Database.Open("Northwind")
    Dim categories = db.Query(
        "SELECT CategoryID, CategoryName FROM Categories")
End Code
```

Now add the markup to show each of the category names in an unordered list. As mentioned earlier, the `CategoryName` property is late-bound and will not appear in Intellisense (code file: `CategoryList-Step01.vbhtml`).

```
<div>
    <h2>Product Categories</h2>
    <ul>
        @For Each category In categories
            @<li>
                @category.CategoryName
            </li>
```

```
        Next
    </ul>
</div>
```

The complete page should look like that in Listing 14-1. If you run the application you should see a page similar to the one shown in Figure 14-25 (code file: categoryList-Step01.vbhtml).

```
@Code
    PageData("Title") = "Category List"
    Layout = "~/_SiteLayout.vbhtml"
End Code

@Code
    Dim db = Database.Open("Northwind")
    Dim categories = db.Query(
        "SELECT CategoryID, CategoryName FROM Categories")
End Code

<div>
    <h2>Product Categories</h2>
    <ul>
        @For Each category In categories
            @<li>
                @category.CategoryName
            </li>
        Next
    </ul>
</div>
```

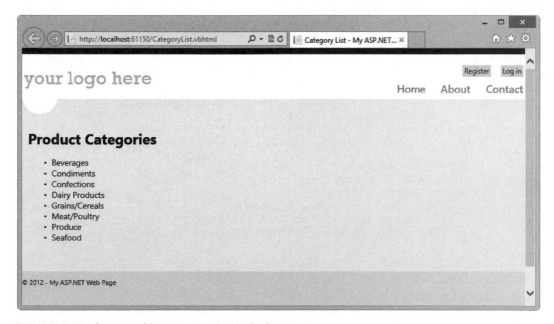

**FIGURE 14-25:** Category List page running in the browser

## Helpers

In lieu of controls, Razor uses Helpers. The two are similar in that they are reusable components that assist you in implementing common functionality, but Helpers are simpler—they do not expose events and do not have a design experience. They weren't identified as such, but the code you used in the Category List page used Database Helpers. Now you'll create a page that uses the WebGrid Helper to show product information.

Add a new Razor content page named ProductList.vbhtml. Set the page title and layout page and then add code to retrieve the ProductID, ProductName, QuantityPerUnit, and UnitPrice from the Products table in the Northwind database. Your code should look something like this (code file: ProductList-Step01.vbhtml):

```
@Code
    Layout = "~/_SiteLayout.vbhtml"
    PageData("Title") = "Product List"
End Code

@Code
    Dim db = Database.Open("Northwind")

    Dim sql = "SELECT ProductID, ProductName, QuantityPerUnit, UnitPrice " +
        "FROM Products "
    Dim products = db.Query(sql)
End Code
```

Now add the following code to create an instance of the WebGrid Helper, and have it generate the HTML markup representing the grid in the page body (code file: ProductList-Step01.vbhtml).

```
@Code
    @* Code removed for brevity *@

    Dim grid As New WebGrid(source:=products, rowsPerPage:=20)
End Code

<div>
    <h2>All Products</h2>
    <br />
    @grid.GetHtml(
        tableStyle:="grid",
        columns:=grid.Columns(
            grid.Column("ProductID", "ID"),
            grid.Column("ProductName", "Name"),
            grid.Column("QuantityPerUnit", "Unit"),
            grid.Column("UnitPrice", "Unit Price")
        )
    )
</div>
```

If you run the application you should see a page similar to the one shown in Figure 14-26.

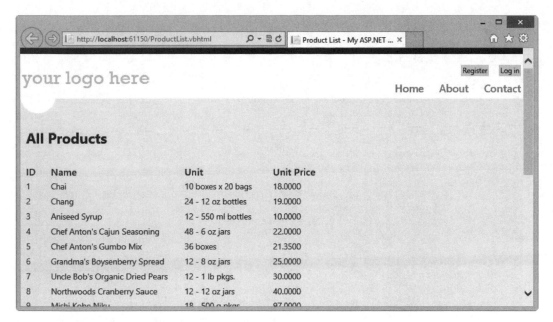

**FIGURE 14-26:** Product List page running in the browser

## Passing Information between Pages

Now that you have both Category and Product List pages, you can tie the two together. You can change the items in the category list to links and, when one of the links is clicked, navigate to the Product List page showing the items in the selected category.

Start by modifying the code and markup in CategoryList.vbhtml to render a link to ProductList (in Web Pages you do not need to include the extension on the page name in the URL). Add a query string parameter named catid and set it to the current category's ID (code file: CategoryList-Step02.vbhtml).

```
@For Each category In categories
    @<li>
        <a href="~/ProductList?catid=@category.CategoryID" />
            @category.CategoryName
        </li>
Next
```

Back in ProductList.vbhtml you need to check to see if a parameter named catid has been passed to you. If it has then you'll show the products for the associated category; if it hasn't then you'll show all products. You can use the Request object to get the value of the query string parameter. You also need to update the <h2> tag above the grid to show the appropriate category name. Modify the code in Products.vbhtml to look like the following (code file: ProductList-Step02.vbhtml):

```
@Code
    Dim categoryID = 0
    Dim categoryName = "All Categories"
    Dim sql = String.Empty

    Dim temp = Request("catid")
    If Not temp.IsEmpty() AndAlso temp.IsInt() Then
        categoryID = temp.AsInt
    End If

    Dim db = Database.Open("Northwind")

    If categoryID > 0 Then
        sql = "SELECT CategoryName FROM Categories WHERE CategoryID = @0"
        Dim category = db.QuerySingle(sql, categoryID)
        categoryName = category.CategoryName
    End If

    sql = "SELECT ProductID, ProductName, QuantityPerUnit, UnitPrice " +
        "FROM Products "
    If categoryID > 0 Then
        sql &= "WHERE CategoryID = " & categoryID
    End If
    Dim products = db.Query(sql)

    Dim grid As New WebGrid(source:=products, rowsPerPage:=20)
End Code

<div>
    <h2>@categoryName</h2>
    <br />
    @* Grid removed for brevity *@
</div>
```

In the Solution Explorer, select CategoryList.vbhtml and press F5. In the Category List page, click the link for Confections. The browser should navigate to the Products List page and the URL should have catid=3 in the query string (see Figure-27).

In this example you used a query string variable to pass information from one page to the other. This is a very simple and common way to perform the task. In Web Pages you can also use UrlData, which is just as simple but more SEO (search engine optimization) friendly. You'll see how to use UrlData in the next section.

## Working with Forms

Repeating what you did in the last sample application, you'll now create a form that will enable you to edit a product. You'll do it in two parts, first retrieving the appropriate product and showing it in the form, and then updating the product when the user chooses to save.

Open ProductList.vbhtml and add one more column to the grid. This column should be a link to ProductDetail.vbhtml (which you will create next) that includes the ID of the product you want to edit. Now, you could pass the ID as a parameter on the query string (like ProductDetail?id=5) but instead you'll include the ID in the URL itself (like ProductDetail/5). You'll be able to retrieve the

ID of the product in the target page using the `UrlData` object (code file: `ProductList-Step03`
`.vbhtml`).

```
@grid.GetHtml(
    tableStyle:="grid",
    columns:=grid.Columns(
        grid.Column("ProductID", "ID"),
        grid.Column("ProductName", "Name"),
        grid.Column("QuantityPerUnit", "Unit"),
        grid.Column("UnitPrice", "Unit Price"),
        grid.Column(format:= _
            @@<a href="~/ProductDetail/@item.ProductID">Edit</a>)
    )
)
```

Now create a new Razor content page named ProductDetail.vbhtml. In this page you are going
to check the `UrlData` object for the ID of the product to edit. `UrlData` is a collection with each
index representing a part of the URL. For example, if the URL was `ProductDetail/5/a/22/`
`foo`, `UrlData(0)` would be 5, `UrlData(1)` would be a, and so on. If there is no item at the index
`UrlData` will return an empty string.

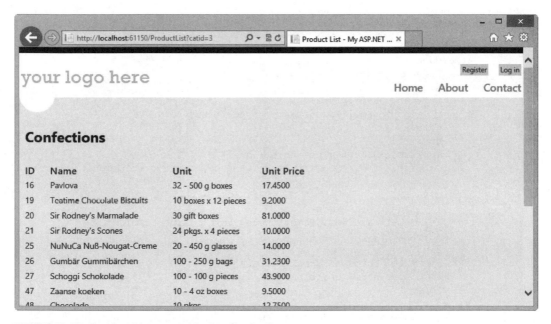

**FIGURE 14-27:** Product List page showing Confections

If you aren't given an ID you'll redirect back to the Product List page. If you are then you'll query
the database for the appropriate product. Finally you'll copy the column values into variables (code
file: `ProductDetail-Step01.vbhtml`).

```
@Code
    Layout = "~/_SiteLayout.vbhtml"
    PageData("Title") = "Product Detail"
End Code
```

```
@Code
    Dim id = UrlData(0)
    If id.IsEmpty() Then
        Response.Redirect("~/ProductList")
    End If

    Dim db = Database.Open("Northwind")
    Dim name, unit, price, stock, order As String

    Dim product = db.QuerySingle("SELECT * FROM Products " + _
        "WHERE ProductID = @0", id)
    name = product.ProductName
    unit = product.QuantityPerUnit
    price = product.UnitPrice
    stock = product.UnitsInStock
    order = product.UnitsOnOrder
End Code
```

Now that you have the data you can create the form used to view and edit it. You could use the TextBox Helper to build the form, but using HTML input tags is just as easy (code file: ProductDetail-Step01.vbhtml).

```
<div>
    <form method="post">
        <fieldset>
            <legend>Product: @id</legend>
            <div>
                <label>Name</label>
                <input name="ProductName" type="text" value="@name" />
            </div>
            <div>
                <label>Quantity per Unit</label>
                <input name="QuantityPerUnit" type="text" value="@unit" />
            </div>
            <div>
                <label>Unit Price</label>
                <input name="UnitPrice" type="text" value="@price" />
            </div>
            <div>
                <label>Units in Stock</label>
                <input name="UnitsInStock" type="text" value="@stock" />
            </div>
            <div>
                <label>Units on Order</label>
                <input name="UnitsOnOrder" type="text" value="@order" />
            </div>
            <div>
                <label> </label>
                <input type="submit" value="Save" />
            </div>
        </fieldset>
    </form>
</div>
```

In the Solution Explorer, select ProductList.vbhtml and press F5 to open the page. Click the Edit link for Ikura (ID 10) and you should be redirected to a page similar to the one shown in Figure 14-28. If you make changes and try to submit the form nothing will happen, because you haven't added the code to deal with user input. You'll do that next.

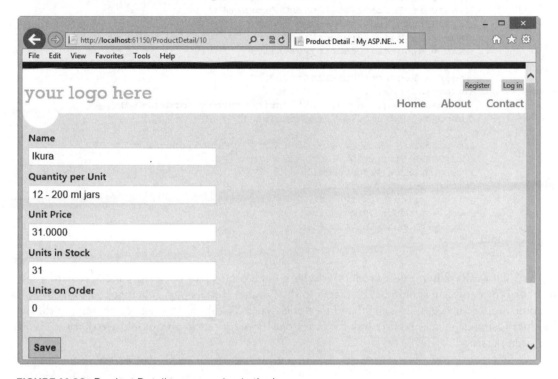

**FIGURE 14-28:** Product Detail page running in the browser

## Handling User Input

When you first request the Product Details page, the browser will issue a HTTP GET to the server. By setting the method attribute of the <form> tag to "post," the browser will issue a HTTP POST with the form data in the body of the request when the Submit button is clicked.

So, in your page you need to check if there was a POST using the IsPost property. If there was, you will retrieve the form data from the Request object and update the appropriate Product in the database. Add the code shown in bold in the following snippet to implement the desired functionality (code file: ProductDetail-Step02.vbhtml):

```
@Code
    Dim id = UrlData(0)
    If id.IsEmpty() Then
        Response.Redirect("~/ProductList")
    End If

    Dim db = Database.Open("Northwind")
```

```
        Dim name, unit, price, stock, order As String

        If IsPost Then
            Dim sql = "UPDATE Products SET ProductName=@0, " + _
                "QuantityPerUnit=@1, UnitPrice=@2, " + _
                "UnitsInStock=@3, UnitsOnOrder=@4 " + _
                "WHERE ProductID=@5"
            name = Request("ProductName")
            unit = Request("QuantityPerUnit")
            price = Request("UnitPrice")
            stock = Request("UnitsInStock")
            order = Request("UnitsOnOrder")
            db.Execute(sql, name, unit, price, stock, order, id)
            Response.Redirect("~/ProductList")
        Else
            Dim product = db.QuerySingle("SELECT * FROM Products " +
                "WHERE ProductID = @0", id)
            name = product.ProductName
            unit = product.QuantityPerUnit
            price = product.UnitPrice
            stock = product.UnitsInStock
            order = product.UnitsOnOrder
        End If
    End Code
```

In the Solution Explorer, select ProductList.vbhtml and press F5 to open the page. Click the Edit link for Ikura and you should be redirected to the Product Details page. Change the Units in Stock to some number between 20 and 50 and then click Save. You should be redirected back to the Product List page. Click the Edit link for Ikura one more time, and you should see that the change has been persisted.

## Validation

To try one more update, in the Solution Explorer, select ProductList.vbhtml and press F5 to open the page. Click the Edit link for Ikura and you should be redirected to the Product Details page. Change the Units in Stock to 100000 and then click Save. You should see an error similar to the one shown in Figure 14-29, because 100000 is too large to fit into the UnitsInStock column.

To help prevent these kinds of errors from happening, you'll add some Validation Helpers to check for data entry errors. You can use these helpers to check that values of submitted form fields meet certain criteria: field is not empty, field is of a certain type, field is in a certain range, etc. Once you've defined the validation rules, you can then check the value of the IsValid method to determine if any of the rules have been broken before trying to update the database. Finally, you can use the ValidationSummary Html Helper to show the error messages for the rules that have been broken.

Note that even if there are validation errors, you still want to populate the controls with the invalid values so the user can see why there were errors, correct the data they entered, and resubmit the form.

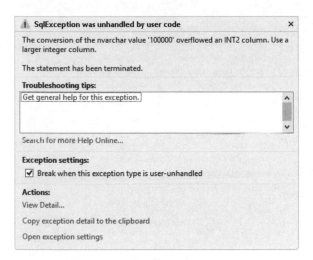

**FIGURE 14-29:** Visual Studio error dialog

Add the code shown in bold below to your page (including the `ValidationSummary` at the bottom) to implement validation for the form (code file: `ProductDetail-Step03.vbhtml`):

```
@Code
    Layout = "~/_SiteLayout.vbhtml"
    PageData("Title") = "Product Detail"
End Code

@Code
    Dim id = UrlData(0)
    If id.IsEmpty() Then
        Response.Redirect("~/ProductList")
    End If

    Validation.RequireField("ProductName",
        "Product name is required")
    Validation.Add("ProductName",
        Validator.StringLength(40, 0,
        "Product name must be 40 characters or less"))
    Validation.Add("QuantityPerUnit",
        Validator.StringLength(20, 0,
        "Quantity per unit must be 20 characters or less"))
    Validation.Add("UnitPrice",
        Validator.Decimal("Unit price must be a number"))
    Validation.Add("UnitsInStock",
        Validator.Range(0, Short.MaxValue,
        "Units in stock must be less than 32767"))
    Validation.Add("UnitsOnOrder",
        Validator.Range(0, Short.MaxValue,
        "Units on order must be less than 32767"))
```

```vb
        Dim db = Database.Open("Northwind")
        Dim name, unit, price, stock, order As String

        If IsPost Then
            Dim sql = "UPDATE Products SET ProductName=@0, " + _
                "QuantityPerUnit=@1, UnitPrice=@2, " + _
                "UnitsInStock=@3, UnitsOnOrder=@4 " + _
                "WHERE ProductID=@5"
            name = Request("ProductName")
            unit = Request("QuantityPerUnit")
            price = Request("UnitPrice")
            stock = Request("UnitsInStock")
            order = Request("UnitsOnOrder")
            If Validation.IsValid() Then
                db.Execute(sql, name, unit, price, stock, order, id)
                Response.Redirect("~/ProductList")
            End If
        Else
            Dim product = db.QuerySingle("SELECT * FROM Products " +
                "WHERE ProductID = @0", id)
            name = product.ProductName
            unit = product.QuantityPerUnit
            price = product.UnitPrice
            stock = product.UnitsInStock
            order = product.UnitsOnOrder
        End If

    End Code

    <div>
        <form method="post">
            <fieldset>
                <!-- Controls removed for brevity  -->
            </fieldset>
        </form>
        @Html.ValidationSummary()
    </div>
```

Run the application and get to the Product Details page for Ikura (ID 10). Enter some invalid values and click the Save button. You should see a result similar to the one shown in Figure 14-30.

# ASP.NET MVC

ASP.NET MVC is a Web framework that was originally released in March 2009 as an alternative to ASP.NET Web Forms. It was designed to limit abstractions and give developers a great deal of control over the creation of pages in an application. Specifically, ASP.NET MVC was designed to do the following:

➤ **Provide complete control over HTML markup**—With Web Forms, the final markup is mostly determined by the server controls on a page.

➤ **Have intuitive website URLs**—With Web Forms, the URL is determined by the location and name of the file being addressed.

> ➤ **Have a clear separation of concerns**—The Web Forms programming model encourages developers to put business logic and database access code in the code-behind for a page.

> ➤ **Be testable by default**—Several aspects of the Web Forms model make it difficult to write unit tests for user interface layer logic.

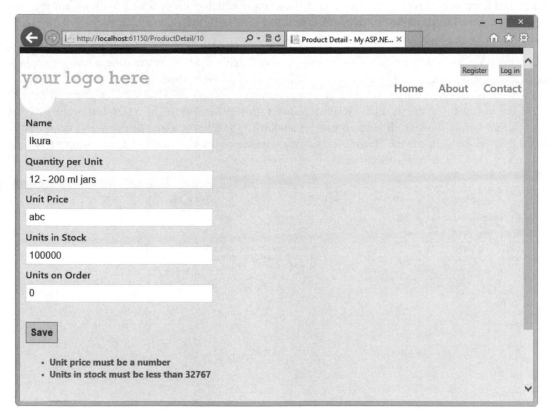

**FIGURE 14-30:** Submitted form with errors

## Model-View-Controller and ASP.NET

The Model-View-Controller pattern was conceived in the late 1970s by Trygve Reenskaug, a Norwegian computer scientist. It provides a powerful and elegant means of separating concerns within an application, and it applies extremely well to Web development.

The pattern separates an application into three components:

1. **Model**—The business objects in the application
2. **View**—The user interface
3. **Controller**—Classes that handle user requests and manage application logic and flow

In the ASP.NET implementation of the pattern, requests are routed to controller classes that generally apply application logic (authorization, for example), interact with the model to retrieve or update data, determine the data that needs to be rendered in the response, and then pass control to a view to format the data and render the final markup to the user.

Another important aspect of the implementation of ASP.NET MVC is the use of convention over configuration. As you build an application you will see that conventions are used to determine the names and locations of files in a project, or to determine which class or file to load at runtime. You are not forced to follow these conventions, but doing so allows for a consistent experience across ASP.NET MVC applications.

In keeping with the practice you've been using, you will explore MVC by creating a sample application. Open Visual Studio and create a new ASP.NET MVC 4 Web Application named MvcDemo. You will be asked three things: what MVC template you want to use, what view-engine you want to use, and if you want to create an associated unit test project (see Figure 14-31). Choose the Internet Application template (this will create a project similar to the ones you saw in the Web Forms and Web Pages demos), choose the Razor view engine, and check the checkbox to create a unit test project keeping the default test project name.

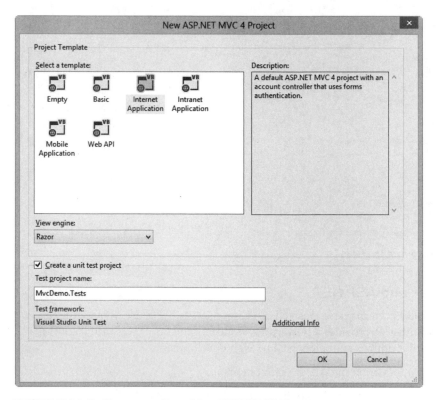

**FIGURE 14-31:** Setting properties of the ASP.NET MVC project

If you look at the MVC project in the Solution Explorer (see Figure 14-32), you'll see that several files and folders have been created by default. Three of the folders should jump out at you immediately: Models, Views, and Controllers. These folders map to the three components of the pattern on which this style of application is based.

As you've seen in the two previous examples, the project template generates a working website. Run the application and take a brief look around (see Figure 14-33).

## Controllers and Actions

In traditional Web application frameworks, requests are mapped to files containing markup for pages. In ASP.NET MVC, requests are mapped to methods on classes. The classes are the previously mentioned controller classes, and the methods are known as actions. Action methods are responsible for receiving user input, retrieving or saving data to the model, and passing control to the appropriate view. The view will typically return the markup for a page, but it could also return other content types such as a binary file or JSON (native JavaScript object) formatted data. Typical actions will handle requests to list, add, edit, or delete entities from the model.

**FIGURE 14-32:** Files included in the MVC Internet Application template

Now you can examine these concepts further by creating a new controller. In the Solution Explorer, right-click on the Controllers folder and select Add ➪ Controller. By convention, the names of controller classes should end with "Controller." The Add Controller dialog even encourages the use of this convention, as shown in Figure 14-34. Set the name to SimpleController and click the Add button.

The class that's created will inherit from the base `Controller` class (`System.Web.Mvc.Controller`) and will have the shell for a default action method named `Index` (code file: `\Controllers\SimpleController.vb`):

```
Namespace MvcDemo
    Public Class SimpleController
        Inherits System.Web.Mvc.Controller

        '
        ' GET: /Simple

        Function Index() As ActionResult
            Return View()
        End Function

    End Class
End Namespace
```

The `Index` action method is about as simple as it gets. When a request comes in for this action it just passes control to a view without any application logic or data access. Because the action method has not specified which view to show, convention states that ASP.NET MVC should look for a file matching the pattern `/Views/{Controller}/{Action}.aspx`. In the case of the `Index` action, that would be `/Views/Simple/Index.aspx`, which does not exist at this point.

The comment above the method (i.e., `GET·  /Simple`) is not required, but it is something you'll typically see in code generated by Visual Studio. It indicates that this action will be accessed via an `HTTP GET` request to `/Simple`. This illustrates another convention. The default routing rules used by MVC expect something in the form of `/{Controller}/{Action}`. If the action is not specified, then ASP. NET MVC will default to calling the `Index` action method, so a request to `/Simple` or `/Simple/Index` will be routed to the `Index` action. You will learn about routing and how to add or modify routing rules later in this chapter.

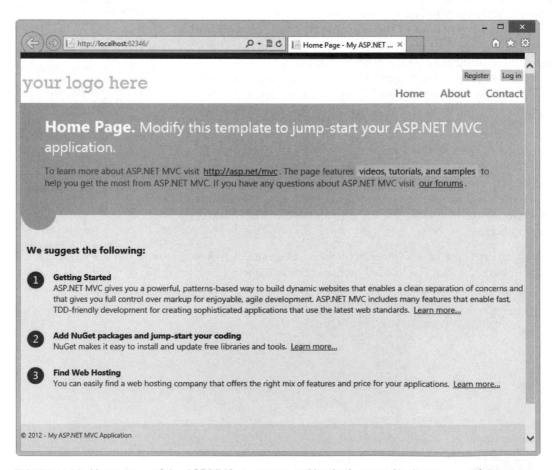

**FIGURE 14-33:** Home page of the ASP.MVC site generated by the Internet Application template

Although the view for the `Index` action does not exist, you can create it. You could do this rather easily by hand, but there's no need to; Visual Studio will create it for us. In the Code Editor, right-click anywhere in the code for the `Index` method and select the Add View option in the context menu.

In the Add View dialog you will use the default values as they are (see Figure 14-35), but before you click the Add button note that the Use layout or master page option is checked but no value has been specified. The comment about leaving the value empty if you want to use the setting in the Razor _ViewStart file applies here. You can find this file in the Views folder. Looking inside you'll see the default layout page has been set to `Views\Shared\_Layout.vbthml`.

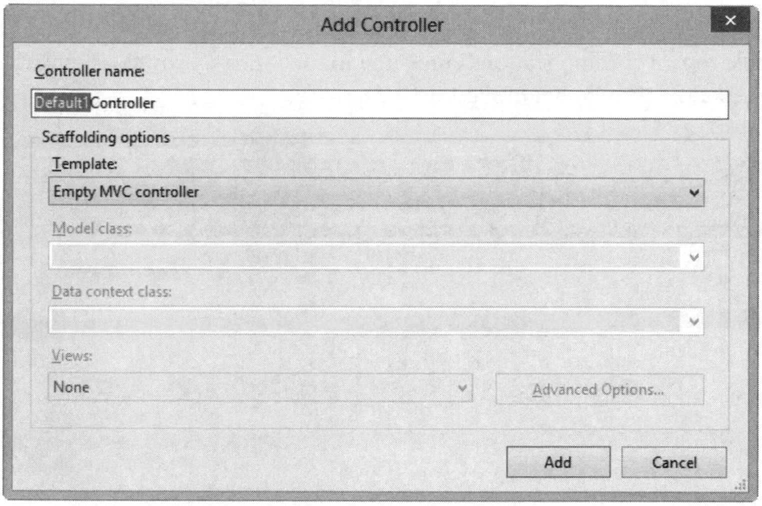

**FIGURE 14-34:** Adding a controller

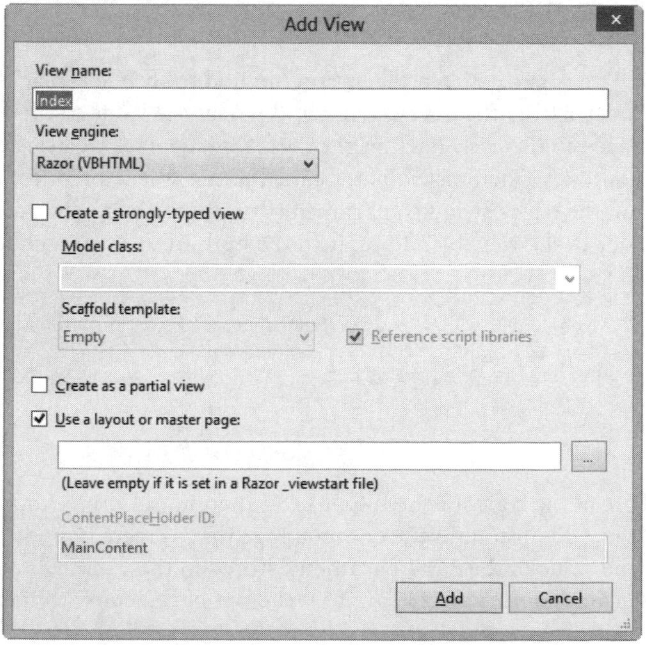

**FIGURE 14-35:** Adding a View for the Index action

After clicking the Add button you will be presented with a new content page that looks something like the following (code file: \Views\Simple\Index.vbhtml):

```
@Code
    ViewData("Title") = "Index"
End Code

<h2>Index</h2>
```

At this point you should be able to run the application. Once it is loaded in the browser, navigate to /Simple and you'll see a page like the one shown in Figure 14-36.

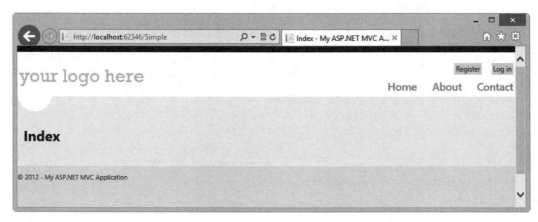

**FIGURE 14-36:** View for the Index action running in the browser

Now you'll look at an example in which data is passed from the action method to the view. You'll create an action that takes the name parameter from the query string and passes the value of this parameter to the view where it will displayed to the user. Back in the SimpleController class, add a new action method called SayHello that takes a string parameter called name. When a request is made, ASP.NET will match parameters on the query string to parameters of the method. The action method can pass the value of the parameter to the view by adding it to the built-in ViewData collection (code file: \Controllers\SimpleController.vb).

```
' GET: /Simple/SayHello?name=Rob

Function SayHello(ByVal name As String) As ActionResult
    ViewData("Name") = name
    Return View()
End Function
```

Create the view by right-clicking anywhere in the code for the SayHello function, selecting Add View in the context menu, and clicking the Add button. In the content page that's created, modify the value of the <h2> element to output the value of the name parameter stored in the ViewData. Note that Razor automatically HTML-encodes output so it's safe to write out parameters from the query string this way (code file: \Views\Simple\SayHello.vbhtml).

```
@Code
    ViewData("Title") = "SayHello"
```

```
End Code

<h2>Hello @ViewData("Name")</h2>
```

If you run the application and navigate to `/Simple/SayHello?name=Rob`, you should see a page similar to the one shown in Figure 14-37.

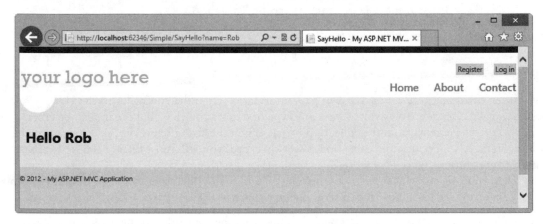

**FIGURE 14-37:** SayHello view showing data passed from the controller

## Adding the Model

In MVC, the model typically refers to the business or domain objects. These are classes that represent the data in the application, along with the corresponding business rules and validation. For your sample application you will use the types in the pre-created Northwind.Services assembly for your model.

Add a reference to this assembly by right-clicking on the project in the Solution Explorer and selecting Add Reference. The assembly should show in the Recent category—check it and click OK. If it isn't there, click the Browse button (at the bottom), navigate to the Northwind.Services.dll, click the Add button, and then click the OK button.

## Views

Now that you have a model, you can create some controllers, actions, and views that are more like those you would create in a traditional business application. To start off, you will look at views that display data from the database; later in the chapter you will add views that let us modify the data.

Create a new controller called `ProductsController`. The `Index` action should be modified to get the list of categories and return a view that will display them (code file: `\Controllers\ProductsController.vb`):

```
Imports Northwind.Services

Namespace MvcDemo
    Public Class ProductsController
        Inherits System.Web.Mvc.Controller
```

```
            Private _catService As New CategoryService()
            Private _prodService As New ProductService()

            '
            ' GET: /Products

            Function Index() As ActionResult
                Dim categories = _catService.GetCategoryList()
                Return View(categories)
            End Function

        End Class
    End Namespace
```

You've seen that you can use `ViewData` to pass information from the controller to the view. `ViewData` is flexible; it enables you to pass any type of data to the view, but it can also be error prone. You retrieve items from the collection by passing in the string name of the key associated with the item. Also, because the collection is weakly typed, you will most likely need to do a cast to perform operations on the values returned from the collection. ASP.NET MVC offers a second mechanism you can use when you know the type of data that will be sent to the view at design time. This mechanism enables us to create a strongly typed view.

When using a strongly typed view you pass the data from the controller to the view using the first parameter to the `View` method. Then you specify the type of data being passed in the wizard that creates the view. In the view there will be a variable named `Model`, which is a strongly typed reference to the data passed from the controller.

Bring up the Add View dialog as before, but this time check the "Create a strongly typed view" check box and select CategoryDto (Northwind.Services) from the Model class drop-down (see Figure 14-38). For now you'll keep the default value of Empty in the Scaffold template drop-down. You'll see the effect of using the other values in this drop-down later in the chapter.

Modify the generated view page to show the category names in an unordered list (code file: \Views\Products\Index.vbhtml).

```
@ModelType IEnumerable(Of Northwind.Services.CategoryDto)

@Code
    ViewData("Title") = "Product Categories"
End Code

<h2>Product Categories</h2>

<ul>
    @For Each category In Model
        @<li>
            @category.CategoryName
        </li>
    Next
</ul>
```

Notice the `@ModelType` at the top of the page has picked up the type you specified in the wizard that created the page. Since you are working with a list of categories instead of an individual category, this needs to be manually changed to `IEnumerable(Of Northwind.Services.CategoryDto)`.

If you run the application and navigate to /Products, you should see a page similar to the one shown in Figure 14-39.

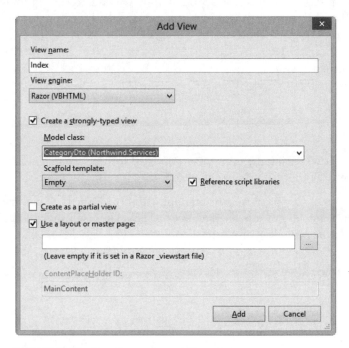

**FIGURE 14-38:** Creating a strongly typed view

**FIGURE 14-39:** Showing a list of categories

Now that you have a way to create a list of categories, you can repeat the process to create a list of products. Because there are a lot of products, you can show them by category to limit the number shown on a page. In the `ProductsController`, create a new action method called `Browse`. It should use the repository to get the products for the category passed in as a parameter and then pass control to the `Browse` view (code file: `\Controllers\ProductsController.vb`):

```
' GET: /Products/Browse?category=beverages

Function Browse(ByVal category As String) As ActionResult
    Dim products = _prodService.GetProducts(category)
    Return View(products.ToList())
End Function
```

Create the strongly typed view for this action using the same steps you used for the `Index` action. In this case, set the Model class option to ProductDto (Northwind.Services).

As before, the `@ModelType` in the generated view page must be manually modified (the type parameter needs to be `IEnumerable(Of Northwind.Services.ProductDto)`). This view will show an unordered list of products and their corresponding unit prices (code file: `\Views\Products\Browse.vbhtml`):

```
@ModelType IEnumerable(Of Northwind.Services.ProductDto)

@Code
    ViewData("Title") = "Browse Products"
End Code

<h2>Browse Products</h2>

<ul>
    @For Each prod In Model
        @Code
        Dim item = String.Format("{0} (${1:F})", _
            prod.ProductName, prod.UnitPrice)
        End Code
        @<li>
            @item
        </li>
    Next
</ul>
```

Running the application and navigating to `/Products/Browse?category=beverages` should render a page similar to the one shown in Figure 14-40.

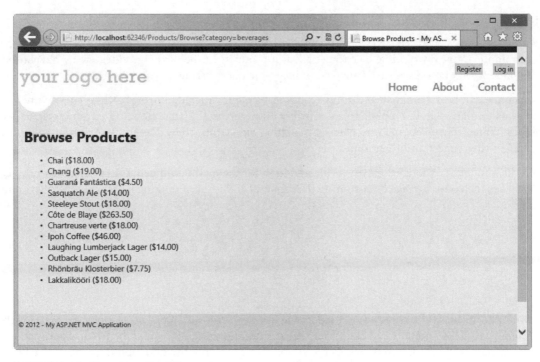

**FIGURE 14-40:** Showing a list of beverages

To complete this section, you'll tie the list of categories and products together. You'll modify the Index view (i.e., the list of categories), changing the items in the unordered list to links that will take us to the page showing the products for the selected category. Instead of creating anchor tags directly, you'll use the ActionLink HTML Helper to build the links for us; specifically, you'll use the overloaded version that takes the link text, the target action, and the parameters to pass to the action (code file: \Views\Products\Index.vbhtml):

```
<ul>
    @For Each category In Model
        @<li>
            @* category.CategoryName *@
            @Html.ActionLink(category.CategoryName, _
                "Browse", New With { .category = category.CategoryName })
        </li>
    Next
</ul>
```

You should now be able to navigate to the list of categories, click one of the links, and get the list of products for the category you selected.

## Routing

One of the goals of ASP.NET MVC is to enable developers to create "friendly" URLs for their users. In your application, it would be nice to get a list of products in the beverage category by navigating to /Products/Browse/Beverages instead of using the query string as you are now.

This change can be accomplished through the routing engine included in ASP.NET. This engine enables us to map a URL template to a controller (and potentially an action and parameters). When a request comes in, the engine uses pattern-matching algorithms to find a template that matches the "shape" of the request and then routes the request to the corresponding controller.

Open the App_Start\RouteConfig.vb file and look for the method named RegisterRoutes. In it you will see the code that has been routing the requests you've been making so far to controllers and actions:

```
routes.MapRoute( _
    name:="Default", _
    url:="{controller}/{action}/{id}", _
    defaults:=New With {.controller = "Home", .action = "Index", _
        .id = UrlParameter.Optional} _
)
```

The first parameter is the route name used as the key in the route table. The second parameter is the URL template. This template indicates there are potentially three segments: the first mapping to the controller name, the second mapping to the action name, and the third mapping to an id. The final parameter is an anonymous type that defines the default values of the segments.

Add the following code (above the existing call to MapRoute) to add a mapping that allows us to include the category name as part of the URL when you browse products (code file: \ App_Start\ RouteConfig.vb):

```
routes.MapRoute( _
    name:="BrowseProducts", _
    url:="Products/Browse/{Category}", _
    defaults:=New With {.controller = "Products", .action = "Browse", _
        .Category = UrlParameter.Optional} _
)
```

You should now be able to run the application and navigate to /Products/Browse/Beverages or /Products/Browse/Condiments to see products in those categories.

## Scaffolding and CRUD Operations

You've used the tooling in Visual Studio to assist us in creating controllers and views, but you haven't explored these tools fully. They have additional functionality to assist in creating the action methods and views for a slightly modified version of the CRUD (create, read, update, and delete) operations.

These tools work in a very similar way to the data server controls in Web Forms. By indicating the type of data to render and the type of view you desire (list, edit, create, etc.), Visual Studio can use reflection to determine the properties of the object being rendered and generate the appropriate markup and code.

To see this in action, create a new controller called `AdminController`, but this time set the scaffolding template to MVC controller with empty read/write actions, as shown in Figure 14-41. The generated code contains base implementations of `Index`, `Details`, `Create`, and `Edit` action methods.

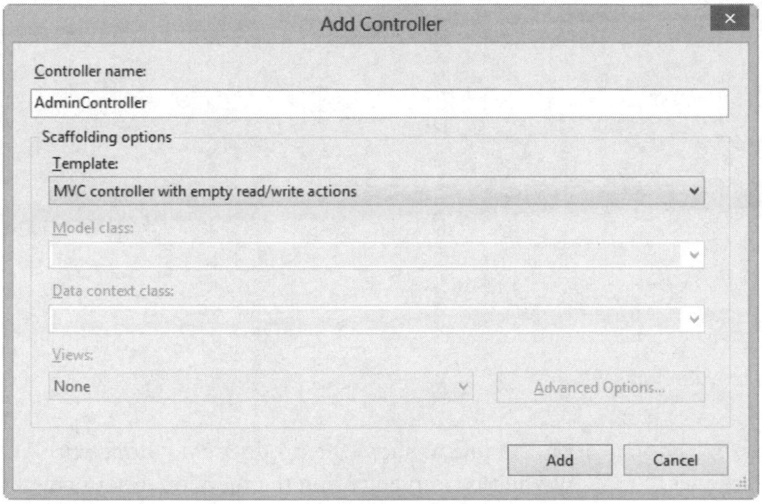

**FIGURE 14-41:** Creating a controller with CRUD operations shelled in

You'll start by modifying the `Index` action method. When it is requested you'll return a view showing a grid with the data for all products. Modify the action method to get all products from the `ProductService` and pass the resulting list to the `Index` view. You'll also need to add `Imports Northwind.Services` at the top of the file (code file: `\Controllers\ AdminController.vb`).

```
Private _prodService As New ProductService()

'
' GET: /Admin

Function Index() As ActionResult
    Dim products = _prodService.GetProducts()
    Return View(products)
End Function
```

Add a strongly typed view for the `Index` action, choosing List from the Scaffold template dropdown, as shown in Figure 14-42.

**FIGURE 14-42:** Adding a view with scaffolding

Choosing List will cause Visual Studio to generate a table to show the product data along with links to create, edit, or display the product data. You won't be implementing the functionality to create or delete products, so comment out the ActionLink helpers for those. For edit and details, the ActionLink helper needs to know what property to pass on the query string so the target controller can retrieve the selected item. The generated code will always use currentItem.PrimaryKey because the actual property cannot be determined during code generation. You'll be retrieving products using the ProductID, so change PrimaryKey to this property for the edit and details links (code file: \Views\Admin\Index.vbhtml).

```
@ModelType IEnumerable(Of Northwind.Services.ProductDto)

@Code
    ViewData("Title") = "Product Index"
End Code

<h2>Product Index</h2>

<p>
    @*Html.ActionLink("Create New", "Create")*@
</p>
<table>
    <tr>
        <th>
            @Html.DisplayNameFor(Function(model) model.ProductID)
        </th>
        <th>
```

```
                    @Html.DisplayNameFor(Function(model) model.ProductName)
                </th>
                <th>
                    @Html.DisplayNameFor(Function(model) model.QuantityPerUnit)
                </th>
                <th>
                    @Html.DisplayNameFor(Function(model) model.UnitPrice)
                </th>
                <th>
                    @IItml.DisplayNameFor(Function(model) model.UnitsInStock)
                </th>
                <th>
                    @Html.DisplayNameFor(Function(model) model.UnitsOnOrder)
                </th>
                <th></th>
            </tr>

        @For Each item In Model
            Dim currentItem = item
            @<tr>
                <td>
                    @Html.DisplayFor(Function(modelItem) currentItem.ProductID)
                </td>
                <td>
                    @Html.DisplayFor(Function(modelItem) currentItem.ProductName)
                </td>
                <td>
                    @Html.DisplayFor(Function(modelItem) currentItem.QuantityPerUnit)
                </td>
                <td>
                    @Html.DisplayFor(Function(modelItem) currentItem.UnitPrice)
                </td>
                <td>
                    @Html.DisplayFor(Function(modelItem) currentItem.UnitsInStock)
                </td>
                <td>
                    @Html.DisplayFor(Function(modelItem) currentItem.UnitsOnOrder)
                </td>
                <td>
                    @Html.ActionLink("Edit", "Edit", New With { _
                        .id = currentItem.ProductID}) |
                    @Html.ActionLink("Details", "Details", New With { _
                        .id = currentItem.ProductID}) |
                    @*@Html.ActionLink("Delete", "Delete", New With { _
                        .id = currentItem.PrimaryKey})*@
                </td>
            </tr>
        Next

    </table>
```

Notice the assumptions based on the ASP.NET MVC conventions. The Create link assumes you will have a Create action method, the Edit link assumes you have an Edit action method, and so on. Without the conventions in place, these links would not be able to be code generated.

Also note the use of the strongly typed `DisplayNameFor` and `DisplayFor` helper methods. These helpers take data of different types and determine how to best display that data on the page.

Running the application and navigating to `/Admin` should render a page similar to the one shown in Figure 14-43.

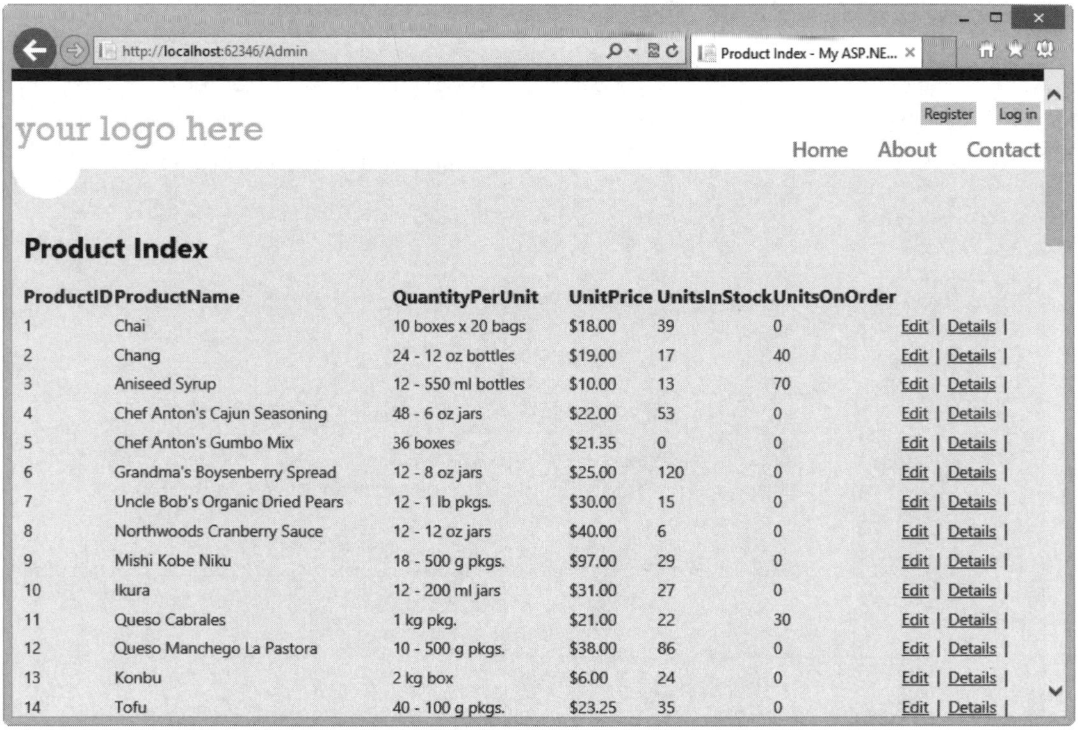

**FIGURE 14-43:** Products shown in a grid

Moving to the `Details` action method, modify the code to get the requested product from the repository and pass it on to the `Details` view (code file: `\Controllers\AdminController.vb`):

```
'
' GET: /Admin/Details/5

Function Details(ByVal id As Integer) As ActionResult
    Dim product = _prodService.GetProduct(id)
    Return View(product)
End Function
```

Generate the strongly typed view, this time selecting Details from the Scaffold template drop-down menu. Update the title and headers in the page as shown in bold below (code file: `\Views\Admin\Details.vbhtml`):

```
@ModelType Northwind.Services.ProductDto

@Code
```

```
    ViewData("Title") = "Product Details"
End Code

<h2>Product Details</h2>

<fieldset>
    <legend>Product</legend>

    <div class="display-label">
        @Html.DisplayNameFor(Function(model) model.ProductID)
    </div>
    <div class="display-field">
        @Html.DisplayFor(Function(model) model.ProductID)
    </div>

    <div class="display-label">
        @Html.DisplayNameFor(Function(model) model.ProductName)
    </div>
    <div class="display-field">
        @Html.DisplayFor(Function(model) model.ProductName)
    </div>

    <div class="display-label">
        @Html.DisplayNameFor(Function(model) model.QuantityPerUnit)
    </div>
    <div class="display-field">
        @Html.DisplayFor(Function(model) model.QuantityPerUnit)
    </div>

    <div class="display-label">
        @Html.DisplayNameFor(Function(model) model.UnitPrice)
    </div>
    <div class="display-field">
        @Html.DisplayFor(Function(model) model.UnitPrice)
    </div>

    <div class="display-label">
        @Html.DisplayNameFor(Function(model) model.UnitsInStock)
    </div>
    <div class="display-field">
        @Html.DisplayFor(Function(model) model.UnitsInStock)
    </div>

    <div class="display-label">
        @Html.DisplayNameFor(Function(model) model.UnitsOnOrder)
    </div>
    <div class="display-field">
        @Html.DisplayFor(Function(model) model.UnitsOnOrder)
    </div>
</fieldset>
<p>
    @*@Html.ActionLink("Edit", "Edit", New With {.id = Model.PrimaryKey}) |*@
    @Html.ActionLink("Back to List", "Index")
</p>
```

Run the application, navigate to /Admin, and click the Details link for one of the items. You should be taken to a page similar to the one shown in Figure 14-44. It's not the prettiest page, but that issue could be fairly easily addressed with the addition of some CSS. Clicking the Back to List link at the bottom of the page will take you back to the list of products.

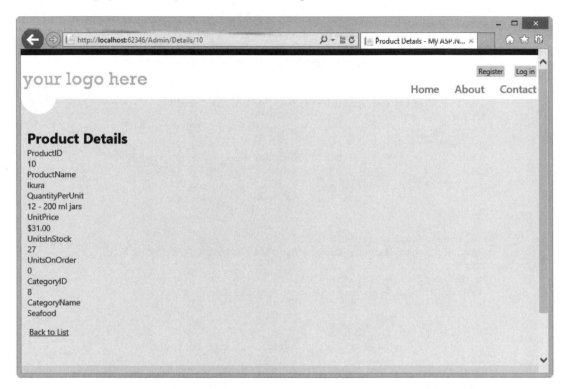

**FIGURE 14-44:** Details for a product

You'll look at the Edit action in two parts. The first part involves generating a form that allows editing of product data; the second involves receiving the updated data when the user submits the form.

The Edit action method will have the same implementation as the Details action method. Modify it so that it retrieves the requested product and returns the appropriate view (code file: \Controllers\AdminController.vb):

```
'
' GET: /Admin/Edit/5

Function Edit(ByVal id As Integer) As ActionResult
    Dim product = _prodService.GetProduct(id)
    Return View(product)
End Function
```

Generate a strongly typed view, selecting Edit from the Scaffold template drop-down (code file: \Views\Admin\Edit.vbhtml).

```
@ModelType Northwind.Services.ProductDto

@Code
    ViewData("Title") = "Edit Product"
End Code

<h2>Edit Product</h2>

@Using Html.BeginForm()
    @Html.ValidationSummary(True)

    @<fieldset>
        <legend>Product</legend>

        <div class="editor-label">
            @Html.LabelFor(Function(model) model.ProductID)
        </div>
        <div class="editor-field">
            @Html.EditorFor(Function(model) model.ProductID)
            @Html.ValidationMessageFor(Function(model) model.ProductID)
        </div>

        <div class="editor-label">
            @Html.LabelFor(Function(model) model.ProductName)
        </div>
        <div class="editor-field">
            @Html.EditorFor(Function(model) model.ProductName)
            @Html.ValidationMessageFor(Function(model) model.ProductName)
        </div>

        <div class="editor-label">
            @Html.LabelFor(Function(model) model.QuantityPerUnit)
        </div>
        <div class="editor-field">
            @Html.EditorFor(Function(model) model.QuantityPerUnit)
            @Html.ValidationMessageFor(Function(model) model.QuantityPerUnit)
        </div>

        <div class="editor-label">
            @Html.LabelFor(Function(model) model.UnitPrice)
        </div>
        <div class="editor-field">
            @Html.EditorFor(Function(model) model.UnitPrice)
            @Html.ValidationMessageFor(Function(model) model.UnitPrice)
        </div>

        <div class="editor-label">
            @Html.LabelFor(Function(model) model.UnitsInStock)
        </div>
        <div class="editor-field">
            @Html.EditorFor(Function(model) model.UnitsInStock)
            @Html.ValidationMessageFor(Function(model) model.UnitsInStock)
        </div>

        <div class="editor-label">
```

```
                @Html.LabelFor(Function(model) model.UnitsOnOrder)
        </div>
        <div class="editor-field">
            @Html.EditorFor(Function(model) model.UnitsOnOrder)
            @Html.ValidationMessageFor(Function(model) model.UnitsOnOrder)
        </div>

        <p>
            <input type="submit" value="Save" />
        </p>
    </fieldset>
End Using

<div>
    @Html.ActionLink("Back to List", "Index")
</div>

@Section Scripts
    @Scripts.Render("~/bundles/jqueryval")
End Section
```

In addition to the strongly typed `DisplayNameFor` and `DisplayFor` helpers you saw earlier, you now see the `EditorFor` and `ValidationMessageFor` helpers. `EditorFor` looks at the type of the data and determines the appropriate UI element to use to let the user edit it. `ValidationMessageFor` looks at the `ModelState` to see if the data entered is invalid and reports any errors.

The final item of note is the `BeginForm` helper. This method is responsible for rendering the HTML form tag that will determine how updated data is sent to the client when the user submits the form. Calling `BeginForm` without any parameters will cause the form data to be sent via an HTTP POST to the current URL.

To handle the POST, you have a second `Edit` action method (code file: `\Controllers\ AdminController.vb`):

```
'
' POST: /Admin/Edit/5

<HttpPost()> _
Function Edit(ByVal id As Integer, ByVal collection As FormCollection) _
    As ActionResult
    Dim product = _prodService.GetProduct(id)
    Try
        UpdateModel(product)
        _prodService.UpdateProduct(product)
        Return RedirectToAction("Index")
    Catch
        Return View(product)
    End Try
End Function
```

Using the `HttpPost` attribute enables differentiation between action methods of the same name. Think of it as an additional form of method overloading.

If you look at the method implementation closely, you should notice that it looks very similar to what you saw in the Web Forms example. ASP.NET MVC uses model binding just like Web Forms does, so the implementation of the method is almost exactly the same. The only difference is that UpdateModel throws an exception if the ModelState is not valid.

Run the application, navigate to /Admin, and click the Edit link for one of the items. You should be taken to a page similar to the one shown in Figure 14-45.

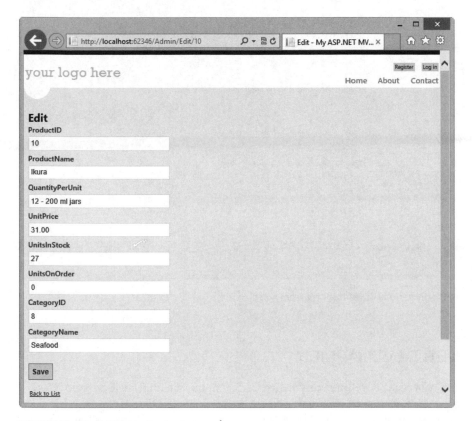

**FIGURE 14-45:** Editing a product

Update a field or two with valid values and click the Save button. Verify the changes were persisted by navigating back to the Edit page for the same item. Now try to enter invalid values and you'll see the validation in action. You should see a page similar to the one shown in Figure 14-46.

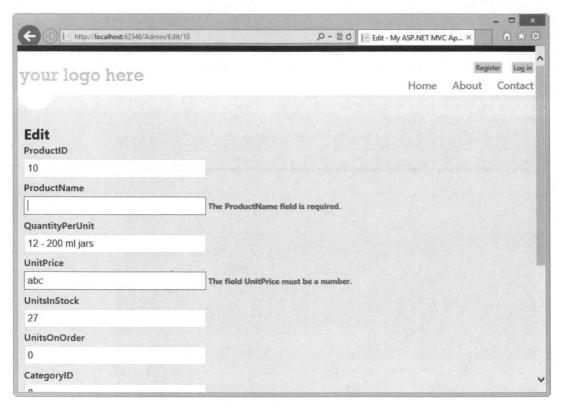

**FIGURE 14-46:** Product edit page with validation errors

# CLIENT-SIDE WEB DEVELOPMENT

When you talk about client-side development you are talking about writing JavaScript code that runs in the user's browser. Client-side Web development uses neither Visual Basic nor .NET (i.e., the focus of this book), but the topic is too important to ignore altogether. While the use of server-side technologies to build Web applications is still very popular, the amount of development being done for the client-side has been growing rapidly and will most likely continue to grow in the foreseeable future.

Just like you did with the server-side technologies, you'll get an overview of the client-side technologies so you can decide if you want to investigate them further.

## Web Development with HTML and JavaScript

You are going to build a sample application using only HTML and JavaScript. As mentioned a moment ago, most developers using Visual Studio to build Web applications are using some server-side technology, so it would be rare to see an application built this way, but doing so gives us the greatest opportunity to explore the topic of this section.

## REST Services and the Web API

Client-side code relies heavily on Web services to communicate with the server to get and update data. While you can call SOAP services from JavaScript, it's much easier to work with REST services. Instead of having to construct an XML document to make a service call as you do with SOAP, you just make a Web request with specific information in the URL in REST. Instead of getting an XML document as a response from a SOAP service call, most REST services will return JSON (native JavaScript objects).

So before you start building your HTML and JavaScript sample application, you'll build a Web service that it can use to communicate with the Northwind database. The operations in the Web service will just be wrappers around the methods in the Northwind.Services data-access layer.

To build the Web service you'll use a new technology called the ASP.NET Web API. Built on top of ASP.NET MVC, the Web API makes it easy to build the kind of RESTful services described above.

Open Visual Studio and create a new ASP.NET MVC 4 Web Application named JavaScriptDemo. Choose the Web API template and click OK (see Figure 14-47).

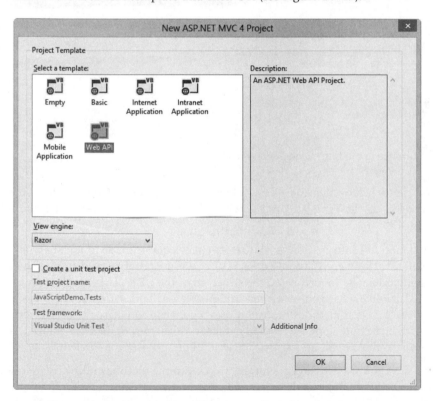

**FIGURE 14-47:** Creating a new Web API project

Now you'll create service operations that map one-to-one with the methods in the `CategoryService` and `ProductService` in the Northwind.Services assembly. Add a reference to this assembly by right-clicking on the project in the Solution Explorer and selecting Add Reference.

The assembly should show in the Recent category—check it and click OK. If it isn't there, click the Browse button (at the bottom), navigate to the Northwind.Services.dll, click the Add button, and then click the OK button (see Figure 14-48).

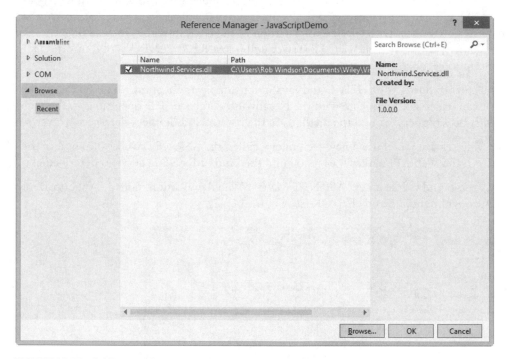

**FIGURE 14-48:** Adding a reference to the Northwind.Services assembly

In the Solution Explorer, right-click on the Controllers folder and select Add ➪ Controller. Set the name to CategoriesController, set the Template drop-down to Empty API Controller, and click the Add button (see Figure 14-49).

The Web API will use two pieces of information to route HTTP GET requests made to api/categories to the GetValue method. The Web API is based on MVC, so it uses routing to determine which controller to call and what parameters to pass based the structure of the URL. The default route is /api/{controller}/{id}. Unlike what you've seen earlier, the Web API does not use attributes to map different HTTP verbs to different methods. Instead it uses a convention where the HTTP verb used in the request maps to the beginning of the method name. So the names of methods implemented in a controller in the Web API will all start with "Get," "Put," "Post," or "Delete."

In this controller and the next you want to add operations that wrap the methods in the two services in the Northwind.Services assembly. Replace the generated code in the CategoriesController with the following (code file: \Controllers\CategoriesController.vb):

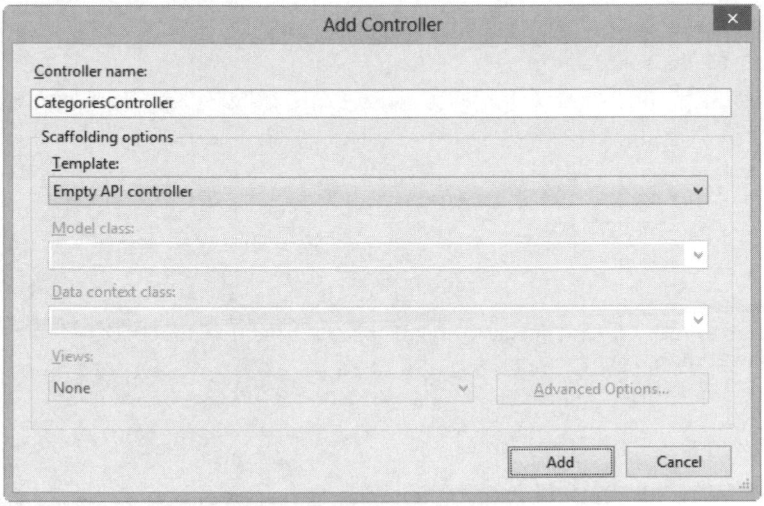

FIGURE 14-49: Adding the CategoriesController

```vb
Imports System.Net
Imports System.Web.Http
Imports Northwind.Services

Public Class CategoriesController
    Inherits ApiController

    Private _service As New CategoryService()

    ' GET api/categories
    Public Function GetValue() As IEnumerable(Of CategoryDto)
        Return _service.GetCategoryList()
    End Function
End Class
```

Now add another controller named `ProductsController.vb` (also using the Empty API Controller template) and replace the generated code with the following (code file: \Controllers \ProductsController.vb):

```vb
Imports System.Net
Imports System.Web.Http
Imports Northwind.Services

Public Class ProductsController
    Inherits ApiController

    Private _service As New ProductService()

    ' GET api/products
    Public Function GetValue() As IEnumerable(Of ProductDto)
        Return _service.GetProducts()
    End Function
```

```
' GET api/products?catid=5
Public Function GetByCategory(ByVal catid As Integer) As _
    IEnumerable(Of ProductDto)
    Return _service.GetProducts(catid)
End Function

' GET api/products/5
Public Function GetValue(ByVal id As Integer) As ProductDto
    Return _service.GetProduct(id)
End Function

' PUT api/products/5
Public Sub PutValue(ByVal id As Integer, ByVal product As ProductDto)
    _service.UpdateProduct(product)
End Sub

End Class
```

IIS Express is not configured to handle PUT or DELETE verbs by default. To enable these verbs you need to update the configuration for IIS Express. The process is documented in the IIS Express FAQ at http:learn.iis.net/page.aspx/901/iis-express-faq/. Look for the question "How do I enable verbs like PUT/DELETE for my web application?"

## Testing REST Services

There are several tools you could use to test the REST service you built; one of the most popular of these is Fiddler. You can download Fiddler for free from www.Fiddler2.com. Once you've downloaded and installed Fiddler, go back to Visual Studio and press F5 to start your Web API application in debug mode. It doesn't matter what page opens in the browser; you just need IIS Express to be listening for requests. Note the host address, as you'll need it for testing. You can also find the host address by selecting the project in the Solution Explorer and looking at the URL property in the Properties Window.

With the Visual Studio project still running, start Fiddler and open the Composer tab on the right. Enter the host address from the Web API application plus /api/categories and press the Execute button (see Figure 14-50).

You should see a new entry in the list on the left with the host address in the Host column and /api/ categories in the URL column. You should also see 200 in the Result column; this indicates that the service call completed successfully. Click on this item in the list and then click on the JSON tab in the bottom section on the right. You should see category information shown in the text box below the tab (see Figure 14-51).

If you have errors you can set breakpoints in Visual Studio to debug the Web service code and use Fiddler to see information about the calls made to the service.

## Building the Website

Now that you have the REST service you can move on to building the site itself. You could do this in a separate Visual Studio project, but keep things simple by continuing to use the same one.

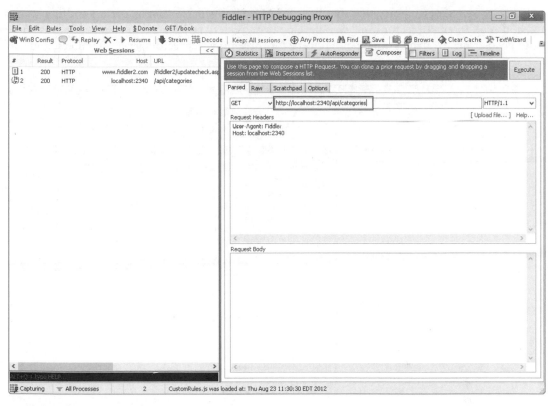

**FIGURE 14-50:** Sending a request to a REST service using Fiddler

Right-click on the project in the Solution Explorer and select Add ➪ New Item. In the Add New
Item dialog select the HTML Page template, set the Name to ProductList.html, and click the Add
button. In the body of the page add a `<select>` element (i.e., a drop-down) to show the categories,
a `<ul>` element to show the products in the selected category, and a `<h2>` element that will serve as
the title for the list of products. When you are done the body of the page should look similar to the
following (code file: `ProductList-Step01.html`):

```
<body>
    <select id="category-select">
        <option value="0">All categories</option>
    </select>
    <br />
    <br />
    <h2 id="product-list-title"></h2>
    <ul id="product-list">
    </ul>
</body>
```

## jQuery

jQuery is an extremely popular JavaScript library. So popular, in fact, that the term *jQuery* has
become synonymous with client-side Web development. From the jQuery website: "jQuery is a fast

and concise JavaScript Library that simplifies HTML document traversing, event handling, animating, and Ajax interactions for rapid web development. jQuery is designed to change the way that you write JavaScript." You are going to use jQuery for three things: selectors, event handlers, and calling web services.

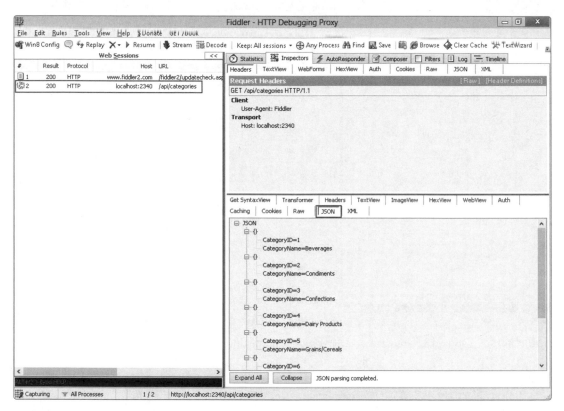

**FIGURE 14-51:** Examining the response from the service call in Fiddler

Version 1.7.1 of the library (`jquery-1.7.1.js`) is included in the project template in the Scripts folder, so you'll start by adding a script reference to the file. With the reference added, you can start using the `jQuery` object. The short form for the name of the jQuery object is the dollar sign, but you use the full name if you want. That is, `$()` is equivalent to `jQuery()`.

Next you'll use jQuery's `$(document).ready()` to detect when the page has loaded and is ready to use. You'll call this the *ready function*. Think of it as the conceptual equivalent of `Page_Load` in a Web Forms page.

Inside the ready function you'll use a jQuery selector to get a reference to the category drop-down (i.e., the `<select>` element.) To do this you'll pass the parameter "#category-select" to the jQuery object. This tells jQuery to find the element with the id set to "category-select." Had you passed in ".foo" to the jQuery object it would have found all the elements with the class set to "foo." The selector syntax used by jQuery is very similar to that used by CSS. Once you have a reference to the categories drop-down, you'll call `getCategories` to populate it.

In `getCategories` you'll use jQuery's `ajax` function to call the REST service you created earlier to get the categories. This call will be made asynchronously, so you won't get the results back immediately. When the results do come back, jQuery will call the `done` method on the object created by the `ajax` method.

Inside the `done` method, you'll loop through the array of JSON objects returned by the service call and create a new `<option>` element for each one and add it to the drop-down.

With all of this done the head for the page should look like the following (code file: `ProductList-Step01.html`):

```
<head>
    <title>Product List</title>

    <!-- jQuery script reference -->
    <script type="text/javascript" src="Scripts/jquery-1.7.1.js"></script>

    <script type="text/javascript">
        // Ready function
        $(document).ready(function () {
            // Get a reference to the categories drop-down
            var select = $("#category-select");

            // Populate the categories drop-down
            getCategories(select);
        });

        function getCategories(select) {
            // Initiate web service call to get categories
            var call = $.ajax("api/categories");

            // Callback when web service call completes
            call.done(function (data) {
                $.each(data, function (i, obj) {
                    // Create a new item to go in categories drop-down
                    var option = $("<option></option>");

                    // Set the value attribute to Category ID
                    option.attr("value", obj.CategoryID);

                    // Set the text of the item
                    option.text(obj.CategoryName);

                    // Add the item to the drop-down
                    select.append(option);
                });
            });
        }
    </script>
</head>
```

To make debugging easier you'll configure the project to open the page that has focus when you run. Open the project properties and select the Web tab. Change the Start Action to Current Page and save (see Figure 14-52).

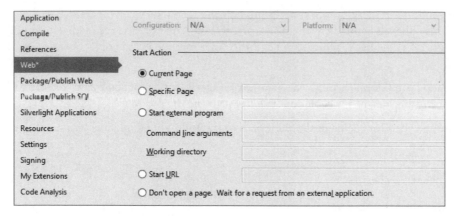

**FIGURE 14-52:** Changing the Start Action for the project

Now select ProductList.html in the Solution Explorer and press F5. You may have to wait a moment for the drop-down to be populated, as your client-side code isn't executing until after the page has been loaded. After waiting, you should see a page that looks like the one in Figure 14-53.

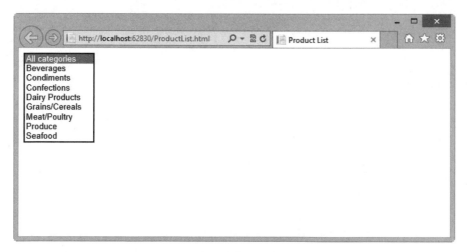

**FIGURE 14-53:** Product list page with the category drop-down populated

## Handling Events

You have the code to populate the categories drop-down. Now you need to write the code that will run when the user selects an item. Inside the ready function you already have a jQuery object that represents the drop-down. You can use the change method on this object to attach an event handler. This will be a new method named getProducts.

Inside getProducts you need to find the selected item in the categories drop-down. You can do this using "#category-select option:selected" selector. Once you have a reference to this <option> element, you can find the ID and the name of the category that has been selected. Then you can call the REST service to get the products in that category and populate the products list. Each item in the list should show the product name as a link to ProductDetails.html (which you will create next) with the product ID added as a query string parameter.

One final step is to add a call to getProducts after you've retrieved the categories to populate the drop-down (near the end of getCategories).

· Add the code shown in bold below to implement the functionality described above (code file: ProductList-Step02.html).

```
$(document).ready(function () {
    var select = $("#category-select");
    getCategories(select);
    select.change(getProducts);
});

function getCategories(select) {
    var call = $.ajax("api/categories");
    call.done(function (data) {
        $.each(data, function (i, obj) {
            var option = $("<option></option>");
            option.attr("value", obj.CategoryID);
            option.text(obj.CategoryName);
            select.append(option);
        });
        getProducts();
    });
}

function getProducts() {
    var selectedItem = $("#category-select option:selected");
    var selectedID = selectedItem.attr("value");
    var selectedText = selectedItem.text();

    var call = $.ajax("api/products?catid=" + selectedID);
    call.done(function (data) {
        var header = $("#product-list-title");
        header.text(selectedText);
        var list = $("#product-list");
        list.empty();
        $.each(data, function (i, obj) {
            var item = $("<li></li>");
            var link = $("<a></a>");
            link.attr("href", "productdetails.html?id=" + obj.ProductID);
            link.text(obj.ProductName);
            item.append(link);
            list.append(item);
        });
    });
}
```

Press F5 to run the page. Now when you select a category from the drop-down you should see the products in that category (see Figure 14-54).

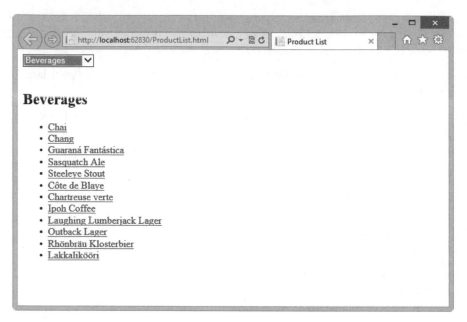

**FIGURE 14-54:** Product list page with product data showing

## Working with Forms

Keeping with the pattern, you'll implement a form to edit products in two parts. Add a new HTML Page named ProductDetails.html to the project. In the body of the page add a form that can be used to view and edit a product. This form will be almost identical to the one you used in the Web Pages example application. The form should look like the one shown below (code file: ProductDetails-Step01.html):

```
<body>
    <div>
        <form id="product-form">
            <input id="ProductID" type="hidden" />
            <fieldset>
                <legend>Product</legend>
                <div>
                    <label>Name</label>
                    <input id="ProductName" type="text" />
                </div>
                <div>
                    <label>Quantity per Unit</label>
                    <input id="QuantityPerUnit" type="text" />
                </div>
                <div>
                    <label>Unit Price</label>
                    <input id="UnitPrice" type="text" />
                </div>
                <div>
                    <label>Units in Stock</label>
```

```
                    <input id="UnitsInStock" type="text" />
                </div>
                <div>
                    <label>Units on Order</label>
                    <input id="UnitsOnOrder" type="text" />
                </div>
                <div>
                    <label> </label>
                    <input type="submit" value="Save" />
                </div>
            </fieldset>
        </form>
    </div>
</body>
```

In the ready function you need to get the "id" parameter from the query string. If it isn't there redirect to the Product List page; if it is then call getProduct to get the product data and show it in the form. Update the head for the page with the code shown below (code file: ProductDetails-Step01.html):

```
<head>
    <title>Product List</title>

    <script type="text/javascript" src="Scripts/jquery-1.7.1.js"></script>
    <script type="text/javascript">
        $(document).ready(function () {
            var qs = parseQueryString();
            var id = qs["id"];
            if (typeof id === "undefined") {
                top.location.href = "productlist.html";
                return;
            }

            getProduct(id);
        });

        function parseQueryString() {
            var nvpair = {};
            var qs = window.location.search.replace('?', '');
            var pairs = qs.split('&');
            $.each(pairs, function (i, v) {
                var pair = v.split('=');
                nvpair[pair[0]] = pair[1];
            });
            return nvpair;
        }

        function getProduct(id) {
            var call = $.ajax("api/products/" + id);
            call.done(function (data) {
                $("#ProductID").val(data.ProductID);
                $("#ProductName").val(data.ProductName);
                $("#QuantityPerUnit").val(data.QuantityPerUnit);
                $("#UnitPrice").val(data.UnitPrice);
                $("#UnitsInStock").val(data.UnitsInStock);
```

```
                    $("#UnitsOnOrder").val(data.UnitsOnOrder);
                });
            }

        </script>
    </head>
```

Select ProductList.html in the Solution Explorer and press F5 to run the page. Select Beverages from the categories in the drop-down and then click the link for Ipoh Coffee. You should be redirected to a page that looks like the one shown in Figure 14-55.

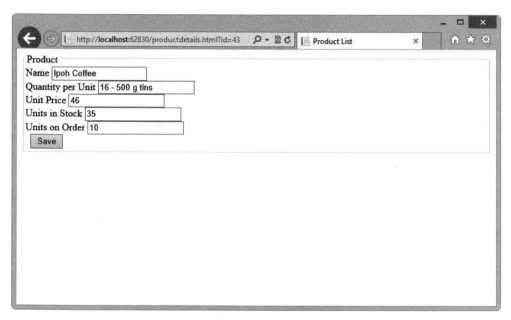

**FIGURE 14-55:** Product details page running in the browser

## Handling User Input

In your previous examples you've always had to worry about posting the page back to the server to perform the update. You don't have to worry about that here because all the code is running in the browser.

In the ready function you'll get a reference to the form and then attach the saveProduct as the event handler for submit. Inside saveProduct you'll construct a new JSON object to represent the product data and then include that information in the body of a HTTP PUT request back to the server. When the request hits the server, the JSON will be de-serialized into a .NET ProductDto object, which will then get saved to the database.

Add the code shown bold below to the page head to implement the functionality described above (code file: ProductDetails-Step02.html).

```
<head>
    <title>Product List</title>

    <script type="text/javascript" src="Scripts/jquery-1.7.1.js"></script>
    <script type="text/javascript">
```

```
$(document).ready(function () {
    var qs = parseQueryString();
    var id = qs["id"];
    if (typeof id === "undefined") {
        top.location.href = "productlist.html";
        return;
    }

    var form = $("#product-form");
    form.submit(saveProduct);

    getProduct(id);
});

function parseQueryString() {
    // removed for brevity
}

function getProduct(id) {
    // removed for brevity
}

function saveProduct() {
    var product = {
        "ProductID": $("#ProductID").val(),
        "ProductName": $("#ProductName").val(),
        "QuantityPerUnit": $("#QuantityPerUnit").val(),
        "UnitPrice": $("#UnitPrice").val(),
        "UnitsInStock": $("#UnitsInStock").val(),
        "UnitsOnOrder": $("#UnitsOnOrder").val()
    }
    var productString = JSON.stringify(product);

    var call = $.ajax({
        url: "api/products/" + product.ProductID,
        cache: false,
        type: "PUT",
        data: productString,
        contentType: 'application/json; charset=utf-8'
    });
    call.done(function () {
        top.location.href = "productlist.html";
    });
}
    </script>
</head>
```

Now when you run the application, you should be able to update and save the product data.

If you are using an older browser you may get an error on the call to JSON.stringify. This means the browser you are using does not have native JSON processing support. A common alternative is to use json2.js, written by Douglas Crockford. This library is available at http:github.com/douglascrockford/JSON-js.

## Validation

You may have noticed that there is no validation being done in the form you created, so if you enter invalid data you'll get exceptions. Validation could be added using jQuery's validation plugin (http:docs.jquery.com/Plugins/Validation). Doing so is left as an exercise for the reader.

# BUILDING WINDOWS 8 STYLE APPS WITH HTML AND JAVASCRIPT

In the previous chapter you saw how to build Windows 8 style apps using Visual Basic and XAML. You can also build these kinds of apps using HTML and JavaScript. You'll take a brief look at how to do so by building a sample application similar to the others you've built in this chapter.

The key to building Windows 8 style apps with Web technologies is the *Windows Library for JavaScript (WinJS)*. Not only does it include a set of controls you can use to build the interface for your applications, but it includes functionality that enables us to call services, interact with Windows, and much more. The sample application demonstrates how to use WinJS controls and how to use WinJS to call Web services and to enable data-binding. Note that you'll only be able to build and run the sample application if you are using Windows 8.

Open Visual Studio and select File ⇨ New ⇨ Project. In the New Project dialog, select the Installed ⇨ Templates ⇨ JavaScript ⇨ Windows Store category on the left, then select the Navigation App template, set the Name to MetroDemo, and click the OK button (see Figure 14-56).

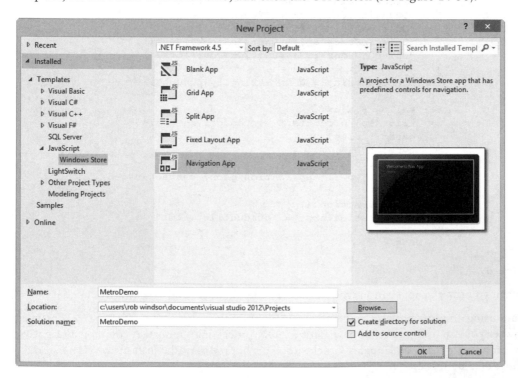

**FIGURE 14-56:** Creating a Windows 8 style app project

When the project has been created, expand the pages and home nodes in the Solution Explorer. You should see something similar to Figure 14-57.

In a navigation app, default.html is the shell page. Home.html and the other custom content you'll create are `PageControls` that get inserted into the shell. It's somewhat analogous to the master and content pages you saw in Web Forms. You'll update home.html to show a list of products grouped by category, and then you'll create a new page control to show the product details when a product is selected.

Before you build your first page, you'll examine how to use WinJS with markup in a little more detail. Instead of having custom tags to represent controls you use `<div>` tags with a `data-win-control` attribute. If you set the value of this attribute to "WinJS. UI.Rating" you get a `Rating` control, if you set it to "WinJS. UI.ListView" you get a `ListView` control, and so on.

**FIGURE 14-57:** Files added by the project template

You use the `win-data-bind` attribute to configure data-binding. The value of this attribute is a set of name value pairs. For example, say you are binding to the Ipoh Coffee product in the Northwind database. Setting the value of `win-data-bind` to "innerText: ProductName; id: ProductID" on an `<h2>` tag would result in `<h2 id="43">Ipoh Coffee</h2>`.

Now that you have an overview of WinS, you can implement your first `PageControl`. Open \pages\ home\home.html and set the text of the `<span>` tag in the header to Products. Then replace the main content section with the contents of the code snippet below. In this markup you have three WinJS controls, a `ListView`, and two `Templates`. The `Templates` are used to represent the markup that will be contained in the `ListView`. You'll configure the `ListView` to use these Templates in the code-behind for the page.

Recall that the product data will be shown grouped by category. The first `Template` defines how the category will be shown. It will be an `<h2>` tag with the category name as the text. The second `Template` defines how each of the products will be shown. It will be in a blue square (a tile) with the name of the product shown inside (code file: \pages\home\home.html).

```
<section aria-label="Main content" role="main">
    <div id="productsHeaderTemplate"
        data-win-control="WinJS.Binding.Template">
        <div>
            <h2 data-win-bind="innerText: category"></h2>
        </div>
    </div>

    <div id="productsTemplate"
        data-win-control="WinJS.Binding.Template">
        <div style="width: 200px; height: 130px; background-color: #557EB9">
            <h4 data-win-bind="innerText:name" />
        </div>
    </div>

    <div id="productsList" data-win-control="WinJS.UI.ListView" />
</section>
```

Now open \pages\home\home.js. This is the code-behind for the page. The first thing to note is this piece of code near the top of the file: WinJS.UI.Pages.define("/pages/home/home.html"); this creates the PageControl and links the code-behind to the markup for the page.

Inside the define method you also have the ready function, which is called after the page control contents have been loaded. This is where you'll put your code. Implement the ready function with the code shown in the code snippet below. There's quite a bit going on here; you'll go through it step by step.

The first thing you'll do is create a variable of type WinJS.Binding.List to store the data you are going to bind to the ListView. Then you'll use WinJS to call the REST service you created in the last part of this chapter to get the product data. The code to do this is very similar to what you saw earlier, except instead of using jQuery's ajax and done functions you're using WinJS's xhr and then methods. Note that you may need to change the host address in the code snippet below to match that used by the REST service. Once you have the data, which comes to us as a string, you'll parse it into an array of JSON objects and use that array to populate the binding list.

You want to show the product data grouped by category, so you'll use the binding list's createGrouped function to do the grouping. The first parameter is used to determine which groups there are, and the second is used to determine which items belong in each group. Once you have the grouped data you can bind it to the ListView.

You get a reference to the ListView using the winControl property of the <div> element that contains it. You can then set the data sources for the items and groups and configure the templates.

Finally you want to attach an event handler for when one of the product tiles is clicked. When this happens you want to navigate to a page that shows the details for the product (you'll create this page control next). When you navigate you want to pass a reference to the item from the binding list associated with the product that was clicked. The target page will use it to retrieve the appropriate item data (code file: \pages\home\home.js).

```
ready: function (element, options) {
    // Create an observable list for data-binding
    var products = new WinJS.Binding.List();

    // Get the product data and populate the binding list
    WinJS.xhr({
        url: "http://localhost:62830/api/products"
    }).then(function (xhr) {
        var data = JSON.parse(xhr.response);
        data.forEach(function (i) {
            var item = {
                id: i.ProductID,
                name: i.ProductName,
                category: i.CategoryName
            }
            products.push(item);
        });
    });

    // Group the product data by category
    var groupedProducts = products.createGrouped(
        function (i) { return i.category; },
        function (i) { return { category: i.category } }
    );
```

```
        // Get a reference to the ListView
        var lstCategories = document.getElementById("productsList").winControl;

        // Set the data sources and templates used by the ListView
        lstCategories.itemDataSource = groupedProducts.dataSource;
        lstCategories.itemTemplate = document.getElementById("productsTemplate");
        lstCategories.groupDataSource = groupedProducts.groups.dataSource;
        lstCategories.groupHeaderTemplate =
            document.getElementById("productsHeaderTemplate");

        // Add an event handler for when a product tile is clicked
        lstCategories.addEventListener("iteminvoked", function (e) {
            var item = groupedProducts.getAt(e.detail.itemIndex);
            WinJS.Navigation.navigate("/pages/detail/detail.html", item);
        });
    }
```

Open another instance of Visual Studio and open the JavaScriptDemo project you created earlier. Press F5 to start this application and leave it running so you can make calls to the REST service. Now switch back to the MetroDemo project and press F5 to run it. You should see something similar to what is shown in Figure 14-58.

Now you'll create the page to show the product details. In the Solution Explorer, right-click on the pages folder and create a new folder named detail. Then right-click on the newly created folder and select Add ⇨ New Item. In the Add New Item dialog select the Page Control template, set the Name to detail.html, and click the Add button (see Figure 14-59).

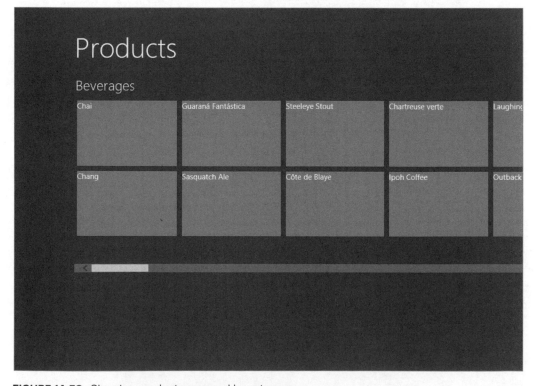

**FIGURE 14-58:** Showing products grouped by category

Open detail.html and set the text of the `<span>` tag in the header to Product Detail. In the main content section add the markup to show the properties of a product in text box controls. You can use a `<fieldset>` as you did in the Web Pages sample or a table as, shown in the following code snippet. You could use data-binding to populate the controls, but it's really unnecessary in such a simple page. You populate the control values the old-fashioned way, with JavaScript code (code file: \pages\detail\detail.html).

```
<section aria-label="Main content" role="main">
    <div style="padding-left:50px; width:80%">
        <table>
            <tr>
                <td>Product:</td>
                <td>
                    <input id="ProductName" type="text" />
                </td>
            </tr>
            <tr>
                <td>Quantity Per Unit:</td>
                <td>
                    <input id="QuantityPerUnit" type="text" />
                </td>
            </tr>
            <tr>
                <td>Unit Price:</td>
                <td>
                    <input id="UnitPrice" type="text" />
                </td>
            </tr>
            <tr>
                <td>Units in Stock:</td>
                <td>
                    <input id="UnitsInStock" type="text" />
                </td>
            </tr>
            <tr>
                <td>Units on Order:</td>
                <td>
                    <input id="UnitsOnOrder" type="text" />
                </td>
            </tr>
        </table>
    </div>
</section>
```

Now open detail.js and implement the ready function as shown in the code snippet below. This code is pretty simple. The options parameter contains a reference to the object from the binding list associated with the product selected by the user. The id property of this object contains the product ID. You'll use this ID in a call to the REST service to get the product data and then use that data to populate the text box controls on the page. Again note that you may have to change the host address used in the service call to match that used by the REST service (code file: \pages\detail\detail. js).

```
ready: function (element, options) {
    WinJS.xhr({
        url: "http://localhost:62830/api/products/" + options.id
    }).then(function (xhr) {
        var data = JSON.parse(xhr.response);
        document.getElementById("ProductName").value = data.ProductName;
        document.getElementById("QuantityPerUnit").value = data.QuantityPerUnit;
        document.getElementById("UnitPrice").value = data.UnitPrice;
        document.getElementById("UnitsInStock").value = data.UnitsInStock;
        document.getElementById("UnitsOnOrder").value = data.UnitsOnOrder;
    });
},
```

Run the JavaScriptDemo application if it's not running and then run the MetroDemo application. When the product list appears, click on one of the product tiles, and you should be redirected to a page that looks similar to the one shown in Figure 14-60.

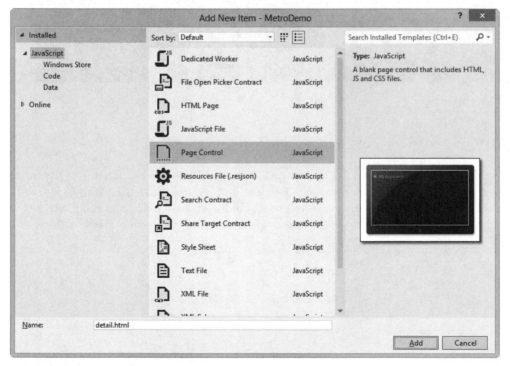

**FIGURE 14-59:** Adding the detail page control

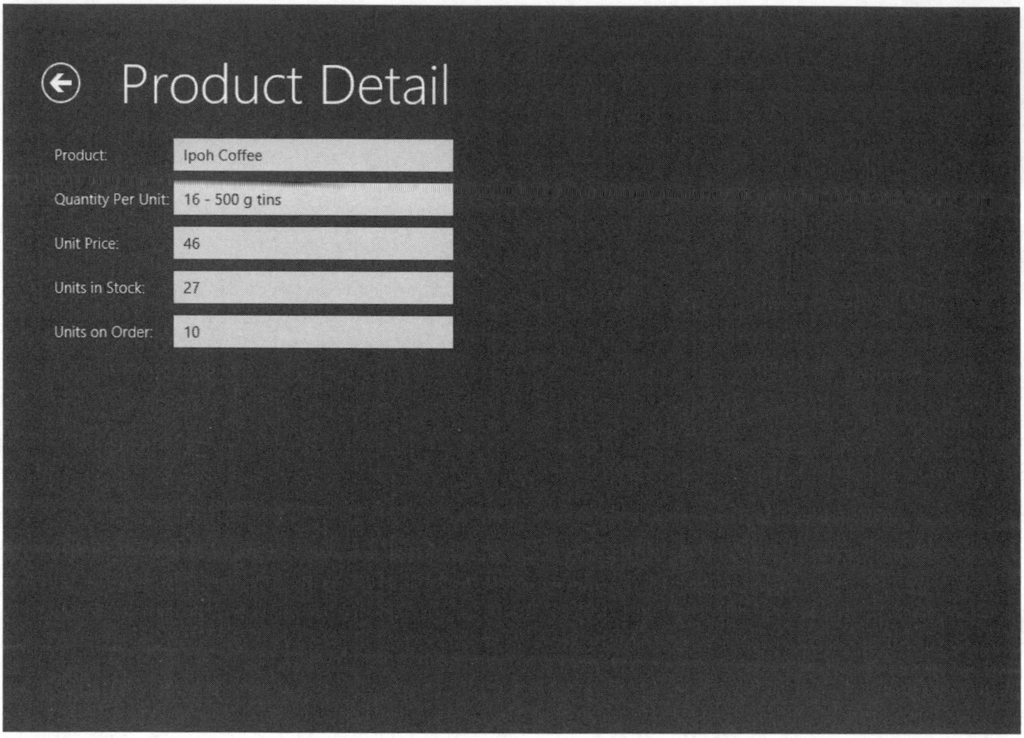

**FIGURE 14-60:** Product details

## SUMMARY

This chapter covered a lot of ground. The goal was to give you an overview of many of the frameworks and technologies available for Web development in ASP.NET and Visual Studio. You didn't cover enough to make you an expert in any one area, but hopefully you covered enough to enable you to decide which parts best suit your style and needs so that you can study them further.

In the next chapter you'll take a look at how to localize your Visual Basic applications.

# 15

# Localization

## WROX.COM CODE DOWNLOADS FOR THIS CHAPTER

The wrox.com code downloads for this chapter are found at www.wrox.com/remtitle .cgi?isbn=9781118314456 on the Download Code tab. The code is in the chapter 15 download and individually named according to the code filenames noted throughout the chapter.

As the audience for an application expands, businesses often realize they need to globalize the application. Of course, the ideal solution is to build the application to handle an international audience right from the start, but in most cases this may not be feasible because building for localized versions requires extra work and cost.

The core of any localization effort is the translation of resources and user interface changes. Such changes are application specific and, therefore, not really open to generic implementation across the multitude of potential cultures for which you might choose to target an application. However, some common elements of localization, such as date support or numeric and currency formats, can be implemented by .NET Framework classes.

The .NET Framework has made a considerable effort to support the internationalization of .NET applications. API support, server controls, and even Visual Studio itself equip you to do the extra work required to bring your application to an international audience. This chapter looks at some of the important items to consider when building your applications for the world.

## CULTURES AND REGIONS

As an example, the ASP.NET page that is pulled up in an end user's browser runs under a specific culture and region setting. When building an ASP.NET application or page, the defined culture in which it runs is dependent upon a culture and region setting specified either in the server in which the application is run or in a setting applied by the client (the end user). By default, ASP.NET runs under a culture setting defined by the server. Stated simply, unless you specifically look for a client's requested culture, your application will run based on the server's culture settings.

The world is made up of a multitude of cultures, each of which has a language and a set of defined ways in which it views and consumes numbers, uses currencies, sorts alphabetically, and so on. The .NET Framework defines languages and regions using the *Request for Comments 1766* standard definition (tags for identification of languages—www.ietf.org/rfc/rfc1766.txt), which specifies a language and region using two-letter codes separated by a dash. The following table provides examples of some culture definitions:

| CULTURE CODE | DESCRIPTION |
| --- | --- |
| en-US | English language; United States |
| en-GB | English language; United Kingdom (Great Britain) |
| en-AU | English language; Australia |
| en-CA | English language; Canada |
| fr-CA | French language; Canada |

The examples in this table define five distinct cultures. These five cultures have some similarities and some differences. Four of the cultures speak the same language (English), so the language code of "en" is used in these culture settings. Following the language setting is the region setting. Even though most of these cultures speak the same language, it is important to distinguish them further by setting their region (such as US for the United States, GB for the United Kingdom, AU for Australia, and CA for Canada). These settings reflect the fact that the English used in the United States is slightly different from the English used in the United Kingdom, and so forth. Beyond language, differences exist in how dates and numerical values are represented. This is why a culture's language and region are presented together.

The differences between the cultures in the table do not break down by region only. Many countries contain more than a single language, and each may have its own preference for notation of dates and other items. For example, en-CA specifies English speakers in Canada. Because Canada is not only an English-speaking country, it also includes the culture setting of fr-CA for French-speaking Canadians.

## Understanding Culture Types

The culture definition just given is called a *specific culture* definition. This definition is as detailed as you can possibly get, defining both the language and the region. The other type of culture definition is a *neutral culture* definition. Each specific culture has a specified neutral culture with which it is associated. For instance, the English language cultures shown in the previous table are separate, but they also belong to one neutral culture: EN (English). The diagram presented in Figure 15-1 illustrates how these culture types relate to one another.

From this diagram, you can see that many specific cultures belong to a neutral culture. Higher in the hierarchy than the neutral culture is an *invariant culture*, which is an agnostic culture setting that should be utilized when passing items (such as dates and numbers) around a network. When performing these kinds of operations, you should make your back-end data flows devoid of user-specific culture settings. Instead, apply these settings in the business and presentation layers of your applications.

In addition, pay attention to neutral culture when working with your applications. In most cases, you are going to build applications with views that are more dependent on a neutral culture than on a specific culture. For instance, if you have a Spanish version of your application, you'll prob-

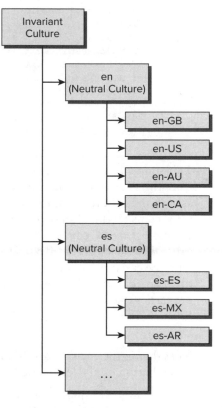

**FIGURE 15-1:** Language and culture relationship

ably make this version available to all Spanish speakers regardless of where they live. In many applications, it won't matter whether the Spanish speaker is from Spain, Mexico, or Argentina. In cases where it does make a difference, use the specific culture settings.

## Looking at Your Thread

When the end user requests an ASP.NET page or runs a Windows Forms dialog, the item is executed on a thread from the thread pool. That thread has a culture associated with it. You can get information about the culture of the thread programmatically and then check for particular details about that culture.

To see an example of working with a thread and reading the culture information of that thread, start with the basic WPF application created in Chapter 1. To reproduce this, create a new project called ProVB2012_Localization, and add the appropriate button and text box controls.

Add a new Sub DisplayCultureInfo and have it called by the Click event handler for the test button on the form. When the TestButton_Click event is fired, the user's culture information is retrieved and displayed in the TextBox control. The code for the new Sub is as follows (code file: MainWindow.xaml.vb):

```
    Private Sub DisplayCultureInfo()
        Dim ci As New System.Globalization.CultureInfo(
```

```
    System.Threading.Thread.CurrentThread.CurrentCulture.ToString())
TextBoxResult.Text = "CURRENT CULTURE'S INFO" & Environment.NewLine
TextBoxResult.Text += "Name: " & ci.Name & Environment.NewLine
TextBoxResult.Text += "Parent Name: " & ci.Parent.Name & Environment.NewLine
TextBoxResult.Text += "Display Name: " & ci.DisplayName & Environment.NewLine
TextBoxResult.Text += "English Name: " & ci.EnglishName & Environment.NewLine
TextBoxResult.Text += "Native Name: " & ci.NativeName & Environment.NewLine
TextBoxResult.Text += "Three Letter ISO Name: " &
    ci.ThreeLetterISOLanguageName & Environment.NewLine
TextBoxResult.Text += "Calendar Type: " &
    ci.Calendar.ToString() & Environment.NewLineEnd Sub
```

This simple form creates a `CultureInfo` object from the `System.Globalization` namespace and assigns the culture from the current thread that is running using the `System.Threading.Thread` `.CurrentThread.CurrentCulture.ToString` call. Once the `CultureInfo` object is populated with the end user's culture, details about that culture can be retrieved using a number of available properties that the `CultureInfo` object offers. Example results of running the form are shown in Figure 15-2.

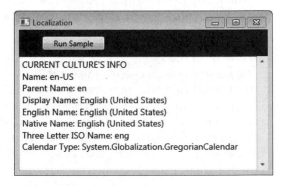

**FIGURE 15-2:** US English culture properties

Note that in the code download there is an additional button on the form based on additional changes that are made to this sample project.

The `CultureInfo` object contains a number of properties that provide you with specific culture information. The items displayed are only a small sampling of what is available from this object. From this figure, you can see that the en-US culture is the default setting in which the thread executes. In addition to this, you can use the `CultureInfo` object to get at a lot of other descriptive information about the culture. You can always change a thread's culture on the overloads provided via a new instantiation of the `CultureInfo` object. The following code illustrates commenting out the original default line of code and replacing it with an explicit change of the current culture to Thailand (code file: `MainWindow.xaml.vb`):

```
Private Sub DisplayCultureInfo()
    System.Threading.Thread.CurrentThread.CurrentCulture =
        New Globalization.CultureInfo("th-TH")
    Dim ci As Globalization.CultureInfo =
        System.Threading.Thread.CurrentThread.CurrentCulture

    ' Dim ci As New System.Globalization.CultureInfo(
    '   System.Threading.Thread.CurrentThread.CurrentCulture.ToString())
    TextBoxResult.Text = "CURRENT CULTURE'S INFO" & Environment.NewLine
    TextBoxResult.Text += "Name: " & ci.Name & Environment.NewLine
    TextBoxResult.Text += "Parent Name: " & ci.Parent.Name & Environment.NewLine
    TextBoxResult.Text += "Display Name: " & ci.DisplayName & Environment.NewLine
    TextBoxResult.Text += "English Name: " & ci.EnglishName & Environment.NewLine
    TextBoxResult.Text += "Native Name: " & ci.NativeName & Environment.NewLine
    TextBoxResult.Text += "Three Letter ISO Name: " &
```

```
          ci.ThreeLetterISOLanguageName & Environment.NewLine
    TextBoxResult.Text += "Calendar Type: " &
          ci.Calendar.ToString() & Environment.NewLineEnd Sub
```

In this example, only a couple of lines of code are changed to assign a new instance of the `CultureInfo` object to the `CurrentCulture` property of the thread being executed by the application. The culture setting enables the `CultureInfo` object to define the culture you want to utilize. In this case, the Thai language of Thailand is assigned. The results produced in the `TextBox` control are illustrated in Figure 15-3.

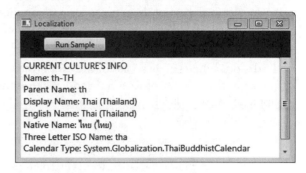

**FIGURE 15-3:** Thailand culture settings

From this figure, you can see that the .NET Framework provides the native name of the language used even if it is not a Latin-based letter style. In this case, the results are presented for the Thai language in Thailand, including some of the properties associated with this culture (such as an entirely different calendar than the one used in Western Europe and the United States).

# Declaring Culture Globally in ASP.NET

ASP.NET enables you to easily define the culture that is used either by your entire ASP.NET application or by a specific page within your Web application, using what are termed *server-side culture declarations*. You can specify the culture for any of your ASP.NET applications by means of the appropriate configuration files. To demonstrate this, close the ProVB2010_Localization application you started with and create a new ASP.NET Empty Web Site called ProVB_Russian. Alternatively, you can open this download folder as a website in Visual Studio 2012. Once the site has been created add a `default.aspx` page. On this blank page add a new `Calendar` control from the toolbox, following the text: Welcome to ASP.NET!

To change the default language used by this control, you can specify culture settings in the `web.config` file of the application itself, as illustrated here (code file: `web.config`):

```
<configuration>
  <system.web>
    <globalization culture="ru-RU" uiCulture="ru-RU" />
  </system.web>
</configuration>
```

Only the `<globalization>` line will need to be added to your default `web.config` file; it should also be noted that based on the following page-specific settings, this line has been commented out in the code download.

Note the two attributes represented: `culture` and `uiCulture`. The `culture` attribute enables you to define the culture to use for processing incoming requests, whereas the `uiCulture` attribute enables you to define the default culture needed to process any resource files in the application (use of these attributes is covered later in the chapter).

Note that one additional option you have when specifying a culture on the server is to define this culture in the root `web.config` file for the server. Thus, if you are setting up a web server that will be used with only a single culture, you can specify that culture at the server level, instead of needing to specify it as part of the settings for each application running on the server. This can be useful if you are installing Web applications created outside of your native culture, but where you want date, currency, sorting, and similar formats to default appropriately.

In the preceding snippet, the culture established for this ASP.NET application is the Russian language in the country of Russia. In addition to setting the culture at either the server-wide or the application-wide level, another option is to set the culture at the page level, as shown in the following snippet.

```
<%@ Page Language="VB"
    AutoEventWireup="false"
    CodeFile="Default.aspx.vb" Inherits="_Default"
    UICulture="ru-RU" Culture="ru-RU"%>
%>
```

This example specifies that the Russian language and culture settings are used for everything on the page. You can see this in action by using this `@Page` directive and a simple `Calendar` control on the page. Figure 15-4 shows the output. Notice that marking the page as using Russian settings does not automatically translate text within the page; it only updates the embedded control added to the page.

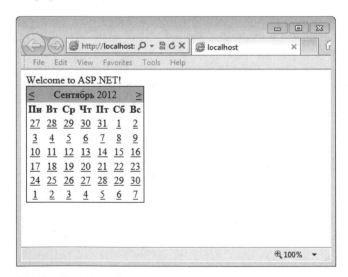

**FIGURE 15-4:** Using the Russian culture settings on a calendar

## Adopting Culture Settings in ASP.NET

In addition to using server-side settings to define the culture for your ASP.NET pages, you also have the option to define the culture according to what the client has set as his or her preference in a browser instance.

When end users install Microsoft's Internet Explorer or some other browser, they have the option to select their preferred cultures in a particular order (if they have selected more than a single culture preference). To see this in action in IE, select Tools ⇨ Internet Options from the IE menu. On the first tab provided (General) is a Languages button at the bottom of the dialog. Select this button and you are provided with the Language Preference dialog shown in Figure 15-5.

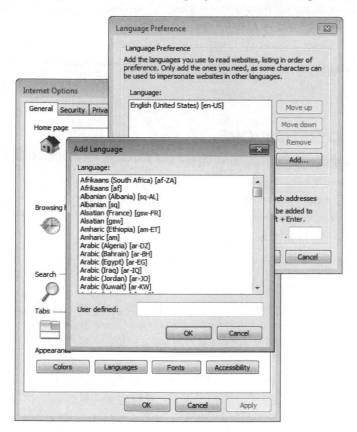

**FIGURE 15-5:** Changing your language preferences in Internet Explorer

To add any additional cultures to the list, click the Add button and select the appropriate culture from the list. After you have selected any cultures present in the list, you can select the order in which you prefer to use them. Thus, a user with multiple settings in this list will have a version of the application with their first language choice before anything else; if a version that supports that language is not available, their second and then consecutive versions are checked. The first available language matching one of their preferences will be presented.

Making language selections, the end user can leverage the automatic culture recognition feature provided in ASP.NET. Instead of specifying a distinct culture in any of the configuration files or from the @Page directive, you can also state that ASP.NET should automatically select the culture provided by the end user requesting the page. This is done using the auto keyword, as illustrated here:

```
<%@ Page UICulture="auto" Culture="auto" %>
```

With this construction in your page, the dates, calendars, and numbers appear in the preferred culture of the requester. What happens if you have translated resources in resource files (shown later in the chapter) that depend on a culture specification? Or what if you have only specific translations and therefore can't handle every possible culture that might be returned to your ASP.NET page? In this case, you can specify the auto option with an additional fallback option if ASP.NET cannot find any of the culture settings of the user (such as culture-specific resource files). This usage is illustrated in the following code:

```
<%@ Page UICulture="auto:en-US" Culture="auto:en-US" %>
```

In this case, the automatic detection is utilized; but if the culture preferred by the end user is not present, then en-US is used.

## TRANSLATING VALUES AND BEHAVIORS

In the process of globalizing your .NET application, you may notice a number of aspects that are handled differently compared to building an application that is devoid of globalization, including how dates are represented and how currencies are shown. This section looks at some of these issues.

## Understanding Differences in Dates

Different cultures specify dates and time very differently. Consider the following date as an example:

```
08/11/2008
```

Is this date August 11, 2008, or is it November 8, 2008? It should be the job of the business logic layer or the presentation layer to convert all date and times for use by the end user. To avoid interpretation errors, always use the same culture (or invariant culture) when storing values, such as dates and times, in a database or other data store.

Setting the culture at the server level in ASP.NET or within a Windows Forms application, as shown in the earlier examples, enables your .NET application to make these conversions for you. You can also simply assign a new culture to the thread in which the code is running. Close out the ASP.NET solution you were looking at in the preceding section and return to the ProVB2012_Localization project. Now consider the following code, which can be called from the `Button_Click_1` event handler. Note that this `Sub` is dependent on the `Imports` statements (code file: `MainWindow .xaml.vb`):

```vb
Imports System.Globalization
Imports System.Threading

Private Sub DisplayCalendarByCulture()
    Dim dt As DateTime = New DateTime(2012, 9, 12, 13, 5, 1, 10)
    Thread.CurrentThread.CurrentCulture = New CultureInfo("pt-br")
    TextBoxResult.Text +=
      Thread.CurrentThread.CurrentCulture.EnglishName & " : " & _
      dt.ToString() & Environment.NewLine

    Thread.CurrentThread.CurrentCulture = New CultureInfo("en-US")
    TextBoxResult.Text +=
```

```
    Thread.CurrentThread.CurrentCulture.EnglishName & " : " & _
    dt.ToString() & Environment.NewLine

Thread.CurrentThread.CurrentCulture = New CultureInfo("es-mx")
TextBoxResult.Text +=
    Thread.CurrentThread.CurrentCulture.EnglishName & " : " & _
    dt.ToString() & Environment.NewLine

Thread.CurrentThread.CurrentCulture = New CultureInfo("es-es")
TextBoxResult.Text +=
    Thread.CurrentThread.CurrentCulture.EnglishName & " : " & _
    dt.ToString() & Environment.NewLine

Thread.CurrentThread.CurrentCulture = New CultureInfo("ru-RU")
TextBoxResult.Text +=
    Thread.CurrentThread.CurrentCulture.EnglishName & " : " & _
    dt.ToString() & Environment.NewLine

Thread.CurrentThread.CurrentCulture = New CultureInfo("fi-FI")
TextBoxResult.Text +=
    Thread.CurrentThread.CurrentCulture.EnglishName & " : " & _
    dt.ToString() & Environment.NewLine

Thread.CurrentThread.CurrentCulture = New CultureInfo("ar-SA")
TextBoxResult.Text +=
    Thread.CurrentThread.CurrentCulture.EnglishName & " : " & _
    dt.ToString() & Environment.NewLine

Thread.CurrentThread.CurrentCulture = New CultureInfo("am-ET")
TextBoxResult.Text +=
    Thread.CurrentThread.CurrentCulture.EnglishName & " : " & _
    dt.ToString() & Environment.NewLine

Thread.CurrentThread.CurrentCulture = New CultureInfo("as-IN")
TextBoxResult.Text +=
    Thread.CurrentThread.CurrentCulture.EnglishName & " : " & _
    dt.ToString() & Environment.NewLine

Thread.CurrentThread.CurrentCulture = New CultureInfo("th-TH")
TextBoxResult.Text +=
    Thread.CurrentThread.CurrentCulture.EnglishName & " : " & _
    dt.ToString() & Environment.NewLine

Thread.CurrentThread.CurrentCulture = New CultureInfo("zh-cn")
TextBoxResult.Text +=
    Thread.CurrentThread.CurrentCulture.EnglishName & " : " & _
    dt.ToString() & Environment.NewLine

Thread.CurrentThread.CurrentCulture = New CultureInfo("zh-tw")
TextBoxResult.Text +=
    Thread.CurrentThread.CurrentCulture.EnglishName & " : " & _
    dt.ToString() & Environment.NewLine

Thread.CurrentThread.CurrentCulture = New CultureInfo("ko-kr")
```

```
TextBoxResult.Text +=
    Thread.CurrentThread.CurrentCulture.EnglishName & " : " & _
    dt.ToString() & Environment.NewLine

Thread.CurrentThread.CurrentCulture = New CultureInfo("zh-hk")
TextBoxResult.Text +=
    Thread.CurrentThread.CurrentCulture.EnglishName & " : " & _
    dt.ToString() & Environment.NewLine
End Sub
```

Using the ProVB2012_Localization test form again, you can test this code. The code snippet captures the current date/time for output, but does so while referencing a dozen or more different cultures, one for each copy output to the screen. The date/time construction used by the defined culture is written to the TextBox control. The result from this code operation is presented in Figure 15-6.

Clearly, the formats used to represent a date/time value can be dramatically different between cultures—some, such as Saudi Arabia (ar-SA) and Thailand, (th-TH) use entirely different calendar baselines.

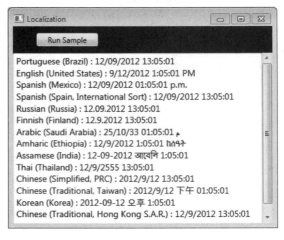

**FIGURE 15-6:** Different Date/Time formats by culture

# Differences in Numbers and Currencies

In addition to date/time values, numbers are displayed quite differently from one culture to the next. How can a number be represented differently in different cultures? Well, it has less to do with the actual number (although certain cultures use different number symbols) and more to do with how the number separators are used for decimals or for showing amounts such as thousands, millions, and more. For instance, in the English culture of the United States (en-US), numbers are represented in the following fashion:

```
5,123,456.00
```

From this example, you can see that the en-US culture uses a comma as a separator for thousands and a period for signifying the start of any decimals that might appear after the number is presented. It is quite different when working with other cultures. The following snippet shows an example of representing numbers in other cultures (code file: MainWindow.xaml.vb):

```
Private Sub Numbers()
    Dim myNumber As Double = 5123456.0

    Thread.CurrentThread.CurrentCulture = New CultureInfo("en-US")
    TextBoxResult.Text += Thread.CurrentThread.CurrentCulture.EnglishName &
        " : " & myNumber.ToString("n") & Environment.NewLine

    Thread.CurrentThread.CurrentCulture = New CultureInfo("vi-VN")
```

```
TextBoxResult.Text += Thread.CurrentThread.CurrentCulture.EnglishName &
    " : " & myNumber.ToString("n") & Environment.NewLine

Thread.CurrentThread.CurrentCulture = New CultureInfo("fi-FI")
TextBoxResult.Text += Thread.CurrentThread.CurrentCulture.EnglishName &
    " : " & myNumber.ToString("n") & Environment.NewLine

Thread.CurrentThread.CurrentCulture = New CultureInfo("fr-CH")
TextBoxResult.Text += Thread.CurrentThread.CurrentCulture.EnglishName &
    " : " & myNumber.ToString("n") & Environment.NewLine

End Sub
```

Adding this code to your project and running it from the click event produces the results shown in Figure 15-7.

As you can see, cultures show numbers in numerous different formats. The second culture listed in the figure, vi-VN (Vietnamese in Vietnam), constructs a number exactly the opposite from the way it is constructed in en-US. The Vietnamese culture uses periods for the thousand separators and a comma for signifying decimals, a somewhat common format around the world. Finnish uses spaces for the thousand separators and a comma for the decimal

**FIGURE 15-7:** Different numeric formats across cultures

separator, whereas the French-speaking Swiss use an apostrophe for separating thousands, and a period for the decimal separator. This demonstrates that not only do you need to consider dates and language constructs, but that it is also important to "translate" numbers to the proper format so that users of your application can properly understand the numbers represented.

Another scenario in which you represent numbers is when working with currencies. It is one thing to *convert* currencies so that end users understand the proper value of an item; it is another to translate the construction of the currency just as you would a basic number.

Each culture has a distinct currency symbol used to signify that a number represented is an actual currency value. For instance, the en-US culture represents currency in the following format:

```
$5,123,456.00
```

The en-US culture uses a U.S. dollar symbol ($), and the location of this symbol is just as important as the symbol itself. For en-US, the $ symbol directly precedes the currency value (with no space in between the symbol and the first character of the number). Other cultures use different symbols to represent currency and often place those currency symbols in different locations.

Create another `Sub` that can be called from the button's click event handler, and this time format the same numbers using the built-in .NET currency formatting shown here (code file: `MainWindow .xaml.vb`):

```
Private Sub Currency()
    Dim myNumber As Double = 5123456.0

    Thread.CurrentThread.CurrentCulture = New CultureInfo("en-US")
    TextBoxResult.Text += Thread.CurrentThread.CurrentCulture.EnglishName &
        " : " & myNumber.ToString("c") & Environment.NewLine
```

```
    Thread.CurrentThread.CurrentCulture = New CultureInfo("vi-VN")
    TextBoxResult.Text += Thread.CurrentThread.CurrentCulture.EnglishName &
        " : " & myNumber.ToString("c") & Environment.NewLine

    Thread.CurrentThread.CurrentCulture = New CultureInfo("fi-FI")
    TextBoxResult.Text += Thread.CurrentThread.CurrentCulture.EnglishName &
        " : " & myNumber.ToString("c") & Environment.NewLine

    Thread.CurrentThread.CurrentCulture = New CultureInfo("fr-CH")
    TextBoxResult.Text += Thread.CurrentThread.CurrentCulture.EnglishName &
        " : " & myNumber.ToString("c") & Environment.NewLine
End Sub
```

Executing this code displays the output shown in Figure 15-8.

Not only are the numbers constructed quite differently from one another, but the currency symbol and the location of the symbol in regard to the number are quite different as well.

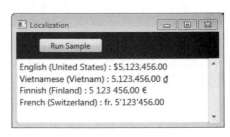

**FIGURE 15-8:** Formatting currency across cultures

Note that when you are using currencies on an ASP.NET page and you have provided an automatic culture setting for the page as a whole (such as setting the culture in the @Page directive), you need to specify a specific culture for the currency that is the same in all cases. Unlike dates, for which the differences are primarily display oriented, with a currency there is an expectation of value conversion. Thus, reformatting a currency can cause expensive errors unless you are actually doing a currency conversion.

For instance, if you are specifying a U.S. dollar currency value in your data, you do not want your ASP.NET page to display that value as something else (for example, the euro) based on translating the remainder of the page information to another language. Of course, if you actually performed a currency conversion and showed the appropriate euro value along with the culture specification of the currency, that makes sense and is the best solution.

Therefore, if you are using an automatic culture setting on your ASP.NET page and you are *not* converting the currency, you should perform something similar to the following code for currency values:

```
Dim myNumber As Double = 5123456.00
Dim usCurr As CultureInfo = New CultureInfo("en-US")
Response.Write(myNumber.ToString("c", usCurr))
```

## Understanding Differences in Sorting

You have learned to translate textual values and alter the construction of the numbers, date/time values, currencies, and more when you are globalizing an application. You should also take care when applying culture settings to some of the programmatic behaviors that you establish for values in your applications. One operation that can change based upon the culture setting applied is how .NET sorts strings. You might think that all cultures sort strings in the same way (and generally they do), but sometimes differences exist. For example, the following snippet shows a sorting operation occurring in the en-US culture (code file: `MainWindow.xaml.vb`):

```
Private Sub Sorting()
    Thread.CurrentThread.CurrentCulture = New CultureInfo("en-US")
    'Thread.CurrentThread.CurrentCulture = New CultureInfo("fi-FI")

    Dim myList As List(Of String) = New List(Of String)

    myList.Add("Washington D.C.")
    myList.Add("Helsinki")
    myList.Add("Moscow")
    myList.Add("Warsaw")
    myList.Add("Vienna")
    myList.Add("Tokyo")

    myList.Sort()

    For Each item As String In myList
        TextBoxResult.Text += item.ToString() & Environment.NewLine
    Next
End Sub
```

For this example to work, you have to reference the `System.Collections` and the `System.Collections.Generic` namespaces, because this example makes use of the `List(Of String)` object.

In this example, a generic list of capitals from various countries of the world is created in random order. Then the `Sort` method of the generic `List(Of String)` object is invoked. This sorting operation sorts the strings according to how sorting is done for the defined culture in which the application thread is running. The preceding code shows the sorting as it is done for the en-US culture. The result of this operation when used within the ProVB2012_Localization form is shown in Figure 15-9.

**FIGURE 15-9:** Typical sorting in English

This is pretty much what you would expect. Now, however, change the previous example so that the culture is set to the Finnish culture. Do this by uncommenting the second line of the `Sub Sorting` and commenting out the first line of the `Sub Sorting` which sets the "en-US" culture settings, in the preceding snippet.

If you run the same bit of code under the Finnish culture setting, you get the results presented in Figure 15-10.

Comparing the Finnish culture sorting shown in Figure 15-10 and the U.S. English culture sorting done in Figure 15-9, you can see that the city of Vienna is in a different place in the Finnish version. This is because in the Finnish language, there is no difference

**FIGURE 15-10:** Finnish cultural setting impact on sorting

between the letter V and the letter W. Therefore, if you are sorting using the Finnish culture setting, Vi comes after Wa, and thus Vienna appears last in the list of strings in the sorting operation.

## ASP.NET RESOURCE FILES

When you work with ASP.NET, resources are handled by resource files. A resource file is an XML-based file that has a `.resx` extension. You can have Visual Studio help you construct this file. Resource files provide a set of items that are utilized by a specified culture. In your ASP.NET applications, you store resource files as either *local resources* or *global resources*. The following sections describe how to use each type of resource.

## Making Use of Local Resources

You might be surprised how easily you can build an ASP.NET page so that it can be *localized* into other languages. In fact, the only thing you need to do is build the ASP.NET page as you normally would and then use some built-in capabilities from Visual Studio to convert the page to a format that enables you to plug in other languages easily.

To see this in action, build an ASP.NET empty web application called ProVB_Localization. Next, add a new web form called a `Default.aspx` page. Note that a few simple controls have been added. This page will be referred to later in this chapter as the "ASP.NET page code block." Keep in mind that the downloaded code will not match the initial code snippet shown here because this chapter modifies this code to support multiple languages (code file: `Default.aspx`):

```
<%@ Page Language="vb" AutoEventWireup="false" CodeBehind="Default.aspx.vb"
                      Inherits="ProVB_Localization._Default" %>
<!DOCTYPE html>
<html xmlns="http://www.w3.org/1999/xhtml">
<head runat="server">
    <title></title>
</head>
<body>
    <form id="form1" runat="server">
    <div>
        <asp:Label ID="Label1" runat="server"
         Text="What is your name?"></asp:Label><br />
        <br />
        <asp:TextBox ID="TextBox1" runat="server"></asp:TextBox> 
        <asp:Button ID="Button1" runat="server" Text="Submit Name" /><br />
        <br />
        <asp:Label ID="Label2" runat="server"></asp:Label>
    </div>
    </form>
</body>
</html>
```

As you can see, there is not much to this page. It is composed of a couple of `Label` controls, as well as `TextBox` and `Button` controls. Update the click event handler for `Button1` to set the `Label2.Text` property text to the `TextBox1.Text` property value. This way, when users enter their name into the text box, the `Label2` server control is populated with the inputted name.

The next step is what makes Visual Studio so great. To change the construction of this page so that it can be localized easily from resource files, ensure that you are on the .aspx page and not the code file. Next, using the Visual Studio menu, select Tools ⇨ Generate Local Resource. Note that you can select this tool only when you are editing the .aspx page.

Selecting Generate Local Resource from the Tools menu causes Visual Studio to create an App_LocalResources folder in your project if you don't have one already. A .resx file based upon this ASP.NET page is then placed in the folder. For instance, if you are working with the Default.aspx page, then the resource file is named Default.aspx.resx (see Figure 15-11).

Right-click on the .resx file; select View Code. If View Code isn't present on your default menu, select Open With; you'll get a dialog with a list of editor options. From the Open With dialog, select the XML (Text) Editor as the program to open this file using the OK button. After doing this, you should find the View Code option on the context menu for this file. When the .resx file opens, you'll notice that the .resx file is nothing more than an XML file with an associated schema at the beginning of the document. The resource

**FIGURE 15-11:** Folder to hold application cultural resources

file that is generated for you takes every possible property of every translatable control on the page and gives each item a key value that can be referenced in your ASP.NET page. Looking at the page's code, note that all the text values you placed in the page have been retained, but they have also been placed inside the resource file. Visual Studio changed the code of the Default.aspx page in two places as follows (code file: Default.aspx):

```
<%@ Page Language="vb" AutoEventWireup="false" CodeBehind="Default.aspx.vb"
        Inherits="ProVB_Localization._Default" culture="auto"
        meta:resourcekey="PageResource1" uiculture="auto" %>


<div>
        <asp:Label ID="Label1" runat="server"
         Text="What is your name?" meta:resourcekey="Label1Resource1">
        </asp:Label><br />
        <br />
        <asp:TextBox ID="TextBox1" runat="server"
                     meta:resourcekey="TextBox1Resource1"></asp:TextBox> 
        <asp:Button ID="Button1" runat="server" Text="Submit Name"
                    meta:resourcekey="Button1Resource1" /><br />
        <br />
        <asp:Label ID="Label2" runat="server" meta:resourcekey="Label2Resource1">
        </asp:Label>
</div>
```

From this bit of code, you can see that the Culture and UICulture attributes have been added to the @Page directive with a value of auto, thus, enabling this application to be localized. In addition, the attribute meta:resourcekey has been added to each of the controls, along with an associated value. This is the key from the .resx file that was created on your behalf. Double-clicking on the Default.aspx.resx file opens the resource file in the Resource Editor, shown in Figure 15-12, built into Visual Studio. Keep in mind the code download will have additional settings not shown if you are working along with the chapter.

**FIGURE 15-12:** Editing default resource mappings

Note that a few properties from each of the server controls have been defined in the resource file. For instance, the Button server control has its Text and ToolTip properties exposed in this resource file, and the Visual Studio localization tool has pulled the default Text property value from the control based on what you placed there. Looking more closely at the Button server control constructions in this file, you can see that both the Text and ToolTip properties have a defining Button1Resource1 value preceding the property name. This is the key that is used in the Button server control shown earlier.

```
<asp:Button ID="Button1" runat="server" Text="Submit Name"
  meta:resourcekey="Button1Resource1" />
```

In the following aspx source, a meta:resourcekey attribute has been added to a Button control. In this case it references Button1Resource1. All the properties using this key in the resource file (for example, the Text and ToolTip properties) are applied to this Button server control at run time.

## Adding Another Language Resource File

The Default.aspx.resx file created in the last section is used by the application as the default or invariant culture. No specific culture is assigned to this resource file. If for a given request no culture can be determined, then this is the resource file that is utilized. To add another resource file for the Default.aspx page that handles another language altogether, right click the App_LocalResources

folder and select Add ➪ Resources File from the context menu. Use the name `Default.aspx.fi-FI`
`.resx` for your new file. Next click on the top left corner of your original `.resx` file, which will
select all, then right-click and select copy. Now return to your newly created file and paste the contents into your file. Finally give the following keys the values shown to make a Finnish-language
resource file:

```
Button1Resource1.Text     Lähetä Nimi
Label1Resource1.Text      Mikä sinun nimi on?
```

Once you have created this file, take an additional step and assign a value to the `Label2Resource1`
`.Text` entry. The `Default.aspx.resx` file should have the following key value pair:

```
Label2Resource1.Text Hello
```

You can add a value to the same key in the `Default.aspx.fi-FI.resx` file as shown here:

```
Label2Resource1.Text Hei
```

You now have resources for specific controls, and a resource that you can access later
programmatically.

## Finalizing the Building of the Default.aspx Page

Finalizing the `Default.aspx` page, you want to add a `Button1_Click` event so that when the end
user enters a name into the text box and clicks the Submit button, the `Label2` server control provides a greeting pulled from the local resource files. When all is said and done, your default page
should have a code-behind element that matches the following snippet:

```
Label2.Text = GetLocalResourceObject("Label2Resource1.Text") &
    " " & TextBox1.Text
```

In addition to pulling local resources using the `meta:resourcekey` attribute in the server controls
on the page to access the exposed attributes, you can also access any property value contained in the
local resource file by using the `GetLocalResourceObject`. When using `GetLocalResourceObject`,
you simply use the name of the key as a parameter, as shown here:

```
GetLocalResourceObject("Label2Resource1.Text")
```

With the code from the `Default.aspx` page in place and the resource files completed, you can
run the page, entering a name in the text box and then clicking the Submit Name button to get a
response, as shown in Figure 15-13.

**FIGURE 15-13:** Displaying the form in English

What happened behind the scenes that caused this page to be constructed in this manner? First, only two resource files—`Default.aspx.resx` and `Default.aspx.fi-FI.resx`—are available. The `Default.aspx.resx` resource file is the invariant culture resource file, whereas the `Default.aspx.fi-FI.resx` resource file is for a specific culture (fi-FI). Because the browser requesting the `Default.aspx` page was set to en-US as the preferred culture, ASP.NET found the local resources for the `Default.aspx` page. From there, ASP.NET checked for an en-US-specific version of the `Default.aspx` page. Because there isn't a specific page for the en-US culture, ASP.NET checked for an EN-(neutral culture)-specific page. Not finding a page for the EN neutral culture, ASP.NET was then forced to use the invariant culture resource file of `Default.aspx.resx`, producing the page shown in Figure 15-13.

If you now set your IE language preference as fi-FI and rerun the `Default.aspx` page, you'll see a Finnish version of the page, as shown in Figure 15-14.

**FIGURE 15-14:** Displaying the form in Finnish

In this case, having set the IE language preference to fi-FI, you are presented with this culture's page instead of the invariant culture page presented earlier. ASP.NET found this specific culture through use of the `Default.aspx.fi-FI.resx` resource file.

You can see that all the control properties that were translated and placed within the resource file are utilized automatically by ASP.NET, including the page title presented in the title bar of IE.

## Neutral Cultures Are Generally Preferred

When you are working with the resource files from this example, note that one of the resources is for a *specific culture*. The `Default.aspx.fi-FI.resx` file is for a specific culture—the Finnish language as spoken in Finland. Another option would be to make this file work not for a specific culture, but instead for a neutral culture. To do so, simply name the file `Default.aspx.FI.resx`. In this case, it doesn't make any difference because no other countries speak Finnish; but it would make sense for languages such as German, Spanish, or French, which are spoken in multiple countries.

For instance, if you are going to have a Spanish version of the `Default.aspx` page, you could definitely build it for a specific culture, such as `Default.aspx.es-MX.resx`. This construction is for the Spanish language as spoken in Mexico. With this in place, if someone requests the `Default.aspx` page with the language setting of es-MX, that user is provided with the contents of this resource file. If the requester has a setting of es-ES, he or she will not get the `Default.aspx.es-MX.resx` resource file, but the invariant culture resource file of `Default.aspx.resx`. If you are going to make only a single translation for your site or any of your pages, construct the resource files to be for neutral cultures, not specific cultures.

If you have the resource file `Default.aspx.ES.resx`, then it won't matter if the end user's preferred setting is set to es-MX, es-ES, or even es-AR—that user gets the appropriate ES neutral-culture version of the page.

## Localization for Windows Store Apps

Rather than having just a generic set of tools, when working with Visual Studio 2012 on Windows 8 Microsoft has created a separate set of language-specific tool kits. Called the "Multilingual App Toolkit for Visual Studio 2012" these kits (which vary by language) provide you the tools to help you localize your Windows Store application. They provide translation support, management of resource files and editor tools.

Before you work at localizing a Windows Store application, you need to install a copy of this toolkit on your Windows 8 development machine. Next load the solution containing the project you want to localize and select that project in the Solution Explorer. With the project selected you'll find that the top option on the Tools menu for Visual Studio is "Enable Multilingual App Toolkit."

Selecting that option will add a new folder to your solution called `MultilingualResources`. By default within this folder you will see a newly created `Pseudo Language` file. This `.xlf` file is used to hold a series of test strings associated with your custom localization efforts. If in a brand new application you double-click on this file you'll find that the Multilingual Editor opens as shown in Figure 15-15.

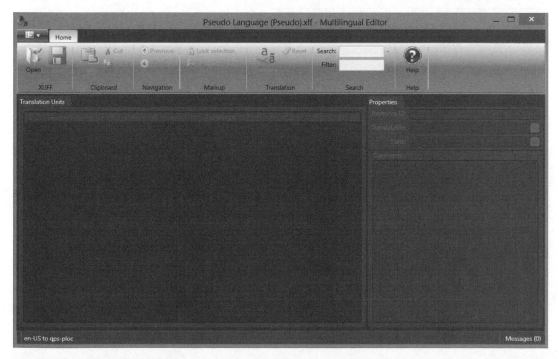

**FIGURE 15-15:** Multilingual Editor for Windows Store apps

Windows Store applications use a combination of `.xlf` file extensions for the language resources and `.resw` files to define the resources. The `.xlf` file extension relates to the industry standard XLIFF localization interchange file format. This format, which is defined on the `www.oasis-open .org` website, describes a standard extensible XML vocabulary that allows for easy interchange of translation files.

These files are assigned a default source and target language. Then they apply `xml` tags within a trans-unit structure to define the source and target strings for translation. Each trans-unit is named and has the potential to include additional alternative language definitions that essentially allow you to provide multiple target translations for each source string.

Unlike the previously described `.resx` files, Windows Store applications use `.resw` files. The good news is that these file formats are very similar, so similar, in fact, that the easiest way to transfer a `.resx` file to a Windows application is to create the necessary folders in your application and then copy in the `.resx` file and rename it as an `.resw` file. That will transfer your resource mappings. However, you will place only a single `.resw` file in your project, because you'll leverage the `.xlf` files and language editors to handle your translations.

Once you've added a `.resw` file to your project, you can then choose to add additional language. Right-click on the project file that you are looking to localize. Within the context menu you will find a new option to "Add Translation Languages." Selecting this option will open the dialog shown in Figure 15-16, from which you can select the languages you would like to support.

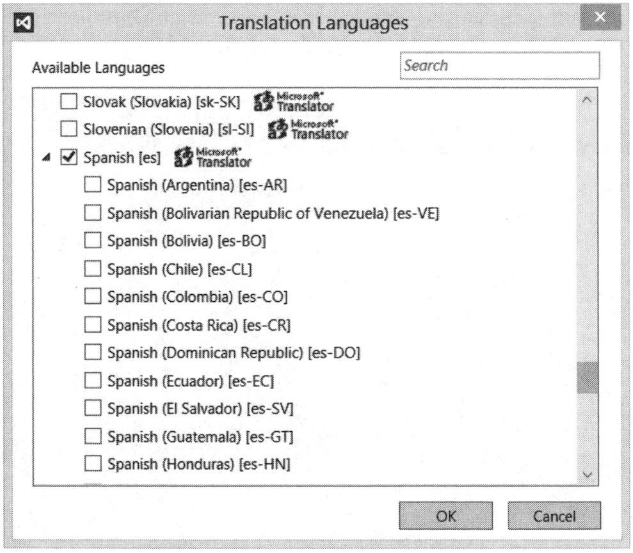

**FIGURE 15-16:** Selecting languages for a Windows Store app

As shown in Figure 15-16, there is the option to select the neutral language (es) or to specify a culture and language that you would like to target. Each language you add will create a separate `.xlf` file to your multilingual resources folder in your project. You can then use the Multilingual Editor to create and maintain your translations.

## SUMMARY

This chapter looked at some of the localization tools available to you. It started with a review of the culture types and how to determine the preferred culture for either a thread or Web request. It looked at understanding how different cultures may treat the same date or number differently for display and, just as important, how .NET can automate this handling for you. It also examined differences with currency with a warning about the need to convert a value and not just swap the display formatting when dealing with currency. The chapter then looked at how .NET supports the use of multiple resource files to provide support for different languages and cultures.

While .NET has provided many tools to help you with this process, you should keep in mind that these tools only make the process easier when looking at the built-in features of controls, not the application specific text and layout; when you want to localize an application, you need to plan to work with someone familiar with the language, and ideally the culture, you will target.

In addition to making many of the changes described in this chapter, localization is a process that requires consideration of multiple different time zones, consideration for information that reads Left to Right versus cultures that expect information to flow Right to Left, and other issues that are outside the scope of the tools you use. While that seems like a lot, you'll note that the same concepts for using resource files exist across the different .NET solution templates.

The next chapter takes you from the topics in this chapter, which focused on how to make your application user interface work with different cultures, to writing service applications that have little or no user interface.

# 16

# Application Services

**WHAT'S IN THIS CHAPTER?**

➤ Choices for implementing application services

➤ Characteristics of one of the most common technologies for application services, namely Windows Services

➤ How to interact with a Windows Service using Visual Studio and the management applets in the Windows Control Panel

➤ How to create, install, and communicate with a Windows Service using Visual Basic

➤ How to debug a Windows Service from Visual Studio

Modern, multitasking operating systems often need to run applications that operate in the background and that are independent of the user who is logged in. For example, an application that provides a service interface to obtain data needs to service external requests for data regardless of whether there is a current user.

Over time, the number of choices to implement application services has increased. Originally, the main choice was Windows Services, but other choices have been added as .NET and Windows have evolved. Keep in mind that Windows Services aren't something you are going to access in a purely client environment like Windows 8 RT.

## USING IIS FOR APPLICATION SERVICES

Depending on the version of Windows in use and the Windows options that have been installed, there are multiple ways to host .NET programs in the background. Chapter 11 covered Web Services and Windows Communication Foundation (WCF) services, both of which are examples of technologies that can use Internet Information Services (IIS) to load programs and run them independent of the user.

If you are using IIS 7.0 or above, you also have the option to run WCF services using the Windows Process Activation Service (normally called WAS). This allows hosting of WCF services using non-HTTP protocols such as TCP. As with IIS, no code needs to be written; only the proper configuration is necessary.

Another option that offers more control over when and how background programs are loaded is called Windows Services. The basic concept goes back to Windows NT, when this capability was called NT Services.

## WINDOWS SERVICES

The tasks carried out by Windows Services are typically long-running tasks and have little or no direct interaction with a user. Many of the constituent parts of Windows and other products use Windows Services to carry out their functions. For example, some versions of Windows install an indexing service to enable searching of the file system. IIS and SQL Server both use Windows Services for important functionality. Such applications may be started when the computer is booted and often continue to run until the computer is shut down.

Example scenarios for creating your own Windows Services would include programs such as the following:

➤ **A file watcher**—Suppose you are running an FTP server that enables users to place files in a particular directory. You could use a Windows Service to monitor and process files within that directory as they arrive. The service runs in the background and detects when files are changed or added within the directory, and then extracts information from these files in order to process orders, or update address and billing information. You will see an example of such a Windows Service later in this chapter.

➤ **An automated stock price reporter**—You could build a system that extracts stock prices from a Web service or website and then e-mails the information to users. You could set thresholds such that an e-mail is sent only when the stock price reaches a certain price. This Windows Service can be automated to extract the information every 10 minutes, every 10 seconds, or whatever time interval you choose. Because a Windows Service can contain any logic that does not require a user interface, you have a lot of flexibility in constructing such applications.

➤ **A system activity logger**—You might want to have a service that monitors a TCP channel and accepts activity log entries. The service could then place the log entries in an appropriate location, such as a database. Having a single service would relieve your application of the responsibility for knowing how activity is logged. They would only need to know how to send an entry to your service.

# CHARACTERISTICS OF A WINDOWS SERVICE

To properly design and develop a Windows Service, it is important to understand how it differs from a typical Windows program. Here are the most important characteristics of a Windows Service:

➤ It can start before a user logs on. The system maintains a list of Windows Services, which can be set to start at boot time. Services can also be installed such that they require a manual startup and will not start at bootup.

➤ It can run under a different account from that of the current user. Most Windows Services provide functionality that needs to be running all the time, and some load before a user logs on, so they cannot depend on a user being logged on to run.

➤ It has its own process. It does not run in the process of a program communicating with it.

➤ It typically has no built-in user interface. This is because the service may be running under a different account from that of the current user, or the service may start at bootup, which means that calls to put up a user interface might fail because they are out of context.

➤ Under certain operating systems, activities permitted in normal programs are not allowed in Windows Services. For example, you can play a sound from a Windows Service in Windows XP, but you cannot do so in Windows Vista, Windows Server 2008, or Windows 7.

➤ User interaction with the service is accomplished either via a built-in Windows program, the *Service Control Manager*, or using a special external program you develop. Creation of such an external program is covered in this chapter. The Service Control Manager can be accessed through the Computer Management section of the Control Panel.

➤ It requires a special installation procedure; just clicking on a compiled Windows service .exe file will not run it. The program must run in a special context in the operating system, and a specific installation process is required to do the configuration necessary for a Windows Service to be run in this special context.

# INTERACTING WITH WINDOWS SERVICES

You can view the services that are used on your computer by opening the Service Control Manager user interface. To do so from the Start menu in Windows 7 or Windows 2008, select Administrative Tools ➪ Services. If the Administrative Tools menu isn't visible from the Start menu go through the Control panel, select Control Panel ➪ Administrative Tools ➪ Services.

Those of you on Windows 8 have two options. The first is to go to the charms bar on the right hand side and select Settings. In the Settings window you will see "Tiles." Select the Tiles option and you will find a single setting for "Show administrative tools." Move this option from the default of "No" to "Yes." At this point your Start screen will repopulate and on the far right side you'll find a new tile for Services.

Alternatively, on Windows 8 you can use the Desktop button that is on the Start screen. From the desktop you can open the Windows File Explorer and look at your Desktop folder. Within the Desktop folder you should see a reference to the Control Panel. Accessing the Control Panel, switch your view to Small icons and then you can select the Administrative Tools folder. A new window will open and you can access the Services dialog. Note that other paths on Windows 8 will also allow you to get here, this is just one such method.

Using the Service Control Manager, a service can be set to automatically start when the system is booted, or it can be started manually. Services can also be stopped or paused. The list of services contained in the Service Control Manager includes the current state for each service. Figure 16-1 shows the Service Control Manager in Windows 7. (Note it looks unchanged on Windows 8.)

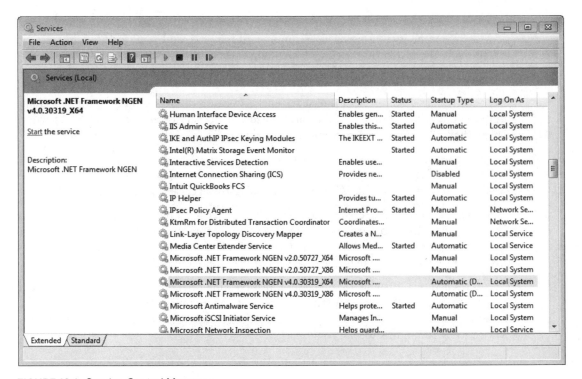

**FIGURE 16-1:** Service Control Manager

The Status column indicates the current state of the service. If this column is blank, then the service is not running. Other possible values for Status are Started and Paused. You can access additional settings and details concerning a service by double-clicking it.

When a service is started, it automatically logs in to the system using one of the following accounts:

➤ **User account**—A regular Windows account that allows the program to interact with the system; in essence, the service impersonates a user.

➤ **LocalSystem account**—Not associated with a particular user. This built-in account has a lot of privileges, and can roughly be thought of as the equivalent of an administrator account for services.

➤ **LocalService account**—Not associated with a particular user. This built-in account has a more limited set of privileges, and is commonly used for routine services.

➤ **NetworkService account**—Not associated with a particular user. This built-in account is similar to LocalService, but is designed for services that communicate across the local network rather than working only on the local system.

The Service Control Manager shown in Figure 16-1 is part of the operating system (OS), which is what supports Windows Services; it is not a part of the .NET Framework. Any service run by the OS is exposed through the Service Control Manager, regardless of how the service was created or installed. You can also examine the installed Windows Services via the Server Explorer in Visual Studio.

## CREATING A WINDOWS SERVICE

Creating a Windows Service in .NET requires using several .NET classes, which provide the necessary interface to the operating system required by a Windows Service.

## The .NET Framework Classes for Windows Services

Several base classes are needed to create a Windows Service:

➤ `System.ServiceProcess.ServiceBase`—Provides the base class for the Windows Service. The class containing the logic that will run in the service inherits from `ServiceBase`. A single executable can contain more than one service, but each service in the executable is a separate class that inherits from `ServiceBase`.

➤ `System.Configuration.Install.Installer`—This is a generic class that performs the installation chores for a variety of components. One class in a Windows Service process must inherit and extend `Installer` in order to provide the interface necessary to install the service under the various Windows operating systems.

Each class that inherits from `Installer` needs to contain an instance of each of the following classes:

➤ `System.ServiceProcess.ServiceProcessInstaller`—This class contains the information needed to install a .NET executable that contains Windows Services (that is, an executable that contains classes that inherit from `ServiceBase`). The .NET installation utility for Windows Services (`InstallUtil.exe`, discussed later) calls this class to get the information it needs to perform the installation.

➤ `System.ServiceProcess.ServiceInstaller`—This class also interacts with the `InstallUtil.exe` installation program. Whereas `ServiceProcessInstaller` contains information needed to install the executable as a whole, `ServiceInstaller` contains information about a specific service in the executable. If an executable contains more than one service, then an instance of `ServiceInstaller` is needed for each one.

For most Windows Services you develop, you can let Visual Studio take care of `Installer`, `ServiceProcessInstaller`, and `ServiceInstaller`. You just need to set a few properties. The class you should thoroughly understand is `ServiceBase`, as this is the class that contains the essential functionality of a Windows Service.

## The ServiceBase Class

The `ServiceBase` class contains several useful properties and methods, but initially it is more important to understand the methods that are fired by the Service Control Manager when the state of the service is changed. Table 16-1 describes the most important of these methods.

**TABLE 16-1:** Important ServiceBase Events

| EVENT | DESCRIPTION |
|---|---|
| OnStart | Occurs when the service is started. This is where the initialization logic for a service is usually placed. |
| OnStop | Occurs when the service is stopped. Cleanup and shutdown logic are generally placed here. |
| OnPause | Occurs when the service is paused. Any logic required to suspend operations during a pause goes here. |
| OnContinue | Occurs when a service continues after being paused. |
| OnShutdown | Occurs when the operating system is being shut down. |
| OnSessionChange | Occurs when a change event is received from a Terminal Session service. This method was new in .NET Framework 2.0. |
| OnPowerEvent | Occurs when the system's power management software causes a change in the power status of the system. This is typically used to change the behavior of a service when a system is entering or leaving a "suspended" power mode. This is more frequent with end users who are working on laptops. |
| OnCustomCommand | Occurs when an external program has told the Service Control Manager that it wants to send a command to the service. The operation of this event is covered in the section "Communicating with the Service." |

The events used most frequently are `OnStart`, `OnStop`, and `OnCustomCommand`. The `OnStart` and `OnStop` events are used in almost every Windows service written in Visual Basic, and the `OnCustomCommand` is used when any special configuration of the service is needed while the service is running.

All of these are `Protected` events, so they are available only to classes that inherit from the `ServiceBase` class. Because of the restricted context in which it runs, a Windows Service component that inherits from `ServiceBase` often lacks a public interface. While you can add public properties and methods to such a component, they are of limited use, because programs running in a normal user context cannot obtain an object reference to running a Windows Service component, which is running in a special system context created by the System Control Manager.

To be active as a Windows Service, an instance of the `ServiceBase` class must be started via the shared `Run` method of the `ServiceBase` class. However, normally you don't have to write code to do this because the template code generated by a Visual Studio Windows Service project places the correct code in the `Main` subroutine of the project for you.

The most commonly used property of the `ServiceBase` class is the `AutoLog` property. This `Boolean` property is set to `True` by default. If `True`, then the Windows service automatically logs the `Start`, `Stop`, `Pause`, and `Continue` events to an event log. The event log used is the Application Event Log and the Source in the log entries is taken from the name of the Windows service. This automatic event logging is stopped by setting the `AutoLog` property to `False`.

Later in this chapter you will create a File Watcher example that will go into more detail about the automatic logging capabilities in a Windows service, and about event logs in general.

## Installation-Oriented Classes

The `Installer`, `ServiceProcessInstaller`, and `ServiceInstaller` classes are quite simple to build and use if you are employing Visual Studio. After you create your Windows Service project, Visual Studio will create a class file called `Service1.vb` for you. To add the `Installer`, `ServiceProcessInstaller`, and `ServiceInstaller` classes to your project, simply right-click the design surface of this `ServiceBase` class, `Service1.vb`, and select Add Installer. This creates the code framework necessary to use them.

The `Installer` class (named `ProjectInstaller.vb` by default in a Windows Service project) generally needs no interaction at all — it is ready to use when created by Visual Studio. However, it may be appropriate to change some properties of the `ServiceProcessInstaller` and `ServiceInstaller` classes. You can do this by simply highlighting these objects on the design surface and changing their properties directly in the Properties window of Visual Studio. The properties that are typically modified for `ServiceProcessInstaller` include the following:

➤ **Account**—This specifies the type of account under which the entire service application will run. Different settings give the services in the application different levels of privilege on the local system. For simplicity, this chapter uses the highest level of privilege, LocalSystem, for most of the examples. If this property is set to `User` (which is the default), then you must supply a username and password when the service is installed. (You'll see more about that when `InstallUtil.exe` is discussed later in the chapter.) That user's account is used to determine privileges for the service. If there is any possibility that a service could access system resources that should be "out of bounds," then using the User setting to restrict privileges is a good idea. Besides LocalSystem and User, other possible settings for the `Account` property include NetworkService and LocalService.

➤ **HelpText**—This specifies information about the service that will be displayed in certain installation options.

If the `Account` property is set to User, then it is good practice to set up a special user account for the service, rather than rely on some existing account intended for a live user. The special account can be set up with exactly the appropriate privileges for the service. This way, it is not as vulnerable to having its password or its privileges inadvertently changed in a way that would cause problems in running the service.

For the `ServiceInstaller` class, the properties you might change include the following:

➤ **DisplayName**—The name of the service displayed in the Service Manager or the Server Explorer can be different from the class name and the executable name if desired, though it is better to make this name the same as the class name for the service.

➤ `StartType`—This specifies how the service is started. The default is Manual, which means you must start the service yourself, as it will not start automatically after the system boots. If you want the service to always start when the system starts, then change this property to Automatic. The Service Manager can be used to override the `StartType` setting.

➤ `ServiceName`—The name of the service that this `ServiceInstaller` handles during installation. If you changed the class name of the service after using the Add Installer option, then you would need to change this property to correspond to the new name for the service.

`ServiceProcessInstaller` and `ServiceInstaller` are used as necessary during the installation process, so there is no need to understand or manipulate the methods of these.

## Multiple Services within One Executable

It is possible to place more than one class that inherits from the `ServiceBase` class in a single Windows Service executable. Each such class then allows for a separate service that can be started, stopped, and so on, independently of the other services in the executable.

If a Windows Service executable contains more than one service, then it must contain one `ServiceInstaller` for each service. Each `ServiceInstaller` is configured with the information used for its associated service, such as the displayed name and the start type (automatic or manual). However, the executable still needs only one `ServiceProcessInstaller`, which works for all the services in the executable. It is configured with the account information that is used for all the services in the executable.

## The ServiceController Class

Another important .NET Framework class used with Windows Services is `System .ServiceProcess.ServiceController`. This class is not used when constructing a service; it is used by external applications to communicate with a running service, enabling operations such as starting and stopping the service. The `ServiceController` class is described in detail in the section "Communicating with the Service."

# Other Types of Windows Services

The `ServiceBase` and `ServiceController` classes can be used to create typical Windows Services that work with high-level system resources such as the file system or performance counters. However, some Windows Services need to interact at a deeper level. For example, a service may work at the kernel level, fulfilling functions such as that of a device driver.

Presently, the .NET Framework classes for Windows Services cannot be used to create such lower-level services, which rules out both Visual Basic and C# as tools to create them. C++ is typically the tool of choice for these types of services. If the C++ is used, the code for such services would typically run in unmanaged mode.

Another type of service that cannot be created with the .NET Framework classes is one that interacts with the Windows desktop. Again, C++ is the preferred tool for such services.

You'll look at the types of services that *are* possible during the discussion of the `ServiceType` property of the `ServiceController` class, in the section "Communicating with the Service."

# CREATING A WINDOWS SERVICE IN VISUAL BASIC

Here is a summary description of the necessary tasks to create a Windows Service. These tasks are demonstrated later in a detailed example:

1. Create a new project of the type Windows Service. By default, the service will be in a module named `Service1.vb`, but it can be renamed, like any other .NET module. The class automatically placed in `Service1.vb` is named `Service1` by default, and it inherits from the `ServiceBase` class.

2. Place any logic that needs to run when the service is started in the `OnStart` event of the service class. You can find the code listing for the `Service1.vb` file by double-clicking this file's design surface.

3. Add any additional logic that the service needs to carry out its operation. Logic can be placed in the class for the service, or in any other class module in the project. Such logic is typically called via some event that is generated by the operating system and passed to the service, such as a file changing in a directory, or a timer tick.

4. Add an installer to the project. This module provides the interface to the Windows operating system to install the module as a Windows Service. The installer is a class that inherits from `System.Configuration.Install.Installer`, and it contains instances of the `ServiceProcessInstaller` and `ServiceInstaller` classes.

5. Set the properties of the installer modules as necessary. The most common settings needed are the account under which the service will run and the name the service will display in the Service Control Manager.

6. Build the project. This results in an .exe file. For example, if the service were named `WindowsService1`, then the executable file would be named `WindowsService1.exe`.

7. Install the Windows Service with a command-line utility named `InstallUtil.exe`. (As previously mentioned, a service cannot be started by just running the .exe file.)

8. Start the Windows Service with the Service Control Manager or with the Server Explorer in Visual Studio.

You can also start a service from the command console if the proper paths to .NET are set. The command is as follows:

```
NET START <servicename>
```

Note that the `<servicename>` used in this command is the name of the service, not the name of the executable in which the service resides.

Depending on the configuration of your system, a service started with any of the aforementioned methods will sometimes fail, resulting in an error message indicating that the service did not start in a timely fashion. This may be because the .NET libraries and other initialization tasks did not finish fast enough to suit the Service Control Manager. If this happens, attempt to start the service again; if it has no actual defects, it usually succeeds the second time.

> **NOTE** *Steps 2 through 5 can be done in any order. It doesn't matter whether the installer is added and configured before or after the logic that does the processing for the service is added.*

At this point, a service is installed and running. The Service Control Manager can stop the service, or it will be automatically stopped when the system is shut down. The command to stop the service in a command console is as follows:

```
NET STOP <servicename>
```

The service does not automatically start the next time the system is booted unless it is configured for that. This can be done by setting the StartType property for the service to Automatic when developing the service, or it can be done in the Service Manager. Right-clicking the service in the Service Manager provides access to this capability.

Developing a Windows Service project is similar to most other Visual Basic projects. There are a few important differences, however:

➤ Even though the result of the development is an .exe file, you should not include any message boxes or other visual elements in the code. A Windows Service executable is more like a component library in that sense, and should not have a visual interface. If you include visual elements such as message boxes, the results can vary. In some cases, the UI code will have no effect. In other cases, the service may hang when attempting to write to the user interface.

➤ You cannot debug the project in the environment as you normally would with any other Visual Basic program. Most important, it is possible to run your application code interactively in a test harness prior to deployment. However, to fully test the service it must be installed and started as a service. In that scenario the debugger is automatically available. To debug a running service you need to attach to the process of the service to do debugging. Details about this are included in the section "Debugging the Service."

➤ Finally, be especially careful to handle all errors within the program. The program is not running in a user context, so a runtime error has no place to report itself visually. Handle all errors with structured exception handling, and use a Trace file, Event Log, or other persistent storage to record runtime errors.

## CREATING A FILE WATCHER SERVICE

To illustrate the outlined steps, the following example monitors a particular directory and reacts when a new or changed file is placed in the directory. The example Windows Service application waits for those files, extracts information from them, and then logs an event to a system log to record the file change.

# Creating a Solution for the Windows Service

First, you need an appropriate solution in place to hold the Windows Service. To do so, follow these steps:

1. Create a new Windows Service project using Visual Studio. Name the project ProVB_FileWatcherService.

2. In the Solution Explorer, rename `Service1.vb` to `FileWatcherService.vb`. You will be prompted to also change the class name.

3. Click the design surface for `FileWatcherService.vb`. In the Properties window, change the `ServiceName` property from `Service1` to `FileWatcherService`. Step 2 changes the name of the class on which the service is based, while the `ServiceName` property changes the name of the service as shown in the Service Control Manager.

4. Add an installer to the project. Go back to the design surface for FileWatcherService and right-click it. Select Add Installer. A new file called `ProjectInstaller.vb` is created and added to the project. The `ProjectInstaller.vb` file has two components added to its design surface: `ServiceProcessInstaller1` and `ServiceInstaller1`.

5. On the `ProjectInstaller.vb` design surface, highlight the `ServiceProcessInstaller1` control. In its Properties window, change the `Account` property to LocalSystem.

6. Highlight the `ServiceInstaller1` control. In its Properties window, type in **FileWatcherService** as the value of the `DisplayName` property. (The `ServiceName` property will already have this value.)

7. Build the project by right-clicking on the solution and selecting Build from the menu. An .exe file named `FileWatcherService.exe` will be created for the service.

At this point, you have a Windows Service that is compiled and ready to be installed, but it doesn't do anything yet. The preceding steps are very similar for every Windows Service you would create; the main points that vary are the name and the type of account you choose to use. The next part, however, is specific to a particular Windows Service: creating the application logic to support the functionality you need in the Windows Service.

# Adding .NET Components to the Service

This example service will have the capability to watch a directory for file changes and log events to report its activity. Two .NET components will facilitate these capabilities: the `FileSystemWatcher` component and the `EventLog` component.

## The FileSystemWatcher Component

The `FileSystemWatcher` component is used to monitor a particular directory. The component implements `Created`, `Changed`, `Deleted`, and `Renamed` events, which are fired when files are placed in the directory, changed, deleted, or renamed, respectively.

The operation that takes place when one of these events is fired is determined by the application developer. Most often, logic is included to read and process the new or changed files. However, you are just going to write a message to a log file.

To implement the component in the project, drag and drop a `FileSystemWatcher` control from the Components tab of the Toolbox onto the design surface of `FileWatcherService.vb`. (Be sure not to drag the component onto `ProjectInstaller.vb`. If `ProjectInstaller.vb` is still the displayed design surface, you'll need to click on the tab for the `FileWatcherService.vb` design surface.) This control is automatically called `FileSystemWatcher1`.

## The EnableRaisingEvents Property

The `FileSystemWatcher` component should not generate any events until the service is initialized and ready to handle them. To prevent this, set the `EnableRaisingEvents` property of `FileSystemWatcher1` to False. This prevents the component from firing any events. You will enable it during the `OnStart` event in the service. These events fired by the `FileSystemWatcher` component are controlled using the `NotifyFilter` property, discussed later.

## The Path Property

The path that you want to monitor is the `TEMP` directory on the C: drive, so set the `Path` property to `C:\TEMP` (be sure to confirm that there is a `TEMP` directory on your C: drive). Of course, this path can be changed to monitor any directory depending on your system, including any network or removable drives.

## The NotifyFilter Property

For this example, you only want to monitor when a file is freshly created or the last modified value of a file has changed. To do this, set the `NotifyFilter` property to `FileName, LastWrite`. Note that you can specify multiple changes to monitor by including a comma-separated list. Even though the property has a drop-down, you'll need to type in the value to get both parts of it.

You could also watch for other changes such as attributes, security, size, and directory name changes as well, just by including those options as part of the `NotifyFilter` property.

## The Filter Property

The types of files that you will look for are text files, so set the `Filter` property to `*.txt`. Note that if you were going to watch for all file types, then the value of the `Filter` property would be set to `*.*` (which is the default).

## The IncludeSubdirectories Property

If you wanted to watch subdirectories, you would set the `IncludeSubdirectories` property to `True`. This example leaves it as `False`, which is the default value. Figure 16-2 shows how the properties should be set.

## Adding FileSystemWatcher Code to OnStart and OnStop

Now that some properties are set, let's add some code to the `OnStart` event for `FileWatcherService.vb`. You want to

**FIGURE 16-2:** Properties for FileSystemWatcher

start the `FileSystemWatcher1` component so it will start triggering events when files are created or copied into the directory you are monitoring, so set the `EnableRaisingEvents` property to `True`. Choose to View Code on `FileWatcherSErvice.vb` and update the `OnStart` handler as shown in the following snippet:

```
Protected Overrides Sub OnStart(ByVal args() As String)
    ' Add code here to start your service. This method should set things
    ' in motion so your service can do its work.
    ' Start monitoring for files
    FileSystemWatcher1.EnableRaisingEvents = True
End Sub
```

After the file monitoring properties are initialized, you are ready to start the monitoring. When the service stops, you need to stop the file monitoring process. Add the following code shown to the `OnStop` event.

```
Protected Overrides Sub OnStop()
    ' Add code here to perform any tear-down necessary to stop your service.
    ' Stop monitoring for files
    FileSystemWatcher1.EnableRaisingEvents = False
End Sub
```

## The EventLog Component

Now you are ready to place an `EventLog` component in the service to facilitate the logging of events. Event logs are available under the Windows operating system, and were discussed in Chapter 6. As with many other system-level features, the use of Event Logs is simplified in .NET because a .NET Framework base class does most of the work for you.

Depending on your system's configuration and installed software, there should be several Event Logs on the system. Normally, your applications should write only to the Application Log. A property of a log entry called `Source` identifies the application writing the message. This property does not have to share the same name as the executable of the application, but it is often given that name to make it easy to identify the source of the message.

You can look at the events in the Event Log by using the Event Viewer. On Windows 7 or Windows Server 2008, select Start ⇨ Control Panel ⇨ System and Maintenance ⇨ Administrative Tools ⇨ Event Viewer. If you are on Windows 8 and turned on the administrative tiles, select the Event Viewer tile from your Start screen.

It was mentioned earlier in the chapter that the `AutoLog` property of the `ServiceBase` class determines whether the service automatically writes events to the Application Log. The `AutoLog` property instructs the service to use the Application event log to report command failures, as well as information for `OnStart`, `OnStop`, `OnPause`, and `OnContinue` events on the service. What is actually logged to the event log is an entry indicating whether the service started successfully and stopped successfully, and any errors that might have occurred.

You can turn off event log reporting by setting the `AutoLog` property to `False` in the Properties window for the service, but leave it set to `True` for this example. That means some events will be logged automatically (without you including any code for them). If desired, you can add some code to the service to log additional events not covered by the `AutoLog` property.

Drag and drop an `EventLog` control from the Components tab of the Toolbox onto the designer surface of `FileWatcherService.vb`. This control is automatically called `EventLog1`. Set the `Log` property for `Eventlog1` to `Application`, and set the `Source` property to `FileWatcherService`.

### The Created Event

Next, you will place some logic in the `Created` event of the `FileSystemWatcher` component to log when a file has been created. This event fires when a file has been placed or created in the directory that you are monitoring. It fires because the information last modified on the file has changed.

Bring up `FileSystemWatcher1.vb` in the code editor. Select `FileSystemWatcher1` from the left-hand drop-down list and then select `Created` from the right-hand drop-down list. The `Created` event will be added to your code. Add the following code to the `Created` event:

```
Public Sub FileSystemWatcher1_Created(ByVal sender As Object, _
        ByVal e As System.IO.FileSystemEventArgs) _
        Handles FileSystemWatcher1.Created
    EventLog1.WriteEntry("File created in directory - file name is " & e.Name)
End Sub
```

Notice that the event argument's object (the `System.IO.FilesSystemEventsArgs` object named "e" in the event parameters) includes a property called `Name`. This property holds the name of the file that generated the event.

At this point, you could add the other events for `FileSystemWatcher` (`Changed`, `Deleted`, `Renamed`) in a similar way and create corresponding log messages for those events. To keep the example simple, you will just use the `Created` event in this service.

Build the service again to compile the new functionality. You are now ready to install the service and test it.

## Installing the Service

The utility for installing the service, `InstallUtil.exe`, must be run from a command line. `InstallUtil.exe` is located in the .NET utilities directory, found at `C:\Windows\Microsoft.NET\Framework\v4.0.xxxxx` ("xxxxx" is a placeholder for the version number of the .NET Framework you have installed).

You'll need a Developer Command Prompt for VS2012 window to access this utility. You can start this by using the start menu and going to All Programs ⇨ Visual Studio 2012 ⇨ Visual Studio Tools. You should right-click on the link for the command window and select Run as Administrator. Note that if on Windows 8, you'll just want to select the "Developer Command Prompt for VS2012" tile that should be on your Start screen near the Visual Studio 2012 tile. Right-clicking that tile will display the option to 'Run as Administrator" at the bottom of your screen.

In the command window, change to the directory that contains `FileWatcherService.exe`. Right click on your project in the solution explorer and select the "Open folder in File Explorer" menu item. From here you'll go to the bin folder. Next, if you are currently using a Debug configuration you will find it in the Debug folder; otherwise, you will find it in the Release folder. After navigating your command window to this location (cd <paste your path here>) run the following command:

```
InstallUtil ProVB_FileWatcherService.exe
```

Check the messages generated by InstallUtil.exe to ensure that installation of the service was successful. The utility generates several lines of information; if successful, the last two lines are as follows:

```
The Commit phase completed successfully.
The transacted install has completed.
```

If the preceding two lines do not appear, then you need to read all the information generated by the utility to find out why the install didn't work. Reasons might include a bad pathname for the executable, or trying to install the service when it is already installed (it must be uninstalled before it can be reinstalled; the uninstall process is described later). Also, if you did not select Run as Administrator for the command window, you may get an error relating to insufficient security privileges.

> **NOTE** *If your service has the Account property of the ServiceProcessInstaller set to User, you will need to arrange for a user name and password during installation. The user name and password to use are passed as parameters in the InstallUtil command. The InstallContext class is then used in code inside your ServiceProcessInstaller to set the UserName and Password properties. The documentation for the InstallContext class includes an example.*

## Starting the Service

Later in this chapter, you will create your own "control panel" screen to start and stop the service. For now, to test the new Windows service, you will use the Service Control Manager built into Windows to start the FileWatcherService service. It was shown previously in Figure 16-1. Open the Service Control Manager and locate the FileWatcherService service. If you already had the Service Control Manager open, you'll need to refresh it after installing the FileWatcherService.

If the FileWatcherService service does not appear in the list, then the installation failed. Try the installation again and check the error messages. Right-click the FileWatcherService service and select the Start menu option.

To test the service, copy or create a .TXT file in the C:/TEMP directory (or any other directory you decided to use). You should be able to see a corresponding event in the event log for your machine, using the Event Viewer as described earlier.

Figure 16-3 shows the Event Viewer with several example messages created by the service. Notice that the message corresponds to the event log message you constructed in the Created event of the FileSystemWatcher control in the service. Play with it a little; notice how if you create a new file and rename it, only the default new filename is shown. Similarly if you rename a file, no message is generated. The only action triggering those events is the creation of new files in that folder.

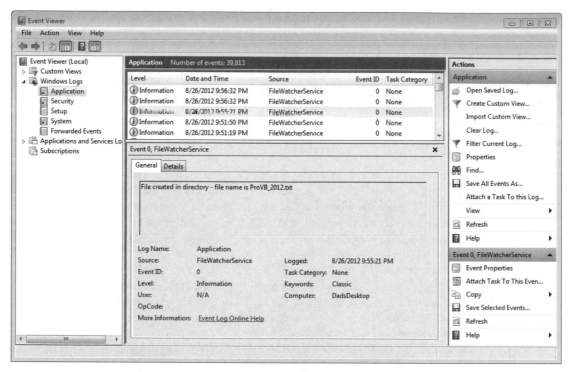

**FIGURE 16-3:** File watcher even for new ProVB_2012.txt file

## Uninstalling the Service

Uninstalling the service is very similar to installing it. The service must be in a stopped state before it can be uninstalled, but the uninstall operation will attempt to stop the service if it is running. The uninstall operation is done in the same command window as the install operation, and the command used is the same as the one for installation, except that the option /u is included just before the name of the service. Remember that you need to navigate to the project folder and go to the \Debug (or the equivalent \Release folder, depending on your current configuration) to run the following command:

```
InstallUtil.exe /u FileWatcherService.exe
```

You can tell the uninstall was successful if the information displayed by the utility contains the following line:

```
Service FileWatcherService was successfully removed from the system.
```

If the uninstall is not successful, then read the rest of the information to determine why. Besides typing in the wrong pathname, another common reason for failure is trying to uninstall a service that is in a running state and could not be stopped in a timely fashion.

Once you have uninstalled FileWatcherService, it will no longer show up in the list of available services to start and stop (at least, after a refresh it won't).

> **NOTE** *A Windows Service must be uninstalled and reinstalled every time you make changes to it.*

## COMMUNICATING WITH THE SERVICE

Up to this point, you have learned how to do the following:

➤ Create a Windows service using Visual Basic

➤ Start and stop a service with the Service Control Manager from the Control Panel

➤ Make a service work with a system-level function such as a FileSystemWatcher

If these procedures are sufficient to start, stop, and check on the service through the Server Explorer or the Service Control Manager, and there is no need for any other communication with the service, then this is all you have to do. However, it is often helpful to create a specialized application to manipulate your service. This application will typically be able to start and stop a service, and check on its status. The application may also need to communicate with the service to change its configuration. Such an application is often referred to as a *control panel* for the service, even though it does not necessarily reside in the operating system's Control Panel. A commonly used example of such an application is the SQL Server Service Manager, whose icon appears in the tray on the taskbar (normally in the lower-right section of the screen) if you have SQL Server installed.

Such an application needs a way to communicate with the service. The .NET Framework base class that is used for such communication is `ServiceController`. It is in the `System.ServiceProcess` namespace. You need to add a reference to `System.ServiceProcess.dll` (which contains this namespace) before a project can use the `ServiceController` class.

The `ServiceController` class provides an interface to the Service Control Manager, which coordinates all communication with Windows Services. However, you do not have to know anything about the Service Control Manager to use the `ServiceController` class. You just manipulate the properties and methods of the `ServiceController` class, and any necessary communication with the Service Control Manager is accomplished on your behalf behind the scenes.

Because multiple instances of `ServiceController` that are communicating with the same service can have timing conflicts, it is a good idea to use exactly *one* instance of the `ServiceController` class for each service you are controlling. Typically, that means using a module-level object variable to hold the reference to the active `ServiceController`, and instantiating the `ServiceController` during the initialization logic for the application. Later in this chapter you will create an example that uses this technique.

### The ServiceController Class

The constructor for the `ServiceController` requires the name of the Windows Service with which it will be communicating. This is the same name that was placed in the `ServiceName` property of the class that defined the service. You will see how to instantiate the `ServiceController` class shortly.

The `ServiceController` class has several members that are useful in manipulating services. Table 16-2 describes the most important methods, followed by the most important properties in Table 16-3.

**TABLE 16-2:** Important ServiceController Methods

| METHOD | DESCRIPTION |
| --- | --- |
| Start | A method to start the service. |
| Stop | A method to stop the service. |
| Refresh | A method to ensure that the `ServiceController` object contains the latest state of the service (needed because the service might be manipulated from another program). |
| ExecuteCommand | A method used to send a custom command to the service. This method is covered later in the section "Custom Commands." |

**TABLE 16-3:** Important ServiceController Properties

| PROPERTY | DESCRIPTION |
| --- | --- |
| CanStop | A property indicating whether the service can be stopped. |
| ServiceName | A property containing the name of the associated service. |
| Status | An enumerated property that indicates whether a service is stopped, started, in the process of being started, and so on. The `ToString` method on this property is useful for getting the status in a string form for text messages. The possible values of the enumeration are:<br><br>`ContinuePending` — The service is attempting to continue.<br>`Paused` — The service is paused.<br>`PausePending` — The service is attempting to go into a paused state.<br>`Running` — The service is running.<br>`StartPending` — The service is starting.<br>`Stopped` — The service is not running.<br>`StopPending` — The service is stopping. |
| ServiceType | A property that indicates the type of service. The result is an enumerated value. The enumerations values are:<br>`Win32OwnProcess` — The service uses its own process (this is the default for a service created in .NET).<br>`Win32ShareProcess` — The service shares a process with another service (this advanced capability is not covered here).<br>`Adapter, FileSystemDriver, InteractiveProcess, KernelDriver, RecognizerDriver` — These are low-level service types that cannot be created with Visual Basic because the `ServiceBase` class does not support them. However, the value of the `ServiceType` property may still have these values for services created with other tools. |

# Integrating a ServiceController into the Example

To manipulate the service, you need to create a program with an appropriate user interface. For simplicity, the example presented will use WPF. Here are step-by-step instructions to create the example:

**1.** Add a new WPF Application project to your current solution and name it **ProVB_FileWatcherPanel**.

**2.** Add three new buttons to the blank `MainWindow` window, with the following names and content properties:

| NAME | CONTENT |
|------|---------|
| ButtonStatus | Check Status |
| ButtonStart | Start Service |
| ButtonStop | Stop Service |

**3.** Add a reference to the `System.ServiceProcess` namespace and click OK.

**4.** Add this line at the top of the code for `MainWindow`:

```
Imports System.ServiceProcess
```

**5.** As discussed, the project needs only one instance of the `ServiceController` class. Create a class property to reference a `ServiceController` instance by adding the following line of code within the `MainWindow` class:

```
Private myController As ServiceController
```

**6.** Create a `Window Loaded` event in `MainWindow`, and place the following line of code in it to instantiate the `ServiceController` class:

```
myController = New ServiceController("FileWatcherService")
```

You now have a `ServiceController` class named `myController` that you can use to manipulate the FileWatcherService Windows service. The next step is to implement the click event handlers for each of the buttons on your form. The following illustrates the resulting code in your `MainWindows`.`xaml`.`vb` file to implement these simple controls.

```vb
Imports System.ServiceProcess

Class MainWindow
    Private myController As ServiceController

    Private Sub Window_Loaded_1(sender As Object, e As RoutedEventArgs)
        myController = New ServiceController("FileWatcherService")
    End Sub

    Private Sub ButtonStatus_Click(sender As Object,
                    e As RoutedEventArgs) Handles ButtonStatus.Click
        Dim sStatus As String
        myController.Refresh()
        sStatus = myController.Status.ToString
        MessageBox.Show(myController.ServiceName & " is in state: " & sStatus)
```

```
        End Sub

        Private Sub ButtonStart_Click(sender As Object,
                    e As RoutedEventArgs) Handles ButtonStart.Click
            Try
                myController.Start()
                MessageBox.Show("Service Started.")
            Catch exp As Exception
                MessageBox.Show("Could not start service or is already running")
            End Try
        End Sub

        Private Sub ButtonStop_Click(sender As Object,
                    e As RoutedEventArgs) Handles ButtonStop.Click
            If myController.CanStop Then
                myController.Stop()
                MessageBox.Show("Service Stopped.")
            Else
                MessageBox.Show("Service cannot be stopped or is already stopped.")
            End If

        End Sub
    End Class
```

You can run and test the program, but remember if you've uninstalled the service you'll first need to reinstall it. Alternatively the service may already be running because of one of your previous tests. If your program cannot stop or start the service, your user account may not have sufficient security privileges. You can recognize this as an error that the application failed to open the service. There are two possible solutions; one is to start/restart Visual Studio with Run as Administrator privileges. The alternative is to navigate to the /bin/debug (or release) folder for your project and directly start your application using the Run as Administrator option.

## More about ServiceController

ServiceController classes can be created for *any* Windows service, not just those created in .NET. For example, you could instantiate a ServiceController class that was associated with the Windows Service for Internet Information Services (IIS) and use it to start, pause, and stop IIS. The code would look just like the code used earlier for the application that controlled the FileWatcherService service. The only difference is that the name of the service would need to be changed in the line that instantiates the ServiceController (step 6).

Keep in mind that the ServiceController is not communicating directly with the service. It is working through the Service Control Manager. That means the requests from the ServiceController to start, stop, or pause a service do not behave synchronously. As soon as the ServiceController has passed the request to the Services Control Manager, it continues to execute its own code without waiting for the Service Control Manager to pass on the request, or for the service to act on the request.

## CUSTOM COMMANDS

Some services need additional operations besides starting and stopping. For example, for the FileWatcherService, you might want to support multiple file extensions, using a different FileSystemWatcher component for each.

With most components, you would implement such functionality through a public interface. That is, you would put public properties and methods on the component. However, you cannot do this with a Windows Service because it has no public interface that you can access from outside the service.

To deal with this need, the interface for a Windows Service contains a special event called OnCustomCommand. The event arguments include a numeric code that can serve as a command sent to the Windows Service. The code can be any number in the range 128 to 255. (The numbers under 128 are reserved for use by the operating system.)

To fire the event and send a custom command to a service, the ExecuteCommand method of the ServiceController is used. The ExecuteCommand method takes the numeric code that needs to be sent to the service as a parameter. When this method is accessed, the ServiceController class tells the Service Control Manager to fire the OnCustomCommand event in the service, and to pass it the numeric code.

You can modify the example code to demonstrate this process in action. Suppose you want to be able to change the file filter being used for the FileWatcherService service. You cannot directly send the filter that you want, but you can pick various values of the filter, and associate a custom command numeric code with each.

For example, assume you want to be able to set filters of *.txt, *.dat, or *.docx. You could set up the following correspondence:

| CUSTOM COMMAND NUMERIC CODE | FILTER FOR FILESYSTEMWATCHER |
| --- | --- |
| 201 | *.txt |
| 203 | *.docx |
| 210 | *.dat |

The correspondences in the table are completely arbitrary. You could use any codes between 128 and 255 to associate with the filters. These were chosen because they are easy to remember.

First, you need to change the FileWatcherService service so that it is able to accept the custom commands for the beep interval. To do that, first make sure the FileWatcherService service is uninstalled from any previous installs.

Create an OnCustomCommand event in the service: Open the code window for FileWatcherService .vb and type **Protected Overrides OnCustomCommand**. By this point, IntelliSense will kick in, and you can press the Tab key to autocomplete the shell event. Notice how it only accepts a single Integer as a parameter:

```
Protected Overrides Sub OnCustomCommand(ByVal command As Integer)
    MyBase.OnCustomCommand(command)
End Sub
```

In the OnCustomCommand event handler, replace the single line that was generated automatically (the one beginning with MyBase) with the following code:

```
Select Case command
    Case 201
        FileSystemWatcher1.Filter = "*.txt"
```

```
        Case 203
            FileSystemWatcher1.Filter = "*.docx"
        Case 210
            FileSystemWatcher1.Filter = "*.dat"
    End Select
```

Build the FileWatcherService service, reinstall it, and start it.

Now you can enhance the FileWatcherPanel application created earlier to set the filter. To enable users to select the file filter, you will use a ComboBox. Add a Label to your window with the text "Select File Extension." Next add a ComboBox control below it. Name it "ComboBoxFileType" then go to the Items property of the ComboBox and use the ellipsis button to add new items. Add three new ListBoxItems to the collection. Set the contents of each using TXT, DOCX, and DAT, respectively. Once you have defined the three items you should set the SelectedIndex property of your ComboBox to 0.

Place a button directly under your ComboBox. Name it ButtonFilter and set its text to Set Filter, as follows:.

```
    Private Sub ButtonFilter_Click(sender As Object,
            e As RoutedEventArgs) Handles ButtonFilter.Click
        Dim s As String = ComboBoxFileType.Text
        Select Case s
            Case "TXT"
                myController.ExecuteCommand(201)
            Case "DOCX"
                myController.ExecuteCommand(203)
            Case Else
                myController.ExecuteCommand(210)
        End Select
    End Sub
```

At this point, the MainWindow should look something like the screen shown in Figure 16-4.

Start the FileWatcherPanel control program and test the capability to change the filter by adding different file types with each filter setting and examining the resulting logged events.

FIGURE 16-4: File Watcher Control Panel

## PASSING STRINGS TO A SERVICE

Because the OnCustomCommand event only takes numeric codes as input parameters, you cannot directly pass strings to the service. For example, if you wanted to reconfigure a directory name for a service, you could not just send the directory name over. Instead, it would be necessary to place the information to be passed to the service in a file in some known location on disk. Then a custom command for the service could instruct it to look at the standard file location and read the information in the file. What the service did with the contents of the file would, of course, be customized for the service.

## DEBUGGING THE SERVICE

Debugging a service is not as straightforward as debugging other application types, because a service must be run from within the context of the Service Control Manager rather than from within Visual Studio. To debug a service, you must start the service and then attach a debugger to the process in which it is running. You can then debug the application using all of the standard debugging functionality of Visual Studio.

> **NOTE** *Don't attach to a process unless you know what the process is and understand the consequences of attaching to and possibly killing that process.*

To avoid going through this extra effort, you may want to test most of the code in your service in a test application. This test-bed application can have the same components (FileSystemWatchers, EventLogs, Timers, and so on) as the Windows Service, and thus be able to run the same logic in events. Once you have checked out the logic in this context, you can just copy and paste it into a Windows Service application.

However, sometimes the service itself needs to be debugged directly, so it is important to understand how to attach to the service's process and do direct debugging. You can only debug a service when it is running. When you attach the debugger to the service, you are interrupting it. The service is suspended for a short period while you attach to it. It is also interrupted when you place breakpoints and step through your code.

Attaching to the service's process enables you to debug most, but not all, of the service's code. For instance, because the service has already been started, you cannot debug the code in the service's `OnStart` method this way, or the code in the `Main` method that is used to load the service. To debug the `OnStart` event or any of the Visual Studio designer code, you have to add a dummy service and start that service first. In the dummy service, you would create an instance of the service that you want to debug. You can place some code in a `Timer` object and create the new instance of the object that you want to debug after 30 seconds or so. Allow enough time to attach to the debugger before the new instance is created. Meanwhile, place breakpoints in your startup code to debug those events, if desired.

Aside from issues with an issue occurring at startup to debug a running service, you'll need to ensure you have the appropriate permissions. This means you need to have started Visual Studio with Administrator privileges. Once you have done that you can perform the following steps:

1. Verify the service is installed and running.

2. Load the solution for the service in Visual Studio. Then select Attach to Process from the Debug menu. The Attach to Process dialogue appears (see Figure 16-5). Be sure to enable the check boxes next to the "Show processes from all users."

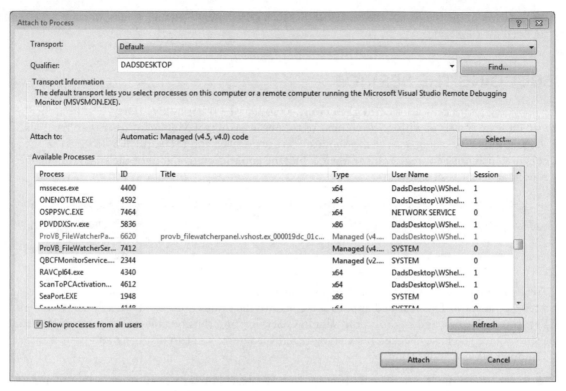

**FIGURE 16-5:** Attach to a running process dialogue

3. In the Available Processes section, click the process indicated by the executable name (`ProVB_FileWatchter.exe`) for the service, and then click Attach.

4. You can now debug your process. Place a breakpoint in the code for the service at the place you want to debug. Cause the code in the service to execute (by placing a file in a monitored directory, for example).

5. When finished, select Stop Debugging from the Debug menu.

## SUMMARY

This chapter presented a general overview of what a Windows Service is and how to create one with Visual Basic. The techniques in this chapter can be used for many different types of background service, including the following:

➤ Automatically moving statistical files from a database server to a Web server

➤ Pushing general files across computers and platforms

➤ A watchdog timer to ensure that a connection is always available

➤ An application to move and process FTP files, or indeed files received from any source

While Visual Basic cannot be used to create every type of Windows Service, it is effective for creating many of the most useful ones. The .NET Framework classes for Windows Services make this creation relatively straightforward. The designers generate much of the routine code needed, enabling you, as a developer, to concentrate on the code specific to your particular Windows Service.

In the next chapter you are going to take a deeper look at how .NET handles assemblies and versioning. The chapter will also go into more detail on leveraging reflection to dynamically load classes.

# 17

# Assemblies and Reflection

## WHAT'S IN THIS CHAPTER?

- ➤ The general structure of an assembly
- ➤ How assemblies can be versioned
- ➤ The global assembly cache (GAC), including how and when to use it
- ➤ How assemblies are located and loaded by the CLR
- ➤ Using reflection to inspect assemblies in order to determine the types they contain and the interfaces of those types
- ➤ Dynamic loading of assemblies, allowing your application to inject functionality that was not available at compile time

## WROX.COM CODE DOWNLOADS FOR THIS CHAPTER

The wrox.com code downloads for this chapter are found at `www.wrox.com/remtitle .cgi?isbn=9781118314456` on the Download Code tab. The code is in the chapter 17 download and individually named according to the code file names throughout the chapter.

.NET-compiled modules, both DLLs and EXEs, are referred to as *assemblies*. Assemblies are the unit of deployment in .NET, containing both compiled code and metadata that is needed by the .NET common language runtime (CLR) to run the code. Metadata includes information such as the code's identity and version, dependencies on other assemblies, and a list of types and resources exposed by the assembly.

Development in .NET doesn't require you to know any more than that. However, as your applications become more complex, and as you begin considering such issues as deployment and maintenance of your code, you may want to understand more about assemblies. For advanced scenarios, you'll also need to know how to inspect assemblies to find out the types they contain and the interfaces of those types. This inspection capability is known as *reflection*.

Keep in mind however, that reflection and these advanced capabilities for examining and dynamically loading assemblies aren't Win RT compatible. This chapter focuses on capabilities that require elevated permissions to function.

## ASSEMBLIES

The assembly is used by the CLR as the smallest unit for the following:

➤ Deployment

➤ Version control

➤ Security

➤ Type grouping

➤ Code reuse

An assembly must contain a *manifest*, which tells the CLR what else is in the assembly. The other elements fall into the following three categories:

**1.** Type metadata

**2.** Microsoft Intermediate Language (MSIL) code

**3.** Resources

An assembly can be just one file. Figure 17-1 details the contents of a single-file assembly. Alternatively, the structure can be split across multiple files.

An assembly can have only one manifest section across all the files that make up the assembly. There is nothing stopping you, however, from having a resource section (or any of the other available section types, such as Metadata and MSIL code) in separate files that make up an assembly.

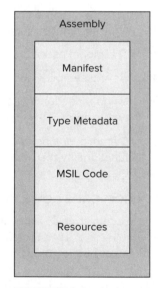

**FIGURE 17-1:** Logical structure of an assembly

## THE MANIFEST

The manifest is the part of the assembly that contains a list of the other elements contained in the assembly and basic identification information for the assembly. The manifest contains the largest part of the information that enables the assembly to be self-describing. Elements listed in the manifest are placed in appropriate sections. The manifest includes the sections displayed in Figure 17-2. These sections are covered later in the chapter.

To look at the manifest for a particular assembly, you can use the IL Disassembler (`Ildasm.exe`), which is included with the Windows SDK installed with Visual Studio. The version of `Ildasm`

`.exe` in the SDK for .NET Framework 4.5 can examine assemblies created with earlier versions of the .NET Framework; in fact, as of release it is the same version that was released with .NET 4.0. A shortcut to `ildasm.exe` is no longer included on the Start menu. Instead use the All Programs ➪ Microsoft Visual Studio 2012 ➪ Visual Studio Tools ➪ Developer Command Prompt for VS2012 to open a command window from which you can start `ILDasm.exe`. It appears that in order to simplify how many items are shown on the Start Menu (or Start screen in Windows RT), this tool has been removed from the list of available selections.

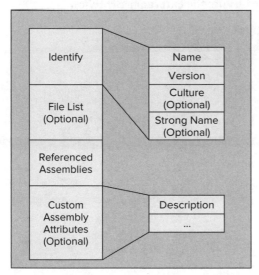

**FIGURE 17-2:** Logical structure of an assembly manifest

When `Ildasm.exe` loads, you can browse for an assembly to view by selecting File ➪ Open. For this example and screenshots the sample code from Chapter 6 will be used. Once an assembly has been loaded into `Ildasm.exe`, it disassembles the metadata contained within the assembly and presents you with a tree-view layout of the data. Initially, the tree view shows only top-level elements, as illustrated in Figure 17-3. This example has only one namespace element in the tree, but if an assembly contains classes in more than one namespace, then additional elements will be shown.

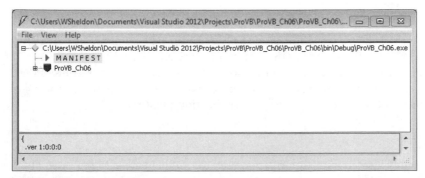

**FIGURE 17-3:** ILDasm window

The full path of the assembly you are viewing represents the root node. The first node below the root is called MANIFEST; and as you've probably guessed, it contains all the information about the assembly's manifest. If you double-click this node, a new window is displayed with the information contained within the manifest. The manifest for a complex assembly can be rather long. For this example, three sections of a manifest are shown in Figures 17-4, 17-5, and 17-6. Figure 17-4 shows the top of the manifest, which contains the external references needed by this assembly, such as other .NET assemblies on which this assembly depends. If the assembly depended on COM libraries, those will be shown as external modules and listed before the external assemblies.

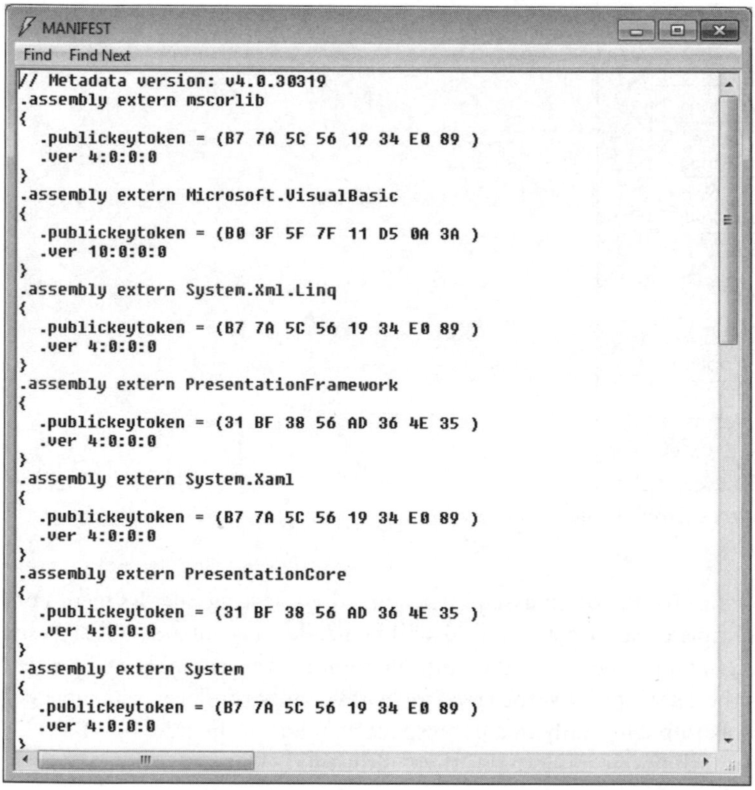


```
// Metadata version: v4.0.30319
.assembly extern mscorlib
{
  .publickeytoken = (B7 7A 5C 56 19 34 E0 89 )
  .ver 4:0:0:0
}
.assembly extern Microsoft.VisualBasic
{
  .publickeytoken = (B0 3F 5F 7F 11 D5 0A 3A )
  .ver 10:0:0:0
}
.assembly extern System.Xml.Linq
{
  .publickeytoken = (B7 7A 5C 56 19 34 E0 89 )
  .ver 4:0:0:0
}
.assembly extern PresentationFramework
{
  .publickeytoken = (31 BF 38 56 AD 36 4E 35 )
  .ver 4:0:0:0
}
.assembly extern System.Xaml
{
  .publickeytoken = (B7 7A 5C 56 19 34 E0 89 )
  .ver 4:0:0:0
}
.assembly extern PresentationCore
{
  .publickeytoken = (31 BF 38 56 AD 36 4E 35 )
  .ver 4:0:0:0
}
.assembly extern System
{
  .publickeytoken = (B7 7A 5C 56 19 34 E0 89 )
  .ver 4:0:0:0
}
```

**FIGURE 17-4:** Accessing the manifest from ILDasm

Figure 17-5 shows a portion of the manifest further down, containing the beginning of the section for the actual assembly. The first items listed in the manifest for the assembly itself are the attributes that apply to the assembly. Further down, shown in Figure 17-6, are items such as resources that reside in the assembly. Keep in mind, however, that the purpose of the IL Disassembler is to allow you to review the various elements that are part of your application identity.

## Assembly Identity

The manifest for an assembly also contains information used to uniquely identify the assembly. This section contains some standard information, such as the version number, and may also contain some optional elements, such as a strong name for the assembly. Assemblies come in two types: *application-private* and *shared* (differences between the two types are covered shortly), and they have slightly different identity information.

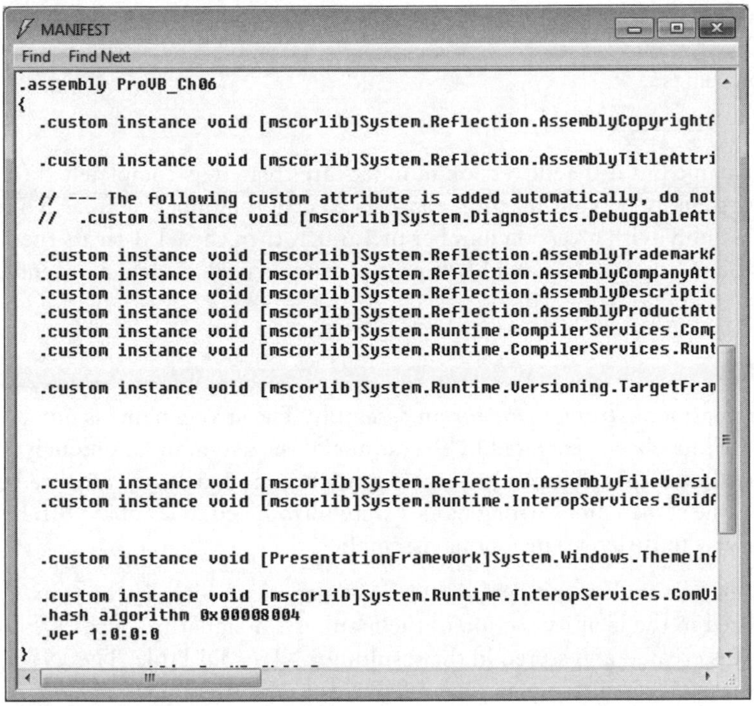

**FIGURE 17-5:** View near the bottom of the manifest

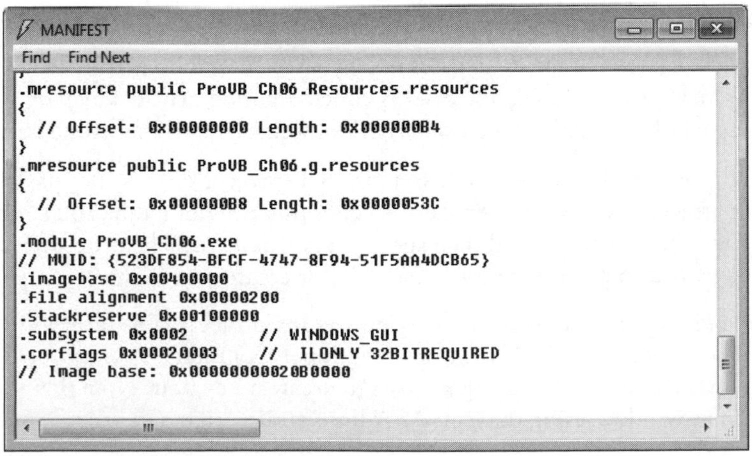

**FIGURE 17-6:** The bottom of the manifest

## The Version Number

The manifest for an assembly contains a version number, which is indicated by the `.ver` directive in `Ildasm.exe`. Figure 17-5, shown earlier, includes a `.ver` directive on the bottom line in the `.assembly` section:

```
.ver 1.0.0.0
```

A version number contains four parts:

```
Major : Minor : Build : Revision
```

Assemblies that have the same name but different version numbers are treated as completely different assemblies. If you have an assembly on your machine that has a version number of 1.5.2.3 and another version of the same assembly with a version number of 1.6.0.1, then the CLR treats them as different assemblies. The version number of an assembly is part of what is used to define dependencies between assemblies.

## Strong Names

A manifest can also contain an optional *strong name* for an assembly. The strong name is not a name per se, but a public key that has been generated by the author of the assembly to uniquely identify it. A strong name is used to ensure that your assembly has a unique signature compared to other assemblies that may have the same name. Strong names were introduced to combat DLL hell by providing an unambiguous way to differentiate among assemblies.

A strong name is based on public-private key encryption and creates a unique identity for your assembly. The public key is stored in the identity section of the manifest. A signature of the file containing the assembly's manifest is created and stored in the resulting EXE or DLL file. The .NET Framework uses these two signatures when resolving type references to ensure that the correct assembly is loaded at run time. A strong name is indicated in the manifest by the `.publickey` directive in the `.assembly` section.

## Signing an Assembly with a Strong Name

As mentioned previously, applying a strong name to an assembly is based on public-private key encryption. The public and private keys are related, and a set is called a public-private *key pair*. Applying a strong name to an assembly is usually called *signing* the assembly with the strong name.

Visual Studio gives you a straightforward way to sign an assembly. The project's Properties page (accessed by right-clicking on a project and choosing Properties) contains a Signing tab. You simply check the CheckBox labeled "Sign the assembly" and then specify a key pair file. The drop-down for the strong name key file allows you to browse for a key pair file, or create a new one.

You can also control the signing process manually for non–Windows RT projects. The utility `sn.exe` can create a key pair. The utility is available from the Developer Command Prompt for VS2012. The following code shows the syntax for using `sn.exe` to create a key pair. Note that you need to start the command prompt window using the Run As Administrator rights in order to successfully create a new key.

```
sn -k pairname.snk
```

You should replace *pairname* with an appropriate name, often the name of your product or system. This will be the name of the file that is created; for example, it might be Ch17Test.snk. Note that the same key pair can be used to apply a strong name to multiple assemblies in your environment.

Once you have a key pair, you need to add it to any projects in Visual Studio that need to generate a strongly named assembly. To do that, just select "browse" from the Choose a strong name key file, then drop down and select your file's name. Figure 17-7 shows an example of the signing properties populated for a sample project.

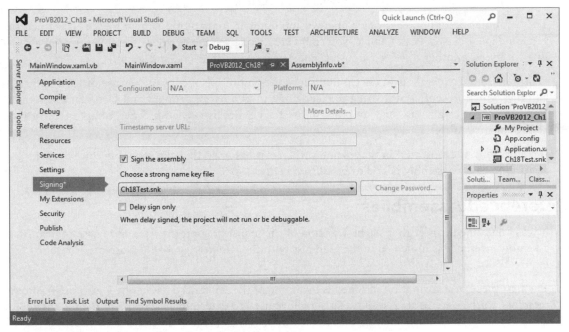

**FIGURE 17-7:** Project Properties — Signing tab

You can also sign an assembly with a strong name by compiling at the command line. This might be the case if you want to sign the assembly outside of Visual Studio. A typical command line to compile and sign a Visual Basic assembly looks like this:

```
vbc /reference:Microsoft.VisualBasic.dll /reference:System.Windows.Forms.dll
/target:library /keyfile:c:\mykeys\keypair.snk /out:MyAssembly.dll
/rootnamespace:MyAssembly *.vb
```

The separate elements of the command line have been placed on different lines for ease of reading, but they should all be on the same line in actual use. The preceding is just a template. You would need to change the /reference options to include any references needed by your assembly. You would also need to specify the correct file path for your own key pair file (.snk file) and apply your assembly and root namespace names.

Finally, strong names can be applied with a technique called *delay signing*. Delayed signing is helpful when assemblies need to be properly strongly named during development (so that any problems with strong names are detected at that point), but it is undesirable for all the developers to have a copy of the key pair that will be used for signing the final compiled version of the assembly. Of course, it comes at the cost of making it impossible to debug the assembly, so using the delay sign option is typically only handled near the end of the development cycle.

## The Culture

The final part of an assembly's identity is its *culture*, which is optional. Cultures are used to define the country/language for which the assembly is targeted.

The combination of name, strong name, version number, and culture is used by the CLR to enforce version dependencies. For example, you could create one version of your assembly targeted at English users, another for German users, another for Finnish users, and so on.

Cultures can be general, as in the case of English, or more specific, as in the case of US-English. Cultures are represented by a string that can contain two parts: primary and secondary (optional). The culture for English is "en," and the culture for US-English is "en-us." See Chapter 15 for more about cultures in .NET.

If a culture is not indicated in the assembly, then it is assumed that the assembly can be used for any culture. Such an assembly is said to be *culture neutral*.

# Referenced Assemblies

It was mentioned earlier that the first section of the manifest contains referenced assemblies. An assembly reference is indicated in the manifest with the `.assembly extern` directive (refer to Figure 17-4).

The first piece of information included is the name of the referenced assembly. Figure 17-4 shows a reference to the `mscorlib` assembly. This name is used to determine the name of the file that contains the actual assembly. The CLR takes the name of the assembly reference and appends `.dll`. For instance, in the last example, the CLR will look for a file called `mscorlib.dll`. The assembly `mscorlib` is a special assembly in .NET that contains all the definitions of the base types used in .NET, and is referenced by all assemblies.

## The .publickeytoken Directive

If the assembly being referenced contains a strong name, then a hash of the public key of the referenced assembly is stored as part of the record to the external reference. This hash is stored in the manifest using the `.publickeytoken` directive as part of the `.assembly extern` section. The assembly reference shown in Figure 17-4 contains a hash of the strong name of the `mscorlib` assembly. The stored hash of the strong name is compared at run time to a hash of the strong name (`.publickey`) contained within the referenced assembly to help ensure that the correct assembly is loaded. The value of the `.publickeytoken` is computed by taking the lower 8 bytes of a hash (`SHA1`) of the strong name of the referenced assemblies.

## The .ver Directive

The version of the assembly being referenced is also stored in the manifest. This version information is used with the rest of the information stored about a reference to ensure that the correct assembly is loaded (this is discussed later). If an application references version 1.1.0.0 of an assembly, it will not load version 2.1.0.0 of the assembly unless a version policy (also discussed later) exists to indicate otherwise. The version of the referenced assembly is stored in the manifest using the `.ver` directive as part of an `.assembly extern` section.

### The .locale Directive

If an assembly that is being referenced has a culture, then the culture information is also stored in the external assembly reference section, using the `.locale` directive. The combination of name, strong name (if it exists), version number, and culture are what constitute a unique version of an assembly.

## ASSEMBLIES AND DEPLOYMENT

The information in the manifest enables the reliable determination of the identity and version of an assembly. This is the basis for the deployment options available in .NET, and for the side-by-side execution of assemblies that helps .NET overcome DLL hell. This section looks at these issues in detail.

## Application-Private Assemblies

Prior to Windows RT, assemblies could be of two types. The first is an application-private assembly. As the name implies, this type of assembly is used by one application only and is not shared. This was the default style of assembly in .NET and is the main mechanism by which an application can be independent of changes to the system. Windows RT, which deploys applications using the Windows store, does not support this type of assembly.

Application-private assemblies are deployed into the application's own directory. Because application-private assemblies are not shared, they do not need a strong name. This means that at a minimum, they need to have only a name and version number in the identity section of the manifest. Because the assemblies are private to the application, the application does not perform version checks on the assemblies, as the application developer has control over the assemblies that are deployed to the application directory. If strong names exist, however, the CLR will verify that they match.

If all the assemblies that an application uses are application-private and the CLR is already installed on the target machine, then deployment is quite simple. Typically, such applications are deployed via simple folder copy, although other deployment models do exist.

## Shared Assemblies

The second type of assembly is the shared assembly. As the name suggests, this type of assembly can be shared among several different applications that reside on the same server. Note this definition isn't focused on assemblies targeting Windows RT. However, for the purposes of this chapter, which is carrying out actions that aren't Windows RT compatible, the concepts are sufficient although the implementation is slightly different.

This type of assembly should be used only when it is important to share assemblies among many applications—for example, if a custom third-party control suite typically purchased as part of a package is packaged this way. The when it is used in multiple applications, it can be installed as a shared version of the assembly. Alternatively, each application would install a separate copy of it. The .NET Framework assemblies themselves are also examples of shared assemblies.

Certain requirements are placed upon shared assemblies. The assembly needs to have a globally unique name, which is not a requirement of application-private assemblies. As mentioned earlier, a strong name is used to create a globally unique name for an assembly. As the assembly is shared, all references to the shared assembly are checked to ensure that the correct version is being used by an application.

Shared assemblies are stored in the global assembly cache (GAC), which is usually located in the assembly folder in the Windows directory (in a typical Windows installation, `C:\Windows\assembly`). However, it's not enough to just copy an assembly into that directory. In fact, if you browse to that directory using Windows Explorer, you'll find that you can't just drag files in and out of it. The process for placing an assembly in the GAC requires registration, a process discussed in detail later in this chapter.

No other changes to the code of the assembly are necessary to differentiate it from that of an application-private assembly. In fact, just because an assembly has a strong name does not mean that it has to be deployed as a shared assembly; it could just as easily be deployed in the application directory as an application-private assembly.

Installing a shared assembly into the GAC requires administrator rights on the machine. This is another factor complicating deployment of shared assemblies. Because of the extra effort involved in the creation and deployment of shared assemblies, you should avoid this type of assembly.

## The Global Assembly Cache

Each computer that has the .NET run time installed has a global assembly cache. However, assemblies in the GAC are always stored in the same folder, no matter which version of .NET you have. The folder is a subfolder of your main Windows folder, and it is named Assembly. If you have multiple versions of the .NET Framework, assemblies in the GAC for all of them are stored in this directory.

As previously noted, a strong name is required for an assembly placed in that GAC. That strong name is used to identify a particular assembly. However, another piece of metadata is also used for verification of an assembly. When an assembly is created, a hash of the assembly is placed in the metadata. If an assembly is changed (with a binary editor, for example), the hash of the assembly will no longer match the hash in the metadata. The metadata hash is checked against the actual hash when an assembly is placed in the GAC with the `gacutil.exe` utility. If the two hash codes do not match, the installation cannot be completed.

The strong name is also used when an application resolves a reference to an external assembly. It checks whether the public key stored in the assembly is equal to the hash of the public key stored as part of the reference in the application. If the two do not match, then the application knows that the external assembly has not been created by the original author of the assembly.

You can view the assemblies contained within the GAC by navigating to the directory using the Windows Explorer. The `gacutil.exe` utility that ships with .NET is used to add and remove assemblies from the GAC. To add an assembly into the GAC with the `gacutil.exe` tool, use the following command line:

```
gacutil.exe /i myassembly.dll
```

Recall that the assembly being loaded must have a strong name.

To remove an assembly, use the `/u` option, like this:

```
gacutil.exe /u myassembly.dll
```

`gacutil.exe` has a number of other options. You can examine them and see examples of their usage by typing in the following command:

```
gacutil.exe /?
```

## VERSIONING ISSUES

In COM, the versioning of DLLs had some significant limitations. For example, a different DLL with the same nominal version number could be indistinguishable from the one desired.

.NET's versioning scheme was specifically designed to alleviate the problems of COM. The major capabilities of .NET that solve versioning issues are as follows:

➤ Application isolation

➤ Side-by-side execution

➤ Self-describing components

## Application Isolation

For an application to be isolated, it should be self-contained and independent. This means that the application should rely on its own dependencies for ActiveX controls, components, or files, and not share those files with other applications. The option of having application isolation is essential for a good solution to versioning problems.

If an application is isolated, components are owned, managed, and used by the parent application alone. If a component is used by another application, even if it is the same version, the other application must have its own copy. This ensures that each application can install and uninstall dependencies and not interfere with other applications.

> **NOTE** *Does this sound familiar? Gray-haired people may recall that this is what most early Windows and DOS applications did until COM required registration of DLLs in the registry and placement of shared DLLs in the system directory.*

The .NET Framework enables application isolation by allowing developers to create application-private assemblies. These are in the application's own directory; and if another application needs the same assembly, it can be duplicated in that application's directory.

This means that each application is independent from the others. This isolation works best for many scenarios. It is sometimes referred to as a *zero-impact deployment* because when you either install or uninstall such an application, you are in no danger of causing problems for any other application.

## Side-By-Side Execution

Side-by-side execution occurs when multiple versions of the same assembly can run at the same time. Side-by-side execution is performed by the CLR. Components that are to execute side by side must be installed within the application directory or a subdirectory of it.

With application assemblies, versioning is not much of an issue. The interfaces are dynamically resolved by the CLR. If you replace an application assembly with a different version, the CLR will load it and make it work with the other assemblies in the application, as long as the new version doesn't have any interface incompatibilities. The new version may even have interface elements that are new and therefore don't exist in the old version (new properties or methods). As long as the existing class interface elements used by the other application assemblies are unchanged, the new version will work fine. In the following discussion of exactly how the CLR locates a referenced assembly, you'll learn more about how this works.

## Self-Describing Components

In the earlier section on the manifest, the self-describing nature of .NET assemblies was mentioned. The term "self-describing" means that all the information the CLR needs to know to load and execute an assembly is inside the assembly itself.

Self-describing components are essential to side-by-side execution. Once the CLR knows which version is needed, everything else about the assembly needed to run side by side is in the assembly itself. Each application can get its own version of an assembly, and all the work to coordinate the versions in memory is performed transparently by the CLR.

Versioning becomes more important with shared assemblies. Without good coordination of versions, .NET applications with shared assemblies are subject to some of the same problems as COM applications. In particular, if a new version of a shared assembly is placed in the GAC, then there must be a means to control which applications get which version of a shared assembly. This is accomplished with a *versioning policy*.

## Version Policies

As discussed earlier, a version number includes four parts: major, minor, build, and revision. The version number is part of the identity of the assembly. When a new version of a shared assembly is created and placed in the GAC, any of these parts can change. Which ones change affects how the CLR views compatibility for the new assembly.

When the version number of a component only changes according to its build and revision parts, it is considered compatible. This is often referred to as *Quick Fix Engineering* (*QFE*). It's only necessary to place the new assembly in the GAC, and it will automatically be considered compatible with applications that were created to use the folder version, even though those applications are expecting a different build number and revision. If either the major or minor build number changes, however, compatibility is over.

When an application comes across a type that is implemented in an external reference, the CLR has to determine what version of the referenced assembly to load. What steps does the CLR go through to ensure that the correct version of an assembly is loaded? To answer this question, you need to understand version policies and how they affect which version of an assembly is loaded.

## The Default Versioning Policy

Let's start by looking at the default versioning policy. This policy is followed in the absence of any configuration files that would modify the versioning policy. The runtime default behavior is to consult the manifest for the name of the referenced assembly and the version of the assembly to use.

If the referenced assembly does not contain a strong name, then it is assumed that the referenced assembly is application-private and is located in the application's directory. The CLR takes the name of the referenced assembly and appends .dll to create the filename that contains the referenced assembly's manifest. The CLR then searches in the application's directory for the filename. If it's found, then it uses the version indicated, even if the version number is different from the one specified in the manifest. Therefore, the version numbers of application-private assemblies are not checked, because the application developer, in theory, has control over which assemblies are deployed to the application's directory. If the file cannot be found, the CLR raises a System .IO.FileNotFoundException.

## Loading Assemblies

Unlike the default policy, which relies on an assembly being located in the local folder, if the referenced assembly contains a strong name, the process by which an assembly is loaded is different. The CLR instead goes through a process of checking multiple possible locations for the correct copy of the assembly to load. This process follows the following steps.

**1.** The three different types of assembly configuration files (discussed later) are consulted, if they exist, to see whether they contain any settings that will modify which version of the assembly the CLR should load.

**2.** The CLR then checks whether the assembly has been requested and loaded in a previous call. If it has, it uses the loaded assembly.

**3.** If the assembly is not already loaded, then the GAC is queried for a match. If a match is found, it is used by the application.

**4.** If any of the configuration files contains a codebase (discussed later) entry for the assembly, then the assembly is looked for in the location specified. If the assembly cannot be found in the location specified in the codebase, then a TypeLoadException is raised to the application.

**5.** If there are no configuration files or no codebase entries for the assembly, then the CLR probes for the assembly starting in the application's base directory.

6. If the assembly still isn't found, then the CLR asks the Windows Installer service if it has the assembly in question. If it does, then the assembly is installed and the application uses it. This is a feature called *on-demand installation*.

If the assembly hasn't been found by the end of this entire process, then a `TypeLoadException` is raised.

Although a referenced assembly contains a strong name, this does not mean that it has to be deployed into the GAC. This enables application developers to install a version with the application that is known to work. The GAC is consulted to see whether it contains a version of an assembly with a higher build revision number to enable administrators to deploy an updated assembly without having to reinstall or rebuild the application.

## Configuration Files

The default versioning policy described earlier may not be the most appropriate policy for your requirements. Fortunately, you can modify this policy through the use of XML configuration files to meet your specific needs. Two types of configuration files can hold versioning information:

1. The first is an *application configuration file*, and it is created in the application directory. As the name implies, this configuration file applies to a single application only. You need to create the application configuration file in the application directory with the same name as the application filename and append `.config`. For example, if you have a Windows Forms application called `HelloWorld.exe` installed in the `C:\HelloWorld` directory, then the application configuration file would be `C:\HelloWorld\HelloWorld.exe.config`. Note the `app.config` file in your project is this file. At compilation that file is copied to the folder you're your application and given the appropriate name.

2. The second type of configuration file is called the *machine configuration file*. It is named `machine.config` and can be found in the `C:\Windows\Microsoft.NET\Framework\v4.0.xxxx\CONFIG` directory. The `machine.config` file overrides any other configuration files on a machine and can be thought of as containing global settings. It is not considered best practice to change this file for a single application.

The main purpose of configuration files is to provide binding-related information to the developer or administrator who wishes to override the default policy handling of the CLR.

The configuration file is in XML and has a root node named `<configuration>`. The configuration file is divided into specific types of nodes that represent different areas of control. These areas are as follows:

➤ Startup

➤ Runtime

➤ Remoting

➤ Crypto

➤ Class API

➤ Security

Although all of these areas are important, this chapter covers only the first two. All of the settings discussed can be added to the application configuration file. Some of the settings (these are pointed out) can also be added to the machine configuration file. If a setting in the application configuration file conflicts with one in the machine configuration file, then the setting in the machine configuration file is used. When talking about assembly references in the following discussion of configuration settings, this refers exclusively to *shared assemblies* (which implies that the assemblies have a strong name, as required by assemblies in the GAC).

## Startup Settings

The `<startup>` node of the application and machine configuration files has a `<supportedRuntime>` node that specifies the runtime version required by the application. This is because different versions of the CLR can run on a machine side by side. The following example shows how Visual Studio uses the configuration file to identify the correct version of the .NET runtime to host the application at runtime.

```
<configuration>
  <startup>
    <supportedRuntime version ="4.0 " sku=".NETFramework,Version=v4.5" />
  </startup>
</configuration>
```

## Runtime Settings

The runtime node, which is written as `<runtime>`, can be used to specify settings that manage how the CLR handles garbage collection and versions of assemblies. With these settings, you can specify which version of an assembly the application requires, or redirect it to another version entirely.

### Loading a Particular Version of an Assembly

The application and machine configuration files can be used to ensure that a particular version of an assembly is loaded. In those situations where the default load order might result in loading an incompatible version of your DLL, you can indicate the specific version that should be loaded. This functionality is supported through the use of the `<assemblyIdentity>` and `<bindingRedirect>` elements in the configuration file. The following snippet demonstrates how these nodes would look within your project's `app.config` file.

```
<configuration>
  <runtime>
    <assemblyBinding xmlns="urn:schemas-microsoft-com:asm.v1">
      <dependentAssembly>
        <assemblyIdentity name="AssemblyName"
                          publickeytoken="b77a5c561934e089"
                          culture="en-us"/>
          <bindingRedirect oldVersion="*"
                           newVersion="2.1.50.0"/>

      </dependentAssembly>
    </assemblyBindings>
  </runtime>
</configuration>
```

The <assemblyBinding> node is used to declare settings for the locations of assemblies and redirections via the <dependentAssembly> node and the <probing> node (which you will look at shortly).

In the last example, when the CLR resolves the reference to the assembly named AssemblyName, it loads version 2.1.50.0 instead of the version that appears in the manifest. If you want to load only version 2.1.50.0 of the assembly when a specific version is referenced, for example version 2.0.25.0 , then you can replace the value of the oldVersion attribute with the version number that you would like to replace. In that situation, if the application was still referencing version 2.0.0.0 by default, the application would still reference that version. The publickeytoken attribute is used to store the hash of the strong name of the assembly to replace. This ensures that the correct assembly is identified. The same is true of the culture attribute.

## Defining the Location of an Assembly

The location of an assembly can also be defined in both the application and machine configuration files. You can use the <codeBase> element to inform the CLR of the location of an assembly. This enables you to distribute an application and have the externally referenced assemblies downloaded the first time they are used (on-demand downloading):

```
<configuration>
  <runtime>
    <assemblyBinding xmlns="urn:schemas-microsoft-com:asm.v1">
      <dependentAssembly>
        <assemblyIdentity name="AssemblyName"
                          publickeytoken="b77a5c561934e089"
                          culture="en-us"/>
        <codeBase version="2.1.50.0"
                  href="http://www.wrox.com/AssemblyName.dll/>
      </dependentAssembly>
    </assemblyBindings>
  </runtime>
</configuration>
```

You can see from this example that whenever a reference to version 2.1.50.0 of the assembly AssemblyName is resolved (and the assembly isn't already on the user's computer), the CLR will try to load the assembly from the location defined in the href attribute. The location defined in the href attribute is a standard URL and can be used to locate a file across the Internet or locally.

If the assembly cannot be found or the details in the manifest of the assembly defined in the href attribute do not match those defined in the configuration file, then the loading of the assembly will fail and you will receive a TypeLoadException. If the version of the assembly in the preceding example were actually 2.1.60.0, then the assembly would load because the version number is only different by build and revision number.

## Providing the Search Path

The final use of configuration files to consider is that of providing the search path to use when locating assemblies in the application's directory. This setting applies only to the application configuration file (AppName.exe.config, for example). By default, the CLR searches for an assembly only in the application's base directory — it will not look in any subdirectories. You can modify this behavior by using the `<probing>` element in an application configuration file, as shown in the following example:

```
<configuration>
  <runtime>
    <assemblyBinding xmlns="urn:schemas-microsoft-com:asm.v1">
      <probing privatePath="regional"/>
    </assemblyBinding>
  </runtime>
</configuration>
```

The `privatePath` attribute can contain a list of directories relative to the application's directory (separated by a semicolon) that you would like the CLR to search when trying to locate an assembly. The `privatePath` attribute cannot contain an absolute pathname.

As part of resolving an assembly reference, the CLR checks in the application's base directory for it. If it cannot find it, then it looks through, in order, all the subdirectories specified in the `privatePath` variable, as well as looking for a subdirectory with the same name as the assembly. If the assembly being resolved is called `AssemblyName`, then the CLR also checks for the assembly in a subdirectory called `AssemblyName`, if it exists.

This isn't the end of the story, though. If the referenced assembly being resolved contains a culture setting, then the CLR also checks for culture-specific subdirectories in each of the directories it searches in. For example, if the CLR is trying to resolve a reference to an assembly named `AssemblyName` with a culture of en and a `privatePath` equal to that in the last example, and the application being run has a home directory of `C:\ExampleApp`, then the CLR will look in the following directories (in the order shown):

➤   `C:\ExampleApp`

➤   `C:\ExampleApp\en`

➤   `C:\ExampleApp\en\AssemblyName`

➤   `C:\ExampleApp\regional\en`

➤   `C:\ExampleApp\regional\en\AssemblyName`

As you can see, the CLR can probe quite a number of directories to locate an assembly. When an external assembly is resolved by the CLR, it consults the configuration files first to determine whether it needs to modify the process by which it resolves an assembly. As discussed, you can modify the resolution process to suit your needs.

## BASICS OF REFLECTION

As mentioned in Chapter 2, you can explore the internals of a given assembly using a process called *reflection*. You can find out what assemblies are loaded into your current application domain. You can discover what types reside in each assembly, and for any given type, the methods and properties exposed by the type. You can even execute a method or change a property value via reflection, even though you might not know the name of the method or property at compile time.

In this section, you'll see the basic code required for each of these operations. The code uses classes in the `System.Reflection` namespace, most notably the `Assembly` class, and each example assumes that the code module has an `Imports` statement to import `System.Reflection`.

Major classes needed to use reflection capabilities include the following:

➤ **`Assembly`**—Contains members to examine an assembly's metadata and even manipulate the assembly

➤ **`AppDomain`**—Contains information about the currently running application domain

➤ **`Type`**—Gives access to information about a .NET type

After this section, you will also see an additional capability provided through reflection: dynamic loading. You'll see how to gain a reference to an assembly on the fly and generate an instance of a type within the assembly.

> **NOTE** *While the process of reflection is powerful and enables you to perform operations that would otherwise be impossible, you should be aware of the performance implications of using reflection heavily. Some reflection operations are rather slow; code that contains many such operations, as in a loop, can cause your program to experience noticeable delays.*

## The Assembly Class

Almost all work with reflection will require you to work with the `Assembly` class. An instance of this class is associated with a .NET assembly.

There are several ways to get a reference to an instance of an `Assembly` class. Several shared methods of the `Assembly` class can return such an instance. The ones most commonly used are:

➤ **`GetAssembly`**—Takes a Type instance and returns a reference to the assembly containing that Type. The assembly must already be available in the current application domain.

➤ **`GetExecutingAssembly`**—Returns the assembly that contains the code currently being executed.

➤ **`LoadFile`**—Loads an assembly using a string containing the filename in which the assembly resides.

➤ **`LoadFrom`**—Loads an assembly from a string containing a filename or URL.

Here is a code example that gets an assembly reference using each of the first three of these methods. The fourth method is covered in the section on dynamic loading later in the chapter.

```
Dim Assembly1 As [Assembly]
Assembly1 = [Assembly].GetAssembly(GetType(System.Boolean))
' This would return a reference to mscorlib

Dim Assembly2 As [Assembly]
```

```
Assembly2 = [Assembly].GetExecutingAssembly
' This would return a reference to the assembly
' containing this code.

Dim Assembly3 As [Assembly]
Dim sFileName As String
sFileName = "C:\Dev\MyProject\bin\Release\MyLibrary.dll"
Assembly3 = [Assembly].LoadFile(sFileName)
```

You can also get a reference to an assembly by first getting a list of the assemblies loaded into an application and then choosing an assembly from that list.

## Getting Currently Loaded Assemblies

The application domain is the context for your current running application. You can work with an application domain using the `AppDomain` class in the `System` namespace. `AppDomain` has a shared property called `CurrentDomain` that will return the application domain in which you are currently running.

An application domain instance has a `GetAssemblies` method to obtain the assemblies currently loaded in the application domain. `GetAssemblies` returns an array of type `Assembly`.

Putting these capabilities together, you can print out the long name of each assembly in the current application domain using the following code:

```
Dim LoadedAssemblies As Assembly()
'Get the list of loaded assemblies from the current AppDomain.
LoadedAssemblies = AppDomain.CurrentDomain.GetAssemblies()

For Each LoadedAssembly In LoadedAssemblies
    ' There are many operations available on
    ' each assembly. This code simply lists the
    ' assembly's full name.
    Console.WriteLine(LoadedAssembly.FullName)
Next
```

## The Type Class

Chapter 2 discussed types in .NET. To recap, a type is a class, structure, or native value type such as a `Double` or `Boolean`.

A type is represented during reflection by an instance of the `Type` class. As Chapter 2 explained, you can get a reference to a type by using the `GetType` method of the type. However, you can also get a reference to a type via a method on an instance of the `Assembly` class that is associated with the assembly containing the type.

### Finding the Types in an Assembly

The `GetTypes` method of an `Assembly` class instance returns an array containing all the types in the assembly. You can also get a reference to a single type in an assembly with the `GetType` method, which takes a string with the fully qualified namespace pathname of the type.

For example, the following code will print out the names of all the types in the assembly containing the currently executing code:

```
Dim CurrentAssembly As [Assembly]
CurrentAssembly = [Assembly].GetExecutingAssembly
For Each IndividualType In CurrentAssembly.GetTypes
    Console.WriteLine(IndividualType.Name)
Next
```

## Finding the Members of a Type

Reflection also allows you to explore a type and discover the members (properties and methods) of the type. The GetProperties method of a type will return an array of property descriptor objects, and the GetMethods method will return an array of method descriptors in the form of MethodInfo instances. The more general GetMembers method will return all the members of a Type, including properties, methods, events, and so forth. The following code, when placed inside a class, will print out all the properties, events, and public methods for the class:

```
For Each Member In Me.GetType.GetMembers
    Console.WriteLine(Member.Name)
Next

For Each IndividualProperty In Me.GetType.GetProperties
    Console.WriteLine(IndividualProperty.Name)
Next
```

There is some redundancy between these two methods. At a binary level, properties are actually pairs of get and set methods. That means you will see the get and set methods for a type's properties when you list out the methods.

Visual Basic Sub and Function routines are both considered methods in reflection. The only difference is that a Sub has no return value. If a method is a Function, and thus does have a return value, reflection allows you to discover the type of that return value.

Methods may have calling parameters. Reflection allows you to discover the calling parameters of a method, if there are any, using the GetParameters method of the MethodInfo instance for the method. The GetParameters method returns an array of ParameterInfo objects.

Using parameters, if any, a method can be invoked with the Invoke method of the MethodInfo instance. Suppose, for example, that the current class has a function named CalculateFee that takes an integer for customer ID and returns a decimal value.

Here is sample code to print the parameters for the method:

```
Dim MyMethodInfo As MethodInfo = Me.GetType.GetMember("CalculateFee")(0)
For Each ParamInfo In MyMethodInfo.GetParameters
    Console.WriteLine("Parameter name:" & ParamInfo.Name)
    Console.WriteLine("Parameter type:" & ParamInfo.ParameterType.Name)
Next
```

To set up the parameter values and invoke the method, the code would look like this:

```
Dim MyMethodInfo2 As MethodInfo = _ Me.GetType.GetMember("CalculateFee")(0)

'Create array of objects to serve as parameters.
'In this case, only one integer is needed.
Dim MyParameters() As Object = {4321}
Dim oReturn As Object
oReturn = MyMethodInfo2.Invoke(Me, MyParameters)
' Now cast oReturn to Decimal
```

The code download for this chapter includes a WPF program (`AssemblyBrowser`) that enables you to locate an assembly on disk and load the types from that assembly. For any type available in the assembly, you can then load all the methods of the type.

# DYNAMIC LOADING OF ASSEMBLIES

The preceding discussion about locating and loading assemblies refers to assemblies that are known at compile time through the application's references. There is an alternative method of locating and loading an assembly that is useful for certain scenarios.

In this technique, the location of the assembly is supplied by the application, using a URL or filename. The normal rules for locating the assembly do not apply — only the location specified by the application is used.

The location is just a string variable, so it may come from a configuration file or a database. In fact, the assembly to be loaded may be newly created, and perhaps did not even exist when the original application was compiled. Because the information to load the assembly can be passed into the application on the fly at run time, this type of assembly loading is called *dynamic loading*.

## The LoadFrom Method of the Assembly Class

The `Assembly` class has a shared method called `LoadFrom` that takes a URL or filename and returns a reference to the assembly at that location. Here's a code example of `LoadFrom` in action, getting an assembly reference from a URL:

```
Dim asmDynamic As [Assembly]
asmDynamic = [Assembly].LoadFrom("http://www.dotnetmasters.com/DynamicWindows.dll")
```

As previously discussed, the brackets around `Assembly` are needed because it is a reserved keyword in Visual Basic. The brackets indicate that the word applies to the `Assembly` class, and the keyword is not being used.

After these lines are executed, the code contains a reference to the assembly at the given location. That enables the reflection operations discussed earlier for finding types in the assembly. Recall that one such operation is getting a reference to a particular type (which could be a class, a structure, or an enumeration) in the assembly.

For dynamic loading, normally the `GetType` method of the `Assembly` class is used to get the reference, using a string that represents the identification of the type. The identification consists of the full namespace path that uniquely identifies the type within the current application. Once a reference to a type is obtained, an instance of the type can be created, even though the assembly was loaded dynamically.

For example, suppose that you wanted to get an instance of a certain form in the assembly, with a namespace path of `MyProject.MainWindow`. The following line of code would get a reference to the type for that form:

```
Dim typMyWindow As Type = formAsm.GetType("MyProject.MainWindow")
```

The type reference can then be used to generate an instance of the type. To do this, you need another class in the `System` namespace called the `Activator` class. This class has a shared method called `CreateInstance`, which takes a type reference and returns an instance of that type. You could, therefore, get an instance of the form with these lines:

```
Dim window As Object
window = Activator.CreateInstance(typeMyWindow)
```

`CreateInstance` always returns a generic object. That means it may be necessary to coerce the returned reference to a particular type to gain access to the type's interface. For example, assuming that you knew the object was actually a WPF window, you could cast the preceding instance into the type of `System.Windows.Window` and then do normal operations available on that window:

```
Dim FormToShow As Form = CType(objForm, Window)
FormToShow.MdiParent = Me
FormToShow.Show()
```

At this point, the form will operate normally. It will behave no differently from a form that was in a referenced assembly.

If the newly loaded form needs to load other classes in the dynamic assembly, nothing special needs to be done. For example, suppose that the form just shown needs to load an instance of another form, named `Window2`, that resides in the same dynamically loaded assembly. The standard code to instantiate a window will work fine. The CLR will automatically load the `Window2` type, because it already has a reference to the assembly containing `Window2`.

Furthermore, suppose that the dynamically loaded form needs to instantiate a class from another DLL that is not referenced by the application. For example, suppose that the form needs to create an instance of a `Customer` object, and the `Customer` class is in a different DLL. As long as that DLL is in the same folder as the dynamically loaded DLL, the CLR will automatically locate and load the second DLL.

## Dynamic Loading Example

To see dynamic loading in action, try the following step-by-step example:

1. Create a new WPF Application project in Visual Studio and name it ProVB2012_Ch17. Place a single button on the window, and change its content to Open Window.

**2.** Double-click the Open Window button to get to its Click event in the Code Editor. Then go to the top of the code module and insert the following `Imports` statement:

```
Imports System.Reflection
```

**3.** Insert the code shown in Listing 17-1 into the button's Click event (code file: `MainWindow .xaml.vb`):

```
Private Sub Button_Click_1(sender As Object, e As RoutedEventArgs)
    Dim sLocation As String = "C:\Temp\ProVB2012_DynamicWindows.dll"
    If My.Computer.FileSystem.FileExists(sLocation) Then
        Dim sType As String = "ProVB2012_DynamicWindows.MainWindow"
        Dim DynamicAssembly As [Assembly] = _
                [Assembly].LoadFrom(sLocation)
        Dim DynamicType As Type = DynamicAssembly.GetType(sType)
        Dim DynamicObject As Object
        DynamicObject = Activator.CreateInstance(DynamicType)
        ' We know it's a form - cast to form type
        Dim WindowToShow As Window = CType(DynamicObject, Window)
        WindowToShow.Show()
    Else
        MsgBox("Unable to load assembly " & sLocation & _
                " because the file does not exist")
    End If
End Sub
```

**4.** Run the program and click the Open Window button. You should get a message box with the message "Unable to load assembly `C:\Temp\ProVB2012_DynamicWindows.dll` because the form does not exist." Leave this program running while you carry out the next few steps.

**5.** Start another separate Visual Studio instance, and create a new Windows Forms Application project named ProVB2012_DynamicWindows. On the blank `MainWindow` that appears, drag over a few controls. It doesn't really matter what controls you drag onto the `MainWindow`. The version that can be downloaded for the book includes some labels, and text boxes.

**6.** In the properties for ProVB2012_DynamicWindows, first be certain to uncheck the check box labeled "Enable application framework." Then change the application type to WPF Class Library.

**7.** Build the ProVB2012_DynamicWindows project by selecting Build ➪ Build ProVB2012_ DynamicWindows from the Visual Studio menu. This will place a file named `ProVB2012_ DynamicWindows.dll` in the project's `\bin\Debug` directory (or the `\bin\Release` directory if you happen to have the Release configuration set in Visual Studio).

**8.** Create a directory named `C:\Temp` and copy the `ProVB2012_DynamicWindows.dll` file to that directory.

**9.** Return to the running program ProVB2012_DynamicWindows. Click the Load button again. This time, it should load the assembly from the DLL you just copied and launch an instance of `Form1` from the ProVB2012_DynamicWindows project.

Notice that the `ProVB2012_DynamicWindows.dll` was created and compiled after the `ProVB2012_ Ch17.exe` project that loaded it. It is not necessary to recompile or even restart `ProVB2012_Ch17`

.exe to load a new assembly dynamically, as long as `ProVB2012_Ch17.exe` knows the location of the assembly and the type to be loaded from it.

## Putting Assemblies to Work

The previous code examples include hard-coded strings for the location of the assembly and the identification of the type. There are uses for such a technique, such as certain types of Internet deployment of an application. However, when using dynamic loading, it is common for these values to be obtained from outside the code. For example, a database table or an XML-based configuration file can be used to store the information.

This enables you to add new capabilities to a .NET application on the fly. A new assembly with new functionality can be written, and then the location of the assembly and the identity of the type to load from the assembly can be added to the configuration file or database table. Of course this same behavior is completely unacceptable in a fully managed environment such as Windows RT.

Unlike application assemblies automatically located by the CLR, which must be in the application's directory or a subdirectory of it, dynamically loaded assemblies can be anywhere the application knows how to access. Possibilities include the following:

- ➤ A website
- ➤ A directory on the local machine
- ➤ A directory on a shared network machine

The security privileges available to code vary, depending on where the assembly was loaded from. Code loaded from a URL via HTTP has a very restricted set of privileges by default compared to code loaded from a local directory.

## SUMMARY

Assemblies are the basic unit of deployment and versioning in .NET. You can write and install simple applications without knowing much about assemblies. More complex applications require an in-depth understanding of the structure of assemblies, the metadata they contain, and how assemblies are located and loaded by the CLR.

You have learned how the identity of an assembly is used to allow multiple versions of an assembly to be installed on a machine and run side by side. This chapter explained how an assembly is versioned, the process by which the CLR resolves an external assembly reference, and how you can modify this process through the use of configuration files.

You also learned about how an assembly stores information, such as version number, strong name, and culture, about any external assemblies that it references, and information checked at run time to ensure that the correct version of the assembly is referenced. You saw how you can use versioning policies to override this in the case of a buggy assembly. The assembly is the single biggest aid in reducing the errors that can occur due to DLL hell, and in helping with deployment.

You've also seen how to examine assemblies to discover the types they contain, and the members of those types. You can even invoke a method on a type using the capabilities of reflection.

The chapter also discussed the capability to load an assembly dynamically, based on a location that is derived at run time. This capability is useful for some special deployment scenarios, such as simple Internet deployment, but completely unavailable in others such as Windows RT. Understanding all these elements helps you understand how to structure an application, when and how to use shared assemblies, and the deployment implications of your choices for assemblies.

Simple applications are usually created with no strong names or shared assemblies, and all assemblies for the application are deployed to the application directory. Versioning issues are rare as long as class interfaces are consistent.

Complex applications may require shared assemblies to be placed in the GAC, which means that those assemblies must have strong names, and you must control your version numbers. You also need to understand your options for allowing an application to load a version of an assembly other than the one it would load by default, or for loading assemblies dynamically using an application-specific technique to determine the assembly's location.

The next chapter looks in more detail at how your application interacts with the operating system's built-in security requirements. It also takes a closer look at the new security models that default to fewer privileges at run time, and how you can interact with and adjust for that behavior.

# 18

# Security in the .NET Framework

**WHAT'S IN THIS CHAPTER?**

- ➤ Concepts and definitions
- ➤ Permissions
- ➤ Roles
- ➤ Principals
- ➤ Code access permissions
- ➤ Role-based permissions
- ➤ Identity permissions
- ➤ User Access Control (UAC)
- ➤ Encryption
- ➤ Hashing
- ➤ Symmetric Key Encryption
- ➤ Asymmetric Key Encryption
- ➤ Digital Signatures
- ➤ X.509 Certificates
- ➤ SSL

**WROX.COM CODE DOWNLOADS FOR THIS CHAPTER**

The wrox.com code downloads for this chapter are found at www.wrox.com/remtitle
.cgi?isbn=9781118314456 on the Download Code tab. The code is in the chapter 18
download and individually named according to the code filenames throughout the chapter.

This chapter covers the basics of security and cryptography. It begins with a brief discussion of the .NET Framework's security architecture, because this affects all the solutions you may choose to implement. Note that this chapter goes into detail on security concepts, which in some cases aren't applicable to applications running under Windows RT. That operating system manages user access and permissions at a different level, and some of the capabilities from the past are simply prohibited.

The .NET Framework provides you with tools, and core functionality with regard to security. You have the `System.Security.Permissions` namespace, which enables you to manage runtime permissions along with role-based and identity permissions. Through your code, you can control access to objects programmatically, as well as receive information on the current permissions of objects. This security framework will assist you in determining whether you have permissions to run your code, instead of getting halfway through execution and having to deal with permission-based exceptions.

Cryptography is the cornerstone of the .NET Web Services security model, so the second half of this chapter discusses the basis of cryptography and how to implement it. Specifically, it covers the following:

➤ Hash algorithms

➤ SHA

➤ MD5

➤ Secret key encryption

➤ Public key cryptography standard

➤ Digital signatures

➤ Certification

➤ Secure Sockets Layer communications

Let's begin by looking at some security concepts and definitions.

## SECURITY CONCEPTS AND DEFINITIONS

Table 18-1 describes the different types of security presented in this chapter and how they relate to real-world scenarios.

There are many approaches to providing security on the machines where your shared code is hosted. If multiple shared code applications are on one machine, each piece of shared code can be called from many front-end applications. Each piece of shared code will have its own security requirements for accessing environment variables—such as the registry, the file system, and other items—on the machine that it is running on. From an NTFS perspective, the administrator of your server can only lock down those items on the machine that are not required to be accessed from any piece of shared code running on it. Therefore, some applications require additional security built in to prevent application code from doing things it is not supposed to do.

To limit your Internet applications' access to the local file system, you create a permission set that limits that access and associates the Internet application group with this permission set. By default, the .NET environment provides one code group named All Code that is associated with the FullTrust permission set.

A permission set creates a combination of security configurations. This set defines what each authorized user has access to and what that user can do on that machine—for instance, whether the user can read environment variables or the file system, or execute other code.

Security that is used within the programming environment also makes use of permission sets. Through code you can control access to files in a file system, environment variables, file dialogues, isolated storage, reflections, registry, sockets, and UI. Isolated storage and virtual file systems are new operating-system-level storage locations that can be used by programs and are governed by the machine security policies. These file systems keep a machine safe from file system intrusion by designating a regulated area for file storage. The main access to these items is controlled through code access permissions.

Although many methods used in Visual Basic provide an identifiable return value, the only time you get a return value from security methods is when the method fails. When a security method succeeds, it does not provide a return value. If it fails, then it returns an exception object reflecting the specific error that occurred.

**TABLE 18-1:** Types of Security

| SECURITY TYPE | RELATED CONCEPT IN SECURITY .PERMISSIONS NAMESPACE | PURPOSE |
|---|---|---|
| NTFS | None | Allows for detailed file system rights, e.g., locking down of specific files. |
| Cryptographic | Strong name and assembly, generation, SignCode.exe utility | Use of public key infrastructure and certificates. |
| Programmatic | Groups and permission sets | For use in pieces of code that are being called into. Provides extra security to prevent users of calling code from violating security measures implemented by the programs that are not provided for on a machine level. |
| User Access Control | Users run without administrative permission | Provided by the operating system to help users protect their system from unexpected changes that might occur when logged in using the machine's administrator account. |

# WINDOWS STORE PROJECTS

One of the ways a Windows RT application are by definition slightly more limited than those of a traditional .NET application are based on limitations imposed by the Windows Store. When you create a Visual Basic application that targets the Windows Store you will have a requirement for an additional set of permission requests.

Figure 18-1 shows a newly created sample Windows Store application. This Visual Basic application includes a `Package.appxmanifest` file. After you open this file for editing, it is possible to modify many of the characteristics associated with your application—from UI elements associated with your application, and Packaging considerations, to a description of key capabilities aka system features—that your application will access.

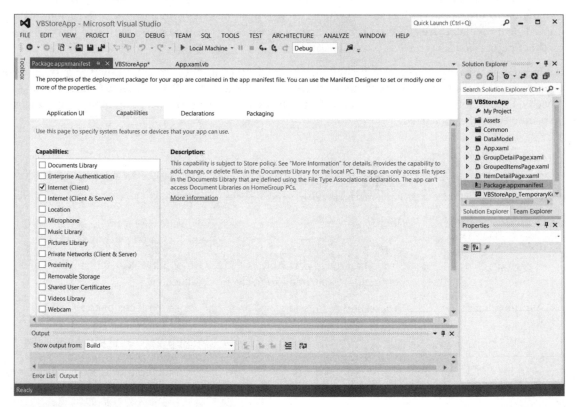

**FIGURE 18-1:** Defining Windows Store app access permissions

The Capabilities tab is selected in Figure 18-1 because it could also be labeled "Permissions." This tab is where you must define what access to the file system and related system features your application will use. Unlike the other security elements that this chapter will discuss, this section defaults to no access with the exception of network access.

More important, because your application will deploy through the Windows Store and as such be tested for compatibility with the selections you make on this page—these become the first level of security within your application. Keep in mind that the Windows Store is going to publish exactly how much permission your application is requesting, so just defaulting to asking for everything isn't going to be well received.

The reality is that when you are developing a Windows Store application you are going to be working with an additional security layer not present for traditional .NET applications. This display is a good reflection of how as Windows moves to a more controlled runtime environment, you will need to be more explicit in providing the metadata that describes what capabilities your application provides and consumes. Of course these new limitations are in addition to the security controls that already exist for .NET applications.

# THE SYSTEM.SECURITY.PERMISSIONS NAMESPACE

The `System.Security.Permissions` namespace is the namespace used in code to establish and use permissions associated with objects, including the file system, environment variables, and the registry. The namespace controls access to both operating-system-level objects as well as code objects. In order to use this namespace in your project, you need to import it. Using this namespace gives you access to the `CodeAccessPermission` and `PrincipalPermission` classes for using role-based permissions and information supplied by identity permissions. `CodeAccessPermission` controls access to the operating-system-level objects. Role-based permissions and identity permissions grant access to objects based on the identity of the user of the program that is running (the user context).

Table 18-2 lists the members of the `System.Security.Permissions` namespace that apply to Windows application programming. While there is a description accompanying each member, those classes that end with `Attribute`, such as `EnvironmentPermissionAttribute`, are classes that enable you to modify the security level at which your code is allowed to interact with each respective object. These objects create a declarative model for setting security that can be leveraged across multiple different implementation models.

**TABLE 18-2:** Members of System.Security.Permissions

| CLASS | DESCRIPTION |
| --- | --- |
| `CodeAccessSecurityAttribute` | Base class for code access security attribute classes. |
| `DataProtectionPermission` | Controls access to the data protection APIs, T. |
| `DataProtectionPermissionAttribute` | Allows declarative control of `DataProtectionPermssion` via code. |
| `EnvironmentPermission` | Controls the capability to see and modify system and user environment variables. |
| `EnvironmentPermissionAttribute` | Allows security actions for environment variables to be added via code. |
| `FileDialogPermission` | Controls the capability to open files via a file dialogue. |

*continues*

**TABLE 18-2** *(continued)*

| CLASS | DESCRIPTION |
|---|---|
| FileDialogPermissionAttribute | Allows security actions to be added for file dialogs via code. |
| FileIOPermission | Controls the capability to read and write files in the file system. |
| FileIOPermissionAttribute | Allows security actions to be added for file access attempts via code. |
| GacIdentityPermission | Defines the identity permissions for files that come from the global assembly cache (GAC). |
| GacIdentityPermissionAttribute | Allows security actions to be added for files that originate from the GAC. |
| HostProtectionAttribute | Allows for the use of security actions to determine host protection requirements. |
| IsolatedStorageFilePermission | Controls access to a private virtual file system within the isolated storage area of an application. |
| IsolatedStorageFilePermissionAttribute | Allows security actions to be added for private virtual file systems via code. |
| IsolatedStoragePermission | Controls access to the isolated storage area of an application. |
| IsolatedStoragePermissionAttribute | Allows security actions to be added for the isolated storage area of an application. |
| KeyContainerPermission | Controls access to key containers. |
| KeyContainerPermissionAccessEntry | Defines the access rights for particular key containers. |
| KeyContainerPermissionAccessEntryCollection | Represents a collection of KeyContainerPermission-AccessEntry objects. |
| KeyContainerPermissionAccessEntryEnumerator | Represents the enumerators for the objects contained in the KeyContainerPermission AccessEntryCollection object. |
| KeyContainerPermissionAttribute | Allows security actions to be added for key containers. |
| MediaPermission | The permission set associated with the capability to access audio, video, and images. WPF leverages this capability. |

| CLASS | DESCRIPTION |
| --- | --- |
| `MediaPermissionAttribute` | Allows code to set permissions related to the `MediaPermission` set. |
| `PermissionSetAttribute` | Allows security actions to be added for a permission set. |
| `PrincipalPermission` | Controls the capability to verity the active principal. |
| `PrincipalPermissionAttribute` | Allows verification of a specific user. Security principals are a user and role combination used to establish security identity. |
| `PublisherIdentityPermission` | Allows access based on the identity of a software publisher. |
| `PublisherIdentityPermissionAttribute` | Allows security to be defined for a software publisher. |
| `ReflectionPermission` | Controls access to nonpublic members of a given type. |
| `ReflectionPermissionAttribute` | Allows security to be defined for public and nonpublic members of a given type. |
| `RegistryPermission` | Controls access to registry keys and values. |
| `RegistryPermissionAttribute` | Allows security to be defined for the registry. |
| `ResourcePermissionBase` | Controls the capability to work with the code access security permissions. |
| `ResourcePermissionBaseEntry` | Allows you to define the smallest part of a code access security permission set. |
| `SecurityAttribute` | Controls which security attributes are representing code; used to control security when creating an assembly. |
| `SecurityPermission` | This collection is used in code to specify a set of permissions for which access will be defined. |
| `SecurityPermissionAttribute` | Allows security actions for the security permission flags. |
| `StorePermission` | Controls access to stores that contain X.509 certificates. |
| `StorePermissionAttribute` | Allows security actions to be added for access stores that contain X.509 certificates. |

*continues*

**TABLE 18-2** *(continued)*

| CLASS | DESCRIPTION |
|---|---|
| `StrongNameIdentityPermission` | Defines the permission level for creating strong names. |
| `StrongNameIdentityPermissionAttribute` | Allows security to be defined on the `StrongNameIdentityPermission` set. |
| `StrongNamePublicKeyBlob` | The public key information associated with a strong name. |
| `TypeDescriptorPermission` | Permission set that controls partial-trust access to the `TypeDescriptor` class. |
| `TypeDescriptorPermissionAttribute` | Allows security to be defined on the `TypeDescriptorPermission` set. |
| `UIPermission` | Controls access to user interfaces and use of the Windows clipboard. |
| `UIPermissionAttribute` | Allows security actions to be added for UI interfaces and the use of the clipboard. |
| `UrlIdentityPermission` | Permission set associated with the identity and related permissions for the URL from which code originates. |
| `UrlIdentityPermissionAttribute` | Allows security to be defined on the `UrlIdentityPermission` set. |
| `WebBrowserPermission` | Controls the capability to create the `WebBrowser` control. |
| `WebBrowserPermissionAttribute` | Allows security to be defined on the `WebBrowser Permission` set. |
| `ZoneIdentityPermission` | Defines the identity permission for the zone from which code originates. |
| `ZoneIdentityPermissionAttribute` | Allows security to be defined on the `ZoneIdentity Permission` set. |

The default environment will provide a given level of access. It is not possible to grant access beyond this level via code access security; however, when working with these classes you can specify exactly what should or should not be available in a given situation. Additionally, these classes have been marked to prevent inheritance. It really wouldn't be a very secure system if you could inherit from one of these classes. Code could be written to override the associated security methods and grant unlimited permissions.

Table 18-2 also deals with security in regard to software publishers. A *software publisher* is a specific entity that is using a digital signature to identify itself in a Web-based scenario.

# Code Access Permissions

Code access permissions are controlled through the CodeAccessPermission class within the System .Security namespace. The code access permissions are used extensively by the common language runtime (CLR) to manage and secure the operating environment.

The code access permissions grant and deny access to portions of the operating system such as the file system, but although your code can request permission changes, there is a key limit. Code using this API can request to reduce the rights of the user currently executing the code, but the API will not grant rights that a user does not have within his or her current context or based on those available from the CLR.

When code is downloaded from a website, and the user then attempts to run the code, the CLR can choose to limit the rights of that code given that it shouldn't by default be trusted. For example, requesting access to the system registry will be denied if the operating system does not trust that code. Thus, the primary use of code access security by application developers is to limit the permissions already available to a user given the current context of what the user is doing. Code access security leverages many of the same core security methods used across the various security categories, many of which are described in Table 18-3.

**TABLE 18-3:** Methods of CodeAccessPermission

| METHOD | DESCRIPTION |
| --- | --- |
| Assert | Sets the permission to full access so that the specific resource can be accessed even if the caller hasn't been granted permission to access the resource. |
| Copy | Copies a permission object. |
| Demand | Returns an exception unless all callers in the call chain have been granted the permission to access the resource in a given manner. |
| Deny | In prior versions of .NET you would use this to explicitly deny access. This will still work, but it's becoming obsolete and should be avoided. |
| Equals | Determines whether a given object is the same instance of the current object. |
| FromXml | Establishes a permission set given a specific XML encoding. This parameter that this method takes is an XML encoding. |
| Intersect | Returns the permissions that two permission objects have in common. |
| IsSubsetOf | Returns a result indicating whether the current permission object is a subset of a specified permission. |

*continues*

**TABLE 18-3** *(continued)*

| METHOD | DESCRIPTION |
|---|---|
| PermitOnly | Specifies that only those rights within this permission set can be accessed even if the user of the assembly has been granted additional permission to the underlying objects. This is one of the more common permission levels when working with custom permission sets. |
| RevertAll | Reverses all previous assert, deny, or permit-only methods. |
| RevertAssert | Reverses all previous assert methods. |
| RevertDeny | Reverses all previous deny methods. |
| RevertPermitOnly | Reverses all previous permit-only methods. |
| Union | Creates a permission that is the union of two permission objects. |

# Identity Permissions

Identity permissions are pieces of information, also called *evidence*, by which an assembly can be identified. Examples of the evidence would be the strong name of the assembly or the digital signature associated with the assembly.

> **NOTE** *A strong name is a combination of the name of a program, its version number, and its associated cryptographic key and digital signature files.*

Identity permissions are granted by the runtime based on information received from the trusted host, or the operating system's loader. Therefore, they are permissions that you don't specifically request. Identity permissions provide additional information to be used by the runtime. The identity information can take the form of a trusted host's URL or can be supplied via a digital signature, the application directory, or the strong name of the assembly. Identity permissions are similar to code access permissions, discussed in the preceding section. They derive from the same base class as the code access permissions.

# Role-Based Permissions

Role-based permissions are permissions granted based on the user and the role that code is being called with. Users are authenticated within the operating system platform and hold a Security Identifier (SID) that is associated within a security context. The SID is associated with one or more roles or group memberships that are established within a security context. .NET supports those users and roles associated within a security context and has support for generic and custom users and roles through the concept of principals.

A *principal* is an object that holds the current caller's credentials. This includes the identity of the user. Principals come in two types: Windows principals and non-Windows principals. Windows-based principal objects are objects that store the Windows SID information regarding the current user context associated with the code that is calling into the module role-based permissions that are being used. Non-Windows principals are principal objects that are created programmatically via a custom login methodology and which are made available to the current thread.

Role-based permissions are not set against objects within your environment like code access permissions. They are checked within the context of the current user and user's role. The concepts of principals and the `PrincipalPermission` class are used to establish and check permissions. If a programmer passes the user and role information during a call as captured from a custom login, then the `PrincipalPermission` class can be used to verify this information as well.

The `PrincipalPermission` class does not grant access to objects, but has methods that determine whether a caller has been given permissions according to the current permission object through the `Demand` method. If a security exception is generated, then the user does not have sufficient permission. As an example of how you might use these methods, the following code snippet captures the current Windows principal information and displays it on the screen in a text box. It is included as part of the ProVB2012_Security project, which has the same basic structure as the ProVB_VS2012 project introduced in Chapter 1. Each element of the principal information could be used in a program to validate against, and thus restrict, code execution based on the values in the principal information. The following code example inserts `Imports System.Security.Principal` and `Imports System.Security.Permissions` lines at the top of `MainWindow.xaml.vb` so you can directly reference identity and principal objects without full namespace qualifiers:

```vb
Imports System.Security.Principal
Imports System.Security.Permissions

    '<PrincipalPermissionAttribute(SecurityAction.Demand,
                            Name:="WSheldon", Role:="Users")> _
    Private Sub DisplayPrincipalIdentity()
        ' The attribute above can be used to check security declaratively
        ' similar to how you would check using WPF or Silverlight.
        ' The code below uses imperative commands to get security information.
        Dim objIdentity As WindowsIdentity = WindowsIdentity.GetCurrent()
        TextBoxResult.Text = "User Name: " & objIdentity.Name &
            Environment.NewLine
        TextBoxResult.Text &= "Is Guest: " & objIdentity.IsGuest.ToString() _
            & Environment.NewLine
        TextBoxResult.Text &= "Is Authenticated: " _
            & objIdentity.IsAuthenticated.ToString() & Environment.NewLine
        Dim objPrincipal As New Security.Principal.WindowsPrincipal(objIdentity)
        ' Determine if the user is part of an authorized group.
        TextBoxResult.Text &= "Is in Role Users? " & objPrincipal.IsInRole("Users") _
            & Environment.NewLine
        TextBoxResult.Text &= "Is in Role Administrators? " _
            & objPrincipal.IsInRole("Administrators")
    End Sub
```

This code illustrates a few of the properties that could be used to validate against when a caller wants to run your code. The attribute at the top of this is commented out at this point by design. It represents a declarative security check similar to what you would use from the XAML in a WPF or Silverlight project. First, however, let's examine this code being run, as shown in Figure 18-2.

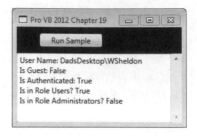

It starts by retrieving the user name of the currently authenticated Windows principal. Pay attention to the fact that this is a fully qualified username with the machine name included.

**FIGURE 18-2:** Details of the current user

It then uses the identity checks to see if the current identity is the Guest account, and ensures that the user was authenticated.

At this point the snippet creates a new `WindowsPrincipal` based on the current user's identity. This object allows you to query to see if the current user is in a role. In this case, our account is in the role of a user as a member of the Users security group, but is not in the role of an administrator even though it is part of the Administrators group.

Roles are typically defined via security groups, but it is important to not say that this method allowed you to determine if a user were in a given group. That's because under Windows Vista and Windows 7, the operating system keeps a user from running in the Administrator role even if they are part of the Administrators group. Thus, the check for whether the code is running in the role Administrators returns false—even though our WSheldon account is in fact a member of the Administrators group on this machine. Only if the user chooses to have their permission elevated will this query return true.

> **NOTE** *The issue of permission elevation in relation to User Access Control (UAC) and the fact that the WSheldon account is in fact an Administrator on the system is discussed later in this chapter.*

Now uncomment the attribute line that precedes this method. Notice that it is making a Demand security query and passing a user name, and a role name as part of this name. Because these are named optional parameters, the code could in theory check only for a role, which is a much more usable check in a real-world application. However, in this case use only a name and do not include the machine as part of the full user name. As a result, when `ButtonTest` is clicked this declarative check fails and the error shown in Figure 18-3 is displayed.

This illustrates how the same objects that have been available since the early versions of .NET are still used within XAML to enable the same level of security to declarative applications. The principal and identity objects are used in verifying the identity or aspects of the identity of the caller attempting to execute your code. Based on this information, your application can either lock down system resources or adjust the options available to users within your custom application. The `Identity` and `Principal` objects make it possible to have your application respond as changes to user roles occur within `Active Directory`. Note you'll want to comment this line back out so that this error isn't present as you work with the sample application later in this chapter.

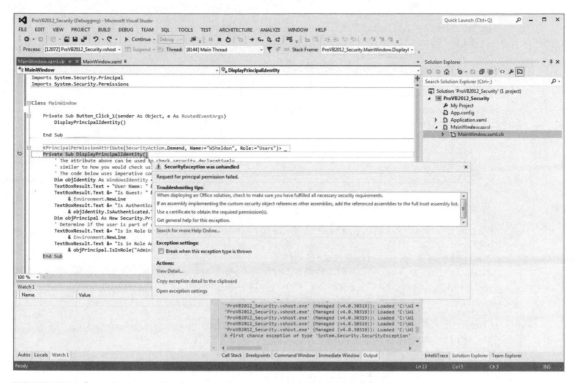

**FIGURE 18-3:** Security exception for nonexistent user running in the debugger

# MANAGING CODE ACCESS PERMISSION SETS

This section looks at programmatic access to permissions. The example extends the ProVB2012_
Security project discussed earlier. This example illustrates how when a method fails, an exception
object containing the result is generated. Note that in the case of a real-world example, you would
be setting up permissions for a calling application. In many instances, you don't want a calling
application to be able to access the registry, or you want a calling application to be able to read
memory variables but not change them. Keep in mind that you can only limit those permissions
which are already available to a user based on their identity. You can't grant access to a portion of
the operating system via code that the user doesn't have access to based on their identity.

The following example first sets up the permission that is wanted and then grants the code the
appropriate access level. Thee code that accesses this security object illustrates the effect of these
new permissions on the code. Note you will need to add the line `Imports System.IO` to the top of
your `MainWindow.xaml.vb` file for the following code to compile.

```
Private Sub TestFileIOPermission()
    Dim oFp = New FileIOPermission(
            FileIOPermissionAccess.AllAccess,
            "C:\Temp")
    oFp.PermitOnly()
```

```
        'Try
        Dim strmWrite As New IO.StreamWriter(
             File.Open("C:\Temp\Permission.txt",
             IO.FileMode.Open))
        strmWrite.WriteLine("Hi there!")
        strmWrite.Flush()
        strmWrite.Close()
        Dim objWriter As New IO.StreamWriter(
             File.Open("C:\Temp\NoPermission.txt",
             IO.FileMode.Open))
        objWriter.WriteLine("Hi there!")
        objWriter.Flush()
        objWriter.Close()

        'Uncomment the lines below (comment those above) to reverse the test.

        'Dim oFp = New FileIOPermission(FileIOPermissionAccess.Read, "C:\")
        'oFp.PermitOnly()
        'Dim temp = oFp.AllFiles.ToString()
        'Dim strmWrite = New IO.StreamWriter(
        '                File.Open("C:\Temp\Permission.txt",
        '                IO.FileMode.Open))
        'strmWrite.WriteLine("Hi there!")
        'strmWrite.Flush()
        'strmWrite.Close()
        'Dim objWriter = New IO.StreamWriter(
        '                File.Open("C:\Temp\NoPermission.txt",
        '                IO.FileMode.Open))
        'objWriter.WriteLine("Hi there!")
        'objWriter.Flush()
        'objWriter.Close()
        ''Catch objA As System.Exception
        ''MessageBox.Show(objA.Message)
        ''End Try
    End Sub
```

The first example attempts to access a file in the file system. This illustrates the use of the `FileIOPermission` class. Within the folder `C:\Temp`, create two new files. The first file, `C:\Temp\Permission.txt`, will use the default permissions assigned when you created the account. The second file, `C:\Temp\NoPermission.txt` (these files are not part of the download), has its permissions modified.

To do this, access the file's properties by right-clicking on the file and choosing Properties. On the Properties dialogue select the Security tab and then use the Advanced button. Within the Advanced Security Settings dialogue use the Change Permission button to open the Advanced Security Settings dialogue. Next go to the bottom of this dialogue and unclick the check box "Include inheritable permissions from this object's parent." You will need to verify that you want to add the security settings for this file to the file itself.

After returning to the original Properties dialogue by clicking the OK buttons you will want to remove the settings for Authorized Users. To do this you will need to use the Edit button to access the Permission dialogue where you can use the Remove button. After having done this you will have removed the default modify permission for authenticated users to this file. The result should be the permission level that is depicted in Figure 18-4. Note that there are only three Groups or usernames assigned permissions.

Looking at the previous code snippet notice that the Sub TestFileIOPermission first grants FileIO write permissions to the current user and attempts to access both files. This will fail for the NoPermissions.txt file, because code access security can't grant additional access to a user at runtime. You can see this result in the error shown in Figure 18-5.

Now to test the reverse, comment out the top half of the preceding method and uncomment the bottom half. Now the method uses the PermitOnly assignment to limit the user to ReadOnly permissions for the FileIO permission set. In this case the code will fail when attempting to write to the Permission.txt file because of the stricter limits of this setting as opposed to what the operating system would allow. You can see this result in the error shown in Figure 18-6.

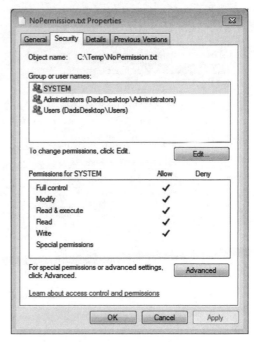

**FIGURE 18-4:** Properties of target file for security checks

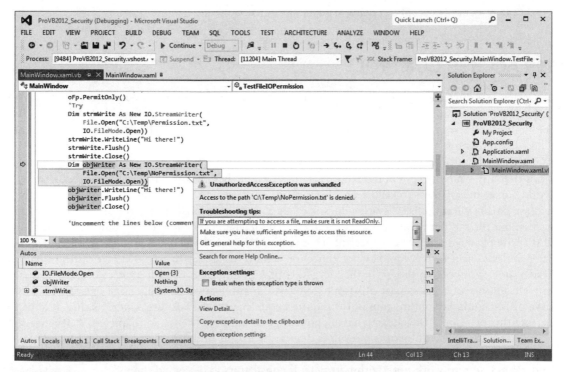

**FIGURE 18-5:** Security access exception in Visual Studio debugger

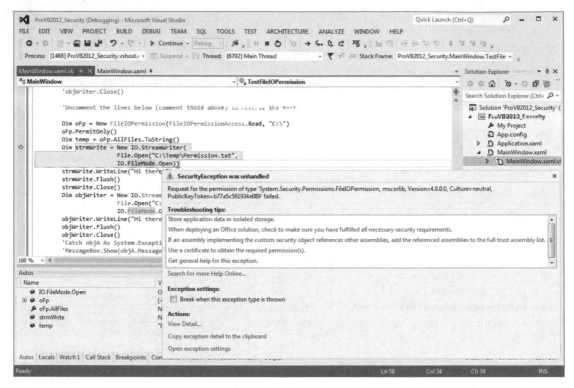

**FIGURE 18-6:** Security exception related to permission not access

# USER ACCESS CONTROL

With the introduction of Windows Vista and continuing with Windows 7, developers became aware of a new security model: User Access Control (UAC). The core premise of UAC is that even a user with administrative rights should normally run in the context of a reduced privilege user account. The concept is quite simply a best practice. Unfortunately, as with any situation where rights are reduced, application developers and users have spent so much time running with elevated permissions that any time the system interrupts what they want they become upset. But for security to work, sometimes its best to keep access limited and force you to recognize when you are granting access. This is what the UAC system does: it locks the access; you still have the ability to grant that access, but the system makes you pause and evaluate if that access should be granted. If you get a UAC prompt when you aren't expecting it, or realize that software you don't fully trust is attempting privileged access that you may not expect or want it to have, you are far better off than had the system not prompted you to grant that access. UAC gets a bit of a bad rap in part because it was introduced to end users as part of Vista before custom application developers, or even Microsoft developers, could get out in front of the required code changes. Thus, users were asking, "Why am I getting this prompt?" Developers, having no real good answers then, had to answer, "Because Vista changed things." The unfortunate result is that many people and organizations have turned off UAC. However, as a developer you should now have it enabled on your desktop and should begin to understand how to work both within its default constraints and beyond them.

# DEFINING YOUR APPLICATION UAC SETTINGS

By default in Visual Studio, your application settings include information related to UAC. It is possible to create your application so that it ships with certain permissions. Within your application manifest you'll find the section `requestedPrivileges`. This section is where the requested UAC execution level for your application is defined. Note that these settings are applicable to Windows Store applications that run on Windows RT.

To get to your application manifest, right-click on your project in Solution Explorer and select Properties. In the Properties pane, select the Application tab and there you'll find a button labeled View Windows Settings. Selecting this button will open your application manifest (`app.manifest`) XML file in the editor window. Within the XML, you'll find the `requestedPrivileges` node, a copy of which is shown in the code block that is part of Listing 18-1.

**LISTING 18-1: Manifest Level Rights—**`My Project\app.manifest`

```
<requestedPrivileges xmlns="urn:schemas-microsoft-com:asm.v3">
  <!-- UAC Manifest Options
      If you want to change the Windows User Account Control level
          replace the
      requestedExecutionLevel node with one of the following.

  <requestedExecutionLevel  level="asInvoker" uiAccess="false" />
  <requestedExecutionLevel  level="requireAdministrator" uiAccess="false" />
  <requestedExecutionLevel  level="highestAvailable" uiAccess="false" />

      Specifying requestedExecutionLevel node will disable file and registry
      virtualization. If you want to utilize File and Registry
          Virtualization
      for backward compatibility then delete the
          requestedExecutionLevel node.-->
  <requestedExecutionLevel level="asInvoker" uiAccess="false" />
</requestedPrivileges>
```

The beauty of this XML is that Microsoft took the time to include meaningful XML comments about the `requestedExecutionLevel` setting. By default, as shown in the preceding snippet, your application requests to run `asInvoker`. Thus, as discussed earlier when looking at which group you are running as, this means you are running as a user, not an administrator.

As the comments make clear, it is possible to change this to `requireAdministrator`, so make this change. Next ensure that you have both the `Sub DisplayPrincipalIdentity()` and the `Sub TestFileIOPermission()` uncommented in the button's click event handler within the ProVB2012_Security project.

Finally, within the `Sub TestFileIOPermission()`, ensure that you have restored which block is commented out; the code should look like the previous listing where the bottom half of the method is commented and the top half is uncommented. Now that you have indicated that this application requires administrator privileges, you can repeat the first test where the user account didn't have permission to write to `NoPermission.txt`, but where the code attempted to grant permission. Note, this test depends on the Administrator having permission to access the file `C:\Test\NoPermission.txt`. Save your change to the `app.manifest` and attempt to run the application. If you are running on Windows 7 and didn't start Visual Studio using Run as Administrator, you should get the error shown in Figure 18-7.

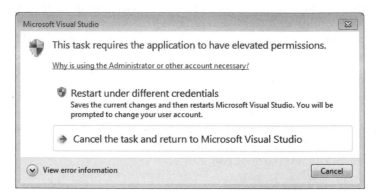

**FIGURE 18-7:** Elevated permissions dialogue

What happened? As noted previously, the error message in Figure 18-7 is dependent on having not started Visual Studio with the Run as Administrator option from the right-click context menu. Since Visual Studio is running under your downgraded rights at the level of user, when it attempts to create a new process with the rights for administrator, the system refuses.

Just as you can't use code access security to grant the running account additional rights, you can't use the application manifest for the same purpose. The operating system knows that the current process has only user rights, so when you attempt to have that process spawn a new debugging process with administrator rights, the operating system throws an error.

You can get around this in one of two ways. The first, obviously, is to start or restart Visual Studio running as Administrator. Alternatively, you can go to the `bin/debug` folder and manually start the `ProVB2012_Security.exe` executable outside of the debugger. In either case you should now be prompted to grant administrator rights to this assembly, because the current code does not sign the assembly. Accepting this grant of elevated privileges, the results should be similar to what is shown in Figure 18-8.

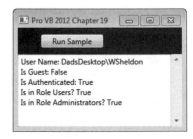

**FIGURE 18-8:** Output when running as an administrator

The successful completion of the Run Code button highlights two important points. First, as shown in Figure 18-8, the fact that the WSheldon account is in fact an administrator is now reflected in the onscreen permission display. Second, no error was thrown in the attempt to write the `NoPermission.txt` because the application is now running with the rights of an Administrator.

Regarding the `uiAccess` setting within the application manifest, this `Boolean` value defaults to false, and in most cases this is the correct setting. Changing this value to true will allow your code to update the user interface that is part of another assembly. However, setting this to true means that the application must be signed and that it must run from a trusted location.

As noted, signing your application will make the elevated privileges warning more meaningful and user friendly. Application signing is typically done during deployment, as discussed in Chapter 17, "Assemblies and Reflection." It is not suggested that you just go in and start marking all of your applications with the `requireAdministrator` flag. Instead, you should elevate a user's rights when those rights are needed. Unfortunately, this option is available only at the time your application starts, but there is an important capability involved. In short, if you mark your application as essentially requiring Administrator rights, only administrators will be able to run the application.

Thus, the third application activation alternative is to use the `highestAvailable` setting. This setting allows both users and administrators to run your application. Within your application code, you'll need to check what privileges are available to the current user. As demonstrated earlier in this chapter, this will allow you to enable or disable application features depending upon whether the current user is an administrator.

## Security Tools

Microsoft provides many security tools in its .NET SDK. Most of these tools are console-based utility applications. These tools can be used to help implement the security processes outlined earlier. They are not described in great detail, though they do deserve a review. Basically, two groups of tools are provided with the SDK:

**1.** Permissions and assembly management tools

**2.** Certificate management tools

Table 18-4 describes the permissions and assembly management tools. Table 18-5 describes the certificate management tools.

**TABLE 18-4:** Permissions and Assembly Management Tools

| PROGRAM NAME | DESCRIPTION |
| --- | --- |
| Storeadm.exe | An administrative tool for isolated storage management. It restricts code access to the file system. |
| Peverify.exe | Checks whether the executable file will pass the runtime test for type-safe coding. |
| Sn.exe | Creates assemblies with strong names—that is, a digitally signed namespace and version information. |

**TABLE 18-5:** Certificate Management Tools

| PROGRAM NAME | DESCRIPTION |
| --- | --- |
| Makecert.exe | Creates an X.509 certificate for testing purposes. |
| Certmgr.exe | Assembles certificates into a CTL (Certificate Trust List). It can also be used for revoking certificates. |
| Cert2spc.exe | Creates an SPC (Software Publisher Certificate) from an X.509 certificate. |

# Exceptions Using the SecurityException Class

Originally, using the .NET Framework versions 1.0/1.1, the `SecurityException` class provided very little information in terms of actually telling you what was wrong and why an exception was thrown. Due to this limitation, the .NET Framework 2.0 added a number of new properties to the `SecurityException` class. Table 18-6 details some of these properties.

**TABLE 18-6:** Common SecurityException Properties

| PROPERTY | DESCRIPTION |
| --- | --- |
| Action | Retrieves the security action that caused the exception to occur |
| Data | Gets a collection of key/value pairs that provide user-defined information about an exception |
| Demanded | Returns the permissions, permission sets, or permission set collections that caused the error to occur |
| DenySetInstance | Returns the denied permissions, permission sets, or permission set collections that caused the security actions to fail |
| FailedAssemblyInfo | Returns information about the failed assembly |
| FirstPermissionThatFailed | Returns the first permission contained in the permission set or permission set collection that failed |
| GrantedSet | Returns the set of permissions that caused the security actions to fail |
| HelpLink | Gets or sets a link to a help file associated with this error |
| InnerException | A reference to an earlier exception that triggered the current exception |
| Method | Returns information about the method connected to the exception |
| PermissionState | Returns the state of the permission that threw the exception |
| PermissionType | Returns the type of the permission that threw the exception |
| PermitOnlySetInstance | Returns a permission set or permission set collection that is part of the permit-only stack frame if a security action has failed |
| RefusedSet | Returns the permissions that were refused by the assembly |
| Source | Gets or sets the name of the application or object that triggered the error |
| Url | Returns the URL of the assembly that caused the exception |
| Zone | Returns the zone of the assembly that caused the exception |

Clearly, you can get your hands on a lot of information if a security exception is thrown in your application. For instance, you can use something similar to the following Catch section of code to check for security errors:

```
Dim myFile as FileInfo

Try
    myFile = _
        My.Computer.FileSystem.GetFileInfo("C:\Test\NoPermission.txt")
Catch ex As Security.SecurityException
    MessageBox.Show(ex.Method.Name.ToString())
End Try
```

# ENCRYPTION BASICS

Rather than present an exposition of cryptography, this section is meant to familiarize you with basic techniques required to deal with .NET security and protect your Web services through encryption. There are four different categories of cryptography: encoding, hashing, and symmetric and asymmetric encryption.

First you will review each of these four different cryptographic categories. The first is encoding, which, as you may already know, if you are at all familiar with encryption, doesn't actually protect information. The most common encodings are things like UTF8, UTF7, and Base64 encoding. These encodings are typically used to take information that might interact with a container and hide the special characters. Thus, if you want to embed binary data within an XML file and want to ensure that the binary data won't interfere with the XML, you can Base64 the data, and it can safely be placed within an XML file.

Encoding is quite common for passing hidden or state data in Web pages, MIME, and XML file formats. For example, in ASP.NET, ViewState is an encoded block of information about the state of an ASP.NET page. However, keep in mind that encoded data, while not immediately humanly readable, uses a public algorithm to create its string. Encoding algorithms are designed to be quickly and easily reversed, and without any form of implied privacy. This means that anyone can reverse the encoded data, so for ASP.NET, ViewState does not protect the data which has been encoded; it just allows for transport of that data. To reiterate, encoding does not protect information.

The next item in the list of cryptography categories is hashing. Hashing algorithms digest sequences of data, creating a "random" output for the input string. A hash has a private key that can be varied by each application using the hash. Using a different key ensures you get different random string representations. While changing a single character will result in an entirely different result, the key to a hash is that there is no way to decrypt the original string from that result. In fact, hashing algorithms are specifically designed to not support the decryption of data once it has been hashed. At the same time, a hash always produces the same result for a given input string.

In terms of degree of security, hash keys are generally judged by the size of the encryption key, with larger keys (512-bit) providing greater security than shorter (128-bit) keys. Two popular hashing algorithms are SHA (Secure Hash Algorithm) and MD5 (Message-Digest algorithm 5). These hash keys are used for everything from saving passwords to signing digital documents; in other words, the hash is generated and encrypted using a private key.

Hashing works for passwords and pass phrases (longer authentication strings, which are far more difficult to guess) by never actually decrypting the password value. In order to validate your protected data, you reenter that data, which is then hashed, and the original hash is compared to the hashing of the newly entered text. If these two hashed values match, then the same text was entered. If the hashed values don't match, it means that the correct password or other information was not entered. In this way the original password can be protected not only from outsiders, but also from insiders who might want to impersonate another user.

Hashing algorithms, unlike other forms of encryption, are meant to be nonreversible. This is an important part of the security they provide. Note that in most cases, complex algorithms can be developed to reverse a hash, the most common being the creation of a dictionary of hashed values. However, the point of a hash is to create a "random" string based on input and ensure that the "random" element is repeatable for the same string. Thus, each password attempt is hashed, and the result is compared to the stored hash value for that user's password or pass phrase; matches mean success, and there is no relationship to "how close" the entered text is to the correct text, because the hashed value is "random" for any given set of characters.

Symmetric encryption is commonly used to protect data such as private messages or data that will be retrieved. Symmetric key encryption is suitable for situations where the encrypted data needs to be accessed by someone in the same organization as the one who protected it. In this scenario, a key might be embedded within an application or stored as part of some device that the organization members control. It is important to keep the key private, as the same key is used to both encrypt and decrypt the data. Private keys work well as long as only those people who are authorized to view the protected data have them. It breaks down when attempting to interchange private data with the world at large. For that you need one key used by outsiders and a different key used by insiders.

Asymmetric public key encryption is most widely used in protecting the data that may be shared with an outside group. It is also used for digital signatures. Public key encryption is based on asymmetric keys, which means you always have a pair of keys. One key is known to all and is called the *public key*. The other key of the pair is kept secret and is known only to the owner. This is called the *private key*. If you use the public key to encrypt data, it can only be decrypted using the corresponding private key of the key pair, and vice versa.

Because the public key is known to all, anyone can decrypt information protected by the private key. However, the private key is known only to the owner, so this process acts as a digital signature. In other words, if the public key decrypts the message, then you know that the sender was the owner of the private key. It is important to remember that when data is protected using the public key, only the holder of the private key can decrypt it; another holder of the public key will be unable to decrypt the protected information.

In some cases an entire set of data is encrypted—for example, HTTPS does this. Similarly, asymmetric encryption is also used for digital signatures. Rather than encrypt the whole document using the private key, a public key and an agreed-upon hash algorithm describing the data is used to "sign" the document. The signature is attached to the document, and the receiver then decrypts it using the private key. The result of the decryption is compared with rerunning the same hash on the key document characteristics that were agreed upon for the hash; if the results match, then the document is considered authentic. The result of this process is a *digital signature* associated with the digital document. This process works bidirectionally, so a document can be signed with the private key and the signature can be checked with the public key.

Because the holder of the private key will be able to read the data, it is very important that when you create a key pair, the private key must be protected and never shared.

## Hash Algorithms

Hash algorithms are also called *one-way functions* because of their mathematical property of nonreversibility. The hash algorithms reduce large strings into a fixed-length binary byte array.

To verify a piece of information, the hash is recomputed and compared against a previously computed hash value. If both values match, then the newly provided data is correct. Cryptographic hashing algorithms map strings of data to a fixed-length result. Thus, two strings of different length will have a hash of the same size.

Although it is theoretically possible for two documents to have the same MD5 hash result, it is computationally impossible to create a meaningful forged document having the same hash key as the original hash value.

## Cryptographic Hash Algorithms

The abstract class System.Security.Cryptography.HashAlgorithm represents the concept of cryptographic hash algorithms within the .NET Framework. The framework provides eight classes that extend the HashAlgorithm abstract class:

1. MD5CryptoServiceProvider (extends abstract class MD5)
2. RIPEMD160Managed (extends abstract class RIPEMD160)
3. SHA1CryptoServiceProvider (extends abstract class SHA1)
4. SHA256Managed (extends abstract class SHA256)
5. SHA384Managed (extends abstract class SHA384)
6. SHA512Managed (extends abstract class SHA512)
7. HMACSHA1 (extends abstract class KeyedHashAlgorithm)
8. MACTripleDES (extends abstract class KeyedHashAlgorithm)

The last two classes belong to a class of algorithm called *keyed hash algorithms*. Keyed hashes extend the concept of the cryptographic hash with the use of a shared secret key. This is used for computing the hash of data transported over an unsecured channel.

To demonstrate this, a hashing example is available as part of the code download. The TestHashKey.vb file is part of the ProVB2012_Security solution. This class can be called using the following line of code in the click event handler that is part of the main window's code-behind:

```
TextBoxResult.Text = TestHashKey.Main("..\..\TestHashKey.vb")
```

Calling the shared method Main using this line of code from the Button_Click_1 event handler will run the example code shown in Listing 18-2, telling it to encrypt a copy of the source file TestHashKey.vb:

---

**LISTING 18-2: Class TestHashKey**—`TestHashKey.vb`

```vb
'TestHashKey.vb
Imports System
Imports System.IO
Imports System.Security.Cryptography
Imports System.Text

Public Class TestHashKey
    Public Shared Function Main(ByVal pathToFileToProtect As String) As String
        Dim key() As Byte = Encoding.ASCII.GetBytes("My Secret Key".ToCharArray())
        Dim hmac As HMACSHA1 = New HMACSHA1(key)
        Dim fs As FileStream = File.OpenRead(pathToFileToProtect)
        Dim hash() As Byte = hmac.ComputeHash(fs)
        Dim b64 As String = Convert.ToBase64String(hash)
        fs.Close()
        Return b64
    End Function
End Class
```

The preceding snippet creates the object instance of the .NET SDK Framework class with a *salt* (a random secret to confuse a snooper). The next four lines compute the hash, encode the binary hash into a printable Base64 format, close the file, and then return the Base64 encoded string. Running this will result in the hashed output shown in 18-9.

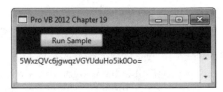

**FIGURE 18-9:** Displaying the hash results

The previous example uses an instance of the `HMACSHA1` class. The output displayed is a Base64 encoding of the binary hash result value. As noted earlier, Base64 encoding is widely used in MIME and XML file formats to represent binary data. To recover the binary data from a Base64-encoded string, you could use the following code fragment:

```vb
Dim orig() As Byte = Convert.FromBase64String(b64)
```

The XML parser, however, does this automatically, as shown in later examples.

## SHA

Secure Hash Algorithm (SHA) is a block cipher that operates on a block size of 64 bits. However, subsequent enhancements of this algorithm have bigger key values, thus, increasing the value range and therefore enhancing the cryptographic utility. Note that the bigger the key value sizes, the longer it takes to compute the hash. Moreover, for relatively smaller data files, smaller hash values are more secure. To put it another way, the hash algorithm's block size should be less than or equal to the size of the data itself.

The hash size for the SHA1 algorithm is 160 bits. Similar to the `HMACSHA1` code discussed previously, the code in Listing 18-3 shows an example of using this algorithm:

---

**LISTING 18-3: Class TestSHA1**—`TestSHA1.vb`

```vb
'TestSHA1.vb
Imports System
```

```
Imports System.IO
Imports System.Security.Cryptography
Imports System.Text

Public Class TestSHA1
    Public Shared Function Main(ByVal pathToFileToProtect As String) As String

        Dim fs As FileStream = File.OpenRead(pathToFileToProtect)
        Dim sha As SHA1 = New SHA1CryptoServiceProvider
        Dim hash() As Byte = sha.ComputeHash(fs)
        Dim b64 As String = Convert.ToBase64String(hash)
        fs.Close()
        Return b64
    End Function
End Class
```

The .NET Framework provides larger key size algorithms as well—namely, SHA256, SHA384, and SHA512. The numbers at the end of the name indicate the block size.

The class `SHA256Managed` extends the abstract class `SHA256`, which in turn extends the abstract class `HashAlgorithm`. The forms authentication module of ASP.NET security (`System.Web.Security.Forms AuthenticationModule`) uses SHA1 as one of its valid formats to store and compare user passwords.

## MD5

Message-Digest algorithm 5 (MD5) is a cryptographic, one-way hash algorithm. The MD5 algorithm competes well with SHA. MD5 is an improved version of MD4, devised by Ronald Rivest of Rivest, Shamir and Adleman (RSA) fame. In fact, FIPS PUB 180-1 states that SHA-1 is based on principles similar to MD4. The salient features of this class of algorithms are as follows:

➤ It is computationally unfeasible to forge an MD5 hash digest.

➤ MD5 is not based on any mathematical assumption such as the difficulty of factoring large binary integers.

➤ MD5 is computationally cheap, and therefore suitable for low-latency requirements.

➤ It is relatively simple to implement.

MD5 was the de facto standard for hash digest computation, due to the popularity of RSA. The .NET Framework provides an implementation of this algorithm through the class `MD5CryptoServiceProvider` in the `System.Security.Cryptography` namespace. This class extends the MD5 abstract class, which in turn extends the abstract class `HashAlgorithm`. This class shares a common base class with SHA1, so the examples previously discussed can be easily replicated by updating the SHA1 source to reference the `MD5CryptoServiceProvider` instead of the SHA1 provider.

```
Dim md5 As MD5 = New MD5CryptoServiceProvider()
Dim hash() As Byte = md5.ComputeHash(fs)
```

## RIPEMD-160

Based on MD5, RIPEMD-160 started as a project in Europe called the RIPE (RACE Integrity Primitives Evaluation) project Message Digest in 1996. By 1997, the design of RIPEMD-160 was finalized. RIPEMD-160 is a 160-bit hash algorithm that is meant to be a replacement for MD4 and MD5.

The .NET Framework 2.0 introduced the RIPEMD160 class to work with this iteration of encryption techniques. As you should recognize from the preceding MD5 example, switching to this provider is also easily accomplished:

```
Dim myRIPEMD As New RIPEMD160Managed()
Dim hash() As Byte = myRIPEMD.ComputeHash(fs)
```

## Symmetric Key Encryption

Symmetric key encryption is widely used to encrypt data files using passwords. The simplest technique is to seed a random number using a password, and then encrypt the files with an XOR operation using this random number generator.

The .NET Framework provides an abstract base class SymmetricAlgorithm. Five concrete implementations of different symmetric key algorithms are provided by default:

1. AesCryptoServiceProvider (extends abstract class Aes)

2. DESCryptoServiceProvider (extends abstract class DES)

3. RC2CryptoServiceProvider (extends abstract class RC2)

4. RijndaelManaged (extends abstract class Rijndael)

5. TripleDESCryptoServiceProvider (extends abstract class TripleDES)

Let's explore the SymmetricAlgorithm design. As indicated by the following example code, two separate methods are provided to access encryption and decryption. You can run a copy of symmetric encryption using the sample code. Uncomment the following line of code in the ButtonTest _Click event handler in MainWindow.xaml.vb. An example of this call is shown here:

```
SymEnc.Main(TextBoxResult, 0, "..\..\SymEnc.vb", "DESencrypted.txt", True)
```

Listing 18-4 illustrates the code that encrypts and decrypts a file, given a secret key:

**LISTING 18-4: Class SymEnc—**SymEnc.vb

```
'SymEnc.vb
Imports System.Security.Cryptography
Imports System.IO
Imports System.Text
Imports System

Public Class SymEnc
    Private Shared algo() As String = {"DES", "RC2", "Rijndael", "TripleDES"}
    Private Shared b64Keys() As String = {"YE32PGCJ/g0=", _
    "vct+rJ09WuUcR61yfxniTQ==", _
    "PHDPqfwE3z25f2UYjwwfwg4XSqxvl8WYmy+2h8t6AUg=", _
    "Q1/lWoraddTH3IXAQUJGDSYDQcYYuOpm"}
    Private Shared b64IVs() As String = {"onQX8hdHeWQ=", _
    "jgetiyz+pIc=", _
```

```
                    "pd5mgMMfDI2Gxm/SKl5I8A==", _
                    "6jpFrUh8FF4="}

        Public Shared Sub Main(ByVal textBox As TextBox, ByVal algoIndex As Integer, _
                      ByVal inputFile As String, ByVal outputFile As String, _
                      ByVal encryptFile As Boolean)

            Dim fin As FileStream = File.OpenRead(inputFile)
            Dim fout As FileStream = File.OpenWrite(outputFile)
            Dim sa As SymmetricAlgorithm = SymmetricAlgorithm.Create(algo(algoIndex))
            sa.IV = Convert.FromBase64String(b64IVs(algoIndex))
            sa.Key = Convert.FromBase64String(b64Keys(algoIndex))
            textBox.Text = "Key length: " & CType(sa.Key.Length, String) & _
                    Environment.NewLine
            textBox.Text &= "Initial Vector length: " & CType(sa.IV.Length, String) & _
                    Environment.NewLine
            textBox.Text &= "KeySize: " & CType(sa.KeySize, String) & _
                    Environment.NewLine
            textBox.Text &= "BlockSize: " & CType(sa.BlockSize, String) & _
                    Environment.NewLine
            textBox.Text &= "Padding: " & CType(sa.Padding, String) & _
                    Environment.NewLine
            If (encryptFile) Then
                Encrypt(sa, fin, fout)
            Else
                Decrypt(sa, fin, fout)
            End If
        End Sub
```

The parameters to Main provide the Textbox where the output will be displayed and the index from the array algo, which is the name of the algorithm to be used. It then looks for the input and output files, and finally a Boolean indicating whether the input should be encrypted or decrypted.

Within the code, first the action is to open the input and output files. The code then creates an instance of the selected algorithm and converts the initial vector and key strings for use by the algorithm. Symmetric algorithms essentially rely on two secret values: one called the key; the other, the initial vector, both of which are used to encrypt and decrypt the data. Both private values are required for either encryption or decryption.

The code then outputs some generic information related to the encryption being used and then checks which operation is required, executing the appropriate static method to encrypt or decrypt the file.

To encrypt, the code gets an instance of the ICryptoTransform interface by calling the CreateEncryptor method of the SymmetricAlgorithm class extender. The encryption itself is done in the following method:

```
        Private Shared Sub Encrypt(ByVal sa As SymmetricAlgorithm, _
        ByVal fin As Stream, _
        ByVal fout As Stream)
            Dim trans As ICryptoTransform = sa.CreateEncryptor()
            Dim buf() As Byte = New Byte(fin.Length) {}
            Dim cs As CryptoStream = _
            New CryptoStream(fout, trans, CryptoStreamMode.Write)
```

```
        Dim Len As Integer
        fin.Position = 0
        Len = fin.Read(buf, 0, buf.Length)
        While (Len > 0)
            cs.Write(buf, 0, Len)
            Len = fin.Read(buf, 0, buf.Length)
        End While
        cs.Close()
        fin.Close()
    End Sub
```

For decryption, the code gets an instance of the `ICryptoTransform` interface by calling the `CreateDecryptor` method of the `SymmetricAlgorithm` class instance. To test this you can uncomment the line of code which follows the method call to encrypt the file using the method `Main` and matches the following line:

```
    SymEnc.Main(TextBoxResult, 0, "DESencrypted.txt", "DESdecrypted.txt", False)
```

The following snippet provides the decryption method:

```
    Private Shared Sub Decrypt(ByVal sa As SymmetricAlgorithm, _
    ByVal fin As Stream, _
    ByVal fout As Stream)
        Dim trans As ICryptoTransform = sa.CreateDecryptor()
        Dim buf() As Byte = New Byte(fin.Length) {}
        Dim cs As CryptoStream = _
        New CryptoStream(fin, trans, CryptoStreamMode.Read)
        Dim Len As Integer
        Len = cs.Read(buf, 0, buf.Length - 1)
        While (Len > 0)
            fout.Write(buf, 0, Len)
            Len = cs.Read(buf, 0, buf.Length)
        End While
        fin.Close()
        fout.Close()
    End Sub
```

The class `CryptoStream` is used for both encryption and decryption. You'll find it listed both in the `Decrypt` method shown in the preceding code snippet and also in the earlier code snippet that showed the `Encrypt` method. Notice, however, that depending on if you are encrypting or decrypting, the parameters to the constructor for the `CryptoStream` differ.

You'll also notice if you review the code in `SymEnc.vb`, that this code supports testing of encryption and decryption using any of the four symmetric key implementations provided by the .NET Framework. The second parameter to `Sub Main` is an index indicating which algorithm to use. The secret keys and associated initialization vectors (IVs) were generated by a simple source code generator, examined shortly.

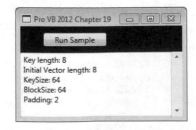

If you haven't done so yet, you should run the application and verify the contents of the `DESencrypted.txt` and `DESdecrypted.txt` files. If the new methods run to completion, the screen display should look similar to what is shown in Figure 18-10.

**FIGURE 18-10:** Symmetric encryption characteristics as output

To generate the keys, a simple code generator is available in the file `SymKey.vb`. You can reference it by adding a call to the button click event as shown in the following line.

```
SymKey.SymKeyMain(TextBoxResult)
```

The code to generate the key and vectors is shown in Listing 18-5.

**LISTING 18-5:** Class SymKey—`SymKey.vb`

```
'SymKey.vb
Imports System.Security.Cryptography
Imports System.Text
Imports System.IO
Imports System
Imports Microsoft.VisualBasic.ControlChars

Public Class SymKey
    Public Shared Sub SymKeyMain(ByVal textBox As TextBox)
        Dim keyz As StringBuilder = New StringBuilder
        Dim ivz As StringBuilder = New StringBuilder
        keyz.Append("Dim b64Keys() As String = { " & vbCrLf)
        ivz.Append(vbCrLf + "Dim b64IVs() As String = { " & vbCrLf)
        Dim algo() As String = {"DES", "RC2", "Rijndael", "TripleDES"}
        For i As Integer = 0 To 3
            Dim sa As SymmetricAlgorithm = SymmetricAlgorithm.Create(algo(i))
            sa.GenerateIV()
            sa.GenerateKey()
            Dim Key As String
            Dim IV As String
            Key = Convert.ToBase64String(sa.Key)
            IV = Convert.ToBase64String(sa.IV)
            keyz.AppendFormat(algo(i) & vbTab & ": """ & Key & """" & vbCrLf)
            ivz.AppendFormat(algo(i) & vbTab & ": """ & IV & """" & vbCrLf)
        Next i
        keyz.Append("}")
        ivz.Append("}")
        textBox.Text = keyz.ToString() & vbCrLf & ivz.ToString()
    End Sub
End Class
```

The preceding program creates a random key and an initializing vector for each algorithm. When run, the result are displayed as shown in Figure 18-11. You can use the output from this call to create unique and thus secure keys that can be copied into the `SymEnc.vb` program.

## PKCS

The Public Key Cryptographic System (PKCS) is a type of asymmetric key encryption. This system uses two keys, one private and the other public. The public key is widely distributed, whereas the

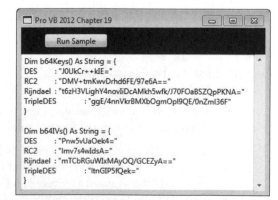

**FIGURE 18-11:** Generating random encryption key values

private key is kept secret. One cannot derive or deduce the private key by knowing the public key, so the public key can be safely distributed.

The keys are different, yet complementary. That is, if you encrypt data using the public key, then only the owner of the private key can decipher it, and vice versa. This forms the basis of PKCS encryption.

If the private key holder encrypts a piece of data using his or her private key, any person with access to the public key can decrypt it. The public key, as the name suggests, is available publicly. This property of the PKCS is exploited along with a hashing algorithm, such as SHA or MD5, to provide a verifiable digital signature process.

The abstract class `System.Security.Cryptography.AsymmetricAlgorithm` represents this concept in the .NET Framework. Four concrete implementations of this class are provided by default:

1. `DSACryptoServiceProvider`, which extends the abstract class `DSA`

2. `ECDiffieHellmanCngCryptoServiceProvider`, which extends the `ECDiffieHellmanCng` abstract class

3. `ECDsaCngCryptoServiceProvider`, which extends the abstract class `ECDsaCng`

4. `RSACryptoServiceProvider`, which extends the abstract class `RSA`

The Digital Signature Algorithm (DSA) was specified by the National Institute of Standards and Technology (NIST) in January 2000. The original DSA standard, however, was issued by NIST much earlier, in August 1991. DSA cannot be used for encryption and is good only for digital signature. Digital signature is discussed in more detail in the next section.

Similarly, the ECDsa algorithm is also an elliptic curve algorithm, in this case combined with the Digital Signature Algorithm. This is then enhanced with a Cryptographic Next Generation algorithm.

RSA algorithms can also be used for encryption as well as digital signatures. RSA is the de facto standard and has much wider acceptance than DSA. RSA is a tiny bit faster than DSA as well.

RSA can be used for both digital signature and data encryption. It is based on the assumption that large numbers are extremely difficult to factor. The use of RSA for digital signatures is approved within the FIPS PUB 186-2 and is defined in the ANSI X9.31 standard document.

## Digital Signature Example

Digital signature is the encryption of a hash digest (for example, MD5 or SHA-1) of data using a public key. The digital signature can be verified by decrypting the hash digest and comparing it against a hash digest computed from the data by the verifier.

As noted earlier, the private key is known only to the owner, so the owner can sign a digital document by encrypting the hash computed from the document. The public key is known to all, so anyone can verify the signature by recomputing the hash and comparing it against the decrypted value, using the public key of the signer.

The .NET Framework provides DSA and RSA digital signature implementations by default. This section considers only DSA, as both implementations extend the same base class, so all programs for DSA discussed here work for RSA as well.

First, you need to produce a key pair. To do this, you'll need the the following method which has been added to the ProVB2012_Security main window. This can be called once from the `Button_Click_1` event handler to generate the necessary files in your application's folder.

```
Private Sub GenDSAKeys()
    Dim dsa As Security.Cryptography.DSACryptoServiceProvider =
        New Security.Cryptography.DSACryptoServiceProvider

    Dim prv As String = dsa.ToXmlString(True)
    Dim pub As String = dsa.ToXmlString(False)
    Dim fileutil As FileUtil = New FileUtil
    fileutil.SaveString("dsa-key.xml", prv)
    fileutil.SaveString("dsa-pub.xml", pub)
End Sub
```

This method generates two XML-formatted files, `dsa-key.xml` and `dsa-pub.xml`, containing private and public keys, respectively. This code is dependent on an additional class, `FileUtil`, that is available in the project to wrap some of the common file I/O operations. This file is shown in Listing 18-6.

**LISTING 18-6:** Class FileUtil—`FileUtil.vb`

```
'FileUtil.vb
Imports System.IO
Imports System.Text
Public Class FileUtil
    Public Sub SaveString(ByVal fname As String, ByVal data As String)
        SaveBytes(fname, (New ASCIIEncoding).GetBytes(data))
    End Sub
    Public Function LoadString(ByVal fname As String)
        Dim buf() As Byte = LoadBytes(fname)
        Return (New ASCIIEncoding).GetString(buf)
    End Function
    Public Function LoadBytes(ByVal fname As String)
        Dim finfo As FileInfo = New FileInfo(fname)
        Dim length As String = CType(finfo.Length, String)
        Dim buf() As Byte = New Byte(length) {}
        Dim fs As FileStream = File.OpenRead(fname)
        fs.Read(buf, 0, buf.Length)
        fs.Close()
        Return buf
    End Function
    Public Sub SaveBytes(ByVal fname As String, ByVal data() As Byte)
        Dim fs As FileStream = File.OpenWrite(fname)
        fs.SetLength(0)
        fs.Write(data, 0, data.Length)
```

*continues*

**LISTING 18-6** *(continued)*

```
            fs.Close()
    End Sub
    Public Function LoadSig(ByVal fname As String)
        Dim fs As FileStream = File.OpenRead(fname)
        ' Need to omit the trailing null from the end of the 0 based buffer
        Dim buf() As Byte = New Byte(39) {}
        fs.Read(buf, 0, buf.Length)
        fs.Close()
        Return buf
    End Function
End Class
```

To create the signature for a data file, call the method `SignMain` in the class `DSASign` from the `Button_Click_1` event handler. Listing 18-7 shows the code that signs the data:

**LISTING 18-7: Class DSASign with Sub SignMain—**`DSASign.vb`

```
'DSASign.vb
Imports System
Imports System.IO
Imports System.Security.Cryptography
Imports System.Text

Public Class DSASign
    Public Shared Sub SignMain()

        Dim fileutil As FileUtil = New FileUtil
        Dim xkey As String = fileutil.LoadString("dsa-key.xml")
        Dim fs As FileStream = File.OpenRead("..\..\FileUtil.vb")
        Dim data(fs.Length) As Byte
        fs.Read(data, 0, fs.Length)
        Dim dsa As DSACryptoServiceProvider = New DSACryptoServiceProvider
        dsa.FromXmlString(xkey)
        Dim sig() As Byte = dsa.SignData(data)
        fs.Close()
        fileutil.SaveBytes("FileUtilSignature.txt", sig)
    End Sub
End Class
```

The two lines of code that reference the `DSACryptoServiceProvider` and `dsa.FromXmlString` method actually create the DSA provider instance and reconstruct the private key from the XML format. Next, the file is signed using the call to `dsa.SignData` while passing the file stream to be signed to this method. The `FileStream` is then cleaned up and the resulting signature is saved into the output file.

Now that you have a data file and a signature, the next step is to verify the signature. The class `DSAVerify` can be leveraged to verify that the signature file created is in fact valid. Listing 18-8 illustrates the contents of this class.

**LISTING 18-8:** Class DSAVerify with Function VerifyMain—`DSAVerify.vb`

```vb
'DSAVerify.vb
Imports System
Imports System.IO
Imports System.Security.Cryptography
Imports System.Text

Public Class DSAVerify

    Public Shared Function VerifyMain() As String

        Dim fileutil As FileUtil = New FileUtil
        Dim xkey As String = fileutil.LoadString("dsa-key.xml")
        Dim fs As FileStream = File.OpenRead("..\..\FileUtil.vb")
        Dim data(fs.Length) As Byte
        fs.Read(data, 0, fs.Length)
        Dim xsig() As Byte = fileutil.LoadSig("FileUtilSignature.txt")
        Dim dsa As DSACryptoServiceProvider = New DSACryptoServiceProvider
        dsa.FromXmlString(xkey)
        Dim verify As Boolean = dsa.VerifyData(data, xsig)
        Return String.Format("Signature Verification is {0}", verify)
    End Function
End Class
```

During testing you may want to ensure that both of these methods are enabled at the same time. This will ensure that you are encrypting and decrypting with the same keys. When working correctly, your display should look similar to what is shown in Figure 18-12.

**FIGURE 18-12:** Validating the signature for a certificate

There are many helper classes in the `System.Security` `.Cryptography` and `System.Security.Cryptography.Xml` namespaces. These classes provide numerous features to help deal with digital signatures and encryption. They also provide overlapping functionality, so there is more than one way of doing the same thing.

## X.509 Certificates

X.509 is a public key certificate exchange framework. A public key certificate is a digitally signed statement by the owner of a private key, trusted by the verifier (usually a certifying authority), that certifies the validity of the public key of another entity. This creates a trust relationship between two unknown entities. X.509 is an ISO standard specified by the document ISO/IEC 9594-8. X.509 certificates are also used in SSL (Secure Sockets Layer), which is covered in the next section.

Many certifying authority services are available over the Internet. VeriSign (`www.verisign.com`) is one of the most popular, and was founded by the RSA trio themselves. Other providers may cost less, but if you intend to make your certificate public, you'll want to investigate if they are default providers within the Windows operating system. Alternatively, at the low-cost end, and during development, you can run your own Certificate Authority (CA) service over an intranet using Microsoft Certificate Services.

The Microsoft .NET Framework SDK also provides tools for generating certificates for testing purposes. Using the Developer Command Prompt for VS2012, the following command generates a test certificate:

```
makecert -n CN=ProVB test.cer
```

The certificate is with the code at the solution directory level.

Three classes dealing with X.509 certificates are provided in the .NET Framework in the namespace `System.Security.Cryptography.X509Certificates`. The code in Listing 18-9 loads and manipulates the certificate created using `makecert`. Note you'll need to adjust the path to that certificate from the sample code.

---

**LISTING 18-9:** Class CertLoad with Sub CertMain—`CertLoad.vb`

```vb
' CertLoad.vb
Imports System
Imports System.Security.Cryptography.X509Certificates

Public Class CertLoad
    Public Shared Sub CertMain(ByVal certFilePath As String,
                               ByVal textbox As TextBox)

        Dim cert As X509Certificate = _
        X509Certificate.CreateFromCertFile(certFilePath)
        textbox.Text = "Hash = " & cert.GetCertHashString() & Environment.NewLine
        textbox.Text &= "Effective Date = " &
            cert.GetEffectiveDateString() & Environment.NewLine
        textbox.Text &= "Expire Date = " &
            cert.GetExpirationDateString() & Environment.NewLine
        textbox.Text &= "Issued By = " & cert.Issuer & Environment.NewLine
        textbox.Text &= "Issued To = " & cert.Subject & Environment.NewLine
        textbox.Text &= "Algorithm = " & cert.GetKeyAlgorithm() &
                        Environment.NewLine
        textbox.Text &= "Pub Key = " & cert.GetPublicKeyString() &
                        Environment.NewLine
    End Sub
End Class
```

The static method loads `CreateFromCertFile` (the certificate file) and creates a new instance of the class `X509Certificate`. When working correctly, the results are displayed in ProVB_Security as shown in Figure 18-13. The next section deals with Secure Sockets Layer (SSL), which uses X.509 certificates to establish the trust relationship.

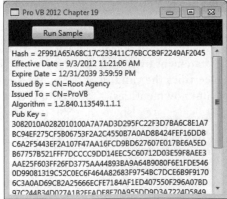

FIGURE 18-13: Displaying the contents of a certificate file

## Secure Sockets Layer

The Secure Sockets Layer (SSL) protocol provides privacy and reliability between two communicating applications over the Internet. SSL is built over the TCP layer. In January 1999, the Internet Engineering Task Force (IETF) adopted an enhanced version of SSL 3.0 called *Transport Layer Security* (*TLS*). TLS is backwardly compatible with SSL, and is defined in RFC 2246. However, the name SSL was retained due to wide acceptance of this Netscape protocol name. This section provides a simplified overview of the SSL algorithm sequence. SSL provides connection-oriented security via the following four properties:

1.  Connection is private and encryption is valid for the current session only.

2.  Symmetric key cryptography, like DES, is used for encryption. However, the session symmetric key is exchanged using public key encryption.

3.  Digital certificates are used to verify the identities of the communicating entities.

4.  Secure hash functions, such as SHA and MD5, are used for message authentication code (MAC).

The SSL protocol provides the following features:

➤ **Cryptographic security**—Using a symmetric key for session data-encryption, and a public key for authentication

➤ **Interoperability**—Interpolates OS and programming languages

➤ **Extensibility**—Adds new data-encryption protocols that are allowed within the SSL framework

➤ **Relative efficiency**—Reduces computation and network activity by using caching techniques

Two entities communicating using SSL protocols must have a public-private key pair, optionally with digital certificates validating their respective public keys.

At the beginning of a session, the client and server exchange information to authenticate each other. This ritual of authentication is called the *handshake protocol*. During this handshake, a session ID, the compression method, and the cipher suite to be used are negotiated. If the certificates exist, then they are exchanged. Although certificates are optional, either the client or the server may refuse to continue with the connection and end the session in the absence of a certificate.

After receiving each other's public keys, a set of secret keys based on a randomly generated number is exchanged by encrypting them with each other's public keys. After this, the application data exchange can commence. The application data is encrypted using a secret key, and a signed hash of the data is sent to verify data integrity.

Microsoft implements the SSL client in the .NET Framework classes. However, the server-side SSL can be used by deploying your service through the IIS Web server.

The following snippet demonstrates a method for accessing a secured URL. It takes care of minor details, such as encoding, and allows you to directly receive the results of a web request.

```
' Cryptography/GetWeb.vb
Imports System
Imports System.IO
Imports System.Net
Imports System.Text
```

```
Public Class GetWeb
    Dim MaxContentLength As Integer = 16384 ' 16k

    Public Shared Function QueryURL(ByVal url As String) As String
        Dim req As WebRequest = WebRequest.Create(url)
        Dim result As WebResponse = req.GetResponse()
        Dim ReceiveStream As Stream = result.GetResponseStream()
        Dim enc As Encoding = System.Text.Encoding.GetEncoding("utf-8")
        Dim sr As StreamReader = New StreamReader(ReceiveStream, enc)
        Dim response As String = sr.ReadToEnd()
        Return response
    End Function

End Class
```

Using this method from the ProVB_Security application allows you to retrieve the information associated with the selected Web page. In this case, you can pass the URL www.amazon.com to the method from the ButtonTest click event handler. The resulting display should be similar to what is shown in Figure 18-14.

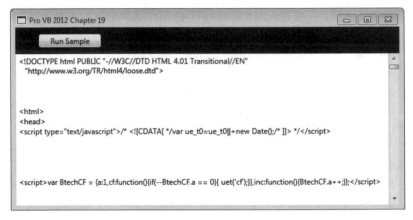

**FIGURE 18-14:** Output from a programmatic HTTP request

## SUMMARY

This chapter covered the basics of security and cryptography. It began with an overview of the security architecture of the .NET Framework and an understanding of how managing access to system capabilities will introduce a new layer of security controls for applications that go through the Windows Store. The chapter introduced the four types of security within Windows and .NET: NTFS, User Access Control (UAC), cryptographic, and programmatic.

It then examined the security tools and functionality that the .NET Framework provides. You looked at the System.Security.Permissions namespace and learned how you can control code access permissions, role-based permissions, and identity permissions. You also learned how to manage code access permissions and UAC for your assembly.

The second half of the chapter looked at cryptography, both the underlying theory and how it can be applied within your applications. You looked at the different types of cryptographic hash algorithms, including SHA, MD5, symmetric key encryption, and PKCS. You should also understand how you can use digital certificates, such as X.509 and Secure Socket Layer (SSL) certificates.

In the next chapter you will move from security to threading. You will dig into how you can use multiple threads and coordinate those threads in your applications.

# 19

# Parallel Programming Using Tasks and Threads

**WROX.COM CODE DOWNLOADS FOR THIS CHAPTER**

The wrox.com code downloads for this chapter are found at `www.wrox.com/remtitle .cgi?isbn=9781118314456` on the Download Code tab. The code is in the chapter 19 download and individually named according to the code file names listed throughout the chapter.

In the last few years, multicore technology has become the mainstream in CPU designs, and microprocessor manufacturers continue to improve their processing power. However, the shift to multicore is an inflexion point for software design philosophy.

This chapter is about the lightweight concurrency model introduced by Visual Basic 2010 with .NET Framework 4 and extended in Visual Basic 2012 with .NET Framework 4.5. A comprehensive treatment of the challenges offered by the new multicore designs could easily fill 600 pages or more, so this chapter attempts to strike a reasonable balance between detail and succinctness.

## LAUNCHING PARALLEL TASKS

It was really difficult to develop applications capable of taking full advantage of multicore microprocessors working with .NET Framework versions prior to .NET Framework 4. It was necessary to launch, control, manage, and synchronize multiple threads using complex structures prepared for some concurrency but not tuned for the modern multicore age.

.NET Framework 4 introduced the new *Task Parallel Library* (*TPL*), and .NET Framework 4.5 expanded its capabilities. The TPL was born in the multicore age and is prepared to work with a new lightweight concurrency model. The TPL provides a lightweight framework that enables developers to work with the following parallelism scenarios, implementing task-based designs instead of working with heavyweight and complex threads:

➤ **Data parallelism**—There is a lot of data and it is necessary to perform the same operations for each piece—for example, encrypting 100 Unicode strings using the Advanced Encryption Standard (*AES*) algorithm with a 256-bits key.

➤ **Task parallelism**—There are many different operations that can run concurrently, taking advantage of parallelism—for example, generating hash codes for files, encrypting Unicode strings, and creating thumbnail representations of images.

➤ **Pipelining**—A mix of task and data parallelism. It is the most complex scenario because it always requires the coordination between multiple concurrent specialized tasks—for example, encrypting 100 Unicode strings using the AES algorithm with a 256-bits key and then generating a hash code for each encrypted string. This pipeline could be implemented running two concurrent tasks, the encryption and the hash code generation. Each encrypted Unicode string would enter into a queue in order to be processed by the hash code generation algorithm.

The easiest way to understand how to work with parallel tasks is by using them. Thus, you can take your first step to creating parallelized code with the methods offered by the `System.Threading.Tasks.Parallel` static class.

## System.Threading.Tasks.Parallel Class

The most important namespace for TPL is `System.Threading.Tasks`. It offers access to classes, structures, and enumerations introduced in .NET Framework 4, including the `System.Threading.Tasks.Parallel` static class. Therefore, it is a good idea to import this namespace whenever you want to work with TPL:

```
Imports System.Threading.Tasks
```

This way, you will avoid large references. For example, instead of writing `System.Threading.Tasks.Parallel.Invoke`, you will be able to write `Parallel.Invoke`. In order to simplify the code, I will assume the aforementioned import is used in all the code snippets. However, remember that you can download the sample code for each code snippet and listing.

The main class is `Task`, representing an asynchronous and potentially concurrent operation. However, it is not necessary to work directly with instances of `Task` in order to create parallel code. Sometimes, the best option is to create parallel loops or regions, especially when the code seems to be appropriate for a sequential loop. In these cases, instead of working with the lower-level `Task` instances, it is possible to work with the methods offered by the `Parallel` static class (`System.Threading.Tasks.Parallel`):

➤ `Parallel.For`—Offers a load-balanced, potentially parallel execution of a fixed number of independent `For` loop iterations

➤ `Parallel.ForEach`—Offers a load-balanced, potentially parallel execution of a fixed number of independent `For Each` loop iterations

➤ `Parallel.Invoke`—Offers the potentially parallel execution of the provided independent actions

These methods are very useful when refactoring existing code to take advantage of potential parallelism. However, it is very important to understand that it is not as simple as replacing a `For` statement with `Parallel.For`. Many techniques to refactor existing loops are covered in detail later in this chapter.

## Parallel.Invoke

One of the easiest ways to try to run many methods in parallel is by using the new `Invoke` method provided by the `Parallel` class. For example, suppose that you have the following four independent subroutines that perform a format conversion, and you are sure it is safe to run them concurrently:

1. `ConvertEllipses`

2. `ConvertRectangles`

3. `ConvertLines`

4. `ConvertText`

You can use the following line in order to launch these subroutines, taking advantage of potential parallelism:

```
Parallel.Invoke(
    AddressOf ConvertEllipses,
    AddressOf ConvertRectangles,
    AddressOf ConvertLines,
    AddressOf ConvertText)
```

In this case, each `AddressOf` operator creates a function delegate that points to each subroutine. The definition of the `Invoke` method receives an array of `Action` (`System.Action()`) to execute in parallel.

The following code produces the same results using single-line lambda expression syntax for the subroutines to run. Instead of using the aforementioned `AddressOf` operator, it adds `Sub()` before each method name.

```
Parallel.Invoke(
    Sub() ConvertEllipses(),
    Sub() ConvertRectangles(),
    Sub() ConvertLines(),
    Sub() ConvertText())
```

The multiline lambda expression syntax makes it easier to understand the code that runs the four subroutines. The following code uses that syntax to produce the same result (code file: `Snippet01.sln`):

```
Parallel.Invoke(Sub()
                    ConvertEllipses()
                    ' Do something else adding more lines
                End Sub,
                Sub()
                    ConvertRectangles()
                    ' Do something else adding more lines
                End Sub,
                Sub()
                    ConvertLines()
                    ' Do something else adding more lines
                End Sub,
                Sub()
                    ConvertText()
                    ' Do something else adding more lines
                End Sub)
```

> **NOTE** *One of the great advantages of using the multiline lambda expression syntax is that it enables you to define and run in parallel more complex multiline subroutines without needing to create additional methods. When working with parallel programming using TPL, it is very important to master delegates and lambda expressions.*

## Lack of Execution Order

The following explanations apply to any of the previously shown code examples. The `Parallel.Invoke` method will not return until each of the four subroutines shown earlier has completed. However, completion could occur even with exceptions.

The method will try to start the four subroutines concurrently, taking advantage of the multiple *logical cores*, also known as *hardware threads*, offered by one or more physical microprocessors. However, their actual parallel execution depends on many factors. In this case, there are four subroutines. This means that `Parallel.Invoke` needs at least four logical cores available to be able to run the four methods concurrently.

In addition, having four logical cores doesn't guarantee that the four subroutines are going to start at the same time. The underlying scheduling logic could delay the initial execution of some of the provided subroutines because one or more cores could be too busy. It is indeed very difficult to make accurate predictions about the execution order because the underlying logic will try to create the most appropriate execution plan according to the available resources at runtime.

Figure 19-1 shows three of the possible concurrent execution scenarios that could take place according to different hardware configurations or diverse workloads. It is very important to keep in mind that the same code doesn't require a fixed time to run. Therefore, sometimes, the `ConvertText` method could take more time than the `ConvertLines` method, even using the same hardware configuration and input data stream.

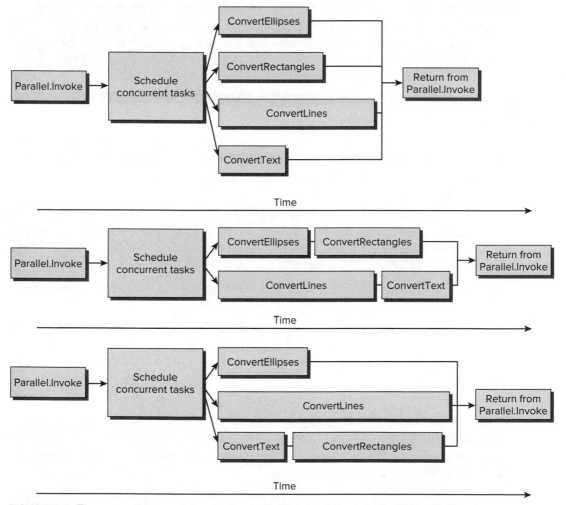

**FIGURE 19-1:** Three possible parallel executions of four methods launched with Parallel.Invoke

The top diagram represents an almost ideal situation: the four subroutines running in parallel. It is very important to consider the necessary time to schedule the concurrent tasks, which adds an initial overhead to the overall time.

The middle diagram shows a scenario with just two concurrent lanes and four subroutines to run. On one lane, once `ConvertEllipses` finishes, `ConvertRectangles` starts. On the other lane, once `ConvertLines` finishes, `ConvertText` starts. `Parallel.Invoke` takes more time than the previous scenario to run all the subroutines.

The bottom diagram shows another scenario with three concurrent lanes. However, it takes almost the same time as the middle scenario, because in this case the `ConvertLines` subroutine takes more time to run. Thus, `Parallel.Invoke` takes almost the same time as the previous scenario to run all the subroutines even using one additional parallel lane.

> **NOTE** *The code written to run concurrently using* `Parallel.Invoke` *doesn't have to rely on a specific execution order. If you have concurrent code that needs a specific execution order, you can work with other mechanisms provided by the TPL. These are covered in detail later in this chapter.*

## Advantages and Disadvantages

The key advantage of using `Parallel.Invoke` is its simplicity; you can run many subroutines in parallel without having to worry about tasks or threads. However, it isn't suitable for all the situations in which it is possible to take advantage of parallel execution. `Parallel.Invoke` has many trade-offs, including the following:

➤ If you use it to launch subroutines that need very different times to run, it will need the longest time to return control. This could mean that many logical cores stay idle for long periods of time. Therefore, it is very important to measure the results of using this method—that is, the speed gain achieved and the logical core usage.

➤ If you use it to launch delegates with different running times, it will need the longest time to return.

➤ It imposes a limit on the parallel scalability, because it calls a fixed number of delegates. In the previous example, if you run it in a computer with 16 logical cores, it will launch only four subroutines in parallel. Therefore, 12 logical cores could remain idle.

➤ Each call to this method adds an overhead before running the potentially parallel subroutines.

➤ Like any parallelized code, the existence of interdependencies or uncontrolled interaction between the different subroutines could lead to concurrency bugs that are difficult to detect and unexpected side effects. However, this trade-off applies to any concurrent code; it isn't a problem limited to using `Parallel.Invoke`.

➤ As there are no guarantees made about the order in which the subroutines are executed, it isn't suitable for running complex algorithms that require a specific execution plan of concurrent methods.

➤ Because exceptions could be thrown by any of the delegates launched with different parallel execution plans, the code to catch and handle these exceptions is more complex than the traditional sequential exception handling code.

> **NOTE** *The aforementioned trade-offs apply to the use of* `Parallel.Invoke` *as explained in the examples. However, it is possible to combine various different techniques to solve many of these trade-offs. You will learn about many of these mechanisms in this chapter.* `Parallel.Invoke` *is ideal to begin working with parallelism and to measure potential speed gains running CPU-intensive methods in parallel. You can improve the code later using the other parallelization methods provided by TPL.*

## Parallelism and Concurrency

The previously explained example provides a good transition to the differences between *parallelism* and *concurrency*, because they aren't the same thing, as shown in Figure 19-2.

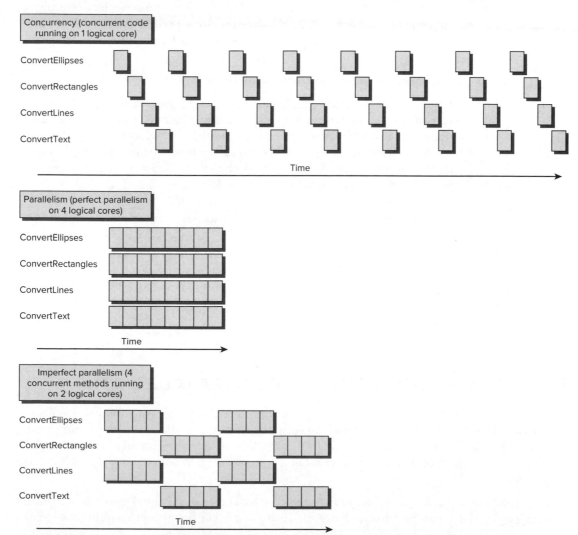

**FIGURE 19-2:** Possible scenarios for the execution of four methods in 1, 4, and 2 cores

Concurrency means that different parts of code can start, run, and complete in overlapping time periods. Concurrency can happen even on computers with a single logical core. When many parts of code run concurrently on a computer with a single logical core, time-slicing mechanisms and fast context switches can offer the impression of parallel execution. However, on this hardware, it requires more time to run many parts of code concurrently than to run a single part of code alone, because the concurrent code is competing for hardware resources (refer to Figure 19-2). You can think of concurrency as many cars sharing a single lane. This is why concurrency is also defined as a form of virtual parallelism, but it isn't real parallelism.

Parallelism means that different parts of code can actually run simultaneously, i.e., at the same time, taking advantage of real parallel processing capabilities found in the underlying hardware. Parallelism isn't possible on computers with a single logical core. You need at least two logical cores in order to run parallel code. When many parts of code run in parallel on a computer with multiple logical cores, time-slicing mechanisms and context switches also occur because typically many other parts of code are trying to use processor time. However, when real parallelism occurs, you can achieve speed gains because many parts of code running in parallel can reduce the overall necessary time to complete certain algorithms. The diagram shown in Figure 19-2 offers two possible parallelism scenarios:

1. An ideal situation: perfect parallelism on four logical cores (four lanes). The instructions for each of the four methods run in a different logical core.

2. A combination of concurrency and parallelism, imperfect parallelism, whereby four methods take advantage of just two logical cores (two lanes). Sometimes the instructions for each of the four methods run in a different logical core, in parallel, and sometimes they have to wait for their time-slice. Therefore, in this case, there is concurrency combined with parallelism. This is the most common situation, because it is indeed very difficult to achieve a perfect parallelism even on real-time operating systems (RTOS).

> **NOTE** *When parts of code run in parallel with other parts, sometimes new bugs are introduced because of parallelism — that is, they appear only when certain parts of code run exactly at the same time. These bugs can be difficult to locate, making parallel programming even more complex than concurrent programming. Luckily, TPL offers many structures and new debugging features that can help to avoid many parallelism nightmares.*

## TRANSFORMING SEQUENTIAL CODE TO PARALLEL CODE

Until recently, most Visual Basic code was written with a sequential and synchronous execution approach. Therefore, a lot of algorithms have been designed with neither concurrency nor parallelism in mind. Typically, you won't find algorithms that can be completely converted to fully parallelized and perfectly scalable code. It could happen, but it represents an ideal situation and it isn't the most common scenario.

When you have sequential code and you want to take advantage of potential parallelism to achieve better performance, you have to find *hotspots*. Then you can convert them to parallel code, measure speedups, identify potential scalability, and ensure that you haven't introduced new bugs while transforming the existing sequential code to parallel code.

> **NOTE** *A hotspot is a part of the code that takes significant time to run. You can achieve speedups if it is split into two or more pieces running in parallel. If part of the code doesn't take significant time to run, the overhead introduced by TPL could reduce the performance improvement to worthless or even make the parallelized code run slower than the sequential version. Once you begin working with the different options offered by TPL, it is going to be easier for you to detect the hotspots in sequential code.*

## Detecting Hotspots

The code discussed in this section is from code file `Listing01.sln` and shows an example of a very simple console application that runs two sequential subroutines:

1. `GenerateAESKeys`—This runs a `For` loop to generate the number of AES keys specified by the `NUM_AES_KEYS` constant. It uses the `GenerateKey` method provided by the `System.Security.Cryptography.AesManaged` class. Once the key is generated, it stores the results of converting the `Byte` array into a hexadecimal string representation (`ConvertToHexString`) in the `hexString` local variable.

2. `GenerateMD5Hashes`—This runs a `For` loop to compute a number of hashes, using the Message-Digest algorithm 5 (MD5 algorithm), specified by the `NUM_MD5_HASHES` constant. It uses a number (`i` variable) converted to string in order to call the `ComputeHash` method provided by the `System.Security.Cryptography.MD5` class. Once the hash is generated, it stores the results of converting the `Byte` array into a hexadecimal string representation (`ConvertToHexString`) in the `hexString` local variable.

The highlighted lines of code that follow are the ones added to measure the time it takes to run each subroutine, and the total elapsed time. It starts a new `Stopwatch`, calling its `StartNew` method at the beginning of each method, and then it writes the elapsed time to the `Console` output.

```
Imports System
Imports System.Text
Imports System.Security.Cryptography
' This import will be used later to run code in parallel
Imports System.Threading.Tasks

Module Module1

    Private Const NUM_AES_KEYS As Integer = 800000
    Private Const NUM_MD5_HASHES As Integer = 900000

    Function ConvertToHexString(ByRef byteArray() As Byte) As String
        ' Convert the byte array to hexadecimal string
        Dim sb As New StringBuilder()
```

```vb
        For i As Integer = 0 To (byteArray.Length() - 1)
            sb.Append(byteArray(i).ToString("X2"))
        Next

        Return sb.ToString()
    End Function

    Sub GenerateAESKeys()
        Dim sw = Stopwatch.StartNew()
        Dim aesM As New AesManaged()
        For i As Integer = 1 To NUM_AES_KEYS
            aesM.GenerateKey()
            Dim result = aesM.Key
            Dim hexString = ConvertToHexString(result)
            ' Console.WriteLine(ConvertToHexString(result))
        Next
        Console.WriteLine("AES: " + sw.Elapsed.ToString())
    End Sub

    Sub GenerateMD5Hashes()
        Dim sw = Stopwatch.StartNew()
        Dim md5M As MD5 = MD5.Create()

        For i As Integer = 1 To NUM_MD5_HASHES
            Dim data = Encoding.Unicode.GetBytes(i.ToString())
            Dim result = md5M.ComputeHash(data)
            Dim hexString = ConvertToHexString(result)
            ' Console.WriteLine(ConvertToHexString(result))
        Next
        Console.WriteLine("MD5: " + sw.Elapsed.ToString())
    End Sub

    Sub Main()
        Dim sw = Stopwatch.StartNew()
        GenerateAESKeys()
        GenerateMD5Hashes()
        Console.WriteLine(sw.Elapsed.ToString())
        ' Display the results and wait for the user to press a key
        Console.ReadLine()
    End Sub
End Module
```

The For loop in the GenerateAESKeys subroutine doesn't use its controlled variable (i) in its code because it just controls the number of times it generates a random AES key. However, the For loop in the GenerateMD5Hashes subroutine uses its controlled variable (i) to convert it to a string. Then, it uses this string as the input data to call the method that computes its hash, as shown here:

```vb
For i As Integer = 1 To NUM_MD5_HASHES
    Dim data = Encoding.Unicode.GetBytes(i.ToString())
    Dim result = md5M.ComputeHash(data)
    Dim hexString = ConvertToHexString(result)
    'Console.WriteLine(ConvertToHexString(result))
Next
```

The lines of code that write the generated keys and hashes to the default console output appear commented in code file `Listing01.sln` because these operations would generate a bottleneck that would distort the accuracy of the time measurement.

Figure 19-3 shows the sequential execution flow for this application and the time it takes to run each of the two aforementioned subroutines in a specific computer with a dual-core microprocessor.

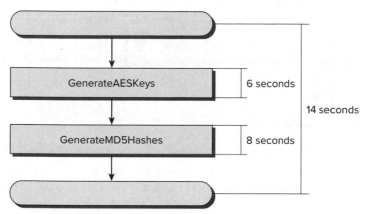

**FIGURE 19-3:** Sequential execution flow of two subroutines

`GenerateAESKeys` and `GenerateMD5Hashes` need approximately 14 seconds to run. The first one takes 6 seconds and the latter 8 seconds. Of course, these times will vary considerably according to the underlying hardware configuration.

There is no interaction between these two subroutines. Thus, they are completely independent from each other. As the subroutines run one after the other, in a sequential way, they aren't taking advantage of the parallel processing capabilities offered by the additional core(s). Therefore, these two subroutines represent a clear hotspot where parallelism could help to achieve a significant speedup over sequential execution. For example, it is possible to run both subroutines in parallel using `Parallel.Invoke`.

## Measuring Speedups Achieved by Parallel Execution

Replace the `Main` subroutine shown in the simple console application with the following new version, launching both `GenerateAESKeys` and `GenerateMD5Hashes` in parallel, using `Parallel.Invoke` (code file: `Snippet02.sln`):

```
Sub Main()
    Dim sw = Stopwatch.StartNew()
    Parallel.Invoke(Sub() GenerateAESKeys(), Sub() GenerateMD5Hashes())
    Console.WriteLine(sw.Elapsed.ToString())
    ' Display the results and wait for the user to press a key
    Console.ReadLine()
End Sub
```

Figure 19-4 shows the parallel execution flow for the new version of this application and the time it takes to run each of the two subroutines in a specific computer with a dual-core microprocessor.

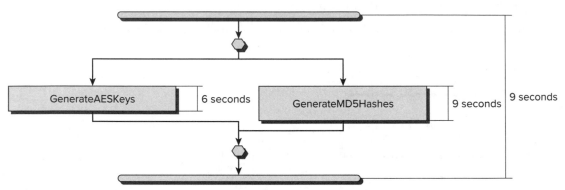

**FIGURE 19-4:** Parallel execution flow for two subroutines with a dual-core microprocessor

Now, `GenerateAESKeys` and `GenerateMD5Hashes` need approximately nine seconds to run because they take advantage of both cores offered by the microprocessor. Thus, it is possible to calculate the speedup achieved using the following formula:

$$\text{Speedup} = (\text{Serial execution time})/(\text{Parallel execution time})$$

In the preceding example, 14/9 = 1.56 times faster, usually expressed as a 1.56x speedup over the sequential version. `GenerateAESKeys` takes more time than `GenerateMD5Hashes` to run, nine seconds versus six seconds. However, `Parallel.Invoke` doesn't continue with the next line until all the delegates finish their execution. Therefore, during approximately three seconds, the application is not taking advantage of one of the cores, as shown in Figure 19-5.

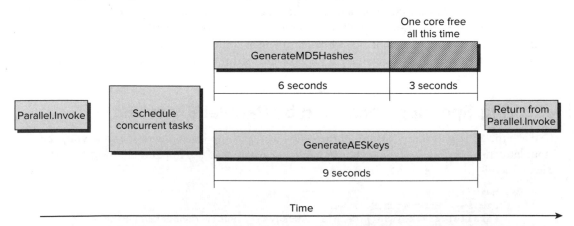

**FIGURE 19-5:** Example of inefficient scheduling when using Parallel.Invoke on a dual-core microprocessor

In addition, if this application runs on a computer with a quad-core microprocessor, its speedup over the sequential version would be nearly the same, as it won't scale to take advantage of the two additional cores found in the underlying hardware.

In this section, you saw how it is possible to detect hotspots by adding some code to measure the elapsed time to run certain methods. By changing just a few lines of code, a noticeable improvement in speed was achieved. Now it is time to learn other TPL structures that can help to achieve better results and offer improved scalability when the number of available cores increases.

> **NOTE** *There is no need to initialize TPL in order to begin working with its classes and methods. TPL does a lot of work under the hood and does its best to optimize its scheduling mechanisms to take advantage of the underlying hardware at runtime. However, choosing the right structure to parallelize a hotspot is a very important task.*

## Understanding Parallel

Now, uncomment the lines that send output to the console in both `GenerateAESKeys` and `GenerateMD5Hashes`:

```
Console.WriteLine(ConvertToHexString(result))
```

Writing to the console will generate a bottleneck for the parallel execution. However, this time, there is no need to measure accurate times. Instead, you can view the output to determine that both methods are running in parallel. The following lines show a sample console output generated by this application. The highlighted lines, the shorter hexadecimal strings, correspond to the MD5 hashes. The others represent AES keys. Each AES key takes less time to generate than each MD5 hash. Remember that the code creates 800,000 AES keys (`NUM_AES_KEYS`) and 900,000 MD5 hashes (`NUM_MD5_HASHES`). Depending on your environment, the code might take a lot of time to complete the execution.

```
0364DBC9A8FA3EAC793FC53AAE6D0193484087634C3033C470D96C72F89D7254
E410BCB82B36729CB7CCCCDFE30746F2DF141CC8275790360E2ED731F8C7113D
66CF85EA8FC77746A7C4A116F68D802D7167AE9E7C5FB0B6B85D44B8929386DE
0421897DCF492380BADF872205AE32D94632C60022A4E965652524D7023C59AD
C3BEF1DFFF5A9CAB11BFF8EA3F7DEFC97D91562A358DB56477AD445ACB4F1DE3
AF521D65489CA5C69517E32E652D464676E5F2487E438124DBF9ACF4157301AA
A641EB67C88A29985CFB0B2097B12CFB9296B4659E0949F20271984A3868E0B3
D7A05587DFDFD0C49BEF613F2EB78A43
90BF115C60B2DECA60C237F3D06E42EE
B3519CBA0137FD814C09371836F90322
1415C19F7F93306D35186721AF6B8DDE56427BB9AF29D22E37B34CB49E96BB49
208B73D3E6468F48B950E5F5006DDF30FE7A1B3BCC46489F7722BD98D54079D7
ACD0312DFF1BF29ECA2721DAFA9B20AB5FBDBD20E76C150C5CCE4026990C9D26
EB68C902145439F2A66514B9D89E9A958F18EE15D491014D3DCB312781F277D1
9DB8ABF087C78091F1E77AC769FF175A
F3EFB2804A969D890AFABCE17E84B26E
B342A8A253003754B752B85C67DA1560F30CD36A1AA759A0010E1F8E5045CBB5
9681656DC08F29AB1911A1CCCFBE6B468D1DF7B9D8722324E5E2BB4A314EC649
7DE56E111213655F54D6F8656238CA5E
196D194BA2B786EADD1B6852645C67C5
BA7AC6B878064E98D98336CA5DE45DEC
875DAB451CCE3B5FBD8E5091BAD1A8ED7DB2FF8C9E3EEA834C6DEA7C2467F27E
C1AA2CB88AB669317CB90CD842BF01DB26C6A655D10660AF01C37ECC7AEDA267
66E1F4F56E04FC9BFF225F68008A129D93F9B277ADAB43FF764FB87FFD098B78
```

Now, comment the lines that send output to the console in both `GenerateAESKeys` and `GenerateMD5Hashes` again.

## PARALLELIZING LOOPS

Both `GenerateAESKeys` and `GenerateMD5Hashes` represent an opportunity to run iterations in parallel. They generate the input data to simplify the example and perform the same operation for each piece. Thus, it represents a data parallelism scenario. It is possible to refactor the loops to run the operations in parallel. This way, instead of running both subroutines in parallel, each one can take full advantage of parallelism and automatically scale according to the number of existing logical cores.

## Parallel.For

You can think of refactoring an existing `For` loop to take advantage of parallelism as a simple replacement of `For` with `Parallel.For`. Unfortunately, it isn't as simple as that.

The following code snippets refactor the subroutines shown in the preceding section, showing the code for both the original loops and the new code with the refactored loops using the imperative syntax to implement the data parallelism offered by `Parallel.For`. The new methods, `ParallelGenerateAESKeys` and `ParallelGenerateMD5Hashes`, try to take advantage of all the cores available, relying on the work done under the hood by `Parallel.For` to optimize its behavior according to the existing hardware at runtime.

**1.** The original `GenerateAESKeys` subroutine with the sequential `For` loop, and its parallelized version

> Original sequential `For` version (code file: `Listing02.sln`):

```
Sub GenerateAESKeys()
    Dim sw = Stopwatch.StartNew()
    Dim aesM As New AesManaged()
    For i As Integer = 1 To NUM_AES_KEYS
        aesM.GenerateKey()
        Dim result = aesM.Key
        Dim hexString = ConvertToHexString(result)
        ' Console.WriteLine(ConvertToHexString(result))
    Next
    Console.WriteLine("AES: " + sw.Elapsed.ToString())
End Sub
```

> Parallelized version using `Parallel.For` (code file: `Listing03.sln`):

```
Sub ParallelGenerateAESKeys()
    Dim sw = Stopwatch.StartNew()
    Parallel.For(1, NUM_AES_KEYS + 1, Sub(i As Integer)
                        Dim aesM As New AesManaged()
                        aesM.GenerateKey()
                        Dim result = aesM.Key
                        Dim hexString = ConvertToHexString(result)
                        ' Console.WriteLine(ConvertToHexString(result))
                    End Sub)
    Console.WriteLine("AES: " + sw.Elapsed.ToString())
End Sub
```

**2.** The original `GenerateMD5Hashes` subroutine with the sequential `For` loop, and its parallelized version

➤ Original sequential `For` version (code file: `Listing02.sln`):

```
Sub GenerateMD5Hashes()
    Dim sw = Stopwatch.StartNew()
    Dim md5M As MD5 = MD5.Create()
    For i As Integer = 1 To NUM_MD5_HASHES
        Dim data = Encoding.Unicode.GetBytes(i.ToString())
        Dim result = md5M.ComputeHash(data)
        Dim hexString = ConvertToHexString(result)
        ' Console.WriteLine(ConvertToHexString(result))
    Next
    Console.WriteLine("MD5: " + sw.Elapsed.ToString())
End Sub
```

➤ Parallelized version using `Parallel.For` (code file: `Listing03.sln`):

```
Sub ParallelGenerateMD5Hashes()
    Dim sw = Stopwatch.StartNew()
    Parallel.For(1, NUM_MD5_HASHES + 1, Sub(i As Integer)
                    Dim md5M As MD5 = MD5.Create()
                    Dim data = Encoding.Unicode.GetBytes(i.ToString())
                    Dim result = md5M.ComputeHash(data)
                    Dim hexString = ConvertToHexString(result)
                    ' Console.WriteLine(ConvertToHexString(result))
                End Sub)
    Console.WriteLine("MD5: " + sw.Elapsed.ToString())
End Sub
```

The most basic version of the class function `Parallel.For` has the following parameters:

➤ `fromInclusive`—The first number for the iteration range (`Integer` or `Long`).

➤ `toExclusive`—The number before which the iteration will stop, an exclusive upper bound (`Integer` or `Long`). The iteration range will be from `fromInclusive` up to `toExclusive - 1`. It is very important to pay attention to this parameter because the classic `For` loop defines the iteration range using an inclusive upper bound. Thus, when converting a `For` loop to a `Parallel.For` loop, the original upper bound has to be converted to an upper bound minus 1.

➤ `body`—The delegate to be invoked, once per iteration, and without a predefined execution plan. It can be of the type `Action(Of Integer)` or `Action(Of Long)` depending on the type used in the iteration range definition.

> **NOTE** `Parallel.For` *supports neither floating-point values nor steps. It works with* `Integer` *and* `Long` *values and it runs adding 1 in each iteration. In addition, it partitions the iteration range according to the available hardware resources at run time and runs the body in parallel tasks. Thus, there are no guarantees made about the order in which the iterations are executed. For example, in an iteration from 1 to 101 – 1 (100 inclusive), the iteration number 50 could begin running before the iteration number 2, which could also be executing in parallel, because the time it takes to run each iteration is unknown and variable. Because the loop could be split into many parallel iterations, it's impossible to predict the execution order. The code has to be prepared for parallel execution, and it must avoid undesired side effects generated by parallel and concurrent executions.*

In addition, `Parallel.For` can return a `ParallelLoopResult` value because parallelized loops, like any parallelized code, are more complex than sequential loops. Because execution is not sequential, you cannot access a variable to determine where the loop stopped its execution. In fact, many chunks are running in parallel.

## Refactoring an Existing Sequential Loop

The code discussed in this section is from code file `Listing03.sln`. The code in the previous section showed the original `GenerateAESKey` subroutine with the sequential `For` loop. It is a good practice to create a new subroutine, function, or method with a different name when refactoring sequential code to create a parallelized version. In this case, `ParallelGenerateAESKeys` is the new subroutine.

The original `For` loop's iteration range definition is as follows:

```
For i As Integer = 1 To NUM_AES_KEYS
```

This means that it will run the loop body `NUM_AES_KEYS` times, from 1 (inclusive) to `NUM_AES_KEYS` (inclusive).

It is necessary to translate this definition to a `Parallel.For`, adding 1 to `NUM_AES_KEYS` because it is an exclusive upper bound:

```
Parallel.For(1, NUM_AES_KEYS + 1,
```

The third parameter is the delegate. In this case, this loop doesn't use the iteration variable. However, the code uses multiline lambda expression syntax to define a subroutine with an `Integer` parameter (`i`) that is going to work as the iteration variable, holding the current number:

```
Parallel.For(1, NUM_AES_KEYS + 1, Sub(i As Integer)
```

An `End Sub)` replaces the previous `Next` statement.

The preceding code was prepared to run alone, or perhaps with other methods running in parallel. However, each iteration was not designed to run in parallel with other iterations of the same loop body. Using `Parallel.For` changes the rules. The code has some problems that need to be solved. The sequential iterations shared the following three local variables:

1. `aesM`
2. `result()`
3. `hexString`

The loop body has code that changes the values of these variables in each iteration—for example, the following lines:

```
aesM.GenerateKey()
Dim result = aesM.Key
Dim hexString = ConvertToHexString(result)
```

First, the key generated by calling the `GenerateKey` method of the `AesManaged` instance, stored in `aesM`, is held in the `Key` property. Then, the code assigns the value stored in this property to the `result` variable. Finally, the last line assigns the product of converting it to a hexadecimal string to `hexString`, the third local variable. It is really difficult to imagine the results of running this code in parallel or concurrently, because it could result in a very large mess. For example, one part of the code could generate a new key, which would be stored in the aesM.Key property that was going to be read in another part of the code running in parallel. Therefore, the value read from the aesM.Key property is corrupted.

One possible solution could be using synchronization structures to protect each value and state that is changing. However, that's not appropriate in this case, because it would add more code and more synchronization overhead. There is another solution that is more scalable: refactoring the loop body, transferring these local variables as local variables inside the subroutine acting as a delegate. In order to do this, it is also necessary to create an instance of AesManaged inside the loop body. This way, it is not going to be shared by all the parallel iterations. This change adds more instructions to run for each iteration, but it removes the undesirable side effects and creates safe and stateless parallel code. The following lines show the new body. The highlighted lines of code are the variables moved inside the delegate:

```
Sub(i As Integer)
    Dim aesM As New AesManaged()

    aesM.GenerateKey()
    Dim result = aesM.Key
    Dim hexString = ConvertToHexString(result)
    ' Console.WriteLine(ConvertToHexString(result))
End Sub)
```

A very similar problem has to be solved in order to transform the original loop body found in GenerateMD5Hashes. The code in file Listing02.sln showed the original subroutine with the sequential For loop. In this case, ParallelGenerateMD5Hashes is the new subroutine. It was necessary to use the same aforementioned refactoring technique, because it is not known whether the MD5 instance holds internal states that could generate problems. It is safer to create a new independent instance for each iteration. The following lines show the new body. The highlighted lines of code are the variables moved inside the delegate:

```
Sub(i As Integer)
    Dim md5M As MD5 = MD5.Create()
    Dim data = Encoding.Unicode.GetBytes(i.ToString())
    Dim result = md5M.ComputeHash(data)
    Dim hexString = ConvertToHexString(result)
    ' Console.WriteLine(ConvertToHexString(result))
End Sub)
```

## Measuring Scalability

Replace the Main subroutine with the following new version, launching first ParallelGenerateAESKeys and then ParallelGenerateMD5Hashes (code file: Listing03.sln):

```
Sub Main()
    Dim sw = Stopwatch.StartNew()
    ParallelGenerateAESKeys()
    ParallelGenerateMD5Hashes()
    Console.WriteLine(sw.Elapsed.ToString())
    ' Display the results and wait for the user to press a key
    Console.ReadLine()
End Sub
```

Now, `ParallelGenerateAESKeys` and `ParallelGenerateMD5Hashes` need approximately 7.5 seconds to run because each one takes full advantage of both cores offered by the microprocessor. Thus, the speedup achieved is 14 / 7.5 = 1.87x over the sequential version. It is better than the previous performance gain achieved using `Parallel.Invoke` (1.56x), because the time wasted in that version is now used to run the loops, using parallel chunks in an attempt to load-balance the work done by each core. `ParallelGenerateAESKeys` takes 2.2 seconds and `ParallelGenerateMD5Hashes` takes 5.3 seconds.

Using `Parallel.For` to parallelize this code has another advantage: The same code can scale when executed with more than two cores. The sequential version of this application running on a computer with a specific quad-core microprocessor needs approximately 11 seconds to run. It is necessary to measure the time needed to run the sequential version again, because each hardware configuration will provide different results with both sequential and parallel code.

In order to measure the achieved speedup, you will always need a baseline calculated on the same hardware configuration. The version optimized using `Parallel.For` needs approximately 4.1 seconds to run. Each subroutine takes full advantage of the four cores offered by the microprocessor. Thus, the speedup achieved is 11 / 4.1 = 2.68x over the sequential version. `ParallelGenerateAESKeys` takes 1.30 seconds and `ParallelGenerateMD5Hashes` takes 2.80 seconds.

> **NOTE** *The parallelized code is capable of scaling as the number of cores increases. That didn't happen with the `Parallel.Invoke` version. However, it doesn't mean that the parallelized code will offer a linear speedup. In fact, most of the time, there is a limit to the scalability — that is, once it reaches a certain number of cores, the parallelized algorithms won't achieve additional speedup.*
>
> *In this case, it was necessary to change the code for the loop's body used in each iteration. Thus, there is an additional overhead in each iteration that wasn't part of each sequential iteration, and calling delegates is more expensive than calling direct methods. In addition, `Parallel.For` and its underlying work adds additional overhead to distribute and coordinate the execution of different chunks with parallel iterations. This is why the speedup is not near 4x and is approximately 2.68x when running with four cores. Typically, the parallelized algorithms won't offer a linear speedup. Furthermore, serial and hardware architecture-related bottlenecks can make it very difficult to scale beyond a certain number of cores.*
>
> *It is very important to measure speedup in order to determine whether the overhead added to parallelize the code brings present and potentially future (further scalability) performance benefits.*

The diagram shown in Figure 19-6 represents one of the possible execution flows, taking advantage of the four cores. Each box shown inside a method represents a chunk, automatically created by `Parallel.For` at run time.

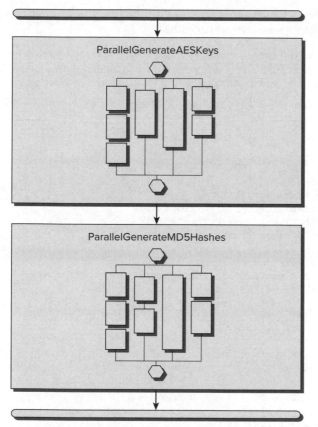

**FIGURE 19-6:** Representation of the execution flows that take advantage of four cores with Parallel.For

## Parallel.ForEach

Sometimes, refactoring an existing For loop, as previously explained, can be a very complex task, and the changes to the code could generate too much overhead for each iteration, reducing the overall performance. Another useful alternative is to partition all the data to be processed into parts that can be run as smaller loops in parallel, defining a *custom partitioner*, a tailored mechanism to split the input data into specific pieces that overrides the default partitioning mechanism. It is possible to use a Parallel.ForEach loop with a custom partitioner in order to create new versions of the sequential loops with a simpler refactoring process.

The code in file Listing05.sln shows the new code with the refactored loops using the imperative syntax to implement data parallelism offered by Parallel.ForEach, combined with a sequential For loop and a custom partitioner created with System.Collections. Concurrent.Partitioner. The new methods, ParallelPartitionGenerateAESKeys and ParallelPartitionGenerateMD5Hashes, also try to take advantage of all the cores available, relying on the work done under the hood by Parallel.ForEach and the range partitioning performed to distribute smaller sequential loops inside as many parallel loops as available cores. The code also optimizes its behavior according to the existing hardware at run time.

The code uses another important namespace for TPL, the new `System.Collections.Concurrent` namespace. This namespace offers access to useful collections prepared for concurrency and custom partitioners introduced for the first time in .NET Framework 4. Therefore, it is a good idea to import this namespace by using `Imports System.Collections.Concurrent` to work with the new examples (code file: `Listing05.sln`):

```
Sub ParallelPartitionGenerateAESKeys()
    Dim sw = Stopwatch.StartNew()
    Parallel.ForEach(Partitioner.Create(1, NUM_AES_KEYS + 1),
            Sub(range)
                Dim aesM As New AesManaged()
                Debug.WriteLine("Range ({0}, {1}. Time: {2})",
                range.Item1, range.Item2, Now().TimeOfDay)
                For i As Integer = range.Item1 To range.Item2 - 1
                    aesM.GenerateKey()
                    Dim result = aesM.Key
                    Dim hexString = ConvertToHexString(result)
                    ' Console.WriteLine("AES: " +
                    '     ConvertToHexString(result))                    Next
            End Sub)
    Console.WriteLine("AES: " + sw.Elapsed.ToString())
End Sub

Sub ParallelPartitionGenerateMD5Hashes()
    Dim sw = Stopwatch.StartNew()
    Parallel.ForEach(Partitioner.Create(1, NUM_MD5_HASHES + 1),
            Sub(range)
                Dim md5M As MD5 = MD5.Create()
                For i As Integer = range.Item1 To range.Item2 - 1
                    Dim data = Encoding.Unicode.GetBytes(i.ToString())
                    Dim result = md5M.ComputeHash(data)
                    Dim hexString = ConvertToHexString(result)
                    ' Console.WriteLine(ConvertToHexString(result))
                Next
            End Sub)
    Console.WriteLine("MD5: " + sw.Elapsed.ToString())
End Sub
```

The class function `Parallel.ForEach` offers 20 overrides. The definition used in this code file has the following parameters:

➤ source—The partitioner that provides the data source split into multiple partitions.

➤ body—The delegate to be invoked, once per iteration, and without a predefined execution plan. It receives each defined partition as a parameter—in this case, `Tuple(Of Integer, Integer)`.

In addition, `Parallel.ForEach` can return a `ParallelLoopResult` value. The information offered in this structure is covered in detail later in this chapter.

## Working with Partitions in a Parallel Loop

The code in file `Listing03.sln` showed the original `GenerateAESKey` subroutine with the sequential `For` loop. The highlighted lines of code shown in file `Listing05.sln` represent the same sequential `For` loop. The only line that changes is the `For` definition, which takes into account the lower bound and the upper bound of the partition assigned by `range.Item1` and `range.Item2`:

```
For i As Integer = range.Item1 To range.Item2 - 1
```

In this case, it is easier to refactor the sequential loop because there is no need to move local variables. The only difference is that instead of working with the entire source data, it splits it into many independent and potentially parallel partitions. Each one works with a sequential inner loop.

The following call to the `Partitioner.Create` method defines the partitions as the first parameter for `Parallel.ForEach`:

```
Partitioner.Create(1, NUM_AES_KEYS + 1)
```

This line splits the range from 1 to NUM_AES_KEYS into many partitions with an upper bound and a lower bound, creating a `Tuple(Of Integer, Integer)`. However, it doesn't specify the number of partitions to create. `ParallelPartitionGenerateAESKeys` includes a line to write the lower and upper bounds of each generated partition and the actual time when it starts to run the sequential loop for this range.

```
Debug.WriteLine("Range ({0}, {1}. Time: {2})",
                range.Item1, range.Item2, Now().TimeOfDay)
```

Replace the `Main` subroutine with the following new version, launching first `ParallelPartitionGenerateAESKeys` and then `ParallelParallelGenerateMD5Hashes` (code file: `Listing05.sln`):

```
Sub Main()
    Dim sw = Stopwatch.StartNew()
    ParallelPartitionGenerateAESKeys()
    ParallelPartitionGenerateMD5Hashes()
    Console.WriteLine(sw.Elapsed.ToString())
    ' Display the results and wait for the user to press a key
    Console.ReadLine()
End Sub
```

As shown in the following lines, the partitioner creates 13 ranges. Thus, the `Parallel.ForEach` will run 13 sequential inner `For` loops with ranges. However, they don't start at the same time, because that wouldn't be a good idea with four cores available. The parallelized loop tries to load-balance the execution, taking into account the available hardware resources. The highlighted line shows the complexity added by both parallelism and concurrency. If you take into account the time, the first partition that reaches the sequential inner `For` loop is (66667, 133333) and not (1, 66667). Remember that the upper bound values shown in the following output are exclusive.

```
Range (133333, 199999. Time: 15:45:38.2205775)
Range (66667, 133333. Time: 15:45:38.2049775)
Range (266665, 333331. Time: 15:45:38.2361775)
Range (199999, 266665. Time: 15:45:38.2205775)
Range (1, 66667. Time: 15:45:38.2205775)
```

```
Range (333331, 399997. Time: 15:45:39.0317789)
Range (399997, 466663. Time: 15:45:39.0317789)
Range (466663, 533329. Time: 15:45:39.1097790)
Range (533329, 599995. Time: 15:45:39.2345793)
Range (599995, 666661. Time: 15:45:39.3281794)
Range (666661, 733327. Time: 15:45:39.9365805)
Range (733327, 799993. Time: 15:45:40.0145806)
Range (799993, 800001. Time: 15:45:40.1705809)
```

In addition, the order in which the data appears in the debug output is different because there are many concurrent calls to `WriteLine`. In fact, when measuring speedups, it is very important to comment these lines before the loop begins, because they affect the overall time by generating a bottleneck.

This new version using `Parallel.ForEach` with custom partitions needs approximately the same time as the previous `Parallel.For` version to run.

## Optimizing Partitions According to Number of Cores

It is possible to tune the generated partitions in order to match them with the number of logical cores found at run time. `System.Environment.ProcessorCount` offers the number of logical cores or logical processors detected by the operating system. Hence, it is possible to use this value to calculate the desired range size for each partition and use it as a third parameter for the call to `Partitioner.Create`, using the following formula:

$$((numberOfElements / numberOfLogicalCores) + 1)$$

`ParallelPartitionGenerateAESKeys` can use the following code to create the partitions:

```
Partitioner.Create(0,
    NUM_AES_KEYS,
    (CInt(NUM_AES_KEYS / Environment.ProcessorCount) + 1))
```

A very similar line can also help to improve `ParallelPartitionGenerateMD5Hashes`:

```
Partitioner.Create(1,
    NUM_MD5_HASHES,
    (CInt(NUM_MD5_HASHES / Environment.ProcessorCount) + 1))
```

As shown in the following lines, now the partitioner creates four ranges because the desired range size is CInt((800000 / 4) + 1) = 200001. Thus, the `Parallel.ForEach` will run four sequential inner `For` loops with ranges, according to the number of available logical cores.

```
Range (1, 200002. Time: 16:32:51.3754528)
Range (600004, 800000. Time: 16:32:51.3754528)
Range (400003, 600004. Time: 16:32:51.3754528)
Range (200002, 400003. Time: 16:32:51.3754528)
```

Now, `ParallelPartitionGenerateAESKeys` and `ParallelPartitionGenerateMD5Hashes` need approximately 3.40 seconds to run, because each one generates as many partitions as cores available and uses a sequential loop in each delegate; therefore, it reduces the previously added overhead. Thus, the speedup achieved is 11 / 3.4 = 3.23x over the sequential version. The reduced overhead makes it possible to reduce the time from 4.1 seconds to 3.4 seconds.

> **NOTE** *Most of the time, the load-balancing schemes used by TPL under the hood are very efficient. However, you know your designs, code, and algorithms better than TPL at run time. Therefore, considering the capabilities offered by modern hardware architectures and using many of the features included in TPL, you can improve overall performance, reducing unnecessary overhead introduced by the first loop parallelization without the custom partitioner.*

The diagram shown in Figure 19-7 represents one of the possible execution flows with the numbers for the lower and upper bounds for each partition, taking advantage of the four cores with the optimized partitioning scheme.

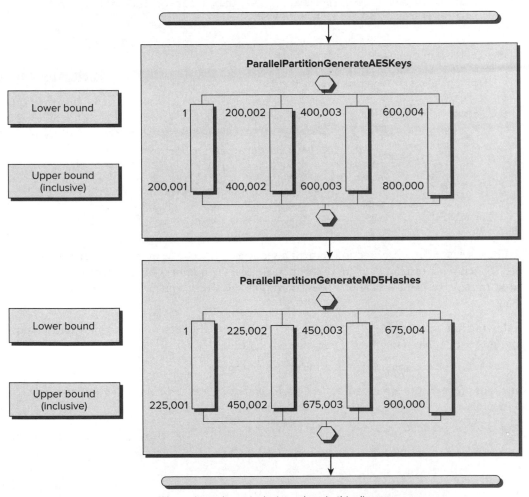

Upper bounds are inclusive values in this diagram.

**FIGURE 19-7:** Lower and upper bounds for each partition when executed on four cores

## Working with IEnumerable Sources of Data

Parallel.ForEach is also useful to refactor existing For Each loops that iterate over a collection that exposes an IEnumerable interface. The simplest definition of the class function Parallel.ForEach, used in the following code (code file: Listing08.sln) to generate a new version of the MD5 hashes generation subroutine, ParallelForEachGenerateMD5Hashes, has the following parameters:

➤ source—The collection that exposes an IEnumerable interface and provides the data source.

➤ body—The delegate to be invoked, once per iteration, and without a predefined execution plan. It receives each element of the source collection—in this case, an Integer.

```
Private Function GenerateMD5InputData() As IEnumerable(Of Integer)
    Return Enumerable.Range(1, NUM_AES_KEYS)
End Function

Sub ParallelForEachGenerateMD5Hashes()
    Dim sw = Stopwatch.StartNew()
    Dim inputData = GenerateMD5InputData()

    Parallel.ForEach(inputData, Sub(number As Integer)
                    Dim md5M As MD5 = MD5.Create()
                    Dim data =
                       Encoding.Unicode.GetBytes(number.ToString())
                    result = md5M.ComputeHash(data)
                    hexString = ConvertToHexString(result)
                    ' Console.WriteLine(ConvertToHexString(result))
                End Sub)
    Debug.WriteLine("MD5: " + sw.Elapsed.ToString())
End Sub
```

The GenerateMD5InputData function returns a sequence of Integer numbers from 1 to NUM_AES_KEYS (inclusive). Instead of using the loop to control the numbers for the iteration, the code in the ParallelForEachGenerateMD5Hashes subroutine saves this sequence in the inputData local variable.

The following line calls Parallel.ForEach with the source (inputData) and a multiline lambda delegate subroutine, receiving the number for each iteration:

```
Parallel.ForEach(inputData, Sub(number As Integer)
```

The line that prepares the input data for the hash computing method also changes to use the value found in number:

```
Dim data = Encoding.Unicode.GetBytes(number.ToString())
```

> **NOTE** *In this case, performance isn't really good compared with the other versions. However, when each iteration performs time-consuming operations, it would improve performance with an IEnumerable collection. It should be obvious that this isn't an optimal implementation, because the code has to iterate the 900,000 items of a sequence. It does it in parallel, but it takes more time than running loops with less overhead. It also consumes more memory. The example isn't intended to be a best practice for this case. The idea is to understand the different opportunities offered by the Parallel class methods and to be able to evaluate them.*

## Exiting from Parallel Loops

If you want to interrupt a sequential loop, you can use `Exit For` or `Exit For Each`. When working with parallel loops, it requires more complex code, because exiting the delegate body sub or function doesn't have any effect on the parallel loop's execution, as it is the one that's being called on each new iteration. In addition, because it is a delegate, it is disconnected from the traditional loop structure.

The following code (code file: `Listing09.sln`) shows a new version of the `ParallelForEachGenerateMD5Hashes` subroutine, called `ParallelForEachGenerateMD5HashesBreak`. Now, the `loopResult` local variable saves the result of calling the `Parallel.ForEach` class function. Moreover, the delegate body subroutine receives a second parameter—a `ParallelLoopState` instance:

```
Dim loopResult = Parallel.ForEach(
    inputData,
    Sub(number As Integer, loopState As ParallelLoopState)
Private Sub DisplayParallelLoopResult(
    ByVal loopResult As ParallelLoopResult)
    Dim text As String
    If loopResult.IsCompleted Then
        text = "The loop ran to completion."
    Else
        If loopResult.LowestBreakIteration.HasValue = False Then
            text = "The loop ended prematurely with a Stop statement."
        Else
            text = "The loop ended by calling the Break statement."
        End If
    End If
    Console.WriteLine(text)
End Sub
```

```
Sub ParallelForEachGenerateMD5HashesBreak()
    Dim sw = Stopwatch.StartNew()
    Dim inputData = GenerateMD5InputData()

    Dim loopResult = Parallel.ForEach(
        inputData,
        Sub(number As Integer,
            loopState As ParallelLoopState)
            'If loopState.ShouldExitCurrentIteration Then
            '    Exit Sub
            'End If
            Dim md5M As MD5 = MD5.Create()
            Dim data = Encoding.Unicode.GetBytes(number.ToString())
            Dim result = md5M.ComputeHash(data)
            Dim hexString = ConvertToHexString(result)
            If (sw.Elapsed.Seconds > 3) Then
                loopState.Break()
                Exit Sub
            End If
            ' Console.WriteLine(ConvertToHexString(result))
        End Sub)
    DisplayParallelLoopResult(loopResult)
    Console.WriteLine("MD5: " + sw.Elapsed.ToString())
End Sub


Private Function GenerateMD5InputData() As IEnumerable(Of Integer)
    Return Enumerable.Range(1, NUM_AES_KEYS)
End Function
```

## Understanding ParallelLoopState

The instance of ParallelLoopState (*loopState*) offers two methods to cease the execution of a Parallel.For or Parallel.ForEach:

**1.** Break—Communicates that the parallel loop should cease the execution beyond the current iteration, as soon as possible

**2.** Stop—Communicates that the parallel loop should cease the execution as soon as possible

> **NOTE** *Using these methods doesn't guarantee that the execution will stop as soon as possible, because parallel loops are complex, and sometimes it is difficult to cease the execution of all the parallel and concurrent iterations. The difference between Break and Stop is that the former tries to cease execution once the current iteration is finished, whereas the latter tries to cease it immediately.*

The code shown previously from file Listing09.sln calls the Break method if the elapsed time is more than 3 seconds:

```
If (sw.Elapsed.Seconds > 3) Then
    loopState.Break()
    Exit Sub
End If
```

It is very important to note that the code in the multiline lambda is accessing the `sw` variable that is defined in `ParallelForEachGenerateMD5HashesBreak`. It reads the value of the `Seconds` read-only property.

It is also possible to check the value of the `ShouldExitCurrentIteration` read-only property in order to make decisions when the current or other concurrent iterations make requests to stop the parallel loop execution. The code line in code file `Listing 09.sln` shows a few commented lines that check whether `ShouldExitConcurrentIteration` is `True`:

```
If loopState.ShouldExitCurrentIteration Then
    Exit Sub
End If
```

If the property is `true`, then it exits the subroutine, avoiding the execution of unnecessary iterations. The lines are commented because in this case an additional iteration isn't a problem; therefore, it isn't necessary to add this additional instruction to each iteration.

## Analyzing the Results of a Parallel Loop Execution

Once the `Parallel.ForEach` finishes its execution, `loopResult` has information about the results, in a `ParallelLoopResult` structure.

The `DisplayParallelLoopResult` subroutine shown in the code file `Listing09.sln` receives a `ParallelLoopResult` structure, evaluates its read-only properties, and outputs the results of executing the `Parallel.ForEach` loop to the console. Table 19-1 explains the three possible results of in this example.

**TABLE 19-1:** ParallelLoopResult Read-only Properties

| CONDITION | DESCRIPTION |
|---|---|
| `IsCompleted = True` | The loop ran to completion. |
| `IsCompleted = False And LowesBreakIteration.HasValue = False` | The loop ended prematurely with a `Stop` statement. |
| `IsCompleted = False And LowesBreakIteration.HasValue = True` | The loop ended by calling the `Break` statement. The `LowestBreakIteration` property holds the value of the lowest iteration that called the `Break` statement. |

> **NOTE** *It is very important to analyze the results of a parallel loop execution, because continuation with the next statement doesn't mean that it completed all the iterations. Thus, it is necessary to check the values of the* `ParallelLoopResult` *properties or to include customized control mechanisms inside the loop bodies. Again, converting sequential code to parallel and concurrent code isn't just replacing a few loops. It is necessary to understand a very different programming paradigm and new structures prepared for this new scenario.*

## Catching Parallel Loop Exceptions

As many iterations run in parallel, many exceptions can occur in parallel. The classic exception management techniques used in sequential code aren't useful with parallel loops.

When the code inside the delegate that is being called in each parallelized iteration throws an exception that isn't captured inside the delegate, it becomes part of a set of exceptions, handled by the new System.AggregateException class.

You have already learned how to handle exceptions in your sequential code in Chapter 6: "Exception Handling and Debugging." You can apply almost the same techniques. The only difference is when an exception is thrown inside the loop body, which is a delegate. The following code (code file: Listing10.sln) shows a new version of the ParallelForEachGenerateMD5Hashes subroutine, called ParallelForEachGenerateMD5HashesException. Now, the body throws a TimeOutException if the elapsed time is more than three seconds:

```
If (sw.Elapsed.Seconds > 3) Then
    Throw New TimeoutException(
        "Parallel.ForEach is taking more than 3 seconds to complete.")
End If
Sub ParallelForEachGenerateMD5HashesExceptions()
    Dim sw = Stopwatch.StartNew()
    Dim inputData = GenerateMD5InputData()
    Dim loopResult As ParallelLoopResult

    Try
        loopResult = Parallel.ForEach(inputData,
            Sub(number As Integer, loopState As ParallelLoopState)
                'If loopState.ShouldExitCurrentIteration Then
                '    Exit Sub
                'End If
                Dim md5M As MD5 = MD5.Create()
                Dim data = Encoding.Unicode.GetBytes(number.ToString())
                Dim result = md5M.ComputeHash(data)
                Dim hexString = ConvertToHexString(result)
                If (sw.Elapsed.Seconds > 3) Then
                    Throw New TimeoutException(
    "Parallel.ForEach is taking more than 3 seconds to complete.")
                End If
                ' Console.WriteLine(ConvertToHexString(result))
            End Sub)
    Catch ex As AggregateException
        For Each innerEx As Exception In ex.InnerExceptions
            Debug.WriteLine(innerEx.ToString())
            ' Do something considering the innerEx Exception
        Next
    End Try
    DisplayParallelLoopResult(loopResult)
    Debug.WriteLine("MD5: " + sw.Elapsed.ToString())
End Sub
```

A Try...Catch...End Try block encloses the call to Parallel.ForEach. Nevertheless, the line that catches the exceptions is

```
Catch ex As AggregateException
```

instead of the classic

```
Catch ex As Exception
```

An `AggregateException` contains one or more exceptions that occurred during the execution of parallel and concurrent code. However, this class isn't specifically for parallel computing; it can be used to represent one or more errors that occur during application execution. Therefore, once it is captured, it is possible to iterate through each individual exception contained in the `InnerExceptions` read-only collection of `Exception`. In this case, the `Parallel.ForEach` without the custom partitioner will display the contents of many exceptions. The loop result will look like it was stopped using the `Stop` keyword. However, as it is possible to catch the `AggregateException`, you can make decisions based on the problems that made it impossible to complete all the iterations. In this case, a sequential `For Each` loop retrieves all the information about each `Exception` in `InnerExceptions`. The following code (code file: `Listing11.sln`) shows the information about the first two exceptions converted to a string and sent to the Debug output:

```
Catch ex As AggregateException
    For Each innerEx As Exception In ex.InnerExceptions
        Debug.WriteLine(innerEx.ToString())
        ' Do something considering the innerEx Exception
    Next
End Try
```

The output looks like this:

```
System.TimeoutException: Parallel.ForEach is taking
more than 3 seconds to complete.
    at ConsoleApplication3.Module1.
_Closure$__2._Lambda$__9(Int32 number,
ParallelLoopState loopState) in
C:\Users\Public\Documents\ConsoleApplication3\
ConsoleApplication3\Module1.vb:line 255
    at System.Threading.Tasks.Parallel.<>c__DisplayClass32`2.
<PartitionerForEachWorker>b__30()
    at System.Threading.Tasks.Task.InnerInvoke()
    at System.Threading.Tasks.Task.InnerInvokeWithArg(Task childTask)
    at System.Threading.Tasks.Task.<>c__DisplayClass7.
<ExecuteSelfReplicating>b__6(Object )
System.TimeoutException: Parallel.ForEach is taking
more than 3 seconds to complete.
    at ConsoleApplication3.Module1._Closure$__2.
_Lambda$__9(Int32 number, ParallelLoopState loopState) in
C:\Users\Public\Documents\ConsoleApplication3\
ConsoleApplication3\Module1.vb:line 255
    at System.Threading.Tasks.Parallel.<>c__DisplayClass32`2.
<PartitionerForEachWorker>b__30()
    at System.Threading.Tasks.Task.InnerInvoke()
    at System.Threading.Tasks.Task.InnerInvokeWithArg(Task childTask)
    at System.Threading.Tasks.Task.<>c__DisplayClass7.
<ExecuteSelfReplicating>b__6(Object )
```

> **NOTE** *As you can see in the previous lines, the two exceptions display the same information to the Debug output. However, most of the time you will use a more sophisticated exception management technique, and you will provide more information about the iteration that is generating the problem. This example focuses on the differences between an* AggregateException *and the traditional* Exception. *It doesn't promote the practice of writing information about errors to the Debug output as a complete exception management technique.*

## SPECIFYING THE DESIRED DEGREE OF PARALLELISM

TPL methods always try to achieve the best results using all the available logical cores. Sometimes, however, you don't want to use all the available cores in a parallel loop, either because you have specific needs, and therefore better plans for the remaining available cores, or you want to leave one core free to create a responsive application and the remaining core can help you run another part of code in parallel. In these cases, you want to specify the *maximum degree of parallelism* for a parallel loop.

## ParallelOptions

TPL enables you to specify a different maximum desired degree of parallelism by creating an instance of the new ParallelOptions class and changing the value of its MaxDegreeOfParallelism property. The code in file Listing 12.sln shows a new version of the two well-known subroutines that use Parallel.For, ParallelGenerateAESKeysMaxDegree, and ParallelGenerateMD5HashesMaxDegree.

Now, they receive an Integer with the maximum desired degree of parallelism, maxDegree. Each subroutine creates a local instance of ParallelOptions and assigns the value received as a parameter to its MaxDegreeOfParallelism property, which is a new parameter for each parallel loop before the body. This way, the loop won't be optimized to take advantage of all the available cores (MaxDegreeOfParallelism = -1). Instead, it will be optimized as if the total number of available cores were equal to the maximum degree of parallelism specified in the property (code file: Listing12.sln):

```
Private Sub ParallelGenerateAESKeysMaxDegree(ByVal maxDegree As Integer)
    Dim parallelOptions As New ParallelOptions()
    parallelOptions.MaxDegreeOfParallelism = maxDegree
    Dim sw = Stopwatch.StartNew()
    Parallel.For(1,
                NUM_AES_KEYS + 1,
                parallelOptions,
        Sub(i As Integer)
                Dim aesM As New AesManaged()
                aesM.GenerateKey()
                Dim result = aesM.Key
                Dim hexString = ConvertToHexString(result)
                ' Console.WriteLine(ConvertToHexString(result))
            End Sub)
```

```vb
        Console.WriteLine("AES: " + sw.Elapsed.ToString())
    End Sub

    Sub ParallelGenerateMD5HashesMaxDegree(ByVal maxDegree As Integer)
        Dim parallelOptions As New ParallelOptions
        parallelOptions.MaxDegreeOfParallelism = maxDegree
        Dim sw = Stopwatch.StartNew()
        Parallel.For(1,
                  NUM_MD5_HASHES + 1,
                  parallelOptions,
            Sub(i As Integer)
                    Dim md5M As MD5 = MD5.Create()
                    Dim data = Encoding.Unicode.GetBytes(i.ToString())
                    Dim result = md5M.ComputeHash(data)
                    Dim hexString = ConvertToHexString(result)
                    ' Console.WriteLine(ConvertToHexString(result))
                End Sub)
        Console.WriteLine("MD5: " + sw.Elapsed.ToString())
    End Sub
```

> **NOTE** *It is not convenient to work with* static *values for the desired degree of parallelism because it can limit scalability when more cores are available. These options should be used carefully; it is best to work with* relative *values according to the number of available logical cores, or consider this number in order to prepare the code for further scalability.*

This way, it is possible to call both subroutines with a dynamic value, considering the number of logical cores at runtime:

```vb
        ParallelGenerateAESKeysMaxDegree(Environment.ProcessorCount - 1)
        ParallelGenerateMD5HashesMaxDegree(Environment.ProcessorCount - 1)
```

Both `Parallel.For` loops are going to try to work with the number of logical cores minus 1. If the code runs with a quad-core microprocessor, then it will use just three cores.

The following is *not* a best practice for final code. However, sometimes you want to know whether two parallelized subroutines offer better performance if they are executed at the same time, limiting the number of cores for each one. You can test this situation using the following line (code file: `Listing12.sln`):

```vb
    Parallel.Invoke(
        Sub() ParallelGenerateAESKeysMaxDegree(2),
        Sub() ParallelGenerateAESKeysMaxDegree(2))
```

The two subroutines will be launched in parallel, and each will try to optimize its execution to use two of the four cores of a quad-core microprocessor. The obvious drawback of the previous line is that it uses a static number of cores. Nonetheless, this is just for performance testing purposes.

`ParallelOptions` also offers two additional properties to control more advanced options:

**1.** `CancellationToken`—Allows assigning a new `System.Threading.CancellationToken` instance in order to propagate notification that parallel operations should be canceled. The usage of this property is covered in detail later in this chapter

2. `TaskScheduler`—Allows assigning a customized `System.Threading.Tasks.
   TaskScheduler` instance. It is usually not necessary to define a customized task scheduler to schedule parallel tasks unless you are working with very specific algorithms.

## Understanding Hardware Threads and Logical Cores

The `Environment.ProcessorCount` property provides the number of logical cores. However, sometimes the number of *logical* cores, also known as *hardware threads*, is different from the number of *physical* cores.

For example, an Intel Core i7 microprocessor with six physical cores offering HyperThreading technology doubles the number to twelve logical cores. Therefore, in this case, `Environment.ProcessorCount` is twelve, not six. The operating system also works with twelve logical processors.

All the code created with TPL runs using multiple software *threads*. Threads are the low-level lanes used to run many parts of code in parallel, taking advantage of the presence of multiple cores in the underlying hardware. However, most of the time, the code running in these lanes has some imperfections. It waits for I/O data or other threads to finish, or it causes latency as it waits for data to be fetched from the different caches available in the microprocessor or the system memory. This means that there are idle execution units.

HyperThreading technology offers an increased degree of instruction-level parallelism, by duplicating the architectural states for each physical core in order to mitigate the imperfections of the parallel code by starting the execution of a second thread when the first one is waiting. This way, it appears to be a microprocessor with two times the real number of physical cores.

> **NOTE** *Logical cores are not the same as real physical cores. Although this technique sometimes improves performance through increased instruction-level parallelism when each physical core has two threads with independent instruction streams, if the software threads don't have many data dependencies, the performance improvements could be less than expected. It depends on the application.*

As TPL uses the number of hardware threads, or logical cores, to optimize its execution, sometimes certain algorithms won't offer the expected scalability as more cores appear because they aren't real physical cores.

For example, if an algorithm offered a 6.5x speedup when executed with eight physical cores, it would offer a more reticent 4.5x speedup with a microprocessor with four physical cores and eight logical cores with HyperThreading technology.

## CREATING AND MANAGING TASKS

TPL introduced the new task-based programming model to translate multicore power into application performance without having to work with low-level, more complex, and heavyweight threads. It is very important to understand that *tasks* aren't threads. Tasks run using threads. However, it doesn't mean they replace threads. In fact, all the parallel loops used in the previous examples run by creating tasks, and their parallel and concurrent execution is supported by underlying threads, as shown in Figure 19-8.

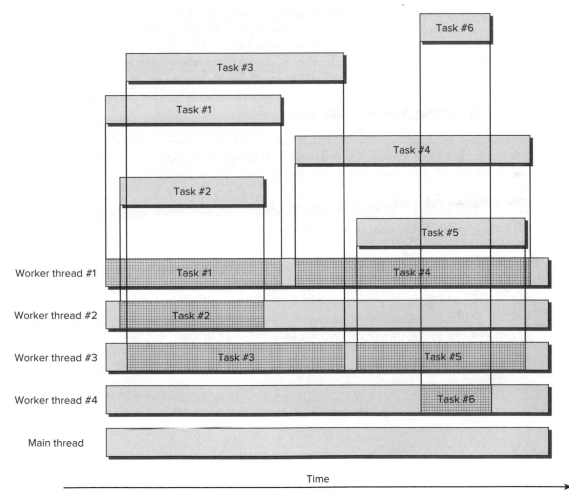

**FIGURE 19-8:** Tasks and their relationship with threads

When you work with tasks, they run their code using underlying threads (software threads, scheduled on certain hardware threads, or logical cores). However, there isn't a one-to-one relationship between tasks and threads. This means you aren't creating a new thread each time you create a new task. The CLR creates the necessary threads to support the tasks' execution needs. Of course, this is a simplified view of what goes on when creating tasks.

Synchronizing code running in multiple threads is indeed complex. Thus, a task-based alternative offers an excellent opportunity to leave some synchronization problems behind, especially those regarding work scheduling mechanisms. The CLR uses *work-stealing queues* to reduce the locks and to schedule small work chunks without adding a significant overhead. Creating a new thread introduces a big overhead, but creating a new task "steals" work from an existing thread whenever possible. Therefore, tasks offer a new lightweight mechanism for parts of code capable of taking advantage of multiple cores.

The default task scheduler relies on an underlying thread pool engine. Thus, when you create a new task, it will use the steal-working queues to find the most appropriate thread to enqueue it. It steals work from an existing thread or creates a new one when necessary. The code included in tasks will run in one thread, but this happens under the hood, and the overhead is smaller than manually creating a new thread.

# System.Threading.Tasks.Task

So far, TPL has been creating instances of `System.Threading.Tasks.Task` under the hood in order to support the parallel execution of the iterations. In addition, calling `Parallel.Invoke` also creates as many instances of `Task` as delegates are called.

A `Task` represents an asynchronous operation. It offers many methods and properties that enable you to control its execution and get information about its status. The creation of a `Task` is independent of its execution. This means that you have complete control over the execution of the associated operation.

> **NOTE** *When you launch many asynchronous operations as Task instances, the task scheduler will try to run them in parallel in order to load-balance all the available logical cores at run time. However, it isn't convenient to use tasks to run any existing piece of code, because tasks add an overhead. Sometimes it doesn't make sense to use tasks. Although this overhead is smaller than that added by a thread, it is still an overhead that has to be considered. For example, it doesn't make sense to create tasks to run two lines of code as two independent asynchronous tasks that solve very simple calculations. Remember to measure the speedups achieved between the parallel execution and the sequential version to decide whether parallelism is appropriate or not.*

Table 19-2 explains the three possible situations considered in this example.

**TABLE 19-2:** Task Read-only Properties

| PROPERTY | DESCRIPTION |
| --- | --- |
| AsyncState | A state `Object` supplied when you created the `Task` instance. |
| CreationOptions | The `TaskCreationOptions` enum value used to provide hints to the task scheduler in order to help it make the best scheduling decisions. |
| CurrentId | The unique ID for the `Task` being executed. It is not equivalent to a thread ID in unmanaged code. |
| Exception | The `AggregateException` that caused the `Task` to end prematurely. It is a null value if the `Task` hasn't thrown exceptions at all or finished without throwing exceptions. |

| Factory | Provides access to the factory methods that allow the creation of `Task` instances with and without results |
|---|---|
| Id | The unique ID for the `Task` instance |
| IsCanceled | A Boolean value indicating whether the `Task` instance was canceled |
| IsCompleted | A Boolean value indicating whether the `Task` has completed its execution |
| IsFaulted | A Boolean value indicating whether the `Task` has aborted its execution due to an unhandled exception |
| Status | The `TaskStatus` value indicating the current stage in the life cycle of a `Task` instance |

## Understanding a Task's Life Cycle

It is very important to understand that each `Task` instance has a life cycle. However, it represents concurrent code potentially running in parallel according to the possibilities offered by the underlying hardware and the availability of resources at run time. Therefore, any information about the `Task` instance could change as soon as you retrieve it, because its states are changing concurrently.

A `Task` instance completes its life cycle just once. After it reaches one of its three possible final states, it doesn't go back to any previous state, as shown in the state diagram in Figure 19-9.

A `Task` instance has three possible initial states, depending on how it was created, as described in Table 19-3.

**TABLE 19-3:** Initial States for a Task Instance

| VALUE | DESCRIPTION |
|---|---|
| `TaskStatus.Created` | A `Task` instance created using the `Task` constructor has this initial state. It will change once there is a call to either `Start` or `RunSynchronously`, or if the task is canceled. |
| `TaskStatus.WaitingForActivation` | This is the initial state for tasks created through methods that allow the definition of continuations—that is, tasks that aren't scheduled until other dependent tasks finish their execution. |
| `TaskStatus.WaitingToRun` | This is the initial state for a task created through `TaskFactory.StartNew`. It is waiting for the specified scheduler to pick it up and run it. |

Next, the task status can transition to the `TaskStatus.Running` state, and finally move to a final state. If it has attached children, it isn't considered complete and will transition to the `TaskStatus.WaitingForChildrenToComplete` state. Once its children tasks complete, the task moves to one of the three possible final states shown in Table 19-4.

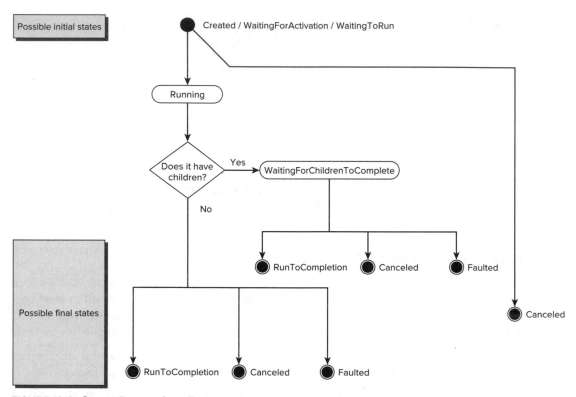

**FIGURE 19-9:** Status diagram for a Task instance

**TABLE 19-4:** Final States for a Task Instance

| VALUE | DESCRIPTION |
| --- | --- |
| `TaskStatus.Canceled` | A cancellation request arrived before the task started its execution or during it. The `IsCanceled` property will be `True`. |
| `TaskStatus.Faulted` | An unhandled exception in its body or the bodies of its children made the task end. The `IsFaulted` property will be `True` and the `Exception` property will be non-null and will hold the `AggregateException` that caused the task or its children to end prematurely. |
| `TaskStatus.RanToCompletion` | The task completed its execution. It ran to the end of its body without being canceled or throwing an unhandled exception. The `IsCompleted` property will be `True`. In addition, `IsCanceled` and `IsFaulted` will be both `False`. |

# Using Tasks to Parallelize Code

In a previous example, you used `Parallel.Invoke` to launch two subroutines in parallel:

```
Parallel.Invoke(Sub() GenerateAESKeys(), Sub() GenerateMD5Hashes())
```

It is possible to do the same job using two instances of `Task`, as shown in the following code (code file: `Listing13.sln`). Working with instances of `Tasks` offers more flexibility to schedule and start independent and chained tasks that can take advantage of multiple cores.

```
' Create the tasks
Dim t1 = New Task(Sub() GenerateAESKeys())
Dim t2 = New Task(Sub() GenerateMD5Hashes())
' Start the tasks
t1.Start()
t2.Start()
' Wait for all the tasks to finish
Task.WaitAll(t1, t2)
```

The first two lines create two instances of `Task` with a lambda expression to create a delegate for `GenerateAESKeys` and `GenerateMD5Hashes`. `t1` is associated with the first subroutine, and `t2` with the second. It is also possible to use multiline lambda expression syntax to define the action that the `Task` constructor receives as a parameter. At this point, the `Status` for both `Task` instances is `TaskStatus.Created`. The subroutines aren't running yet, but the code continues with the next line.

## Starting Tasks

Then, the following line starts the *asynchronous execution* of `t1`:

```
t1.Start()
```

The `Start` method initiates the execution of the delegate in an independent way, and the program flow continues with the instruction after this method, even though the delegate has not finished its execution. The code in the delegate associated with the task runs concurrently and potentially in parallel with the main program flow, the *main thread*. This means that at this point, there is a main thread and another thread or threads supporting the execution of this new task.

The execution of the main program flow, the main thread, is synchronous. This means that it will continue with the next instruction, the line that starts the *asynchronous execution* of `t2`:

```
t2.Start()
```

Now the `Start` method initiates the execution of the delegate in another independent way and the program flow continues with the instruction after this method, even though this other delegate has not finished its execution. The code in the delegate associated with the task runs concurrently and potentially in parallel with the main thread and the code inside `GenerateAESKeys` that is already running. This means that at this point, there is a main thread and other threads supporting the execution of the two tasks.

> **NOTE** *It is indeed easy to run asynchronous code using Task instances and the latest language improvements added to Visual Basic. With just a few lines, you can create code that runs asynchronously, control its execution flow, and take advantage of multicore microprocessors or multiple processors. Microsoft .NET Framework 4.5 went a step forward with the addition of the Async and Await modifiers to simplify their usage in asynchronous operations.*

The sequence diagram in Figure 19-10 shows the parallel and asynchronous execution flow for the main thread and the two tasks.

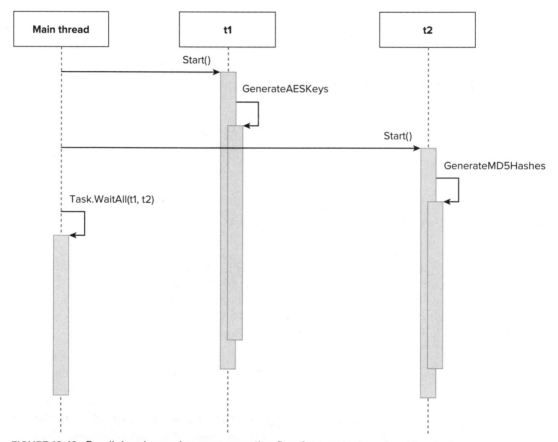

**FIGURE 19-10:** Parallel and asynchronous execution flow for a main thread and two tasks

## Visualizing Tasks Using Parallel Tasks and Parallel Stacks

The Visual Basic 2012 IDE improves the two debugging windows introduced in Visual Basic 2010: Parallel Tasks and Parallel Stacks. These windows offer information about the tasks that are running, including their status and their relationship with the underlying threads. It is very easy to understand the relationship between the tasks and the underlying threads in .NET Framework 4.5 when debugging simple parallelized code and running it step-by-step using the debugging windows, which enable you to monitor what is going on under the hood. By running the code step-by-step, you can see the differences between synchronous and asynchronous execution.

For example, if you insert a breakpoint on the line `Task.WaitAll(t1, t2)` and your microprocessor has at least two cores, you will be able to see two tasks running in parallel while debugging. To do so, select Debug ⇨ Windows ⇨ Parallel Tasks (Ctrl + Shift + D, K) while debugging the application. The IDE will display the Parallel Tasks dialogue shown in Figure 19-11, which includes a list of all the tasks and their status (Active).

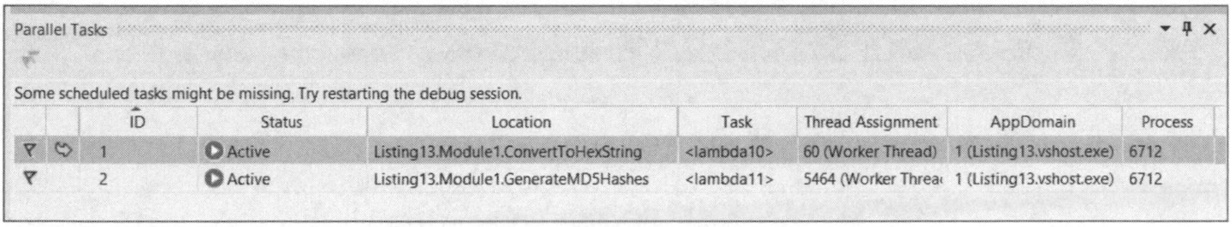

| | | ID | Status | Location | Task | Thread Assignment | AppDomain | Process |
|---|---|---|---|---|---|---|---|---|
| | | | | **Parallel Tasks** | | | | ▾ ⊣ × |
| | | | | Some scheduled tasks might be missing. Try restarting the debug session. | | | | |
| ⚑ | ⇨ | 1 | ▶ Active | Listing13.Module1.ConvertToHexString | <lambda10> | 60 (Worker Thread) | 1 (Listing13.vshost.exe) | 6712 |
| ⚑ | | 2 | ▶ Active | Listing13.Module1.GenerateMD5Hashes | <lambda11> | 5464 (Worker Threa‹ | 1 (Listing13.vshost.exe) | 6712 |

**FIGURE 19-11:** Parallel Tasks dialogue with two active tasks

There are two tasks:

➤ Task ID 1: `<lambda10>()` — Assigned to Worker thread ID 60

➤ Task ID 2: `<lambda11>()` — Assigned to Worker thread ID 5464

Each of the two tasks is assigned to a different thread. The status for both tasks is Running, and they are identified by an auto-generated lambda name and number, `<lambda10>()` and `<lambda11>()`. This happens because the code uses lambda expressions to generate the delegates associated with each task.

If you double-click on a task name, the IDE will display the next statement that is going to run for the selected task. Remember that the threads assigned to these tasks and the main thread are running concurrently and potentially in different logical cores, according to the available hardware resources and the decisions taken by the schedulers.

> **NOTE** *The CLR task scheduler tries to steal work from the most appropriate underlying thread, by consuming time from an idle one. It can also decide to create a new thread to support the task's execution. The operating system scheduler distributes the cores between the dozens or hundreds of threads scheduled to receive processor time from the available cores. This is why the same code can run with different parallelism levels and different concurrent times on the same hardware configuration.*

You can check what is going on with each different concurrent task. You have similar options to those offered by previous Visual Basic versions with threads, but the information is better because you can check whether a task is scheduled or waiting-deadlocked. You can also order and group the information shown in the windows, as you can with any other Visual Basic IDE feature.

The Parallel Tasks grid includes a column named Thread Assignment. This number is the ID shown in the Threads window. Thus, you know which managed thread is supporting the execution of a certain task while debugging. You can also check the next statement and additional detailed information for each different thread. To do so, select Debug ➪ Windows ➪ Threads (Ctrl + Alt + H) while debugging the application. The IDE will display the Threads dialog shown in Figure 19-12, which includes a list of all the threads, their category, and their locations.

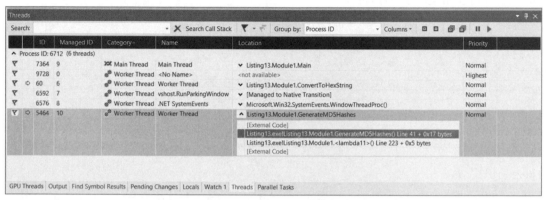

**FIGURE 19-12:** Threads dialog with 5 worker threads and the main thread

> **NOTE** *There is a simpler way to visualize the relationship between tasks and threads. You can select Debug ➪ Windows ➪ Parallel Stacks (Ctrl + Shift + D, S). The IDE will display the Parallel Stacks window shown in Figure 19-13, which includes a diagram with all the tasks or threads, their status, and their relationships. The default view is Threads.*

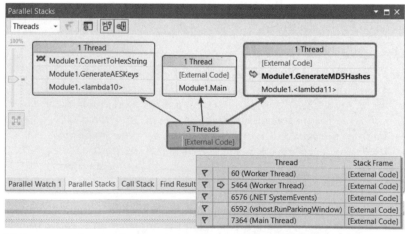

**FIGURE 19-13:** Parallel Stacks window displaying the default Threads view

The two threads on the right side of the diagram are running the code scheduled by the two tasks. Each thread shows its call stack. The thread that supports `Module1.<lambda10>` is running the `GenerateAESKeys` subroutine — specifically, code inside the call to the `ConvertToHexString` subroutine. The thread that supports `Module1.<lambda11>` is running the `GenerateMD5Hashes` subroutine. This diagram indicates what each thread is doing with a great level of detail.

You can change the value for the combo box in the upper-left corner from Threads to Tasks, and the IDE will display a diagram with all the tasks, including their status, relationships, and the call stack, as shown in Figure 19-14.

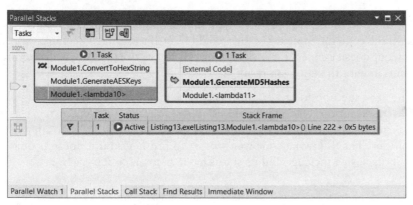

**FIGURE 19-14:** Parallel Stacks window displaying the Tasks view

## Waiting for Tasks to Finish

At some point, you need to wait for certain tasks, started with an asynchronous execution, to finish. The following line calls the `Task.WaitAll` method, which will wait for the `Task` instances received as a `ParamArray`, separated by commas. This method has a synchronous execution, which means that the main thread won't continue with the next statement until the `Task` instances received as parameters finish their execution.

```
Task.WaitAll(t1, t2)
```

Here, `t1` and `t2` have to finish their execution. The current thread—in this case, the main thread—will wait until both tasks finish their execution. However, it is very important that this time waiting for the tasks to finish is not a loop continuously checking a status and consuming a lot of CPU cycles. The `WaitAll` method uses a lightweight mechanism to reduce the need for CPU cycles as much as possible. This way, once these tasks finish their execution, the next statement will run.

Because the `WaitAll` method uses a synchronous execution, if the tasks take one minute to run, then the thread where this method was called (in this case, the main thread) will be waiting for this amount of time. Therefore, sometimes you want to limit the number of milliseconds to wait for the tasks to finish. You can use another definition for the `Task.WaitAll` method that accepts an array of `Task` instances and the number of milliseconds to wait. The method returns a `Boolean` value indicating whether the tasks where able to finish within the specified timeout. The following code waits for `t1` and `t2` to finish their execution with a three-second timeout (code file: `Snippet03.sln`):

```
If Task.WaitAll(New Task() {t1, t2}, 3000) = False Then
    Console.WriteLine(
"GenerateAESKeys and GenerateMD5Hashes are taking
more than 3 seconds to complete.")
    Console.WriteLine(t1.Status.ToString())
    Console.WriteLine(t2.Status.ToString())
End If
```

If `t1` and `t2` don't finish in three seconds, the code displays a message and the status for both tasks. If no exceptions occurred in the code for these tasks, they could be still running. The `Task.WaitAll` method with a specific timeout doesn't cancel the tasks if they take more time to run; it just returns from its synchronous execution with the `Boolean` result.

It is also possible to call the `Wait` method for a `Task` instance. In this case, the current thread will wait until that task finishes its execution. Of course, there is no need to send the task instance as a parameter because the `Wait` method is an instance method. The `Task.Wait` method also supports a timeout in one of its definitions. The following code waits for `t1` to finish, and if it doesn't complete its work in three seconds, it displays a message and its status (code file: `Snippet04.sln`):

```
If t1.Wait (3000) = False Then
    Console.WriteLine("GenerateAESKeys is taking more than 3 seconds to complete.")
    Console.WriteLine(t1.Status.ToString())
End If
```

## Cancelling Tasks Using Tokens

You can interrupt the execution of `Task` instances through the use of *cancellation tokens*. To do so, it is necessary to add some code in the delegate, in order to create an cancelable operation that is capable of terminating in a timely manner.

The following code (code file: `Listing14.sln`) shows two new versions of the AES keys and MD5 hash generators. The changes made in order to support cancellation appear in bold. The new `GenerateAESKeysCancel`, replacing the old `GenerateAESKeys`, receives a `System.Threading.CancellationToken` instance and throws an `OperationCanceledException` calling the `ThrowIfCancellationRequested` method. This way, the `Task` instance transitions to the `TaskStatus.Canceled` state and the `IsCanceled` property will be `True`.

```
Private Sub GenerateAESKeysCancel(ByVal ct As System.Threading.CancellationToken)
    ct.ThrowIfCancellationRequested()
    Dim sw = Stopwatch.StartNew()
    Dim aesM As New AesManaged()
    For i As Integer = 1 To NUM_AES_KEYS
        aesM.GenerateKey()
        Dim result = aesM.Key
        Dim hexString = ConvertToHexString(result)
        ' Console.WriteLine("AES: " + ConvertToHexString(result))
        If ct.IsCancellationRequested Then
            ct.ThrowIfCancellationRequested()
        End If
```

```vbnet
        Next
        Console.WriteLine("AES: " + sw.Elapsed.ToString())
    End Sub

    Private Sub GenerateMD5HashesCancel(ByVal ct As System.Threading.CancellationToken)
        ct.ThrowIfCancellationRequested()
        Dim sw = Stopwatch.StartNew()
        Dim md5M As MD5 = MD5.Create()
        For i As Integer = 1 To NUM_MD5_HASHES
            Dim data = Encoding.Unicode.GetBytes(i.ToString())
            Dim result = md5M.ComputeHash(data)
            Dim hexString = ConvertToHexString(result)
            ' Console.WriteLine(ConvertToHexString(result))
            If ct.IsCancellationRequested Then
                ct.ThrowIfCancellationRequested()
            End If
        Next
        Debug.WriteLine("MD5: " + sw.Elapsed.ToString())
    End Sub

    Sub Main()
        Dim cts As New System.Threading.CancellationTokenSource()
        Dim ct As System.Threading.CancellationToken = cts.Token

        Dim t1 = Task.Factory.StartNew(Sub() GenerateAESKeysCancel(ct), ct)
        Dim t2 = Task.Factory.StartNew(Sub() GenerateMD5HashesCancel(ct), ct)

        ' Sleep the main thread for 1 second
        Threading.Thread.Sleep(1000)

        cts.Cancel()

        Try
            If Task.WaitAll(New Task() {t1, t2}, 1000) = False Then
                Console.WriteLine(
"GenerateAESKeys and GenerateMD5Hashes are taking
more than 1 second to complete.")
                Console.WriteLine(t1.Status.ToString())
                Console.WriteLine(t2.Status.ToString())
            End If
        Catch ex As AggregateException
            For Each innerEx As Exception In ex.InnerExceptions
                Debug.WriteLine(innerEx.ToString())
                ' Do something else considering the innerEx Exception
            Next
        End Try
        If t1.IsCanceled Then
            Console.WriteLine("The task running GenerateAESKeysCancel was canceled.")
        End If
        If t2.IsCanceled Then
            Console.WriteLine(
"The task running GenerateMD5HashesCancel was canceled.")
        End If
            ' Display the results and wait for the user to press a key
```

```
        Console.ReadLine()
    End Sub
```

The first line of `GenerateAESKeysCancel` will throw the aforementioned exception if its cancellation was already requested at that time. This way, it won't start the loop if unnecessary at that point.

```
ct.ThrowIfCancellationRequested()
```

In addition, after each iteration of the loop, new code checks the token's `IsCancellationRequested`. If it is `True`, it calls the `ThrowIfCancellationRequested` method. Before calling this method, when `IsCancellationRequested` is `True`, it is possible to add cleanup code when necessary:

```
If ct.IsCancellationRequested Then
    ' It is important to add cleanup code here when necessary
    ct.ThrowIfCancellationRequested()
End If
```

Doing this adds a small amount of overhead to each iteration of the loop, but it is capable of observing an `OperationCanceledException` and compares its token to the `Task` instance's associated one. If they are the same and its `IsCancelled` property is `True`, the `Task` instance understands that there is a request for cancellation and makes the transition to the `Canceled` state, interrupting its execution. When there is code waiting for the canceled `Task` instance, this also generates an automatic `TaskCanceledException`, which is wrapped in an `AggregateException`.

In this case, the main subroutine creates a `CancellationTokenSource`, *cts*, and a `Cancellation Token`, *ct*:

```
        Dim cts As New System.Threading.CancellationTokenSource()
        Dim ct As System.Threading.CancellationToken = cts.Token
```

`CancellationTokenSource` is capable of initiating cancellation requests, and `CancellationToken` communicates it to asynchronous operations.

It is necessary to send a `CancellationToken` as a parameter to each task delegate; therefore, the code uses one of the definitions of the `TaskFactory.StartNew` method. The following lines create and start two `Task` instances with associated actions and the same `CancellationToken` instance (ct) as parameters:

```
        Dim t1 = Task.Factory.StartNew(Sub() GenerateAESKeysCancel(ct), ct)
        Dim t2 = Task.Factory.StartNew(Sub() GenerateMD5HashesCancel(ct), ct)
```

The preceding lines use the `Task` class `Factory` property to retrieve a `TaskFactory` instance that can be used to create tasks with more options than those offered by direct instantiation of the `Task` class. In this case, it uses the `StartNew` method, which is functionally equivalent to creating a `Task` using one of its constructors and then calling `Start` to schedule it for execution.

Then, the code calls the `Sleep` method to make the main thread sleep for one second. This method suspends the current thread for the indicated time—in this case, specified as an `Integer` in milliseconds:

```
    Threading.Thread.Sleep(1000)
```

> **NOTE** *The main thread remains suspended for one second, but the threads that are supporting the tasks' execution won't be suspended. Therefore, the tasks will be scheduled to begin their execution.*

One second later, the main thread communicates a request for cancellation for both tasks through the `CancellationTokenSource` instance's `Cancel` method:

```
cts.Cancel()
```

The cancellation token is evaluated in the two delegates launched by the `Task` instances, as previously explained.

Adding a few lines, it is indeed easy to cancel asynchronous actions. However, it is very important to add the necessary cleanup code.

A `Try...Catch...End Try` block encloses the call to `Task.WaitAll`. Because there was a request for cancellation for both tasks, there will be two benign exceptions of type `OperationCanceledException`.

The `IsCanceled` property for both tasks is going to be `True`. Checking this property, you can add code whenever a task was canceled.

## Handling Exceptions Thrown by Tasks

As many tasks run in parallel, many exceptions can occur in parallel. Task instances also work with a set of exceptions, handled by the previously explained `System.AggregateException` class.

The following code (code file: `Listing15.sln`) shows the highlighted lines that add an unhandled exception in the `GenerateAESKeysCancel` subroutine.

Comment the code that requested cancellation for both tasks:

```
' cts.Cancel()
Private Sub GenerateAESKeysCancel(ByVal ct As System.Threading.CancellationToken)
    ct.ThrowIfCancellationRequested()
    Dim sw = Stopwatch.StartNew()
    Dim aesM As New AesManaged()
    For i As Integer = 1 To NUM_AES_KEYS
        aesM.GenerateKey()
        Dim result = aesM.Key
        Dim hexString = ConvertToHexString(result)
        ' Console.WriteLine("AES: " + ConvertToHexString(result))
        If (sw.Elapsed.Seconds > 0.5) Then
            Throw New TimeoutException(
"GenerateAESKeysCancel is taking
more than 0.5 seconds to complete.")
        End If
        If ct.IsCancellationRequested Then
            ct.ThrowIfCancellationRequested()
        End If
    Next
    Console.WriteLine("AES: " + sw.Elapsed.ToString())
End Sub
```

Add the following lines to the `Main` subroutine:

```
If t1.IsFaulted Then
    For Each innerEx As Exception In t1.Exception.InnerExceptions
        Debug.WriteLine(innerEx.ToString())
        ' Do something else considering the innerEx Exception
    Next
End If
```

Because there is an unhandled exception in `t1`, its `IsFaulted` property is `True`. Therefore, `t1.Exception`, an `AggregateException`, contains one or more exceptions that occurred during the execution of its associated delegate. After checking the `IsFaulted` property, it is possible to iterate through each individual exception contained in the `InnerExceptions` read-only collection of `Exception`. You can make decisions according to the problems that made it impossible to complete the task. The following lines show the information about the unhandled exception converted to a string and sent to the Debug output.

```
System.TimeoutException: GenerateAESKeysCancel
is taking more than 0.5 seconds to complete.
   at ConsoleApplication3.Module1.GenerateAESKeysCancel(CancellationToken ct)
in C:\Wrox\Professional_VB_2012\ConsoleApplication3\
ConsoleApplication3\Module1.vb:line 427
   at ConsoleApplication3.Module1._Closure$__3._Lambda$__11()
in C:\Wrox\Professional_VB_2012\ConsoleApplication3\
ConsoleApplication3\Module1.vb:line 337
   at System.Threading.Tasks.Task.InnerInvoke()
   at System.Threading.Tasks.Task.Execute()
```

> **NOTE** *Unhandled exceptions inside asynchronous operations are usually complex problems, because sometimes you need to perform important cleanup operations. For example, when an exception occurs, you can have partial results, and you could have to remove these values if the job doesn't complete because of an exception. Thus, you have to consider cleanup operations when working with tasks.*

## Returning Values from Tasks

So far, task instances did not return values; they were delegates running subroutines. However, it is also possible to return values from tasks, invoking functions and using `Task(Of TResult)` instances, where `TResult` has to be replaced by the returned type.

The following code (code file: `Listing17.sln`) shows the code for a new function that generates the well-known AES keys and then returns a list of the ones that begin with the character prefix received as one of the parameters (*prefix*). `GenerateAESKeysWithCharPrefix` returns a `List` of `String`.

The `Main` subroutine uses the definition of the `TaskFactory.StartNew` method, but this time it calls it from a `Task(Of TResult)` instance and not a `Task` instance. Specifically, it creates a

`Task(Of List(Of String))` instance, sending it a `CancellationToken` as a parameter to the task delegate:

```
Dim t1 = Task(Of List(Of String)).Factory.StartNew(
    Function() GenerateAESKeysWithCharPrefix(ct, "A"), ct)
```

The delegate is a function that returns a `List(Of String)`, which is going to be available in the `Task(Of Result)` instance (`t1`) through its `Result` property after the associated delegate completes its execution and the function returns a value.

The main thread waits for `t1` to finish and then checks whether it completed its execution, checking the previously explained `Task` instance properties. Then, it iterates through each string in the list, returned by the function called in the previous task, and displays the results on the console. It does this job running a new asynchronous task, `t2` (code file: `Listing17.sln`).

```
Private Function GenerateAESKeysWithCharPrefix(
    ByVal ct As System.Threading.CancellationToken,
    ByVal prefix As Char) As List(Of String)

    ct.ThrowIfCancellationRequested()
    Dim sw = Stopwatch.StartNew()
    Dim aesM As New AesManaged()
    Dim keysList As New List(Of String)
    For i As Integer = 1 To NUM_AES_KEYS
        aesM.GenerateKey()
        Dim result = aesM.Key
        Dim hexString = ConvertToHexString(result)
        If Left(hexString, 1) = prefix Then
            keysList.Add(hexString)
        End If
        If ct.IsCancellationRequested Then
            ' It is important to add cleanup code here
            ct.ThrowIfCancellationRequested()
        End If
    Next
    Return keysList
    Console.WriteLine("AES: " + sw.Elapsed.ToString())
End Function

Sub Main()
    Dim sw = Stopwatch.StartNew()
    Dim cts As New System.Threading.CancellationTokenSource()
    Dim ct As System.Threading.CancellationToken = cts.Token

    Dim t1 = Task(Of List(Of String)).Factory.StartNew(
        Function() GenerateAESKeysWithCharPrefix(ct, "A"), ct)

    Try
        t1.Wait()
    Catch ex As AggregateException
        For Each innerEx As Exception In ex.InnerExceptions
            Debug.WriteLine(innerEx.ToString())
            ' Do something else considering the innerEx Exception
```

```
            Next
        End Try
        If t1.IsCanceled Then
            Console.WriteLine(
    "The task running GenerateAESKeysWithCharPrefix was canceled.")
            Exit Sub
        End If
        If t1.IsFaulted Then
            For Each innerEx As Exception In t1.Exception.InnerExceptions
                Debug.WriteLine(innerEx.ToString())
                ' Do something else considering the innerEx Exception
            Next
            Exit Sub
        End If

        Dim t2 = Task.Factory.StartNew(Sub()
            ' Do something with the result
            ' returned by the task's delegate
            For i As Integer = 0 To t1.Result.Count - 1
                Console.WriteLine(t1.Result(i))
            Next
          End Sub, TaskCreationOptions.LongRunning)

        ' Wait for the user to press a key while t2 is displaying the results
        Console.ReadLine()
    End Sub
```

## TaskCreationOptions

The code creates and starts the second task, t2, using the StarNew method and multiline lambda expression syntax. However, in this case, it uses a different definition that receives a TaskCreationOptions parameter that specifies flags to control optional behavior for the creation, scheduling, and execution of tasks.

The TaskCreationOptions enumeration has the four members described in Table 19-5.

**TABLE 19-5:** Optional Behaviors for Tasks

| VALUE | DESCRIPTION |
| --- | --- |
| TaskCreationOptions.AttachedToParent | The task is attached to a parent task. You can create tasks inside other tasks. |
| TaskCreationOptions.None | The task can use the default behavior. |
| TaskCreationOptions.LongRunning | The task will take a long time to run. Therefore, the scheduler can work with it as a coarse-grained operation. You can use this option if the task is likely to take many seconds to run. It is not advisable to use this option when a task takes less than one second to run. |
| TaskCreationOptions.PreferFairness | This option tells the scheduler that tasks scheduled sooner should be run sooner and tasks scheduled later should be run later. |

> **NOTE** *It is possible to combine multiple TaskCreationOptions enum values using bitwise operations.*

### Chaining Two Tasks Using Continuations

Clearly, the previous case shows an example of chained tasks. Task t1 produces a result, and t2 needs it as an input in order to start processing it. In these cases, instead of adding many lines that check for the successful completion of a precedent task and then schedule a new task, TPL enables you to chain tasks using continuations.

You can call the ContinueWith method for any task instance and create a continuation that executes when this task successfully completes its execution. It has many definitions, the simplest of which defines an action as done when creating Task instances.

The following lines show a simplified version of the code used in the previous example to display the results generated by t1 (code file: Snippet05.sln):

```
Dim t1 = Task(Of List(Of String)).Factory.StartNew(
    Function() GenerateAESKeysWithCharPrefix(ct, "A"), ct)

Dim t2 = t1.ContinueWith(Sub(t)
                            ' Do something with the result returned
                            ' by the task's delegate
                            For i As Integer = 0 To t.Result.Count - 1
                                Console.WriteLine(t.Result(i))
                            Next
                        End Sub)
```

It is possible to chain many tasks and then wait for the last task to be executed. However, you have to be careful with the continuous changes in the states when checking their values for all these asynchronous operations. In addition, it is very important to consider all the potential exceptions that could be thrown.

## Preparing the Code for Parallelism

Parallel programming applied to certain complex algorithms is not as simple as shown in the previously explained examples. Sometimes, the differences between a reliable and bug-free parallelized version and its sequential counterpart could reveal an initially unexpected complexity. The code can become too complex, even when taking advantage of the new features offered by TPL. In fact, a complex sequential algorithm is probably going to be a more complex parallel algorithm. Therefore, TPL offers many new data structures for parallel programming that simplify many complex synchronization problems:

➤ Concurrent collection classes

➤ Lightweight synchronization primitives

➤ Types for lazy initialization

The aforementioned data structures were designed to avoid *locks* wherever possible, and use fine-grained locking when they are necessary on their different shared resources. Locks generate many potential bugs and can significantly reduce scalability. However, sometimes they are necessary because writing lock-free code isn't always possible.

These new data structures enable you to forget about complex lock mechanisms in certain situations because they already include all the necessary lightweight synchronization under the hood. Therefore, it is a good idea to use these data structures whenever possible.

## Synchronization Primitives

Furthermore, .NET Framework 4.5 offers synchronization primitives for managing and controlling the interactions between different tasks and their underlying threads, including the following operations:

➤ **Locking**—As with relational databases, sometimes you need to ensure that only one piece of code is working with a variable at that time. Unfortunately, the same problems that appear when working with concurrent access in a relational database are also present in concurrent and parallel codes.

➤ **Signaling**—It provides a waiting and signaling mechanism to simplify the communication between different tasks and their underlying threads. The previously explained cancellation token is a clear example of signaling among many tasks. The mechanisms to wait for certain tasks to complete and the continuations are also examples of signaling implementations.

➤ **Lock constructors (interlocked operations)**—These provide a mechanism to perform *atomic operations*, such as addition, increment, decrement, exchange, or conditional exchange, depending on the results of a comparison operation and a read operation.

## Synchronization Problems

The aforementioned synchronization primitives are advanced topics that require an in-depth analysis in order to determine the most convenient primitive to apply in a given situation. Nowadays, it is important to use the right synchronization primitive in order to avoid potential pitfalls, explained in the following list, while still keeping the code scalable.

Many techniques and new debugging tools can simplify the most complex problems, such as the following:

➤ **Deadlock**—At least two tasks are waiting for each other but the wait never ends because they won't continue with other instructions until the other task releases the protection held over certain resources. The other task is also waiting for resources held by its counterpart to resume its execution. As no task is willing to release its protection, none of them make any progress, and the tasks continue to wait for each other forever. Consider the following situation, task `t1` holds a protection over resource A and is waiting to gain exclusive access over resource B. However, at the same time, task `t2` holds a protection over resource B and is waiting to gain exclusive access over resource A. This is one of the most horrible bugs.

➤ **Race conditions**—Many tasks read from and write to the same variable without the appropriate synchronization mechanism. It is a correctness problem. Erroneous parallelized code could generate wrong results under certain concurrency or parallel execution scenarios. However, when executed in some circumstances it could generate the expected results because the race may finish correctly. Consider the following situation: Task `t1` writes a value to public variable A. Then, task *t2* writes another value to public variable A. When task *t1* reads the value for the public variable A, it will hold a different value than the one that it had originally written to it.

# Understanding Concurrent Collection Features

Lists, collections, and arrays are excellent examples of when complex synchronization management is needed to access them concurrently and in parallel. If you have to write a parallel loop that adds elements in an unordered way into a shared collection, you have to add a synchronization mechanism to generate a *thread-safe* collection. The classic lists, collections, and arrays are not thread-safe because they aren't prepared to receive concurrent instructions to add or remove elements. Therefore, creating a thread-safe collection is indeed a very complex job.

## Systems.Collections.Concurrent

Luckily, TPL offers a new namespace, System.Collections.Concurrent, for dealing with thread-safe issues. As previously explained, this namespace provides access to the custom partitioners for parallelized loops. However, it also offers access to the following collections prepared for concurrency:

➤ BlockingCollection(Of T)—Similar to the classic blocking queue data structure—in this case, prepared for producer-consumer scenarios in which many tasks add and remove data. It is a wrapper of an IProducerConsumer(Of T) instance, providing blocking and bounding capabilities.

➤ ConcurrentBag(Of T)—Offers an unordered collection of objects. It is useful when ordering doesn't matter.

➤ ConcurrentDictionary(Of TKey, TValue)—Similar to a classic dictionary, with key-value pairs that can be accessed concurrently.

➤ ConcurrentQueue(Of T)—A FIFO (First In, First Out) collection whereby many tasks can enqueue and dequeue elements concurrently.

➤ ConcurrentStack(Of T)—A LIFO (Last In, First Out) collection whereby many tasks can push and pop elements concurrently.

> **NOTE** *You don't have to worry about locks and synchronization primitives while using the aforementioned collections in many tasks because they are already prepared to receive concurrent and parallel methods calls. They solve potential deadlocks and race conditions, and they make it easier to work with parallelized code in many advanced scenarios.*

## ConcurrentQueue

It would be difficult to use a classic shared list to add elements from many independent tasks created by the Parallel.ForEach method. You would need to add synchronization code, which would be a great challenge without restricting the overall scalability. However, it is possible to add strings to a queue (enqueue strings) in a shared `ConcurrentCollection` inside the parallelized code, because it is prepared for adding elements concurrently.

The following code (code file `Listing18.sln`) uses a shared `ConcurrentQueue(Of String)`, *Keys*, in order to hold the strings that contain the AES keys that begin with a certain prefix, generated in a parallelized loop with the custom partitioner. All the tasks created automatically by `Parallel.ForEach` are going to call the `Enqueue` method to add the elements that comply with the condition.

```
Keys.Enqueue(hexString)
```

It is indeed simple to work with a `ConcurrentQueue`. There is no need to worry about synchronization problems because everything is controlled under the hood.

```
Private Keys As Concurrent.ConcurrentQueue(Of String)

Private Sub ParallelPartitionGenerateAESKeysWCP(
    ByVal ct As System.Threading.CancellationToken,
    ByVal prefix As Char)
    ct.ThrowIfCancellationRequested()
    Dim sw = Stopwatch.StartNew()
    Dim parallelOptions As New ParallelOptions()
    ' Set the CancellationToken for the ParallelOptions instance
    parallelOptions.CancellationToken = ct
    Parallel.ForEach(Partitioner.Create(1, NUM_AES_KEYS + 1), parallelOptions,
        Sub(range)
            Dim aesM As New AesManaged()
            'Debug.WriteLine("Range ({0}, {1}. Time: {2})",
            '                   range.Item1, range.Item2, Now().TimeOfDay)
            For i As Integer = range.Item1 To range.Item2 - 1
                aesM.GenerateKey()
                Dim result = aesM.Key
                Dim hexString = ConvertToHexString(result)
                ' Console.WriteLine("AES: " + ConvertToHexString(result))
                If Left(hexString, 1) = prefix Then
                    Keys.Enqueue(hexString)
                End If
                parallelOptions.CancellationToken.ThrowIfCancellationRequested()
            Next
        End Sub)
    Console.WriteLine("AES: " + sw.Elapsed.ToString())
End Sub

Sub Main()
    Dim cts As New System.Threading.CancellationTokenSource()
    Dim ct As System.Threading.CancellationToken = cts.Token
    Keys = New ConcurrentQueue(Of String)

    Dim tAsync = New Task(Sub() ParallelPartitionGenerateAESKeysWCP(ct, "A"))
    tAsync.Start()

    ' Do something else
    ' Wait for tAsync to finish
    tAsync.Wait()

    Console.ReadLine()
End Sub
```

For example, it is possible to run many LINQ queries to display partial statistics while running the task that is adding elements to the `ConcurrentQueue` (Keys). The following code (code file: `Listing19.sln`) shows a new `Main` subroutine that checks whether the task (`tAsync`) is running or waiting to run, and while this happens it runs a LINQ query to show the number of keys that contain an `F` in the shared `ConcurrentQueue` (Keys).

```
Sub Main()
    Dim cts As New System.Threading.CancellationTokenSource()
    Dim ct As System.Threading.CancellationToken = cts.Token

    Keys = New ConcurrentQueue(Of String)
    Dim tAsync = Task.Factory.StartNew(
        Sub() ParallelPartitionGenerateAESKeysWCP(ct, "A"))

    Do While (tAsync.Status = TaskStatus.Running) Or
             (tAsync.Status = TaskStatus.WaitingToRun)
        ' Display partial results
        Dim countQuery = Aggregate key In Keys
                         Where key.Contains("F")
                         Into Count()

        Console.WriteLine("So far, the number of keys
that contain an F is: {0}", countQuery)
        ' Sleep the main thread for 0.5 seconds
        Threading.Thread.Sleep(500)
    Loop

    tAsync.Wait()

    ' Do something else

    Console.ReadLine()
End Sub
```

Another useful feature is the capability to remove an element at the beginning of the queue in a safe way using its `TryDequeue` method:

```
Dim firstKey As String
If Keys.TryDequeue(firstKey) Then
    ' firstKey has the first key added to the ConcurrentQueue
Else
    ' It wasn't possible to remove an element from the ConcurrentQueue
End If
```

`TryDequeue` returns a `Boolean` value indicating whether the operation was successful. It returns the element using an output attribute—in this case, a `String` received by reference (`firstKey`).

It is possible to add and remove elements in different tasks.

## ConcurrentStack

`ConcurrentStack` is very similar to the previously explained `ConcurrentQueue` but it uses different method names to better represent a stack (a LIFO collection). Its most important methods are `Push` and `TryPop`.

Push inserts an element at the top of the ConcurrentStack. If Keys were a ConcurrentStack(Of String), the following lines would add *hexString* at the top of the stack:

```
If Left(hexString, 1) = prefix Then
    Keys.Push(hexString)
End If
```

You can remove an element at the top of the stack in a safe way using its TryPop method. However, in this case, the method will return the last element added because it is a stack and not a queue:

```
Dim firstKey As String
If Keys.TryPop(firstKey) Then
    ' firstKey has the last key added to the ConcurrentStack
Else
    ' It wasn't possible to remove an element from the ConcurrentStack
End If
```

TryPop also returns a Boolean value indicating whether the operation was successful.

## Transforming LINQ into PLINQ

You already learned that LINQ is very useful to query and process different data sources. If you are using LINQ to Objects, it is possible to take advantage of parallelism using its parallel implementation, *Parallel LINQ (PLINQ)*.

> **NOTE** *PLINQ implements the full set of LINQ query operators and adds new additional operators for parallel execution. PLINQ can achieve significant speedups over its LINQ counterpart, but it depends on the scenario, as always with parallelism. If the query involves an appreciable number of calculations and memory-intensive operations and ordering doesn't matter, the speedups could be significant. However, when ordering matters, the speedups could be reduced.*

As you might have expected, LINQ and PLINQ can work with the previously explained concurrent collections. The following code defines a simple but intensive function to count and return the number of letters in a string received as a parameter (code file: Snippet06.sln):

```
Function CountLetters(ByVal key As String) As Integer
    Dim letters As Integer = 0
    For i As Integer = 0 To key.Length() - 1
        If Char.IsLetter(key, i) Then letters += 1
    Next
    Return letters
End Function
```

A simple LINQ expression to return all the AES keys with at least 10 letters containing an A, an F, a 9, and not a B, would look like the following:

```
Dim keysWith10Letters = From key In Keys
                        Where CountLetters(key) >= 10
                        And key.Contains("A")
                        And key.Contains("F")
                        And key.Contains("9")
                        And Not key.Contains("B")
```

In order to transform the aforementioned LINQ expression into a PLINQ expression that can take advantage of parallelism, it is necessary to use the `AsParallel` method, as shown here:

```
Dim keysWith10Letters = From key In Keys.AsParallel()
                        Where CountLetters(key) >= 10
                        And key.Contains("A")
                        And key.Contains("F")
                        And key.Contains("9")
                        And Not key.Contains("B")
```

This way, the query will try to take advantage of all the available logical cores at run time in order to run faster than its sequential version.

It is possible to add code at the end of the `Main` subroutine to return some results according to the PLINQ query (code file: `Snippet06.sln`):

```
Dim sw = Stopwatch.StartNew()

Dim keysWith10Letters = From key In Keys.AsParallel()
                        Where CountLetters(key) >= 10
                        And key.Contains("A")
                        And key.Contains("F")
                        And key.Contains("9")
                        And Not key.Contains("B")

Console.WriteLine("The code generated {0} keys
with at least ten letters, A, F and 9
but no B in the hexadecimal code.", keysWith10Letters.Count())
Console.WriteLine("First key {0}: ", keysWith10Letters(0))
Console.WriteLine("Last key {0}: ",
    keysWith10Letters(keysWith10Letters.Count() - 1))
Debug.WriteLine(sw.Elapsed.ToString())

Console.ReadLine()
```

This code shows the number of keys that comply with the conditions, the first one and the last one, stored in the results of the PLINQ query that worked against the `ConcurrentQueue(Of String)`.

## ParallelEnumerable and Its AsParallel Method

The `System.Linq.ParallelEnumerable` class is responsible for exposing most of PLINQ's additional functionality, including its most important one: the `AsParallel` method. Table 19-6 summarizes the PLINQ-specific methods.

**TABLE 19-6:** PLINQ Operators Exposed by ParallelEnumerable

| VALUE | DESCRIPTION |
| --- | --- |
| AsOrdered() | PLINQ must preserve the ordering of the source sequence for the rest of the query or until it changes using an `Order By` clause. |
| AsParallel() | The rest of the query should be parallelized, whenever possible. |

*continues*

**TABLE 19-6:** *(continued)*

| VALUE | DESCRIPTION |
|---|---|
| AsSequential() | The rest of the query should run sequentially, as traditional LINQ. |
| AsUnordered() | PLINQ doesn't have to preserve the ordering of the source sequence. |
| ForAll() | An enumeration method that enables the results to be processed in parallel, using multiple tasks. |
| WithCancellation | Enables working with a cancellation token to permit cancellation of the query execution as previously explained with tasks. |
| WithDegreeOfParallelism | PLINQ will be optimized as if the total number of available cores were equal to the degree of parallelism specified as a parameter for this method. |
| WithExecutionMode | This can force parallel execution when the default behavior would be to run it sequentially as traditional LINQ. |
| WithMergeOptions | This can provide hints about the way PLINQ should merge the parallel pieces of the result on the thread that is consuming the query. |

In addition, `AsParallel` offers an `Aggregate` overload that enables the implementation of parallel reduction algorithms. It enables intermediate aggregation on each parallelized part of the query and a final aggregation function that is capable of providing the logic to combine the results of all the generated partitions.

Sometimes it is useful to run a PLINQ query with many different degrees of parallelism in order to measure its scalability. For example, the following line runs the previously shown PLINQ query to take advantage of no more than three cores:

```
Dim keysWith10Letters = From key In Keys.AsParallel().WithDegreeOfParallelism(3)
                        Where CountLetters(key) >= 10
                        And key.Contains("A")
                        And key.Contains("F")
                        And key.Contains("9")
                        And Not key.Contains("B")
```

## AsOrdered and Order By

Because using `AsOrdered` and the `Order By` clause in PLINQ queries can reduce any speed gains, it is very important to compare the speedup achieved against the sequential version before requesting ordered results.

If a PLINQ query doesn't achieve significant performance improvements, you have another interesting option to take advantage of parallelism: running many LINQ queries in independent tasks or using `Parallel.Invoke`.

## Working with ForAll and a ConcurrentBag

The `ForAll` extension method is very useful to process the results of a query in parallel without having to write a parallel loop. It receives an action as a parameter, offering the same possibilities as the same parameter received by the Task constructors. Therefore, using lambda expressions, you can combine parallelized processing actions from the results of a PLINQ query. The following lines add elements in parallel to a new `ConcurrentBag` (*keysBag*), an unordered collection of `Integer`, counting the letters for each of the keys in the results of the previous PLINQ query (code file: `Snippet07.sln`):

```
Dim keysWith10Letters = From key In Keys.AsParallel()
                        Where CountLetters(key) >= 10
                        And key.Contains("A")
                        And key.Contains("F")
                        And key.Contains("9")
                        And Not key.Contains("B")

Dim keysBag As New ConcurrentBag(Of Integer)
keysWith10Letters.ForAll(Sub(i) keysBag.Add(CountLetters(i)))
```

> **NOTE** *This parallel processing is possible because ConcurrentBag is one of the concurrent collections that allows many elements to be added by multiple tasks running in parallel.*

# SUMMARY

This chapter provided an overview of the task-based programming model introduced with .NET Framework 4 and improved in .NET Framework 4.5. The chapter introduced some of its classes, structures, and enumerations. In order to help you tackle the multicore revolution, it also explained several related concepts used in basic concurrent and parallel programming designs, including the following key points:

➤   You have to plan and design with concurrency and parallelism in mind. TPL offers structures that simplify the process of creating code that takes advantage of multicore architectures.

➤   You don't need to recompile your code in order to take advantage of additional cores. TPL optimizes the parallel loops and the distributions of tasks in underlying threads using load-balancing scheduling according to the available hardware resources at run time.

➤ You can parallelize existing loops and measure the achieved performance gains.

➤ You can launch tasks and combine everything you learned so far about lists and arrays to work with multiple tasks and manage their execution.

➤ Concurrent collections provide a way to update collections in parallel and concurrent tasks without worrying about complex synchronization mechanisms.

➤ You can transform a LINQ query into PLINQ in order to test the speedup achieved with multicore architectures.

➤ Backward compatibility is possible with threaded code written in previous versions of Visual Basic and .NET Framework.

The next chapter will dive deep into the different deployment options for .NET applications. You will learn to easily select the most convenient deployment mechanism according to the kind of application you have developed and your target environments.

# 20

# Deploying XAML Applications via the Windows 8 Windows Store

The deployment mechanism for Windows 8 apps is a radical departure from previous platforms. In this chapter, you will see why these radical changes were made, and get an introduction to the main deployment option in Windows 8, which is the Windows Store.

## A NEW DEPLOYMENT OPTION FOR WINDOWS 8 APPS

Your applications must be deployed to be used. Deployment options have varied over the years. All have had advantages and disadvantages, and they have evolved to meet the needs of a given era.

Older deployment options are still available for applications based on .NET Framework 4.5, and you can continue to use those options for server and desktop applications. Those include xcopy deployment, ClickOnce, and creation of .msi files. There are also third-party products that package and install applications. Most experienced developers who use Microsoft technologies are familiar with one or more of these options.

Changes in the last few years have highlighted some disadvantages of these older options. In particular, the most common way to acquire applications has changed from inserting physical media into a computer to downloading applications straight from the Internet. While this certainly simplifies buying and installing applications, it also opens up computer users to a serious threat: having deployment mechanisms hijacked by malware.

Estimates of the cost of malware go into the billions, and the problem is rapidly getting worse. Malware authors have shifted to attempting to acquire information and credentials to manipulate financial accounts, which threatens to dramatically inflate the damages due to malware.

One model that has evolved over the last few years to address that problem is the "app store." Many users will be familiar with app stores for other platforms, and Microsoft has made an app store a built-in and significant part of Windows 8.

In the app store model, applications are required to go through a central point of deployment. Applications can be vetted in several ways before being placed in the store. This raises the bar for distribution of malware, and offers a fast way to chop off the distribution of malware when it is discovered.

App stores have additional benefits. For line-of-business applications, app stores provide a secure, widely available deployment mechanism with minimal investment by the IT departments involved. For consumer applications, which are often written by small teams and organizations, app stores help monetize applications. The app store relieves small organizations of creating the infrastructure to sell their apps and collect the payments. The Windows 8 app store is called the Windows Store.

# Deployment of WinRT Apps

The app store model and its associated technologies restricts the deployment of applications that will run on WinRT. There are currently two channels by which apps can be deployed:

1. The Windows Store
2. Side-loading

## Windows Store

The online Windows Store is owned and managed by Microsoft. It provides a searchable catalog of apps. When a user chooses to acquire an app, if it has a purchase price, then Microsoft collects the money and deposits it (after taking a fee, of course) in the account for the organization that placed the app in the store.

The Windows Store also provides a mechanism to update apps to new versions and arrange to download those new versions to previous purchasers of the app.

The Windows Store includes some features for allowing businesses to distribute software through the app store to both internal and external users. However, this chapter concentrates on what developers need to know about the Windows Store in general, and does not discuss those features.

As mentioned earlier, applications must be approved before they can be placed in the store. The section "Requirements for Apps in the Windows Store" below goes into details. These requirements are not merely guidelines; apps uploaded to the store are subject to testing by human testers to see if each app meets the requirements for the store.

### Side-loading

Applications can bypass the Windows Store and be directly installed on Windows 8 machines under some fairly restrictive conditions. This process is called *side-loading*. Apps to be side-loaded must be signed, and the certificate needed to validate the signing must be available on the machine where the app will run. Additional details on the process of side-loading are in the section below "Side-loading for LOB Apps in an organization."

## Developer License

It's not necessary to deploy an application through the Windows Store to test it during development. Instead, Visual Studio enables a special form of side-loading, which requires a special type of license.

When you begin using Visual Studio 2012 on Windows 8, you will automatically be offered an option to obtain what is called a *developer license*. This license is required to develop and test Windows 8 style applications. Without it, your installation of Visual Studio 2012 will be restricted to the development of applications for versions of the .NET Framework.

A developer license is free, and is created for a particular machine and for a limited time. As such, you can expect to acquire such licenses as necessary on various machines. Note that you can't install such a license when you are running a machine via remote desktop—you must be running directly on a machine to install it.

The dialog in Visual Studio 2012 to obtain a developer license comes up the first time you run it. You simply agree to the license terms, and give permission to install in the User Account Control dialog.

Visual Studio 2012 has a menu option to renew a developer license. It is at Project ➪ Store ➪ Acquire Developer License.

You can also get a dialog to obtain developer license with a command prompt, with the command `Show-WindowsDeveloperLicenseRegistration`. In the unlikely event that you need to remove a developer license, the command `Unregister-WindowsDeveloperLicense` will do that.

## Working with the Windows Store

One of the protection layers of the Windows Store is that applications are associated with an account at the Windows Store. To place an application in the store, you must have such an account. Getting an account is a multistep process, and it is discussed in the next section.

## GETTING AN ACCOUNT AT THE WINDOWS STORE

Before getting an account for the app store, you need to understand some of the options you will be offered and a few of the choices you will be making.

## Microsoft Account is Required

You will need a Microsoft account, which used to be known as a Windows Live ID. You probably have one already; it's an email address plus a special password you gave to Microsoft. If you use a Microsoft email provider, such as Hotmail (hotmail.com), Windows Live (live.com), or Outlook. com, then that email+password will serve as a Microsoft account. If you have multiple Microsoft accounts, ensure that you have logged into the one you want to use before starting the process of acquiring an app store account.

## Windows Store Account Types

There are two account types in the Windows Store: Individual and Company. Both require a registration fee, though Microsoft is making codes available through various channels to reduce or eliminate the fee.

As of this writing, Individual accounts are available only to those testing the app store, and require a registration code straight from Microsoft. However, it is expected that these accounts will be generally available once Windows 8 goes into general release.

Company accounts require additional verification. Two email addresses are needed, and a verification process will be performed involving both of them. Both email addresses can be yours, or the second email address can be a different person in your organization.

Company accounts have some extra features and cost a bit more for the registration fee. Company accounts can submit Windows 7 style desktop applications as well as Windows 8 style apps. Two important additional features for Windows 8 style apps deployed via Company accounts are:

1. The app can access the user's Documents library to add, change or delete files.
2. The app can use Windows credentials to access a corporate intranet.

For your own purposes when learning about Windows 8 apps and investigating the Windows Store, an Individual account should be sufficient. If you are confident that you will be selling apps through the Windows Store, or if you expect to use the account to deploy apps for a business, the small additional cost for a Company account is probably a good investment.

## Steps to Obtain an Account

The steps to obtaining an account at the Windows Store can vary somewhat, but the following steps are typical.

### Step 1 — Account Registration

To start the process of getting an account, you can access a Visual Studio 2012 menu option: Project ➪ Store ➪ Open Developer Account. You can also start the process through a web browser, using the starting URL of `https://appdev.microsoft.com/StorePortals`. If you are not logged in to a Microsoft account, the first step will be to do so.

As mentioned earlier, make sure you log in with the email address you want to be associated with the app store account. If you log in with one email address and then later enter a different email address in the screen in Step 3, you'll just have to start over.

Microsoft has made some recent changes in the switch from the Windows Live ID system, and you may be requested to provide additional validation of your Microsoft account via a number that is emailed to you. This is a one-time process; if you've already done it, you will not need to do it again.

## Step 2 — Configure Account Type

The first screen in the process of registering an account looks like Figure 20-1.

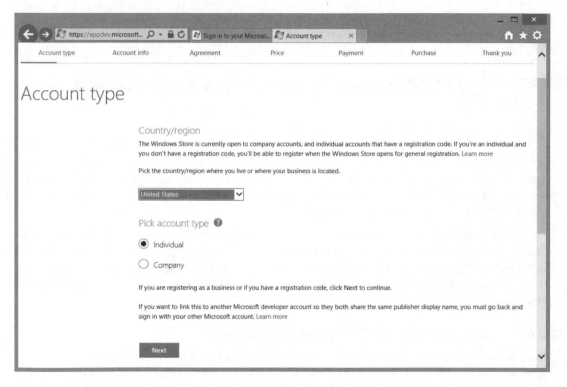

**FIGURE 20-1:** Choosing the account type to set up a Windows Store account

The only choices you make at this point are the country or region in which your business is located, and the type of account you want. Company accounts require some extra information, so the account type is needed before the next steps.

As discussed previously, when you are first starting out and just learning how the app store works, you might want an Individual account. It's somewhat simpler to acquire. However, when you get ready to actually sell apps or distribute apps for a company, you'll probably want a Company account. That requires additional verification and has an associated account for the money that comes in for the app.

## Step 3 — Enter Demographic Information and Publisher Name

In this step, you'll put in your demographic information—name, address, etc. The email address you use in this step should be the same email with which you logged into your Microsoft account.

You also need to supply a "Publisher display name" as the last item on the page. This area of the screen is shown in Figure 20-2. Naturally, this is the name the Windows Store will display as the publisher of the app.

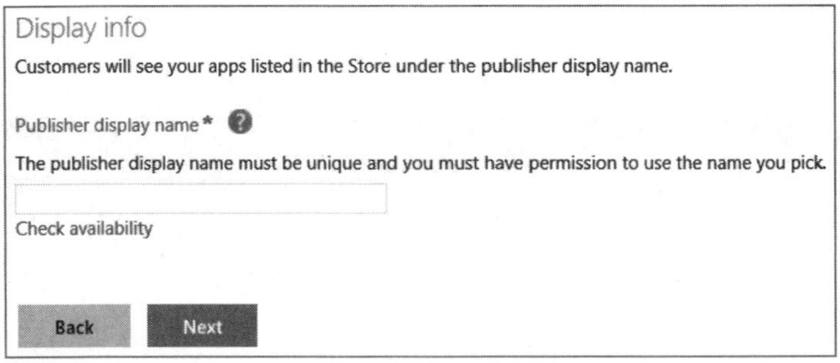

**FIGURE 20-2:** Specifying the Publisher display name for a Windows Store account

The Publisher display name must be unique. If you are getting a Company account for your organization, and you know this will be the main account to deploy your organization's apps, you should use your organization's name. If you work for a large organization, you may want to check with any appropriate parties before using the name.

If you are creating an Individual account, or a Company account for yourself or some small entity, choose a name you have control over and which you don't need any special permission to use. If you have a personal corporation, such as an LLC, that name would be a good choice. The screen will let you check the availability of your chosen name, and you must enter a unique name before you proceed.

## Step 4 — Accept Application Developer Agreement

Given the complexity of what happens in the Windows Store, including transfer of money, it's no surprise that a detailed agreement is required to get a Windows Store account. In this step, you will indicate that you have read and accept the agreement.

Read it first—don't just treat it as just another EULA. It's a binding legal agreement that designates the terms of selling and supporting your application, and such aspects as what to do if someone else is infringing on your app. There are a number of constraints in it to be aware of, particularly the Certification Requirements, which can be seen at `http://bit.ly/Win8CertRequirements`. The section below on "Checking to See if an App Meets Requirements" discusses some of the more important aspects of certification for Windows 8.

## Step 5 — Supply a Registration Code and/or Pay a Registration Fee

The next step is where you commit to getting the account and, if necessary, paying a fee for it. As of the time this is written, Individual accounts have a list price of $49US, and Company accounts have a list price of $99US. However, the page also allows you to enter a registration code, which may reduce or eliminate the fee.

For developers acquiring an Individual account, Microsoft has various mechanisms for distributing registration codes. These will likely vary over time, so this chapter will not detail the precise mechanisms in place at the moment.

### Step 6 — Confirm Identity

The procedure for confirming identity varies depending on the type of account. Company accounts require more confirmation. You will need to carry out the instructions on the registration screens for your particular case. Once this step is done, you should have an active account at the app store.

## REQUIREMENTS FOR APPS IN THE WINDOWS STORE

Microsoft has rarely imposed any significant constraints on the applications produced by their tools. User interface guidelines are also rare in the Microsoft arena. Early versions of Windows had some very general guidelines back in the 1990s, but they were not made detailed and prescriptive as the Windows ecosystem grew.

That is changing with Windows 8. With applications that will run on WinRT, which are currently called Windows 8 Style Apps, there are both firm constraints and detailed, prescriptive user interface guidelines.

During the beta period of Windows 8, you may have heard a different word used to describe Windows 8 Style Apps: "Metro." This term was first used for Windows Phone 7. However, legal restrictions barred Microsoft from using the term in production for Windows 8.

The user interface design guidelines for Windows 8 style apps were discussed in chapter 13. This chapter concentrates on the technical and content requirements for app certification, which your application must meet to be deployed via the Windows Store.

The app certification requirements for Windows 8 are quite detailed. They are also expected to evolve steadily. This chapter will therefore not attempt to cover all the details. The URL noted earlier, `http://bit.ly/Win8CertRequirements`, should guide you to the most current version of the requirements.

However, this chapter summarizes some of the most important requirements you will need to know as you begin development of Windows 8 style apps. It's very important that you know and understand these requirements. When you place an app in the store, it is subject to being tested by human testers who will verify whether or not your app meets the requirements. If it doesn't, it won't be made available in the store.

In the section on "Checking to See if an App Meets Requirements," you will look at the process you use for checking to see if you app meets the requirements. Some requirements are rather specific, and it's easy to see if you meet them. These can be validated before you attempt to place your app in the store. Other requirements are more general, and whether you meet them is open to interpretation once your apps have been placed in the store. However, you would be wise to understand those requirements and attempt to meet them before placing your app in the store.

# Specific Requirements

Here are some of the specific requirements for an app to be certified for the Windows Store. This list isn't intended to be comprehensive; it simply highlights some of the requirements you will want to know about right away. You should still look at the entire set of requirements at http://bit.ly/ Win8CertRequirements to become acquainted with the entire list.

### Restricted APIs

Apps in the store can access only a restricted set of APIs. The certification requirements have the details, but you are basically restricted to a set of namespaces in the Windows 8 runtime libraries, a set of namespaces in the .NET libraries for Windows 8 style apps, and the Live Connect API for authentication.

This obviously means you can't use any version of the general .NET Framework libraries. Those libraries are intended for applications that run in the desktop mode.

### Support for Windows 8 Interaction

Your app must support touch input to be certified, but this is usually handled by the controls you use to build the interface. More importantly, your application must not violate conventions for visual elements, including the bottom app bar and top navigation panel. Your app isn't required to use these elements, but if it does, it must use them correctly. For example, the app bar has to appear with a bottom swipe.

These requirements are easy to meet. One that's a bit harder is that your app must support a snapped view. This usually means special design for the view that is shown in the snapped view. Chapter 13 covered an example.

### Performance Criteria

As you might expect, your app can't lock up. But it also can't run too slowly. The current certification criteria, for example, specify that the app has to start up in five seconds or less, and suspend in two seconds or less, even on a low-powered computer.

# General Requirements

Some requirements are open to interpretation by the testers at the Windows Store. However, for the typical business application, it's unlikely an application would fail certification for such requirements.

### Provide Customer Value

There are several listed requirements about providing value to the customer. Those requirements mean your app has to actually do something worthwhile, which means you probably won't be able to deploy a "Hello, World" app to the store. Also, if your app has a trial version, it has to look and act a lot like the full version.

There are a number of requirements that apply to any advertising you place in your apps. There are certain parts of Windows 8, such as the app bar, where you are not allowed to place ads. And of course, there are content policies prohibiting inappropriate ads.

### Privacy and Consent

A number of requirements detail what you must do if you collect personal information. Certain privacy guidelines must be observed by your application.

Windows Store Apps also have some restrictions on the content they can access and display. As you might expect, there are restrictions on adult content, and on content that is discriminatory. Given the proclivities of some developers, it's worthwhile to mention that excessive or gratuitous profanity is not allowed. The Windows Store includes an age rating system, and your app is required to have an age rating that accurately matches your app.

## WORKING WITH THE WINDOWS STORE IN VISUAL STUDIO 2012

Visual Studio has a menu of items associated with functions concerning the Windows Store. It is accessed by choosing Project ⇨ Store, and is shown in Figure 20-3.

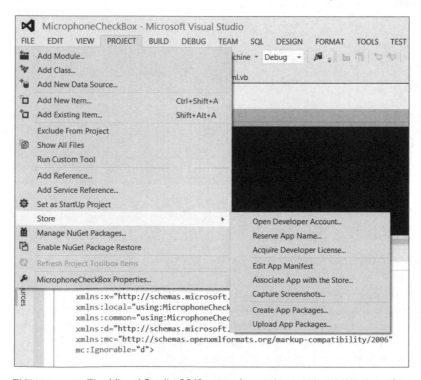

**FIGURE 20-3:** The Visual Studio 2012 menu for working with the Windows Store

## Options on the Store Menu

You saw earlier in the chapter the first option on the Store menu, which is used to get a Windows Store account using "Open Developer Account…" Other options cover additional steps in the process of testing and deploying the app. Some of these options link to the Window Store Dev Center, which includes options for configuring your apps in the Windows Store.

For example, one of the earliest options you'll want to use if you intend to sell an app is "Reserve App Name…" That will open a browser window with the title "Submit an app" and several options associated with submission. The top option is "App name." The window is shown in Figure 20-4.

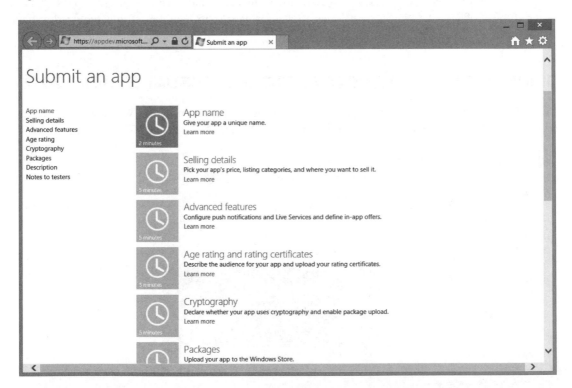

**FIGURE 20-4:** Options associated with submitting an app to the Windows Store

Most of the options on this screen are easy to figure out. For example, the App name option simply requires you to enter a name you intend to use, which should be a unique name for your app. The reservation on the name is good for up to one year. Therefore, if you have a clever name you intend to use and can't develop the app right away, you should go ahead and reserve your name. You can also reserve a name at the point that you create an app package.

Since most of the options are straightforward, the details will not be discussed here. You will see the last option, Packages, discussed later. It is used to upload your app the Windows Store.

The "Capture Screenshots…" is the recommended way to capture screenshots used in the Windows Store. At least one screenshot is required for an uploaded app.

The last two options on the menu are both quite important. They allow you to create an app package for testing or to upload to the store, and to upload the app package to the store.

## Creating an App Package

After you have finished much or all of the functionality of your app, you will want to test it to see if it meets Windows Store requirements. This requires that a package be created for the app using the Create App Packages menu option.

The first step is to reserve a name for the app, unless you have done that previously. The dialog will show you the names you have reserved and allow you to choose one. The dialog is shown in Figure 20-5.

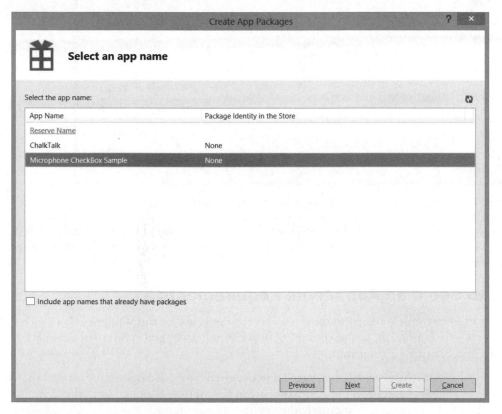

**FIGURE 20-5:** Choosing an app for which to generate a package

In the next step, you'll supply a version number and specify the architectures you want to support. That's usually Neutral, unless your app has special needs or features that tie it to a particular platform. After supplying that information, press the Create button, and your package will be created. The resulting screen will look much like Figure 20-6.

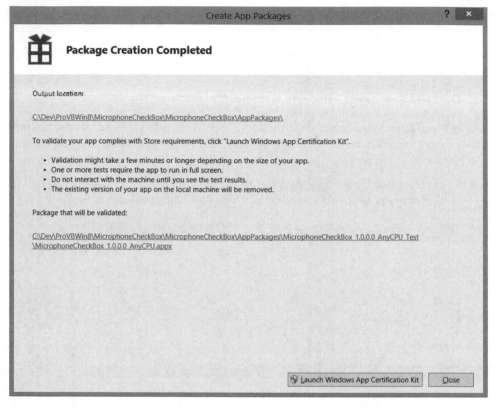

**FIGURE 20-6:** The dialog that displays once an app has been packaged

In addition to a Close button, the dialog also contains a button that says "Launch Windows App Certification Kit." This is one way to launch the app that checks to see if your app meets Windows Store requirements.

## Checking to See if an App Meets Requirements

The software used to check your app to see if it meets requirements for the Windows Store is the Windows App Certification Kit. It is part of the SDK for Windows 8, and is installed automatically as a part of a Visual Studio 2012 install.

Before an app can be tested, it must be packaged and deployed on the local machine, as just shown. As mentioned in chapter 13, the app must be based on an appropriate template so that it contains the items needed to be packaged, particularly the application manifest.

If you wish, you can start the Windows App Certification Kit as soon as your app is packaged, as shown in Figure 20-6 above. The app that was just packaged will automatically become the app to be validated.

You can also start the kit by accessing it directly from Windows Explorer or the command line. The default directory that contains the kit is one of the following directories, depending on whether you have a 32-bit version of Windows 8 or a 64-bit version:

```
C:\Program Files\Windows Kits\8.0\App Certification Kit

C:\Program Files (x86)\Windows Kits\8.0\App Certification Kit
```

The executable is appcertui.exe. If you navigate to the above directory and run that executable, you will get a screen asking you what kind of app you want to validate. In this case, you're only concerned with Windows Store Apps, which is the first option.

The program then scans the system to find all the Windows 8 style apps. It presents a list and allows you to choose the app you want to check. That list looks like Figure 20-7.

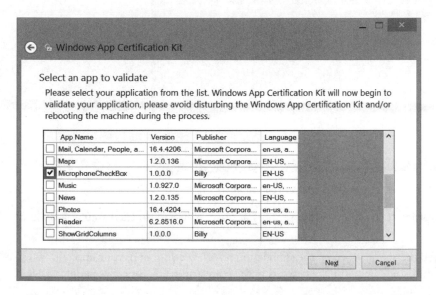

**FIGURE 20-7:** Choosing the app to be validated by the Windows App Certification Kit

Once you start the validation process, it's best to leave your machine alone while it's going on. You'll see a progress screen that looks like Figure 20-8, but it will be replaced from time to time with the app being checked, and you're not supposed to interact with the app during the validation process.

When the validation process is finished, you'll see a screen indicating whether the app has passed, and a link to a detailed report. Remember, the validation process doesn't check everything the Windows Store requires. A "Hello World" application will pass the Windows App Certification Kit tests, but it doesn't deliver any value, so the human testers at the Windows Store will likely turn it down.

## Deploying the App to the Windows Store

Once you have an app that has passed the Windows App Certification Kit tests, you are almost ready to upload the app to the Windows Store. However, you need to carry out several preliminary steps to configure the app in the store, and then do the actual upload step.

If you select the Project ➪ Store ➪ Upload App Packages option, you'll get the same screen you saw in Figure 20-4. You'll need to step through the unfinished options there, probably starting with

"Selling details." As mentioned earlier, these steps are straightforward, and this chapter won't cover the details.

**FIGURE 20-8:** The progress screen shown during app validation

By the way, it isn't necessary to complete all these steps at once. You can do each step at a different time if need be.

Once you have completed the steps shown on the submission screen for your app, your app will be vetted by the Windows Store, and you'll be notified when it is in the store and ready for other people to get it.

Your main interaction with your app in the app store from this point is using the Dashboard. It contains the apps you have placed in the store, and those in the process of being put in the store. Figure 20-9 shows the Dashboard.

The Dashboard helps you see metrics for how your app is doing, including a financial summary. It also lets you delete or edit an app.

## SIDE-LOADING FOR LOB APPS IN AN ORGANIZATION

As mentioned earlier, the main alternative to the Windows Store is side-loading of apps. That process is simpler in some respects than placing an app in the store. For example, it isn't necessary to supply the information that people need when shopping in the store.

Keep in mind, though, that you can distribute your line of business apps through the store if you like. The benefits of the store, such as the updating pipeline, are then available to you. The Windows Store includes a Business category for such apps. However, if you have an IT department that desires a higher degree of control over the app, then side-loading is probably the option that you want.

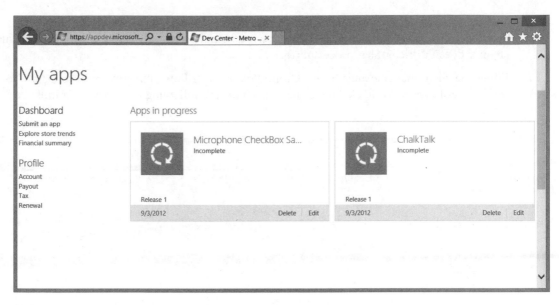

**FIGURE 20-9:** The Dashboard for a Windows Store account

## Packaging and Validation

For a side-loaded app, you can use the same process shown earlier for packaging and validating the app with the Windows App Certification Kit. The principle additional requirement for side-loaded apps is that the app must be signed.

This requires a valid certificate, and the Publisher Name in the certificate used to sign the app must match the Publisher Name in the package manifest for the app. Discussing acquisition and deployment of certificates is beyond the scope of this book, but in any large organization, it's likely that you have IT personnel familiar with certificates.

You can use a special certificate provided by Visual Studio to test the application internally. The certificate is generated when your project is created. The file name for the certificate is constructed from the project name plus "TemporaryKey," and the file has an extension of .pfx. There's nothing stopping you from using that certificate to deploy the app as broadly as you like, but that is not recommended.

To supply a different certificate for signing, open the `Package.appmanifest` item in the Solution Explorer, and select the Packaging tab at the top of the dialog. The screen will look like Figure 20-10. The dialog contains a button with "Choose Certificate…," which is highlighted in Figure 20-10.

## Preparing Client Machines for Side-loading

Once your app is signed and you have located the packages for any dependencies of your app, the next step is to prepare the Windows 8 client machines that will receive the side-loaded app. There are two requirements for client machines that need to receive side-loaded apps:

1.   The appropriate certificate must be installed locally. This is the certificate used to sign the app. Again, your IT staff should be familiar with the nuances of managing certificates, so this chapter doesn't discuss that process further.

2.   Either the client machine must have a Group Policy for "Allow all trusted apps to install" or, if Group Policy is unavailable on the client machine, the following registry setting must be made:

```
HKEY_LOCAL_MACHINE\Software\Policies\Microsoft\Windows\Appx\AllowAllTrustedApps = 1
```

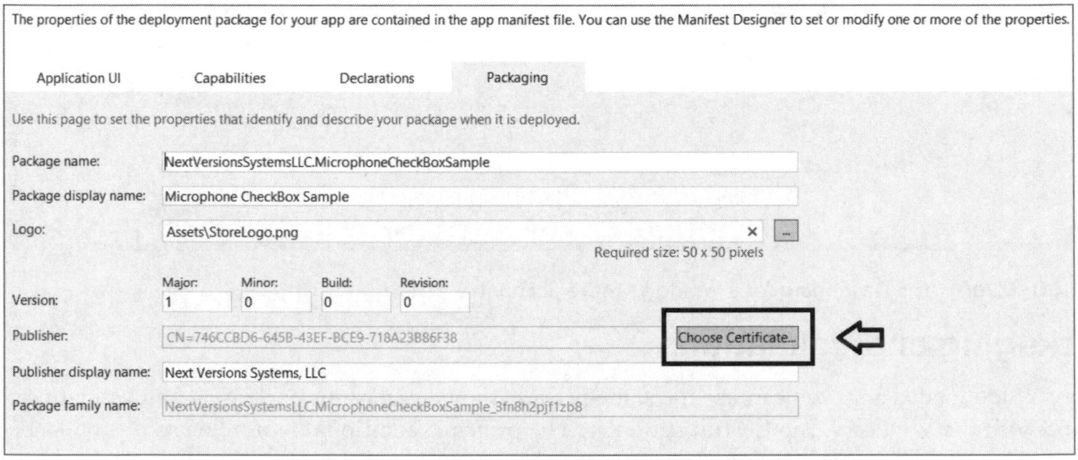

The properties of the deployment package for your app are contained in the app manifest file. You can use the Manifest Designer to set or modify one or more of the properties.

Application UI   Capabilities   Declarations   **Packaging**

Use this page to set the properties that identify and describe your package when it is deployed.

| | |
|---|---|
| Package name: | NextVersionsSystemsLLC.MicrophoneCheckBoxSample |
| Package display name: | Microphone CheckBox Sample |
| Logo: | Assets\StoreLogo.png |

Required size: 50 x 50 pixels

| | Major: | Minor: | Build: | Revision: |
|---|---|---|---|---|
| Version: | 1 | 0 | 0 | 0 |

| | |
|---|---|
| Publisher: | CN=746CCBD6-645B-43EF-BCE9-718A23B86F38   Choose Certificate... |
| Publisher display name: | Next Versions Systems, LLC |
| Package family name: | NextVersionsSystemsLLC.MicrophoneCheckBoxSample_3fn8h2pjf1zb8 |

**FIGURE 20-10:** Selecting a different certificate for signing the app

There is one last requirement, but it varies based on which version of Windows 8 is in use on the client machine and whether the client machine is on a domain. For Windows 8 Enterprise Edition and Windows 8 ARM Edition, if the machine is on a domain, the client machine is ready for side-loading. For other editions, or for client machines not on a domain, a script must be run on the client machine. At the time this is being written, the script and the process for running it is not yet available.

## The Side-loading Operation

Once the prerequisites for the client machine are accomplished, the actual side-loading operation is simple. From a PowerShell command prompt that is started with "Run as Administrator," just use a command similar to this:

```
add-appxpackage C:\MyDeploymentDir\MyAppName.appx
```

The .appx package is the one that was generated during the earlier packaging operation. The same command is also used to deploy updates.

# SUMMARY

The Windows Store represents a huge shift in application deployment. The process is far more complex and restrictive than older deployment options. You must follow carefully prescribed guidelines for your application to be considered valid for placement in the Windows Store.

However, the benefits are major. The Windows Store provides the infrastructure to locate, deploy, and update an app once you have placed your app in the store. That reduces your responsibilities, and gives you a lot of instrumentation that you likely did not have with earlier options.

And, of course, the threat of malware is significantly reduced. Even for applications that do not go through the Windows Store, the process requires a level of trust via certificates that will be hard for malware to routinely overcome.

This chapter has told you the basics, but given that the Windows Store is rather new, you can expect evolution and refinement of the process in short order. Once you understand the concepts, you'll want to invest some time in online resources to be aware of changes over time.

# INDEX

**F**

nHibernate, 408

NIST. *See* National Institute of Standards and Technology

NodeType, 332

nondeterministic finalization, 73

nonvirtual methods, 195–202

Not operator, 115

Nothing, 6, 8, 294–295

NotifyFilter property, 678

NT Services, 668

NTFS, 720, 721

Nullable, 294–295

nullable types, 294–295

numbers and currencies, cultural differences, 654–656

**O**

obfuscator, 70–71

Object Browser, 86

Object class, 125–126

object interfaces, 216–217

object memory allocation, 77–79

ObjectContext, 418–419

ObjectDataSource, 361, 581

object-oriented languages, 104

object-oriented programming, 179–180
  inheritance hierarchies, 199

object-oriented terminology, 105–109

Object-Relational Mapping (ORM), 408

objects
  composition, 105–108
  CultureInfo, 648–649
  DataAdapter, 382, 389–394
  DataReader, 372–373, 381, 385–386, 389, 400
  DataSet, 397–398
  DataTable, 398–401
  Debug, 275–278
  declaration, 134–135
  defining, 105

EventLog, 274–275

events, 152

exception, 264

generic, 125–126

instantiation, 134–135

mapping to entities, 419–426

references, 135–136

Request, 595

scope, 209–211

ServiceHost, 441

single table for multiple, 422–425

Trace, 275–278

working with, 134–143

ODBC data providers, 380

Office projects, 13

OLE DB data providers, 380, 394–395

OLE DB session pooling, 403

OleDbConnection, 380–381

OnContinue, 672

OnCustomCommand, 672, 687–688

on-demand installation, 706

one-way functions, 741

OnPause, 672

OnPowerEvent, 672

OnSessionChange, 672

OnShutdown, 672

OnStart, 672, 678–679, 689

OnStop, 672, 678–679

OpenAccess, 408

OperationCanceledException, 798, 801

Operator keyword, 169

operator overloading, 169–172

operators
  binary, 170, 171
  classes supporting, 169
  comparison, 115–116, 170
  data type support, 169
  equality, 171
  inequality, 171
  unary, 170, 171
  Visual Basic, 171

## X